ITIL®

ITIL® Service Strategy

London: TSO

information & publishing solutions

Published by TSO (The Stationery Office) and available from:

Online
www.tsoshop.co.uk

Mail, Telephone, Fax & E-mail
TSO
PO Box 29, Norwich, NR3 1GN
Telephone orders/General enquiries: 0870 600 5522
Fax orders: 0870 600 5533
E-mail: customer.services@tso.co.uk
Textphone: 0870 240 3701

TSO@Blackwell and other Accredited Agents

Customers can also order publications from:
TSO Ireland
16 Arthur Street, Belfast BT1 4GD
Tel: 028 9023 8451 Fax: 028 9023 5401

First edition Crown Copyright 2007
Second edition Crown Copyright 2011

First published 2011

ISBN 9780113313044

Printed in the United Kingdom for The Stationery Office
Material is FSC certified and produced using ECF pulp. Sourced from fully sustainable forests
P002425494   70   07/11

Contents

List of figures

List of tables

Foreword

Back in the 1980s no one truly understood IT service management (ITSM), although it was clear that it was a concept that needed to be explored. Hence a UK government initiative was instigated and ITIL® was born. Over the years, ITIL has evolved and, arguably, is now the most widely adopted approach in ITSM. It is globally recognized as the best-practice framework. ITIL's universal appeal is that it continues to provide a set of processes and procedures that are efficient, reliable and adaptable to organizations of all sizes, enabling them to improve their own service provision.

In the modern world the concept of having a strategy to drive the business forward with adequate planning and design transitioning into day-to-day operation is compelling. In this ever-changing world the provision of a clear and precise strategy that aligns the business requirements with IT, ensuring that IT becomes a strategic partner, has never been more important. This publication explores how to ensure synergy exists between the business and IT and explains the supporting processes and procedures.

The principles contained within *ITIL Service Strategy* have been proven countless times in the real world. We encourage feedback from business and the ITSM community, as well as other experts in the field, to ensure that ITIL remains relevant. This practice of continual service improvement is one of the cornerstones of the ITIL framework and the fruits of this labour are here before you in this updated edition.

There is an associated qualification scheme so that individuals can demonstrate their understanding and application of the ITIL practices. So whether you are starting out or continuing along the ITIL path, you are joining a legion of individuals and organizations who have recognized the benefits of good quality service and have a genuine resolve to improve their service level provision.

ITIL is not a panacea to all problems. It is, however, a tried and tested approach that has been proven to work.

I wish you every success in your service management journey.

Frances Scarff

Head of Best Management Practice
Cabinet Office

Preface

'In strategy it is important to see distant things as if they were close and to take a distanced view of close things.' Miyamoto Musashi

This is the first book in the series of five ITIL core publications containing advice and guidance around the activities and processes associated with the five stages of the service lifecycle. The primary purpose of the service strategy stage of the service lifecycle is to set and manage the correct overall strategy for IT, based upon the organization's overall business strategy, so that appropriate IT services can be provided to meet the current and future needs of the business. Therefore strategic thinking must be applied to service management and service management must itself be regarded as a strategic asset of an IT organization.

Service strategy agrees and defines the service portfolio and any new additions to it, and provides the input to service design so that the appropriate IT services can be designed and delivered to meet required business outcomes. Establishing a viable strategy is the first step but it is also essential to successfully communicate, market and sell that strategy to all customers, internal staff and suppliers to ensure that the design, transition and operation of IT services consistently meet required business outcomes. This involves close collaboration with continual service improvement to set up the appropriate monitoring, measurement, analysis, reporting and implementation of corrective actions. In this way the IT services being provided; the processes, tools and suppliers that deliver and operate them; and the overall strategy itself will remain fit for purpose (or will be updated as required).

Strategy requires academic thinking, but should not remain as an academic exercise – it must be applied to the real business world in order to influence and drive successful business outcomes. *ITIL Service Strategy* provides practical guidance on how service strategy should be formulated and applied to provide business value.

Contact information

Full details of the range of material published under the ITIL banner can be found at:

www.best-management-practice.com/IT-Service-Management-ITIL/

If you would like to inform us of any changes that may be required to this publication, please log them at:

www.best-management-practice.com/changelog/

For further information on qualifications and training accreditation, please visit:

www.itil-officialsite.com

Alternatively, please contact:

APM Group – The Accreditor Service Desk
Sword House
Totteridge Road
High Wycombe
Buckinghamshire
HP13 6DG
UK

Tel: +44 (0) 1494 458948
Email: servicedesk@apmgroupltd.com

Acknowledgements

2011 EDITION

Authors and mentors

David Cannon (HP)	Author
David Wheeldon (David Wheeldon IT Service Management)	Mentor
Shirley Lacy (ConnectSphere)	Project mentor
Ashley Hanna (HP)	Technical continuity editor

Other members of the ITIL authoring team

Thanks are due to the authors and mentors who have worked on all the publications in the lifecycle suite and contributed to the content in this publication and consistency across the suite. They are:

Lou Hunnebeck (Third Sky), Vernon Lloyd (Fox IT), Anthony T. Orr (BMC Software), Stuart Rance (HP), Colin Rudd (IT Enterprise Management Services Ltd (ITEMS)) and Randy Steinberg (Migration Technologies Inc.).

Project governance

Members of the project governance team included:

Jessica Barry, APM Group, project assurance (examinations); Marianna Billington, itSMFI, senior user; Emily Egle, TSO, team manager; Janine Eves, TSO, senior supplier; Phil Hearsum, Cabinet Office, project assurance (quality); Tony Jackson, TSO, project manager; Paul Martini, itSMFI, senior user; Richard Pharro, APM Group, senior supplier; Frances Scarff, Cabinet Office, project executive; Rob Stroud, itSMFI, senior user; Sharon Taylor, Aspect Group Inc., adviser to the project board (technical) and the ATO sub-group, and adviser to the project board (training).

For more information on the ATO sub-group see:

www.itil-officialsite.com/News/ ATOSubGroupAppointed.aspx

For a full list of acknowledgements of the ATO sub-group at the time of publication, please visit:

www.itil-officialsite.com/Publications/ PublicationAcknowledgements.aspx

Wider team

Change advisory board

The change advisory board (CAB) spent considerable time and effort reviewing all the comments submitted through the change control log and their hard work was essential to this project. Members of the CAB involved in this review included:

David Cannon, Emily Egle, David Favelle, Ashley Hanna, Kevin Holland, Stuart Rance, Frances Scarff and Sharon Taylor.

Once authors and mentors were selected for the 2011 update, a revised CAB was appointed and now includes:

Emily Egle, David Favelle, Phil Hearsum, Kevin Holland and Frances Scarff.

Further contributions

The author would specifically like to thank Greg Morrison of Progressive Insurance for his assistance, and Rob England for his presentation on governance at the 2010 itSMF New Zealand conference.

Reviewers

Claire Agutter, IT Training Zone; Ernest R. Brewster, Independent; David M. Brink, Solutions3; Jeroen Bronkhorst, HP; Tony Brough, DHL Supply Chain; Janaki Chakravarthy, Independent; Collin Chan, Dell Inc.; Christiane Chung Ah Pong, NCS Pte Ltd, Singapore; Federico Corradi, Cogitek; Catalin Danila, ITAcademy; Michael Davies, ProActive Services Pty Ltd; James Doss, General Dynamics Information Technology; Jenny Dugmore, Service Matters; Frank Eggert, MATERNA GmbH; David Favelle, UXC Consulting/Lucid IT; Ryan Fraser, HP; Ian Head, Gartner Inc; Björn Hinrichs, SERVIEW GmbH; Kevin Holland, NHS Connecting for Health; Steve Ingall, iCore-ltd; Andreas Knaus, santix AG; Maggie Kneller; Brad Laatsch, HP; Chandrika Labru, Tata Consultancy Services; Reginald Lo, Third Sky; Hank Marquis, Lowe's Companies Inc.;

Jane McNamara, Lilliard Associates Ltd; Christian F. Nissen, CFN People; Dalibor Petrovic, Deloitte & Touche LLP, Canada; Judit Pongracz, ITeal Consulting; Noel Scott, Symantec; Joy Shewring, JS Project Services Ltd; Arun Simha, L-3 Communications STRATIS; John A. Sowerby, DP DHL IT Services; Thorsten Steiling, EJOT Holding GmbH & Co. KG; Helen Sussex, Logica; J.R. Tietsort, Micron Technology; Steve Tremblay, Excelsa Technologies Consulting Inc.; Ken Turbitt, Service Management Consultancy (SMCG) Ltd; John Windebank, Oracle Corporation.

2007 EDITION

Chief architect and authors

Thanks are still due to those who contributed to the 2007 edition of Service Strategy, upon which this updated edition is based.

Sharon Taylor (Aspect Group Inc)	Chief architect
Majid Iqbal (Carnegie Mellon University)	Author
Michael Nieves (Accenture)	Author

All names and organizations were correct at publication in 2007.

For a full list of all those who contributed to the 2007 and 2011 editions of *Service Strategy, Service Design, Service Transition, Service Operation* and *Continual Service Improvement*, please go to

www.itil-officialsite.com/Publications/ PublicationAcknowledgements.aspx

Introduction

1

1 Introduction

ITIL is part of a suite of best-practice publications for IT service management (ITSM).[1] ITIL provides guidance to service providers on the provision of quality IT services, and on the processes, functions and other capabilities needed to support them. ITIL is used by many hundreds of organizations around the world and offers best-practice guidance to all types of organization that provide services. ITIL is not a standard that has to be followed; it is guidance that should be read and understood, and used to create value for the service provider and its customers. Organizations are encouraged to adopt ITIL best practices and to adapt them to work in their specific environments in ways that meet their needs.

ITIL is the most widely recognized framework for ITSM in the world. In the 20 years since it was created, ITIL has evolved and changed its breadth and depth as technologies and business practices have developed. ISO/IEC 20000 provides a formal and universal standard for organizations seeking to have their service management capabilities audited and certified. While ISO/IEC 20000 is a standard to be achieved and maintained, ITIL offers a body of knowledge useful for achieving the standard.

In 2007, the second major refresh of ITIL was published in response to significant advancements in technology and emerging challenges for IT service providers. New models and architectures such as outsourcing, shared services, utility computing, cloud computing, virtualization, web services and mobile commerce have become widespread within IT. The process-based approach of ITIL was augmented with the service lifecycle to address these additional service management challenges. In 2011, as part of its commitment to continual improvement, the Cabinet Office published this update to improve consistency across the core publications.

The ITIL framework is based on the five stages of the service lifecycle as shown in Figure 1.1, with a core publication providing best-practice guidance for each stage. This guidance includes key principles, required processes and activities,

organization and roles, technology, associated challenges, critical success factors and risks. The service lifecycle uses a hub-and-spoke design, with service strategy at the hub, and service design, transition and operation as the revolving lifecycle stages or 'spokes'. Continual service improvement surrounds and supports all stages of the service lifecycle. Each stage of the lifecycle exerts influence on the others and relies on them for inputs and feedback. In this way, a constant set of checks and balances throughout the service lifecycle ensures that as business demand changes with business need, the services can adapt and respond effectively.

In addition to the core publications, there is also a complementary set of ITIL publications providing guidance specific to industry sectors, organization types, operating models and technology architectures.

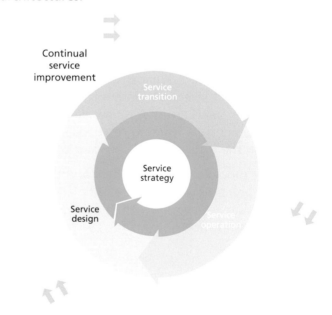

Figure 1.1 The ITIL service lifecycle

1.1 OVERVIEW

ITIL Service Strategy provides best-practice guidance for the service strategy stage of the ITIL service lifecycle. Although this publication can be read in isolation, it is recommended that it is used in conjunction with the other core ITIL publications.

---

1 ITSM and other concepts from this chapter are described in more detail in Chapter 2.

1.1.1 Purpose and objectives of service strategy

The purpose of the service strategy stage of the service lifecycle is to define the perspective, position, plans and patterns that a service provider needs to be able to execute to meet an organization's business outcomes.

The objectives of service strategy include providing:

■ An understanding of what strategy is
■ A clear identification of the definition of services and the customers who use them
■ The ability to define how value is created and delivered
■ A means to identify opportunities to provide services and how to exploit them
■ A clear service provision model, that articulates how services will be delivered and funded, and to whom they will be delivered and for what purpose
■ The means to understand the organizational capability required to deliver the strategy
■ Documentation and coordination of how service assets are used to deliver services, and how to optimize their performance
■ Processes that define the strategy of the organization, which services will achieve the strategy, what level of investment will be required, at what levels of demand, and the means to ensure a working relationship exists between the customer and service provider.

The reader should be able to understand the most important practices related to defining and executing a service strategy within a service provider organization.

1.1.2 Scope

ITIL Service Strategy starts by defining and discussing the generic principles and processes of service management, and these generic principles are then applied consistently to the management of IT services.

This publication is intended for use by both internal and external service providers, and includes guidance for organizations which are required to offer IT services as a profitable business, as well as those which are required to offer IT services to other business units within the same organization – at no profit.

Two aspects of strategy are covered in *ITIL Service Strategy*:

■ Defining a strategy whereby a service provider will deliver services to meet a customer's business outcomes
■ Defining a strategy for how to manage those services.

1.1.3 Usage

ITIL Service Strategy provides access to proven best practice based on the skill and knowledge of experienced industry practitioners in adopting a standardized and controlled approach to service management. Although this publication can be used and applied in isolation, it is recommended that it is used in conjunction with the other core ITIL publications. All of the core publications need to be read to fully appreciate and understand the overall lifecycle of services and IT service management.

1.1.4 Value to business

Selecting and adopting the best practice as recommended in this publication will assist organizations in delivering significant benefits. Adopting and implementing standard and consistent approaches for service strategy will:

■ Support the ability to link activities performed by the service provider to outcomes that are critical to internal or external customers. As a result, the service provider will be seen to be contributing to the value (and not just the costs) of the organization.
■ Enable the service provider to have a clear understanding of what types and levels of service will make its customers successful and then organize itself optimally to deliver and support those services. The service provider will achieve this through a process of defining strategies and services, ensuring a consistent, repeatable approach to defining how value will be built and delivered that is accessible to all stakeholders.
■ Enable the service provider to respond quickly and effectively to changes in the business environment, ensuring increased competitive advantage over time.
■ Support the creation and maintenance of a portfolio of quantified services that will enable

the business to achieve positive return on its investment in services.

■ Facilitate functional and transparent communication between the customer and the service provider, so that both have a consistent understanding of what is required and how it will be delivered.

■ Provide the means for the service provider to organize itself so that it can provide services in an efficient and effective manner.

1.1.5 Target audience

ITIL Service Strategy is aimed at executives and managers who are responsible for defining the strategy of a service provider.

Customers and business unit leaders who interact with service providers as part of their responsibilities will also find this publication helpful in providing a perspective about how service providers work, and how they can facilitate a more constructive interface with the service provider. The more a customer understands the context of service provision, the better they are able to articulate their needs in a way that the service provider is able to fulfil.

ITIL Service Strategy will also be valuable to owners of more strategic processes such as strategy management for IT services, service portfolio management, demand management, financial management and business relationship management. Indeed, service management professionals working in any part of the service lifecycle will find this publication helpful in identifying the context for the activities they are performing, which will help to improve their ability to define and deliver quality services, and to build appropriate structures to manage those services.

1.2 CONTEXT

The context of this publication is the ITIL service lifecycle as shown in Figure 1.1.

The ITIL core consists of five lifecycle publications. Each provides part of the guidance necessary for an integrated approach as required by the ISO/IEC 20000 standard specification. The five publications are:

■ *ITIL Service Strategy*
■ *ITIL Service Design*
■ *ITIL Service Transition*

■ *ITIL Service Operation*
■ *ITIL Continual Service Improvement*

Each one addresses capabilities having direct impact on a service provider's performance. The core is expected to provide structure, stability and strength to service management capabilities, with durable principles, methods and tools. This serves to protect investments and provide the necessary basis for measurement, learning and improvement. The introductory guide, *Introduction to the ITIL Service Lifecycle*, provides an overview of the lifecycle stages described in the ITIL core.

ITIL guidance can be adapted to support various business environments and organizational strategies. Complementary ITIL publications provide flexibility to implement the core in a diverse range of environments. Practitioners can select complementary publications as needed to provide traction for the ITIL core in a given context, in much the same way as tyres are selected based on the type of vehicle, purpose and road conditions. This is to increase the durability and portability of knowledge assets and to protect investments in service management capabilities.

1.2.1 Service strategy

At the centre of the service lifecycle is service strategy. Value creation begins here with understanding organizational objectives and customer needs. Every organizational asset including people, processes and products should support the strategy.

ITIL Service Strategy (this publication) provides guidance on how to view service management not only as an organizational capability but as a strategic asset. It describes the principles underpinning the practice of service management which are useful for developing service management policies, guidelines and processes across the ITIL service lifecycle.

Topics covered in *ITIL Service Strategy* include the development of market spaces, characteristics of internal and external provider types, service assets, the service portfolio and implementation of strategy through the service lifecycle. Business relationship management, demand management, financial management, organizational development and strategic risks are among the other major topics.

Organizations should use *ITIL Service Strategy* to set objectives and expectations of performance towards serving customers and market spaces, and to identify, select and prioritize opportunities. Service strategy is about ensuring that organizations are in a position to handle the costs and risks associated with their service portfolios, and are set up not just for operational effectiveness but for distinctive performance.

Organizations already practising ITIL can use *ITIL Service Strategy* to guide a strategic review of their ITIL-based service management capabilities and to improve the alignment between those capabilities and their business strategies. *ITIL Service Strategy* will encourage readers to stop and think about why something is to be done before thinking of how.

1.2.2 Service design

For services to provide true value to the business, they must be designed with the business objectives in mind. Design encompasses the whole IT organization, for it is the organization as a whole that delivers and supports the services. Service design is the stage in the lifecycle that turns a service strategy into a plan for delivering the business objectives.

ITIL Service Design provides guidance for the design and development of services and service management practices. It covers design principles and methods for converting strategic objectives into portfolios of services and service assets. The scope of *ITIL Service Design* is not limited to new services. It includes the changes and improvements necessary to increase or maintain value to customers over the lifecycle of services, the continuity of services, achievement of service levels, and conformance to standards and regulations. It guides organizations on how to develop design capabilities for service management.

Other topics in *ITIL Service Design* include design coordination, service catalogue management, service level management, availability management, capacity management, IT service continuity management, information security management and supplier management.

1.2.3 Service transition

ITIL Service Transition provides guidance for the development and improvement of capabilities for introducing new and changed services into supported environments. It describes how to transition an organization from one state to another while controlling risk and supporting organizational knowledge for decision support. It ensures that the value(s) identified in the service strategy, and encoded in service design, are effectively transitioned so that they can be realized in service operation.

ITIL Service Transition describes best practice in transition planning and support, change management, service asset and configuration management, release and deployment management, service validation and testing, change evaluation and knowledge management. It provides guidance on managing the complexity related to changes to services and service management processes, preventing undesired consequences while allowing for innovation.

ITIL Service Transition also introduces the service knowledge management system, which can support organizational learning and help to improve the overall efficiency and effectiveness of all stages of the service lifecycle. This will enable people to benefit from the knowledge and experience of others, support informed decision-making, and improve the management of services.

1.2.4 Service operation

ITIL Service Operation describes best practice for managing services in supported environments. It includes guidance on achieving effectiveness and efficiency in the delivery and support of services to ensure value for the customer, the users and the service provider.

Strategic objectives are ultimately realized through service operation, therefore making it a critical capability. *ITIL Service Operation* provides guidance on how to maintain stability in service operation, allowing for changes in design, scale, scope and service levels. Organizations are provided with detailed process guidelines, methods and tools for use in two major control perspectives: reactive and proactive. Managers and practitioners are provided with knowledge allowing them to make better decisions in areas such as managing the availability of services, controlling demand, optimizing capacity utilization, scheduling of operations, and avoiding or resolving service incidents and managing problems. New models and architectures such as shared services, utility computing, web services and mobile commerce to support service operation are described.

Other topics in *ITIL Service Operation* include event management, incident management, request fulfilment, problem management and access management processes; as well as the service desk, technical management, IT operations management and application management functions.

1.2.5 Continual service improvement

ITIL Continual Service Improvement provides guidance on creating and maintaining value for customers through better strategy, design, transition and operation of services. It combines principles, practices and methods from quality management, change management and capability improvement.

ITIL Continual Service Improvement describes best practice for achieving incremental and large-scale improvements in service quality, operational efficiency and business continuity, and for ensuring that the service portfolio continues to be aligned to business needs. Guidance is provided for linking improvement efforts and outcomes with service strategy, design, transition and operation. A closed loop feedback system, based on the Plan-Do-Check-

Act (PDCA) cycle, is established. Feedback from any stage of the service lifecycle can be used to identify improvement opportunities for any other stage of the lifecycle.

Other topics in *ITIL Continual Service Improvement* include service measurement, demonstrating value with metrics, developing baselines and maturity assessments.

1.3 ITIL IN RELATION TO OTHER PUBLICATIONS IN THE BEST MANAGEMENT PRACTICE PORTFOLIO

ITIL is part of a portfolio of best-practice publications (known collectively as Best Management Practice or BMP) aimed at helping organizations and individuals manage projects, programmes and services consistently and effectively (see Figure 1.2). ITIL can be used in harmony with other BMP products, and international or internal organization standards. Where appropriate, BMP guidance is supported by a qualification scheme and accredited training and consultancy services. All BMP guidance is intended to be tailored for use by individual organizations.

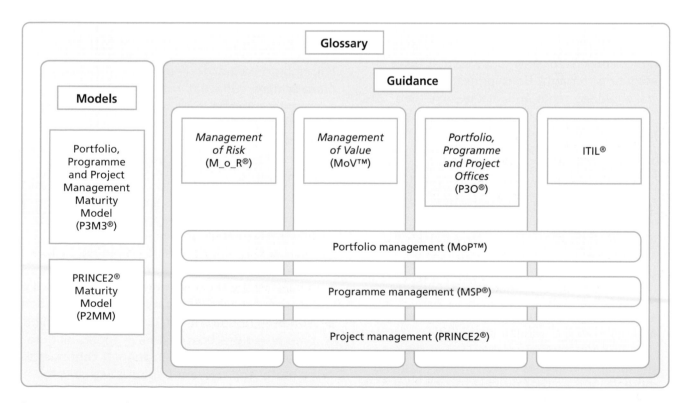

Figure 1.2 ITIL's relationship with other Best Management Practice guides

BMP publications include:

- **Management of Portfolios (MoP™)** Portfolio management concerns the twin issues of how to do the 'right' projects and programmes in the context of the organization's strategic objectives, and how to do them 'correctly' in terms of achieving delivery and benefits at a collective level. MoP encompasses consideration of the principles upon which effective portfolio management is based; the key practices in the portfolio definition and delivery cycles, including examples of how they have been applied in real life; and guidance on how to implement portfolio management and sustain progress in a wide variety of organizations. Office of Government Commerce (2011). *Management of Portfolios*. TSO, London.

- **Management of Risk (M_o_R®)** M_o_R offers an effective framework for taking informed decisions about the risks that affect performance objectives. The framework allows organizations to assess risk accurately (selecting the correct responses to threats and opportunities created by uncertainty) and thereby improve their service delivery. Office of Government Commerce (2010). *Management of Risk: Guidance for Practitioners*. TSO, London.

- **Management of Value (MoV™)** MoV provides a cross-sector and universally applicable guide on how to maximize value in a way that takes account of organizations' priorities, differing stakeholders' needs and, at the same time, uses resources as efficiently and effectively as possible. It will help organizations to put in place effective methods to deliver enhanced value across their portfolio, programmes, projects and operational activities to meet the challenges of ever-more competitive and resource-constrained environments. Office of Government Commerce (2010). *Management of Value*. TSO, London.

- **Managing Successful Programmes (MSP®)** MSP provides a framework to enable the achievement of high-quality change outcomes and benefits that fundamentally affect the way in which organizations work. One of the core themes in MSP is that a programme must add more value than that provided by the sum of its constituent project and major activities.

Cabinet Office (2011). *Managing Successful Programmes*. TSO, London.

- **Managing Successful Projects with PRINCE2®** PRINCE2 (PRojects IN Controlled Environments, V2) is a structured method to help effective project management via clearly defined products. Key themes that feature throughout PRINCE2 are the dependence on a viable business case confirming the delivery of measurable benefits that are aligned to an organization's objectives and strategy, while ensuring the management of risks, costs and quality. Office of Government Commerce (2009). *Managing Successful Projects with PRINCE2*. TSO, London.

- **Portfolio, Programme and Project Offices (P3O®)** P3O provides universally applicable guidance, including principles, processes and techniques, to successfully establish, develop and maintain appropriate support structures. These structures will facilitate delivery of business objectives (portfolios), programmes and projects within time, cost, quality and other organizational constraints. Office of Government Commerce (2008). *Portfolio, Programme and Project Offices*. TSO, London.

1.4 WHY IS ITIL SO SUCCESSFUL?

ITIL embraces a practical approach to service management – do what works. And what works is adapting a common framework of practices that unite all areas of IT service provision towards a single aim – that of delivering value to the business. The following list defines the key characteristics of ITIL that contribute to its global success:

- **Vendor-neutral** ITIL service management practices are applicable in any IT organization because they are not based on any particular technology platform or industry type. ITIL is owned by the UK government and is not tied to any commercial proprietary practice or solution.
- **Non-prescriptive** ITIL offers robust, mature and time-tested practices that have applicability to all types of service organization. It continues to be useful and relevant in public and private sectors, internal and external service providers,

small, medium and large enterprises, and within any technical environment. Organizations should adopt ITIL and adapt it to meet the needs of the IT organization and their customers.

- **Best practice** ITIL represents the learning experiences and thought leadership of the world's best-in-class service providers.

ITIL is successful because it describes practices that enable organizations to deliver benefits, return on investment and sustained success. ITIL is adopted by organizations to enable them to:

- Deliver value for customers through services
- Integrate the strategy for services with the business strategy and customer needs
- Measure, monitor and optimize IT services and service provider performance
- Manage the IT investment and budget
- Manage risk
- Manage knowledge
- Manage capabilities and resources to deliver services effectively and efficiently
- Enable adoption of a standard approach to service management across the enterprise
- Change the organizational culture to support the achievement of sustained success
- Improve the interaction and relationship with customers
- Coordinate the delivery of goods and services across the value network
- Optimize and reduce costs.

1.5 CHAPTER SUMMARY

ITIL Service Strategy comprises:

- Chapter 2 Service management as a practice
  This chapter explains the concepts of service management and services, and describes how these can be used to create value. It also summarizes a number of generic ITIL concepts that the rest of the publication depends on.

- Chapter 3 Service strategy principles
  This chapter describes the terminology and key principles which form the building blocks of service strategy best practice. These principles are the policies and governance aspects of the service strategy lifecycle stage that anchor the tactical processes and activities to achieving their objectives. It concludes with a table

showing the major inputs and outputs for the service strategy lifecycle stage.

- Chapter 4 Service strategy processes
  Chapter 4 sets out the processes and activities on which effective service strategy depends and how they integrate with the other stages of the lifecycle.

- Chapter 5 Service strategy, governance, architecture and ITSM implementation strategies
  Chapter 5 deals with some of the major strategic interfaces between service strategy, the business context and service management. Specifically, it looks at the interface between the overarching organization strategy, the strategy of the service provider, and the service provider's IT service management strategy. It also considers the relationship between service management, enterprise architecture and application development.

- Chapter 6 Organizing for service strategy
  This chapter identifies the organizational roles and responsibilities that are needed to manage the service strategy lifecycle stage and processes. These roles are provided as guidelines and can be combined to fit into a variety of organizational structures. Examples of organizational structures are also provided.

- Chapter 7 Technology considerations
  ITIL service management practices gain momentum when the right type of technical automation is applied. This chapter provides recommendations for the use of technology in service strategy and the basic requirements a service provider will need to consider when choosing service management tools.

- Chapter 8 Implementing service strategy
  For organizations new to ITIL, or those wishing to improve their maturity and service capability, this chapter outlines effective ways to implement the service strategy lifecycle stage.

- Chapter 9 Challenges, risks and critical success factors
  It is important for any organization to understand the challenges, risks and critical success factors that could influence their success. This chapter discusses typical examples of these for the service strategy lifecycle stage.

- Appendix A Present value of an annuity

- Appendix B Description of asset types
  This appendix describes the key asset types of management, organization, process, knowledge, people, information, applications, infrastructure and financial capital.

- Appendix C Service strategy and the cloud
  Included here is a brief overview of the major themes and issues surrounding the complex area of cloud services.

- Appendix D Related guidance
  This contains a list of some of the many external methods, practices and frameworks that align well with ITIL best practice. Notes are provided on how they integrate into the ITIL service lifecycle, and when and how they are useful.

- Appendix E Risk assessment and management
  This appendix contains basic information about several commonly used approaches to the assessment and management of risk.

- Appendix F Examples of inputs and outputs across the service lifecycle
  This appendix identifies some of the major inputs and outputs between each stage of the service lifecycle.

- References and further reading
  This provides a list of other sources of information that both informed the writing of this publication and can be used for further study and exploration by readers.

- Abbreviations and glossary
  This contains a list of abbreviations and a selected glossary of terms.

Service management as a practice

2

2   Service management as a practice

2.1   SERVICES AND SERVICE MANAGEMENT

2.1.1   Services

Services are a means of delivering value to customers by facilitating the outcomes customers want to achieve without the ownership of specific costs and risks. Services facilitate outcomes by enhancing the performance of associated tasks and reducing the effect of constraints. These constraints may include regulation, lack of funding or capacity, or technology limitations. The end result is an increase in the probability of desired outcomes. While some services enhance performance of tasks, others have a more direct impact – they perform the task itself.

The preceding paragraph is not just a definition, as it is a recurring pattern found in a wide range of services. Patterns are useful for managing complexity, costs, flexibility and variety. They are generic structures useful to make an idea applicable in a wide range of environments and situations. In each instance the pattern is applied with variations that make the idea effective, economical or simply useful in that particular case.

Definition: outcome

The result of carrying out an activity, following a process, or delivering an IT service etc. The term is used to refer to intended results, as well as to actual results.

An outcome-based definition of service moves IT organizations beyond business–IT alignment towards business–IT integration. Internal dialogue and discussion on the meaning of services is an elementary step towards alignment and integration with a customer's business (Figure 2.1). Customer outcomes become the ultimate concern of business relationship managers instead of the gathering of requirements, which is necessary but not sufficient. Requirements are generated for internal coordination and control only after customer outcomes are well understood.

Customers seek outcomes but do not wish to have accountability or ownership of all the associated costs and risks. All services must have a budget when they go live and this must be managed. The service cost is reflected in financial terms such as return on investment (ROI) and total cost of ownership (TCO). The customer will only be exposed to the overall cost or price of a service, which will include all the provider's costs and risk mitigation measures (and any profit margin if appropriate). The customer can then judge the value of a service based on a comparison of cost or price and reliability with the desired outcome.

Definitions

Service: A means of delivering value to customers by facilitating outcomes customers want to achieve without the ownership of specific costs and risks.

IT service: A service provided by an IT service provider. An IT service is made up of a combination of information technology, people and processes. A customer-facing IT service directly supports the business processes of one or more customers and its service level targets should be defined in a service level agreement. Other IT services, called supporting services, are not directly used by the business but are required by the service provider to deliver customer-facing services.

Customer satisfaction is also important. Customers need to be satisfied with the level of service and feel confident in the ability of the service provider to continue providing that level of service – or even improving it over time. The difficulty is that customer expectations keep shifting, and a service provider that does not track this will soon find itself losing business. *ITIL Service Strategy* is helpful in understanding how this happens, and how a service provider can adapt its services to meet the changing customer environment.

Services can be discussed in terms of how they relate to one another and their customers, and can be classified as core, enabling or enhancing.

Core services deliver the basic outcomes desired by one or more customers. They represent the value that the customer wants and for which they are willing to pay. Core services anchor the value

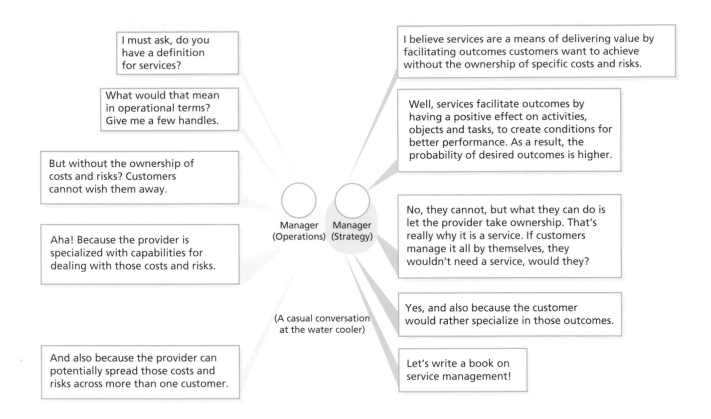

Figure 2.1 Conversation about the definition and meaning of services

proposition for the customer and provide the basis for their continued utilization and satisfaction.

Enabling services are services that are needed in order for a core service to be delivered. Enabling services may or may not be visible to the customer, but the customer does not perceive them as services in their own right. They are 'basic factors' which enable the customer to receive the 'real' (core) service.

Enhancing services are services that are added to a core service to make it more exciting or enticing to the customer. Enhancing services are not essential to the delivery of a core service, and are added to a core service as 'excitement' factors, which will encourage customers to use the core service more (or to choose the core service provided by one company over those of its competitors).

Services may be as simple as allowing a user to complete a single transaction, but most services are complex. They consist of a range of deliverables and functionality. If each individual aspect of these complex services were defined independently, the service provider would soon find it impossible to track and record all services.

Most service providers will follow a strategy where they can deliver a set of more generic services to a broad range of customers, thus achieving economies of scale and competing on the basis of price and a certain amount of flexibility. One way of achieving this is by using service packages. A service package is a collection of two or more services that have been combined to offer a solution to a specific type of customer need or to underpin specific business outcomes. A service package can consist of a combination of core services, enabling services and enhancing services.

Where a service or service package needs to be differentiated for different types of customer, one or more components of the package can be changed, or offered at different levels of utility and warranty, to create service options. These different service options can then be offered to customers and are sometimes called service level packages.

2.1.2 Service management

When we turn on a water tap, we expect to see water flow from it. When we turn on a light switch, we expect to see light fill the room. Not so many years ago, these very basic things were not as reliable as they are today. We know instinctively that the advances in technology have made them reliable enough to be considered a utility. But it isn't just the technology that makes the services reliable. It is how they are managed.

The use of IT today has become the utility of business. Business today wants IT services that behave like other utilities such as water, electricity or the telephone. Simply having the best technology will not ensure that IT provides utility-like reliability. Professional, responsive, value-driven service management is what brings this quality of service to the business.

Service management is a set of specialized organizational capabilities for providing value to customers in the form of services. The more mature a service provider's capabilities are, the greater is their ability to consistently produce quality services that meet the needs of the customer in a timely and cost-effective manner. The act of transforming capabilities and resources into valuable services is at the core of service management. Without these capabilities, a service organization is merely a bundle of resources that by itself has relatively low intrinsic value for customers.

Definitions

Service management: A set of specialized organizational capabilities for providing value to customers in the form of services.

Service provider: An organization supplying services to one or more internal or external customers.

Organizational capabilities are shaped by the challenges they are expected to overcome. An example of this is provided by Toyota in the 1950s when it developed unique capabilities to overcome the challenge of smaller scale and financial capital compared to its American rivals. Toyota developed new capabilities in production engineering, operations management and managing suppliers to compensate for its inability to afford large inventories, make components, produce raw materials or own the companies that produced them (Magretta, 2002).

Service management capabilities are similarly influenced by the following challenges that distinguish services from other systems of value creation, such as manufacturing, mining and agriculture:

- Intangible nature of the output and intermediate products of service processes: they are difficult to measure, control and validate (or prove).
- Demand is tightly coupled with the customer's assets: users and other customer assets such as processes, applications, documents and transactions arrive with demand and stimulate service production.
- High level of contact for producers and consumers of services: there is little or no buffer between the service provider's creation of the service and the customer's consumption of that service.
- The perishable nature of service output and service capacity: there is value for the customer from assurance on the continued supply of consistent quality. Providers need to secure a steady supply of demand from customers.

Service management is more than just a set of capabilities. It is also a professional practice supported by an extensive body of knowledge, experience and skills. A global community of individuals and organizations in the public and private sectors fosters its growth and maturity. Formal schemes exist for the education, training and certification of practising organizations, and individuals influence its quality. Industry best practices, academic research and formal standards contribute to and draw from its intellectual capital.

The origins of service management are in traditional service businesses such as airlines, banks, hotels and phone companies. Its practice has grown with the adoption by IT organizations of a service-oriented approach to managing IT applications, infrastructure and processes. Solutions to business problems and support for business models, strategies and operations are increasingly in the form of services. The popularity of shared services and outsourcing has contributed to the increase in the number of organizations that behave as service providers, including internal IT organizations. This in turn has strengthened the practice of service management while at the same time imposed greater challenges.

2.1.3 IT service management

Information technology (IT) is a commonly used term that changes meaning depending on the different perspectives that a business organization or people may have of it. A key challenge is to recognize and balance these perspectives when communicating the value of IT service management (ITSM) and understanding the context for how the business sees the IT organization. Some of these meanings are:

- IT is a collection of systems, applications and infrastructures which are components or sub-assemblies of a larger product. They enable or are embedded in processes and services.
- IT is an organization with its own set of capabilities and resources. IT organizations can be of various types such as business functions, shared services units and enterprise-level core units.
- IT is a category of services utilized by business. The services are typically IT applications and infrastructure that are packaged and offered by internal IT organizations or external service providers. IT costs are treated as business expenses.
- IT is a category of business assets that provide a stream of benefits for their owners, including, but not limited to, revenue, income and profit. IT costs are treated as investments.

Every IT organization should act as a service provider, using the principles of service management to ensure that they deliver the outcomes required by their customers.

Definitions

IT service management (ITSM): The implementation and management of quality IT services that meet the needs of the business. IT service management is performed by IT service providers through an appropriate mix of people, process and information technology.

IT service provider: A service provider that provides IT services to internal or external customers.

ITSM must be carried out effectively and efficiently. Managing IT from the business perspective enables organizational high performance and value creation.

A good relationship between an IT service provider and its customers relies on the customer receiving an IT service that meets its needs, at an acceptable level of performance and at a cost that the customer can afford. The IT service provider needs to work out how to achieve a balance between these three areas, and communicate with the customer if there is anything which prevents it from being able to deliver the required IT service at the agreed level of performance or price.

A service level agreement (SLA) is used to document agreements between an IT service provider and a customer. An SLA describes the IT service, documents service level targets, and specifies the responsibilities of the IT service provider and the customer. A single agreement may cover multiple IT services or multiple customers.

2.1.4 Service providers

There are three main types of service provider. While most aspects of service management apply equally to all types of service provider, other aspects such as customers, contracts, competition, market spaces, revenue and strategy take on different meanings depending on the specific type. The three types are:

- **Type I – internal service provider** An internal service provider that is embedded within a business unit. There may be several Type I service providers within an organization.
- **Type II – shared services unit** An internal service provider that provides shared IT services to more than one business unit.
- **Type III – external service provider** A service provider that provides IT services to external customers.

ITSM concepts are often described in the context of only one of these types and as if only one type of IT service provider exists or is used by a given organization. In reality most organizations have a combination of IT service providers. In a single organization it is possible that some IT units are dedicated to a single business unit, others provide shared services, and yet others have been outsourced or depend on external service providers.

Many IT organizations who traditionally provide services to internal customers find that they are dealing directly with external users because of the online services that they provide. *ITIL Service Strategy* provides guidance on how the IT organization interacts with these users, and who owns and manages the relationship with them.

2.1.5 Stakeholders in service management

Stakeholders have an interest in an organization, project or service etc. and may be interested in the activities, targets, resources or deliverables from service management. Examples include organizations, service providers, customers, consumers, users, partners, employees, shareholders, owners and suppliers. The term 'organization' is used to define a company, legal entity or other institution. It is also used to refer to any entity that has people, resources and budgets – for example, a project or business.

Within the service provider organization there are many different stakeholders including the functions, groups and teams that deliver the services. There are also many stakeholders external to the service provider organization, for example:

- **Customers** Those who buy goods or services. The customer of an IT service provider is the person or group who defines and agrees the service level targets. This term is also sometimes used informally to mean user – for example, 'This is a customer-focused organization.'
- **Users** Those who use the service on a day-to-day basis. Users are distinct from customers, as some customers do not use the IT service directly.
- **Suppliers** Third parties responsible for supplying goods or services that are required to deliver IT services. Examples of suppliers include commodity hardware and software vendors, network and telecom providers, and outsourcing organizations.

There is a difference between customers who work in the same organization as the IT service provider, and customers who work for other organizations. They are distinguished as follows:

- **Internal customers** These are customers who work for the same business as the IT service provider. For example, the marketing department is an internal customer of the IT organization because it uses IT services. The head of marketing and the chief information officer both report to the chief executive

officer. If IT charges for its services, the money paid is an internal transaction in the organization's accounting system, not real revenue.
- **External customers** These are customers who work for a different business from the IT service provider. External customers typically purchase services from the service provider by means of a legally binding contract or agreement.

2.1.6 Utility and warranty

The value of a service can be considered to be the level to which that service meets a customer's expectations. It is often measured by how much the customer is willing to pay for the service, rather than the cost to the service provider of providing the service or any other intrinsic attribute of the service itself.

Unlike products, services do not have much intrinsic value. The value of a service comes from what it enables someone to do. The value of a service is not determined by the provider, but by the person who receives it – because they decide what they will do with the service, and what type of return they will achieve by using the service. Services contribute value to an organization only when their value is perceived to be higher than the cost of obtaining the service.

From the customer's perspective, value consists of achieving business objectives. The value of a service is created by combining two primary elements: utility (fitness for purpose) and warranty (fitness for use). These two elements work together to achieve the desired outcomes upon which the customer and the business base their perceptions of a service.

Utility is the functionality offered by a product or service to meet a particular need. Utility can be summarized as 'what the service does', and can be used to determine whether a service is able to meet its required outcomes, or is 'fit for purpose'. Utility refers to those aspects of a service that contribute to tasks associated with achieving outcomes. For example, a service that enables a business unit to process orders should allow sales people to access customer details, stock availability, shipping information etc. Any aspect of the service that improves the ability of sales people to improve the performance of the task of processing sales orders would be considered utility. Utility can therefore represent any attribute of a service that removes, or reduces the effect of, constraints on the performance of a task.

Warranty is an assurance that a product or service will meet its agreed requirements. This may be a formal agreement such as a service level agreement or contract, or a marketing message or brand image. Warranty refers to the ability of a service to be available when needed, to provide the required capacity, and to provide the required reliability in terms of continuity and security. Warranty can be summarized as 'how the service is delivered', and can be used to determine whether a service is 'fit for use'. For example, any aspect of the service that increases the availability or speed of the service would be considered warranty. Warranty can therefore represent any attribute of a service that increases the potential of the business to be able to perform a task. Warranty refers to any means by which utility is made available to the users.

Utility is *what* the service does, and warranty is *how* it is delivered.

Customers cannot benefit from something that is fit for purpose but not fit for use, and vice versa. The value of a service is therefore only delivered when both utility and warranty are designed and delivered. Figure 2.2 illustrates the logic that a service has to have both utility and warranty to create value. Utility is used to improve the performance of the tasks required to achieve an outcome, or to remove constraints that prevent the task from being performed adequately (or both). Warranty requires the service to be available, continuous and secure and to have sufficient capacity for the service to perform at the required

level. If the service is both fit for purpose and fit for use, it will create value.

It should be noted that the elements of warranty in Figure 2.2 are not exclusive. It is possible to define other components of warranty, such as usability, which refers to how easy it is for the user to access and use the features of the service to achieve the desired outcomes.

The warranty aspect of the service needs to be designed at the same time as the utility aspect in order to deliver the required value to the business. Attempts to design warranty aspects after a service has been deployed can be expensive and disruptive.

Information about the desired business outcomes, opportunities, customers, utility and warranty of the service is used to develop the definition of a service. Using an outcome-based definition helps to ensure that managers plan and execute all aspects of service management from the perspective of what is valuable to the customer.

2.1.7 Best practices in the public domain

Organizations benchmark themselves against peers and seek to close gaps in capabilities. This enables them to become more competitive by improving their ability to deliver quality services that meet the needs of their customers at a price their customers can afford. One way to close such gaps is the adoption of best practices in wide industry use. There are several sources for best practice including public frameworks, standards and the proprietary knowledge of organizations and individuals (Figure 2.3). ITIL is the most widely recognized and trusted

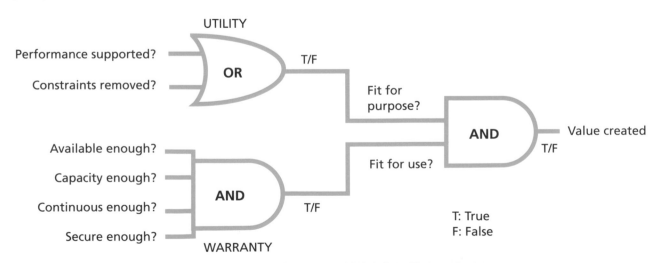

Figure 2.2 Services are designed, built and delivered with both utility and warranty

source of best-practice guidance in the area of ITSM.

Public frameworks and standards are attractive when compared with proprietary knowledge for the following reasons:

■ Proprietary knowledge is deeply embedded in organizations and therefore difficult to adopt, replicate or even transfer with the cooperation of the owners. Such knowledge is often in the form of tacit knowledge which is inextricable and poorly documented.

■ Proprietary knowledge is customized for the local context and the specific needs of the business to the point of being idiosyncratic. Unless the recipients of such knowledge have matching circumstances, the knowledge may not be as effective in use.

■ Owners of proprietary knowledge expect to be rewarded for their investments. They may make such knowledge available only under commercial terms through purchases and licensing agreements.

■ Publicly available frameworks and standards such as ITIL, LEAN, Six Sigma, COBIT, CMMI, PRINCE2, PMBOK®, ISO 9000, ISO/IEC 20000 and ISO/IEC 27001 are validated across a diverse set of environments and situations rather than the limited experience of a single organization. They are subject to broad review across multiple organizations and disciplines, and vetted by diverse sets of partners, suppliers and competitors.

■ The knowledge of public frameworks is more likely to be widely distributed among a large community of professionals through publicly available training and certification. It is easier for organizations to acquire such knowledge through the labour market.

Ignoring public frameworks and standards can needlessly place an organization at a disadvantage. Organizations should cultivate their own proprietary knowledge on top of a body of knowledge based on public frameworks and standards. Collaboration and coordination across organizations become easier on the basis of shared practices and standards. Further information on

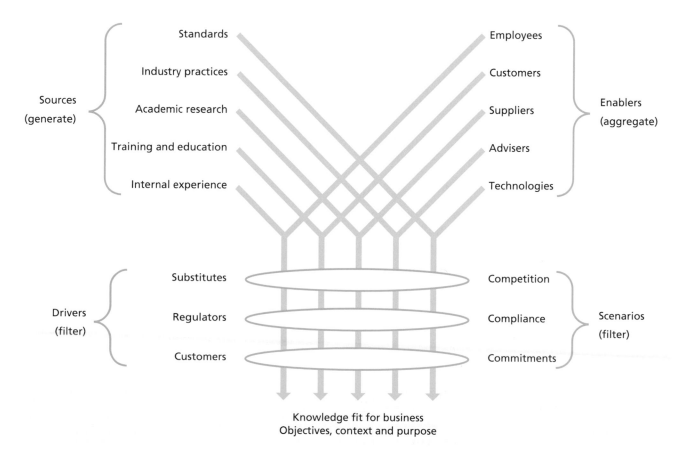

Figure 2.3 Sources of service management best practice

best practice in the public domain is provided in Appendix D.

2.2 BASIC CONCEPTS

2.2.1 Assets, resources and capabilities

The service relationship between service providers and their customers revolves around the use of assets – both those of the service provider and those of the customer. Each relationship involves an interaction between the assets of each party.

Many customers use the service they receive from a service provider to build and deliver services or products of their own and then deliver them on to their own customers. In these cases, what the service provider considers to be the customer asset would be considered to be a service asset by their customer.

Without customer assets, there is no basis for defining the value of a service. The performance of customer assets is therefore a primary concern for service management.

Definitions

Asset: Any resource or capability.

Customer asset: Any resource or capability used by a customer to achieve a business outcome.

Service asset: Any resource or capability used by a service provider to deliver services to a customer.

There are two types of asset used by both service providers and customers – resources and capabilities. Organizations use them to create value in the form of goods and services. Resources are direct inputs for production. Capabilities represent an organization's ability to coordinate, control and deploy resources to produce value. Capabilities are typically experience-driven, knowledge-intensive, information-based and firmly embedded within an organization's people, systems, processes and technologies. It is relatively easy to acquire resources compared to capabilities (see Figure 2.4 for examples of capabilities and resources).

Service providers need to develop distinctive capabilities to retain customers with value propositions that are hard for competitors to duplicate. For example, two service providers may have similar resources such as applications,

infrastructure and access to finance. Their capabilities, however, differ in terms of management systems, organization structure, processes and knowledge assets. This difference is reflected in actual performance.

Capabilities by themselves cannot produce value without adequate and appropriate resources. The productive capacity of a service provider is dependent on the resources under its control. Capabilities are used to develop, deploy and coordinate this productive capacity. For example, capabilities such as capacity management and availability management are used to manage the performance and utilization of processes, applications and infrastructure, ensuring service levels are effectively delivered.

2.2.2 Processes

Definition: process

A process is a structured set of activities designed to accomplish a specific objective. A process takes one or more defined inputs and turns them into defined outputs.

Processes define actions, dependencies and sequence. Well-defined processes can improve productivity within and across organizations and functions. Process characteristics include:

- **Measurability** We are able to measure the process in a relevant manner. It is performance-driven. Managers want to measure cost, quality and other variables while practitioners are concerned with duration and productivity.
- **Specific results** The reason a process exists is to deliver a specific result. This result must be individually identifiable and countable.
- **Customers** Every process delivers its primary results to a customer or stakeholder. Customers may be internal or external to the organization, but the process must meet their expectations.
- **Responsiveness to specific triggers** While a process may be ongoing or iterative, it should be traceable to a specific trigger.

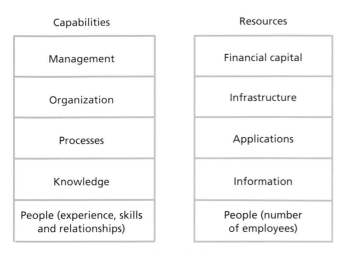

Capabilities	Resources
Management	Financial capital
Organization	Infrastructure
Processes	Applications
Knowledge	Information
People (experience, skills and relationships)	People (number of employees)

Figure 2.4 Examples of capabilities and resources

A process is organized around a set of objectives. The main outputs from the process should be driven by the objectives and should include process measurements (metrics), reports and process improvement.

The output produced by a process has to conform to operational norms that are derived from business objectives. If products conform to the set norm, the process can be considered effective (because it can be repeated, measured and managed, and achieves the required outcome). If the activities of the process are carried out with a minimum use of resources, the process can also be considered efficient.

Inputs are data or information used by the process and may be the output from another process.

A process, or an activity within a process, is initiated by a trigger. A trigger may be the arrival of an input or other event. For example, the failure of a server may trigger the event management and incident management processes.

A process may include any of the roles, responsibilities, tools and management controls required to deliver the outputs reliably. A process may define policies, standards, guidelines, activities and work instructions if they are needed.

Processes, once defined, should be documented and controlled. Once under control, they can be repeated and managed. Process measurement and metrics can be built into the process to control and improve the process as illustrated in Figure 2.5. Process analysis, results and metrics should be

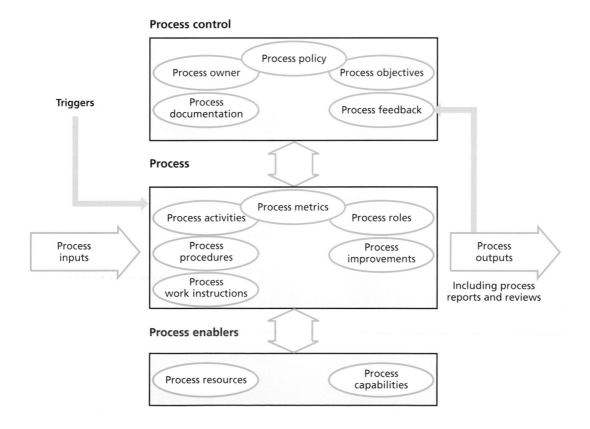

Figure 2.5 Process model

incorporated in regular management reports and process improvements.

2.2.3 Organizing for service management

There is no single best way to organize, and best practices described in ITIL need to be tailored to suit individual organizations and situations. Any changes made will need to take into account resource constraints and the size, nature and needs of the business and customers. The starting point for organizational design is strategy. Organizational development for service management is described in more detail in Chapter 6.

2.2.3.1 Functions

A function is a team or group of people and the tools or other resources they use to carry out one or more processes or activities. In larger organizations, a function may be broken out and performed by several departments, teams and groups, or it may be embodied within a single organizational unit (e.g. the service desk). In smaller organizations, one person or group can perform multiple functions – for example, a technical management department could also incorporate the service desk function.

For the service lifecycle to be successful, an organization will need to clearly define the roles and responsibilities required to undertake the processes and activities involved in each lifecycle stage. These roles will need to be assigned to individuals, and an appropriate organization structure of teams, groups or functions will need to be established and managed. These are defined as follows:

- **Group** A group is a number of people who are similar in some way. In ITIL, groups refer to people who perform similar activities – even though they may work on different technologies or report into different organizational structures or even different companies. Groups are usually not formal organizational structures, but are very useful in defining common processes across the organization – for example, ensuring that all people who resolve incidents complete the incident record in the same way.
- **Team** A team is a more formal type of group. These are people who work together to achieve a common objective, but not necessarily in the same organizational structure. Team members can be co-located, or work in multiple locations and operate virtually. Teams are useful for collaboration, or for dealing with a situation of a temporary or transitional nature. Examples of teams include project teams, application development teams (often consisting of people from several different business units) and incident or problem resolution teams.
- **Department** Departments are formal organizational structures which exist to perform a specific set of defined activities on an ongoing basis. Departments have a hierarchical reporting structure with managers who are usually responsible for the execution of the activities and also for day-to-day management of the staff in the department.
- **Division** A division refers to a number of departments that have been grouped together, often by geography or product line. A division is normally self-contained.

ITIL Service Operation describes the following functions in detail:

- **Service desk** The single point of contact for users when there is a service disruption, for service requests, or even for some categories of request for change. The service desk provides a point of communication to the users and a point of coordination for several IT groups and processes.
- **Technical management** Provides detailed technical skills and resources needed to support the ongoing operation of IT services and the management of the IT infrastructure. Technical management also plays an important role in the design, testing, release and improvement of IT services.
- **IT operations management** Executes the daily operational activities needed to manage IT services and the supporting IT infrastructure. This is done according to the performance standards defined during service design. IT operations management has two sub-functions that are generally organizationally distinct. These are IT operations control and facilities management.
- **Application management** Is responsible for managing applications throughout their lifecycle. The application management function

supports and maintains operational applications and also plays an important role in the design, testing and improvement of applications that form part of IT services.

The other core ITIL publications do not define any functions in detail, but they do rely on the technical and application management functions described in *ITIL Service Operation*. Technical and application management provide the technical resources and expertise to manage the whole service lifecycle, and practitioner roles within a particular lifecycle stage may be performed by members of these functions.

2.2.3.2 Roles

A number of roles need to be performed during the service lifecycle. The core ITIL publications provide guidelines and examples of role descriptions. These are not exhaustive or prescriptive, and in many cases roles will need to be combined or separated. Organizations should take care to apply this guidance in a way that suits their own structure and objectives.

Definition: role

A role is a set of responsibilities, activities and authorities granted to a person or team. A role is defined in a process or function. One person or team may have multiple roles – for example, the roles of configuration manager and change manager may be carried out by a single person.

Roles are often confused with job titles but it is important to realize that they are not the same. Each organization will define appropriate job titles and job descriptions which suit their needs, and individuals holding these job titles can perform one or more of the required roles.

It should also be recognized that a person may, as part of their job assignment, perform a single task that represents participation in more than one process. For example, a technical analyst who submits a request for change (RFC) to add memory to a server to resolve a performance problem is participating in activities of the change management process at the same time as taking part in activities of the capacity management and problem management processes.

See Chapter 6 for more details about the roles and responsibilities described *ITIL Service Strategy*.

2.2.3.3 Organizational culture and behaviour

Organizational culture is the set of shared values and norms that control the service provider's interactions with all stakeholders, including customers, users, suppliers, internal staff etc. An organization's values are desired modes of behaviour that affect its culture. Examples of organizational values include high standards, customer care, respecting tradition and authority, acting cautiously and conservatively, and being frugal.

High-performing service providers continually align the value network for efficiency and effectiveness. Culture through the value network is transmitted to staff through socialization, training programmes, stories, ceremonies and language.

Constraints such as governance, capabilities, standards, resources, values and ethics play a significant role in organization culture and behaviour. Organizational culture can also be affected by structure or management styles resulting in a positive or negative impact on performance. Organizational structures and management styles contribute to the behaviour of people, process, technology and partners. These are important aspects in adopting service management practices and ITIL.

Change related to service management programmes will affect organizational culture and it is important to prepare people with effective communication plans, training, policies and procedures to achieve the desired performance outcomes. Establishing cultural change is also an important factor for collaborative working between the many different people involved in service management. Managing people through service transitions is discussed at more length in Chapter 5 of *ITIL Service Transition*.

2.2.4 The service portfolio

The service portfolio is the complete set of services that is managed by a service provider and it represents the service provider's commitments and investments across all customers and market spaces. It also represents present contractual commitments, new service development, and ongoing service improvement plans initiated by continual service improvement. The portfolio may include third-party services, which are an integral part of service offerings to customers.

The service portfolio represents all the resources presently engaged or being released in various stages of the service lifecycle. It is a database or structured document in three parts:

- **Service pipeline** All services that are under consideration or development, but are not yet available to customers. It includes major investment opportunities that have to be traced to the delivery of services, and the value that will be realized. The service pipeline provides a business view of possible future services and is part of the service portfolio that is not normally published to customers.
- **Service catalogue** All live IT services, including those available for deployment. It is the only part of the service portfolio published to customers, and is used to support the sale and delivery of IT services. It includes a customer-facing view (or views) of the IT services in use, how they are intended to be used, the business processes they enable, and the levels and quality of service the customer can expect for each service. The service catalogue also includes information about supporting services required by the service provider to deliver customer-facing services. Information about services can only enter the service catalogue after due diligence has been performed on related costs and risks.
- **Retired services** All services that have been phased out or retired. Retired services are not available to new customers or contracts unless a special business case is made.

Service providers often find it useful to distinguish customer-facing services from supporting services:

- **Customer-facing services** IT services that are visible to the customer. These are normally services that support the customer's business processes and facilitate one or more outcomes desired by the customer.
- **Supporting services** IT services that support or 'underpin' the customer-facing services. These are typically invisible to the customer, but are essential to the delivery of customer-facing IT services.

Figure 2.6 illustrates the components of the service portfolio, which are discussed in detail in section 4.2. These are important components of the service knowledge management system (SKMS) described in section 2.2.5.

2.2.5 Knowledge management and the SKMS

Quality knowledge and information enable people to perform process activities and support the flow of information between service lifecycle stages and processes. Understanding, defining, establishing and maintaining information is a responsibility of the knowledge management process.

Implementing an SKMS enables effective decision support and reduces the risks that arise from a lack of proper mechanisms. However, implementing an SKMS can involve a large investment in tools to store and manage data, information and knowledge. Every organization will start this work in a different place, and have their own vision of where they want to be, so there is no simple answer to the question 'What tools and systems are needed to support knowledge management?' Data, information and knowledge need to be interrelated across the organization. A document management system and/or a configuration management system (CMS) can be used as a foundation for implementation of the SKMS.

Figure 2.7 illustrates an architecture for service knowledge management that has four layers including examples of possible content at each layer. These are:

- **Presentation layer** Enables searching, browsing, retrieving, updating, subscribing and collaboration. The different views onto the other layers are suitable for different audiences. Each view should be protected to ensure that only authorized people can see or modify the underlying knowledge, information and data.
- **Knowledge processing layer** Is where the information is converted into useful knowledge which enables decision-making.
- **Information integration layer** Provides integrated information that may be gathered from data in multiple sources in the data layer.
- **Data layer** Includes tools for data discovery and data collection, and data items in unstructured and structured forms.

In practice, an SKMS is likely to consist of multiple tools and repositories. For example, there may be a tool that provides all four layers for the support of different processes or combinations of processes. Various tools providing a range of perspectives will be used by different stakeholders to access this

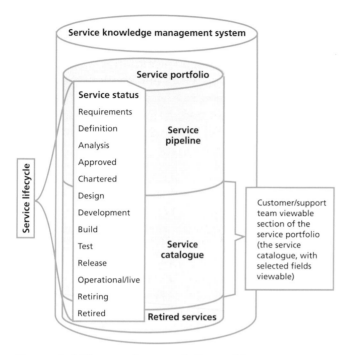

Figure 2.6 The service portfolio and its contents

common repository for collaborative decision support.

This architecture is applicable for many of the management information systems in ITIL. A primary component of the SKMS is the service portfolio, covered in section 2.2.4. Other examples include the CMS, the availability management information system (AMIS) and the capacity management information system (CMIS).

2.3 GOVERNANCE AND MANAGEMENT SYSTEMS

2.3.1 Governance

Governance is the single overarching area that ties IT and the business together, and services are one way of ensuring that the organization is able to execute that governance. Governance is what defines the common directions, policies and rules that both the business and IT use to conduct business.

Many ITSM strategies fail because they try to build a structure or processes according to how they would like the organization to work instead of working within the existing governance structures.

Definition: governance

Ensures that policies and strategy are actually implemented, and that required processes are correctly followed. Governance includes defining roles and responsibilities, measuring and reporting, and taking actions to resolve any issues identified.

Governance works to apply a consistently managed approach at all levels of the organization – first by ensuring a clear strategy is set, then by defining the policies whereby the strategy will be achieved. The policies also define boundaries, or what the organization may not do as part of its operations.

Governance needs to be able to evaluate, direct and monitor the strategy, policies and plans. Further information on governance and service management is provided in Chapter 5. The international standard for corporate governance of IT is ISO/IEC 38500, described in Appendix D.

2.3.2 Management systems

A system is a number of related things that work together to achieve an overall objective. Systems should be self-regulating for agility and timeliness. In order to accomplish this, the relationships within the system must influence one another for the sake of the whole. Key components of the system are the structure and processes that work together.

A systems approach to service management ensures learning and improvement through a big-picture view of services and service management. It extends the management horizon and provides a sustainable long-term approach.

By understanding the system structure, the interconnections between all the assets and service components, and how changes in any area will affect the whole system and its constituent parts over time, a service provider can deliver benefits such as:

■ Ability to adapt to the changing needs of customers and markets
■ Sustainable performance
■ Better approach to managing services, risks, costs and value delivery
■ Effective and efficient service management
■ Simplified approach that is easier for people to use
■ Less conflict between processes
■ Reduced duplication and bureaucracy.

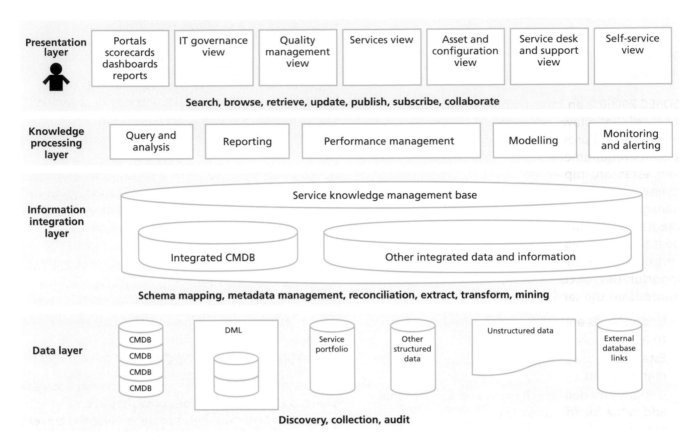

Figure 2.7 Architectural layers of an SKMS

Many businesses have adopted management system standards for competitive advantage and to ensure a consistent approach in implementing service management across their value network. Implementation of a management system also provides support for governance (see section 2.3.1).

Definition: management system (ISO 9001)

The framework of policy, processes, functions, standards, guidelines and tools that ensures an organization or part of an organization can achieve its objectives.

A management system of an organization can adopt multiple management system standards, such as:

■ A quality management system (ISO 9001)
■ An environmental management system (ISO 14000)
■ An service management system (ISO/IEC 20000)
■ An information security management system (ISO/IEC 27001)
■ A management system for software asset management (ISO/IEC 19770).

Service providers are increasingly adopting these standards to be able to demonstrate their service management capability. As there are common elements between such management systems, they should be managed in an integrated way rather than having separate management systems. To meet the requirements of a specific management system standard, an organization needs to analyse the requirements of the relevant standard in detail and compare them with those that have already been incorporated in the existing integrated management system. Appendix D provides further information on these standards.

ISO management system standards use the Plan-Do-Check-Act (PDCA) cycle shown in Figure 2.8. The ITIL service lifecycle approach embraces and enhances the interpretation of the PDCA cycle. You will see the PDCA cycle used in the structure of the guidance provided in each of the core ITIL publications. This guidance recognizes the need to drive governance, organizational design and management systems from the business strategy, service strategy and service requirements.

Definition: ISO/IEC 20000

An international standard for IT service management.

ISO/IEC 20000 is an internationally recognized standard that allows organizations to demonstrate excellence and prove best practice in ITSM. Part 1 specifies requirements for the service provider to plan, establish, implement, operate, monitor, review, maintain and improve a service management system (SMS). Coordinated integration and implementation of an SMS, to meet the Part 1 requirements, provides ongoing control, greater effectiveness, efficiency and opportunities for continual improvement. It ensures that the service provider:

- Understands and fulfils the service requirements to achieve customer satisfaction
- Establishes the policy and objectives for service management
- Designs and delivers changes and services that add value for the customer
- Monitors, measures and reviews performance of the SMS and the services
- Continually improves the SMS and the services based on objective measurements.

Service providers across the world have successfully established an SMS to direct and control their service management activities. The adoption of an SMS should be a strategic decision for an organization.

One of the most common routes for an organization to achieve the requirements of ISO/IEC 20000 is by adopting ITIL service management best practices and using the ITIL qualification scheme for professional development.

Certification to ISO/IEC 20000-1 by an accredited certification body shows that a service provider is committed to delivering value to its customers and continual service improvement. It demonstrates the existence of an effective SMS that satisfies the requirements of an independent external audit. Certification gives a service provider a competitive edge in marketing. Many organizations specify a requirement to comply with ISO/IEC 20000 in their contracts and agreements.

2.4 THE SERVICE LIFECYCLE

Services and processes describe how things change, whereas structure describes how they are connected. Structure helps to determine the correct behaviours required for service management.

Structure describes how process, people, technology and partners are connected. Structure is essential for organizing information. Without structure, our service management knowledge is merely a collection of observations, practices and conflicting goals. The structure of the service lifecycle is an organizing framework, supported by

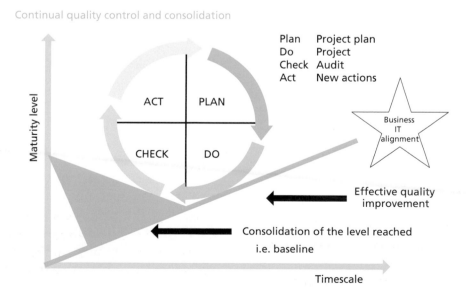

Figure 2.8 Plan-Do-Check-Act cycle

Table 2.1 The processes described in each core ITIL publication

Core ITIL lifecycle publication	Processes described in the publication
ITIL Service Strategy	Strategy management for IT services
	Service portfolio management
	Financial management for IT services
	Demand management
	Business relationship management
ITIL Service Design	Design coordination
	Service catalogue management
	Service level management
	Availability management
	Capacity management
	IT service continuity management
	Information security management
	Supplier management
ITIL Service Transition	Transition planning and support
	Change management
	Service asset and configuration management
	Release and deployment management
	Service validation and testing
	Change evaluation
	Knowledge management
ITIL Service Operation	Event management
	Incident management
	Request fulfilment
	Problem management
	Access management
ITIL Continual Service Improvement	Seven-step improvement process

the organizational structure, service portfolio and service models within an organization. Structure can influence or determine the behaviour of the organization and people. Altering the structure of service management can be more effective than simply controlling discrete events.

Without structure, it is difficult to learn from experience. It is difficult to use the past to educate for the future. We can learn from experience but we also need to confront directly many of the most important consequences of our actions.

See Chapter 1 for an introduction to each ITIL service lifecycle stage.

2.4.1 Specialization and coordination across the lifecycle

Organizations need a collaborative approach for the management of assets which are used to deliver and support services for their customers.

Organizations should function in the same manner as a high-performing sports team. Each player in a team and each member of the team's organization who are not players position themselves to support the goal of the team. Each player and team member has a different specialization that contributes to the whole. The team matures over time taking into account feedback from experience, best practice, current process and procedures to become an agile high-performing team.

Specialization and coordination are necessary in the lifecycle approach. Specialization allows for expert focus on components of the service but components of the service also need to work together for value. Specialization combined with coordination helps to manage expertise, improve focus and reduce overlaps and gaps in processes. Specialization and coordination together help to create a collaborative and agile organizational architecture that maximizes utilization of assets.

Coordination across the lifecycle creates an environment focused on business and customer outcomes instead of just IT objectives and projects. Coordination is also essential between functional groups, across the value network, and between processes and technology.

Feedback and control between organizational assets helps to enable operational efficiency, organizational effectiveness and economies of scale.

2.4.2 Processes through the service lifecycle

Each core ITIL lifecycle publication includes guidance on service management processes as shown in Table 2.1.

Service management is more effective if people have a clear understanding of how processes interact throughout the service lifecycle, within the organization and with other parties (users, customers, suppliers).

Process integration across the service lifecycle depends on the service owner, process owners, process practitioners and other stakeholders understanding:

■ The context of use, scope, purpose and limits of each process
■ The strategies, policies and standards that apply to the processes and to the management of interfaces between processes
■ Authorities and responsibilities of those involved in each process
■ The information provided by each process that flows from one process to another; who produces it; and how it is used by integrated processes.

Integrating service management processes depends on the flow of information across process and organizational boundaries. This in turn depends on implementing supporting technology and management information systems across organizational boundaries, rather than in silos. If service management processes are implemented, followed or changed in isolation, they can become a bureaucratic overhead that does not deliver value for money. They could also damage or negate the operation or value of other processes and services.

As discussed in section 2.2.2, each process has a clear scope with a structured set of activities that transform inputs to deliver the outputs reliably. A process interface is the boundary of the process. Process integration is the linking of processes by ensuring that information flows from one process to another effectively and efficiently. If there is management commitment to process integration, processes are generally easier to implement and there will be fewer conflicts between processes.

Stages of the lifecycle work together as an integrated system to support the ultimate objective of service management for business value realization. Every stage is interdependent as shown in Figure 2.9. See Appendix F for examples of inputs and outputs across the service lifecycle.

The SKMS, described in section 2.2.5, enables integration across the service lifecycle stages. It provides secure and controlled access to the knowledge, information and data that are needed to manage and deliver services. The service portfolio represents all the assets presently engaged or being released in various stages of the lifecycle.

Chapter 1 provides a summary of each stage in the service lifecycle but it is also important to understand how the lifecycle stages work together.

Service strategy establishes policies and principles that provide guidance for the whole service lifecycle. The service portfolio is defined in this lifecycle stage, and new or changed services are chartered.

During the service design stage of the lifecycle, everything needed to transition and operate the new or changed service is documented in a service design package. This lifecycle stage also designs everything needed to create, transition and operate the services, including management

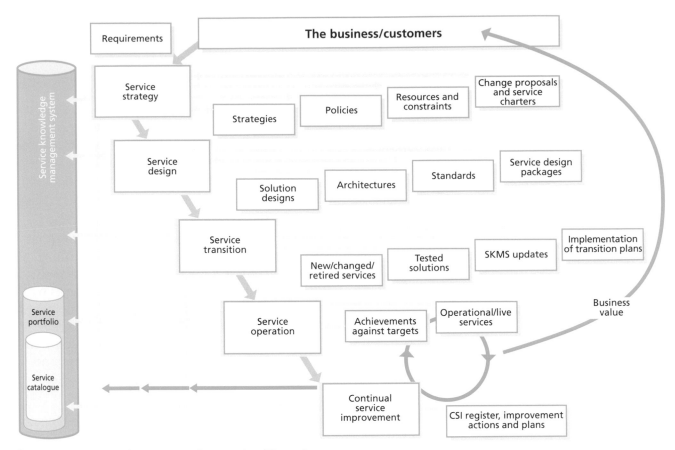

Figure 2.9 Integration across the service lifecycle

information systems and tools, architectures, processes, measurement methods and metrics.

The activities of the service transition and service operation stages of the lifecycle are defined during service design. Service transition ensures that the requirements of the service strategy, developed in service design, are effectively realized in service operation while controlling the risks of failure and disruption.

The service operation stage of the service lifecycle carries out the activities and processes required to deliver the agreed services. During this stage of the lifecycle, the value defined in the service strategy is realized.

Continual service improvement acts in tandem with all the other lifecycle stages. All processes, activities, roles, services and technology should be measured and subjected to continual improvement.

Most ITIL processes and functions have activities that take place across multiple stages of the service lifecycle. For example:

■ The service validation and testing process may design tests during the service design stage and perform these tests during service transition.
■ The technical management function may provide input to strategic decisions about technology, as well as assisting in the design and transition of infrastructure components.
■ Business relationship managers may assist in gathering detailed requirements during the service design stage of the lifecycle, or take part in the management of major incidents during the service operation stage.
■ All service lifecycle stages contribute to the seven-step improvement process.

Appendix F identifies some of the major inputs and outputs between each stage of the service lifecycle. Chapter 3 of each core ITIL publication provides more detail on the inputs and outputs of the specific lifecycle stage it describes.

The strength of the service lifecycle rests upon continual feedback throughout each stage of the lifecycle. This feedback ensures that service optimization is managed from a business

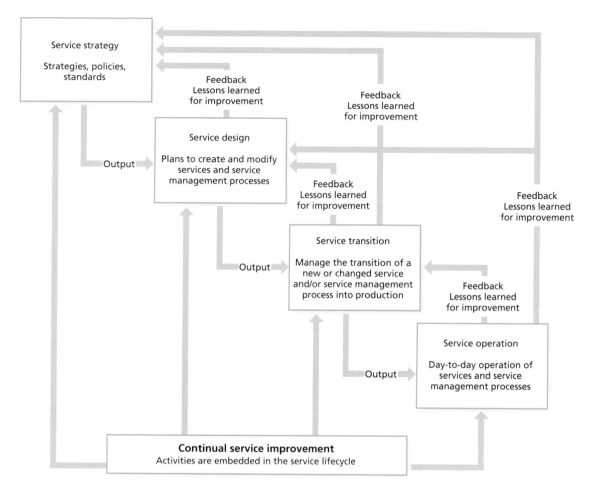

Figure 2.10 Continual service improvement and the service lifecycle

perspective and is measured in terms of the value the business derives from services at any point in time during the service lifecycle. The service lifecycle is non-linear in design. At every point in the service lifecycle, the process of monitoring, assessment and feedback between each stage drives decisions about the need for minor course corrections or major service improvement initiatives.

Figure 2.10 illustrates some examples of the continual feedback system built into the service lifecycle.

Adopting appropriate technology to automate the processes and provide management with the information that supports the processes is also important for effective and efficient service management.

Service strategy principles

3

3 Service strategy principles

'People do not want quarter-inch drills. They want quarter-inch holes.' Professor Emeritus Theodore Levitt, Harvard Business School

3.1 STRATEGY

'The essence of strategy is choosing what not to do.' (Porter, 1996)

Case study: security services

At some time in 2001, a global network security services provider lost a major customer due to quality concerns materially affecting revenues and profits. Senior executives demanded that something be done – either cut costs or find a replacement customer.

While a replacement customer was sought, service operations dutifully reduced costs. Service quality was impacted, prompting three recently acquired customers to depart – further negatively affecting revenues and profits.

Senior executives again demanded that something be done – either cut costs or find replacement customers.

Solution

Surprisingly, the solution was to suspend new sales. The chief information officer (CIO) understood that:

- Service operations were caught in a vicious cycle with disastrous long-term consequences
- Customers were leaving due to a strategic weakness. Customers differentiated the value of security services through service quality. Strategies based on cost and technology were incorrect.

By re-focusing staff and budget on service operations, the organization repaired and rebuilt its distinctive quality capabilities for remaining customers. Customer churn was halted.

The solution, while painful in the short term, allowed the provider to break the vicious cycle and pave a long-term strategy for regaining customers. The counter-intuitive breakthrough was based on (a) a big picture view of services, and (b) the precept of superior performance versus competing alternatives.

At the most simple level, a strategy is a plan that outlines how an organization will meet a designed set of objectives. As will be seen in this publication, strategies are rarely as simple as a single plan. A strategy is a complex set of planning activities in which an organization seeks to move from one situation to another in response to a number of internal and external variables.

A service strategy specifically defines how a service provider will use services to achieve the business outcomes of its customers, thereby enabling the service provider (whether internal or external) to meet its objectives. *ITIL Service Strategy* outlines the concepts necessary to define a successful service strategy, but specifically focuses on defining an IT service strategy.

An IT strategy focuses on how an organization intends to use and organize technology to meet its business objectives. An IT strategy typically includes an IT service strategy.

3.1.1 Fundamental aspects of strategy

Carl von Clausewitz remarked, 'Everything in strategy is very simple, but that does not mean that everything is very easy'. Strategic thought and action can be difficult for the following reasons:

- Defining and executing even a simple strategy involves complex issues such as organizational impact, uncertainty and conflicting priorities and objectives. Experience and codes of practice alone are often not enough to deal with these.
- They involve using complex analysis models to analyse current patterns, project future trends and then estimate the probability of each trend becoming reality.
- They focus on all factors regarding the organization and its environment and the interactions between them. The scope of even simple strategies can appear to be intimidating, but it is still important to take these areas into account.
- Since strategists are dealing with uncertainty, they may spend significant effort investigating the underlying principles of the strategy, only to find that there is so much uncertainty that they have to fall back on basic theory.

3.1.1.1 Using theory to support strategy

Theory is often discounted because of associations with the abstract or impractical. Theory, however, is the basis of best practice. Engineers use theory to solve practical problems. Investment banks use portfolio theory to validate investments. Key methods of Six Sigma are based on the theories of probability and statistics.

Managers rely on mental models that will assure them that they will indeed achieve desired outcomes. Trouble occurs when they use the wrong mental model for the problem at hand. What appears as unfixable or random often looks that way because of a misunderstanding of a process or system. Without underlying principles, it is not possible to explain why a perfectly good solution fails in one instance after tremendous success in another.

3.1.1.2 Strategy must enable service providers to deliver value

A good business model describes the means of fulfilling an organization's objectives. However, without a strategy that in some way makes a service provider uniquely valuable to the customer, there is little to prevent alternatives from displacing the provider, degrading its mission or entering its market space. A service strategy therefore defines a unique approach for delivering better value. The need for having a service strategy is not limited to service providers who are commercial enterprises. Internal service providers need just as much to have a clear perspective, positioning and plans to ensure they remain relevant to the business strategies of their enterprises.

Customers continually seek to improve their business models and strategies. They want solutions that break through performance barriers – and achieve higher quality of outcomes in business processes with little or no increase in cost. Such solutions are usually made available through innovative products and services. If such solutions are not available within a customer's existing span of control, service contracts or value network, they are compelled to look elsewhere.

Service providers should not take for granted their position and role within their customer's plans even though they have the advantage of being incumbents. The value of services from a customer's perspective may change over time due to conditions, events and factors outside a provider's control. A strategic view of service management means a carefully considered approach to the relationships with customers and a state of readiness in dealing with the uncertainties in the value that defines that relationship.

3.1.1.3 A basic approach to deciding a strategy

Imagine you have been given responsibility for an IT organization. This organization could be internal or external, commercial or not-for-profit. How would you go about deciding on a strategy to serve customers?

Firstly, acknowledge that there exist other organizations whose aim is to compete with your organization. Even government agencies are subject to competitive forces. While the value they create can sometimes be difficult to define and measure, these forces demand that an organization should perform its mission better than the alternatives as efficiently as possible.

Secondly, decide on an objective or end-state that differentiates the value of what you do, or how you do it, so that customers do not perceive greater value could be generated from any other alternative. The form of value may be monetary, as in higher profits or lower expenses, or social, as in saving lives or collecting taxes. The differentiation can come in the form of barriers to entry, such as your organization's know-how of your customer's business or the broadness of your service offerings. Or it may be in the form of raising switching costs, such as lower cost structures generated through specialization or service sourcing. Either way, it is a means of doing better by being different. This is often expressed in the vision and mission – which are important in articulating how the service provider differentiates itself and provides unique value to its customers.

The basic premise of service strategy is that service providers must meet objectives defined in terms of their customers' business outcomes while subject to a system of constraints. In a world of constrained resources and capabilities, they must hold their positions against competing alternatives. By understanding the trade-offs involved in its strategic choices, such as services to offer or markets to serve, an organization can better serve customers and outperform its competitors. The goal of a service strategy can be summed up very simply: superior performance versus competing alternatives.

3.1.1.4 Service management as a strategic asset

Case study: use of service management as a strategic asset

At some time in the mid-1990s, a line manager for a leading internet service provider (ISP) noticed a large amount of increased traffic on the bulletin board folders for two satiric stock analysts. The ISP had adopted the strategic perspective of, 'Consumer connectivity first – anytime, anywhere'.

Rather than caution the subscribers about the abnormal increase in capacity usage, the manager took an alternative path.

Solution

The manager used service management as a strategic asset. Rather than caution the subscribers about the marked increase in capacity usage, the manager offered the irreverent analysts the chance to create their own site. The site, now called the Motley Fool, continues to be a heavily trafficked destination for financial advice. The line manager eventually became president of programming.

The manager understood the service provider's strategic intent: deeper consumer connectivity or broader distribution.

Successful strategies are based on the ability to take advantage of a set of distinct capabilities in offering superior value to customers through services. Such capabilities are viewed as strategic assets because a service provider can depend on them for success. Success comes from not only delivering value to customers but also being able to generate returns on investments. Strategic assets are carefully developed bundles of tangibles and intangibles, most notably knowledge, experience, systems and processes. Service management is a strategic asset because it constitutes the core capabilities for service providers. Service management acts as an operating system for service assets in effectively deploying them to provide services.

3.1.1.5 Strategy synthesizes opposing dynamics

A service strategy is sometimes thought of as a future course of action. When senior managers are asked to craft a strategy, the frequent response is a strategic plan detailing how the organization moves from its current state to a desired future state. But there are shortcomings with this understanding of service strategy.

The first opposing dynamic is future versus present. The pace of business change is quickening, no matter how large or specific the organization or in what industry it competes. Opportunities arise while others disappear. What was good about a plan today may be rendered a liability tomorrow. A service strategy resolves big issues so that staff can get on with the small details – how best to provide services, for example, rather than debating what services to offer. But focusing on a strategic plan impedes the organization's ability to respond to changing conditions. Organizations with a high reliance on consistency and formalized procedures, for example, may lose flexibility, the ability to innovate or the ability to adapt quickly to unforeseen conditions. It turns out that a planning approach, while necessary, is insufficient – a service strategy requires more than a plan or direction.

The second dynamic is operational effectiveness versus improvements in functionality that lead to increased competitive advantage. Organizations that have a constant focus on improving operational effectiveness are often not able to improve their competitive advantage. While operational effectiveness is absolutely necessary, it is often not enough to remain competitive. For example, an organization may be able to achieve minimal defects in quality, but if it does not deliver the service that the customer expects, it will not be able to retain its customers. A service strategy explains how a service provider will do better – either in what it does or how it does it – not only compared to itself but against competing alternatives. If a provider's strategy focuses on operational effectiveness at the expense of distinctiveness, it will not prosper for long. Sooner or later every organization runs into competitors. This is true even for public sector organizations, where a one-sided focus on efficiency or effectiveness may cause their organization to reconsider outsourcing IT to an organization that is better able to differentiate itself in the public sector.

The third dynamic is 'value capture' when innovations are launched versus the value captured during ongoing operations. Plans are not well suited to provide the ongoing insight needed to maintain a value capture capability. Value capture is that portion of value creation that a provider is able to keep. While a service provider may create value through distinctiveness, it may not be able to keep any of it – since each innovation is costly. Moreover, the conditions for capturing value do not last indefinitely. There is a very small window between the time the innovation is launched and the time when the next competitor has the same capability. The more competitors, the lower the costs will be driven, and the more difficult it will be to capture value. Each innovation becomes standard operation after it is deployed, and strategy needs to find a balance between entrenching the current innovation and looking for the next opportunity.

> **Note on value capture**
>
> Value capture may not always be possible, especially in public sector organizations. In these cases it is important to focus on demonstrating value for money, to ensure continued allocation of the budget to cover innovation and ongoing improvement.

Strategic failure is often the result of an organization failing to recognize and manage these opposing dynamics. For an IT executive to be a strategist means not just holding opposing views but having the ability to synthesize them. They include the ability to react *and* predict, adapt *and* plan. In fact, high-performing service providers are skilled in blending frames of reference when crafting service strategy. This is illustrated in Figure 3.1.

3.1.1.6 Strategy as a means to outperform competitors

Service providers must meet objectives defined in terms of their customers' business outcomes while subject to a system of constraints. By understanding the trade-offs involved in its strategic choices, such as services to offer or markets to serve, an organization can better serve customers and outperform its competitors. The goal of a service

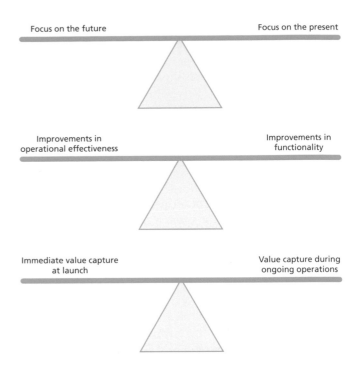

Figure 3.1 Achieving a balance between opposing strategic dynamics

strategy can be summed up as superior performance versus competing alternatives.

A high-performance service strategy, therefore, is one that enables a service provider to consistently outperform competing alternatives over time, across business cycles, industry disruptions and changes in leadership. It comprises both the ability to succeed today and positioning for the future.

3.1.1.7 Government and non-profit organizations

At first glance, it might seem that government and non-profit organizations are not affected by the pressures of competition and markets. The ethics of social-sector services are about helping people, not beating them. However, government and non-profit organizations must also operate under limited and constrained resources and capabilities. Stakeholders and customers demand as much social return as possible for money invested. Eventually, these constituents will consider competing alternatives.

A government or non-profit organization's strategy, much like that of its commercial counterparts, explains how its unique service approach will deliver better results for society. When the need for social-sector services is so demanding, superior performance versus competing alternatives is very important. No commercial enterprise can succeed by attempting to be all things to all people. Similarly, governments and non-profit organizations should make choices in what they will and, just as importantly, will not do.

Finally, it should be noted that government and non-profit organizations can and do compete with private sector organizations. Policy makers often look at economies of alternative delivery models, which may lead to outsourcing elements, or complete services. Therefore, even governments and non-profit organizations need to view themselves in a constantly competitive environment.

3.1.2 The four Ps of strategy

Mintzberg (1994) introduced four forms of strategy that should be present whenever a strategy is defined. These are illustrated in Figure 3.2 (after Simons, 1995).

The four Ps are:

- **Perspective** Describes the vision and direction of the organization. A strategic perspective articulates what the business of the organization is, how it interacts with the customer and how its services or products will be provided. A perspective cements a service provider's distinctiveness in the minds of the employees and customers.
- **Positions** Describe how the service provider intends to compete against other service providers in the market. The position refers to the attributes and capabilities that the service provider has that sets them apart from their competitors. Positions could be based on value or low cost, specialized services or providing an inclusive range of services, knowledge of a customer environment or industry variables.
- **Plans** Describe how the service provider will transition from their current situation to their desired situation. Plans describe the activities that the service provider will need to take to be able to achieve their perspective and positions.
- **Patterns** Describe the ongoing, repeatable actions that a service provider will have to perform in order to continue to meet its strategic objectives.

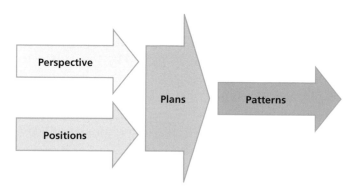

Figure 3.2 Perspective, positions, plans and patterns

A service provider may begin with any one of the four Ps and evolve to another. For example, a service provider might begin with a perspective: a vision and direction for the organization. The service provider might then decide to adopt a position articulated through policies, capabilities and resources. This position may be achieved through the execution of a carefully crafted plan. Once achieved, the service provider may maintain its position through a series of well-understood decisions and action over time: a pattern.

The sequence is not as important as using all four Ps. In this way the strategy is able to be adjusted to enable the service provider to deal with strategies that are already being executed together with those that are just being conceived. It will also ensure that a balance is maintained between the 'big picture' and the detailed execution.

The four Ps are introduced in more detail here and described in section 4.1.5, where they are specifically related to the strategy management for IT services process.

3.1.2.1 Perspective

The perspective of an organization expresses how it sees itself in terms of its context. It describes what the organization is, what it does, who it does it for and how it works, and it does this in a way that makes it easy to communicate internally and externally.

The perspective reminds employees, customers and suppliers about the beliefs, values and purpose of the organization. It sets an overall direction for the organization and articulates how it will fulfil its purpose. Some examples of perspective include:

- 'Focus on the user and all else will follow'
- 'It's all about growth, innovation and the dependency of technology, led by the greatest people anywhere'
- 'Consumer connectivity first – anytime, anywhere'
- '[Our] purpose is to improve the quality of life of the communities we serve'
- 'We will be a best-in-class service provider in [our] industry'.

Or take the real-world service providers who hold a perspective of:

- 'Highly efficient back-office operations' during the emergence of service outsourcing
- 'Low-cost service provider' during the emergence of offshore skilled labour
- 'Technology-specific expertise' with the emergence of open systems and software.

Defining the perspective is discussed in more detail in section 4.1.5.8.

3.1.2.2 Position

Strategy as a position is expressed as distinctiveness in the minds of customers. This often means competing in the same space as others but with a differentiated value proposition that is attractive to the customer. Whether it is about offering a wide range of services to a particular type of customer, or being the lowest-cost option, it is a strategic position.

There are four broad types of position, and these are discussed in detail in section 4.1.5.9. For ease of reference, a brief overview of each is given here:

- **Variety-based positioning** The service provider differentiates itself by offering a narrow range of services to a variety of customers with varied needs. For example, a mobile phone company offers a range of pre-defined packages based on time and type of usage. Customers choose the package that suits them, even though customers may use the same package differently.
- **Needs-based positioning** The service provider differentiates themselves by offering a wide range of services to a small number of customers. This type of positioning is also called 'customer intimacy', where the service provider identifies opportunities in a customer, develops services for them, and then continues to

develop services for new opportunities, or simply continues to provide valuable services that keep other competitors out. The service provider's relationship with and knowledge about the customer is key in needs-based positioning.

- **Access-based positioning** The service provider offers highly tailored services to a very specific target market, usually based on location, special interest or some other category. Only people in that group will typically have access to the service. For example, branded motorcycle accessories can only be purchased from stores that sell that brand of motorcycle.
- **Demand-based positioning** This is an emerging type of positioning in which the service provider uses a variety-based approach to appeal to a broad range of customers, but allows each customer to customize exactly which components of the service they will use, and how much of it they will use. Online service providers are exploring this form of positioning at the time of writing.

3.1.2.3 Plan

The most tangible form of a strategy is a set of documents referred to as the strategic plan, and in many organizations this is what is referred to as 'the strategy'. The plan contains details about how the organization will achieve its strategic objectives, and how much it is prepared to invest in order to do so.

Since the future is uncertain, plans usually contain several scenarios, each one containing a strategic response and level of investment. Throughout the year, the plans are compared with actual events and adjustments made to adapt to the emerging scenario.

Some plans are high-level, such as the overall strategy, while others are more detailed, such as the execution plans for a particular new service, or process. All plans are coordinated and follow the same strategic framework. More detail on crafting strategic plans is contained in section 4.1.5.10.

3.1.2.4 Pattern

Patterns are the ways in which an organization organizes itself to meet its objectives. These patterns could be organizational hierarchies, processes, inter-departmental collaboration, services etc.

Some patterns involve the way the organization works internally. Other patterns involve the way in which the organization interacts with its customers and suppliers. Patterns are important because they ensure that the service provider does not continuously react to demand in a new way every time. Patterns enable the service provider to predict how a strategy will be met, and what investment will be needed.

In some cases the organization will define the patterns it needs in its strategy and then require that everyone complies with the patterns. In other cases, patterns that have been successful in the past will be formalized into the strategy of the organization (emergent strategies).

More information on establishing patterns and emergent strategies can be found in section 4.1.5.11.

3.1.2.5 The relationship between the four Ps

As stated in section 3.1.2, a service provider's perspective and position will allow it to develop plans that, if executed, will ensure that the service provider achieves its strategic objectives.

However, planning deals with the future, which is anything but certain. With the best intent, no plan can be fully reliable. Changes to the organization, its customers and their respective environments can impact the successful execution of a plan. Instead of sticking rigidly to a plan that is no longer valid, the service provider must alter the plan, defer it or abandon it. In some cases they may have to merge plans or even create new ones.

Figure 3.3 illustrates the dynamic nature of plans identified by Mintzberg. In this diagram, one plan is executed (albeit with some adjustment), another is deferred and yet another emerges to respond to a strategy-impacting change. The net result of the executed plan plus the emergent plan is the new patterns for the organization.

In this way, the strategy is not a rigid application of plans in a changing environment, but a continually adapting process whereby the business stays relevant to its changing environment.

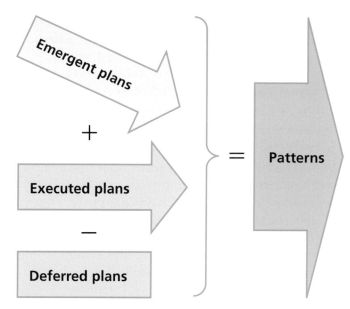

Figure 3.3 Strategic plans result in patterns

3.2 CUSTOMERS AND SERVICES

3.2.1 Customers

The concept of customers has been introduced in section 2.1.5, but is repeated and expanded here.

Customers are those who buy goods or services. The customer of an IT service provider is the person or group who defines and agrees the service level targets. The term is also sometimes used informally to mean user – for example, 'This is a customer-focused organization.'

Users are those who use an IT service on a day-to-day basis. Although some customers are also users, the role of a user is distinct from that of a customer, as some customers do not use the IT service directly. In contexts such as retail, the term 'consumer' is used instead of user.

3.2.1.1 How do customers differ from users and consumers?

IT service providers often talk in generic terms about 'the customer' as anyone who receives a service of some kind. It is important that all IT staff treat people to whom they deliver services as customers. This ensures that IT staff members demonstrate good customer-service behaviour, and that both users and customers are satisfied with the level of service that they receive. This, in turn, promotes customer retention.

However, not all people who receive a service are actually customers. While this should not make a difference in how IT treats them, it is a very important distinction when it comes to responding to requests and demands. Not all users have the authority or responsibility to request services, demand a certain level of service or request changes to existing services.

In the context of retail, the role of the consumer is well understood. For example, advertising for toys is aimed at the consumer (children) not the customer (parents). Toy commercials are aired during children's television programming. Toy stores are designed to make the toys accessible and attractive to children, not necessarily the people who actually make the purchase. Furthermore, the design of toys is done with significant input from children, while parents are consulted about pricing, safety and whether the toy is culturally and morally appropriate.

In retail, the consumer is powerful and plays a very influential role – often more so than the role of the customer. For example, a customer may make a purchase on behalf of a family (the consumers), but if the family do not like the item, it is unlikely that the customer will purchase it again. Consumers form part of focus groups aimed at product and service development.

The same dynamic operates with IT services. While customers actually pay for and negotiate the level of services with the service provider, they usually do so on behalf of a number of users (consumers). It is critical for the service provider to actively engage with these users to ensure that the services meet the needs of both customers and users. Formal interaction with both customers and users needs to be designed into processes such as service level management, business relationship management, service portfolio management etc.

Some service providers specialize in providing service to individual consumers, who are also the customers (for example, mobile-phone providers, or wireless broadband internet connectivity providers). The number of customers is usually large, and the services highly standardized. This means that interaction with customers is also standardized, relying on broad marketing and centralized support.

3.2.1.2 Internal and external customers

Regardless of how consistently customers and consumers are treated, they are not all the same. There is a difference between customers who work in the same organization as the IT service provider, and customers who work for another organization.

Internal customers are people or departments who work in the same organization as the service provider. For example, the marketing department is an internal customer of the IT organization because it uses IT services. The head of marketing and the CIO both report to the chief executive officer (CEO). If IT charges for its services, the money paid is an internal transaction in the organization's accounting system – i.e. not real revenue.

External customers are people who are not employed by the organization, or organizations that are separate legal entities, that purchase services from the service provider in terms of a legally binding contract or agreement. When the service provider charges for services they are paid with 'real' money, or through an exchange of services or products. For example, an airline might obtain consulting services from a large consulting firm. Two-thirds of the contract value is paid in cash, and one-third is paid in air tickets at an equivalent value.

Dealing with external customers

Many IT organizations who traditionally provide services to internal customers find that they are dealing directly with external customers because of the online services that they provide. It is important that the service strategy clearly identifies how the IT organization interacts with these customers, and who owns and manages the relationship with them.

It is very important to note that both internal and external customers must be provided with the agreed level of service, with the same levels of customer service. The way in which services are designed, transitioned, delivered and improved, however, is often quite different. Table 3.1 shows the major differences between internal and external customers.

The difference between internal and external customers is a theme throughout this publication, and the differences between them will be

Table 3.1 Differences between internal and external customers

	Internal customers	External customers
Funding	Funding for IT services is provided internally – so IT is a cost that needs to be recovered. In commercial organizations the internal customer has to use the IT service to generate revenue which has to cover the cost of the IT service and all other costs. Many internal IT service providers fail to quantify the cost of individual IT services and link these to external revenue sources. These service providers risk the situation where multiple internal customers demand services from a limited pool of staff and technology, believing that they have already 'paid' for them through central IT budget allocation. The resulting competition for IT resources can be damaging to the organization's ability to achieve its strategic objectives. In non-profit or government organizations the IT service has to support activities that will ensure that donors or government budget bodies allocate funds to the organization, which are used to cover IT and other costs.	External customers fund the service directly in the form of revenue. IT becomes a generator of income for the organization. The cost of the service, plus a margin, must be recovered from the customer. The ability to provide service to multiple customers is funded by the incremental revenue obtained from each new contract. As revenue increases, so too does the funding for staff and technology to provide the service.
Link to business strategy and objectives	The service provider has the same overall organizational objectives and strategy as its customers. Ideally, the service provider and customer work together to deliver external services and optimize operational efficiency and effectiveness. The term 'customer' is used to ensure that the business outcomes are placed first, and that the service provider prioritizes its activities appropriately, but the term 'colleague' may be more accurate in describing how two internal groups are related to one another.	It is helpful for the service provider to understand what outcomes the customer wants to achieve, so that the service can be properly designed to meet the expected levels of performance and functionality. This will ensure customer satisfaction and retention. The objectives and strategies of the service provider and the customer, though, are different. The customer's objectives are set by their executives and are appropriate for their business. The service provider's objective is to sustain its business by providing IT services. The service provider and customer are typically in different businesses, otherwise they would be competitors.

Table continues

Table 3.1 continued

	Internal customers	External customers
Accounting	The cost of service is the primary driver. It is possible to build a 'profit' margin into services, but this is always subject to enterprise financial management policies. The aim of providing services to internal customers is to provide an optimal balance between the cost and quality of the service – to support the organization in achieving its objectives.	The cost of the service is normally not disclosed to the customer. The price of the service is the primary driver. In a commercial organization, the service provider must ensure that the price of the service is higher than the cost of the service. The aim of the service provider is to maximize profitability while still remaining competitive with pricing. In non-profit and government organizations, the aim of providing services is to achieve the objectives of the organization while covering costs – partially by donations or taxes, and partly by recovering some portion of the costs from the customers.
Involvement in service design	Service design is dependent on enterprise policies, resource constraints and expected return on investment. Customers tend to be involved in detailed design specifications, often covering both functionality and manageability of the service – since both of these impact the level of investment required.	Where a customer purchases pre-defined services they might be asked for feedback about their experience, which is used to improve the service design. If each service is designed for each specific customer, the focus is on the functionality of the service, and the price to ensure that it performs to expectation. Customers may get involved in design work during needs-based and demand-based positioning. Otherwise customers typically do not get involved in design work and the service provider does not typically get involved in calculating the customer's return on investment.
Involvement in service transition and operation	Customers are often involved in building, testing and deploying services. Changes have to be assessed and authorized by customers as well as IT managers. Customers are involved in defining deployment procedures, mechanisms and schedules.	Customer involvement in change management is clearly documented in the contract, along with clauses about how changes will impact service pricing. Requests for change are assessed by the customer in terms of impact and price. Customers are generally not involved in detailed design and testing of services, and have little visibility into the processes whereby these are managed. Involvement in deployment is usually carefully scripted, and customers are trained in how to execute their deployment activities.

	Internal customers	External customers
Drivers for improvement	Improvements are driven by impact on the business, specifically optimizing the balance between cost and quality and the ability to help business units meet their objectives. Improvements are also aimed at improving the way services are designed, delivered and managed. Customers are often involved in the detail of service improvement plans, as they have skills which could help IT become better service providers.	Improvements are driven by the need to retain customers that contribute to the profitability of the service provider, and to remain competitive in the market. Changes that impact pricing and profitability drive measures that reduce cost while providing competitive service levels. Customers are not often involved in defining and executing service improvement plans, instead focusing on the expected results. How the service provider achieves those results is generally not important to the customer. At the same time, it should be noted that customers can be involved in defining service improvement plans – especially where a relationship with the service provider (typically outsourcer) is in difficulty.

referenced and described in more detail in various contexts.

Can a customer ever be wrong?

Customer service training has touted phrases like 'The customer is king' and 'The customer is always right'. Well-meaning IT service providers have taken these phrases to heart, only to find their organizations in some difficulty because they delivered the exact service that their 'customer' requested.

The reality of the situation is that there are circumstances in which the customer is not right, or in which the customer ceases to be a customer. A customer ceases to be a customer when they refuse to pay for a service, or if they require the service provider to do something illegal, or when they use the service for illegal purposes. For example, shoppers become criminals when they steal items from a store.

IT management becomes an accessory to fraud when it follows directions from a customer to destroy certain records. IT is negligent if it agrees to provide a service that is contrary to its business objectives, or damaging to the profitability of the business (even if a customer told them to do it).

There is another very important distinction between internal and external customers here, and that is what factors get taken into account when deciding whether to deliver a new service. For

example, a customer is involved in sensitive and confidential research and development work. They require that all processing be performed in a secure data centre, which has to be built in a virtually inaccessible location that they have identified. This is an extremely expensive requirement, and will require the service provider to make several new investments.

The service provider initiates an investigation and discovers an alternative location that meets all the customer's requirements, and is just as secure. The alternative would reduce the costs of the new service by 25%. The customer insists on going ahead with the original plan. Is the customer right?

The answer is not simple, since there may be other factors involved. If the customer is an external customer, however, the service provider will probably sign the contract and then start designing and building the new facility. This new service requires significant investment, but if the undertaking is legal and possible, and if the customer is willing to pay enough for the service provider to make a profit, it looks like a good opportunity. The key here is that the end result is based on external revenue being generated from the customer.

If the customer is an internal customer, the service provider has a responsibility to question the decision in more detail – since they are both responsible for the money that will be used to make the investments. It is money that belongs to the organization they both work for, and is not revenue. What business outcomes will this investment drive, and how will this specific location achieve these objectives more effectively than the cheaper location? In this case the service provider has an important check-and-balance role to play, while the customer is required to demonstrate what the return will be on the investment, and to justify to senior management why the cheaper alternative is not acceptable.

In addition, this distinction imposes responsibilities on the internal customer. The customer is responsible for providing the appropriate funding for the required level of service. They are committed to not using external competitors as long as the services are delivered as required.

Important note on customer service

ITIL Service Strategy is not suggesting for one moment that IT organizations should start to question the idea of good customer service. Customers, whether internal or external, are the reason a service provider exists. A responsible IT service provider should do everything within their power to ensure that services are appropriately agreed, funded and delivered to ensure customer satisfaction.

However, a responsible service provider also performs due diligence when agreeing to provide the service to a customer, to ensure that it is a legitimate request from an authorized person. If a due diligence exercise is not possible, a responsible service provider may well specify that they have not carried out 'due diligence' (often because the customer is not able or willing to provide sufficient access to information and time to achieve true due diligence, or is not willing to fund a true due diligence exercise). It should also be noted that it is the legal responsibility of the customer to ensure that local laws are obeyed. This becomes an issue with items like local storage, e.g. data protection legislation varies from country to country and it is often the client, not the service provider, who is responsible in law.

3.2.1.3 Business units as customers

In the IT service management model the relationship between an IT organization and other business units is characterized as a service provider–customer relationship. This is a useful model to explain the interactions between different parts of an organization and also to explain the dynamic nature of the IT organization's outputs and activities.

It is appropriate for IT to view other business units as customers, thus making the business objectives the highest priority. While the model of service provider–customer is constructive, the role of IT in the business is a lot more complex.

Theoretically, IT and the other business units are all focused on achieving the same objectives. However, it often happens that IT has to deal with business units that have different or opposing objectives. Sometimes this is a deliberate overall corporate strategy, other times it is just poor implementation of corporate strategy. In either event, the IT organization can find itself between the conflicting demands of the 'corporation' as a whole and each individual business unit. The strategy should clearly identify how to deal with these situations, and obtain the support of the organization's executives for the tactics used to deal with conflicting demands. In some cases this will mean accommodating the conflicting requirements (which will need additional funding), and in others it will mean that IT sometimes has to impose corporate objectives onto business units that do not wish to comply.

As IT matures, and technology becomes more pervasive, more IT organizations find themselves delivering revenue-producing services to external customers. Increasingly, IT is both an internal service provider and a strategic business unit in its own right.

ITIL Service Strategy explores this dual role in each chapter, and identifies how a number of organizations are dealing with the challenges it brings.

3.2.1.4 Other IT organizations as customers

Some IT organizations encourage their staff to view every IT organization as a customer. The reason for doing this is to ensure higher quality work and more positive interactions between departments. While the objective is commendable, it is important to avoid any negative behaviour resulting from a contrived customer–supplier relationship.

For example, in one organization the application hosting and networking departments spent significant time and energy negotiating and trying to improve service levels. The impact of these negotiations on the quality and cost of service was negligible, but the relationship between the two departments became adversarial. The 'customer' accused the 'service provider' of poor quality and a lack of understanding of the way the 'customer' worked. The 'service provider' complained that the 'customer' was too demanding, considering the fact that they did not pay for the service. Neither department ever considered the real customer they were both supposed to be supporting and the quality of service began to suffer as incidents and problems remained unresolved, and joint projects were delayed.

The management of quality between different departments in the service provider is better achieved through focusing on both the actual customer and the associated business objectives. Specific requirements of each department can be specified and measured in standard operating procedures and operational level agreements, reinforced by strong leadership from their managers.

Who is the real customer?

In many organizations, especially manufacturing-related companies, customers are defined as anyone who receives an output from someone else. The aim is to make each person responsible for quality at every step in the process. The supplier will take greater care producing the output, since the customer will not accept sub-standard work.

In reality, this approach only works if all the links in the process chain are managed according to a common end objective. The judgement about what constitutes good service is not defined by the individuals in the process; it is defined by the desired business outcomes that will be achieved if the whole process works properly.

The same is true of several IT organizations working together. While they might view each other as customers, the overall objective of the organization should always be foremost in their relationship. This can be achieved by concerted communications and internal marketing, as well as properly constructed processes and internal agreements.

3.2.1.5 IT as an external service provider

Most of the examples used above refer to IT as an internal service provider, but many organizations are in the business of providing IT services. *ITIL Service Strategy* is also about service providers that provide services such as internet service providers, hosting services and outsourcing companies. Throughout this publication, reference is made to both 'internal' and 'external' service providers.

3.2.2 Services

A service is a means of delivering value to customers by facilitating outcomes customers want to achieve without the ownership of specific costs and risks.

This definition sets the context for managing IT. The chief characteristic of IT is that it focuses on delivering a set of services that contribute to value for its customers. It does not focus on the output as much as on what the customer is able to do with the output.

The approach of managing IT as a set of services is different from the approach where IT is managed as a type of manufacturing environment that produces a set of 'products' or outputs. The key differences between these approaches are summarized in Table 3.2.

It should also be noted that many services are sold or made available when a product is delivered. For example, the price of a server includes shipping and an installation service. Also some 'products' are manufactured from raw materials, but delivered in real time and sometimes called services – for example, electricity. In terms of the definitions given in Table 3.2, these are neither products nor services, but are referred to as utilities.

The appropriate approach for managing IT is therefore the approach of managing a set of services, rather than a set of products. Although there may be a number of products used to deliver services (e.g. desktop PCs), it is not the end objective of IT to produce them. Rather they will deploy products as assets that are used to deliver services. These assets are managed as components of services, not as services in and of themselves.

Table 3.2 Differences between services and manufactured products

Services	Manufactured products
Services are dynamic interactions between a service provider and customer.	Products are physical entities that are produced by processing raw materials or assembling components.
Services are delivered in real time as customers need and use them.	Products are created ahead of time and stored before distribution to the customer. Just In Time production seeks to reduce the amount of time between production and delivery, but it relies on the ability to access the necessary components, assemble them and deliver the finished item to the customer.
Services are produced and consumed at the same time and cannot be separated from their providers.	Products are produced by one entity and can be stored, distributed and sold by different entities at different times.
The output of a service is volatile, often changing in real time depending on the customer's environment. For example, even a simple transaction can vary in size and output depending on the input from a user.	The output of production is predictable, and products should not deviate from a pre-defined norm by more than specific levels, or the product is not even delivered to the customer.
The way in which services are delivered can vary with every iteration of service delivery. For example, in a virtualized environment a transaction can be processed by any number of devices, and routed over any network component. This means that similar transactions are often processed differently.	Most products are produced using a fixed route through a fixed production line with specific equipment. Although there are some cases where variable production methods are used, each type of product generally follows exactly the same route through the factory.
A service's success can only be determined if the customer has been able to achieve a desired outcome. The output is secondary (see section 3.2.2.1).	A product's success is determined by the quality and delivery of the product itself.
The value of a service is only realized when it is actually being used by a customer. It retains no value after it has been used, and cannot be re-sold after it has been used.	Value is created and realized every time a product changes hands. A product retains value over time, and can be purchased and sold several times over its lifetime.
The value of a service is carried in the relationship between the customer and service provider. If either party leaves the relationship, the service has no value, since it cannot be delivered.	The value of a product is carried in the product itself. Even if the producer goes out of business, the product will still retain some (if not all) of its value.
Quality of a service is usually defined by the level of customer satisfaction based on their subjective experience of the service.	Quality is first based on whether the product meets certain pre-defined physical criteria, and only then on the customer's experience of whether the product does what was claimed by the vendor.

Are there any aspects of IT that are delivered as products rather than services?

Some organizations find it helpful to categorize certain IT components as products rather than services. For example, users are provided with desktop computers. Each desktop computer is built and configured according to strict specifications for each type of user, and must be maintained at an approved configuration baseline in order to perform correctly.

However, it is important to remember that these computers are simply a means for the service provider to deliver services to the user. They are not services in and of themselves. If an IT supplier only builds and delivers computers, they are not a service provider, but a computer manufacturer or reseller.

So, while IT may view certain configuration items as products, these must be linked to the services that they are used to provide, and the outcomes that the customer achieves by using them.

3.2.2.1 Outcomes

An outcome is the result of carrying out an activity, following a process, or delivering an IT service etc. The term is used to refer to intended results, as well as to actual results. Please note that in this publication, outcomes are referred to as 'business outcomes' and 'customer outcomes'. There is no real difference in the actual outcome – but the context is often different:

- Business outcomes usually refer to the context of internal customers, where the outcome for the customer represents the overall business objectives of both the business unit and the service provider.
- Customer outcomes usually refer to the context of external service providers, where the service provider's outcomes are based on the customer's outcomes, but are different. For example, the external service provider's primary outcome is to deliver a profitable service. Their customer uses that service to achieve a specific outcome that is important to them, but is not part of the service provider's business. If the customer achieves their outcome, they will be willing to pay the service provider to continue to deliver the service, thus enabling the service provider to achieve its desired outcome of profitability.

The definition of a service specifically refers to outcomes and not outputs. The difference is important. When a service provider focuses on outputs alone, they are able to demonstrate that they delivered a specific level of service, but they do not know whether the service actually achieved the intended results. This is often characterized by situations where the IT service provider meets its service level agreements consistently, but has a low customer satisfaction rating. In other words IT is able to deliver a consistent output, but it is not enabling customers to meet their intended outcomes.

Focusing purely on achieving outputs also makes it difficult for the service provider to track changes to the customer's environment and adjust services accordingly. In addition, the potential for customer dissatisfaction is much higher, since any complaints about the service not meeting requirements is met with the standard answer 'but we delivered what was in the service level agreement'. Instead, the service provider should continually take into account whether the service is meeting the customer's needs, especially when those needs change. This is one of the reasons for holding frequent service level reviews.

Outcomes are achieved when the business is able to perform activities which meet business objectives. Outcomes can be limited by the presence of constraints – for example, manual processes take too long and are too expensive for the organization to be competitive. Services enhance the performance of key activities and reduce the limits of constraints. The result is an increase in the possibility of achieving desired outcomes. While some services enhance performance of tasks (for example, email), others have a more direct impact. These services can perform the task itself – for example, an automated online ordering service which replaces time-consuming manual processes.

Business outcomes are defined in practical, measurable terms. Although some business outcomes refer to strategic results (e.g. growing the business by 15% over the next three years), most of the outcomes referred to in this publication are more tactical and operational. Examples include:

- A business unit processes a sales order
- A product or service is delivered to a customer
- An employee's salary is paid
- A financial report is submitted to a regulatory body
- A sales person is able to obtain information about a customer and use it to identify opportunities
- A driver's licence is issued to a member of the public
- Taxes are collected
- A driver is able to pay a toll and drive on a toll road
- Cargo is shipped on a ship or aeroplane
- An airline passenger makes a reservation, and receives a boarding pass.

The task of defining and documenting outcomes lies with the business units that achieve them. Business relationship management can assist in defining these and communicating them to the service provider. Even when the service provider is a different company, it is helpful for them to understand what the customers will use the services for. This assists them in prioritizing their activities, adjusting the services over time and contributing to customer satisfaction.

To summarize this discussion, examples of the differences between outputs and outcomes have been provided in Table 3.3.

Table 3.3 Differences between outputs and outcomes

Output	Outcome
What a service provider delivers (e.g. a standard report)	What the customer does with the output (e.g. the report is used to track inventory levels)
Measured in terms of performance (e.g. uptime)	Measured in terms of whether the outcome was achieved
Was the service delivered?	Could the service be used to achieve the outcome?
Compliance to a standard level of performance	Outcome may need variable levels of performance

3.2.2.2 Responsibility for specific costs and risks

Customers are concerned about what a service will cost them, and how reliable it will be. Good customer relationships do not, however, depend on the customer knowing every expenditure item and risk mitigation measure made by the service provider.

The customer is primarily interested in the outcome it will receive, and does not need to be concerned with specific costs and specific risks that the service provider will have to incur in order to deliver the service. The customer will only be exposed to the sum total price of the service, which will include all the provider's costs and risk mitigation measures (and any profit margin if appropriate). The customer can then judge the value of service based on a comparison of price and reliability with the desired outcome.

A good relationship between a service provider and its customers relies on the customer receiving a service that meets their needs, at an acceptable level of performance and at a cost that they can afford. The service provider needs to work out how to achieve a balance between these three areas, and communicate with the customer if there is anything that prevents them being able to deliver the required service at the required level of performance or price. This is illustrated in Figure 3.4.

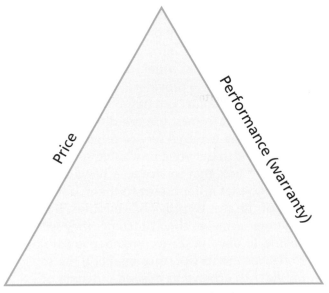

Figure 3.4 The service triangle

Figure 3.4 shows how each service is based on a balance between price, functionality (what the service does) and performance. Customers who wish to pay less money will have to sacrifice performance or functionality, or both. Conversely, if they wish to improve performance or increase functionality, they will have to pay more. Every customer will require a different balance between these three areas. For example, a customer may want a service that does only one thing, but it needs to be highly available and reliable. Another customer may want a service that supports a range of activities, but it is not business critical, so price can be reduced by having lower performance.

It is important to note that just cutting performance or functionality on its own does not necessarily result in a significant price decrease. Cutting down on performance will decrease the amount of money spent on higher performance systems, but it may increase the cost of reactive

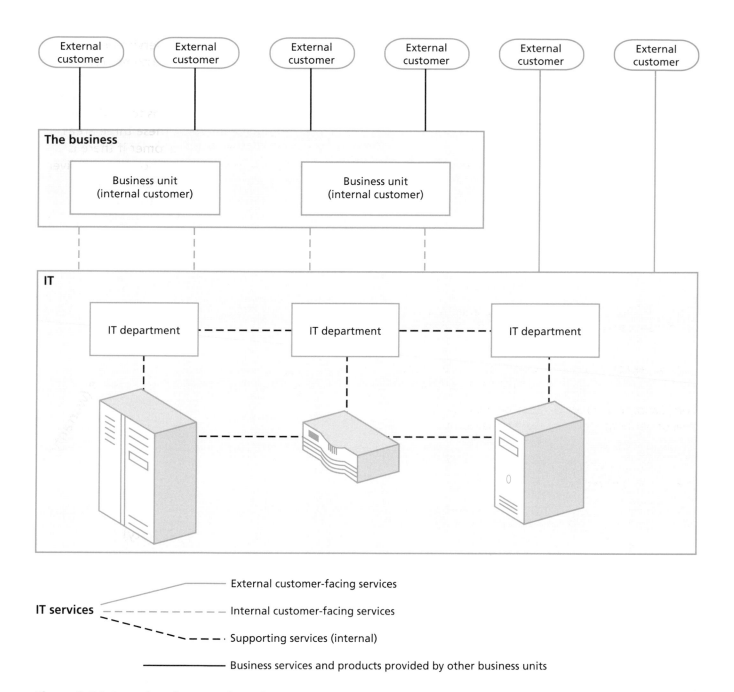

Figure 3.5 Internal and external services

support and downtime. Decreasing the functionality may save development and procurement costs, but if the level of performance remains high, the unit cost of the service will be higher. Most cost reductions result from a reduction in both functionality and performance.

Other than stating their requirements, and selecting the optimal balance between price, functionality and performance, customers should not be involved in specifying the technical details of risk mitigation and expenditure. It is the service provider's responsibility to work out the most

efficient and effective way of providing the service, and then communicating the cost of the service. If the customer wants a lower cost, then they should be prepared to reduce their requirements for functionality or performance, or else forgo the service altogether.

There are times when a service provider needs to reassure the customer of the level of performance or safety of a product or service. In these cases the service provider might provide some information to reassure the customer. For example, cars are tested by safety assurance organizations and given

Table 3.4 Types of IT service

Type of service	Definition	Description
Supporting service, sometimes called an infrastructure service, although they are often broader than just infrastructure	A service that is not directly used by the business, but is required by the IT service provider so they can provide other IT services – for example, directory services, naming services, the network or communication services.	Supporting services are defined to allow IT teams to identify the interdependencies between IT components. They will also show how these components are used to deliver internal and external customer-facing services. Supporting services enable IT processes and services, but are not directly visible to the customer. Some IT teams view recipients of supporting services as 'customers'. Although this promotes good service quality, it is also misleading. Supporting services only exist to be combined with other supporting services to produce customer-facing services. If they cannot, they are of no value and their existence should be questioned. There can be no service level agreements for supporting services as they are all internal to the same department. Instead, the performance of supporting services should be managed using operational level agreements. It should be noted that Figure 3.5 only refers to services originating inside the organization. In some cases supporting services are sourced from outside the organization. In these cases they are managed in the same way as other supporting services, but using underpinning contracts rather than operational level agreements.
Internal customer-facing service	An IT service that directly supports a business process managed by another business unit – for example, sales reporting service, enterprise resource management.	An internal customer-facing service is identified and defined by the business. If it cannot be perceived by the business as a service, then it is probably a supporting service. Internal customer-facing services rely on an integrated set of supporting services, although these are often not seen or understood by the customer or user. Internal customer-facing services are managed according to service level agreements.
External customer-facing service	An IT service that is directly provided by IT to an external customer – for example, internet access at an airport.	An external customer-facing service is available to external customers and is offered to meet business objectives defined in the organization's strategy. An external customer-facing IT service is also a business service in its own right, since it is used to conduct the business of the organization with external customers. Depending on the strategy of the organization, the service is either provided free of charge (many government agencies provide services to the public for no fee), or it is billed directly to the person or organization using the service. In other cases, the service may be provided free to the customer, but paid for by a third party, such as an advertiser or sponsor. These services are managed using a contract – even a simple online agreement constitutes a contract of sale and purchase with terms and conditions.

a safety rating. Customers will consider the rating and some basic safety features when purchasing a car, but they will not have to understand every risk mitigation factor the car manufacturer has designed and built into the car.

An example of this is a business unit that needs a terabyte of secure storage to support its online shopping system. From a strategic perspective, it wants the staff, equipment, facilities and infrastructure for a terabyte of storage to remain within its span of control. It does not want, however, to be accountable for all the associated costs and risks, real or nominal, actual or perceived. Fortunately, there is an IT group within the business with specialized knowledge and experience in large-scale storage systems, and the confidence to control the associated costs and risks. The business unit agrees to pay for the storage service provided by the group under specific terms and conditions.

The business unit remains responsible for the fulfilment of online purchase orders. It is not responsible for the operation and maintenance of fault-tolerant configurations of storage devices, dedicated and redundant power supplies, qualified personnel, or the security of the building perimeter, administrative expenses, insurance, compliance with safety regulations, contingency measures or the optimization problem of idle capacity for unexpected surges in demand. The design complexity, operational uncertainties and technical trade-offs associated with maintaining reliable high-performance storage systems lead to costs and risks the business unit is simply not willing to own. The service provider assumes ownership and allocates those costs and risks to every unit of storage utilized by the business and any other customers of the storage service.

3.2.2.3 Internal and external services

Just as there are internal and external customers, there are internal and external services. Internal services are delivered between departments or business units in the same organization. External services are delivered to external customers.

The reason for differentiating between internal and external services is to differentiate between services that support an internal activity, and those that actually achieve business outcomes. The difference may not appear to be significant at first, since the activity to deliver the services is often similar. However, it is important to recognize that internal services have to be linked to external services before their contribution to business outcomes can be understood and measured. This is especially important when measuring the return on investment of services (see section 3.6.1).

Figure 3.5 shows the difference between internal and external services for an IT service provider. These are described in more detail in the next two sections.

IT services

An IT service is a service that is provided to one or more customers by an IT service provider. An IT service is based on the use of information technology and supports the customer's business processes. It is made up of a combination of people, processes and technology.

There are three types of IT service, as shown in Table 3.4.

Table 3.5 Examples of core, enabling and enhancing services

	Core service	Enabling service	Enhancing service
IT services (office automation)	Word processing	Download and installation of updates	Document publication to professional printer for high-quality brochure
IT services (benefits tracking)	Employees of a company can monitor the status of their benefits (such as health insurance and retirement accounts).	A portal that provides a user-friendly front-end access to the benefits tracking service.	Customers can create and manage a fitness or weight-loss programme. Customers who show progress in their programme are awarded a discount on their premiums.

in section 4.4 on availability management in *ITIL Service Design*.

Note on external customer-facing services

Internal IT organizations are not the only providers of external services to customers. Outsourcers, internet service providers and cloud service providers are all examples of organizations that are in the business of providing external services – and the technology departments providing these services are business units, supported by internal IT service providers.

A business process can be distributed across technologies and applications, span geographies, have many users and yet still reside wholly in the data centre. To integrate business processes, IT frequently employs bottom-up integration, stitching together a patchwork of technology and application components that were never designed to interact at the business process layer. What begins as an elegant top-down business design frequently deteriorates into a disjointed and inflexible IT solution, disconnected from the goals of the business.

A better strategy for supporting these business processes is to start by defining the outcomes (see next section) and then identifying the IT services that support them, and after that defining how supporting services will be aligned to support the entire chain of dependencies.

Business services and products provided by other business units

A business service is defined as a service that is delivered to business customers by business units; for example, delivery of financial services to customers of a bank, or goods to the customers of a retail store. Successful delivery of business services often depends on one or more IT services.

Although IT is not directly responsible for the business's services and products, it is responsible for providing IT services which will enable the outcomes to be met. Thus it is important that IT knows what these services are, how the business uses IT services and how these services are measured. This will directly impact the way in which IT's contribution to the organization is met.

One way of doing this is to define the business activities needed to produce the outcomes as vital business functions. These are discussed more fully

3.2.2.4 Core, enabling and enhancing services

All services, whether internal or external, can be further classified in terms of how they relate to one another and their customers. Services can be classified as core, enabling or enhancing, and are defined in section 2.1.1. Examples of these services are provided in Table 3.5.

To illustrate this in another context, the core services of a bank could be providing financial capital to small and medium enterprises. Value is created for the bank's customers only when the bank can provide financial capital in a timely manner (after having evaluated all the costs and risk of financing the borrower).

Enabling services could be:

- Aid offered by loan officers in assessing working capital needs and collateral
- The application-processing service
- Flexible disbursement of loan funds
- A bank account into which the borrower can electronically transfer funds.

As basic factors, enabling services only give the provider an opportunity to serve the customer. Enabling services are necessary for customers to use the core services satisfactorily. Customers generally take such services for granted, and do not expect to be additionally charged for the value of such services. Examples of commonly offered enabling services are service desks, payment, registration and directory services.

In most markets, enabling services will allow the minimum requirements for operation, although many provide the foundation for differentiation, but it is the enhancing services that will provide the differentiation itself – the 'excitement factor'.

Examples of enhancing services are more difficult to provide, particularly because they tend to drift over time to be subsumed into core or enabling services. In other words, what is exciting to a customer today becomes expected if it is always delivered.

An example is the provision of a broadband internet service in a hotel room. A few years ago the provision of a chargeable broadband service might have been regarded as a differentiator (this hotel offers this service, other comparative hotels do not). As more and more hotels started to offer this service, customers came to regard it as essential – so it became an enabling service. Hotels then started to offer 'free' broadband internet services – so for a time this was an enhancing service, but that is now more common, and is quickly becoming a necessary (and thus enabling) service. For some travellers this service has actually become part of the core, in the same way, say, as an en-suite bathroom.

3.2.3 Value

The value of a service can be considered to be the level to which that service meets a customer's expectations. It is often measured by how much the customer is willing to pay for the service, rather than the cost of the service or any other intrinsic attribute of the service itself.

Unlike products, services do not have much intrinsic value. The value of a service comes from what it enables someone to do. The value of a service is not determined by the provider, but by the person who receives it – because they decide what they will do with the service, and what type of return they will achieve by using the service.

Following this reasoning, the characteristics of value are:

- **Value is defined by customers** No matter how much the service provider advertises the worth of their services, the ultimate decision about whether that service is valuable or not rests with the customer.
- **Affordable mix of features** It is possible to influence the customer's perception of value through communication and negotiation, but that still does not change the fact that the customer will still make the final choice about what is valuable to them. A good sales person can convince a customer to change the priorities influencing their purchase, but the customer will select the service or product that represents the best mix of features at the price they are willing to pay.
- **Achievement of objectives** Customers do not always measure value in financial terms, even though they may indicate how much they are prepared to pay for a service that helps them to realize the desired outcome. Many services are

not designed to produce revenue, but to meet some other organizational objective, such as social responsibility programmes, or human resource management. While commercial organizations tend to measure most services by financial returns, government organizations tend to focus on other objectives. For example, police might focus on reduction in crime or apprehension of criminals; social welfare departments might focus on the amount of funding disbursed to needy families; a mountain rescue organization might focus on the number of people warned about, or rescued from, avalanches.

- **Value changes over time and circumstance** What is valuable to a customer today might not be valuable in two years. As each customer changes to meet the challenges of their environment, so too do their service needs and values. For example, retail outlets might focus on selling a higher percentage of luxury goods when the economy is good, but during a recession they shift the focus to budget product lines and fewer luxury goods.

Services contribute value to an organization only when their value is perceived to be higher than the cost of obtaining the service. Therefore, understanding the value of IT requires three pieces of information:

- **What service(s) did IT provide?** If IT is only perceived as managing a set of servers, networks and PCs it will be very difficult for the customer to understand how these contributed to value. In order for a customer to calculate the value of a service, they must be able to discern a specific, discrete service and link it directly to specific business activities and outcomes. For example, an IT organization claims that application hosting delivers value to the business. The business, however, does not know what application hosting is, or what applications are hosted. If the IT organization wants to communicate its value, it must be able to identify what the customer actually perceives, and then link their activities to that service. The service portfolio, and the service catalogue in particular, will help IT to quantify this.
- **What did the service(s) achieve?** The customer will identify what they were able to do with

the service, and just how important that was to them and their organization.

- **How much did the service(s) cost – or what is the price of the service(s)?** When a customer compares the cost or price of a service with what the service enabled them to achieve, they will be able to judge how valuable the service actually was. If IT is unable to determine the cost of the service, it will be very difficult for them to claim that they delivered value, and very difficult for the customer to perceive IT as 'valuable'.

3.2.3.1 Creating value

Calculating the value of a service can sometimes be straightforward in financial terms. For example, a customer needs a service to support the selling of a new line of products. If the service does what is required, and its cost does not negatively impact the profitability of the product line, and the price remains competitive, the customer will most likely perceive it to be valuable.

In instances where the outcomes are not financial it is harder to quantify the value although it may still be possible to qualify it. For example, a city management department needs a service to enable them to track traffic in a city centre so that they can adjust traffic signals to improve the flow of traffic. If the service enables them to do this, and it fits within the city's budget, it will most likely be perceived to be valuable.

However, there is more to value than just the function of the service and its cost. Value needs to be defined in terms of three areas: the business outcomes achieved, the customer's preferences and the customer's perception of what was delivered. This is illustrated in Figure 3.6.

Value is defined not only strictly in terms of the customer's business outcomes; it is also highly dependent on customer's perceptions and preferences. Perceptions are influenced by attributes of a service, present or prior experiences with similar attributes and relative capability of competitors and other peers. Perceptions are also influenced by the customer's self-image or actual position in the market, such as those of being an innovator, market leader and risk-taker. The value of a service takes on many forms, and customers have preferences influenced by their perceptions. The preferences and perceptions of customers will affect how they differentiate the value of one offering or service provider over another.

The more intangible the value, the more important the definitions and differentiation of value become. Customers are reluctant to buy when there is ambiguity in the cause-and-effect relationship between the utilization of a service and the realization of benefits. The service providers need to provide customers with information to influence their perception of value, by influencing perceptions, and responding to preferences.

Understanding customer perception of value

Although a service provider is not able to decide the value of a service, it is able to influence how the value of the service is perceived by the customers. Figure 3.7 illustrates how customers perceive value (after Nagle and Holden, 2002). In this diagram the starting point for customer perception is the reference value. This could be based on what the customer has heard about the service, or the fact that the customer is currently doing the activity themselves, or some previous experience of that or a similar service.

The reference value may be vaguely defined or based on hard facts. An example of reference value is the baseline that customers maintain on the cost of in-house functions or services (the DIY, or do-it-yourself, strategy). It is important for the service provider to understand and get a sense of what this reference value is. This may be obtained through extensive dialogue with the customer, prior experience with the same or a similar customer or research and analysis available in the market.

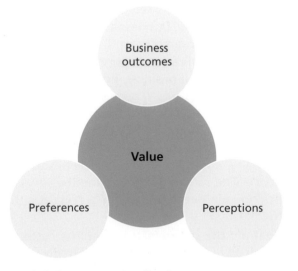

Figure 3.6 Components of value

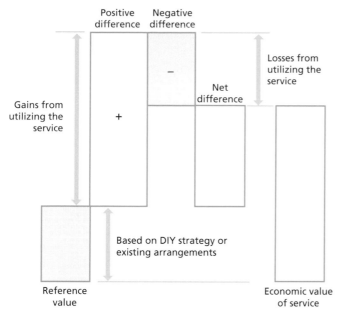

Figure 3.7 How customers perceive value

The positive difference of the service is based on the perceived additional benefits and gains provided by the service provider. These differences are based on the additional warranty and utility that the service provider is able to deliver. This is where the service provider is able to influence the customer's perception most. This requires a marketing approach, which is discussed in the next section.

The negative difference of the service is the perception of what the customer would lose by investing in the service. For example, they might perceive some quality issues or hidden costs. The service might not have the full functionality that they would like at the asking price. The service provider can also influence this area by listening to the customer requirements and matching the service features to them. They can also seek to influence the customer's priorities by emphasizing the service's strengths.

The net difference is the actual perception that the customer has of how much better (or worse) the service is than the reference value after discounting the negative difference. This is the area that will drive the customer's decision to invest in the service or not.

The economic value is the total value that the customer perceives the service to deliver. It includes the reference value plus (or minus) the net difference of the service they receive, and is measured by the customer in the ability to meet their desired outcomes.

Focus on business outcomes over everything else is a critical advance in outlook for many service providers. It represents a shift of emphasis from efficient utilization of resources to the effective realization of outcomes. Efficiency in operations is driven by the need for effectiveness in helping customers realize outcomes. Customers do not buy services; they buy the fulfilment of particular needs. This distinction explains the frequent disconnection between IT organizations and the businesses they serve. What the customer values is frequently different from what the IT organization believes it provides.

Marketing mindset

Understanding and communicating value requires that the service provider approaches the relationship with a marketing mindset. Marketing in this context refers not only to advertising services to influence customer perception, but also to understanding the customer's context and requirements, and ensuring that services are geared to meeting the outcomes that are important to the customer.

What are the outcomes that matter? How are they identified and ranked in terms of customer perceptions and preferences? Effectiveness in answering such questions requires a marketing mindset, which is quite different from engineering and operations mindsets. Rather than focusing inward on the production of services, there is a need to look from the outside in, from the customer's perspective. A marketing mindset begins with simple questions:

- What is our business?
- Who is our customer?
- What does the customer value?
- Who depends on our services?
- How do they use our services?
- Why are they valuable to them?

Value can be added at different levels. What matters is the net difference (Figure 3.7). For example, service providers differentiate themselves from equipment vendors purely through added value even while using the equipment from those same vendors as assets. Differentiation can arise from providing communication services instead of routers and servers. Further differentiation may be

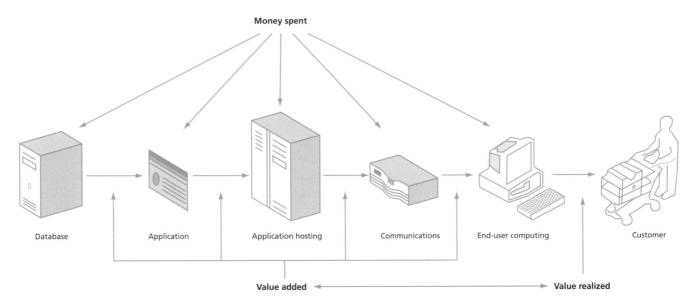

Money spent

Database   Application   Application hosting   Communications   End-user computing   Customer

Value added   Value realized

Figure 3.8 Money spent, value added and value realized

gained from providing collaboration services instead of simply operating email and voicemail services. The focus shifts from service attributes to the fulfilment of outcomes. With a marketing mindset it is possible to understand the components of value from the customer's perspective.

3.2.3.2 Value added and value realized

To better describe the relationship between costs and value, Porter (1996) introduced the concept of value chains. A value chain is a sequence of processes that creates a product or service that is of value to a customer. Each step of the sequence builds on the previous steps and contributes to the overall product or service. A simple IT value chain is represented in Figure 3.8.

In Figure 3.8 a number of components are used to deliver a service, and each component is managed by a department in IT. The database is managed by the database administration department, the application is managed by the application management department, application hosting is carried out by the application hosting department etc.

Money is spent on procuring, developing and maintaining each component, and each department spends money on salaries, office space, benefits etc. As each department manages its component and makes sure it is working effectively, it adds value to the service. For

example, a database on its own has relatively little value, but an application combined with a database has a value that is higher than just the cost of the two components. When combined with application hosting, the service becomes even more valuable.

The secret to adding value is that every time another step is added to the service the value of the service must grow at a higher rate than the amount of money spent (on both initial investment and incremental ongoing costs added at each step). In other words after each step in the value chain the service provider should be able to ask, 'If we sold what we have now, would it be of greater value than what we have spent on it?'.

An analogy might be helpful here. A restaurant buys raw ingredients. It might be able to sell those ingredients for a small profit if there are no other providers in the area. If the restaurant spends some money on combining and cooking the raw materials into tasty dishes, they will be able to charge far more for the food than the actual cost of the ingredients, electricity etc. Serving drinks that complement the meals will increase the value even more.

An important feature of a value chain is that the true value of a service can only be calculated after the value has been realized. In Figure 3.8 this happens when the customer achieves their desired outcome. In a commercial model the service provider can only confirm that value was added if the customer paid more for the service than it actually cost. In the public sector the external customer is usually the tax payer. There are some rules to adding value, as follows:

- The amount of value added can only be calculated once value has been realized (once the service has achieved the desired outcome).
- The value realized has to be greater than the money spent. This is true whether measured in financial terms (for example, how much money the customer paid for the service) or in non-financial terms (for example, could the government agency process the planned number of driver's licence applications per day?). In these cases the non-financial value of the outcome is compared with the financial costs of the service. A decision is then made as to whether the service is worthwhile or not.
- If the value realized is not greater than the money spent, then the service provider has not added any value. Rather they have simply spent money (and made a loss).

These rules also apply to IT organizations. Specifically:

- If IT wants to show that it has added value, it must link its activities to where the business realizes value.
- If IT is unable to do this, it will be perceived as a money-spending organization, not a value-adding organization.
- The only way a money-spending organization can demonstrate value is by cutting costs (thus assumedly increasing the profit margin). This results in a vicious circle. IT is not perceived as adding value, so the business demands that they cut costs. When they cut costs their ability to add value is reduced even more, and the business demands even more cost cutting.

So how does IT ensure that it is perceived as a value adder, rather than a money spender? The secret is in being able to link IT activities to services, and then link those services to outcomes. In other words, IT should not be undertaking activities unless they can show that each activity helps to achieve the business outcome. This is described in the next section.

Important note about value chains

Figure 3.8 shows a very simple value chain to demonstrate the basic principles of value added and value realized. In reality the creation and realization of value in organizations (especially larger organizations) is far more complex, with multiple value chains operating at the same time and across common components. This complexity is better represented by using the concept of value networks, which is discussed in more detail in section 3.8.

3.2.3.3 Linking 'value added' to 'value realized'

Since the infrastructure, applications and staff used to deliver services are generally not visible to the customer, it is difficult for them to understand just how much value has been added to their service. Attempts to describe their investment to the customer will be perceived as defensive, and an attempt to drive up the price of the service. Instead, the service provider should focus on building a model whereby they can measure the contribution of each internal service, and then link it to the achievement of the customer's business outcome.

Figure 3.9 shows the internal and external services provided to internal and external customers by an IT service provider in terms of their value. This is the same diagram as Figure 3.5, but instead of showing the type of service, it shows which of these services add or realize value, and which are classified as 'money spent'.

Value is realized when a service is provided to an external customer and meets their expectations. Value is measured in terms of whether a business outcome has been met. In commercial organizations, this is usually measured as profit or margin. In non-profit and government agencies this is more often measured in non-financial terms, as described in section 3.2.3.1.

In Figure 3.9 value-added services will only be identified as such if they can be linked to a service to an external customer. If there is no linkage to an external service, it will be viewed as a 'money spent'. Supporting services are at least one more step removed from the external services. To be considered valuable, the service provider must be able to link them to an internal or external IT

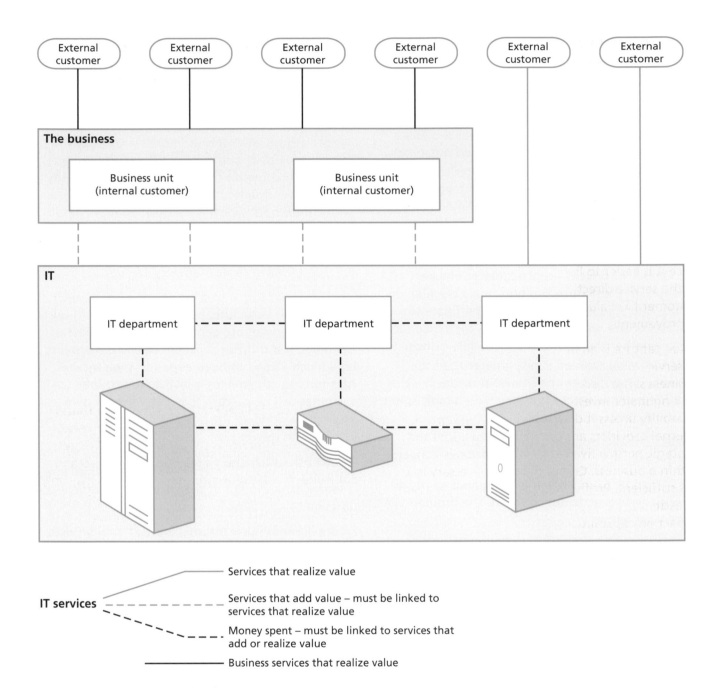

Figure 3.9 IT services and value

service. This does not mean that the service provider should disclose all internal services to the customer. Rather it means that the service provider will be able to measure the contribution of each internal service to the business (or government department's) outcome.

This will enable them to effectively communicate the warranty and utility of the service (section 3.2.4), which will increase the customer's perception of the value of services. Additional information about linking services can be found in section 4.2.4.3.

Value and service packages

The concepts of value added and value realized are two of the major drivers for how service packages are defined, built and delivered. Sections 3.4.7 and 3.4.8 describe these concepts in detail, but it should be noted here that the same dynamics of value apply.

For example, a service package facing an external customer can be defined in the service catalogue (value realized). This external service package may include one or more internal services or service packages provided by internal service providers (value added). These may again include service packages consisting of supporting services provided by internal IT organizations (money spent).

3.2.3.4 Value capture

Value capture is the ability of a service provider to retain a portion of the value that has been created and realized. The ability of a service provider to differentiate themselves and offer more value over time depends on whether they are able to obtain funding to develop and improve services, over and above the cost of operating the services. Value capture is a good way of obtaining this funding since it is easier to link the cost of this development to the service directly, and therefore easier for the customer to evaluate the value of service improvements.

Value capture is an important notion for all types of service providers, internal and external. Good business sense discourages stakeholders from making major investments in any organizational capability unless it demonstrates value capture. Internal providers are encouraged to adopt this strategic perspective to continue as viable concerns within a business. Cost recovery is necessary but not sufficient. Profits or surpluses allow continued investments in service assets that have a direct impact on capabilities.

It should be noted, however, that whether value is captured by the IT organization, or what the rules and boundaries of value capture are, are strategic decisions to be made by the organization's executives. Some organizations, especially internal IT organizations, are not allowed to capture value, and have to operate at a break-even level. In these cases funding has to be obtained on a case-by-case basis, usually from a central budget.

Linking value creation to value capture is a difficult but worthwhile endeavour. In simplest terms customers buy services as part of plans for achieving certain business outcomes. Say, for example, the use of a wireless messaging service allows the customer's sales staff to connect securely to the sales force automation system and complete critical tasks in the sales cycle. This has a positive impact on cash flows from payments brought forward in time. By linking purchase orders and invoices expedited from use of the wireless service it is possible to sense the impact of the service on business outcomes. They can be measured in terms

such as Days Sales Outstanding (DSO) and average time of the Order-to-Cash cycle. The total cost of utilizing the service can then be weighed against the impact on business outcomes.

It is difficult to establish the cause-and-effect relationship between the use of the service and the changes in cash flows. Quite often, there are several degrees of separation between the utilization of the service and the benefits customers ultimately realize. While absolute certainty is difficult to achieve, decision-making nevertheless improves.

3.2.4 Utility and warranty

From the customer's perspective, value consists of achieving business objectives. The value of a service is created by combining two primary elements: utility (fitness for purpose) and warranty (fitness for use). Utility and warranty are defined in section 2.1.6.

Customers cannot benefit from something that is fit for purpose but not fit for use, and vice versa. The value of a service is therefore only delivered when both utility and warranty are designed and delivered. It is tempting for customers to focus only on the utility aspects of a service, while ignoring warranty. For example, why is one service or product more expensive than another when they do exactly the same thing? The answer is often in the reliability or lifespan of the product or the availability of support from the supplier.

In many IT organizations the development of services is often separated from the operation of services. For example, customers will deal only with application developers to ensure that they have the functionality that they need, and assume that the manageability of the application is being taken care of. If the operational teams only get involved when the application is deployed, there is a strong possibility that some key operational considerations have been omitted, and additional funding is required. From a customer perspective, they have already paid for the functionality that they need, and the request for funding from operations seems to add no value.

In reality, however, warranty is an essential element of the design of the service, and needs to be designed and built together with the utility. Failure to do so often results in a limited ability to deliver the utility, and attempts to design warranty after a service has been deployed can be expensive and disruptive. Increasingly, service strategies emphasize the importance of designing and building both functionality (which provides utility) and manageability (which enables warranty) into the service – and funding both together. This ensures that value is not only created and added, but fully realized. Figure 2.2 in Chapter 2 illustrates the logic of utility and warranty as necessary components of a service.

Figure 2.2 illustrates the logic that a service has to have both utility and warranty to create value. Utility is used to improve the performance of the tasks used to achieve an outcome, or to remove constraints that prevent the task from being performed adequately (or both). Warranty requires the service to be available, continuous and secure and to have sufficient capacity for the service to perform at the required level. If the service is both fit for purpose and fit for use, it will create value.

It should be noted that the elements of warranty in Figure 2.2 are not exclusive. It is possible to define other components of warranty, such as usability, which refers to how easy it is for the user to access and use the features of the service to achieve the desired outcomes.

It is doubtful that full value can be realized from services when there is uncertainty in the service output. When the utility of a service is not backed up by warranty, customers think about possible losses due to poor service quality more than they do about the gains from receiving the promised utility. Customers tend to think that if a service provider promises utility, it will automatically deliver warranty. Put differently, customers often don't think about warranty until it is not there – and then it can be expensive to retro-fit the warranty aspects of the service, resulting in even more loss of perceived value.

To allay such concerns and influence customer perceptions of possible gains and losses, it is important that the value of a service is fully described in terms of utility and warranty. Table 3.6 provides examples of how the value of a 'Mobile Sales Order Processing (MoSOP)' service is described in terms of utility and warranty. In this case the value of the service is dependent on sales people achieving the business outcome of processing sales within five minutes of the customer agreeing to make the purchase.

3.2.4.1 The effect of improved utility on a service

Improving the utility of a service has the effect of increasing the functionality of a service or what it does for the customer, thus increasing the type and range of outcomes that can be achieved.

Figure 3.10 illustrates an example of an airline baggage handling service, which is able to complete the loading of baggage onto an aircraft within 15 minutes, 80% of the time. This is shown by the light-coloured curve. With new security legislation, they will be required to perform additional security checks, and to record the location of each bag in the aircraft hold. These additional activities require changes to the utility of the services.

The airline changes the service to be able to do the additional work and is still able to load baggage onto the aircraft within 15 minutes, 80% of the time. This new level of utility is shown by the dark-coloured curve. Note that the standard deviation remains the same since the warranty has not changed.

Figure 3.10 represents the standard distribution of the items being measured (in this case the x-axis represents the utility of the service, while the y-axis refers to the number of data points used to measure the service).

It is important to note that warranty does not automatically stay the same when utility is increased. In fact, maintaining consistent levels of warranty when increasing utility generally requires good planning and increased investment. This investment is required for making changes to existing processes and tools, training, hiring additional employees to do the increased work, additional tools to perform newly automated activities etc.

Thus the utility effect means that, although the customer assets perform better, and the range of outcomes is increased, the probability of achieving those outcomes remains the same (i.e. the shape of the graph, and space under the line, remains the same).

Table 3.6 Examples of utility and warranty statements

Utility	Sales people will be able to submit orders for processing during or immediately after a customer meeting, using data-enabled mobile telephones.
	The customer and sales person will receive a confirmation of the order by email as soon as the order has been accepted.
	Sales assistants must be able to submit sales orders on behalf of sales people if the sales people are unable to submit them themselves.
Warranty	Each sales person will be provided with a data-enabled wireless mobile telephone, with the MoSOP client installed.
	The software will operate over 2G, 3G and 4G mobile phone networks.
	The service will be available from 7.00 a.m. to 7.00 p.m.
	A sales order will be transmitted within 15 seconds after 'Send' is selected.
	The sales order will be processed within 2 minutes of receipt.
	The sales confirmation will be emailed within 30 seconds of sales order processing.
	The sales order processing system will be able to process up to 1,000 sales orders per hour.
	If a mobile signal is not available, the sales person will use a landline to contact a sales assistant to process the order. Once the order has been submitted, the processing and emailing of the sales confirmation will take the same amount of time.

3.2.4.2 The effect of improved warranty on a service

The effect of improving warranty of a service means that the service will continue to do the same things, but more reliably. Therefore there is a higher probability that the desired outcomes will be achieved, along with a decreased risk that the customer will suffer losses due to variations in service performance. Improved warranty also results in an increase in the number of times a task can be performed within an acceptable level of cost, time and activity.

Figure 3.11 shows how the standard deviation of the performance of a service changes when warranty is improved. The lighter line shows that a significant percentage of service delivery is outside of the acceptable range. By making various improvements (e.g. training, process and tool

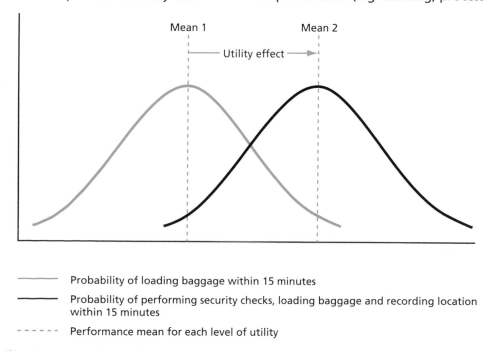

Probability of loading baggage within 15 minutes

Probability of performing security checks, loading baggage and recording location within 15 minutes

Performance mean for each level of utility

Figure 3.10 Utility increases the performance average

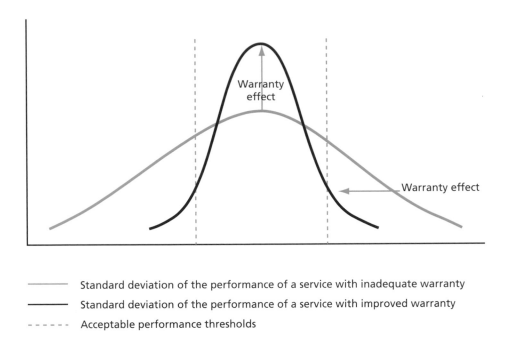

Standard deviation of the performance of a service with inadequate warranty

Standard deviation of the performance of a service with improved warranty

- - - - - - Acceptable performance thresholds

Figure 3.11 Warranty reduces the performance variation

improvement, new tools or processes, automation etc.) the service provider is able to increase the probability that the service will be performed within an acceptable range.

Using the airline baggage handling example, one year after adding the new utility, the airline would like to increase its 'on-time departure' rate. Achieving this means that baggage handling needs to improve its performance. Without adding any new utility, the baggage handling service finds a better way of scanning and recording the location of bags. As a result, the baggage handling service is able to complete the loading of baggage onto the aircraft within 15 minutes, 90% of the time – a significant improvement.

In Figure 3.11 the warranty is increased so that, although the service does exactly the same thing, it is more reliable since the performance of the service assets is improved. The improvement in service asset performance results in the ability to achieve the business outcomes more consistently. For example, a slow network sometimes results in poor processing times for a point-of-sales system, and items that are not properly scanned. The network is upgraded and the point-of-sales system results in consistently fast and more accurate processing. Overall the warranty of the service has improved, although it does exactly the same thing

as before – in other words the utility remains the same.

Figure 3.11 represents the standard distribution of the items being measured (in this case the x-axis represents the warranty of the service, while the y-axis refers to the number of data points used to measure the service). The warranty effect means that the performance of the *service assets* is improved. The utility effect means that the performance of the *customer assets* is improved.

For a definition of customer and service assets, please refer to section 2.2.1.

3.2.4.3 The combined effect of warranty and utility on a service

As stated above, both warranty and utility are required to create and realize value. Improving one or the other will result in improvements, but is often not enough. For example, increasing the warranty of a service that only meets 60% of customer requirements will continue to meet 60% of customer requirements more reliably. Increasing the utility of a service that experiences frequent outages is likely to make the customer even more frustrated than they were before, since the service is able to do more, but it still fails frequently.

Figure 3.12 shows the effect of improving both the utility and warranty of a service. In this diagram the original service is shown in the light colour, and

Table 3.7 Investment strategies for utility and warranty

Quadrant	Description	Challenge	Investment
Bottom left	These services have low business impact and range between a utility and warranty bias.	These services are of little value even when they provide both utility and warranty. They do not support high-value business outcomes.	Minimal investment is justified, since the value to the business is low. Where there is a warranty or utility bias, there is little value in creating a balance, and it might be preferable to retire the service altogether.
Top left	Low impact on customer outcomes, but with high levels of warranty and low levels of utility These services are very reliable, but are of little value to the business. In addition the level of utility is low.	Services with low utility do not provide value because they do not do what the business needs them to do, regardless of how reliable they are. In addition, services in this quadrant do not address high-value business requirements.	The current investment in these services is disproportionate. The value of the services is low, since the ongoing investment to keep the service assets performing is probably higher than it should be. Any investment should be re-allocated to improving the utility of these services.
Bottom right	Services in this quadrant have a high impact on customer outcomes, but with high levels of utility and low levels of warranty.	The value of these services is low since, although they have been designed to meet high-priority customer requirements, they are unable to do so due to poor performance of the service assets.	Investment is needed to improve the level of service provided by the service provider, and this investment is likely to take a high priority.
Top right	Services in this quadrant have a good balance between utility and warranty, and have a high business impact for the customer. Customer perception of service quality and value are highest in the zone of balance.	Shortcomings in services that are skewed towards either a utility or warranty bias in this quadrant tend to have more visibility – since the business outcomes are more valuable to the business.	The optimum levels of investment are in the 'zone of balance' since this represents services that meet both utility and warranty levels. It is much easier to justify investments required to move a service into the zone of balance.

the improved service is shown in the dark colour. In this case the range and number of outcomes is increased (shifting the line to the right) at the same time as improving the probability of outcomes (narrowing the standard distribution).

Figure 3.12 shows a service at its initial range of outcomes supported, and performance (light colour). After improving the utility and warranty, it is now able to support a wider range of outcomes, more reliably.

The most effective service improvement projects will ensure that there is a balance between the utility and warranty of the services. This is illustrated in Figure 3.13.

Figure 3.13 shows a quadrant where services can be ranked according to their levels of warranty and utility. Services are placed in the quadrant according to their warranty and utility levels, as well as their value to the customer. The chart shows services that have a higher utility (services have functionality that meets the customer requirements), but a lower warranty (services are unreliable, unavailable or not secure). These services have a utility bias.

Figure 3.13 also shows services that have lower utility than warranty (services that are reliable, but their functionality does not meet customer requirements fully). These services have a warranty bias. Services that have the appropriate levels of

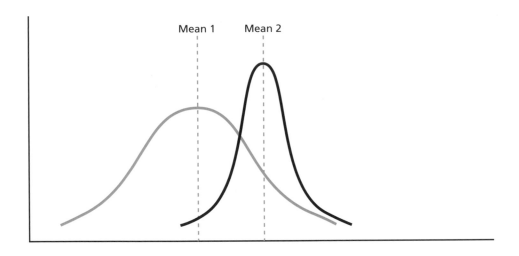

── Standard deviation of the performance of a service with basic utility and warranty

── Standard deviation of the performance of a service with improved utility and warranty

----- Performance mean achieved at each level of utility

Figure 3.12 A service with improved utility and warranty

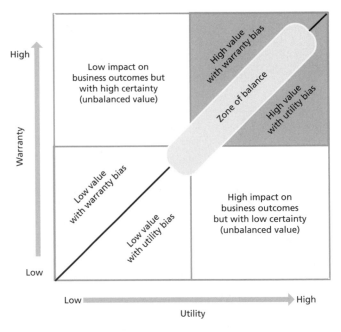

Figure 3.13 Combined effects of utility and warranty on customer assets

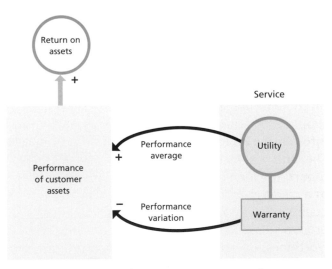

Figure 3.14 Value of a service in terms of return on assets for the customer

both warranty and utility are balanced. These services have functionality that meets the customer requirements and they do so consistently.

Figure 3.13 helps to identify how investments should be made in improving services. These are summarized in Table 3.7.

At the appropriate balance between utility and warranty customers will see a strong link between the utilization of a service and the positive effect

on the performance of their own assets, leading to higher return on assets (Figure 3.14).

The arrows marked with a '+' in Figure 3.14 indicate a directly proportional relationship – here the higher the utility, the higher the performance average. The arrow with a '–' indicates an inversely proportional relationship – here the higher the level of warranty, the lower the performance variation.

In Figure 3.14 services with a balance between utility and warranty increase the average performance of the customer assets (in other words result in higher value outcomes), while reducing the performance variation (in other words increasing the reliability of the service). The combined effects of utility and warranty will enable the customer assets to achieve the customer's business outcomes, and result in a return on their assets. In other words, value is realized.

3.2.4.4 Communicating utility

Communicating utility and warranty is important for customers to be able to calculate the value of a service. Communicating utility will enable the customer to determine the extent to which utility is matched to their functionality requirements.

In terms of outcomes supported

Take the example of a bank that earns profit from lending money to credit-worthy customers who pay fees and interest on loans. The bank would like to disburse as many good loans as possible within a time period (desired outcome). The bank has a lending process that includes the activity of determining the credit rating of loan applicants. The bank uses a commercial credit-reporting service, which is available to order by phone and on the internet. The service provider undertakes to supply accurate, comprehensive and current information on loan applicants in under a minute. The lending process is the consumer of the credit report, the loan officer being the user. The utility of a credit-reporting service is from the high quality of information it provides to the lending process (customer asset) to determine the credit-worthiness of borrowers, so that loan applications may be approved in a timely manner after calculating all the risks for the applicant. By reducing the time it takes to obtain good quality of information, the bank is able to have a high-performance asset in the lending process.

Figure 3.15 illustrates how the utility helps the customer achieve their outcomes by enabling outcomes directly, while at the same time reducing the impact of constraints that could prevent these outcomes being achieved.

In terms of ownership costs and risks avoided

Communicating utility in terms of ownership costs and risks avoided means that the service provider should be able to articulate:

- That the service enables the business to achieve the desired outcomes more efficiently. This allows the business to reduce its costs (and in commercial organizations, to increase its profit margins).
- That the service improves the reliability of outcome achievement. In other words, the service mitigates the risk of the business not being able to achieve its outcomes.

Using the same banking example as the previous section, the value of the credit-reporting service also comes from the lending division being able to avoid certain costs and risks it would incur from operating a credit-enquiry system on its own instead of using the reporting service. For example, the costs of maintaining capabilities and resources required to operate a credit-reporting system would be borne entirely by the lending division. The cost per credit report would become prohibitive within the scope of the loan approval process, and would have to be passed on to the cost of the loan or be absorbed elsewhere within the banking system. Under prevailing conditions, buying the service turns out to be a good decision for the bank. It increases gains and reduces losses.

An alternative strategy is for the lending division to convince other divisions within the same bank, financial services group or industry to use its credit reporting system. This may be a viable option in which the lending division would now offer a credit-reporting service to lenders along with its core service to borrowers. This is a strategic choice that has to be made by the senior managers of the lending division and their leadership at the bank. The risks of such a choice include the lending division straying from its core capabilities, inability to convince others of its competence and attracting too little demand to make the credit-reporting service economically viable.

By *using* a credit-reporting service rather than *operating* a credit-reporting system, the lending division is deliberately *avoiding* specific risks and costs. In effect, the lending division frees itself from certain business constraints. Sets of constraints are often traded for others, provided the overall performance of the business is not lessened.

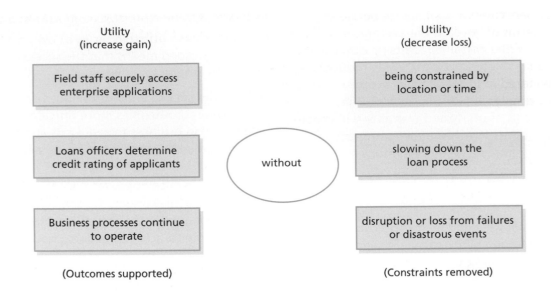

Figure 3.15 Utility described in terms of outcomes supported and constraints removed

Such trade-offs are made by the senior leadership of customers who are in the best position to decide. The senior leadership of service providers become business partners when they are able to support their counterparts in managing constraints on business strategies.

From the business perspective in the example above, service providers support the business strategies of their customers by removing or reducing the impact of certain types of constraints on business models and strategies. The constraints are of the type that imposes specific costs and risks that customers wish to avoid, as follows:

- **Maintaining non-core and under-utilized assets** Customers would like to avoid ownership and control of assets which drain financial resources from core assets, and those used rarely or sporadically. In such cases the return on assets is typically low or uncertain, making the investments risky.
- **Opportunity costs due to limited capacity and overloaded assets** Assets that are overloaded are unable to serve additional units of demand or accommodate unexpected surges in demand. Insufficient capacity also means that new opportunities cannot be pursued with a high probability of success.

3.2.4.5 Communicating warranty

Warranty ensures the utility of the service is available as needed with sufficient capacity, continuity and security – at the agreed cost or price. Customers cannot realize the promised value of a service that is fit for purpose when it is not fit for use.

Warranty in general is part of the value proposition that influences customers to buy. For customers to realize the expected benefits of manufactured goods utility is necessary but not sufficient. Defects and malfunctions make a product either unavailable for use or diminish its functional capacity. Warranties assure the products will retain form and function for a specified period under certain specified conditions of use and maintenance. Warranties are void outside such conditions. Normal wear and tear is not covered. Most importantly, customers are owners and operators of purchased goods.

In the case of services, the customers are neither the owners nor the operators of service assets that provide utility. That responsibility, along with maintenance and improvements, belongs to the service provider. Customers simply utilize the service. There is no wear and tear, misuse, neglect or damage of service assets limiting the validity of warranty. Even when a customer outsources the management of equipment that they own, the resources and capabilities of the outsourcing company to manage that equipment are not dictated by the customer.

Service providers communicate the value of warranty in terms of levels of certainty. Their ability to manage service assets instils confidence in the customer about the support for business outcomes. Warranty is stated in terms of the availability, capacity, continuity and security of the utilization of services.

An example is that an internal IT organization chooses to outsource the management of their web hosting services. The organization reduces the cost of the dedicated resources and under-utilized capacity by using a supplier that has achieved better economies of scale. The supplier also has extensive continuity capabilities, which means that the organization's website is less likely to fail.

Availability

Availability is at the core of customer and user satisfaction and is the most elementary aspect of assuring value to customers. It assures the customer that services will be available for use under agreed terms and conditions. The availability of a service is its most readily perceived attribute from a user's perspective. A service is available only if users can access it in an agreed manner. Perceptions and preferences vary by customer and by business context. The customer is responsible for managing the expectations and needs of its users. Within specified conditions, such as area of coverage, periods and delivery channels, services are expected to be available to users that the customer authorizes.

Availability of a service is more subtle than a binary evaluation of available and unavailable. The customer's tolerance for gradual degradation of availability should be determined and factored into service design. For example, if a subset of users is responsible for a vital business function, service instances for these users can be hosted on dedicated resources with fault tolerance so that the customer retains some critical capability to operate.

In addition, the agreed service hours are an important part of defining the warranty of the service. For example, services may need to be 100% available at certain times, while at other times they may not be needed at all. Using blanket availability metrics and strategies are not helpful for these services. For example, month-end reporting is only needed for a few days a month. At other times, trial reports can be queued and provided only as and when system resources are available. Using the overall availability of the service over the month is a meaningless metric – and providing for 100% (or even 98%) availability at all times of the month would be unnecessarily expensive.

Capacity

Capacity is an assurance that the service will support a specified level of business activity or demand at a specified level of quality. Customers drive business activity with the assurance of adequate capacity. Variations in demand are accommodated within an agreed range. Service providers undertake to maintain resources to give customers freedom from capacity shortfalls and under-utilized assets. Capacity is of particular importance where the utility of the service arises from access to shared resources. Service providers help customers with shortages during periods of peak demand.

Guaranteed capacity during particular periods or at particular locations is also valuable to customers who need to start up new or expanded operations with time-to-market as a critical success factor. Such business plans require low set-up costs and lead times. Additionally, due to the high risks of new or expanded operations, customers may prefer not to make the investments required to own and operate business assets. Businesses that face highly uncertain demand from their own customers also find value in services on demand with little or no latency. Opportunity costs are high in terms of lost customers.

Without effective management of capacity, service providers will not be able to deliver most services. Capacity management is a critical aspect of service management because it has a direct impact on the availability of services. A service that is performing poorly might as well not be delivered at all – for example, an automated teller machine that takes 15 minutes to dispense cash will be viewed by customers as not available. The capacity available to support services also has an impact on the level of service continuity committed to or delivered.

Reliability

Reliability ensures that both the service provider and customers know the level of performance that can be expected under the agreed conditions of delivery. Customers cannot expect consistently high levels of performance if a service is over-subscribed, or if it is used in a way in which it was not designed to be used. For example, a service will perform at a consistent level during service hours, provided that there are no more than 500 concurrent users, and provided the maintenance windows are used to perform the necessary maintenance (and not ignored in favour of providing higher-than-agreed levels of availability).

Continuity

Continuity assures the service will continue to support the business through major failures or disruptive events. The service provider undertakes to maintain service assets that will provide a sufficient level of contingency and recovery. Specialized systems and processes will kick in to ensure that the service levels received by the customer's assets do not fall below a pre-defined level. Continuity is assured primarily through redundancy and providing alternative resources that are dedicated to delivering services during contingencies and that are not impacted by the original event.

Key message

Continuity is not just about ensuring continuity of services, but is also about ensuring continuity of the vital business functions being performed by the customer.

Security

Security assures that services are provided to authorized customers, and that the confidentiality of information and intellectual property is protected when services are delivered. This means that customer assets will be protected from certain threats. Service security covers the following aspects of reducing risks:

■ Authorized and accountable usage of services as specified by customer
■ Protection of customers' assets from unauthorized or malicious access
■ Security zones between customer assets and service assets
■ Ensuring the integrity and confidentiality of information used by the organization and its customers
■ Users of services are guaranteed protected access to services through authentication and non-repudiation.

Service security has to recognize and incorporate the general properties of the security of physical

and human assets, and intangibles such as data, information, coordination and communication. Service security has challenges imposed by the following characteristics of service management:

■ Service assets are typically shared by more than one customer entity
■ Value is delivered just-in-time through the orchestration of several service assets
■ Customer action or inaction is a source of security risks.

Other elements of warranty

The elements of warranty discussed above are not an exhaustive list. Other components that may be considered as part of warranty are usability and affordability (whether customers are able to pay for or fund the service).

Usability refers to whether users can actually perform the required actions and access the information they need in order to be able to achieve the desired outcomes. Factors of usability include readability of text, whether data entry is straightforward and logical etc.

3.2.4.6 Communicating the combined effect of utility and warranty

The ability to deliver a certain level of warranty to customers by itself is a basis of competitive advantage for service providers. This is particularly true where services are commoditized or standardized. In such cases, it is hard to differentiate value largely in terms of utility for customers. When customers have a choice between service providers whose services provide more or less the same utility but different levels of warranty, then they prefer the greater certainty in the support of business outcomes, provided it is offered at a competitive price and by a service provider with a reputation for being able to deliver what is promised.

'Fewest calls dropped on average' is the value proposition of one major provider of mobile communication services expressed in its advertisements. An equally large competitor counteracts with the value proposition of best available coverage in the majority of urban areas. The other perpetual basis of differentiation is the number of calls made for a flat fee within peak hours of usage. This is an indirect measure of the capacity of over-subscribed service assets that service providers are assuring for the exclusive use of their customers. Of course, when competitive action leads to reduced differentiation based on warranty, service providers respond with service packages that offer additional utility, such as GPS navigation or wireless email on mobile phones.

Certain parcel delivery firms and retailers are market leaders in highly commoditized businesses simply because they offer a level of certainty unsurpassed by their peers. Their services guarantee delivery of goods on time regardless of location, time zone or size of shipments. They are able to guarantee these levels of service because they have invested in capabilities and resources that make them confident in their ability to deliver the agreed utility and warranty.

However, service providers emulate each other, leading to situations where providers offer similar levels of utility or warranty. Service providers must continually improve their value propositions to break away from the pack. The improvements can drive through one or more of the service management processes.

Guidance is contained in all the core ITIL publications about how utility and warranty are designed, transitioned and operated to support the competitive advantage of organizations. Desired outcomes are translated into requirements for utility and warranty in the service portfolio. Service design will focus on how to provide the new or improved utility and warranty at optimal cost and acceptable levels of risk. These services, with details about their utility and warranty, are documented in the service catalogue and transitioned into operation.

One point to bear in mind when defining both utility and warranty is the affordability of the service. A service provider can build a perfect service, but the utility and warranty need to be balanced against what the customer can afford to pay. Affordability is a good way for customers to prioritize the elements of warranty and utility, given the outcomes they want to achieve.

3.2.5 Customer assets, service assets and strategic assets

'A basic code of good business behaviour is a bit like oxygen: We take an interest in its presence only when it is absent.' Amartya Sen, Nobel Laureate in Economics

3.2.5.1 Assets, resources and capabilities

Assets, resources and capabilities are defined in section 2.2.1. Supplementary guidance on capabilities and resources is presented in Appendix B (description of asset types).

Capabilities are developed over time. The development of distinctive capabilities is enhanced by the breadth and depth of experience gained from the number and variety of customers, market spaces, contracts and services. Experience is similarly enriched from solving problems, handling situations, managing risks and analysing failures. For example, the combination of experience in a market space, reputation among customers, long-term contracts, subject matter experts, mature processes and infrastructure in key locations results in distinctive capabilities that are difficult for competitors to offer. This assumes the organization captures knowledge and feeds it back into its management systems and processes. Investments in learning capabilities are particularly important for service providers for the development of strategic assets.

Case study: financial services

At some time in the late 1990s, a leading financial services company launched a direct banking service. The service offered an internet-based savings and loans service.

After eight days, the company received almost 2 million website hits and over 100,000 enquiries. After five weeks, demand was so high that the company warned customers of delays of up to 28 days.

Solution

Don't overlook customer assets!

The constraint, it turns out, was not infrastructure capacity or availability, but a customer asset shortcoming in the form of 250 staff members. Once this chokepoint was resolved (250 hires), the company went on to win over 500,000 new customers and £5 billion in deposits in less than six months.

The performance or growth of a service will ultimately be limited by either limits in a resource or capability, or limits in its own potential. Attempts to push a service beyond a resource or capability limit can have strong consequences – often negating any benefits achieved.

The constraint, in this case, did not appear to be technology-related. They were account processors. The CIO missed it because he only considered service assets, overlooking the constraining effect of customer assets on the performance of his organization's services. The CIO's customer, in this case, includes the processing department.

3.2.5.2 Business units and service providers

This section examines the relationship between assets that are used by business units and those used by service providers. Specifically it shows how these assets are related to services and the creation of value.

The business unit

A business unit is an organizational entity, under a manager, that performs a defined set of business activities that create value for customers in the form of goods and services. The goods or services are produced and delivered using a set of assets, referred to as customer assets. Customers pay for the value they receive, which ensures that the business unit maintains an adequate return on assets. The relationship is good as long as the customer receives value and the business unit recovers costs and receives some form of compensation or profit.

Figure 3.16 provides a simple representation of the dynamics of service within a business unit. Customer assets are used to drive the achievement of business outcomes. The better the customer assets perform, the more business outcomes can be achieved. The smooth operation of the customer assets, however, is slowed by constraints. These could be internal constraints such as a lack of knowledge or funding, or external constraints such a weak economy or regulations.

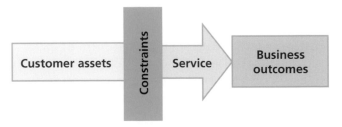

Figure 3.16 Customer assets drive business outcomes

The business unit's capabilities coordinate, control and deploy its resources to create value. Value is always defined in the context of customers and customer assets. Some services simply increase the resources available to the customer. For example, a storage service may assure that a customer's business systems can achieve a particular level of throughput in transaction processing with the availability of adequate, error-free and secure storage of transaction data. The storage service simply increases the capacity of the system, although one might argue that it actually enables the capability of high-volume transaction processing. Other services increase the performance of a customer's management, organization, people and processes. For example, a news-feed service provides real-time market data to be used by traders to make better and quicker decisions on trades.

The relationship with customers becomes strong when there is a balance between value created and returns generated. This relationship is an escalating cycle. The more a customer uses a particular service or product, the more the business unit focuses on what the customer is purchasing. The more the business unit focuses on the goods and services, the stronger their capabilities and resources become. The better the services become the more customers are prepared to purchase them. The better the returns or cost recovery the more the business unit will increase its investment in capabilities and resources.

The business unit could be part of an organization in the public or private sectors. Instead of revenue from sales there could be revenue from taxes collected or achievement of other government objectives. Instead of profits there could be surpluses. The customers of the business unit could be internal or external to the organization.

The service provider

While some units in an organization are business units, others are clearly internal service providers. These departments are organizational entities, under a manager, that perform a defined set of activities to create and deliver services that support the activities of business units. Services define the relationship between business units and their service provider counterparts.

Service providers and their relationship to the business units are illustrated in Figure 3.17. Service providers use service assets to deliver services (in this case, IT services) to the business unit. These services are designed to enhance the performance of the customer assets and/or to reduce the effect of constraints.

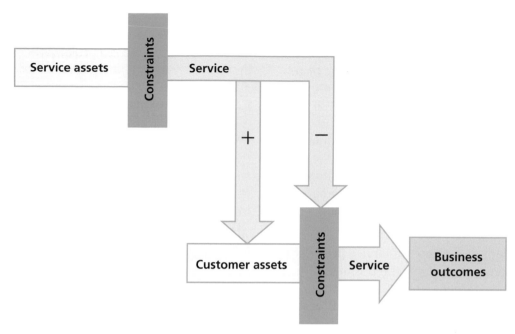

Figure 3.17 Service assets drive services to achieve business outcomes

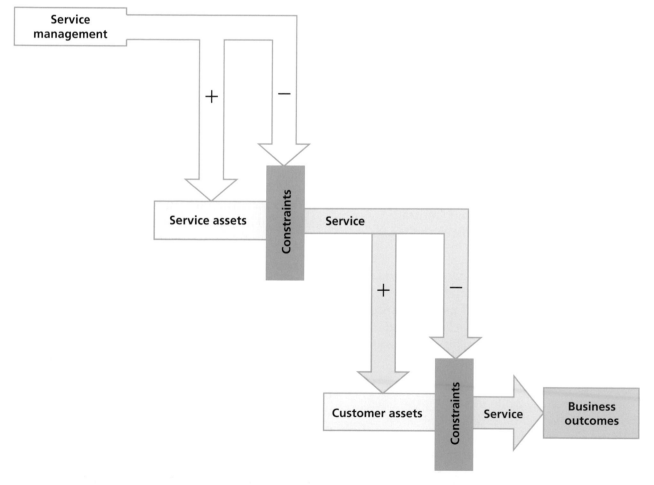

Figure 3.18 Service management optimizes the performance of service assets

Just as customer assets are subject to constraints, so too are the service assets. These constraints may be similar, e.g. funding or limited capacity. The service provider may invest in services from a supplier to help reduce these constraints or to improve the performance of the service assets. In this case the supplier would view the service assets as customer assets, and the IT services as business outcomes. The supplier would have to invest in the appropriate resources and capabilities to support its customer. In this way the chain of customers and service providers could extend upward and downward through several iterations.

In service strategy, however, the service provider is generally only concerned with the business outcome of its customer – assuming that these customers are doing the same for their customers.

IT service management

In the context of customer and service assets, IT service management is the management of the service assets (resources and capabilities) used to deliver services that support the achievement of the customer's business outcomes. Customers could be external or internal.

Figure 3.18 illustrates how service management enables the service assets to perform according to customer requirements, while identifying and reducing the impact of constraints on the service assets. IT service management does this by managing IT's capabilities and resources. This is done either internally, or through the support of external service providers and technology vendors. Achieving this is not straightforward, and often takes several years of hard work and cultural change. The basic approach to achieve this is outlined below.

Most IT service providers start out by organizing their departments according to technical specialization. This is an important principle since each type of technology is very specialized and requires people with specialized skills to manage it. A very simple IT organization is shown in Figure 3.19.

This organization chart, while indicating the lines of authority and the technical specialization of each department, does not indicate how it relates to its customers. In addition, it does not show how

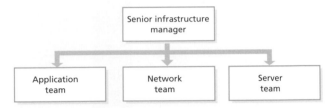

Figure 3.19 Simple view of an IT organization

the services are provided. A simple organization chart does not show what the organization does, how it does it and for whom it does it.

A further drawback of this type of organization is that goal setting and reporting are done in silos. Employees are hired based on expertise for a specific technology or role, rather than competencies in strategic planning, business expertise, forecasting or managing metrics. Each technology or functional manager perceives the other as a competitor rather than a partner; positioning themselves for priority for resources, budget and advancement.

This type of organization prevents cross-silo issues from being resolved at low levels. Instead, the issues have to be escalated to functional managers, who then address the issues with other functional managers, who sometimes do not wish to cooperate with their rivals. In other words, managers are continually forced to resolve low-level issues, taking time away from high-level customer issues. Low-level contributors, rather than resolving these issues, then see themselves as passive implementers, merely taking orders and providing technical information. Cross-functional issues frequently do not get addressed, often falling through the organizational cracks.

The opportunity for improving an organization often lies in these cracks: the white space of the organization chart (the 'white space' of the organization chart is examined in Rummler, 1995). It is the points at which the boxes interface and pass information.

IT service management needs to be able to ensure that technical expertise is focused on its competencies, but it also needs to align the departments to better deliver and support IT services. Processes map the activities, knowledge, information and data that need to cross the 'white space' to meet the organization's objectives.

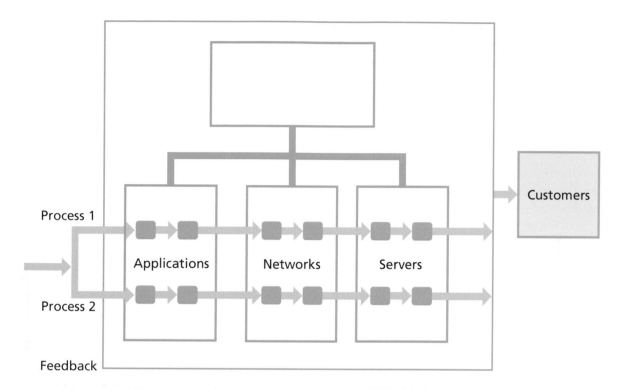

Figure 3.20 Process as a means for managing the silos of the organization chart

Figure 3.20 shows how processes link organizational silos and align them to the customer's requirements.

Some processes can be self-contained within a functional area, while others are cross-functional. Some processes manage and produce a product or service received by a customer external to IT. Organizational performance improves as these processes allow. The discipline of these processes is commonly known as IT service management (ITSM). ITSM means thinking of IT as a cohesive set of business resources and capabilities. These resources and capabilities are managed through processes and ultimately represented as services.

It is important, however, not just to implement processes and assume that the service will be delivered. Focusing on outputs alone will mean that the IT organization is delivering measurable services, but it does not guarantee that these services meet the customers' business outcomes.

IT service management as a service provider to internal and external customers

From a business point of view, IT service management enables the delivery of services which are used to achieve business outcomes (Figure 3.21).

Section 3.2.2.3 shows how IT provides customer-facing services and supports business services. This means that IT needs to look beyond just delivering an output to the business. Rather IT priorities must be clearly aligned with other drivers of business value. In order for IT to organize its activities around business objectives, the organization must link to business processes and services – not just observe them. IT leadership must engage in a meaningful dialogue with line-of-business owners and communicate in terms of desired outcomes.

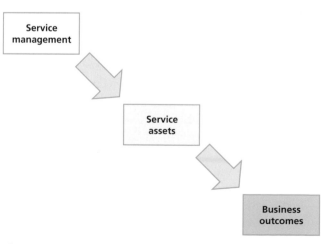

Figure 3.21 Service management enables business outcomes

Organizations are becoming less focused on the IT infrastructure, and more on how to automate end-to-end business processes and deliver business services. The challenge is to understand the operational objectives of the business process, and translate that into activities that can be provided by the IT infrastructure.

Overcoming this problem is the objective of the processes described in Chapter 4. Figure 3.22 illustrates the relationship between the service provider, the business unit and the customer's business outcomes.

In Figure 3.22 an IT service provider delivers services to an internal business unit, which enables it to achieve its desired business outcomes. In this diagram the nature of the business outcomes determines what customer assets the business unit will need. The service provider uses its service assets to deliver a service that meets the needs of the business unit. The dynamics of this service relationship are illustrated in Figure 3.22 and are as follows (an arrow with a '+' represents a directly proportional relationship; and an arrow with a '–' represents an inversely proportional relationship):

■ In order to achieve the outcomes, the business unit needs a minimum level of service. The performance potential of the service indicates what utility and warranty the service will have. This will indicate, in business unit terms, the performance that the service will be capable of. The business unit can then determine whether that will be suitable to enable its customer assets to produce the desired level of outcomes. The more utility and warranty, the higher the performance potential will be.

■ The higher the levels of utility and warranty, the lower the risk that the service will not meet the customer's requirements; and that the business outcomes will not be met.

■ The requirements for utility and warranty are translated back to IT (based on the level of risk acceptable to the business, and the service potential they require). IT uses this information to decide how it will use its service assets to deliver the service. The more capabilities and resources the service provider has (or builds or procures), the higher the level of service it is capable of delivering. This is called the service potential.

■ The higher the service potential, and the lower the risk, the higher the cost of the service. This cost must be covered or justified by the outcomes that are achieved.

■ The more successfully the service performs, the more it is likely to be used by the business unit, thus increasing demand on the service.

■ The higher the demand on the service, the more it will place demands on the service assets, thus reducing the amount of idle capacity.

■ If utilization rises too high and exceeds the service potential, the business will need to decide if it is prepared to fund an increase in performance potential, otherwise it will be at increased risk of service failure.

Figure 3.22 illustrates and reinforces the need for the IT service provider to look beyond the service to understand how business outcomes will impact the strategy for a service. The ability to increase service potential and performance potential is discussed below.

Increasing the service potential

In Figure 3.22 the capabilities and resources (service assets) of a service provider represent the service potential or the productive capacity available to customers through a set of services. Projects that develop or improve capabilities and resources increase the service potential. There is greater efficiency in the utilization of those assets and therefore service potential because of capability improvements in configuration management. Similar examples are given in Table 3.8. One of the key objectives of service management is to improve the service potential of its capabilities and resources.

Through configuration management, all service assets should be tagged with the name of the services to which they add service potential. This helps decisions related to service improvement and asset management. Clear relationships make it easier to ascertain the impact of changes, make business cases for investments in service assets and identify opportunities for scale and scope economies. It identifies critical service assets across the service portfolio for a given customer or market space.

Increasing performance potential

Figure 3.22 shows that the services offered by a service provider represent the potential to increase

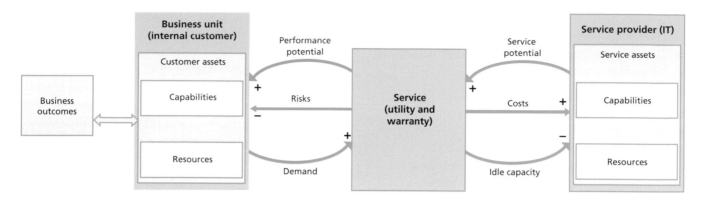

Figure 3.22 How a service provider enables a business unit's outcomes

the performance of customer assets. Without this potential there is no justification for customers to procure the services. Visualize and define the performance potential of services so that all decisions made by managers are rooted in the creation of value for customers. This approach avoids many of the problems of service businesses where value for customers is created in intangible forms and therefore harder to define and control. Working backwards from the performance potential of customers ensures that service providers are always aligned with business needs regardless of how often those needs change.

The performance potential of services is increased primarily by having the right mix of services to offer to customers, and designing those services to

have an impact on the customer's business. The key questions to be asked are:

- Who are our customers?
- What do those customers want?
- Can we offer anything unique to those customers?
- Are the opportunities already saturated with good solutions?
- Do we have the right portfolio of services developed for given opportunities?
- Do we have the right catalogue of services offered to a given customer?
- Is every service designed to support the required outcomes?

Table 3.8 Examples of how service potential is increased

Service management initiative	Increasing service potential from capabilities	Increasing service potential from resources
Data centre rationalization	Better control over service operations Lower complexity in infrastructure Development of infrastructure and technology assets	Increases the capacity of assets Increases economies of scale and scope Capacity building in service assets
Training and certification	Knowledgeable staff in control of service lifecycle Improved analysis and decisions	Staffing of key competencies Extension of service desk hours
Implement incident management process	Better response to service incidents Prioritization of recovery activities	Reducing losses in resource utilization
Develop service design process	Systematic design of services Enrichment of design portfolio	Re-use of service components Fewer service failures through design
Thin client computing	Increased flexibility in work locations Enhanced service continuity capabilities	Standardization and control of configurations Centralization of admin functions

- Is every service operated to support the required outcomes?
- Do we have the right models and structures to be a service provider?

The productive capacity of service assets is transformed into the productive capacity of customer assets. An important aspect of delivering value for customers through services is the reduction of risks for customers. By deciding to utilize a service, customers are often seeking to avoid owning certain risks and costs. Therefore the performance potential of services also arises from the removal of costs and risks from the customer's businesses.

For example, a service that securely processes payments or transfer of funds for the customer reduces the risks of financial losses through error and fraud and at the same time reduces the cost per transaction by leveraging economies of scale and scope on behalf of the customer. The service provider can deploy the same set of service assets to process a large volume of transactions and free the customer from having to own and operate such assets. For certain business functions such as payroll, finance and administration, the customer may face the financial risk of under-utilized or over-utilized assets and may therefore prefer a service offered by a separate service provider.

Demand, capacity and cost

When services are effective in increasing the performance potential of customer assets there is an increase in the demand for the services (Figure 3.22). The demand for services is accompanied by compensation from customers for the service levels received. The form of payment received depends on the type of agreement between the service provider and business unit. The higher the service levels, the greater the compensation that services providers can expect to achieve.

As the maturity of service management increases, it is possible to deliver higher levels of utility and warranty without a proportional increase in costs. Due to the effect of fixed costs and overheads, the costs of providing additional units of service output can decrease with an increase in the demand for services. Service assets are in a productive state when they are engaged in supporting customer assets. In every demand cycle of the customer, value is created by a corresponding delivery cycle.

Value creation for the customer is matched by value capture for the service provider.

3.2.5.3 Strategic assets

A strategic asset is any asset (customer or service) that provides the basis for core competence, distinctive performance or sustainable competitive advantage, or which qualifies a business unit to participate in business opportunities. Strategic assets are dynamic in nature. They are expected to continue to perform well under changing business conditions and objectives of their organization. That requires strategic assets to have learning capabilities. Performance in the immediate future should benefit from knowledge and experience gained from the past.

Part of service strategy is to identify how IT can be viewed as a strategic asset rather than an internal administrative function. As discussed in section 3.2.3 it is important that IT is able to link its services to business outcomes, which in turn will contribute to the organization's competitive advantage and market differentiation.

Perceiving IT as a valuable and trusted strategic business enabler does not happen overnight. It takes a concerted and formal effort in which IT demonstrates its contribution one area at a time. Each new challenge that IT enables the business to overcome, and each new market space IT allows the business to master, provides additional credibility for IT as a strategic service provider. This is illustrated in Figure 3.23.

In Figure 3.23 the service provider moves through three cycles of building trust and the perception of value. The first cycle is indicated by the white shapes, the second by the light-coloured shapes and the third by the dark-coloured shapes. For most IT service providers, this cycle has to be initiated while existing services are being delivered.

The cycle works as follows (the number of each point is referenced in Figure 3.23):

1 Within an existing IT service provider the cycle begins when the service provider and business have selected an opportunity – which could be an existing service(s) or an initiative that has already been defined. The value of this opportunity is defined in terms of outcomes that need to be achieved and the investment required to meet them. The opportunity will

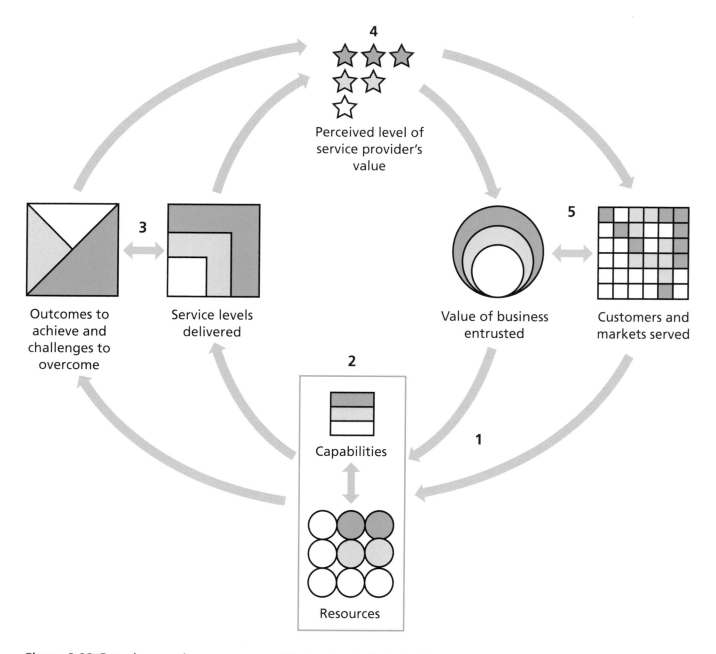

Figure 3.23 Growing service management into a trusted strategic asset

also specify which customers and market spaces the opportunity addresses

2 The service provider ensures that the capabilities and resources are in place to deliver the service(s)

3 When delivered at the agreed levels, these services enable the business to achieve its objectives, or overcome the defined challenge. It is important that these achievements are documented and reported to the stakeholders

4 The customer perceives that the IT service provider has delivered value

5 As a result, the customer is willing to entrust even more opportunities to the service provider.

Only three iterations of the cycle are shown here, but in reality the cycle is repeated many more times over a significant time (often up to three years) before the internal IT service provider is viewed as a fully trusted and strategic business unit.

Service management as a strategic asset

Service management is viewed as a strategic asset (rather than a set of purely operational processes) when it can demonstrate how it enables the service provider to compete and differentiate itself effectively. Service management does this by:

- Establishing a catalogue of services that contribute to strategic business objectives and outcomes
- Identifying in which market spaces IT enables the business to compete
- Defining how these services meet business challenges and then measuring them to ensure that this is achieved
- Building capabilities and resources to deliver these services and overcome identified challenges
- Communicating with the business about delivery achievements.

3.3 SERVICE PROVIDERS

'There is no such thing as a service industry. There are only industries whose service components are greater or less than those of other industries. Everybody is in service.' Professor Emeritus Theodore Levitt, Harvard Business School

It is necessary to distinguish between different types of service provider. While most aspects of service management apply equally to all types of service provider, others aspects such as customers, contracts, competition, market spaces, revenue and strategy take on different meanings depending on the specific type. There are three main types of service provider:

- Type I – internal service provider
- Type II – shared services unit
- Type III – external service provider.

For the sake of simplicity each one is defined below as if it were the only option used in a single organization. In reality most organizations have a combination of IT service providers. In a single organization it is possible that some IT units are dedicated to a single business unit, others provide shared services and yet others have been outsourced.

3.3.1 Type I (internal service provider)

Type I providers are service providers that are dedicated to, and often embedded within, an individual business unit. The business units themselves may be part of a larger enterprise or parent organization. Business functions such as

finance, administration, logistics, human resources and IT provide services required by various parts of the business. They are funded by overheads and are required to operate strictly within the mandates of the business. Type I providers have the benefit of tight coupling with their owner-customers, avoiding certain costs and risks associated with conducting business with external parties.

Since Type I service providers are dedicated to specific business units they are required to have an in-depth knowledge of the business and its goals, plans and operations. They are usually highly specialized, often focusing on designing, customizing and supporting specific applications, or on supporting a specific type of business process.

The primary objectives of Type I providers are to achieve functional excellence and cost effectiveness for their business units (Goold and Campbell, 2002). They specialize in serving a relatively narrow set of business needs. Services can be highly customized and resources are dedicated to providing relatively high service levels. The governance and administration of business functions are relatively straightforward. The decision rights are restricted in terms of the business unit's strategies and operating models. The general managers of business units make all key decisions such as the portfolio of services to offer, the investments in capabilities and resources and the metrics for measuring performance and outcomes.

Type I providers operate within internal market spaces. Their growth is limited by the growth of the business unit they belong to. Each business unit (BU) may have its own Type I provider. The success of Type I providers is not measured in terms of revenues or profits because they tend to operate on a cost-recovery basis with internal funding. All costs are borne by the owning business unit or enterprise.

Figure 3.24 shows three business units (BU) with Type I service providers. Each IT unit is dedicated to a single business unit, and delivers specialized services to that business unit only.

Competition for Type I providers is from providers outside the business unit, such as corporate business functions, who wield advantages such as scale, scope and autonomy. In general, service providers serving more than one customer face much lower risk of market failure. With multiple

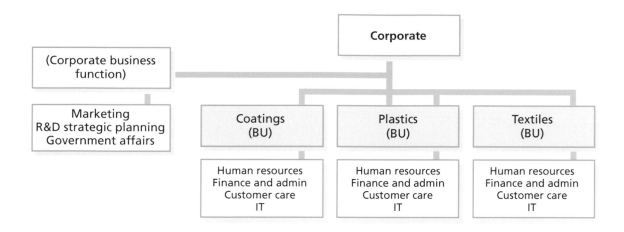

Figure 3.24 Type I providers

sources of demand, peak demand from one source can be offset by low demand from another. There is duplication and waste when Type I providers are replicated within the enterprise. This is especially true when multiple business units need to use data that is maintained by other business units. This results in duplication (in which no two data sets are the same) or complex system integration, which often results in performance issues, and difficulties in maintaining currency of systems.

To leverage economies of scale and scope, Type I providers are often consolidated into a corporate business function when there is a high degree of similarity in their capabilities and resources. At this level of aggregation Type I providers balance enterprise needs with those at the business unit level. The trade-offs can be complex and require a significant amount of attention and control by senior executives. As such, consolidated Type I providers are more appropriate where classes of assets such as IT, R&D, marketing or manufacturing are at the core of the organization's competitive advantage and therefore need careful control.

3.3.2 Type II (shared services unit)

Functions such as finance, IT, human resources and logistics are not always at the core of an organization's competitive advantage. Hence, they need not be maintained at the corporate level where they demand the attention of the chief executive's team (Goold and Campbell, 2002). Instead, the services of such shared functions are consolidated into an autonomous special unit called a shared services unit (SSU) (shown in Figure 3.25). In this diagram IT is shown as a single

department with a service catalogue that is available to multiple business units.

The model in Figure 3.25 allows a more devolved governing structure under which SSUs can focus on serving business units as direct customers. SSUs can create, grow and sustain an internal market for their services and model themselves along the lines of service providers in the open market. Like corporate business functions, they can leverage opportunities across the enterprise and spread their costs and risks across a wider base. Unlike corporate business functions, they have fewer protections under the banner of strategic value and core competence. They are subject to comparisons with external service providers whose business practices, operating models and strategies they must emulate and whose performance they should approximate, if not exceed.

Although Figure 3.25 shows different types of shared service in the SSU, many IT organizations are separate Type II units, and are not combined with other corporate services. When using the term Type II, this publication refers primarily to the IT service provider (whether it is part of an SSU or a separate department).

Customers of Type II are business units under a corporate parent, common stakeholders and an enterprise-level strategy. What may be sub-optimal for a particular business unit may be justified by advantages reaped at the corporate level for which the business unit may be compensated. Type II can offer lower prices compared to external service providers by leveraging corporate advantage, internal agreements and accounting policies. With

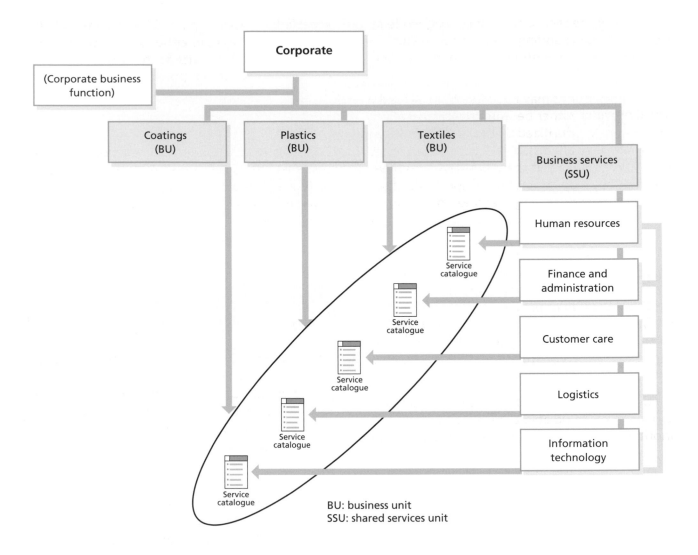

Figure 3.25 Common Type II providers

the autonomy to function like a business unit, Type II providers can make decisions outside the constraints of business unit level policies. They can standardize their service offerings across business units and use market-based pricing to influence demand patterns.

A successful Type II service provider can find itself in a position where it is able to provide its services externally as well as internally. In these cases they are both Type II and Type III service providers. In these cases it is important to make a strategic decision to provide services both externally and internally, and to set up the appropriate governance and management structures. This is not just a case of delivering existing services externally.

Market-based pricing

Market-based pricing refers to the approach of defining the cost of IT to the business in terms of what external organizations would charge for a similar service. With market-based pricing there is minimal need for complex discussions and negotiations over specific requirements, technologies, resource allocations, architectures and designs (that would be necessary with Type I arrangements) because the prices would drive adjustments, self-corrections and optimization on both sides of the value equation.

Strategic and governance decisions include how the organization will account for the revenue, whether the IT organization will be divided into two units (one internal and one external), how IT will sell its services, ensuring that the original objectives of the service can still be met, while at the same time expanding their use to external customers (e.g. who gets priority when there are capacity issues?).

Some business units may not be satisfied with the Type II provider, either because their expectations have not been prioritized by the overall business, or because they are dissatisfied with some aspect of the service quality. If these business units have funding, they may attempt to compete with the Type II provider directly by creating 'rogue' or 'shadow' IT organizations within the business unit. This is a governance issue, and is often not enforced by the organization's executives since the service structure of the organization is not well understood. This should not be confused with a formal hybrid service provider, in which Type I and II service providers co-exist within the same organization, one focusing on shared services, and the other focusing on BU-specific applications and services.

In a hybrid Type I and II context, a key required competency is to be able to meet competing priorities and keep close to those departments who are not getting priority and to work with them to set expectations and provide what services are possible within their budgets.

Industry-leading shared services units have successfully been spun off by their parents as independent businesses competing in the external market. They become a source of revenues from the initial charter of simply providing a cost advantage.

3.3.3 Type III (external service provider)

A Type III service provider is a service provider that provides IT services to external customers.

The business strategies of customers sometimes require capabilities readily available from a Type III provider. The additional risks that Type III providers assume over Type I and Type II are justified by increased flexibility and freedom to pursue opportunities. Type III providers can offer competitive prices and drive down unit costs by consolidating demand.

Certain business strategies are not adequately served by internal service providers such as Type I and Type II. Customers may pursue sourcing strategies requiring services from external providers. The motivation may be access to

knowledge, experience, scale, scope, capabilities and resources that are either beyond the reach of the organization or outside the scope of a carefully considered investment portfolio. Business strategies often require reductions in the asset base, fixed costs and operational risks, or the redeployment of financial assets.

Competitive business environments often require customers to have flexible and lean structures. In such cases it is better to buy services rather than own and operate the assets necessary to execute certain business functions and processes. For such customers, Type III is the best choice for a given set of services.

Figure 3.26 illustrates an organization that has outsourced several IT services and components to Type III suppliers, each with a catalogue of services that can be selected by the business units.

Although this is not shown in Figure 3.26, it should be noted that organizations using Type III service providers will still need an internal IT function or functions to manage the specification of services, coordinate the contracts and ensure that business outcomes are met.

The experience of Type III providers is often not limited to any one enterprise or market. The breadth and depth of such experience is often the single most distinctive source of value for customers. The breadth comes from serving multiple types of customer or market. The depth comes from serving multiples of the same type.

From a certain perspective, Type III providers are operating under an extended large-scale shared services model. They assume a greater level of risk from their customers compared to Type I and Type II. But their capabilities and resources are shared by their customers – some of whom may be rivals. This means that rival customers have access to the same bundle of assets, thereby diminishing any competitive advantage those assets bestowed.

At the same time, Type III service providers have greater freedom to select the business they want to be in. They are able to define their portfolio of services as narrowly or as broadly as they wish, and to decide not to offer certain type of service, or engage with certain types of customer. This allows them to be more agile and allows them to turn away business that might be risky.

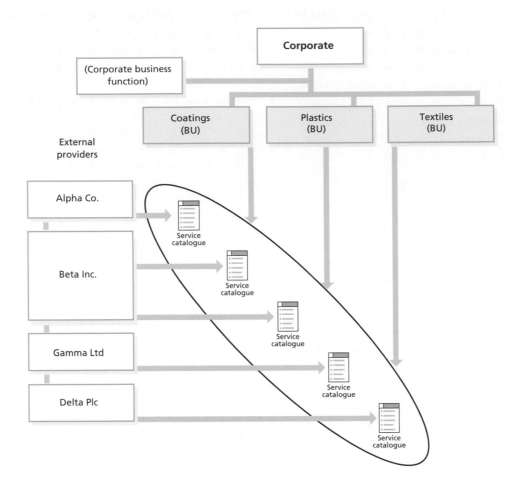

Figure 3.26 Type III providers

A further aspect of Type III service providers also needs to be noted. Many Type III service providers provide specific capabilities or activities that are used by a Type I or II service provider to support their services. For example, an IT organization may engage server administration services, so that they can focus on managing the applications.

Important note about Type III service providers

It is very important not to outsource any aspect of IT services and service management that are core to managing suppliers or the relationships between IT and their customers. Organizations that outsource supplier management, for example, lose the ability to negotiate with suppliers, specify what they need and manage supplier performance. Beyond this, it is unethical for a service provider to manage the contract under which they are engaged by the customer.

An outsourcing company is not well positioned to manage relationships with its customer's customers either. This relationship is key to creating and delivering value and therefore only the business, not the outsourcer, is responsible and accountable for managing that relationship. This means that neither business relationship management nor service level management should ever be outsourced.

Security is always an issue in shared services environments. But when the environment is shared with competitors, security becomes a larger concern. This is a driver of additional costs for Type III providers. As a counter-balance, Type III providers mitigate a type of risk inherent to Types I and II: business functions and shared service providers are subject to the same system of risks as their business unit or enterprise parent. This sets up a vicious cycle, whereby risks faced by the business units or the enterprise are transferred to the service provider and then fed back with amplification through the services utilized. Customers may reduce systemic risks by transferring them to external service providers who spread those risks across a larger value network.

3.3.4 How do customers choose between types?

From a customer's perspective there are advantages and disadvantages with each type of provider. Services, infrastructure, applications etc. may be sourced from each type of service provider with decisions based on transaction costs, strategic industry factors, core competence and the risk management capabilities of the customer.

Case study: sourcing

The internal IT service provider for a global conglomerate decided to outsource all data centre operations to external service providers. The primary driver was lower costs. Five years and several mergers and acquisitions later, and despite having achieved its cost reductions, the internal provider is considering insourcing all data centre operations. The reason for this was as follows.

The Type II provider for the conglomerate had achieved its cost reductions through a relationship with a Type III service provider. As a result of mergers and acquisitions activity, however, the company grew to include additional Type I providers. When the company re-examined its service strategy, it realized it could insource and consolidate all service providers into a single Type II – at a lower cost and with an enhanced technological distinctiveness unavailable from any Type III.

The principle of transaction costs is useful for explaining why customers may prefer one type of

provider to another. Transaction costs are overall costs of conducting a business with a service provider. Over and above the purchasing cost of services sold, they include but are not limited to the cost of finding and selecting qualified providers, defining requirements, negotiating agreements, measuring performance, managing the relationship with suppliers, cost of resolving disputes and making changes or amends to agreements. The more difficult it is (and the more inefficient the process is), the less likely the customer will choose that service provider.

Additionally, whether customers keep a business activity in-house (aggregate), separate it out for dedicated management (disaggregate) or source it from outside (outsource) depends on answers to the following questions (Milgrom and Roberts, 1992):

- Does the activity require assets that are highly specialized? Will those assets be idle or obsolete if that activity is no longer performed? (If yes, then disaggregate and/or outsource)
- How frequently is the activity performed within a period or business cycle? Is it infrequent or sporadic? (If yes, then outsource)
- Does the activity require knowledge specific to a particular business unit, even if the activity is infrequent and/or specialized? (If yes, then disaggregate or insource)
- How complex is the activity? Is it simple and routine? Is it stable over time with few changes? (If yes, then outsource). If it is complex and volatile, it might need to be disaggregated.
- Is it hard to define good performance? (If yes, then aggregate)
- Is it hard to measure good performance? (If yes, then aggregate)
- Is it tightly coupled with other activities or assets in the business? Would separating it increase complexity and cause problems of coordination? (If yes, then aggregate)

Based on the answers to those questions, customers may decide to switch between types of service providers (Table 3.9). Answers to the questions themselves may change over time depending on new economic conditions, regulations and technological innovation.

Table 3.9 Customer decisions on service provider types

From/ to	Type I	Type II	Type III
Type I	Functional reorganization	Aggregation	Outsourcing
Type II	Disaggregation	Corporate reorganization	Outsourcing
Type III	Insourcing	Insourcing	Value net reconfiguration

In Table 3.9, the following types of decision are indicated:

- **Functional reorganization** In this strategy, the business has undergone a functional reorganization, which requires a new structure of Type I service providers, thus the current service provider is reorganized to be able to provide better or more cost-effective services.
- **Corporate reorganization** In this strategy, a Type II service provider model is retained, but the shared services units are reorganized to provide better or more cost-effective services.
- **Value net reconfiguration** This strategy requires a reorganization of the current way in which value is delivered and created by external service providers. Some new providers are integrated into the value network, others are moved out, and yet others will play a different role. An example of this is the emergence of cloud computing models.
- **Aggregation** In this strategy, services are centralized (combined) under a single Type II provider.
- **Disaggregation** This strategy involves decentralizing (unbundling) the shared services unit so that the service is provided by a dedicated service provider for each BU, service or activity.
- **Outsourcing** This strategy involves using a Type III service provider to provide a service that was previously delivered by an internal service provider. Please note that it may first be necessary to disaggregate since it may not always be possible to outsource all activities or functions together.
- **Insourcing** This strategy requires an internal service provider to begin providing a service that was previously provided by an external service provider.

Customers may adopt a sourcing strategy that combines the advantages and mitigates the risks of all three types of service provider. In such cases, the value network supporting a customer cuts across the boundaries of more than one organization. As part of a carefully considered sourcing strategy, customers may allocate their needs across the different types of service providers based on whichever type best provides the business outcomes they desire. Core (often specialized) services, infrastructure, applications etc. are sought from Type I or Type II providers, while supplementary services enhancing core services are sought from Type II or Type III providers.

In a multi-sourced environment, the centre of gravity of a value network rests with the type of service provider dominating the sourcing portfolio. Outsourcing or disaggregating decisions move the centre of gravity away from the corporate core. Aggregation or insourcing decisions move the centre of gravity closer to the corporate core and are driven by the need to maintain firm-specific advantages unavailable to competitors. Certain decisions do not shift the centre of gravity but rather re-allocate services between service providers of the same type.

The sourcing structure may be altered due to changes in the business fundamentals of the customer, making one type of service provider more desirable than the other. For example, a customer merger or acquisition may dramatically alter the economics that underpin a hitherto sound sourcing strategy.

3.3.5 The relative advantage of incumbency

Lasting relationships with customers allow organizations to learn and improve. Fewer errors are made, investments are recovered and the resulting cost advantage can be leveraged to increase the gap with competitors.

Customers find it less attractive to turn away from well-performing incumbents because of switching costs. Experience can be used to improve assets such as processes, knowledge and the competencies that are strategic in nature.

Service providers must therefore focus on providing the basis for a lasting relationship with customers. It requires them to exercise strategic planning and control to ensure that common objectives drive everything, knowledge is shared effectively between units and experience is fed back into future plans and actions for a less steep learning curve.

3.4 HOW TO DEFINE SERVICES

The previous sections in this chapter described services, customers, value and service providers. Understanding these concepts and how the organization relates to them helps to define which services will be delivered, and to which customers.

This section discusses how to identify customers and their requirements, and whether there is an opportunity that the service provider can fulfil. It will then discuss the actual definition of services that will address each opportunity.

These steps will typically happen as part of service portfolio management (discussed in section 4.2), but are discussed here to illustrate the application of the principles contained in the previous section. The steps are listed here and discussed below:

- Step 1 – Define the market and identify customers
- Step 2 – Understand the customer
- Step 3 – Quantify the outcomes
- Step 4 – Classify and visualize the service
- Step 5 – Understand the opportunities (market spaces)
- Step 6 – Define services based on outcomes
- Step 7 – Service models
- Step 8 – Define service units and packages.

3.4.1 Step 1 – Define the market and identify customers

In this context a market can be defined as the group of customers that are interested in and can afford to purchase the service a service provider offers, and to whom the service provider is able legally and logistically to supply those services.

The first step in defining services is to understand the market in which the service provider operates. This will help to narrow down the options open to the service provider. For example:

- A Type I service provider will typically only serve one business unit. Their entire market consists of a single internal customer.
- A Type II service provider's market will consist of several business units. They will not typically define and provide IT services outside of the organization. If they do, they are usually automated business services.
- A Type III service provider cannot provide limitless numbers of services to every market. They typically either provide a generic service to several markets (e.g. internet services to residential users and small businesses), or they provide specialized service(s) to a single market (e.g. monitoring and control for manufacturing).

Markets can be defined by one or more criteria such as the following:

- **Industry** (e.g. manufacturing, retail, financial services, healthcare, transportation etc.)
- **Geographical** (e.g. a specific country or region) A service provider may provide a best-in-class service, but decide to limit its availability to a single geographical region. A different service provider may provide a lower standard of service, but delivers it consistently across multiple regions, making it easier for customers to standardize on a single provider for all regions.
- **Demographic** The service provider may deliver a service geared towards a specific cultural group (e.g. television programming for a Spanish-speaking customer in the USA) or a group of customers with similar incomes (e.g. luxury or economy services).
- **Corporate relationships** Some service providers have specifically been set up to provide services to a group of companies with a common shareholding, and may not market those services to competitors of those companies.

In all cases identifying the market(s) in which the service provider is active is an important part of identifying which services the service provider will deliver, and to which customers.

In some cases identifying the customer will be the same as identifying the market. For example, a Type I service provider, or a supplier that provides support for a specialized system in a specific location. If they are the only service provider of this type in the location, then all organizations using the system are potential customers.

In other cases the market is large and will require further research and analysis to identify potential customers, or customer types (e.g. mobile phone services aimed at families that need multiple lines). Identifying each customer would be impossible, but understanding that 60% of people in a particular region could potentially use the service will determine that the market is viable, and will also help to mould the marketing plans.

3.4.2 Step 2 – Understand the customer

For internal service providers, understanding the customer means understanding the overall business strategies and objectives of the organization, and how each business unit meets those. It also means understanding the business outcomes that each business unit needs to achieve.

For an external service provider, understanding the customer means understanding why they need the service they are purchasing. The service provider does not have to understand the detailed strategy, tactics and operations of the customer, but they do need to understand the reasons the customer needs the service and what features are important.

Understanding the customer involves understanding:

- **Desired business outcomes** The customers use their assets to achieve specific outcomes. Understanding what these outcomes are will help the service provider to define the warranty and utility of the services, and to prioritize service needs.
- **Customer assets** Services enable and support the performance of the assets the customer uses to achieve their business outcomes. Therefore, it is necessary when defining services to understand the linkage between the service and the customer assets.
- **Constraints** Every customer asset will be limited by some form of constraint – a lack of funding, lack of knowledge, regulations, legislation etc. Understanding those constraints will enable the service provider to define boundaries for the service, and also help the customer overcome, or work within, many of them.

- **How value will be perceived and measured** Customers always measure performance, quality and value. Many service providers set up complex monitoring and measurement systems without understanding how the customers measure the service. This results in a misalignment between the customer's expectations and the service provider's actual delivery. It is therefore vital that the service provider understands how the customer measures the service – even if the service provider is not able to measure the service in the same way.

Business managers are given the responsibility, authority and resources necessary to deliver certain outcomes using the best possible means. Services are a means for managers to enable or enhance the performance of business assets leading to better outcomes. The value of a service is best measured in terms of the improvement in outcomes that can be attributed to the impact of the service on the performance of business assets. Some services increase the performance of customer assets, some services maintain performance, and yet others restore performance following adverse events. A major aspect of providing value is preventing or reducing the variation in the performance of customer assets.

In a trading system, for example, it is not enough for the service to feed the trading system with real-time market data. To minimize trading losses the data feed must be available without interruption during trading hours, and at as many trading desks as necessary with a contingency system in place. An investment bank is therefore willing to pay a premium for a news-feed service providing a higher level of warranty than a service used by a competitor. The difference translates into greater trading gains.

Focus on customer assets

The performance of customer assets should be a primary concern of service management professionals because without customer assets there is no basis for defining the value of a service.

3.4.3 Step 3 – Quantify the outcomes

In this step the service provider will work with the customer to identify their desired outcomes. These definitions need to be clear and measurable and they need to be something that can be linked to the service.

In the following example, a lending bank creates value by achieving the outcome of processing a loan application on time. Customers receiving the loan will have access to the required financial capital and the lender benefits from the onset and accrual of interest. The lending process is therefore a business asset whose performance leads to specific business outcomes. Processing the loan application in time makes the process easier for the customer, and creates a competitive advantage.

This is illustrated in Figure 3.27 (after Ulwick, 2005), in which the outcome desired by the bank is to process the loan application on time. The measurement to be used is the number of loan applications that were able to be processed on time. The objective of the service is not only to enable these outcomes to be achieved, but also to increase the number that will be achieved. In this case, a marketing campaign has been launched and the current service needs to be upgraded to deal with the expected increase in loan applications.

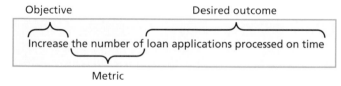

Figure 3.27 Analysing how a service will impact an outcome

Defining outcomes is an important part of defining services, but customers often take it for granted that everyone understands their particular outcomes because they work on them as a matter of routine. It is therefore important that the service provider works with the customer to quantify each outcome, and document it as part of the service description that will be entered into the service pipeline (see section 4.2).

Understanding how services impact outcomes, and therefore what type and level of service is needed, will require the service provider to map the services and outcomes. Although this might be more difficult for external service providers, a good business relationship management process will help the service provider define and document the outcomes in terms that can be measured by the service provider. The valuation of services and service assets becomes easier when it is possible to

visualize the type of outcomes they facilitate. Mapping of outcomes to services and service assets can be accomplished as part of a configuration management system (CMS) and the service portfolio (see section 4.2).

Any outcome that is not well supported represents an opportunity for the service provider. Therefore it is important to review achievement of outcomes regularly, both to ensure that the service provider is not missing an opportunity, and also to ensure that current outcomes are being delivered, so as not to open doors for a competitor. Outcomes for review will be found in the following locations:

- **The service catalogue** Each service in the service catalogue should be clearly linked to defined and quantified outcomes. The service level review or business relationship management surveys should regularly check to ensure that these outcomes are still valid, and that additional outcomes are identified and documented through service portfolio management.
- **The service pipeline** These are outcomes that a new service, or major change to an existing service, needs to be able to support. These will be used as a criterion for the success of the service design and validation.
- **Service level agreement** Many service level agreements will specify the service as well as the outcome it has been designed to support. This will ensure that linkage between the two is maintained and consciously measured.

Gaining insight into the customer's business and having good knowledge of customer outcomes is essential to developing a strong business relationship with customers. This is a key activity within business relationship management (see section 4.5).

An outcome-based definition of services ensures that managers plan and execute all aspects of service management entirely from the perspective of what is valuable to the customer. Such an approach ensures that services not only create value for customers but also capture value for the service provider.

3.4.4 Step 4 – Classify and visualize the service

Every service is unique, but many have similar characteristics. If a new service shares common

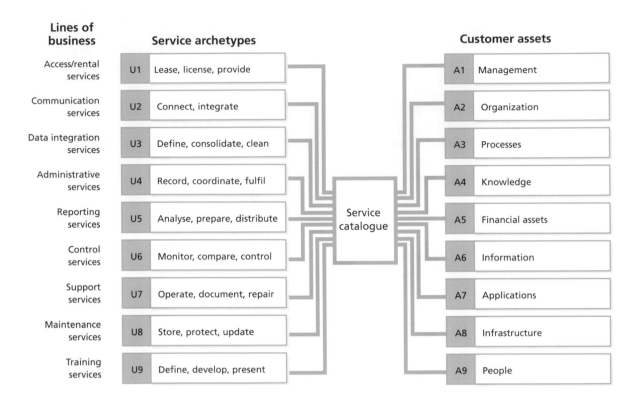

Figure 3.28 Classifying services using service archetypes and customer assets

characteristics with an existing service, it will be easier to determine what it will take to deliver the service. If it has no characteristics in common with existing services, this means that the service will need to be evaluated and designed from the beginning.

Creating a way to classify services and represent them visually will help in identifying whether a new service requirement fits within the current strategy, or whether it will represent an expansion of that strategy. It might also assist the service provider to decide not to make an investment in a service that moves them away from their strategy.

One way to classify services is to use service archetypes, or basic building blocks for services. In Figure 3.28 a number of service archetypes are identified in the boxes on the left of the diagram – labelled U1–9. The 'U' is used to represent the utility of the service, and the archetypes are based on the service provider's current set of resources and capabilities. The right side of the diagram represents the customer assets that are supported by each service (either by enhancing the asset's performance or reducing the impact of constraints) – labelled A1–9. Services are created when a service archetype is used to support a customer asset.

For example, U3×A3 would indicate a service that is used to define, consolidate and clean the data used to support one or more processes. This means that the service provider has the generic skills to manage data integration tasks, and in this case they have applied those skills to support a particular process or processes. For example, IT ensures that the data required from several different sources can be consolidated into a single interface and used by the business to check on stock levels, place orders and deliver goods to customers.

Mapping service archetypes and customer assets can also be useful to define strategies or to reveal patterns of demand or competence that have been built over time. This is especially helpful for those service providers who were required to deliver whatever services the business demanded in the past, without having a clear strategy. This type of mapping will provide a baseline from which they can identify future opportunities and services.

For example, the service provider may learn that many services are based on the same service archetype. They may learn that their resources and capabilities are mainly targeted at supporting business processes. This would be an asset-based

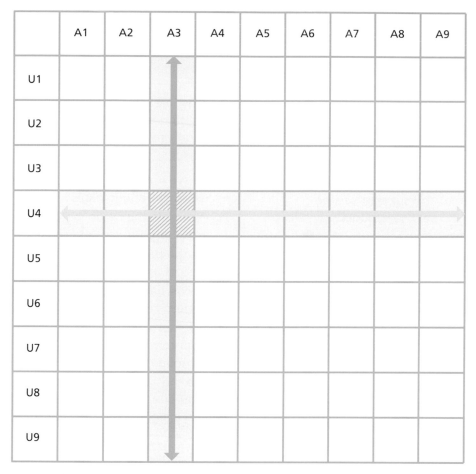

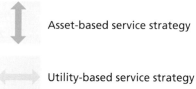

Asset-based service strategy

Utility-based service strategy

Figure 3.29 Asset-based and utility-based strategies

service strategy – represented by the vertical arrow in Figure 3.29.

Alternatively, they may learn that what differentiates them is the ability to provide administrative services that support a wide range of customer assets. This is shown by the horizontal arrow in Figure 3.29, which represents a utility-based strategy.

Most organizations have a combination of utility- and asset-based service patterns, but the visualization of services helps them to understand where they are strongest in each, and where they need to strengthen their portfolio, resources or capabilities.

This combination of service archetypes and customer assets often results in a series of patterns that indicate the positions where the service provider is strong. Services with closely matching patterns indicate opportunity for consolidation or packaging as shared services. If the applications asset type appears in many patterns, then service providers can have more investments in capabilities and resources that support services related to applications. Similarly, if many patterns include the support archetype, it is an indication that support has emerged as a core capability. These are just simple examples of how the service catalogue can be visualized as a collection of useful patterns. Service strategy can result in a particular collection of patterns (intended strategy) or a collection of patterns can make a particular service strategy attractive (emergent strategy).

Figure 3.30 shows examples of patterns of services as described above. In this diagram, a single service may be constructed from one or more service archetypes and may support one or more customer assets, as follows:

- Service A is a utility-based communication service, which supports three types of customer asset: organization, processes and knowledge.
- Service B is largely an asset-based process service, in which processes are supported by reporting, control and support service archetypes. In this service support services are also provided to support the organization asset.
- Service C is a support service archetype that supports financial assets, information and applications.
- Service D is a range of service archetypes (administrative, reporting, control and support) that support application assets. It also includes reporting support for infrastructure assets.

This visual method can be useful in communication and coordination between functions and processes of service management. These visualizations are the basis of more formal definitions of services. Proper matching of the value-creating context (customer assets) with the value-creating concept (service archetype) can avoid shortfalls in performance. For example, the customer's business may involve reviewing and processing of application forms, requests and account registrations. Questions of the following type can be useful:

- Do we have the capabilities to support workflow applications?
- What are the recurring patterns in processing application forms and requests?
- Do the patterns vary based on time of year, type of applicants or around specific events?
- Do we have adequate resources to support the patterns of business activity?
- Are there potential conflicts in fulfilling service level commitments? Are there opportunities for consolidation or shared resources?
- Are the applications and requests subject to regulatory compliance? Do we have knowledge and experience of regulatory compliance?

	A1	A2	A3	A4	A5	A6	A7	A8	A9
U1									
U2		Service A							
U3									
U4							Service D		
U5			Service B				Service D	Service D	
U6			Service B				Service D		
U7		Service B	Service B		Service C	Service C	Service C		
U8									
U9									

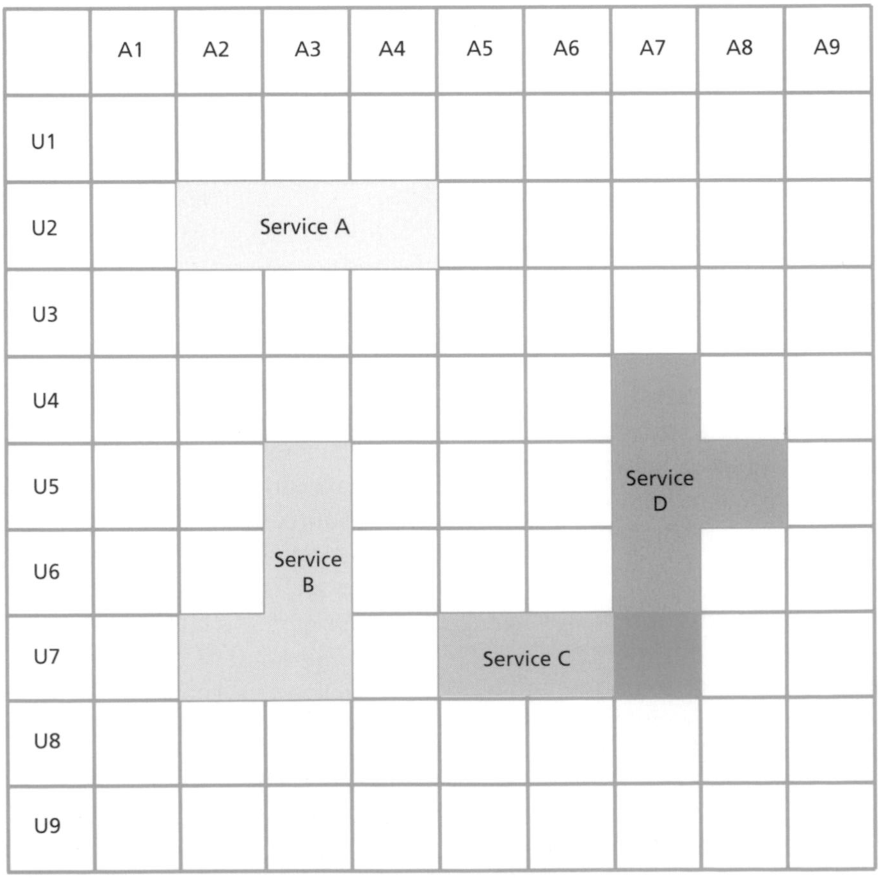

Figure 3.30 Visualization of services as value-creating patterns

- Do we come in direct contact with the customers of the business? If yes, are there adequate controls to manage user interactions and information?

3.4.5 Step 5 – Understand the opportunities (market spaces)

The service provider now has a good understanding of the customer and their assets, and is able to map existing capabilities and resources to existing customer assets to understand what service they are able to provide.

Each customer has a number of requirements, and each service provider has a number of competencies. How does the service provider understand where its competencies will be able to meet the customer's requirements? These intersections between the service provider's competencies and the customer's requirements are called market spaces.

More formally, market spaces are the opportunities that an IT service provider could exploit to meet the business needs of customers. Market spaces identify the possible IT services that an IT service provider may wish to consider delivering.

A market space is defined by a set of business outcomes, which can be facilitated by a service. The opportunity to facilitate those outcomes defines a market space. The following are examples of business outcomes that can be the bases of one or more market spaces:

- Sales teams are productive with sales management system on wireless computers.
- E-commerce website is linked to the warehouse management system.
- Key business applications are monitored and secure.
- Loan officers have faster access to information required on loan applicants.
- Online bill payment service offers more options for shoppers to pay.
- Business continuity is assured.

Each of the outcomes is related to one or more categories of customer assets, such as people, infrastructure, information, accounts receivable and purchase orders, and can then be linked to the services that make them possible. Each outcome can be met in multiple ways, although customers normally prefer those with lower costs and risks. Service providers create the conditions under which outcomes can be met through the services they deliver.

3.4.6 Step 6 – Define services based on outcomes

An outcome-based definition of services ensures that managers plan and execute all aspects of service management entirely from the perspective of what is valuable to the customer. Such an approach ensures that services not only create value for customers but also capture value for the service provider.

Solutions that enable or enhance the performance of the customer assets indirectly support the achievement of the outcomes generated by those assets. Such solutions and propositions hold utility for the business. When that utility is backed by a suitable warranty customers are ready to buy.

Customers can express dissatisfaction with a service provider even when terms and conditions of service level agreements (SLAs) are fulfilled. Often this is because it is not clear how services create value for customers. In these cases services are often defined in the terms of resources made available for use by customers. Service definitions lack clarity on the context in which such resources are useful, and the business outcomes that justify the expense of a service from a customer's perspective. This problem leads to poor designs, ineffective operation and lacklustre performance in service contracts. Service improvements are difficult when it is not clear where improvements are truly required. Customers can understand and appreciate improvements only within the context of their own business assets, performances and outcomes. A proper definition of services takes into account the context in which customers perceive value from the services.

Well-formed service definitions lead to effective and efficient service management processes. Generic examples are given below:

- **Example 1** Collaboration services provide value to the customer when cooperative business communications are conducted without the constraints of location or device. Value is created when the provider operates for the customer store-and-forward and real-time methods of electronic messaging, so that (the customer's) employees can compose, send, store and receive communications in a convenient, reliable and secure manner, for a specified community of users.

■ **Example 2** Application-hosting services provide value to the business when business function services and processes continue to operate without the need to invest capital in a non-core business capability. Value is created when the provider maintains for the business an application software platform system and assures that employees and business systems can work continuously in a convenient, secure and reliable manner, for a specified portfolio of services.

■ **Example 3** Mobile workplace services provide value to the customer when business activity is conducted without the constraints of fixed location. Value is created when the provider operates for the customer a wireless messaging system and assures that (the customer's) employees and business systems can exchange voice and data messages in a convenient, reliable and secure manner, within a specified area of coverage.

■ **Example 4** Order-to-cash services provide value to the business when purchase orders are converted to cash flows without the need to invest capital in a non-core business capability. Value is created when the provider licenses to the business an order fulfilment system and

assures that the sales teams and online shoppers can enter or modify purchase orders in a convenient, fast and secure manner within a specified time schedule.

Two examples of outcome-based service definitions are given in Figures 3.31 and 3.32. Notice how the service archetypes and specific customer assets from step 4 are used in these definitions.

The first example (Figure 3.31) shows outcomes based on the utility of three different lines of service. In this case the outcomes are expressed in terms of the outcomes achieved and the constraints removed (please note that utility can be achieved without having both outcomes achieved *and* constraints removed).

The second example (Figure 3.32) shows the same services expressed in terms of warranty.

Well-constructed definitions make it easier to visualize patterns across service catalogues and portfolios that earlier were hidden due to unstructured definitions. Patterns bring clarity to decisions across the service lifecycle.

Actionable service definitions are useful when they are broken down into discrete elements that can then be assigned to different groups, who will manage them in a coordinated manner to control the overall effect of delivering value to customers.

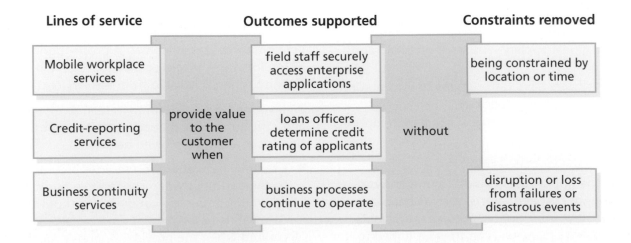

Figure 3.31 Defining services with utility components

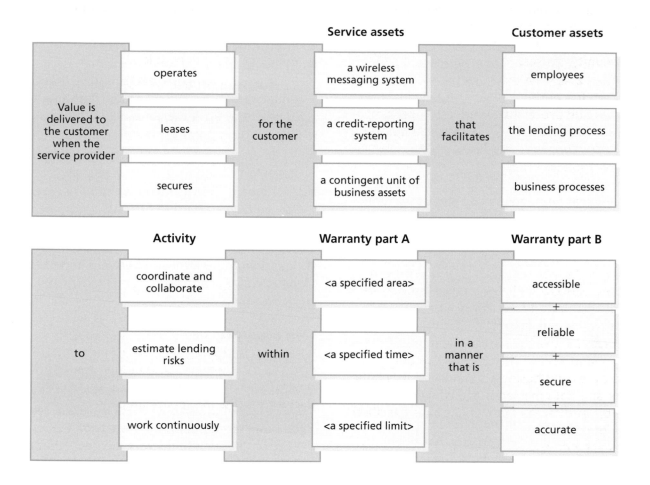

Figure 3.32 Defining services with warranty components

Being able to define services in an actionable manner has its advantages from a strategic perspective. It removes ambiguity from decision-making and avoids misalignment between what customers want and what service providers are organized and capable enough to deliver. Without the context in which the customers use services it is difficult to completely define value. Without complete definition of value, there cannot be complete production of value. As a result, outcomes are not fulfilled to the customer's satisfaction.

However, it is not to say that a service cannot be developed without a customer in hand. It simply means that the story of a service begins either with the needs of a specific customer or a category of customers (i.e. market space). Customer needs exist and are fulfilled independent of service providers or their services. However, value for a customer rests on not only fulfilment of these needs, but also

how they are fulfilled, and often at what risks and costs. Certain services create value by preventing or recovering from undesirable conditions or states. In such cases customers may desire a change in the risks to which their assets may be exposed. In either case, the second-order effect of services is that the changes they produce, or prevent, have a positive and usually measurable effect on the performance and outcomes of the customer's business.

Questions that can be helpful in defining the services in an actionable manner are listed in Table 3.10.

These types of questions are crucial for an organization to consider in the implementation of a strategic approach to service management. They are applied by all types of service providers, internal and external. What changes is the context and meaning of certain ideas such as customers, contracts, competition, market spaces, revenue and

Table 3.10 Defining actionable service components

Service type	Utility (Part A and B)
What services do we provide?	What outcomes do we support?
Who are our customers?	How do they create value for their customers?
	What constraints do our customers face?
Customer assets	Service assets
Which customer assets do we support?	What assets do we deploy to provide value?
Who are the users of our services?	How do we deploy our assets?
Activity or task	Warranty
What type of activity do we support?	How do we create value for them?
How do we track performance?	What assurances do we provide?

strategy. In fact, these clarifying questions are particularly important for internal service providers who typically operate within the realm of an enterprise or government agency, have customers who are also owners and whose strategic objectives may not always be clear.

3.4.7 Step 7 – Service models

The definition of a service model is 'a model that shows how service assets interact with customer assets to create value. Service models describe the structure of a service (how the configuration items fit together) and the dynamics of the service (activities, flow of resources and interactions). A service model can be used as a template or blueprint for multiple services.'

Service models can take many forms, from a simple logical chart showing the different components and their dependencies, to a complex analytical model analysing the dynamics of a service under different configurations and demand patterns.

Service models have a number of uses, especially in service portfolio management (see section 4.2), including:

- Understanding what it will take to deliver a new service
- Identifying critical service components, customer assets or service assets – and then

ensuring that they are designed to cope with the required demand
- Illustrating how value is created
- Mapping the teams and assets that are involved in delivering a service, and ensuring that they understand their impact on the customer's ability to achieve their business outcomes
- As a starting point for designing new services
- As an assessment tool for understanding the impact of changes to existing services
- As a means of identifying whether new services can be delivered using existing assets
- If not, then assessing what type of investment would be required to deliver the service
- Identifying the interface between technology, people and processes required to develop and deliver the service.

Key message

A service model is not a design. A service model is a list or diagram of items that will be needed in order to be able to deliver the service. The service model shows how these items are related and how they are used by the service.

Service models are the blueprints for service management processes and functions to communicate and collaborate on value creation. Service models describe how service assets interact with customer assets and create value for a given portfolio of contracts. Interaction means demand connects with the capacity to serve. Service level agreements specify the terms and conditions in which such interaction occurs with commitments and expectations on each side. The outcomes define the value to be created for the customer, which itself rests on the utility provided to customers and the warranty.

Service models also represent the structure and dynamics of services, which in turn are influenced by the customer's utility and warranty requirements. The structure and dynamics are influenced by factors of utility and warranty to be delivered to customers. Structure is defined in terms of particular service assets needed and the patterns in which they are configured. Dynamics are defined in terms of activities, flow of resources, coordination and interactions. This includes the cooperation and communication between users and service providers. The dynamics of a service include patterns of business activity, demand patterns, exceptions and variations.

Figure 3.33 provides an example of how the dynamics of a service can be represented in a service model. In this case a retail service is illustrated. In this example, each component of the service is listed on a separate leg (or part), and each activity is numbered in the sequence in which the service is normally delivered. Each component of the service is listed in relation to the other components, dependencies identified and flows of communication and data indicated.

The methods and tools of systems engineering and workflow management are useful for developing the process maps, workflow diagrams, queuing models and activity patterns necessary for completeness of service models. Service transition evaluates detailed service models to ensure they are fit for purpose and fit for use before entering service operation through the service catalogue. It is necessary for service models to be under change control because the utility and warranty of a service can have undesired variation if there are changes to the service assets or their configuration.

Service models are very useful during service transition and service operation to help communicate how the components interact to create the service. This will facilitate more thorough testing, building and the communication of changes to stakeholders. During service operation it helps operational teams to perform incident management and problem management better since dependencies and impacts are clearly indicated. They also help operational teams manage performance of the service through a better understanding of all the components that could affect performance.

Service models are useful for effectiveness in continual service improvement (CSI). Improvements can be made to the structure or the dynamics of a model. Service transition evaluates the options or paths for improvements and recommends solutions that are cost-effective and low-risk. Service models continually evolve, based on external feedback received from customers and internal feedback from service management processes. CSI activities ensure that feedback is passed to all service lifecycle stages.

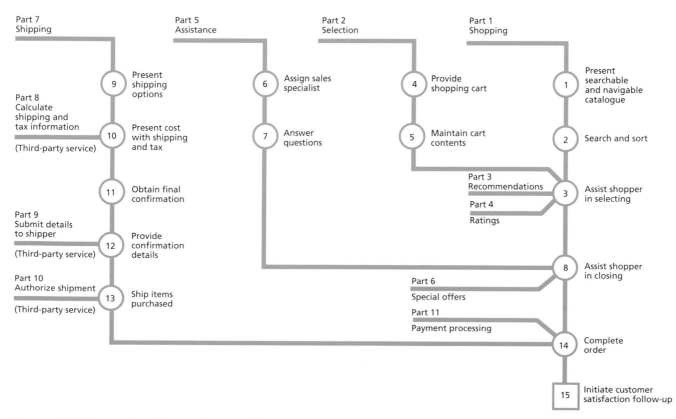

Figure 3.33 Dynamics of a service model

3.4.8 Step 8 – Define service units and packages

Services may be as simple as allowing a user to complete a single transaction, but most services are complex. They consist of a range of deliverables and functionality. If each individual aspect of these complex services were defined independently, the service provider would soon find it impossible to track and record all services.

Some services can be delivered on their own, but others require additional services to make them work. For example, buying a book is straightforward, but to buy an electronic book requires that the customer has a reading device, a means to connect to the service provider and a means to track licensing of the intellectual property.

When a single service is delivered to a customer it is viewed by the service provider as a service. When two or more services are bundled and sold or delivered together they are viewed by the service provider as a service package. Service packages are created for two main reasons:

- If the core service is not able to be delivered without enabling services being present
- To create additional value for the customer, which translates to additional revenue and customer loyalty for the service provider.

Packaging services requires an understanding of the different types of services and how they can be marketed and sold. The three basic types of services that can be delivered are core services, enabling services and enhancing services (these are described in section 2.1.1). These services can, in some cases, be delivered on their own, and in other cases packaged together with other services.

3.4.8.1 Service packages

One strategy is for a service provider to have a small number of customers, and design unique services for each one. Since these services will be expensive (due to high development costs and dedicated resources), there is a very small number of service providers that will be able to make a commercial success of this strategy (since there is a limited number of customers willing to pay the premium for the tailored service).

Most service providers will follow a strategy where they can deliver a set of more generic services to a broad range of customers, thus achieving

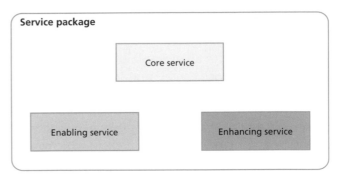

Figure 3.34 A service package

economies of scale and competing on the basis of price and a certain amount of flexibility. One way of achieving this is by using service packages. A service package is a collection of two or more services that have been combined to offer a solution to a specific type of customer need or to underpin specific business outcomes. Service packages can consist of a combination of core, enabling and enhancing services, as illustrated in Figure 3.34. Please note that a service package does not need to have all three types of service – it only needs to have more than one service of any type to be a service package.

It should be noted that service packages can consist of multiple services of each type, as illustrated in Figure 3.35. Also service packages can include one or more service packages as in Figure 3.36. It is important to ensure that services and service packages are grouped so that customers can relate to them better, thus making them easier to buy and use.

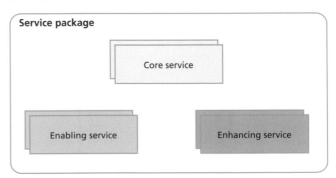

Figure 3.35 Service packages can consist of multiple individual services of any type

> **Key message**
>
> Customers do not always see the layers of service packages – rather they focus on the services that they use without needing to understand how these are constructed.

Packages are constructed so that instead of a bewildering number of individual services being offered to customers, services can be combined in logical groupings to produce products that can then be marketed, sold and consumed to best meet customers' needs.

Media companies provide good examples of service packaging. An example could be a company that provides the following residential services:

- Television channels (cable or satellite)
- Broadband internet
- Digital telephone
- Online storage
- Messaging.

Media companies (and their customers) would find it very difficult if every television channel had to be ordered separately, or if customers had to order, and be billed for, each type of service separately. Imagine the frustration if a customer had to contact the company five times, open five accounts and receive five bills because they wanted to use the full range of services offered.

Instead the media company identifies typical customer groups (e.g. young families, sports fans, retired couples, entertainment venues etc.) and then packages attractive service options to best meet the requirements of each group. In this way the provider can meet most customers' needs in a commercially effective way. This identification of customer groups is sometimes referred to as 'segmentation' (see section 3.4.8.4).

In the world of IT, many organizations have adopted a similar approach by packaging services so as to meet customer demands but in a way that allows a high degree of standardization with a reduction in maintenance complexity and costs. A service package could take the form of a standard desktop image, including all of the service components the users need whilst providing a standard environment that is much easier to support and maintain.

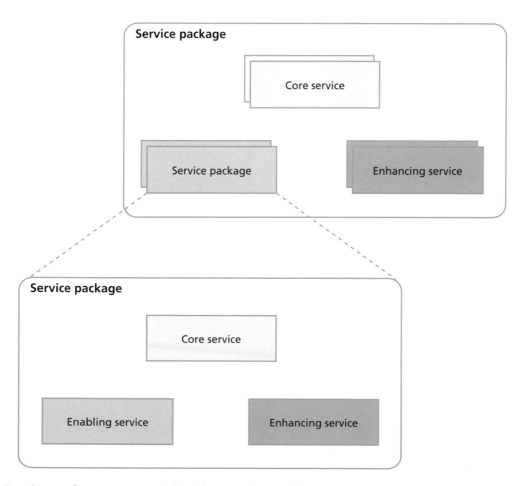

Figure 3.36 Service packages can contain other service packages

3.4.8.2 Services and service packages can include options

In many cases – especially when providing services to a large number and diversity of customers – service packages of the same type may need to be differentiated from one another. For example, a mobile telecommunications company will provide one type of service – mobile phone communication – but they may gear the types of telephone, number of lines, data limits etc. towards different types of consumer, such as business users, families and rural communities. Although the service is essentially the same, each type of consumer will require a different level of warranty and utility.

Where a service or service package needs to be differentiated for different types of customer, one or more components of the package can be changed, or offered at different levels of utility and warranty, to create service options. These different service options can then be offered to customers and are sometimes called service level packages.

Using the media company as an example, each service can be broken down into a number of options, each offering higher or lower levels of service for different types of customer. For example, when considering a core service of television channels (cable or satellite):

■ Option A includes 100 channels
■ Option B includes 200 channels
■ Option C includes only channels appropriate for families with young children
■ Option D includes 300 channels and 5 pay-per-view sporting events per month.

Each of the services above has a defined level of utility and warranty. These levels of utility and warranty will be documented in the service catalogue, thus allowing the customer to choose the option that best suits their needs.

Service packages may be created to offer a number of different options to the customer – for example, a network provider may offer a range of service packages, each with a different amount of storage available (e.g. 5 GB, 10 GB, 20 GB), together with a standard email service. This will allow the customer to choose the service package for their preferred option.

3.4.8.3 Cloud computing

In the case of cloud computing the customer is able to pick and choose their own combinations of services and service levels, so in effect they are choosing their own packages and options. This could be the result of customers being driven to standardized, lower cost services that are widely available on the internet, rather than investing in customized service contracts.

Case study involving a large IT company

Over 10 years the IT services provided by a large IT company had grown in number to over 2,000. Many of these services did exactly the same thing, but on different hardware models. Some of the services had names that included technical jargon, which were used to communicate to the delivery engineers what it was that they needed to do – even though the customer had no idea what they meant.

When selling hardware, sales people tended to avoid selling related services because the list of services in the catalogue was too long and complex for them to find the exact service they needed. As a result, customers would generally find a third party to provide these higher margin services.

The manager of this portfolio needed to simplify the catalogue of services without sacrificing the ability to track what services were delivered on which hardware platform.

The result was a new catalogue of services. The portfolio manager assessed which services were being sold, and in what combination. The most popular combinations were bundled together and sold as packages – the thousands of individual services were consolidated down to fewer than 200 service packages. Salespeople were trained on how to sell the new packages. All they had to do was select the service package, specify which hardware it was being sold with, and the delivery team would deliver the individual services that made up the package – without the customer having to be concerned about understanding the 20 to 30 line items on the invoice with names that only the vendor could understand.

The result was a simpler set of services, that was easier to sell, and customers that had a clear understanding of what they were buying.

IT example of service packages

To help summarize and clarify the use of packaging, here is an example based on the delivery of an email service.

A banking organization builds an email service that provides basic email utility and warranty for all the users in the bank. It also has a networking service and a troubleshooting service. The organization encapsulated these services into a basic email service product (service package) ready for consumption by bank users.

The basic option for this service consists of the basic levels of utility and warranty for the email service that anyone in the bank can use. The basic service package can be offered to any bank user.

A different option of the email service package (consisting of the same core services, but with higher levels of warranty and utility) is designed for commodity traders in the bank (in the US, email for this customer segment must comply to SEC rules, ensure secure logging of emails and instant text messages, support audit requests etc.).

The service provider constructs yet another option of this service package that represents advanced levels of utility and warranty for senior executives of the bank (i.e. higher response priorities, differing channels to receive emails on etc.).

Note: Service packages must not be confused with service design packages and release packages – these are used for very different purposes. The way in which services are packaged for marketing, sales and consumption may be completely different from the way in which they are packaged for design, building, distribution and release.

An example of this is illustrated as follows. A cloud service provider offers a range of service packages. Each service package is offered at three levels of service, at three different price levels. Customers will choose which services they will use, and at what level. In this way they will choose multiple services and service packages to create their own service package, consisting of three options:

■ Online PC backup (100 GB, 200 GB, 500 GB)

■ Email: (50 messages per day, 250 messages per day, unlimited messages)
■ Web page hosting: (5 pages, 10 pages, 50 pages).

3.4.8.4 Segmentation

As briefly mentioned earlier, an organization may choose to categorize its customers, so as to be able to package services targeted to the needs of each category. This is sometimes referred to as segmentation.

In its simplest form this could, for example, be a golf club or leisure centre offering different membership packages (e.g. individual, family, junior, senior etc.) but may be more sophisticated, such as the example of the media company offering entertainment and communication packages, mentioned above.

Segmentation can be extremely valuable for targeting marketing, sales campaigns etc. – as well as for defining service packages aimed at different segments. IT providers can use the same technique to segment IT users. This will allow service packages to be developed to meet the needs of each user type, while giving the following advantages:

■ Maximization of standardization
■ Minimization of different and diverse services
■ Easier distribution
■ Simplification of support issue.

Table 3.11 gives a simplified example of how an IT organization might segment its users and the service packages they might provide.

The segmentation processes will require close consultation with the customers to fully understand their requirements, and with the technical groups to devise the exact packaged solutions.

3.4.8.5 Designing and transitioning service packages

The design and transition of service packages follows exactly the same process as any other service. A suggestion or request for a new service package (or change to an existing service package) is submitted through service portfolio management. The service package is modelled and assessed, and a change proposal submitted. Once authorized, the required levels of utility and warranty for the service package and its options

Table 3.11 User segmentation and user packages

User type	Packages
Standard office worker (2,500 staff)	Standard package (standard desktop hardware configuration plus basic desktop service package)
Office-based security specialist (50 staff)	Standard package (standard desktop hardware configuration plus basic desktop service package) plus security service package
Office-based health and safety specialist (50 staff)	Standard package (standard desktop hardware configuration plus basic desktop service package) plus H&S service package
Standard office and occasional home worker (300 staff)	Standard package (standard desktop hardware configuration plus basic service package) plus VPN service package
Home worker (200 staff)	Home package (home worker hardware configuration plus basic service package plus home service package)
Mobile worker	Mobile package (standard laptop configuration plus basic service package) plus mobile service package
VIP	VIP package (VIP laptop configuration plus basic service package) plus VIP service package

will be documented in the service charter and submitted to design coordination (please refer to section 4.2 for a detailed description of this process).

A service design package (SDP) will be created to support the design, transition and operation of the service package throughout the service lifecycle. The service transition processes will build, test and deploy the service packages, just as they would for any individual service, using the service charter and SDP as a basis for this activity.

The service package and its options will be documented in the service catalogue.

3.5 STRATEGIES FOR CUSTOMER SATISFACTION

It is often not enough for a service to meet a customer's business outcome. Especially in a competitive environment, it is necessary for customers to feel satisfied with the level of service they have received. They also need to feel confident in the ability of the service provider to continue providing that level of service – or even improving it over time.

The only difficulty is that customer expectations keep shifting, and a service provider that does not track this will soon lose business. The following discussion on service attributes and the Kano model is helpful in understanding how this

happens, and how a service provider can adapt its services to meet the changing customer environment.

Attributes of a service are the characteristics that provide form and function to the service from a utilization perspective. The attributes are traced from business outcomes to be supported by the service. Certain attributes must be present for value creation to begin. Others add value on a sliding scale determined by how customers evaluate increments in utility and warranty. Service level agreements commonly provide for differentiated levels of service quality for different sets of users.

Some attributes are more important to customers than others. They have a direct impact on the performance of customer assets and therefore the realization of basic outcomes. Such attributes are 'must-have' attributes (Kano et al., 1984). Table 3.12 describes the type of attributes that influence the customer's perception of utility from a service. A factor that is linear means that the level of customer satisfaction is directly related to the degree to which customer needs are met. Non-linear factors are those where even though a fraction of customer needs are met, they result in high levels of customer satisfaction.

3.5.1 The Kano model

Figure 3.37 illustrates the Kano model (Kano et al., 1984) of customer perceptions of utility. This figure

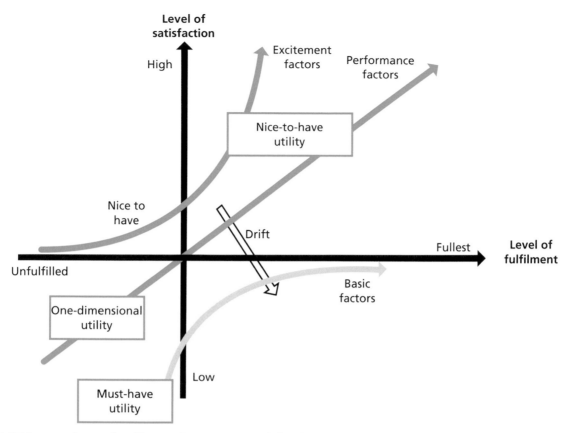

Figure 3.37 Perceptions of utility and customer satisfaction

Table 3.12 The Kano model and service attributes (after Kano *et al.*, 1984)

Type of attribute	Fulfilment and perceptions of utility (gain/loss)
Basic factors (B) (must-have, non-linear)	Attributes of the service expected or taken for granted. Not fulfilling these will cause perceptions of utility loss. Fulfilling them results in utility gain but only until the neutral zone after which there is no gain.
Excitement factors (E) (attractive utility, non-linear)	Attributes of the service that drive perceptions of utility gain but when not fulfilled do not cause perceptions of utility loss.
Performance factors (P) (attractive utility, linear)	Attributes of the service that result in perceptions of utility gain when fulfilled and utility loss when not fulfilled in an almost linear one-dimensional pattern.
Indifferent attributes (I)	Cause neither gains nor losses in perceptions of utility regardless of whether they are fulfilled or not.
Reversed attributes (R)	Cause gains in perceptions of utility when not fulfilled and losses when fulfilled. Assumptions need to be reversed.
Questionable response (Q)	Responses are questionable possibly because questions were not clear or were misinterpreted.

shows a relationship between the level of fulfilment of customer needs that a service offers, and the level of satisfaction that a customer feels.

The Kano model shows that there are three different types of factors involved in customer satisfaction:

- **Basic factors** These are aspects of the service that have to be in place for the customer to receive the service. In many cases these basic factors are taken for granted. Sometimes they don't offer any overt value, but if they fail, or are not delivered, customers will become very dissatisfied. For example, nobody eats at a restaurant because it has lights, but if there is a power failure and customers cannot see what they are eating, they will probably leave. In the same way, a user does not come to work because they have a personal computer connected to the network; but if the network or PC is not working, they will not be able to access email and other key services. These factors are sometimes called 'must-have utility', or the very least the service provider can deliver for a particular service. As shown in Figure 3.37, basic factors are not responsible for high levels of satisfaction, unless they alone fulfil the customer's requirements completely.

- **Performance factors** These are factors that enable a customer to get more of something that they need, or a higher level of service quality. The more a customer wants of each performance factor, the more they will expect to pay, thus the greater value it must contribute. These are also called one-dimensional utilities since each factor is increased or decreased along a predictable line based on customer demand. The higher the level of performance that fulfils a higher percentage of the customer's requirements, the more satisfied a customer will be, although extremely high levels of performance may be perceived as 'nice to have'. An example of performance factors is where a restaurant offers a discount to frequent diners, or to tables that order two or more of the daily special. IT examples may include providing additional storage, bandwidth or other resource allocation for high priority services.

- **Excitement factors** These are attributes of a service that are generous, and which customers do not expect. When they are offered (within

reason) they cause higher levels of satisfaction. The service provider is seen to be 'going the extra mile'. For example, the restaurant offers a free drink with every main course. While excitement factors result in the quickest and highest levels of customer satisfaction, they are expensive to maintain, since the service provider is offering more than necessary at the same price. These factors may be exciting, but they are not essential to the service, and are therefore also referred to as 'nice-to-have utility'. Internal service providers should be careful of introducing excitement factors in the interest of 'customer satisfaction' without doing a proper business case to justify the additional costs.

Excitement factors and performance factors are the basis for market segmentation and differentiated service levels. They are used to fulfil the needs of particular types of customers. Such attributes are necessary for any strategy involving the segmenting of customers into groups and serving them with an appropriate utility package. Basic factors are the cost of entry into the market space. Without basic factors the service provider cannot enter the market space. As time passes, excitement factors become commonly available, losing their ability to differentiate. Competition, changes in customer perceptions and new innovations can cause excitement factors to drift towards becoming performance or basic factors.

Drift

Many service providers fall into the trap of believing that they should deliver the highest level of service possible, regardless of the level of fulfilment that is required. While this might result in higher levels of customer satisfaction in the short term (see Figure 3.37), it does not last very long, for two reasons:

- Firstly, it is expensive to maintain, and after a while the service provider must either increase the price of the service, or stop offering the excitement factors.
- Secondly, generous levels of service quickly become expected. So a nice-to-have becomes a performance factor, and then a must-have.

Excitement factors should only be offered under three circumstances:

■ If the service provider has a strategy to attract customers, and intends to keep these factors as a permanent feature of the service (and they have the funding to continue doing so).
■ If the service provider uses them as part of a marketing campaign and will only be offering them for a limited time. The end date is clearly identified, and the customers know that these attributes will not be available after that date.
■ If the service provider has disappointed the customer due to a service failure or because of not meeting expectations. The nice-to-have may be offered once in order to make up for the error, but both the service provider and the customer clearly understand that this is a special exception.

An IT example may help to clarify the nature of basic, performance and excitement factors and customer satisfaction.

Take the example of an online storage service with synchronized backup and restore capabilities. It must provide round-the-clock access, with high upload and download speeds. It must protect from corruption, unauthorized access and accidental disclosure. At the same time, it must be very accessible to the authorized users. There is utility gain from having access to the storage service on a public network through a secure browser. The service is a substitute for a portable storage device, which needs careful handling and transport by the users to maintain access to the stored data. To an extent, security and accessibility are basic factors. Their provision does not result in utility gains for the customer. Although they don't provide any level of excitement, not providing them would cause a dramatic drop in customer satisfaction.

Some users have need for a greater amount of storage than others. Within a certain range, they value an increasing amount of storage and are willing to pay a proportionally higher price. The size of storage is a performance factor with one-dimensional utility, along with which it is meaningful to offer options. Within the range, the relationship between utility and storage space is approximately linear. Outside this range, the customers have diminishing utility on additional storage or the lack of it. Another type of one-dimensional utility could be the number of 'sub-accounts' so that customers can assign different storage boxes for different purposes such as projects, media type and personal information. More sub-accounts mean greater utility with diminishing utility after a particular number of sub-accounts.

Services can have excitement attributes, which customers do not expect but are happy to have, given a reasonable offer. The storage service may offer attributes such as scheduled backups and notification, administrator-style privileges, multiple sub-accounts, metering, access control, account administration and secure file transfer protocols. Some customers may view these as performance factors with one-dimensional utility. For others these are excitement factors. Their absence does not cause dissatisfaction. Their presence causes a dramatic increase in satisfaction at a reasonable price.

Table 3.13 The Kano evaluation table (Kano et al., 1984)

Customers are asked:	Dysfunctional form (–) →	How would you feel if the service does not have attribute X?				
Functional form (+) ↓	Customers respond ↓ →	Like it	Expect it	Neutral	Accept it	Dislike it
How would you feel if the service has attribute X?	Like it	Q	E	E	E	P
	Expect it	R	I	I	I	B
	Neutral	R	I	I	I	B
	Accept it	R	I	I	I	B
	Dislike it	R	R	R	R	Q

B = basic; E = excitement; P = performance; I = indifferent; R = reversed; Q = questionable

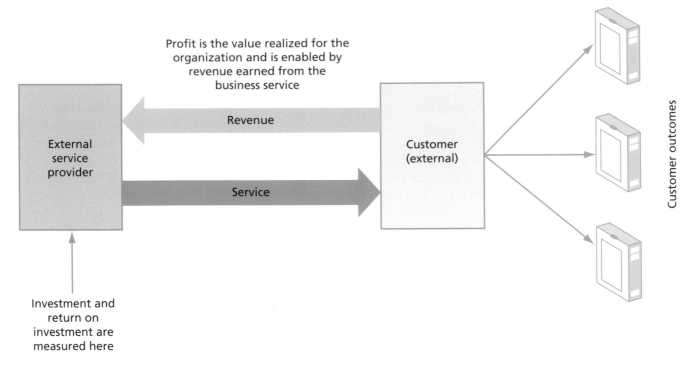

Figure 3.38 Service economic dynamics for external service providers

Extensive dialogue is required with targeted customers or segments of market spaces to determine the attributes a service must have, should have and could have in terms of must-have utility. Questionnaires are used to elicit responses from customers from which further analysis is possible. The Kano evaluation table is a useful method (Table 3.13).

A well-designed service provides a combination of basic, performance and excitement attributes to deliver an appropriate level of utility for the customer. Different customers will place different weights or importance on the same combination of attributes. Furthermore, even if a particular type of customer values a particular combination, they may not find justification to pay for additional charges.

3.6 SERVICE ECONOMICS

Service economics relate to the balance between the cost of providing services, the value of the outcomes achieved and the returns that the services enable the service provider to achieve.

The dynamics of service economics for external service providers are different from those for internal service providers. This is because the returns of internal service providers are mainly measured by their internal customers and do not

accrue directly to the service provider. This is illustrated in Figures 3.38 and 3.39.

In Figure 3.38 the Type III service provider delivers a service to an external customer for payment. The service provider calculates the total investment required to deliver that service, and measures it against the total revenue obtained from delivering the service. The success of the service provider is measured by its return on its investment (ROI).

By contrast, the return on investment cannot be measured by an internal service provider in isolation from their internal customers. In Figure 3.39 an IT service provider delivers a service to another business unit, which covers the costs of the IT service. Therefore the investment in the IT service is carried by the business unit, and not the service provider. The funding provided to the IT service provider cannot be viewed as a return on investment, since the investment is being made by the business unit. Instead the return is in the form of the profitability generated by the business unit, and the ROI calculation is performed by the business unit.

If the IT service provider attempts to demonstrate its ROI without referring to the business unit's revenue, the only time it will be able to demonstrate an actual return is when it reduces its costs. As a result many IT organizations find

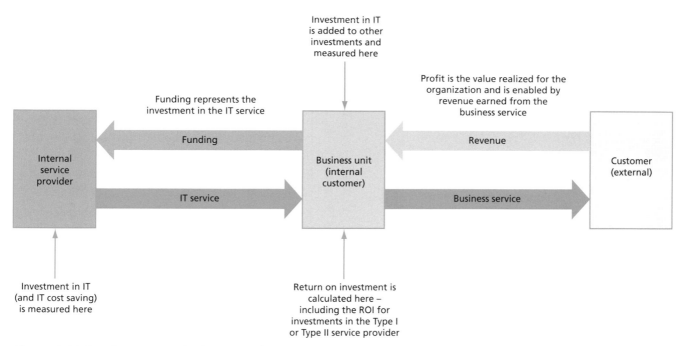

Figure 3.39 Service economic dynamics for internal service providers

themselves being asked by the business to cut costs, even when their services are critical for the business to achieve its outcomes. This is covered in more detail in section 3.2.3, where the importance of linking IT investments to business outcomes is discussed.

Service economics relies on four main areas:

■ **Service portfolio management** The process that defines the outcomes the business desires to achieve, and the services that will be used to achieve them. This is covered in detail in section 4.2.

■ **Financial management for IT services** The process by which service providers (and other business units) calculate, forecast and track costs and income related to services. This is covered in detail in section 4.3.

■ **Return on investment** (ROI) A measurement of the expected or actual benefit of an investment. Section 3.6.1 will focus on how ROI is used, together with service portfolio management and financial management for IT services to build healthy service economics for the service provider's organization.

■ **Business impact analysis** (BIA) This allows an organization to establish the relative priorities of services based on their effect on the business if they are not available for a period of time. This is a key method used in IT service continuity management and is discussed in detail in *ITIL Service Design*. An overview is provided here to explain the role of BIA in service strategy.

In addition to these four areas, a special note needs to be made of demand management (described in section 4.4). This is the process whereby vital business functions are identified and resources deployed to ensure that the appropriate levels of business performance can be met. Demand management works to gear IT resources to meet the changing demands of business as it responds to its environment. Changes in demand reflect a potential change to the value of services, and their ongoing ability to enable the business to meet its objectives. For this reason demand management plays an important role in the ongoing evaluation of the economics of services.

3.6.1 Return on investment

Return on investment (ROI) is a concept for quantifying the value of an investment, and the calculation is normally performed by financial management. The term is not always used consistently. Sometimes it is used by financial officers to indicate the ROIC (return on invested capital), a measure of business performance. In service management, ROI is used as a measure of the ability to use assets to generate additional value. In the simplest sense, it is the net profit of an investment divided by the net worth of the assets invested. The resulting percentage is applied to either additional top-line revenue or the elimination of bottom-line cost. In economic terms, a good investment is one that exceeds the rate of return on the capital market.

A very simple ROI calculation would look something like the following:

$$\text{ROI} = \frac{\text{Increase in profit resulting from the service}}{\text{Total investment in the service}}$$

Although this calculation seems to be straightforward, it is somewhat simplistic since customer perception is subjective, and there are many intangible factors involved in delivering the services. It is even more difficult to quantify the value of service management – since it is not delivered directly to a customer, and does not directly deliver business outcomes for the customer.

While ROI calculations can be helpful in indicating the success of a service or a service management implementation, there are a number of factors that must be taken into account, including:

■ ROI exercises that focus purely on financial metrics do not indicate the full potential return. For example, some services have little direct return, but provide the basis whereby other services can be delivered.
■ The ROI calculation should include some measure of how much the service, or service management project, moved the organization

closer to achieving its strategy. These will often be qualitative statements about the service or project – for example, increased levels of customer loyalty.
■ ROI that is only based on cost savings for the service provider will not be perceived by the business as a return on their investment if there is no corresponding impact on the cost per unit of business service or product.
■ ROI calculations that only focus on the short-term results will often yield negative figures. For example, many service management processes are focused on improving the capability and resources of the service provider. These may take some time to design and build (and significant investment) before they yield any returns.

The limits of many traditional ROI calculations have led to the emergence of calculations aimed at including more of the intangible results expected from a service. These calculations are often referred to as Value on Investment calculations, and are covered in more detail in *ITIL Continual Service Improvement*. Nevertheless, ROI remains the primary business tool for assessing the value of a service, and will therefore be covered in detail below.

While a service can be directly linked and justified through specific business imperatives, few companies can readily identify the financial return for the specific aspects of service management. It is often an investment that companies must make in advance of any return. Service management by itself does not provide any of the tactical benefits that business managers typically budget for. One of the greatest challenges for those seeking funding

Table 3.14 Sample business case structure

A. Introduction	Presents the business objectives addressed by the service.
B. Methods and assumptions	Defines the boundaries of the business case, such as time period, and which organizational context is being used to define costs and benefits.
C. Business impacts	The financial and non-financial results anticipated for the service or service management initiative. Please bear in mind that many non-financial results can also be expressed in financial terms. For example, an increase in staff morale can result in lower staff turnover, and therefore less expenditure on hiring and training.
D. Risks and contingencies	The probability that alternative results will emerge.
E. Recommendations	Specific actions recommended.

Table 3.15 Common business objectives

Operational	Financial	Strategic	Industry
Shorten development time	Improve return on assets	Establish or enhance strategic positioning	Increase market share
Increase productivity	Avoid costs	Introduce competitive products	Improve market position
Increase capacity	Increase discretionary spending as a percentage of budget	Improve professionalism of organization	Increase repeat business
Increase reliability	Decrease non-discretionary spending	Improve customer satisfaction	Take market leadership
Minimize risks	Increase revenues	Provide better quality	Recognized as producer of reliable or quality products or services
Improve resource utilization	Increase margins	Provide customized offerings	Recognized as low-price leader
Improve efficiencies	Keep spending to within budget	Introduce new products or services	Recognized as compliant to industry standards
Meet contractual obligations	Ensure that performance supports revenue generation	Deliver to meet objectives and obligations	Recognized as a reliable provider
Reduce customer complaints	Reduce the cost of rework	Improve customer retention	Recognized as a provider of quality goods and services

for ITIL projects is identifying a specific business imperative that depends on service management. For these reasons, this discussion on ROI focuses on three areas:

■ **Business case** A means to identify business imperatives that depend on service management
■ **Pre-programme ROI** Techniques for quantitatively analysing an investment in service management
■ **Post-programme ROI** Techniques for retroactively analysing an investment in service management.

3.6.1.1 Business case

A business case is a decision support and planning tool that projects the likely consequences of a business action. The consequences can take on qualitative and quantitative dimensions. A financial analysis, for example, is frequently central to a good business case.

An example of a business case structure is provided in Table 3.14.

Business objectives

The structure of a business case varies from organization to organization. What they all have in common is a detailed analysis of business impact or benefits. Business impact is in turn linked to business objectives. A business objective is the reason for considering a service management initiative in the first place. Objectives should start broadly. For example:

■ The business objectives for commercial provider organizations are usually the objectives of the business itself, including financial and organizational performance.
■ The business objectives of an internal service provider should be linked to the business objectives of the business unit to which the service is being provided, and the overall corporate objectives.
■ The business objectives for not-for-profit organizations are usually the objectives for the constituents, population or membership served as well as financial and organizational performance.

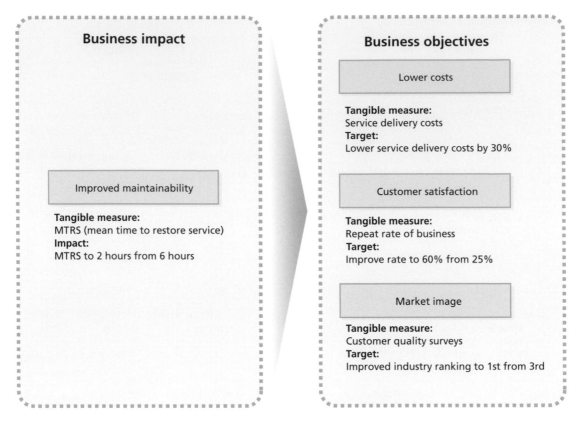

Figure 3.40 Single business impact can affect multiple business objectives

Table 3.15 illustrates possible business objectives.

Business impact

While most of a business case argument relies on cost analysis, there is much more to a service management initiative than financials. A non-financial business impact can be identified by how the achievement of one or more business objectives is affected. For example, an organization changes its sales order service to track individual customer transactions, and report on purchasing trends for each customer. The financial impact for the business is not immediately obvious, but becomes clearer once the non-financial impacts are defined. These include the ability to engage in targeted (and more effective) marketing, better anticipation of stock levels (resulting in lower cost of procurement and storage) and higher customer loyalty. Further examples are given in Figures 3.40 and 3.41.

In Figure 3.40 the business impact of improved maintainability could result in reduced costs (since the service requires less staff time to resolve incidents), which in turn results in a lower investment in the service from the business, and increased profitability. At the same time, customer satisfaction is increased because the business is able to improve its quality of delivery, which in turn results in an increase in the percentage of customers that return to the organization for repeat business. The market image of the organization is improved, since service quality results in higher customer satisfaction and company performance, which in turn results in an improved ranking in industry survey results.

When the term 'business case' is used, it often creates the impression that it is appropriate only to include financial aspects of the service or project. This is not true. Successful businesses understand that their customers are not only interested in paying money; they need to be comfortable with the supplier and their ability to deliver what they have promised. This means that every business should focus on both the financial and non-financial impacts of the proposed project or service.

3.6.1.2 Pre-programme ROI

The term capital budgeting is used to describe how managers plan significant outlays on projects that have long-term implications. A service management initiative may sometimes require capital budgeting to fund the project or service.

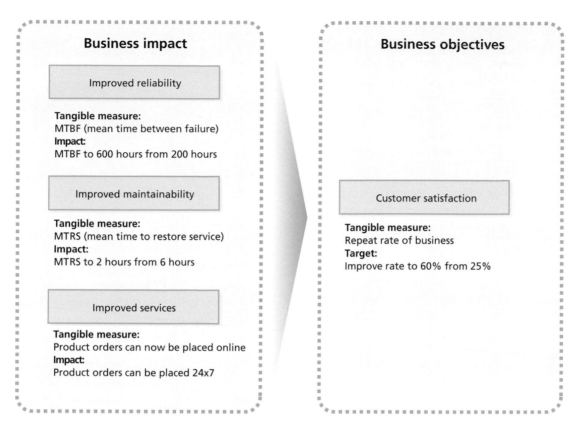

Figure 3.41 Multiple business impacts can affect a single business objective

Definition: capital budgeting

Capital budgeting is the present commitment of funds in order to receive a return in the future in the form of additional cash inflows or reduced cash outflows.

An additional factor to remember when performing pre-programme ROI is the relative value of the investment over time. An investment typically occurs early, while returns do not occur until some time later. The value of the money spent today will probably change over time due to inflation, currency fluctuations etc.

It is therefore not safe to assume that any future income can be calculated at the same value. For example, if an investment of £1,000 is made today, and the rate of inflation and currency exchange rates devalue the currency by 25% over a year, just to recover the investment will mean an income of over £1,250 by the end of the year (assuming that the money was not borrowed, as that would require a calculation of interest be taken into account as well). This fluctuation in the value of income and expenditure over a period of time is called the *discounted cash flow*.

ROI calculations need to take into account these discounted cash flows when calculating the return over a period of time. Fortunately, the science of accountancy has well-established methods to do this, and the following sections are provided for reference for IT specialists so that they can communicate effectively with financial experts and the business.

Capital budgeting decisions fall into two broad categories. These are screening and preference decisions:

- Screening decisions relate to whether a proposed service management initiative passes a predetermined hurdle – for example, a minimum return. Screening decisions are usually made using a discounted cash flow method of net present value (NPV).
- Preference decisions relate to choosing from among several competing alternatives – for example, electing between an internal service improvement plan (SIP) and a service sourcing programme. Preference decisions are usually made using a discounted cash flow method of internal rate of return (IRR).

Screening decisions (using net present value)

Under the NPV method, the programme's cash inflows are compared to the cash outflows over time (discounted cash flows – see previous section). The difference, called net present value, determines whether or not the investment is suitable (Table 3.16). Whenever the net present value is negative, the investment is unlikely to be suitable.

Please note, however, that the organization does not have to use the discount rate as the minimum. These are two separate things, though for various reasons they might choose to use the same figure. When talking about NPV the discount rate used needs to be a reasonable estimate of inflation/ interest rates from other sources etc. so that it reflects with some accuracy the value of the money now that will be spent taking into account what it could have been worth in the future. But the rate a company uses as a minimum before they will spend capital could be set at a higher rate, just to include various risk factors, or because they are not interested in ventures that don't give them a high yield. Although there may be reasons why the two could be similar, they are not the same thing.

Table 3.16 NPV decisions

If the NPV is:	Then the programme is:
Positive	Acceptable. It promises a return greater than the required rate of return.
Zero	Acceptable. It promises a return equal to the required rate of return.
Negative	Unacceptable. It promises a return less than the required rate of return.

Table 3.17 provides a simple but effective expression of an NPV screening analysis for the case study example in this section:

- The projected cost saving is £16,500. This inflow is multiplied by 2.991 (the present value of a series of 5 payments of £1 at yearly intervals. This factor can be found in Table A.1 in Appendix A).
- The initial investment is subtracted from the savings, providing the net present value.

Case study: net present value

A Type I provider for a small company in South America considers investing in a service management programme. The programme is estimated to cost £50,000. The programme is expected to reduce labour costs by £16,500 per year. The company requires a minimum pre-tax return of 20% on all investment programmes. A 5-year window is used for investment return. For simplicity, ignore inflation and taxes.

Should the investment be made?

Answer: no

At first glance the answer seems to be positive since the savings (£82,500 = 5 years × £16,500) exceed investment (£50,000). However, it is not enough that the cost reductions cover the investment. It must also yield a return of at least 20%.

To determine the suitability of the investment, the £16,500 annual savings should be discounted to its present value. Since the company uses a 20% minimum hurdle, this rate is used in the discounting process and is called the discount rate (see Table 3.17). Deducting the present value of the required investment from the present value of the cost savings gives the net present value of –£648. According to the analysis, the company should not proceed.

Please note that the company might also have used a different (higher) minimum rate from the discounted rate, following the explanation given above. In either case, the answer would still be 'no'.

What is an organization's discount rate? The cost of capital is typically considered the minimum required rate of return for an organization. This is the average rate of return the company must pay to its long-term shareholders or creditors for use of their funds. Therefore, the cost of capital serves as a minimum screening device.

For service management programmes, the NPV method has several advantages over the IRR method:

- NPV is generally easier to use.
- IRR may require searching for a discount rate resulting in an NPV of zero.

Table 3.17 Example of NPV of a proposed service management programme

	Years	Amount of cash flow (£)	Discount of 20%	Present value of cash flow (£)
	1 to 5	16,500	2.991*	49,352
Initial investment	Now	(50,000)	1	−50,000
Net present value				−648

Initial investment: £50,000; investment window: 5 years; annual cost savings: £16,500; salvage value: 0; required rate of return: 20%

*Present value of an annuity of £1 in 5 years arrears.

Table 3.18 Types of cash flow

Typical outflows	Typical inflows
Initial investment in assets, including installation costs	Incremental revenues
Periodic outlays for maintenance	Reduced costs
Training and consulting	Salvage the investment in old assets, either from operational retirement or project end
Incremental operating costs	Release of working capital
Increase in working capital	

- IRR assumes the rate of return is the rate of return on the programme, an assumption which may not hold true for environments with minimal service management programme experience.
- When NPV and IRR disagree on the attractiveness of the project, it is best to go with NPV. It makes the more realistic assumption about the rate of return.

There are other methods used for making capital budgeting decisions such as pay-back and simple rate of return. Neither method is covered, as pay-back is not a true measure of the profitability of an investment while simple rate of return does not consider the time value of money.

In a service management NPV, the focus remains on cash flows and not on accounting net income. Managers should look for the types of cash flows shown in Table 3.18.

Although it has an effect on taxes, depreciation is not deducted. Discounted cash flow methods automatically provide for return of the original investment, thereby making a deduction for depreciation unnecessary.

Intangible benefits

There are a number of techniques available when service management cash flows are uncertain. Some are very technical as they involve computer simulations and advanced skills in mathematics.

Process improvement and automation are common examples of difficult-to-estimate cash flows. The up-front and tangible costs are easy to estimate. The intangible benefits, such as lessened risk, greater reliability, quality and speed are much more difficult to estimate. They are very real in impact but nonetheless challenging in estimating cash flows. Fortunately, there is a simple procedure available.

Take, for example, the organization seeking to purchase service management process-automation software. The organization has an 8% discount rate. The useful life of the software is set to 5 years. A prior NPV analysis of the tangible costs and benefits shows an NPV of −£139,755. If the intangible benefits are large enough, the NPV could go from negative to positive. To compute the benefit required (inflow), first find the present value factor in Table A.1, Appendix A. A look in column 8%, row 5-year period, reveals a factor of

3.993 (rounded to three decimal places). Now perform the following calculation:

$$\frac{\text{NPV excluding intangible benefits}\ (\pounds 139,755)}{\text{Present value factor (8\%, 5-year period),}\ 3.993} = \pounds 35,000$$

The result serves as a subjective guideline for estimation. If the intangible benefits are at least £35,000, then the NPV is acceptable. The process automation should be performed. If in the judgement of senior managers, the intangible benefits are not worth £35,000, then the process automation should not be performed.

Preference decisions (using internal rate of return)

While many opportunities pass the screening decision process, not all can be acted on. Financial or resource constraints may preclude investing in every opportunity. Preference decisions, sometimes called rationing or ranking decisions, must be made. The competing alternatives are ranked.

Simply calculating and comparing the NPV of one project with that of another does not compare the actual size of the investment and returns. As a result, the internal rate of return (IRR) is widely used for preference decisions. The higher the internal rate of return, the more desirable the initiative.

The IRR, sometimes called the yield, is the rate of return over the life of an initiative. IRR is computed by finding the discount rate that equates the present value of a project's cash outflows with the present value of its inflows. That is, the IRR is the discount rate resulting in an NPV of zero (or the exact time when the project will break even and start producing a positive contribution).

In the previous case study example, the following steps would be taken to compute the IRR:

Firstly, find the discount rate that will result in a net present value of zero. The simplest approach is to divide the investment in the project by the expected net annual cash flow. This will yield a factor from which the IRR can be calculated.

$$\frac{\text{Investment required}\ (\pounds 50,000)}{\text{Net annual cash inflow}\ (\pounds 16,500)} = 3.03$$

Secondly, locate the IRR factor (in this case 3.03) in Table A.1, Appendix A, to determine the rate of return it represents. Use the 5-year period line since the programme has a 5-year window. A scan on the 5-year period line reveals that an IRR factor of 3.03 represents a rate of return between 19% and 20%.

Third, once the IRR is computed, compare against the required rate of return. In this case, the required rate of return is 20%. Since the IRR is slightly less, it would likely be rejected during a screening decision. A summary is given in Table 3.19.

The IRR for successful candidates can be directly compared to other successful candidates. Viable projects can then be ranked by their respective IRR. The projects with the highest rank are those with the highest IRR percentages.

3.6.1.3 Post-programme ROI

Many companies successfully justify service management implementations through qualitative arguments, without a business case or plan, often ranking cost savings as a low business driver. But without clearly defined financial objectives, companies cannot measure the added value brought about by service management, thereby introducing future risk in the form of strong opposition from business leaders.

Table 3.19 Example of the IRR of a proposed service management programme

	Years	Amount of cash flow (£)	Discount of 19–20%	Present value of cash flow (£)
Annual cost savings	1 to 5	16,500	3.0303	50,000
Initial investment	Now	(50,000)	1	−50,000
Net present value				0

Initial investment: £50,000; investment window: 5 years; annual cost savings: £16,500; salvage value: 0; required rate of return: 20%

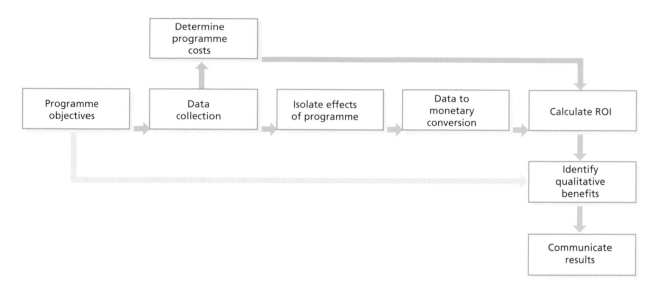

Figure 3.42 Post-programme ROI approach

Having experienced a history of shortfalls in past frameworks, stakeholders may question the resultant value of a service management programme. Without proof of value, executives may cease further investments. Therefore all significant projects should be subjected to a post-programme ROI analysis. However, if a service management initiative is initiated without prior ROI analysis, it is even more important that an analysis be conducted at an appropriate time afterwards (when the anticipated returns can reasonably be measured). The calculation of a service management ROI is illustrated in the basic model shown in Figure 3.42 and explained below.

Programme objectives

Objectives should be clear and measurable, as they serve to guide the depth and scope of the ROI analysis. Objectives can range from simple terminology to the adoption of industry practices:

■ Deliver consistent and repeatable service
■ Lower the overall total cost of ownership
■ Improve quality of service
■ Implement industry-wide best practices
■ Provide an overall structure and process
■ Facilitate the use of common concepts and terminology.

Data collection

The collection of appropriate data is vital for a valid and quantifiable ROI result. The scope and objectives of the initiative should indicate what data is appropriate. Data collected prior to

implementation should be compared with that collected after the implementation to enable a comparison of the two baselines. Examples of data to be collected include:

■ Metrics for quality of service
■ Costs for service transactions
■ Questionnaires for customer satisfaction.

Note that the data collection for process transactions will differ from data collection for a function.

Isolate the effects of the programme

By this stage, the results of the service management programme are becoming evident. By isolating the effects, there should be little doubt that the results should be attributed to the programme. There are many techniques available:

■ **Forecast analysis** A trend-line analysis or another forecasting model is used to project data points had the programme not taken place. An example is given in Figure 3.43.
■ **Impact estimates** When a forecasting approach is not feasible, due to either lack of data or inconsistencies in measurements, an alternative approach in the form of estimations is performed. Simply put, customers and stakeholders estimate the level of improvements. Input is sought from organizational managers, independent experts and external assessments.

■ **Control group** In this technique, a pilot implementation takes place in a subset of the enterprise. That subset may be based on geography, delivery centre or organizational branch. The resultant performance is compared with a similar but unaffected subset.

Data to monetary conversion

To calculate ROI, it is essential to convert the impact data to monetary values. Only then can those values be compared to programme costs. The challenge is in assigning a value to each unit of data. The technique applied will vary and will often depend on the nature of the data:

■ A quality measure, such as a complaint or violation, is assigned or calculated, and reported as a standard value.

■ Staff reductions or efficiency improvements, in the form of loaded costs, are reported as a standard value.

■ Improvements in business performance, in the form of lessened impacts, are reported as a standard value.

■ Internal or external experts are used to establish the value of a measure.

Determine programme costs

This requires tracking all the related costs of the service management programme. It can include:

■ The planning, design and implementation costs. These are pro-rated over the expected life of the programme

■ The technology acquisition costs

■ The education expenses

■ Opportunity costs (or the potential returns lost by choosing one option over another).

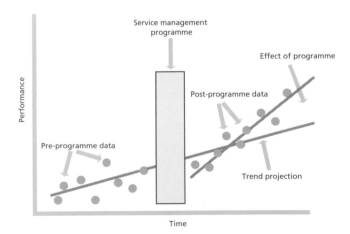

Figure 3.43 Forecast analysis

Calculate ROI

Once the benefits and costs of the programme have been determined, the actual ROI can be calculated and compared to the projected ROI in the original business case.

Identify qualitative benefits

Qualitative benefits begin with those detailed in the business case, as described in a previous section. A second look at service management qualitative benefits is found in *ITIL Continual Service Improvement*.

3.6.2 Business impact analysis

Business impact analysis (BIA) is a method used to evaluate the relative value of services, and is usually performed as part of service portfolio management. Instead of analysing the positive returns of the services, BIA examines what would happen if the service was not available, or only partially available, over different periods of time. The value of this method is that it is easy for the customer to express the value of the service in terms that are meaningful to it – both financial and non-financial.

An advantage of this approach for internal service providers is that it is an excellent communication tool – helping them to share with the wider organization how they have understood their priorities and therefore how they have allocated their resources.

This focus on assessing the outages of services, combined with assessing the severity of the outage, makes it a useful method for IT service continuity management and other related service management processes and functions, for example:

■ It can help to identify risks and prioritize counter-measures – resulting in optimum levels of availability and assurance.

■ It helps the service provider to make better decisions about how to prioritize incidents.

■ It helps problem management to narrow its focus to those areas that provide the best impact for the amount of effort required.

■ Projects can be better prioritized based on what will impact the business most positively.

■ Operational performance can be enhanced by focusing resources and capabilities where they will have the most positive effect (without defocusing on important areas – resulting in a negative impact).

■ It serves as an excellent input to the IT service continuity management process.

Most important, however, is that it enables the business to decide on the priorities of service provision in a meaningful way – by comparing the investment in the service with the cost of not having it (or having access at a reduced level).

BIA identifies the cost of service outage to a company, and the relative worth of a service. These two concepts are not identical:

■ The cost of service outage is a financial value placed on a specific service, and is meant to reflect the value of lost productivity and revenue over a specific period of time.

■ The worth of a service relative to other services in a portfolio may not result exclusively from financial characteristics. Service value, as discussed earlier, is derived from characteristics that may go beyond financial management considerations, and represent aspects such as the ability to complete work or communicate with clients that may not be directly related to revenue generation.

A number of steps need to be completed while generating a BIA. Although there are a number of approaches and methods available in the industry, they all involve the following activities:

■ Arrange resources from the business and IT that will work together on the analysis.

■ Identify all of the top candidate services for designation as critical, secondary and tertiary (you do not need to designate them at this point).

■ Identify the core analysis points for use in assessing risk and impact, such as:

● Lost sales revenue
● Fines
● Failure risk
● Lost productivity
● Lost opportunity
● Number of users impacted
● Visibility to shareholders, management etc.
● Risk of service obsolescence
● Harm to reputation among customers, shareholders and regulatory authorities

● Penalties incurred as a result of not meeting contractual obligations.

■ With the business, weigh and estimate the probability of the identified elements of risk and impact.

■ Score the candidate services against the weighted elements of risk and impact, and total their individual risk scores (Failure Modes and Effects Analysis – FMEA – can be used for additional input here).

■ Generate a list of services in order of risk profile.

■ Decide on a universal time period with which to standardize the translation of service outage to cost (1 minute, 1 hour, 1 day etc.).

■ Calculate the impact of each service being analysed within the BIA using agreed methods, formulae and assumptions. Generally the impact will be financial, but there could also be other impacts. For example, a government department concerned with healthcare could estimate the impact on the health of a particular community.

■ Generate a list of services in order of impact.

■ Utilize the risk and impact data generated to create charts that illustrate the company's highest risk applications that also carry the greatest impact. This data can also be used to justify the investment in service management, since this will ensure greater availability and reliability of key services.

The challenges of performing BIA involve getting buy-in from a wide range of people, each with their own differing perspective of the nature of risks and impact. Each group might also have a different idea of which risks are more probable, and the result might be to neglect a particular threat simply because it was not agreed to be 'likely'.

Some business impacts and mitigation measures may not be based on real risk, but on what is currently in the headlines, or is a 'fashionable' thing to do.

3.7 SOURCING STRATEGY

'The next layers of value creation – whether in technology, marketing, biomedicine or manufacturing – are becoming so complex that no

single firm or department is going to be able to master them alone.' Thomas L. Friedman

Sourcing is about analysing how to most effectively source and deploy the resources and capabilities required to deliver outcomes to customers. It is about deciding on the best combination of supplier types to support the objectives of the organization and the effective and efficient delivery of services.

A service strategy should enhance an organization's special strengths and core competencies. Each component should reinforce the other. Change any one and the whole model changes. As organizations seek to improve their performance, they should consider which competencies are essential and know when to extend their capabilities by partnering in areas both inside and outside their enterprise.

Outsourcing moves a value-creating activity that was performed inside the organization to outside the organization where it is performed by another company. What prompts an organization to outsource an activity is the same logic that determines whether an organization makes or buys inputs. Namely, does the extra value generated from performing an activity inside the organization outweigh the costs of managing it internally? This decision can change over time.

IT services are increasingly delivered by service providers outside the enterprise. Making an informed service sourcing decision requires finding a balance between thorough qualitative and quantitative considerations.

Historically, the financial business case is the primary basis for most sourcing decisions. These analyses include pure cost savings, lower capital investments, investment redirections and long-term cost containment. Unfortunately, most financial analyses do not include all the costs related to sourcing options, leading to difficult relationships with service providers, involving unexpected costs and service issues. If costs are a primary driver for a sourcing decision, include financials for service transition, relationship management, legal support, incentives, training, tools licensing implications and process rationalization, among others.

3.7.1 Deciding what to source

Deciding to outsource is about finding ways to improve competitive differentiation by redeploying resources and capabilities. Any capabilities and

Case study: sourcing strategy

During the early 2000s, companies rushed to implement a service strategy based on labour arbitrage: service providers decrease labour costs by making use of less expensive offshore resources. The strategic intent is to make a provider's value proposition more compelling through lower cost structures.

While costs did indeed decrease for customers, providers were unable to make long-term gains to their financial bottom line.

Why?

Answer: The inability to capture value

Early adopters of a labour arbitrage strategy made great gains because, for a while, the costs of services they offered were lower than any competing alternatives. But as more and more service providers made use of offshore resources, the cost of services was lowered for everyone. This was great for customers but bad for providers – this distinctiveness was eventually eliminated. Value was created for customers but service providers were not able to keep any of it. This ability of a service provider to keep a portion of any value created is known as 'value capture'.

The sourcing strategy was vitally important for fending off competing alternatives. However, service providers who focused solely on this strategy, at the expense of other distinctive capabilities, soon encountered strategic failure in the form 'mediocre performance versus competing alternatives'.

resources that are only peripherally related to the organization's core strategy and differentiation should be considered for outsourcing. Once candidates for sourcing are identified, the following questions can be used to clarify matters:

- Do the candidate services improve the business's resources and capabilities?
- How closely are the candidate services connected to the business's competitive and strategic resources and capabilities?
- Do the candidate services require extensive interactions between the service providers and the business's competitive and strategic resources and capabilities?

If the responses uncover minimal dependencies and infrequent interactions between the sourced services and the business's competitive and strategic positioning, then the candidates are strong contenders. If candidates for sourcing are closely related to the business's competitive or strategic positioning, then care must be taken. Such sourcing structures are particularly vulnerable to:

- **Substitution** 'Why do I need the service provider when its supplier can offer the same services?' The sourced vendor develops competing capabilities and replaces the sourcing organization.
- **Disruption** The sourced vendor has a direct impact on quality or reputation of the sourcing organization.
- **Distinctiveness** The sourced vendor is the source of distinctiveness for the sourcing organization. The sourcing organization then becomes particularly dependent on the continued development and success of the second organization.

Care should be taken to distinguish between distinctive activities and critical activities. Critical activities do not necessarily refer to activities that may be distinctive to the service provider. For example, although customer service is most likely critical, if it does not differentiate the provider from competing alternatives then it is not distinctive, referred to here as 'context'.

This does not mean critical activities are less important than distinctive activities. It means they do not provide the differentiating benefit that generates value. One service provider's context may be another's distinctiveness. What is distinctive today may over time become context. Contextual processes may be recombined into distinctive processes. Here is a basic test:

- Does the customer or market space expect the service provider to do this activity? (context)
- Does the customer or market space give the service provider credit for performing this activity exceptionally well? (distinctiveness)

Early adopters of airline kiosks, for example, differentiated themselves through self-service technology. While kiosks were a distinctive activity central to the service strategy, it was hardly critical. Years later, customers expect kiosks at all airport locations for every airline. Every major airline considers it a critical activity but not distinctive – it no longer differentiates. Hence airlines consolidate or outsource this critical activity. They collaborate with partner airlines to provide kiosks any member airline may use. They source kiosks from external service providers who can place them in other locations, such as hotel lobbies and corporate offices.

3.7.2 Sourcing structures

Regardless of where services, capabilities or resources are sourced from, the organization retains responsibility for their adequacy. Outsourcing does not mean that a service or its performance are no longer important. In most cases, it often means that the service is so important that it should be provided by a service provider that can do a better (or more cost-effective) job. In other words, outsourcing a capability, resource or service does not mean outsourcing the governance of what that item does.

The organization should adopt a formal governance approach to manage its outsourced services as well as assuring the delivery of value. This includes planning for the organizational change initiated by the sourcing strategy and a formal and verifiable description as to how decisions on services are made. An overview of the predominant sourcing structures is provided in Table 3.20. These sourcing structures also represent the strategy that the organization is using to deliver its services.

The selection of a sourcing structure should be balanced with acceptable risks and levels of control. The method an organization uses to manage a sourcing relationship depends greatly on the sourcing organization's characteristics such as degrees of centralization, standards and process maturity. This will require a dedicated function to manage the relationship. In general, the sourcing organization should excel in establishing a set of relationship standards and processes. Other key responsibilities are to:

- Monitor the performance of the agreements and the overall relationship with providers
- Manage the sourcing agreements
- Provide an escalation level for issues and problems

Table 3.20 Main sourcing structures (delivery strategies)

Sourcing structure	Description
Insourcing	This approach relies on utilizing internal organizational resources in the design, development, transition, maintenance, operation and/or support of new, changed or revised services.
Outsourcing	This approach utilizes the resources of an external organization or organizations in a formal arrangement to provide a well-defined portion of a service's design, development, maintenance, operations and/or support. This includes the consumption of services from application service providers (ASPs) described below.
Co-sourcing or multi-sourcing	Often a combination of insourcing and outsourcing, using a number of organizations working together to co-source key elements within the lifecycle. This generally involves using a number of external organizations working together to design, develop, transition, maintain, operate and/or support a portion of a service.
Partnership	Formal arrangements between two or more organizations to work together to design, develop, transition, maintain, operate and/or support IT service(s). The focus here tends to be on strategic partnerships that leverage critical expertise or market opportunities.
Business process outsourcing (BPO)	The increasing trend of relocating entire business functions using formal arrangements between organizations where one organization provides and manages the other organization's entire business process(es) or function(s) in a low-cost location. Common examples are accounting, payroll and call centre operations.
Application service provision	Involves formal arrangements with an application service provider (ASP) organization that will provide shared computer-based services to customer organizations over a network from the service provider's premises. Applications offered in this way are also sometimes referred to as on-demand software/applications. Through ASPs, the complexities and costs of such shared software can be reduced and provided to organizations that could otherwise not justify the investment.
Knowledge process outsourcing (KPO)	KPO is a step ahead of BPO in one respect. KPO organizations provide domain-based processes and business expertise rather than just process expertise. In other words the organization is not only required to execute a process, but also to make certain low-level decisions based on knowledge of local conditions or industry-specific information. One example is the outsourcing of credit risk assessment, where the outsourcing organization has historical information that they have analysed to create knowledge which in turn enables them to provide a service. For every credit card company to collect and analyse this data for themselves would not be as cost-effective as using KPO.
'Cloud'	Cloud service providers offer specific pre-defined services, usually on demand. Services are usually standard, but can be customized to a specific organization if there is enough demand for the service. Cloud services can be offered internally, but generally refer to outsourced service provision.
Multi-vendor sourcing	This type of sourcing involves sourcing different sources from different vendors, often representing different sourcing options from the above.

■ Ensure that providers understand the organization's service priorities.

When sourcing services, organizations should focus on clearly defining exactly what the service provider is expected to do. All too often the primary focus is on the reporting structures and the resources aligned to those structures. Resource alignment and organizational structures should be analysed and adjusted only after understanding the dynamics of the new or enhanced services.

Once the resource and organizational discussion begins, the organization must be sure to account for the introduction of new critical skills. These competencies generally fall into three categories: business, technical and behavioural. For example, the greater the level of outsourcing, the greater the need for business and behavioural skills. The greater the level of insourcing, the greater the need for technical skills.

3.7.3 Multi-vendor sourcing

Sourcing services from multiple providers has become the norm rather than the exception. This approach has been delivering benefits and gaining increasing support. The organization maintains a strong relationship with each provider, spreading the risk and reducing costs. It should also be noted that each provider may represent a different type of sourcing option from Table 3.20.

Governance and managing multiple providers, who often have little to do with each other outside of the common customer, can be challenging. When sourcing multiple providers, the following issues should be carefully evaluated:

■ **Technical complexity** Sourcing services from external service providers is useful for standardized service processes (although as

customization increases it is more difficult to achieve the desired efficiencies).

■ **Organizational interdependencies** Contractual vehicles should be carefully structured to address the dynamics of multiple organizations, ensuring that all providers undergo consistent training in the customer organization's processes etc. Also, contracts should include incentives designed to encourage consistency in contractual performance between providers.

■ **Integration planning** The processes, data and tools of each organization may be different or they may be duplicated. Either case will require the integration of certain processes, data and tools. In addition, it is critical that the reporting of each organization is integrated so that governance can be performed consistently across each organization.

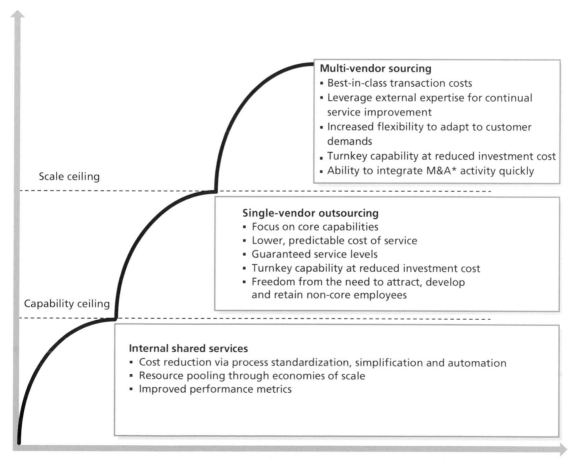

* = mergers and acquisitions

Figure 3.44 The service sourcing staircase

■ **Managed sourcing** This refers to the need for a single interface to the multiple vendors wherever appropriate. A sure recipe for failure in a multi-sourced environment that requires collaboration between service providers is to have each contract negotiated and managed by different groups within the organization.

There are multiple approaches and varying degrees in sourcing. How far up an organization is willing to go with sourcing depends on the business objectives to be achieved and constraints to overcome. Figure 3.44 illustrates the limitations experienced at each of three levels of sourcing and then indicates the additional benefits or features that can be gained by moving to the next level. Please note that this figure does not imply that any single form of sourcing is better than another, merely that there are different potential benefits as the organization moves up the staircase. Whether or not these benefits can be achieved by each organization for each service will need to be assessed.

In Figure 3.44 an organization with limitations in internal capability might move to an outsourcing model where a single outsourcing organization is used to augment current capabilities through

economies of scale (for example, specialized, expensive capabilities can be shared across more than one customer, making them available at a lower overall cost to all customers). A single-vendor outsourcing contract will eventually be limited in what it can provide to a large, complex customer base, requiring customers to source services from multiple providers.

Regardless of the sourcing approach, senior executives must carefully evaluate provider attributes. The following is a useful checklist:

■ **Demonstrated competencies** In terms of staff, use of technologies, innovation, industry experience and certifications (for example, ISO/IEC 20000)
■ **Past achievements** In terms of service quality attained, financial value created and demonstrated commitment to continual improvement
■ **Relationship dynamics** In terms of vision and strategy, the cultural fit, relative size of contract in their portfolio and quality of relationship management

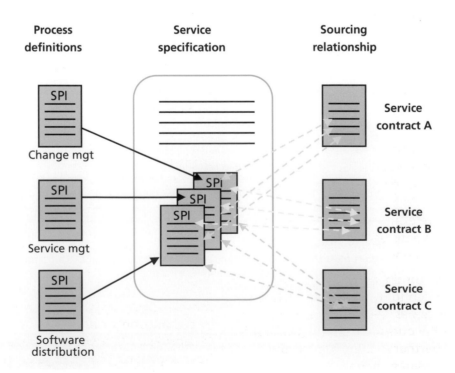

Figure 3.45 Using service provider interfaces

- **Quality of solutions** Relevance of services to your requirements, risk management and performance benchmarks
- **Overall capabilities** In terms of financial strength, resources, management systems and scope and range of services
- **Commitment to transferred personnel** In terms of their longer-term retention, personal development and career opportunities.

3.7.4 Service provider interfaces

To support development of sourcing relationships in a multi-vendor environment, guidelines and reference points (technical, procedural, organizational) are needed between the various service providers. These reference points could refer to technology, procedures or organization structures. One method of formalizing these reference points is the use of service provider interfaces (SPI).

A service provider interface is a formally defined reference point which identifies some interaction between a service provider and a user, customer, process or one or more suppliers. SPIs are generally used to ensure that multiple parties in a business relationship have the same points of reference for defining, delivering and reporting services.

SPIs help coordinate end-to-end management of critical services. The service catalogue drives the service specifications, which are part of standard process definitions. Responsibilities and service levels are negotiated at the time that the sourcing relationship is established, and include:

- Identification of integration points between various management processes of the client and service provider
- Identification of specific roles and responsibilities for managing the ongoing systems management relationship with both parties
- Identification of relevant systems management information that needs to be communicated to the customer on an ongoing basis.

The SPIs also have to consider more than live services. There is a need for management, strategy and transition activities as well as live services. This is especially true if the outsource service provider is seen as a strategic partner in transforming the client's business or business model.

Figure 3.45 illustrates how SPIs could be used. On the left of this diagram are a number of activities or processes that an organization performs. On the right of the diagram are a number of sourcing contracts. Each supplier needs to be able to interface with each of the three activities on the left side of the diagram, but they do not need to be involved in the end-to-end process of each. To resolve this situation, an SPI is defined for each activity, identifying what the supplier needs to know about each activity, and how it interfaces with it. These SPIs are used to identify what will be included in the contract.

Process SPI definitions consist of:

- Technology prerequisites (e.g. management tool standards or prescribed protocols)
- Data requirements (e.g. specific events or records), formats (i.e. data layouts), interfaces (e.g. APIs, firewall ports) and protocols (e.g. SNMP, XML)
- Non-negotiable requirements (e.g. practices, activities, operating procedures)
- Required roles/responsibilities within the service provider and customer organizations
- Response times and escalations.

SPIs are defined, maintained and owned by process owners. Others involved in the definition include:

- Business representatives, who negotiate the SPI requirements and are responsible for managing the strategic relationships with and between service providers
- Service provider process coordinator(s), who take operational responsibility for ensuring the operational processes are synchronized.

3.7.5 Sourcing governance

Sourcing governance is a complex area. In addition, creating a sourcing strategy is a significant task, and will be more demanding than this section is able to articulate. This section highlights the need for undertaking these activities and provides a high-level overview of the area.

There is a frequent misunderstanding of the definition of governance, particularly in a sourcing context. Companies have used the word interchangeably with 'vendor management', 'retained staff', 'supplier management' and 'sourcing management organization'. Governance is none of these.

Governance is covered in detail in section 5.1, but for ease of reference, governance refers to the rules, policies, processes (and in some cases, laws) by which businesses are operated, regulated and controlled. These are often defined by the board or shareholders, or the constitution of the organization; but they can also be defined by legislation, regulation or consumer groups.

Management and governance are different disciplines. Management deals with making decisions and executing processes. Governance is the framework of decision rights that encourage desired behaviours in the sourcing and the sourced organization. When companies confuse management and governance, they inevitably focus on execution at the expense of strategic decision-making. Both are vitally important.

Governance is invariably the weakest link in a service sourcing strategy. The following areas have been shown to be effective at improving that weakness:

- **A governance body** By forming a manageably sized governance body with a clear understanding of the service sourcing strategy, decisions can be made without escalating to the highest levels of senior management. By including representation from each service provider, stronger decisions can be made.
- **Governance domains** Domains can cover decision-making for a specific area of the service sourcing strategy. Domains can cover, for example, service delivery, communication, sourcing strategy or contract management. A governance domain does not include the responsibility for its execution, only its strategic decision-making.
- **Creation of a decision-rights matrix** This ties all the recommendations together. RACI charts are common forms of a decision-rights matrix (see section 6.9).
- **Supplier management** (see *ITIL Service Design*) This ensures that contracts and external service providers are managed according to the organization's governance policies, standards and controls.

Partnering with providers who are ISO/IEC 20000 compliant could be an important element in selecting the appropriate outsourcer. Organizations who have achieved this certification have demonstrated compliance to a consistent standard

of service management. This credential is particularly important in multi-sourced environments where a common framework promotes better integration. Multi-sourced environments require common language, integrated processes and a management structure between internal and external providers. Although ITIL provides common terminology and process definitions, there is no guarantee that an organization will use these as part of its standard operations – even if its employees are ITIL certified. ISO/IEC 20000 provides a means to determine whether a service provider has truly adopted the standard framework.

ISO/IEC 20000 is the first formal international standard specific to IT service management. An organization comfortable with ITIL will find no difficulty in interpreting ISO/IEC 20000. Further details on ISO/IEC 20000 can be found in Appendix D, section D.6.

In addition, the framework of control objectives defined in COBIT provides a good source for defining governance practices. More information on COBIT can be found in Appendix D, section D.5.

3.7.6 Critical success factors

It is important to understand the costs and risks associated with changing from one sourcing model to another. The costs of change can sometimes overshadow any benefit, and the additional management of an outsourced contract can eat into expected savings. In addition, the risk of moving critical operational activities from one entity to another can be disruptive, and can be irrevocably damaging if this disruption is felt over an extended time. It is thus important to consider the following critical success factors when making the decision to ensure a successful sourcing strategy.

The factors for a service sourcing strategy frequently depend on:

- Desired outcomes, such as cost reduction, improved service quality or diminished business risk
- The optimal model for delivering the service
- The best location to deliver the service, such as local, onshore, near-shore or offshore.

The recommended approach to deciding on a strategy includes:

- Analyse the organization's internal service management competencies
- Compare those findings with industry benchmarks
- Assess the organization's ability to deliver strategic value.

The approach will likely lead to these scenarios:

- If the organization's internal service management competence is high and also provides strategic value, then an internal or shared services strategy is the most likely option. The organization should continue to invest internally, leveraging high-value expert providers to refine and enhance the service management competencies.
- If the organization's internal service management competence is low but provides strategic value, then outsourcing is an option provided services can be maintained or improved through the use of high-value providers.
- If the organization's internal service management competence is high but does not provide strategic value, then there are multiple options. The business may want to invest in its service capabilities so that they do provide strategic value or it may sell off this service capability, because it may be of greater value to a third party.
- If the organization's internal service management competence and strategic value are low, then they should be considered candidates for outsourcing.

Prior to any implementation, an organization should establish and maintain a baseline of its performance metrics. Without such metrics, it will be difficult to assess the true impact and trends of a service sourcing implementation. Measurement can take two forms:

- Business metrics: financial savings, service level improvements, business process efficiency
- Customer metrics: availability and consistency of services, increased offerings, quality of service.

3.8 SERVICE STRUCTURES IN THE VALUE NETWORK

'All models are wrong, but some of them are useful.' George Box, statistician

3.8.1 From value chains to value networks

Business executives have long described the process of creating value as links in a value chain. This model is based on the industrial age production line: a series of value-adding activities connecting an organization's supply side with its demand side. Each service provides value through a sequence of events leading to the delivery, consumption and maintenance of that particular service. By analysing each stage in the chain, senior executives presumably find opportunities for improvements.

Much of the value of service management, however, is intangible and complex. It includes knowledge and benefits such as technical expertise, strategic information, process knowledge and collaborative design. Often the value lies in how these intangibles are combined, packaged and exchanged. Linear models have shown themselves to be inadequate for describing and understanding the complexities of value for service management, often treating information as a supporting element rather than as a source of value. Information is used to monitor and control rather than to create new value.

Value chains remain an important tool. They provide a strategy for vertically integrating and coordinating the dedicated assets required for product development. They do not, however, reflect the dynamic situation of services.

It is important to understand the most powerful force to disrupt conventional value chains: the low cost of information. Information was the glue that held the vertical integration together. Getting the necessary information to suppliers and service providers has historically been expensive, requiring dedicated assets and proprietary systems. These barriers to entry gave value chains their competitive advantage. Through the exchange of open and inexpensive information, however, businesses can now make use of resources and capabilities without owning them.

Lower transaction costs allow organizations to control and track information that would have been too costly to capture and process just years ago. Transaction costs still exist, but are increasingly more burdensome within the organization than without. This in turn has created new opportunities for collaboration between service providers and suppliers. The end result is a flexible mix of mechanisms that undermine the rigid vertical integration.

Case study: commerce services

A web-commerce company thrives despite a severe economic slowdown. The business model, based on online auctions, is profitable. However, the business model does not explain why its services succeed in creating sustainable value as other sites fail.

Process flows fail to provide insight. A value net analysis, however, reveals the distinctiveness between the auctioneer and its competitors.

What did the value net reveal about the services that a process flow could not?

Answer

Most services focus on making a profit or performing social benefits. A value net analysis revealed that the online auctioneer did both.

The value net revealed a hidden participant and their intangible exchanges: hobbyists. Hobbyists discovered they could take part in the auctioneer's micro-economy. They became professional participants with their own value capture. They created a sense of community, loyalty, feedback mechanisms and referrals. By indirectly creating prosperity for the hobbyists, the auctioneer created prosperity for itself. The auctioneer used this insight to create a new class of services directed at hobbyists.

New strategies are now available to service providers:

- **Marshal external talent** No single organization can organically produce all the resources and capabilities required within an industry. Most innovation occurs outside the organization.
- **Reduce costs** Produce more robust services in less time and for less expense than possible through conventional value-chain approaches. If it is less expensive to perform a transaction within the organization, keep it there. If it is cheaper to source externally, take a second look. An organization should contract until the cost of an internal transaction no longer

exceeds the cost of performing the transaction externally. This is a corollary to 'Coase's law': a firm tends to expand until the costs of organizing an extra transaction within the firm become equal to the costs of carrying out the same transaction on the open market. The concept of Coase's law was first developed by Tapscott *et al.* (2000).

- **Change the focal point of distinctiveness** By harnessing external talent, an organization can redeploy its own resources and capabilities to enhance services better suited to its customer or market space. Take the case of a popular North American sports league and its Type I service provider. By harnessing the capabilities of Type III infrastructure service providers, the Type I is free to redeploy its capabilities to enhance its new media services, namely web-based services with state-of-the-art streaming video, ticket sales, statistics, fantasy leagues and promotions.
- **Increase demand for complementary services** An organization, particularly a Type I, may lack the breadth of services offered by Type II and Type III service providers. By acting as a service integrator, such organizations not only remedy the gap but also boost demand through complementary offerings.
- **Collaborate** As transaction costs drop, collaboration is less optional. There are always more smart people outside an organization than inside.

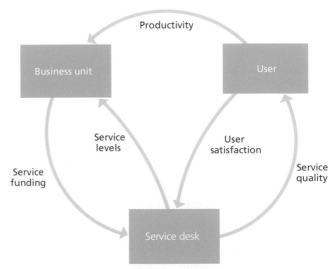

Figure 3.46 Example of a value network

An effective service provider will view service management as patterns of collaborative exchanges, rather than an assembly line. From a systems thinking perspective it is more useful to think of service management as a value network or net.

A value network is a web of relationships that generates tangible and intangible value through complex dynamic exchanges through two or more organizations. A simple example of this is shown in Figure 3.46.

In a value net diagram, an arrow designates a transaction. The direction of the arrow denotes the direction of the transaction or impact on a participant: service provider or customer. Transactions can be temporary. They may include deliverables, tangible or intangible. Dotted arrows can be used to distinguish intangible transactions. Figure 3.46 shows that the traditional model of supplier–service provider–business unit is not adequate to show the complexity of real transactions in a service management situation.

3.8.2 Using value networks

Services are often characterized by complex networks of value flows and forms of value, often involving many parties that influence each other in many ways. Value networks serve to communicate the model in a clear and simple way.

They are designed to leverage external capabilities. Drawing a value network will therefore identify the key role players, and how they contribute to value within the core enterprise. Despite many actors, value networks can help the services operate with the efficiency of a self-contained enterprise, operating on a process rather than an organizational basis. The core enterprise is the central point of execution, rather than one actor in a chain, and is responsible for the whole value network. This includes the infrastructure by which other business partners can collaborate to deliver goods and services.

Firstly consider customer expectation. Only then consider the resources and capabilities required to deliver services. This model requires high-performance information flows, not rigid supply chains. Not too long ago, business employees were the only consumers of its IT services. The pervasive examples of banking ATMs, airport kiosks and online reservation systems illustrate this is no longer the case. Collaborative services such as

Wikipedia, YouTube and Second Life suggest increasing levels of sophistication in customer interactions. As customers and suppliers become the direct users of IT services, the expectations and requirements become more demanding – requiring a value network approach.

The following questions are useful in constructing and analysing the dynamics of a service model in a value network.

Case study: service desk

An internal service provider for a healthcare business unit performed an assessment of their service desk. A map of the service desk process was developed, as depicted in Figure 3.47. This flow chart described how the service desk function worked. While the flow chart looked orderly, the experience of the staff did not match the documented flow. A value net analysis was subsequently performed.

The staff described informal processes used to manoeuvre around the constraints of the process model. The informal processes were needed in order to be effective. Newcomers to the staff predictably took longer to become effective as they learned these undocumented ways to do things.

The analysis moved the focus away from the linear depiction of the process. Rather, it focused on the people who were fulfilling different roles. It became apparent that simple steps on the flowchart were actually complex. They involved multiple staff members and required continuing activities throughout the entire process (Figure 3.48).

The value net appeared messy. But staff agreed that it accurately described how the service desk really worked. The analysis captured the intangibles for which staff were accountable but were not reflected in the flow chart.

The goal was not to replace process modelling or to map the entire organization. The method was used to describe a complex, non-linear process that had been artificially forced into the linear flow diagram.

As Figures 3.47 and 3.48 (both adapted from Allee, 2003) demonstrate, what looks like a simple process in reality is often a far more complex set of interactions.

- Who are all the participants in the service?
- What are the overall patterns of exchange or transactions?
- What are the impacts or deliverables of each transaction on each participant?
- What is the best way to generate value?

Value net diagrams are tools for service analysis, rather than flow charts for work instructions. They show what an organization does, how it is done and for whom. They can help to simplify the way the organization works, making it more efficient. They need not be overly complex to be useful.

3.9 SERVICE STRATEGY INPUTS AND OUTPUTS

The main outputs from service strategy are the vision and mission, strategies and strategic plans, the service portfolio, change proposals and financial information. Table 3.21 shows the major service strategy inputs and outputs, by lifecycle stage. Appendix F provides a summary of the major inputs and outputs between each stage of the service lifecycle.

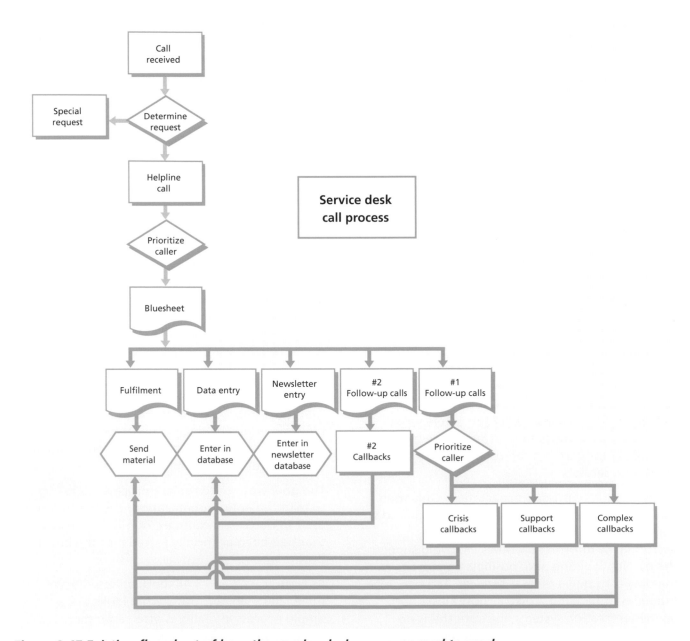

Figure 3.47 Existing flowchart of how the service desk was supposed to work

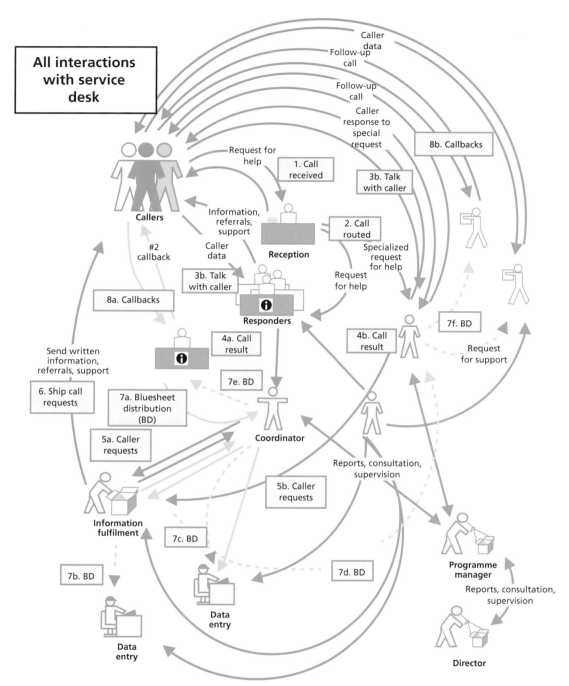

Figure 3.48 Value net exchanges showing how things really worked

Table 3.21 Service strategy inputs and outputs by lifecycle stage

Lifecycle stage	Service strategy inputs (from the lifecycle stages in the first column)	Service strategy outputs (to the lifecycle stages in the first column)
Service design	Input to business cases and the service portfolio Service design packages Updated service models Service portfolio updates including the service catalogue Financial estimates and reports Design-related knowledge and information in the service knowledge management system (SKMS) Designs for service strategy processes and procedures	Vision and mission Service portfolio Policies Strategies and strategic plans Priorities Service charters including service packages and details of utility and warranty Financial information and budgets Documented patterns of business activity and user profiles Service models
Service transition	Transitioned services Information and feedback for business cases and service portfolio Response to change proposals Service portfolio updates Change schedule Feedback on strategies and policies Financial information for input to budgets Financial reports Knowledge and information in the SKMS	Vision and mission Service portfolio Policies Strategies and strategic plans Priorities Change proposals, including utility and warranty requirements and expected timescales Financial information and budgets Input to change evaluation and change advisory board (CAB) meetings
Service operation	Operating risks Operating cost information for total cost of ownership (TCO) calculations Actual performance data	Vision and mission Service portfolio Policies Strategies and strategic plans Priorities Financial information and budgets Demand forecasts and strategies Strategic risks
Continual service improvement	Results of customer and user satisfaction surveys Input to business cases and the service portfolio Feedback on strategies and policies Financial information regarding improvement initiatives for input to budgets Data required for metrics, key performance indicators (KPIs) and critical success factors (CSFs) Service reports Requests for change (RFCs) for implementing improvements	Vision and mission Service portfolio Policies Strategies and strategic plans Priorities Financial information and budgets Patterns of business activity Achievements against metrics, KPIs and CSFs Improvement opportunities logged in the CSI register

Service strategy
processes

4

4 Service strategy processes

This chapter sets out the processes and activities on which effective service strategy depends. These comprise both lifecycle processes and those almost wholly contained within service strategy. Each is described in detail, setting out the key elements of that process or activity.

The processes and activities specifically addressed in this chapter are:

- Strategy management for IT services
- Service portfolio management
- Financial management for IT services
- Demand management
- Business relationship management.

Most of these processes are used throughout the service lifecycle, but are addressed in *ITIL Service Strategy* since they are central to effective service strategy.

The purpose and scope of service strategy as a whole are set out in section 1.1.

4.1 STRATEGY MANAGEMENT FOR IT SERVICES

This section describes a process for strategy management for an enterprise and shows how it is applied to managing a strategy for IT services. Although senior IT executives will participate in this level of strategy management, most IT organizations use this process to manage a service strategy which forms part of the overall enterprise strategy. Section 4.1.5 will focus on describing the generic process of strategy management, and section 4.1.5.20 will explain how this is applied within internal service providers.

4.1.1 Purpose and objectives

Strategy management for IT services is the process of defining and maintaining an organization's perspective, position, plans and patterns with regard to its services and the management of those services. The purpose of a service strategy is to articulate how a service provider will enable an organization to achieve its business outcomes; it establishes the criteria and mechanisms to decide which services will be best suited to meet the business outcomes and the most effective and

efficient way to manage these services. Strategy management for IT services is the process that ensures that the strategy is defined, maintained and achieves its purpose.

The objectives of strategy management for IT services are to:

- Analyse the internal and external environments in which the service provider exists, to identify opportunities that will benefit the organization.
- Identify constraints that might prevent the achievement of business outcomes, the delivery of services or the management of services; and define how those constraints could be removed or their effects reduced.
- Agree the service provider's perspective and review regularly to ensure continued relevance. This will result in a clear statement of the vision and mission of the service provider.
- Establish the position of the service provider relative to its customers and other service providers. This includes defining which services will be delivered to which market spaces, and how to maintain a competitive advantage.
- Produce and maintain strategy planning documents and ensure that all relevant stakeholders have updated copies of the appropriate documents. This will include the IT strategy, the service management strategy and the strategy plans for each service where appropriate.
- Ensure that strategic plans have been translated into tactical and operational plans for each organizational unit that is expected to deliver on the strategy.
- Manage changes to the strategies and related documents, ensuring that strategies keep pace with changes to the internal and external environments.

4.1.2 Scope

Strategy management is the responsibility of the executives of an organization. It enables them to set the objectives of the organization, to specify how the organization will meet those objectives and to prioritize investments required to meet them. However, in medium to large organizations it is unlikely that the executives themselves will conduct the assessments, draft the strategy documents and manage the execution. This is normally performed by a dedicated strategy and planning manager reporting directly into the board of directors.

An organization's strategy is not limited to a single document or department. The overall strategy of an organization will be broken down into a strategy for each unit of the business. Figure 4.1 gives an example of how a business strategy might be broken down into strategies for IT and for manufacturing. There are likely to be several strategies within each organization. Strategy management for the enterprise has to ensure that these are all linked and consistent with one another. Strategy management for IT services has to ensure that the services and the way they are managed support the overall strategy of the enterprise.

Strategy management is described above as a generic process that could be applied to the

business as a whole, or to any of the business units. However, this publication is specifically concerned with how this process is applied to IT as a service provider. Please note that in an external service provider, the business strategy might be related to IT services delivered to an external customer, and the IT strategy would be related to how those services will be delivered and supported. At the same time, external service providers do not just provide IT services to customers. They are also consumers of their own (and potentially other third-party) IT services. External service providers also have internal IT service requirements that must be met to enable them to survive.

Key message

A service strategy is a subset of the overall strategy for the organization. In the case of an IT organization, the IT strategy will encompass the IT service strategy.

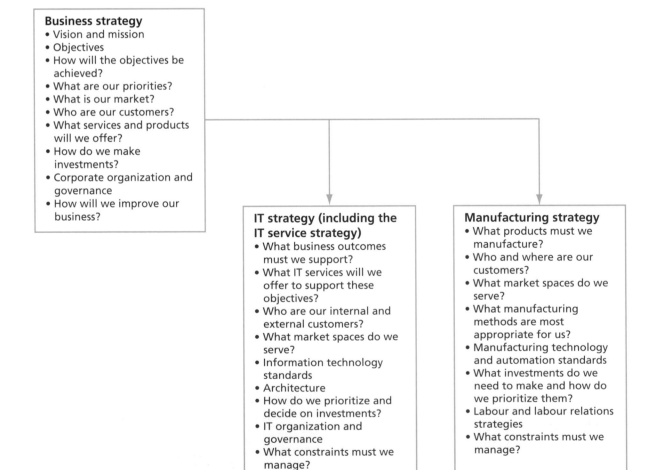

Business strategy
- Vision and mission
- Objectives
- How will the objectives be achieved?
- What are our priorities?
- What is our market?
- Who are our customers?
- What services and products will we offer?
- How do we make investments?
- Corporate organization and governance
- How will we improve our business?

IT strategy (including the IT service strategy)
- What business outcomes must we support?
- What IT services will we offer to support these objectives?
- Who are our internal and external customers?
- What market spaces do we serve?
- Information technology standards
- Architecture
- How do we prioritize and decide on investments?
- IT organization and governance
- What constraints must we manage?

Manufacturing strategy
- What products must we manufacture?
- Who and where are our customers?
- What market spaces do we serve?
- What manufacturing methods are most appropriate for us?
- Manufacturing technology and automation standards
- What investments do we need to make and how do we prioritize them?
- Labour and labour relations strategies
- What constraints must we manage?

Figure 4.1 Overall business strategy and the strategies of business units

The scope of strategy management in *ITIL Service Strategy* is illustrated in Figure 4.2. This diagram shows how a business strategy is used to develop a set of tactics (detailed approaches, processes and techniques that will be used to achieve strategic objectives) and operations (specific procedures, technologies and activities that will be executed by individuals and teams). The IT strategy (and therefore also the strategy for IT services) is derived from the business strategy, but it also provides validation of the business strategy. The IT strategy can determine whether a strategic objective is technologically possible, and what level of investment would be required to meet that objective. The business is then able to decide on whether the objective should be included and at what priority.

IT tactics are partly determined by the IT strategy, but also by the business tactics. For example, if a business tactic requires compliance with a regulation or standard, then IT will have to ensure that its tactics support this. If they do not, the business and IT can then decide what level of investment is required to address the situation. IT tactics can also help the business determine whether its tactics are appropriate. For example, defining how a sales team will work will partly depend on what type of sales automation services are provided by IT. Again, if the limits imposed by IT are too rigid, then the business and IT can

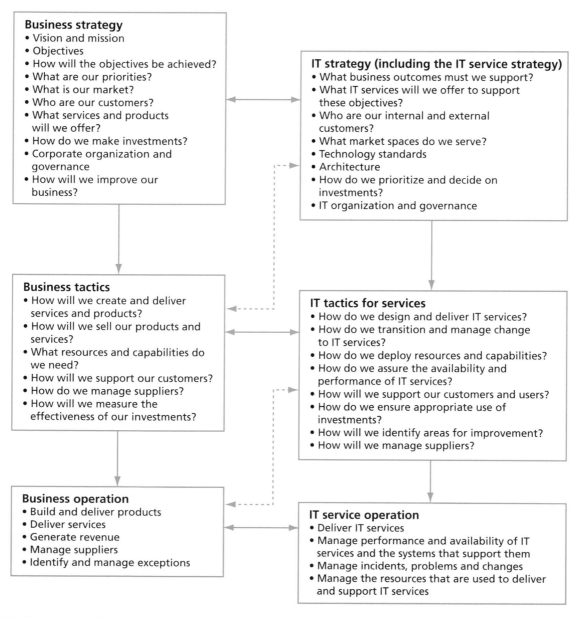

Business strategy
- Vision and mission
- Objectives
- How will the objectives be achieved?
- What are our priorities?
- What is our market?
- Who are our customers?
- What services and products will we offer?
- How do we make investments?
- Corporate organization and governance
- How will we improve our business?

IT strategy (including the IT service strategy)
- What business outcomes must we support?
- What IT services will we offer to support these objectives?
- Who are our internal and external customers?
- What market spaces do we serve?
- Technology standards
- Architecture
- How do we prioritize and decide on investments?
- IT organization and governance

Business tactics
- How will we create and deliver services and products?
- How will we sell our products and services?
- What resources and capabilities do we need?
- How will we support our customers?
- How do we manage suppliers?
- How will we measure the effectiveness of our investments?

IT tactics for services
- How do we design and deliver IT services?
- How do we transition and manage change to IT services?
- How do we deploy resources and capabilities?
- How do we assure the availability and performance of IT services?
- How will we support our customers and users?
- How do we ensure appropriate use of investments?
- How will we identify areas for improvement?
- How will we manage suppliers?

Business operation
- Build and deliver products
- Deliver services
- Generate revenue
- Manage suppliers
- Identify and manage exceptions

IT service operation
- Deliver IT services
- Manage performance and availability of IT services and the systems that support them
- Manage incidents, problems and changes
- Manage the resources that are used to deliver and support IT services

Figure 4.2 The scope of strategy management

investigate what level of investment would resolve the situation, and whether this is appropriate.

IT operations are derived from the IT tactics, but also by the requirements of business operations. The way in which the different operational environments are coordinated and how they interact is very important to strategy management for IT services. It is only once a strategy has been executed that it can be validated. Assessment of the actual performance of activities and services can indicate whether the parameters used in setting the strategy were accurate, and can also validate any assumptions made.

Also in Figure 4.2 IT strategy is related (using a dotted line) to business tactics. Since both IT strategy and business tactics are derived from the business strategy, they have to be checked to ensure consistency. IT should not define a strategy that clashes with the business tactics. Also, the business tactics should not make a tactical decision about how IT services are going to be used if the IT strategy does not allow for that type of usage.

A similar relationship exists between business operation and IT tactics. Since IT exists to support the business, it is important that any tactic they deploy needs to be valid for business operation.

It is important to note, furthermore, that a service strategy is not the same as an ITSM strategy – which is really a tactical plan. The difference can be summed up as follows:

- **Service strategy** The strategy that a service provider will follow to define and execute services that meet a customer's business objectives. For an IT service provider the service strategy is a subset of the IT strategy.
- **Service management (ITSM) strategy** The plan for identifying, implementing and executing the processes used to manage services identified in a service strategy. In an IT service provider, the ITSM strategy will be a subset of the service strategy.

4.1.3 Value to business

The strategy of an organization articulates its objectives, and defines how it will meet those objectives and how it will know it has met those objectives. Without a strategy the organization will only be able to react to demands placed by various stakeholders, with little ability to assess each

Note on strategy for services

Strategy management for IT services is intended for managing the strategy of a service provider. It will include a specification of the type of services it will deliver, the customers of those services and the overall business outcomes to be achieved when the service provider executes the strategy. The IT service strategy is a subset of the IT strategy that, in addition to the IT service strategy, includes strategies for IT architecture, portfolio management (other than services), application management, infrastructure management, project management, technological direction etc.

The strategy of an individual service is defined during the service portfolio management process and documented in the service portfolio. This will include a description of the specific business outcomes that the service will support, and also define how the service will be delivered. The information in the service portfolio (see section 4.2) will be used as input into the process of defining the service provider's strategy.

demand and how it will impact the organization. In these cases the actions of the organizations tend to be led by whoever is making the loudest demands, rather than by what is best for the organization. Strategy becomes a function of organizational politics and self-interest, rather than the overall achievement of its objectives.

A well-defined and managed strategy ensures that the resources and capabilities of the organization are aligned to achieving its business outcomes, and that investments match the organization's intended development and growth.

Strategy management ensures that all stakeholders are represented in deciding the appropriate direction for the organization and that they all agree on its objectives and the means whereby resources, capabilities and investment are prioritized. Strategy management also ensures that the resources, capabilities and investments are appropriately managed to achieve the strategy.

For a service provider, strategy management for IT services ensures that it has the appropriate set of services in its service portfolio, that all of its services have a clear purpose, and that everyone in the service provider organization knows their role in achieving that purpose. Strategy management for IT services further encourages appropriate levels of investment, which will result in one or more of the following:

- Cost savings, since investments and expenditure are matched to achievement of validated business objectives, rather than unsubstantiated demands
- Increased levels of investment for key projects or service improvements
- Shifting investment priorities. The service provider will be able to de-focus attention from one service, and re-focus on another, ensuring that its efforts and budget are spent on the areas with the highest level of business impact.

For the customer of the service provider, strategy management for IT services enables them to articulate clearly their business priorities in a way that is understandable to the service provider. The service provider is then able to make a decision about how to respond to the customer. In some cases, the customer demand represents a departure from the service provider's strategy. The service provider will use strategy management for IT services to make a decision about whether to change its strategy, or whether to turn down the business. Where the service provider is an internal IT organization the second option is not always possible, and in these cases it will use strategy management for IT services to work with the business units to make them aware of the impact of their demand on the current strategy. The business executives will be able to work with IT either to change the existing strategy, or to decline the opportunity.

In other cases, customer demands do not change the service provider's strategy, but will require it to change its priorities. Strategy management for IT services enables the service provider to determine the best way to change its priorities and balance its resources, capabilities and investments.

4.1.4 Policies, principles and basic concepts

Strategy has been defined and explained in detail in Chapter 3. This section defines a generic model for defining, executing and measuring service strategy. This can be applied at the most senior level of the organization, or as the strategy for a part of the organization.

Case study: Strategy management in action

A government department consisted of five agencies, each with a different mission, services, applications and infrastructure. The central office was expected to provide shared services for all agencies, but investments were usually prioritized for the agency that happened to have excess budget, or those that happened to be experiencing the most serious outages. None of the agencies were satisfied with the central office's services, since the agencies receiving investment thought they were reactive, while the other agencies thought they were unresponsive. The central office's staff were always severely overworked as they tried to keep up with the ever-shifting priorities.

The CIO created a steering group with the IT manager of each agency, which met weekly to define the role and objectives of the central office and to agree priorities for investments. The agencies were able to state their objectives and requirements, and prioritize their demands in relation to one another, and the central office was able to define a clear strategy, and keep it up to date with changes in the agencies.

The end result was a significant increase in customer satisfaction, along with substantial cost savings and fewer outages to critical systems in the agencies.

As has been frequently stated, an organization's strategy is defined by its executives. If the organization is an external service provider with a core business of providing services, the service strategy will be the central component of the organization's strategy.

In internal service providers, the service strategy will support the overall enterprise strategy, and provide a tactical plan for the internal service provider. In other words, while the IT strategy is strategic to the IT organization, the board of directors would consider it to be more tactical from their point of view. It is therefore vital that the IT strategy be defined in terms of the organization's overall strategy.

If the IT strategy is unable to support the organization's overall strategy (for example, due to a lack of funding), this must be fed back to the organization's senior leadership, which will need to alter the organization's strategy or to make the necessary funding available.

Chapter 5 contains a discussion on governance and the role of senior executives in defining and executing strategy.

4.1.4.1 Cautionary note

Strategy management should not be undertaken lightly. Simply launching into a strategy exercise for the entire organization, where little has been in place previously, will quickly result in the team being inundated with data and information, before they can produce anything that can be signed off by senior management.

Teams that will be essential to generate and execute the strategy might be hesitant to support the initiative – especially if they perceive that it will impact them negatively.

It is crucial that the strategy is correctly scoped the first time this process is used, and it is even more important that senior executives are seen to be behind the initiative. There is a need for incremental progress to get an organization up to the point of addressing service strategy in the comprehensive manner described in this section.

4.1.5 Process activities, methods and techniques

The process for strategy management is illustrated in Figure 4.3.

4.1.5.1 Strategic assessment

No organization exists in isolation, and every organization is defined by how it interacts with its ever-changing environment. The purpose of the strategic assessment is to determine the service provider's current situation and what changes are likely to impact it in the foreseeable future. The assessment will also highlight constraints that will limit or prevent the service provider from being able to progress its current goals, or to adapt to change.

The strategic assessment analyses both the internal environment (the service provider's own organization) and the external environment (the world with which the service provider's organization interacts), and then arrives at a set of objectives which will be used to define the actual strategy.

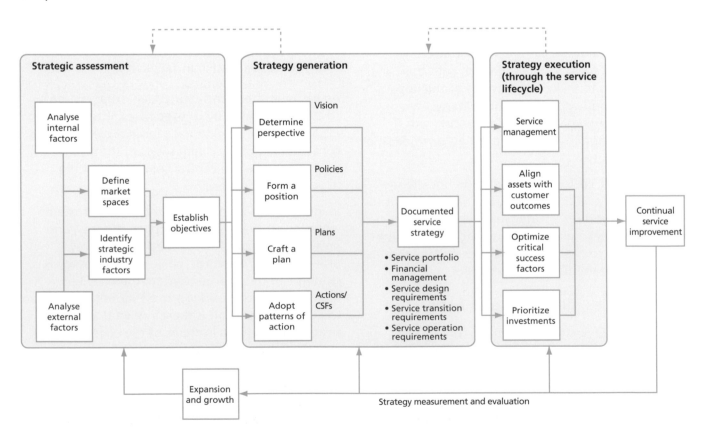

Figure 4.3 The strategy management process

Table 4.1 Questions to assess existing services as differentiators

Which of our services or service varieties are the most distinctive? Are there services that the business or customer cannot easily substitute?	Are there barriers to entry which prevent other service providers from offering the same services? Barriers to entry could be the service provider's knowledge of the customer's business or the broadness of service offerings.
	Would it be expensive to switch to another service provider for the same services? The service provider might have lower cost structures because of specialization or service sourcing.
	Do we offer a particular attribute not readily found elsewhere? These could include product knowledge, regulatory compliance, provisioning speeds, technical capabilities or global support structures.
Which of our services are the most profitable?	The form of value may be monetary, as in higher profits or lower expenses, or social, as in saving lives or collecting taxes. For non-profit organizations, are there services that allow the organization to perform its mission better? Substitute 'profit' with 'benefits realized'.
Which of our customers and stakeholders are the most satisfied?	The answer to this question will indicate services that are high quality, low cost, unique to a specific customer's requirements, or some combination of the three.
Which customers, channels or purchase occasions are the most profitable?	Again, the form of value can be monetary, social or other.
Which of our activities in our value chain or value network are the most different and effective?	These activities will be viewed by the business as a core competency, and therefore will ensure that the service provider is seen as strategic.

4.1.5.2 Strategic assessment: analyse the internal environment

In crafting a service strategy, a provider should first take a careful look at what it does already. The starting point is to identify the service provider's strengths and weaknesses through an internal analysis. This information will help to define the strategy by identifying which strengths can be leveraged, and which weaknesses need to be strengthened. Although internal analysis has sometimes been reduced to a brainstorming session between senior managers, it should be a conscious activity based on careful assessment of the organization over a period of time.

Typical categories of analysing strengths and weaknesses include:

■ **Existing services** It is likely that the service provider already has a basis for differentiating themselves, although established service providers often do not recognize their own unique differentiators. The questions in Table 4.1 can help to identify a service provider's distinctive capabilities and core competencies.

■ **Financial analysis** This will indicate the cost of services, and the return on investment in the service provider. Financial assessment will need to take into account how the service provider contributes to the achievement of business outcomes. Care should be taken here because some large investments will take time to yield a return. This is not necessarily a weakness, since the investment may actually have resulted in a significant differentiator for the service provider, and will result in high future returns (see section 3.6.1).

■ **Human resources** It is important to know what skills and capabilities the service provider has, and where these are sourced. Skills that are contracted in, but are critical to the business, represent a significant risk. This part of the assessment will also focus on the quality of training, recruitment, management, compensation, succession planning, labour relations (e.g. the role of trade unions).

■ **Operations** This part of the analysis focuses on how efficient and effective the organization is at actually supporting and delivering services, and how it manages the technology upon which those services are based. It will look for things such as duplication of effort or technology, level of control, impact of incidents, ability to manage change etc.

- **Relationship with the business units** (for internal service providers) A good strategy requires a good understanding of the overall strategy and requirements of the customer (in this case internal customers), and how the service provider is currently meeting those requirements and enabling that strategy.

- **Resources and capabilities** Those that currently exist to provide services, as well as how they are currently utilized.

- **Existing projects** Projects that will change any of the above aspects of the organization.

4.1.5.3 Strategic assessment: analyse the external environment

There are several publications that provide detailed guidance on analysing the external environment. Some of these are referenced at the end in the section entitled 'References and Further Reading'. This current section summarizes the most important external factors for a service provider to consider. Whereas internal analysis focuses on analysing strengths and weaknesses, the external analysis focuses on opportunities and threats, and especially how they will develop in the future. The aim in defining a strategy will be to identify which opportunities to exploit and which threats to defend against. External factors include:

- **Industry and market analysis** This focuses on trends and practices in the service provider's industry. For example, are organizations spending more on a particular type of service or investing in a new type of technology? What kind of sourcing models are they using (e.g. is there a trend in outsourcing specific types of service?). What kind of management methods are they using?

- **Customers** Who are the customers? What challenges and opportunities are they facing? What are their strategies? How good is the service provider's relationship with them? What services are they using and why, and will this change?

- **Suppliers** Who are the suppliers? What changes are they forecasting for their products and

services? How will these impact the service provider's current services and architectures?

- **Partners** Is the organization partnered with other organizations? What opportunities and strengths do they offer? Are they still relevant? What are the organization's obligations and responsibilities in respect of these partnerships?

- **Competitors** How have competitors differentiated themselves? Have they found a more cost-effective way of doing business? Do they offer higher quality or lower cost services than we do? Are they gaining or losing ground in the market?

- **Legislation and regulation** What legislation or standard will impact the way we work (for example, Sarbanes-Oxley (SOX), ISO/IEC 27001)? Do competitors face the same constraints? Could we use our compliance with these as differentiators?

- **Political** How are our current practices and strategies impacted by political changes? Will changes in fiscal policy enhance or limit our ability to provide services? How will we (or will we) continue to offer services in politically volatile areas?

- **Socio-economic** What is the economic forecast, and will it impact our current situation? For example, during the recession of 2009, companies were put under a huge amount of pressure to reduce employment, which forced service providers to continue to provide services with fewer people. This resulted in reduction in the number of projects, increased telecommunications due to travel restrictions and increased automation and reliance on vendors due to staff cutbacks. Also, what is our policy and actions regarding social responsibility, and how are we impacted by social responsibility groups?

- **Technology** How will new technology change the services provided, and how will it change the way services are provided? It is important to note that technology changes do not just impact the IT environment. Many IT changes have led to radical and direct changes to the way in which the business itself operates. For example, the use of email and the internet are not just services provided by an IT service provider, they are a fundamental set of business tools. The business defines how they will be used, often without input from their IT service provider.

The technique used here that assesses the organization's relationship to both internal and external factors is called SWOT analysis (which stands for strengths, weaknesses, opportunities and threats). This is discussed in detail in *ITIL Continual Service Improvement*.

4.1.5.4 Strategic assessment: define market spaces

The concept of market spaces is described in section 3.4. In summary, market spaces define opportunities where a service provider can deliver value to its customer(s). They identify opportunities by matching service archetypes with customer assets.

In strategy management, this step results in documentation of all current market spaces and any potential new market spaces that were identified from the internal and external analysis.

When the strategy is generated, the service provider will use this information to decide whether to continue servicing existing market spaces and, if so, whether any changes are needed to ensure successful retention of the market space. This might be because competitors are able to provide the same services at a lower cost or increased quality, or if they are using a new technology that effectively changes the way in which the market space is serviced, making the competitor more attractive than the current service provider. For example, most hotel chains have moved from wired to wireless internet access which enables guests to access email and business applications from anywhere in the hotel. Since all laptops are equipped with wireless cards, this means that these hotel chains will be more attractive to travellers who need internet access during their stay.

Exploring business potential

Service providers can be present in more than one market space. As part of strategic planning, both internal and external service providers should analyse their presence across various market spaces. Strategic reviews include the analysis of strengths, weaknesses, opportunities and threats in each market space. Service providers also analyse their business potential based on unserved or under-served market spaces.

This analysis identifies opportunities with current and prospective customers. It also prioritizes

investments in service assets based on their potential to serve market spaces of interest. For example, if a service provider has strong capabilities and resources in service recovery, it explores all those market spaces where such assets can deliver value for customers.

Begin with a broad set of outcomes such as business asset productivity. This defines a broad market space. Unserved and under-served customer needs are identified within this context and focus is applied based on existing strengths and opportunities. This defines narrower market spaces with specialization based on the categories of business assets and the manner in which they are supported by services.

Providers decide which customer needs are effectively and efficiently served through services, while choosing to serve certain market spaces and avoid others. This essential aspect of service strategy is broken down into the following decisions. Firstly, identify:

- Market spaces that are best served by existing service assets
- Market spaces to avoid with existing service assets.

Then for each market space to be served decisions are made with respect to:

- Services to offer (service portfolio – see section 4.2.4.1)
- Customers to serve (customer portfolio – see section 4.2.4.7)
- Critical success factors (CSFs)
- Service models and service assets
- Service pipeline and service catalogue.

Market space analysis for internal service providers follows similar principles to those for external service providers. Differences are in terms of the extent to which decisions are influenced by:

- Priority and strategic value
- Investments required
- Financial objectives (including profit motive)
- Risks involved
- Policy constraints.

4.1.5.5 Strategic assessment: identify strategic industry factors

For every market space there are critical factors that determine the success or failure of a service strategy. In business literature these factors are called strategic industry factors (Amit and Schoemaker, 1993). These are influenced by customer needs, business trends, competition, regulatory environment, suppliers, standards, industry best practices and technologies.

For example, a service provider who wishes to provide IT services to the healthcare industry in the USA needs to comply with complex privacy laws and regulations, such as HIPAA (Health Insurance Portability and Accountability Act) privacy and security regulations.

Strategic industry factors are translated into a set of executable critical success factors for each market space. These critical success factors require a combination of several service assets such as financial assets, experience, competencies, intellectual property, processes, infrastructure and scale of operations. For example, in the market space for high-volume real-time data processing, such as those required by the financial services industry, service providers must have large-scale computer systems, highly reliable network infrastructure, secure facilities, knowledge of industry regulations and a very high level of contingency. Without these assets, it would not be possible for service providers to provide the utility and warranty demanded by customers in that market space.

Critical success factors determine the service assets required to implement a service strategy successfully. For example, if a strategy requires services to be made available across a large network of locations or a wide area of coverage, the service provider must not only build capacity at key locations, but must also operate the network as a system of nodes so that the cost of serving all customers is roughly identical to and within a price point consistent with a strategic position in a market space.

Not all critical success factors need favour large organizations or economy of scale in operations. Some strategies favour organizations small in size but highly competitive because of the knowledge they have of customers and related market spaces. Managers must therefore conduct evaluation exercises to ascertain the critical success factors in force.

Strategic industry factors have the following general characteristics:

- They are defined in terms of capabilities and resources.
- They are proven to be key determinants of success by industry leaders.
- They are defined by market space levels, not peculiar to any one firm.
- They are the basis for competition among rivals.
- They change over time, so they are dynamic not static.
- They usually require significant investments and time to develop.

Critical success factors by themselves are altered or influenced by one or more of the following factors:

- Customers
- Competitors
- Partners
- Suppliers
- Regulators.

The dynamic nature of markets, business strategies and organizations requires strategic industry factors to be reviewed periodically or at significant events such as changes to customer portfolios, expansion into new market spaces, changes in the regulatory environment and disruptive technologies. For example, new legislation for the healthcare industry on the portability and privacy of patient data would alter the set of critical success factors for all service providers operating in market spaces related to healthcare.

Since they are determinants of success in a market space, strategic industry factors are also useful in evaluating a service provider's strategic position in a market space and driving changes to existing positions. For example, being competitive in a market space may require very high levels of availability, fail-safe operation of IT infrastructure, and adequate capacity to support business continuity of services. In many market spaces cost effectiveness is a common critical success factor, while in others it may be specialized domain knowledge or reliability of infrastructure. Customer satisfaction, richness of service offerings, compliance with standards and global presence are also common critical success factors. Internal service providers tend to score well on familiarity with the customer's business.

This part of the strategy management process involves conducting an analysis of every market space, major customer and the existing service portfolio to determine current strategic positions and desired strategic positions for success. This analysis requires service providers to gather data from customer surveys, service level reviews, industry benchmarks and competitive analysis conducted by third parties or internal research teams. Each strategic industry factor is measured on a meaningful index or scale. It is best to adopt indices and scales that are commonly used within a market space or industry to facilitate benchmarking and comparative analysis.

Strategic industry factors are used to define playing fields, which serve as reference frameworks for evaluation of strategic positions and competitive scenarios (Figure 4.4).

A playing field will have the following benchmarks, determining the various zones in which a service provider is currently positioned or plans to be:

- **Entry level** Performance below this level is not acceptable to customers (grey in Figure 4.4).
- **Industry average** Performance at this level is acceptable to customers, but will not differentiate the service provider (white in Figure 4.4).
- **Industry best** Performance above this level signifies leadership (coloured in Figure 4.4).

These benchmarks are not absolute and their values on an index may vary over time. For example, in a new market space with fewer competitors it might be quite easy to cross the initial entry-level cost benchmark. Over time, the costs required to enter that market space may increase or decrease. For example, if the first service provider in that market space develops a new technology innovation as a differentiator, it will be more expensive for competitors to enter that market space. If, on the other hand, the entry benchmark is set by having specialized skills, and there is an over-supply of people with that skill, it might be less costly to enter the market space. Strategic analysis should take into account not only the current benchmarks for a playing field but also the direction in which they are expected to move (higher or lower), the magnitude of change and the related probabilities.

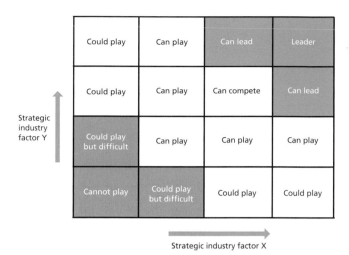

Figure 4.4 Strategic industry factors and competitive positions in playing fields

This analysis is necessary for service providers to avoid being surprised by changes in the market space that can completely destroy their value proposition. Internal service providers may be particularly vulnerable to such blind spots if they are not accustomed to the business analysis found in external service providers. Internal service providers also face competition even if they have captive customers within their enterprise. The playing field is used to conduct strategic analysis of market spaces, customer portfolios (Figure 4.5), service portfolios and customer agreement portfolios. Managers decide the required scenarios to construct using applicable strategic industry factors, scales and indices.

In Figure 4.5, four customers are positioned in relation to two strategic industry factors. This service provider is currently focused on providing industry average services to these customers. However, the services provided to the customer with the highest contract value are approaching market leadership. What strategy will the service provider follow? Some options are listed as follows and illustrated in Figure 4.6:

- For customer 1, it is important that the service provider invest in assets that will solidify their position and enable further growth into the market leadership position.
- After the analysis it was learned that customer 2 was especially focused on strategic industry factor Y. In future the service provider would need to invest in assets that make them more competitive in strategic industry factor Y.

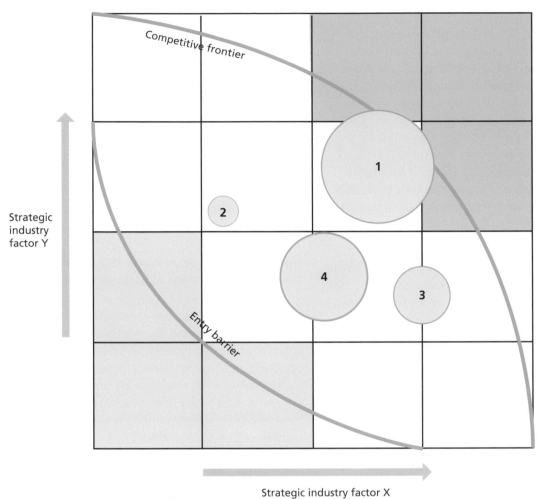

Strategic industry factor Y

Competitive frontier

Entry barrier

Strategic industry factor X

(N) Size of bubble indicates the contract value with customer N

Figure 4.5 Strategic analysis of customer portfolio

■ As the service provider invests in assets to meet strategic industry factors X and Y its overall capabilities will grow. This means that the service provider will be able to offer customer 3 a broader range and quality of services.

■ Customer 4 is using similar services to customer 1, so the service provider could leverage the same or similar assets to reposition customer 4 and ensure retention. Any investment for customer 1 should be evaluated and leveraged for use by customer 4.

■ *Caution*: Just because it is possible to reposition or expand a service it does not follow that every customer will want to do this. Care should be taken not to alienate these customers by forcing them to accept levels and types of services that they do not need, or by increasing prices to levels they might think of as unreasonable.

■ If a service has been repositioned there is a significant chance that the customers previously targeted for this service may no longer be the target market place. Therefore it is also important for the service provider to make clear decisions on which customers it wants to retain. If a customer does not want to take the repositioned service, then they may not be a customer that the IT service provider wishes to retain.

4.1.5.6 Strategic assessment: establish objectives

The objectives defined as an output of the strategic assessment are the results the service provider expects to achieve by pursuing a strategy. Once the objectives have been defined, the service provider will need to define how it will achieve the anticipated results. This is the strategy (or strategies).

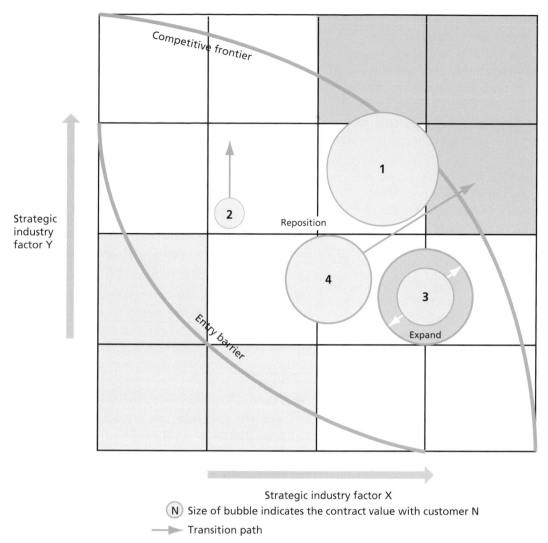

Figure 4.6 Strategic options for the service provider

Clear objectives facilitate consistent decision-making, minimizing later conflicts. They set forth priorities and serve as standards.

When an organization avoids rigorous analysis and objective setting, or where they do not have a good understanding of their services and customers, they tend to use the following strategies (or ways of 'not managing by objectives'). These are surprisingly common, but organizations should not mistake them for valid strategies:

■ **Managing by crisis** The belief that the ability to solve problems effectively is a good strategy. This approach allows events to dictate management decisions, and is highly risky because it assumes that they will always be able to solve problems, and that they will be able to do so without significant business impact. Even more, every time the service provider reacts to a

strategy it potentially takes them in a different direction. When there is some kind of crisis, the organization reacts to the crisis, and then instead of using the opportunity to re-assess the strategy, it waits for the next crisis (which is more likely to occur since the situation has not been rectified).

■ **Managing by customer demand** This type of organization does not seek to understand its customers or their business outcomes. It will make basic services available, such as storage or application hosting, and keep spending money to upgrade capacity whenever users complain about poor performance. It never questions the validity of the demand and it can never quantify the value of its investment.

■ **Managing by extrapolation** Continuing the same activities in the same manner because things are going well. This type of organization will be caught unawares by changes in its customers or in the industry, many of which have been happening slowly over several years, and then suddenly realize that it is unable to continue to provide relevant services, unless it makes huge investments and drastic changes. Many service providers will not survive this level of change.

- **Managing by hope** Making decisions on the belief they will ultimately work out. Most businesses are driven to achieve tangible, measurable results. If the service provider fails to link to these, it will find itself less and less relevant.

- **Managing by best effort** Doing one's best to accomplish what should be done. There is no general plan. There is also no clear understanding of the actual investment required, and so no ability to demonstrate the value of the hard work. In addition, customer expectations for 'best effort' services are generally higher than when the services are quantified and costs explained.

Meaningful objectives are based on the outcomes customers desire to achieve. Objectives must be capable of determining how best to satisfy these outcomes, especially those that are currently under-served. This is how metrics are determined for measuring how well a service is performing. It is therefore important that objectives are not only derived from the overall strategic assessments, but must also take into account specific input from customers. Customer input for creating objectives consists of three distinct types of data, and will help the service provider to identify exactly how they create value (see Table 4.2).

As valuable as this data is, however, it can become very detailed. It is important to distinguish between the level of detail required for strategic objectives and that required to define the strategy or purpose of an individual service. For strategic objectives data about tasks, outcomes and constraints should be at a strategic level, and the service provider should not get swamped with specific requirements for individual services. This type of requirement is defined during the service portfolio management process.

Although this might sound trite, a workable set of guidelines that is frequently used to ensure definition of meaningful objectives is contained in the 'SMART' acronym. This stands for:

- **Specific** Objectives should clearly state what the strategy is or is not going to achieve (e.g. stating that a strategy will result in improved services does not state which services or what is meant by improvement, e.g. cost, response times, availability).

- **Measurable** Managers should be able to assess whether the objective has been met. Ideally, they should be able to measure progress towards the objective as well (e.g. what percentage of this objective has been reached?).

- **Achievable** It must be possible to meet the objective (e.g. totally automating all of service management is not feasible).

- **Relevant** This checks to ensure that the objective is consistent with the culture, structure and direction of the organization; and that it follows from the findings of the assessments.

Table 4.2 Customer data inputs for creating objectives

Type of customer data	Description
Customer tasks	What task or activity is the service to carry out? What job is the customer seeking to execute?
Customer outcomes	What outcomes is the customer attempting to obtain? What is the desired outcome?
Customer constraints	What constraints may prevent the customer from achieving the desired outcome? How can the provider remove these constraints?

- **Time-bound** The timing for the strategy as a whole should be contained in the vision statement, but each objective may have different timing. This should be clearly stated.

While these are good guidelines, experience has shown that they may not be enough. The following are some additional guidelines to bear in mind when setting objectives:

- **Don't have too many** The ideal number of objectives seems to be in the range of 5 to 7. After initial drafting it is common to have somewhere between 20 and 40 objectives. Most of these can be grouped together into a higher-level objective, although the person who raised each objective should be satisfied that their objective can be met (or if not included, should be satisfied that it is not).
- **Use primary and secondary objectives** Where some people are not prepared to let their objective go, it is possible to create a hierarchy of objectives with each of the 5 to 7 high-level objectives being expanded to incorporate clarifications or more detailed descriptions of the main objective. Even so, there should not be more than 3 secondary objectives per primary objective.
- **Keep them simple** Each objective should be easy to read and understand. This will help keep the service provider focused, and will also make it easier to sell the strategy to other stakeholders.
- **Avoid ambiguity** When simplifying objectives, it is important not to create ambiguous statements. When deciding between brevity and clarity, clarity should always be favoured.
- **Be positive, but state the negative** Objectives will state what the strategy is going to achieve, but it is sometimes clearer and less ambiguous to state what the organization is not going achieve. This will help in setting expectations.

Even with well-stated and clear objectives, many are not achieved. There are a number of reasons for this, including:

- **The objective was not well designed** This means that it did not take into account the guidelines outlined above. If an objective is not measurable or achievable it cannot be met.
- **Differing expectations** Where an objective is understood differently by different groups, one may believe that they have met the objective, while another believes that there is still work to be done. This happens even when the objective is stated clearly, and is usually the result of different group contexts or differing ideas as to why the strategy was defined in the first place. For example, IT designed higher availability of the sales order service by reducing failure rates, but when the users requested higher availability they meant extended service hours, not less downtime.
- **Organizational changes** The more complex a strategy and the longer it takes to execute, the more likely it is to be affected by a change in stakeholders. With each organizational change comes a shift in priorities and requirements. What was agreed by the stakeholders when the strategy was defined may not be as relevant to the new stakeholders.
- **Lack of ownership of the objective** It sometimes occurs that the team defines an objective, but there is no stakeholder ownership. This could be the result of miscommunication, or an assumption that somebody else was responsible. It is important that each objective has clear ownership. If ownership is shared, this must be clearly stated, and the respective implications of ownership accepted by each stakeholder.
- **Politics** It is never wise to assume that because a stakeholder signed off on an objective, he or she truly agreed with or supported it. Many decisions made in business are not logical at all, but determined by the complex inter-relationships between people, groups and conflicting sets of objectives. These politics may change the objectives or even result in the strategy being derailed and a new leadership team being appointed. A successful strategy requires that these relationships are monitored carefully and that management keeps reporting on the agreed objectives to as wide an audience as necessary to ensure that stakeholders have more realistic expectations.
- **Environmental changes** Some objectives cannot be met simply because of a change to something the team has no control over. For example, a strategy includes moving to a particular software architecture, but the software company is purchased and the software replaced by the purchaser's suite. This will require a re-evaluation of the strategy and resetting the objectives with all stakeholders.

- **Other factors** The organization has had to change its strategy due to external or internal factors, and the existing strategy is no longer valid.

The most important point to remember about meeting objectives is that they are only met when all parties agree that they have been met. This has some clear implications:

- When setting an objective, ensure that all parties understand how it will be measured and what the terms of acceptance are.
- Any achievements or outcomes identified in the strategy must be linked to an objective. If management can prove that the deliverable was delivered, then it is easier to prove that the objective was met.
- If a requirement is expressed that cannot be linked to an objective, management has two options – reject the requirement, or add a new objective, effectively changing the strategy.
- If a requirement is rejected, this must be done in writing under the signature of the most senior executive. This will reduce the amount of change to the strategy and will also ensure that any politics are handled at the executive level, thus leaving the organization to move forward with executing the strategy with as little ill-will as possible.
- If accepted, the new requirement and objective have to be handled as a change to the strategy and must be signed off by all stakeholders.
- When the strategy is executed, managers should not only focus on what milestones have been reached, they should also include information on how the objectives are being met. Any activity which contributes to or detracts from an objective should be reported specifically.

4.1.5.7 Strategy generation, evaluation and selection

Once the assessment has been completed and the service provider has defined the objectives of the strategy, it is possible to generate the actual strategy in terms of the 'four Ps' described in section 3.1.2.

4.1.5.8 Strategy generation: determine perspective

The perspective of a service provider defines its overall direction, values, beliefs and purpose; and, at a high level, how it intends to achieve these. The most common forms of perspective statements are vision and mission statements.

The vision statement articulates what it is the service provider aims to achieve. Vision statements look at a desired state that will be achieved at some time in the future. Mission statements articulate the basic purpose and values of the organization and its operation. Mission statements are more about how the organization will make its vision a reality.

A clear perspective enables the service provider and its customers to understand its direction and value. A good perspective has four main purposes:

- To clarify the direction of the service provider
- To motivate people to take action that moves the organization to make the vision reality
- To coordinate the actions of different people or groups
- To represent the view of senior management as they direct the organization towards its overall objectives.

From these points it is clear that the perspective does not just articulate the objectives and core business of the organization, but it also forms the basis for its culture. The perspective provides a basis for setting common goals throughout the organization and ensuring that the appropriate actions and behaviour are encouraged at all levels.

The implication is that a successful perspective is at the root of an organization's culture. A change to perspective is thus not just a case of re-defining the vision and mission, and then making structural changes to implement them. Just creating and communicating these statements is not enough to ensure acceptance. A change in perspective will require a significant effort to change the current culture and way of thinking of the organization. *ITIL Service Transition* discusses organizational and stakeholder change in some detail.

The actual process of defining the perspective is valuable in getting people on the management team to align their agendas and thinking. It is not uncommon for the team to spend proportionately longer on defining the vision than on defining the rest of the strategy.

Generally, it is helpful to define or update the perspective at a face-to-face meeting of senior managers, where any disagreements or clarifications can be dealt with immediately. This also helps to deal directly with any interpersonal agendas or politics which could impact the outcome.

Well-defined perspectives serve as a reference for subsequent positions, plans or patterns of action. Public assertions made by a service provider are usually based on strategy as a perspective and reflected in its value proposition to customers. The value proposition may be implicit in the customers it serves, the services it offers, and the particular perspective of service quality it adopts. A clear perspective helps make this value proposition explicit. The perspective is defined at the highest level of abstraction and maintains the organization's farthest planning horizon. It drives other control views of strategy (the other 'Ps') and is modified based on feedback from those views.

Despite its high-level abstraction, perspective should not be ignored or trivialized. Unlike plans or patterns, perspectives are not easily changed. Take the perspective of Swiss watchmakers, for example, when confronted with the emergence of quartz technology – a Swiss invention. Dismissing the technology as a novelty incompatible with the perspective of skill-intensive craftsmanship, the Swiss watch industry was nearly decimated by Japanese companies. That is, until it adopted the technology for major market niches and reclaimed market share through a perspective centred on fashion rather than workmanship.

Once a perspective has been attained, it can be tested by asking the following questions:

- Does it capture what the service provider intends to do for only the next three to five years, or does it capture a more timeless essence of the organization's distinctiveness?
- Is it clear and memorable?
- Does it have the ability to promote and guide action?
- Does it set boundaries within which people are free to experiment?

The distillation of an organization's strategy into a memorable and prescriptive phrase is important.

A sound strategy is of little use unless people understand it well enough to apply it during unforeseen or ambiguous opportunities.

Example of a perspective

Vision

The IT organization contributes to the competitive advantage of Company X by delivering IT services that meet defined business outcomes of other business units.

Mission

The IT organization understands the business outcomes that allow Company X to be successful. It builds, sources and delivers IT services to other business units to achieve these outcomes. The IT organization enables Company X to operate efficiently and with minimal disruption, and it also helps each business unit to innovate new ways of creating and delivering value to external customers.

4.1.5.9 Strategy generation: form a position

The strategic position defines how the service provider will be differentiated from other service providers in the industry. For example, positioning could be based on the type or range of services offered, or providing services at the lowest cost. Positioning is based on the output of the strategic assessment, especially the analysis of market spaces and strategic industry factors.

The position of a service provider is frequently expressed through policies about what services will be provided, to what level and to which customers. These policies will also define any standards or criteria that are used to ensure that differentiation is properly designed and built into the services, operations and organization. The policies defined during this stage of the process will be used as input into the other service lifecycle stages.

Apart from the cost and quality of services, there are four broad types of position for service providers. These are outlined below:

Variety-based positioning

Variety-based positioning focuses on delivering a narrow catalogue of services to a variety of customers and types of customer. Although the catalogue of services is narrow, there is usually more depth in terms of service options, levels and packages. Service assets are highly specialized to deliver this narrow catalogue. Service providers do not try to meet all the needs of any given customer segment. Success is measured in terms of performing exceptionally well in meeting a subset of needs (Figure 4.7). It is possible to leverage economies of scale, since the service provider manages similar types of demand from different customers, and fulfils demand with a small and stable catalogue of services. Growth is based predominantly on new opportunities for the same catalogue of services. For example, a service provider may specialize in payroll services for several groups within a business unit, several business units within an enterprise or several enterprises within a region.

Needs-based positioning

This is sometimes called a 'customer intimate' approach because it focuses on a single customer or customer type and provides a range of services to meet a broad number of customer needs (Figure 4.7). The catalogue of services is relatively broad since the service provider is addressing a broader range of services. Needs-based positioning reflects the traditional approach of grouping customers into segments and then aiming to best serve the needs of one or more targeted segments. Service providers do not aim to gain market share by expanding their services to an unlimited number of potential customers. Rather, they differentiate themselves by performing exceptionally well in meeting most of the needs of a particular customer or segment. Their capabilities are based on being able to leverage economies of scope, managing

different demands from the same customers, and fulfilling them with a flexible catalogue of services. Growth is based predominantly on new services in the catalogue from the same source of demand.

For example, a service provider may specialize in supporting most or all of the business needs of a group of hospitals. It may offer a catalogue of services that covers infrastructure services, application maintenance, information security, document management and disaster recovery services specialized for the healthcare industry. It maintains expertise on electronic medical records, privacy issues, medical equipment and claims processing. Similarly, a provider focusing on the financial services industry has deep insight into the peculiar challenges and opportunities faced by investment banks, insurers and brokerage firms.

Internal service providers are often positioned to serve a customer segment of one. They have only one customer at the enterprise level even if there are several at the business unit level. Many internal IT organizations are expected to meet all the IT needs of the business that owns them. They do not worry about meeting the needs of other enterprises and can therefore organize their service assets to best serve one enterprise customer.

Access-based positioning

Access-based positioning does not (as the name might suggest) have to do with how customers apply for or receive a service. It refers to providing a service, or range of services, to multiple customers who have something in common – usually their location, scale or structure (Figure 4.8

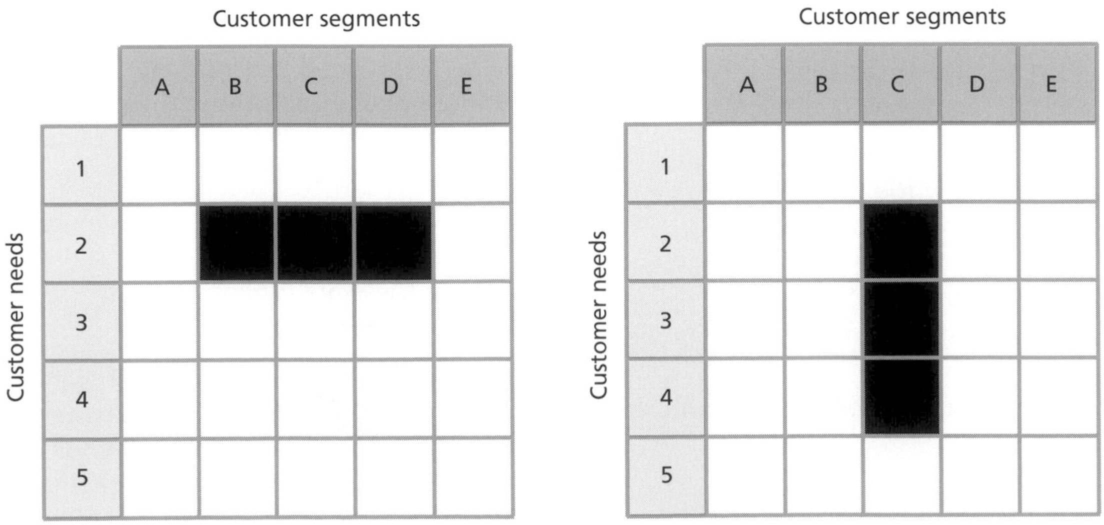

Figure 4.7 Variety-based (left) and needs-based (right) positioning

with the axis on the right to show its relationship to Figure 4.9): for example, a PC support company that only provides support for small businesses in a single city; or a company that only provides point-of-sale solutions for convenience stores. These service providers are typically very specialized and deploy business assets according to the specific business and customer profile that they have targeted. This is in contrast to variety-based positioning where a narrow catalogue of services is available to any type of customer or needs-based positioning where a broad range of services is provided to a specific customer or customer segment.

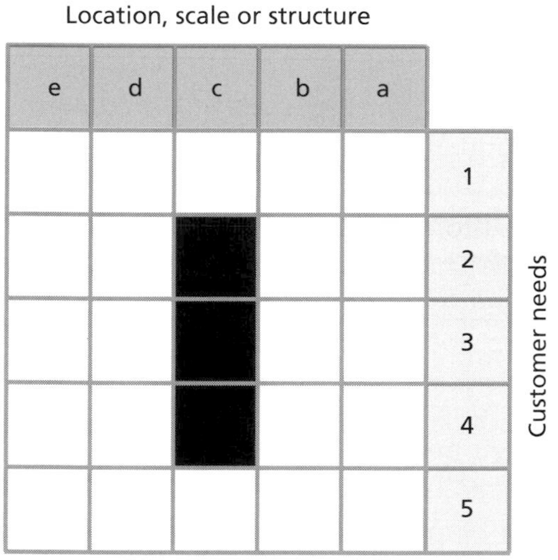

Figure 4.8 Access-based positioning

An insurance company offers to initiate the claims process at the site of an accident. It does so by dispatching claims handling staff to the accident site with all the resources necessary for the claims process. This strategy not only provides distinctive value to its policyholders but also speeds processes and reduces administrative costs from lengthy cases. It puts an office-based clerical job out on the front line in vehicles specially equipped with the necessary business applications. The insurance company itself adopts an access-based strategy to distinguish itself from competing insurers.

Other service providers in turn may compete to win the business of this progressive insurer by offering mobile workplace services that automate and integrate the claims processing vehicles with back-office systems. Service providers with knowledge and experience in mobile systems and applications, similar to those used by emergency medical services, would have a distinctive advantage.

Demand-based positioning

This type of positioning contains features of both variety- and needs-based positioning in that it offers a broad range of services to a potentially unlimited number of customers. It has been made possible by the convergence of infrastructure, applications and services. One example of this type of positioning is 'cloud' services. In this positioning, companies use IT to engage directly with a huge variety of customers and individual consumers. There is no pre-defined standard service, rather a range of service options that can be combined in

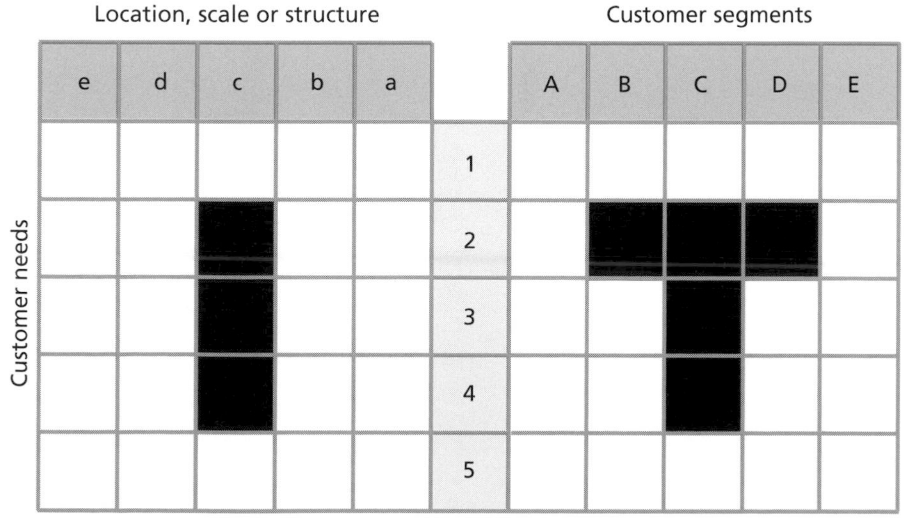

Figure 4.9 Combining variety-based, needs-based and access-based positioning

any number of service packages – all driven by the consumer directly. For example, consumers enter a website, and create an account. They create profiles and select the combination of services that suits their particular needs. For example, an online bookseller can track purchases and preferences and automatically notify the consumer of new products or special pricing available to them, put them in touch with other consumers with similar tastes, allow them to sell used copies of the books, provide shipping services and more.

The main capabilities of the service provider are in being able to have a number of standard services in a catalogue, which can be selected in any combination and linked to each consumer. Demand is highly volatile and the service provider needs to be able to move workloads around so that they can maintain performance. Operationally, they need to monitor capacity and gear it to the demand very quickly. One of the key focuses is on anticipating and staying ahead of the demand.

Service providers may adopt one or more of these generic types of positioning (Figure 4.9). There are no universal rules for these positioning strategies, simply plans and patterns that work, or definitions to comply with. Once a position has been determined, however, the service provider will need concrete plans to maintain strategic positions from which the mission and objectives are achieved. A sound position guides the organization in what to do and, just as important, in what not to do.

The type of positioning chosen will determine how service assets will be specialized and deployed. Each type of positioning will have typical patterns of demand generated by business activities, cycles and events of the target market spaces. The architecture and configuration of service assets will need to be structured appropriately for these demand patterns. This is an opportunity to consolidate, stabilize, learn and grow into a high-performing service provider with focus. Specialization of service assets allows service providers to deliver greater levels of utility to targeted segments. On the other hand, specialization may also expose the service provider to risk of being unable to respond to sudden or drastic changes in the market space. If the service provider does not maintain a balance between specialization and agility, they may not recover from this type of change.

Level of asset specialization

The more specialized an asset gets, the lower its usefulness for other purposes. A point-of-sale terminal has higher asset-specificity than a PC workstation or storage device that can be re-purposed. The level of asset specialization applies to organization and people assets as well. Internal service providers who have never served more than one customer find it difficult to adjust to corporate mergers and acquisitions.

Demand-based positioning requires less specialization. In fact it exists only because converging infrastructures make it possible to manage workloads across multiple linked applications and systems. The more converged and generic the infrastructure becomes the easier it is to interchange systems, move workloads from one area to another, host services anywhere in the organization and provide them anywhere consumers can access the internet. Infrastructure becomes a generic investment, and the service assets become the modules of services themselves.

Once a position has been determined, it can be tested by asking the following questions:

- Does it guide the organization in making decisions between competing resource and capability investments?
- Does it help managers test the appropriateness of a particular course of action?
- Does it set clear boundaries within which staff should and should not operate?
- Does it allow freedom to experiment within these constraints?

4.1.5.10 Strategy generation: craft a plan

A strategic plan identifies how the organization will achieve its objectives, vision and position. The plan is a deliberate course of action towards strategic objectives and describes how the organization will move from one point to another within a specific scenario. Although a strategic plan could be a single document, more often it could comprise several plans – especially when the service provider is pursuing more than one position or more than one market.

Planning horizons are typically longer term, although lengths may vary across organizations, industries and strategic context. Plans typically focus on financial budgets, portfolio of services, new service development, investments in service assets and improvement plans.

Although this section talks about crafting a plan, in reality the strategy for a particular organization is often a collection of plans, each aimed at achieving a specific set of objectives, or a specific position. For example, there might be one plan aimed at growing the number of services offered, and a separate plan aimed at increasing the number of locations in which the organization does business. It is critical that these plans are linked and that their objectives are aligned. It would not be good if the number of locations increased, but the organization was unable to offer key services to its new customers.

Plans should be linked by the need to achieve certain strategic objectives. For example, building infrastructure capacity, consolidating staff at key locations, licensing a new set of software applications and complying with an industry standard may all be parts of the same strategic plan to reach a distinctive position.

The plan should be a concise and readable document. Many strategies have failed simply because they were too complicated for anyone, outside the people who created the plan, to understand. Complex spreadsheets and financial modelling should be placed in appendices or separate documents, and only the results published in the plan, with references to where the workings can be found.

In one sense, service management can be viewed as facilitating a coordinated set of plans with which service providers plan and execute their service strategies. The difference between success and failure in strategic leadership and direction is largely dependent on how well this coordinated set is put together, put to work and controlled in execution. Two service providers with equal sets of resources may achieve different degrees of success simply because of their strategic plans.

It is important to note that strategic plans are confidential documents because they have sensitive information about how the organization maintains a differentiated or competitive position, and what its investment priorities are. At the same time, the plan also contains information that the organization may want to be public, such as the mission, vision and certain aspects of its positioning

– for example, what type of service it will offer. The plan should clearly identify which information is confidential and which should be communicated externally, and to whom.

Although the plans are confidential, they should not be kept from key staff members. It is very difficult to execute a strategy if the people doing the work do not have an understanding of why the work is being done. One company had information about sales patterns and online shopping demand cycles, but refused to share it with the capacity manager because it was confidential. The capacity manager attempted to forecast demand using modelling tools, but was not always able to predict heavy demand cycles. The organization was not prepared to share strategic information with a key employee, but spent millions on additional capacity to avoid the occasional downtime.

Typical contents of a strategic plan

The typical contents of a strategic plan could include:

- **Executive summary** This should outline the strategy at a high level, giving a summary of the mission and vision, major goals and key strategies. The idea is that someone who has not been involved in writing the plan can get an understanding of the overall intent and contents of the document quickly. In most cases it should be enough information for an executive to understand the overall direction and impact of the plan, and direct them to more detailed information that is relevant to them.
- **Authorization** It is important to know who signed off on the plan, as this indicates ownership of the plan. This will lend weight to the plan when it is being executed, audited or measured. It will also identify key stakeholders for plan revisions and updates.
- **Background** This is a brief description of the events leading up to the current strategy. It might be a regular strategy review, but more likely there were some specific triggers that initiated the current plan. These could be positive or negative – for example, unforeseen decline or growth in the business, new customer demands, flaws in the previous strategy which resulted in high-profile failures, a change in the economy etc. It is very important for executives to understand the

context and reasons for the new strategy. This makes it easier to achieve their support and to execute the plan.

- **Situational analysis** This section of the plan could be combined with the background, but contains more specific and detailed information about the situation that gave rise to the current strategy. It will also describe which methods were used to do the analysis (e.g. benchmarking or standards compliance) and any alternative strategies that were rejected, together with the reasons for rejection.

- **Vision, mission and value statements** This section describes the overall perspective of the organization. It acts as a yardstick against which the rest of the plan and any resulting actions should be measured. Although it may seem that many values (such as integrity or fairness) are intangible, they encourage those who execute the strategy to make the values part of their tactical decision-making process. For example, one of the regions where the organization wishes to grow new opportunities requires them to pay substantial bribes to government officials – will that be supported?

- **Objectives** These are the objectives as defined in section 4.1.5.6.

- **Strategies** This section outlines the strategic positioning, services and key milestones. It is important to know what the strategy is, as well as how to know that it has been successful.

- **Appendices** These are documents used to generate and execute the strategy. Many of them are working documents which are used to fine-tune the strategy throughout strategy measurement and evaluation. Appendices could include the following:

  - *Strategy analysis method and data* This is the data that was used to generate the objectives and strategy. It is important to include this so that any incorrect assumptions or data can be detected and the strategy adjusted in time.

  - *Action plans* These are detailed plans about the actions that will be taken in executing the strategy, outlining roles and responsibilities, or identifying projects that have been initiated as a result of the strategy, together with dates, costs and specifications of what will be delivered or achieved.

  - *Resource and budget planning* Many organizations will use the strategy as an input into resource plans and budgets. It is important that these are properly coordinated. In a smaller organization these could be included in the plan. In larger organizations this might be too detailed, in which case the strategy needs to identify which documents contain this information, where they are stored and who is responsible for them. This will also help in coordinating actions to execute the strategy and to ensure that the anticipated investments and returns are achievable.

  - *Board/IT steering group responsibilities* It is sometimes worthwhile to separate out the actions that are required of the executives. This ensures accessibility and focus from a group of managers who have to juggle multiple responsibilities.

  - *Communication plan* This will contain information about who needs to know about the plan and what they need to know. It will also contain details about education or awareness activities and who should attend those events. A good communication plan will also define how to ensure that the message has been understood by its recipients – including surveys, interviews and group sessions in which individuals are asked to articulate how they understand the strategy and its impact on them.

Example of inadequate resource and budget planning

An insurance company decided on a strategy to move all its services from batch processing to real-time online services over three years and at a cost of £80 million. Six years and £240 million later, they are about two-thirds complete and the anticipated returns have not yet materialized. What started as a good idea has turned into a situation where the organization has changed too much to go back, and the IT organization simply has to react to whichever business unit has the most political influence or budget.

The strategy assessment included the identification of strategic industry factors related to the identified market spaces. An output of this activity is a set of critical success factors that need to be in place for the service provider to be able to execute the strategy. As stated in section 4.1.5.5, in the context of strategy management, these critical success factors are typically a combination of several service assets such as financial assets, experience, competencies, intellectual property, processes, infrastructure and scale of operations.

One way to identify critical success factors is to map customer assets and service archetypes (Figure 4.10). For example, in healthcare, IT service providers have extensive knowledge of hospital procedures, medical equipment, interactions between physicians, clinicians and pharmacists, insurance policies and privacy regulations. Service providers present in market spaces related to the quality of outcomes in healthcare typically have physicians and clinicians on their payroll. Service strategies for the healthcare market spaces take into account the need to deal with users with highly specialized skills, special-purpose equipment, low tolerance for error and the need to balance security with usability of services. These are critical success factors for a cluster of market spaces related to healthcare.

A subset of these critical success factors is shared by other market spaces such as military applications. Critical success factors can therefore span more than one market space. They represent opportunities for leveraging economies of scale and scope.

Defining critical success factors for strategy is important because it forms the basis for execution. Critical success factors identify what exists and what needs to be built. They provide a set of requirements for the execution of the plans to be successful.

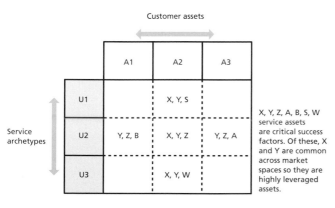

Figure 4.10 Critical success factors leveraged across market spaces

4.1.5.11 Strategy generation: adopt patterns of action

A pattern of action is how an organization works. Formal hierarchies show one view of the organization, but the interactions between these hierarchies, the exchange of information, the handover of units of work and the exchange of money all contribute to a network of activity that gets things done.

Patterns of action work in two ways. On the one hand, the strategy defines patterns that executives believe will be efficient and effective means of achieving objectives. These patterns are discernible and are usually defined and documented in the form of management systems, organizational structures, policies, processes, procedures, budgets, schedules etc. Patterns are also defined in the formal interactions between service provider staff and their customers. The organization makes investments in tools and training to ensure that these patterns are supported and understood, so they can be executed as anticipated.

On the other hand, patterns of action are a way of dealing with the dynamic nature of organizations. As the organization and its environment change, so the strategy needs to be adapted and strengthened. People find better ways to do things, see new opportunities and detect new customer needs or innovative technologies. Strategy needs to be able to take this into account and evolve along with the organization and its environment. These patterns of action are less formal, and are often not tangible. For example, people in the organization use informal networks based on whether someone has tacit knowledge of some task or subject or the organization.

Another example of how working patterns can change or adapt a strategy is if an error was made in defining the organization, processes or tools. Working patterns can change as people in the organization find a more successful way of achieving the objectives. In these cases, patterns of action become the way in which an organization overcomes obstacles introduced by the current strategy or culture.

In this way, patterns of action result in 'emergent strategies', or distinctive patterns in action reinforced over time by repeated success. For example, rather than pursuing a plan to cut service costs through complete outsourcing, the provider makes sourcing decisions one at a time – testing the validity of the idea. Firstly it may source telecommunication services, then application hosting, then security services, and so on, until a strategic pattern has emerged.

However, there is a fine line between innovative behaviour and chaos. Patterns of action may result in an agile and learning organization, but they still need to be aligned to the overall strategy of the organization. If they do not, it is the responsibility of the executives to either change the behaviour or adjust the strategy. A successful pattern of action should always be properly documented, the impact on the strategy quantified and, if necessary, the strategy itself updated.

If patterns of action are properly aligned to the organization's objectives, and are well executed, they are likely to be a signature of the organization and a source of competitive advantage. While industry practices and standards are available to all, signature processes can truly distinguish the value provided by a service provider (Gratton and Ghoshal, 2005). Best practices are patterns of action which document prevalent practice in a particular industry or situation. A successful organization will be able to leverage these, but a superior organization uses them to create its own unique patterns of action, which maximize both the best practice and the organization's own culture and unique position.

If patterns are successful, they can be replicated in other parts of the business, cutting down on development costs, and increasing effectiveness. For example, a department in one service provider found a way of selling their services through partners, but delivering them themselves. In effect they created a whole new sales force, at a fraction of the cost of employing sales people. Within six months, three more departments had positioned themselves to do the same thing. This 'create once, use many times' principle is a fundamental component to many of the models to be found in ITIL – for example, change models, incident models, operations models etc.

When patterns of action become systems and processes, they are placed under configuration management so they can be stabilized, standardized and improved. Each formal pattern of action becomes a baseline from which improvements can be made, and new opportunities

realized. In this way service management can be viewed as an adaptive network of patterns through which strategic objectives are realized.

Types of patterns of action that are helpful in defining and executing service management strategies are shown in Table 4.3.

4.1.5.12 Strategy execution

Once a strategy has been agreed, it needs to be put into action. The question of how to execute the strategy is answered in a set of more detailed tactical plans. Tactical plans describe what approaches and methods will be used to achieve the strategy. If a strategy answers the question 'where are we going?' then tactics answer the question 'how will we get there?'.

All service management processes have a role to play in executing a strategy since they are all about achieving the vision, objectives and plans defined in strategy management. In a very real sense, the other stages of the service lifecycle all have to do with strategy execution. In addition, all services and business outcomes should be in line with the strategy. If they are not then the strategy management process was ineffectual, was not updated regularly enough or was simply bypassed by parts of the organization.

While existing processes and functions will execute strategy as part of their mandate, many of the initiatives will need to be managed as projects. It is usual for a strategy to be linked to a set of projects, managed by a project management office (PMO) and coordinated using the project portfolio (see section 4.2.4.9). In addition, many of these will be initiated as service improvement plans (logged in the CSI register) discussed in detail in *ITIL Continual Service Improvement.* For more information on how to establish, develop and maintain appropriate support structures for portfolios, programmes and projects, see *Portfolio, Programme and Project Offices* (OGC, 2008).

A more detailed description of the interfaces with other service management processes is contained in section 4.1.6.4. In general, however, there are several generic areas that these processes contribute to or that need to be addressed when the strategy is executed. These are illustrated in Figure 4.3 and discussed in the following sections.

Table 4.3 Examples of service management patterns

Patterns of action	Description
'How-to' patterns	Set the operating style of the organization. The framing of how activities are performed, for example: ■ R&D staff must rotate through operations ■ All customer questions must be answered on the first email or call ■ Operations staff must have obtained a minimum level of training and certification.
Boundary patterns	Set the focal point of the organization. The body of opportunities that should, or should not, be pursued, for example: ■ Hardware acquisitions must be done through strategic vendors ■ New technologies must conform to a certain standard ■ New projects must follow a standard methodology.
Priority patterns	Set the allocation of resources. The ranking of new opportunities, for example: ■ Service stability outweighs speed of deployment ■ Service quality outweighs cost savings.
Timing patterns	Set the rhythm of the organization. Staff are synchronized with customer and business cycles, for example: ■ End-of-quarter and end-of-year required enhanced service levels ■ When legislature is in session, no changes are allowed.

Communicating the strategic plan

Ensuring that the strategic plan is communicated to the right people is an important prerequisite for implementing the strategy. The plan is typically communicated as follows:

■ Distribute a copy of the plan to every executive and key stakeholder.

■ Although parts of the plan are confidential, it may be helpful to produce a summary of the plan or a presentation for everyone in the organization.

■ Board members or IT steering group members should be trained on how to talk about the strategy, what points to emphasize and how to ensure compliance in their area of the organization. It should never be assumed that the executives who were part of the strategic planning process will know how to communicate it. This is because they have lived through the plan production, and take information and wording for granted – where a person from outside the process might find it confusing.

■ Key aspects of the strategy, such as vision, mission and main objectives, should be visible throughout the workplace. Posters, screensavers etc. can remind employees of the core strategy throughout the working day.

■ Relevant parts of the strategy should be included in policies, procedures and employee manuals. One large organization requires every manager to use strategic objectives to define goals and key performance indicators (KPIs) for their staff, which are then used as part of ongoing performance measurement.

■ It might also be helpful to provide key strategic partners, such as vendors and investors, with a summary of plans, with briefing about how they expect them to use them.

4.1.5.13 Strategy execution: other service management processes

For a service provider, no strategy can be executed without being able to manage the services that it will be providing. Service management processes enable the service provider to achieve alignment between the services and the desired outcomes on an ongoing basis. Without service management processes the very best the service provider can do is to react promptly to customers, but it will often not be able to follow through to deliver high-quality services over time.

Other service management processes contribute to strategy execution in three ways:

- They provide a management system that formalizes how the service provider will manage services. It is therefore a crucial part of how the strategy will be executed.
- The strategy defines a number of opportunities. Other service management processes define the services to meet those opportunities. Processes in service strategy align the strategy and investment of every service to the overall strategic objectives and investment strategy. Service design processes ensure that services are designed to meet these objectives, and that they can be managed effectively. Service transition processes build, test and validate the services and define exactly what information needs to be recorded to ensure that they can be tracked and managed. Service operation procedures ensure that the services are appropriately delivered and supported. Continual service improvement (CSI) processes measure the actual achievements of services, identify any gaps between requirements and actual delivery, and recommend remediation.
- They define an action plan for how services will be managed. Service management processes not only manage services, they manage the activities, tools and people that deliver and support the services. Service management is a management system that determines not only what services will be used to achieve the strategy, but also how those services will be managed.

Where other components of service management have not been formally implemented, or where it only addresses a sub-set of the aspects of service management, the strategy must include a project or programme to rectify the situation. This strategic project must be formally recognized, approved and supported by the organization's executives as part of the overall organizational strategy.

4.1.5.14 Strategy execution: align assets with customer outcomes

The service provider needs to ensure that its service assets are coordinated, controlled and deployed so that they can provide the appropriate levels of service at the agreed levels. Strategy execution relies on the ability of the service provider to know what service assets they have, where they are located and how they are deployed.

Firstly the service provider needs to be able to articulate the services being provided, and to which customers. The service portfolio has this information, along with information about which business outcomes each service enables. The service portfolio also identifies who the service owner is and who is involved in delivering and supporting the service.

Secondly, the service provider needs to be able to decide how these services will be delivered. Architecture and service models are produced and processes such as capacity management, availability management, service level management, service asset and configuration management all work together to define the optimal design and configuration of the service assets. The aim is to increase productive use of the assets, while optimizing costs.

The way in which service providers manage their assets often reflects the way customers manage theirs. For example, a service provider delivers a wireless email service. This increases the performance of one of the most critical and expensive types of customer assets: managers and staff. Using wireless email, the customer deploys these assets in a manner that gets the most out of their productive capacities.

In this way, sales managers spend more time on-site with clients, technicians are quickly dispatched to cover equipment failures in the field and administrative staff members are consolidated at strategic locations to improve operational effectiveness. To support the customer, the service provider configures and deploys its assets in a manner that effectively supports the customer's own deployments. It may require the design, deployment, operation and maintenance of highly available and secure messaging on wireless phones or computers. What matters is that the customer's employees are able to coordinate business activities, access business applications and control business processes.

4.1.5.15 Strategy execution: optimize critical success factors

The term 'critical success factor' refers to any aspect of a strategy, process, project or initiative that needs to be present in order for it to succeed.

Critical success factors could be specific skills, tools, circumstances, finances, executive support or the completion of another activity or project.

The core ITIL publications describe the critical success factors that are required for each process and each stage of the lifecycle to succeed.

In *ITIL Service Strategy* an additional level of critical success factors is defined. In this context critical success factors specifically relate to those areas that need to be in place for the organization to compete in a specific industry or market space. The strategy assessment identified a number of strategic industry factors. Critical success factors in this context are any aspects or properties of the organization which enable it to achieve or comply with the strategic industry factors.

In this stage of strategy execution the existing organization, services, processes, skills, tools etc. will be compared to the strategic industry factors, and any shortcomings identified. If the organization is not positioned to meet a strategic industry factor, a project will be initiated to implement the critical success factors required. If the organization has been in business for some time it is likely that most of the critical success factors exist already, but they may need to be optimized to deal with changes to the external or internal environment.

Each project must be linked to the strategy, and formally approved and funded by the organization's executives. If this is not done, the importance and relevance of the project might be lost and the project de-prioritized.

4.1.5.16 Strategy execution: prioritize investments

Each new service or project will require funding. It is not unusual for a strategy to be established, and then amended after reviewing the detailed investment analysis, simply because there is insufficient funding set aside, or because the anticipated return does not support the investment.

Service portfolio management will ensure that every proposed new service, or any strategic change to an existing service, is analysed to determine the level of investment required and the proposed return on that investment.

The PMO will ensure that the same is done for any projects that have been proposed as part of strategy execution. Service portfolio management will also identify whether any services are dependent on the proposed projects. This will ensure that any decision to cancel a project is made with a full understanding of the impact, and not just because of a need to cut costs.

Once an investment analysis has been performed for all new services and projects and strategic changes to existing services, they are submitted to the executives of the organization for a final decision. All projects and services will be approved and supported by the executives, together with a commitment to funding. If funding is withdrawn in future, this will need to be done by the executives directly and they will be able to assess the impact of their decision on the strategy execution.

Prioritizing strategic investments based on customer needs

One common problem service providers have is prioritizing investments and managerial attention on the right set of opportunities. The best opportunities for service providers lie in areas where an important customer need remains poorly satisfied.

This is illustrated in Figure 4.11 (after Ulwick, 2005). In this diagram a range of customer requirements and services is illustrated. The bottom left of the chart shows requirements that would have little business impact if fulfilled, and which are not being fulfilled well (or not at all). The top right of the chart shows requirements that have a high impact on the business when fulfilled, and are being fulfilled very well.

Any services that fit into the triangle of Figure 4.11 would be providing the appropriate level of service for the degree of business impact. Any services to the left of the triangle would be providing too high a level of service (at a potentially higher than necessary cost). Any services to the right of the triangle are inadequate for the business requirements.

Service portfolios should be extended to support the areas of opportunity to the right of the chart. This typically means there is a need for services to provide additional levels of utility and warranty. However, managers should not overlook the costs and risks in such areas. There are usually strong reasons why certain needs of customers remain

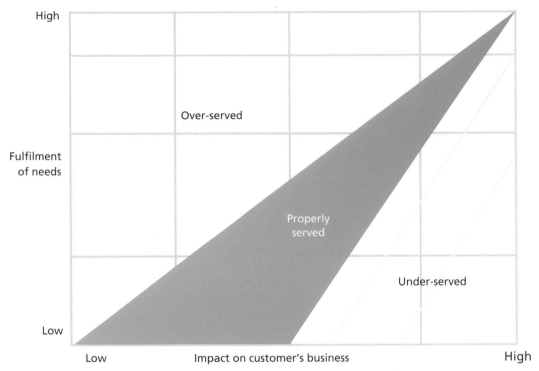

Figure 4.11 Prioritizing strategic investments based on customer needs

unfulfilled (for example, it would cost more than the returns anticipated, or the technology may simply not exist to meet that need). Breakthrough performance and innovation are usually required to successfully deliver value in under-served areas of opportunity.

4.1.5.17 Measurement and evaluation

This stage of strategy management is performed by a number of different areas, including:

- **Customers and users** The customers and users of services will often be the first to determine whether a strategy is being achieved or not, since they are monitoring the performance of business outcomes.
- **Service management processes** If each process has been designed to execute and enable the strategy of the organization, their metrics can be used to measure the effectiveness of the strategy.
- **Continual service improvement** Continual measurement of the performance of services and service management processes will show any deviation from forecast results. These can be related back to specific strategic areas, and opportunities for improvement can be logged

in the CSI register for later consideration for inclusion within service improvement plans.
- **The organization's executives** Executives will need a dashboard to indicate the organization's performance relative to its strategy. They will be able to determine if there are areas that are not performing to the required level, or that require more than the agreed levels of investment, and investigate these in more detail.

4.1.5.18 Measurement and evaluation: continual service improvement

CSI activities measure and evaluate the achievement of strategy over time. CSI contributes to strategy measurement and evaluation in two main ways.

Firstly, CSI activities identify areas that are not performing to expectation, and therefore threaten the achievement of the strategy. CSI activities provide feedback into the strategy generation and execution phases of the process. Specifically, they provide feedback on:

- Adherence to policies defined as part of positioning.

The importance of customers and users in measuring services

Although service providers rely on metrics and measurement to be proactive in delivering and supporting services, the reality is that there is a significant set of metrics that they have no control over. Regardless of how well services have been instrumented and how well they are delivered, the user of the service will still measure them – often using criteria and techniques that are foreign to the service provider.

For example, an online retailer conducted over 100,000 transactions per day. All customers paid by credit card, and all transactions were processed by a third-party financial service company. Approximately 1% of all transactions went missing between the retailer and the financial services company.

It was impossible for the financial services company (the service provider) to detect the missing transactions, because they never arrived. An agreement was reached whereby the retail company (their customer) did a reconciliation of all transactions at the end of the day and provided the missing information for overnight processing.

Service providers should be aware that in many cases they will not be able to measure something that is important to the customer. In these cases what is important is that the customer takes responsibility for performing the measurement, and the service provider will agree to an appropriate response to any exceptions.

■ Whether plans are being met, in terms of time, budget and objectives. Although CSI activities are not responsible for whether projects are completed on time, to budget and specification, they are able to quantify the overall impact of deviations from the plans. This feedback can be used to alter the plans, or expedite actions to complete projects.
■ Whether the patterns of action identified were appropriate and whether they are being used effectively.
■ Achievement of outcomes and performance of the assets that support them. This information can be used to improve alignment of assets to

outcomes, or to improve the overall performance of those assets.
■ Effective definition and achievement of critical success factors.
■ Achievement of return on investment targets for each project, initiative or service.

Secondly, CSI activities set the baseline for the next round of strategy assessments. Since the organization exists in (and is itself) a continuously changing environment, the strategy needs to be continually assessed and revised. CSI activities assist in this process by monitoring and reporting on changes to relevant aspects of the internal environment, the ability to expand market space opportunities and the ability to meet strategic industry factors.

As there is an entire publication dedicated to the subject, this section will not provide detail, except to point out the main areas covered. *ITIL Continual Service Improvement* provides detailed guidance about the following areas:

■ Defining what needs to be measured. This area focuses on understanding what items are important for achieving the strategy and whether they can, in fact, be measured.
■ Defining how to measure these items, where to obtain data and what tools are required to perform the measurement.
■ Establishing monitoring to enable the collection of data.
■ Defining how the measures are to be reported, to whom and what they are expected to do with the reports.
■ Identifying improvement opportunities and logging them in the CSI register.
■ Drafting and executing service improvement plans that resolve deviations from the strategy.

4.1.5.19 Measurement and evaluation: expansion and growth

As the organization achieves its existing strategy, it gets better at being able to deliver services to its existing market spaces. This raises questions such as: 'Can we provide the same services to new customers? 'Can we provide new services to existing customers?' and 'Can we deliver new services to new customers?'

Once service strategies are linked to market spaces, it is easier to make decisions on service portfolios,

	A1	A2	A3	A4	A5	A6	A7	A8
U1								
U2						▓	▓	▓
U3					▓			
U4					▓			
U5					▓		▓	
U6							▓	
U7							▓	
U8								

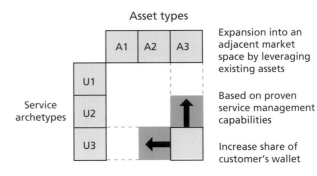

Figure 4.12 Expansion into adjacent market spaces

designs, operations and long-term improvements. Investments in service assets such as skills sets, knowledge, processes and infrastructure are driven by the critical success factors for a given market space. The growth and expansion of any business is less risky when anchored by core capabilities and demonstrated performance.

Successful expansion strategies are often based on leveraging existing service assets and customer portfolios to drive new growth and profitability. Figure 4.12 illustrates how an organization expands its business by moving into adjacent market spaces. In this case the organization is able to use existing service assets (resources and capabilities) to leverage opportunities related to those they are currently serving.

In Figure 4.12 the organization has chosen to expand into a number of market spaces. Following the examples used in section 3.4.4, the organization has chosen to move from U2.A7 (connect and integrate applications) to U2.A6 and U2.A8 connect and integrate information and infrastructure in addition to applications). In this example the organization has developed a solid approach for managing, operating and maintaining applications, and has found a way to use that approach for other technologies.

The exposure to costs and risks is far lower in this approach compared to *ad hoc* expansions, which are opportunistic in nature. This is because expanding into adjacent market spaces leverages service assets that are common across market spaces. This means that additional investments are hedged across new and existing market spaces. If, for any reason, the expansion fails or business opportunities do not materialize, it will be possible to salvage the investment for the new investments made. To further reduce the risks of expansion strategies, it is best to leverage the presence in market spaces that have achieved sufficient growth. Growth and maturity could mean either improving results in existing market spaces or expanding the portfolio to other market spaces with a high potential for success.

Expansion and growth also occur within a single market space or customer – for example, by expanding to new customers in the market spaces already being served by the organization; or by expanding the services offered to existing customers. Expansion within a single market space could involve:

■ Extensions to existing contracts
■ Increases in customer demand for an existing service
■ Providing complementary services (for example, provide early life support for all new software releases).

Figure 4.13 illustrates how it is possible to expand and grow a business within a single customer or market space. In the first example the business expands by providing additional services to the same customer. Each new opportunity that arises within that customer is a new strategic direction, since it will require new services, or applying the same services to a new area within the customer. In this example the organization's historic ability to understand and meet the customer's unique requirements is most important for growth. The biggest risk is that the organization may not have the appropriate skills and capabilities to design and deliver each new service. The lack of the appropriate service assets is therefore a potential constraint.

In the second example, the organization attracts new customers with similar requirements to existing customers, by offering them similar services. In this case the organization's record of service quality is most important for growth. The greatest risk in this type of growth is that the organization may not be able to deal with the increased demand for services, and capacity becomes a major constraint.

4.1.5.20 Strategy management for internal IT service providers

The process described in section 4.1.5 applies directly to external service provider organizations, but it also has to be applied to internal (Types I and

II) service providers. Internal IT organizations often make the mistake of thinking that they do not play a strategic role in the organization, and that they should confine their activities to tactical planning and execution. In many organizations even senior technical staff members have no insight into the organizational strategy, and are caught unawares by fluctuations in business activity and demand.

However, IT is a strategic part of most businesses, and it is important that the IT organization strategy is closely aligned and measured with the business strategy. This is done in two ways:

- Ensuring that the IT strategy is closely linked to the business strategy. For example, action plans devised during the business strategy will include actions for the internal IT service providers. Also, many of the activities in strategy execution rely on IT.
- Following the same steps as in section 4.1.5 to define the IT strategy, but using a narrower scope, specific inputs and defined parameters.

Whereas the organization's overall strategy is the responsibility of its executives, the strategy of internal service providers is the responsibility of the IT executives, led by the CIO. In larger organizations it is likely that strategy management is executed by a dedicated person or team reporting into the CIO.

Strategic assessment for internal service providers

Strategic assessment is similar to the strategy management process described above but it defines its environment more specifically, and uses information gathered by other business units to provide information about their external environments. For example, it is unlikely that IT will need to conduct an investigation into socio-economic environment if this has already been done during the business strategic assessment. Senior IT executives should obtain this information and ensure that the IT steering group (or at least senior IT managers) understand the meaning and implications of this information.

The purpose of the strategic assessment is to determine the IT organization's current situation and what changes are likely to impact it in the foreseeable future. The assessment will also highlight areas which will limit or prevent them from being able to progress its current goals, or to adapt to change.

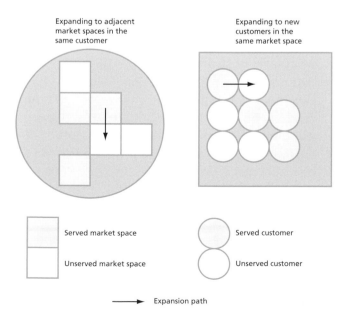

Figure 4.13 Expansion within single customers and market spaces

The internal environment that should be assessed by IT organizations includes:

- **The organization's business strategy** This is the most important framework for IT strategy management, since it provides the parameters within which IT must work. At the same time, new technologies and practices in the industry may make it possible for the organization to stretch the boundaries of its existing strategy. For example, cloud solutions make it possible for the business to change its positioning, rework its service portfolio and reach new customers. In this way the IT strategy helps to mould the business strategy, even while being moulded by the business strategy.

- **Existing services** These reflect the current positioning, differentiation and strategy of the IT organization, and will also form a baseline for potential growth.

- **Existing technologies** Including current architectures, application portfolio, assets, resources etc. This information will help the IT organization to understand what its capabilities are and, if growth is required, where it will need to develop.

- **IT service management** An assessment of the current level of IT service management maturity will highlight any limitations or boundaries for defining how services are defined, built and managed. For example, if financial management for IT services is only able to track general expenses and allocate them to business units, the IT organization will find it difficult to quantify the value of individual services. The IT strategy may need to change the way in which IT costs are tracked and reported.

- **Human resources** The current skills and knowledge of the people that work in the organization are key to whether an opportunity can be exploited or not.

- **Relationship with the business units** For internal service providers, this is an interesting exercise, because they have already assessed the business units as customers; now they also need to assess the dependencies between IT and other business units as partners in the same organization, each striving to meet the same objectives. This part of the assessment will focus on the quality of the relationship between the business units. For example, many departments have to spend as much time trying to sell themselves to other business units as they do to the external customers.

The external environment that should be assessed by IT organizations specifically includes:

- **Other organizations** How other organizations are managing and using IT

- **Industry IT spending rates** This should not be used to set a spending target, but is a good indicator of how money is being spent and why. (There may be a trend that indicates a change in the environment – for example, increased spending on virtualization may indicate that more organizations are turning towards converging infrastructure to achieve greater efficiency or agility.)

- **Vendor strategies and product roadmaps** It is important to know if the technology that supports your current strategy is going to continue to do so. Changes to the vendor's service or product catalogue could be the result of changes in licensing, mergers and acquisitions (where the current product set is no longer supported and an alternative purchase is forced), technology becoming obsolete, unbundling (e.g. where a product suite's components now have to be purchased separately) etc. IT organizations that do not take account of vendor strategies could find themselves dealing with unexpected expenditure or disruption.

- **Partners** It is important that the existing commitments and obligations to and from partners are identified. These may need to be changed, or they may place a boundary on what level of strategic change is possible.

- **Technology trends** For example, what are the implications of converging technologies? Will they make it easier to deliver and support services or will they offer new opportunities, or both?

- **Customers** This is a complex situation for internal service providers because there are two types of customers that they service. On the one hand they provide services to other business units ('internal customers'), who in turn use them to provide services to 'external customers'. IT has to assess the needs of their business unit customers based on what business outcomes the business unit is trying to achieve, and how IT enables those outcomes. This will help IT to prioritize their strategic action plan and also to ensure that their plans have adequate coverage of customer needs. However, most IT organizations also deliver strategic (often revenue-producing) services directly to external customers – for example, online ordering or tax return submission. In a very real sense these are customers of both IT and other business units – and the strategy of both should reflect this.

- **Standards or regulatory requirements for IT** Although legislation like SOX or Basel II is aimed at the business, IT has a very important role to play in ensuring its implementation and the organization's compliance. Other standards, such as ISO/IEC 27001, are directly applicable to IT, and if this is a requirement, the cost of compliance and certification should be reflected in both the IT and business strategies.

- **Operations** The current maturity, effectiveness and efficiency of IT operations are assessed. ITIL can be used as a 'checklist' to ensure that the processes and functions necessary to support the strategy are in place.

- **The relationship between application development and operations** A dysfunctional relationship between these two groups is more than just a political conflict; it represents an organization that has not yet reached a balance between focus on functionality and focus on manageability (or utility and warranty). Although both are essential, many organizations are fraught with situations where each group tries to own the relationship with customers (and their budgets).

Strategy generation for internal service providers

Generating an IT strategy should ideally be done in concert with the business strategic and tactical planning (see Figure 4.2). As the business defines its perspective and position, this information should be communicated to the IT executives preparing the IT strategy.

The IT organization(s) can then start to formulate their own perspective and positions, and start to provide input back into the business strategy development. As the business strategy starts to prepare its plans, these are communicated to the IT executives, who test and validate them, or offer more alternatives. At the same time as this is being done for IT, it is also being done for other business units, such as manufacturing, marketing etc. All of the business units participate in the ongoing communication and refinement of one another's strategy.

Once the business strategic decisions have been made and strategic plans have been finalized and coordinated with all the business units, the IT strategic plan will go through a check to ensure that it is consistent with the business strategy.

An IT strategic plan is produced and the patterns of action needed to ensure its success are defined. As the business strategy is translated into tactical plans for execution, the IT strategic plan and patterns of action will be validated again to ensure that business plans will be supported. The IT tactical plans are drafted, compared with business tactical plans and finalized.

The IT strategic plan will be similar in structure and content to the business strategic plan, but its contents will be specific to the IT organization.

Strategy execution for internal service providers

As with external service providers, strategy execution will be a combination of the normal activities of service management processes, and the initiation of a number of projects – usually coordinated through the PMO.

Measurement and evaluation for internal service providers

Continual service improvement is the primary mechanism for measurement and evaluation, using the same techniques and processes as for external service providers.

The activities around business growth and expansion, however, are very different. In external service providers, the objective is to identify new market spaces and customers that can expand the strategy (and in commercial organizations, the revenue) of the organization. In the public sector, the ability to demonstrate value for money is critical.

Internal service providers should not try to grow their business, rather they should try to find better ways of achieving the desired business outcomes of the organization they work for, or to reduce the cost of service provision. The concept of expanding to adjacent market spaces, or finding new customers in existing market spaces, might be helpful to frame IT's thinking, but it sometimes results in IT organizations that try to implement their own strategies, instead of enabling that of the organization they support.

IT is, however, a very important part of business growth and expansion, since the business uses IT services to increase its capabilities. Each time the business decides to grow or expand, IT will be part of that process – either directly through the business's strategy management process, or indirectly through service portfolio management.

> **When does an internal service provider change business strategy?**
>
> Although the role of internal service providers is to support the strategy of the organization they are part of, there are times when they can take the lead in defining business strategy.
>
> This happens when a new technology becomes available that enables the business to change its strategy – through opening new markets, making new services possible or changing the way the organization works.
>
> Some examples have included email, the internet, Electronic Data Interchanges (EDI) and cloud computing. If the IT organization understands, and is integrated into, the business, they are very well positioned to research and propose these innovations as the basis of a new business strategy. This type of research is usually performed as part of the capacity management process (see *ITIL Service Design*).

4.1.6 Triggers, inputs, outputs and interfaces

4.1.6.1 Triggers

Triggers of strategy management for IT services include:

- **Annual planning cycles** Strategy management for IT services is used to review and plan on an annual basis.
- **New business opportunity** Strategy management for IT services is used to analyse, set objectives, perspectives, positions, plans and patterns for new business or service opportunities.
- **Changes to internal or external environments** Strategy management for IT services will assess the impact of environmental changes on the existing strategic and tactical plans.
- **Mergers or acquisitions** The merger with or acquisition of another company will trigger a detailed analysis and definition of the strategy of the new organization.

4.1.6.2 Inputs

Inputs to strategy management for IT services include:

- Existing plans
- Research on aspects of the environment by specialized research organizations
- Vendor strategies and product roadmaps, that indicate the impact (and possible opportunities) of new or changing technology
- Customer interviews and strategic plans to indicate potential future requirements
- Service portfolio to indicate the current and planned future service commitments
- Service reporting to indicate the effectiveness of the strategy
- Audit reports that indicate compliance with (or deviation from) the organization's strategy.

4.1.6.3 Outputs

Outputs of strategy management for IT services include:

- Strategic plans – in this context especially the service strategy
- Tactical plans that identify how the strategy will be executed
- Strategy review schedules and documentation
- Mission and vision statements
- Policies that show how the plans should be executed, how services will be designed, transitioned, operated and improved
- Strategic requirements for new services, and input into which existing services need to be changed. Strategy management for IT services will also articulate what business outcomes need to be met and how services will accomplish this.

4.1.6.4 Interfaces

Major strategy management for IT services interfaces include:

- Strategy management for IT services interfaces with and directs all service management processes, either directly or indirectly. Chapter 8 defines this in detail. Instead of discussing the interfaces with every process, this section will highlight the major interfaces – as shown in Figure 4.3.
- Strategy management for IT services provides the guidelines and framework within which the

service portfolio will be defined and managed. Specifically, strategy management for IT services provides the objectives, policies and limits which must be used to evaluate every new service, or strategic change to an existing service. The service portfolio provides strategy management for IT services with important information about the type of services currently in the service pipeline or service catalogue, and what strategic objectives they have been designed to meet. This will assist in the strategic assessment and also in evaluating current and future market spaces.

■ Strategy management for IT services provides input to financial management to indicate what types of returns are required and where investments need to be made. Financial management, in turn, provides the financial information and tools to enable strategy management for IT services to prioritize actions and plans.

■ Although strategy management for IT services does not define detailed service design requirements, it does provide input to service design. Specifically, it identifies any policies that must be taken into account when designing services, any constraints within which the design teams must work and a clear prioritization of work. Service design processes will provide feedback into strategy management for IT services to enable measurement and evaluation of the services being designed.

■ Strategy management for IT services enables service transition to prioritize and evaluate the services that are built to ensure that they meet the original intent and strategic requirements of the services. If any variation is detected during service transition this will need to be fed back to strategy management for IT services so that the existing strategy can be reviewed, or so that a decision can be made about the priority and validity of the service.

■ Knowledge management plays an important part in structuring information that is used to make strategic decisions. It allows strategic planners to understand the existing environment, its history and its dynamics, and to make informed decisions about the future.

■ Although strategy management for IT services is quite far removed from daily operations, there

are some important linkages, especially in terms of the execution of strategic priorities, and in the ability to measure whether the strategy is being met. Operational tools and processes must ensure that they have been aligned to the strategic objectives and desired business outcomes. Additionally, the monitoring of operational environments should be instrumented so that the execution of operational activities indicates whether or not the strategy is effective. For example, if a strategic objective is that a new opportunity can result in 10,000 new customers per month, the operational activity required to meet this demand should match what was anticipated.

■ Continual service improvement will help to evaluate whether the strategy has been executed effectively, and whether it has met its objectives (i.e. CSI activities will measure compliance with the strategic plans and policies, and they will also measure whether the anticipated results were achieved). Any deviation will be reported to strategy management for IT services, which will work on improving the process, or on adjusting the strategy.

4.1.7 Information management

The documentation and information required for effective strategy management for IT services have been described throughout section 4.1, but an overview of the main sources is as follows:

■ Information about the external environment, including market research, research of competitors' practices, economic and political trends, technology directions and innovations, industry benchmarks, regulatory requirements etc. Of special importance is any factor indicating that the organization needs to invest in being able to meet a particular strategic industry factor.

■ Results of assessments of the internal environment, which includes formal assessment reports, self-evaluation, interviews, polls of employee opinion etc.

■ Information about customer needs and satisfaction levels, current service capabilities and performance levels.

■ Strategy management for IT services documentation, including the strategic, tactical and operational plans. The plans from the previous planning period provide valuable input to the current period. All plans are important for ensuring concerted activity between organizational units. They provide a valuable tool in educating staff, and managing their performance towards meeting organizational objectives.

- The service portfolio provides valuable information about the current capabilities and resources available in the organization, and how they are currently deployed. It also provides information about proposed future investment, which will need to be assessed in the light of changes from a previous strategy to a new strategy.

- Financial management information is critical for evaluating potential market spaces, and whether it is feasible for the service provider to invest in services aimed at those opportunities.

- Business relationship management and demand management are critical sources of information about what customers need, why they need it and how they will use it. This information is useful, not only for defining the position and plans, but also for understanding the patterns of action that will ensure a successful strategy.

- Continual service improvement provides feedback that is vital to evaluating the effectiveness of strategies, and which enables strategy management for IT services to make changes to strategies as quickly as necessary, thus making the service provider agile and responsive.

4.1.8 Critical success factors and key performance indicators

This section provides examples of critical success factors (CSFs). These are the conditions that need to be in place, or things that need to happen, if the strategy management for IT services process is to be considered successful. Each CSF will include examples of key performance indicators (KPIs). These are metrics that are used to evaluate factors that are crucial to the success of the process. KPIs, as differentiated from general metrics, should be related to CSFs.

The following list includes some sample CSFs for strategy management for IT services. Each organization should identify appropriate CSFs based on its objectives for the process. Each sample CSF is followed by a small number of typical KPIs

that support the CSF. These KPIs should not be adopted without careful consideration. Each organization should develop KPIs that are appropriate for its level of maturity, its CSFs and its particular circumstances. Achievement against KPIs should be monitored and used to identify opportunities for improvement, which should be logged in the CSI register for evaluation and possible implementation.

- **CSF** Access to structured information about the internal and external environments in which the service provider exists, and which can be used to define the components of the organization's strategy.
  - **KPI** Every market space in the strategy is supported by documented evidence of the opportunity.
  - **KPI** Every finding or recommendation in the strategic assessment is based on validated information.
  - **KPI** Forecasts and findings from external research are validated at the end of the planning period and found to be accurate within 5%.

- **CSF** The ability to identify constraints on the ability of the service provider to meet business outcomes, and to deliver and manage services – and the ability to eliminate these constraints or reduce their impact.
  - **KPI** Number of corrective actions taken to remove constraints, and the result of those actions on the achievement of strategic objectives.

- **CSF** The service provider has a clear understanding of their perspective, and it is reviewed regularly to ensure ongoing relevance.
  - **KPI** Vision and mission statements have been defined and all staff members have been trained on what they mean in terms of their roles and jobs within the organization.
  - **KPI** Each business unit has a strategic plan that clearly shows how the business unit's activities are linked to the objectives, vision and mission of the organization.

- **CSF** The service provider has a clear understanding of how it positions itself to ensure competitive advantage. The service strategy clearly identifies which services are delivered to which market spaces, and how the service provider will maintain its competitive advantage.

- **KPI** Every strategic and tactical plan contains a statement of how the contents of the plan support the competitive advantage of the service provider.
- **KPI** (for external service providers) The organization wins a defined percentage of all proposed business deals within the identified market space.
- **KPI** (for internal service providers) Funding is made available to support the strategic initiatives, and a return on investment can be demonstrated by the business units.
- **KPI** Each service in the service portfolio has a statement about which business outcomes it meets, and is measured in terms of these outcomes.
- **KPI** Every service in the service portfolio has an explanation about which market spaces it is delivered to, and what opportunities it will meet. A set of metrics has been defined and reported against, which show that the service is meeting the identified opportunity.

- **CSF** The ability to produce, store, maintain and communicate strategy planning documents.
  - **KPI** Audit results show that each stakeholder has an updated copy of the appropriate planning document.
  - **KPI** Stakeholders can provide an overview of the content of the strategy documents relevant to their business unit.
  - **KPI** All documents are under document control and changes to the documents have been made through the appropriate change control measures.

- **CSF** The ability to translate strategic plans into tactical and operational plans that are executed by each organizational unit.
  - **KPI** Every organizational unit lead can identify the plans for their unit, and provide an overview of the contents of the plan.
  - **KPI** Each tactical and operational plan is identified by the strategic plans they support, and changes to the strategy are managed through change control to ensure that tactical and operational plans are aligned.

- **CSF** Changes to the internal and external environments are identified and adjustments made to strategies and related documents.
  - **KPI** Number of strategic objectives that are not met – identified by CSI activities.

- **KPI** Deviation from activities and patterns identified in the strategy.
- **KPI** Number of changes to internal and external environments identified, compared with the number of changes made to strategy documents.

4.1.9 Challenges and risks

4.1.9.1 Challenges

Challenges for strategy management for IT services include:

- Strategy management for IT services is conducted at the wrong level in the organization – it should be driven by senior executives, and each organizational unit should follow through with the production of a strategic, tactical and operational plan that is a subset of the enterprise strategy.
- Lack of accurate information about the external environment.
- Lack of support by stakeholders.
- Lack of the appropriate tools or a lack of understanding of how to use the tools and techniques identified in this section.
- Lack of the appropriate document control mechanisms and procedures.
- Operational targets need to be matched to the strategic objectives. Failure to do so will result in operational managers striving to achieve targets that are not in support of the strategy.

4.1.9.2 Risks

Risks to strategy management for IT services include:

- A flawed governance model that allows managers to decide on whether to implement all aspects of a strategy, or which allows them to deviate from the strategy for shorter-term goals.
- Short-term priorities override the directives of the strategy. For example, a shortfall in sales for one quarter may encourage managers to implement incentives and measures that move the organization away from its stated policies and strategic objectives.
- Making strategic decisions when there is missing information about the internal or external environments, or using information that is incorrect or misleading (i.e. information

that has not been validated). It is easier to evaluate whether information is accurate than to ascertain whether it is complete. The organization should seriously consider how to verify their sources, and should include a validity check as part of the strategic review.

- The risk of choosing the wrong strategy. It is very important to evaluate and provide feedback to the service management process at all stages so that incorrect decisions can be detected early and corrected.

- Strategies are seen as an exercise that happens once a year and that has no bearing on what happens for the rest of the year. It is critical to align the metrics of each organizational unit to those of the strategies, and to ensure that managers and staff alike are educated about the contents and objectives of the strategies at the appropriate level of detail. Performance reviews should be linked to the achievement of strategic objectives.

4.2 SERVICE PORTFOLIO MANAGEMENT

A service portfolio describes a provider's services in terms of business value. It articulates business needs and the provider's response to those needs. By definition, business value terms correspond to marketing terms, providing a means for comparing service competitiveness across alternative providers. By acting as the basis of a decision framework, a service portfolio either clarifies or helps to clarify the following strategic questions:

- Why should a customer buy these services?
- Why should they buy these services from us?
- What are the pricing or chargeback models?
- What are our strengths and weaknesses, priorities and risks?
- How should our resources and capabilities be allocated?

The service portfolio is the complete set of services that is managed by a service provider. The service portfolio is used to manage the entire lifecycle of all services. It includes three categories of service: service pipeline (proposed or in development), service catalogue (live or available for deployment) and retired services. The service portfolio represents the investment made in an organization's services, and also articulates the value that services help it to realize.

Service portfolio management is responsible for managing the service portfolio. It is therefore also the process that is responsible for defining which services will be entered into the service portfolio and how those services are tracked and progressed through their lifecycle. In other words service portfolio management acts as a gatekeeper for the service provider, ensuring that they only provide services that contribute to strategic objectives and meet the agreed business outcomes.

4.2.1 Purpose and objectives

The purpose of service portfolio management is to ensure that the service provider has the right mix of services to balance the investment in IT with the ability to meet business outcomes. It tracks the investment in services throughout their lifecycle and works with other service management processes to ensure that the appropriate returns are being achieved. In addition, it ensures that services are clearly defined and linked to the achievement of business outcomes, thus ensuring that all design, transition and operation activities are aligned to the value of the services.

The objectives of service portfolio management are to:

- Provide a process and mechanisms to enable an organization to investigate and decide on which services to provide, based on an analysis of the potential return and acceptable level of risk.

- Maintain the definitive portfolio of services provided, articulating the business needs each service meets and the business outcomes it supports.

- Provide a mechanism for the organization to evaluate how services enable it to achieve its strategy, and to respond to changes in its internal or external environments.

- Control which services are offered, under what conditions and at what level of investment.

- Track the investment in services throughout their lifecycle, thus enabling the organization to evaluate its strategy, as well as its ability to execute against that strategy.

- Analyse which services are no longer viable and when they should be retired.

4.2.2 Scope

The scope of service portfolio management is all services a service provider plans to deliver, those currently delivered and those that have been withdrawn from service. The primary concern of service portfolio management is whether the service provider is able to generate value from the services. Service portfolio management will therefore track investments in services and compare them to the desired business outcomes.

Internal service providers will need to work with the business units in the organization to link each service to the business outcomes before they can compare investment with returns. External service providers tend to evaluate value more directly, as each service needs to be able to generate revenue directly, or support revenue-generating services. The generation of revenue in an efficient manner will, in turn, facilitate profitability.

Service portfolio management evaluates the value of services throughout their lifecycles, and must be able to compare what newer services have offered over the retired services they have replaced.

4.2.3 Value to business

Service portfolio management enables the business to make sound decisions about investments. Services cannot be implemented because they are a good idea or because they are an industry standard. They are implemented only if there is a good business case demonstrating a clear return on investment. Service portfolio management does this by comparing the outcomes that are expected by the customer with the investment required to build and deliver the service.

Customers are able to understand exactly what the service provider will deliver to them and under what conditions, enabling them to make decisions about whether the service is a good or bad investment, and to evaluate additional opportunities that the service will open. In this way service portfolio management can also be a tool for innovation for the organization.

The service provider is viewed as a steward of service assets that are key to the customer's success and, provided the service provider delivers what they promised, the service provider can equip their customers to build their strategies.

4.2.4 Policies, principles and basic concepts

Organizations embarking on a service orientation journey have a tendency to view it as a series of tactical programmes. As long as each service is aligned with the business outcomes, the reasoning goes, the overall strategy will take care of itself. Armed with a conceptual understanding of services, organizations frequently rush to industrialize service outcomes. The impulse is to launch initiatives in organizational change or process redesign. While these might be important fulfilment elements, it is important to understand first the overall business of the service provider before launching tactical programmes for single services or small groups of services.

Service portfolio management ensures that the service provider has an understanding of all services that it provides, the investments in those services and the strategy and objectives of each service before it makes tactical plans for how to manage those services. Service portfolio management plays a role in strategy generation, and follows through the service lifecycle to ensure that the agreed strategy is appropriately executed at each stage.

This approach serves two purposes. Firstly, it prevents missteps such as performing organizational design before knowing what services to offer, or performing a tool selection before optimizing processes. Secondly, it ensures continuity between the high-level intent and the detailed-level execution.

Personal finance managers tailor a portfolio of investments based on their customer's risk and reward profile. Regardless of the profile, the objective is the same: maximize return at an acceptable risk level. When conditions change, appropriate changes are made to the portfolio. For IT services, the service portfolio management approach helps managers prioritize investments and improve the allocation of resources. Changes to portfolios are governed by policies and procedures. Portfolios instil a certain financial discipline necessary to avoid making investments that will not yield value. Service portfolios represent the ability and readiness of a service provider to serve customers and market spaces.

4.2.4.1 The service portfolio

The service portfolio represents the commitments and investments made by a service provider across all customers and market spaces. It represents present contractual commitments, new service development and ongoing service improvement plans initiated by CSI. The portfolio also includes third-party services, which are an integral part of service offerings to customers. Some third-party services are visible to the customers (e.g. desktop repairs) while others are not (e.g. wide area networking services).

In other words, the service portfolio is the complete set of services that is managed by a service provider. The service portfolio also identifies those services in a conceptual stage, namely all services the organization would provide if it had unlimited resources, capabilities and funding. This documentation exercise facilitates understanding of the opportunity costs of the existing portfolio and better fiscal discipline. If a service provider understands what it cannot do, then it is better able to assess if it should keep doing what it is doing or re-allocate its resources and capabilities.

The service portfolio represents all the resources presently engaged or being released in various stages of the service lifecycle. Each stage requires resources for completion of projects, initiatives and contracts. This is a very important governance aspect of service portfolio management (SPM). Entry, progress and exit are approved only with approved funding and a financial plan for recovering costs or showing profit as necessary. The service portfolio should have the right mix of services in the pipeline and catalogue to secure the financial viability of the service provider, since the service catalogue is the only part of the portfolio that lists services that recover costs or earn profits.

Figure 4.14 illustrates the components of the service portfolio, which are discussed in detail in the following sections.

4.2.4.2 Service pipeline

The service pipeline is a database or structured document listing all services that are under consideration or development, but are not yet available to customers. It also includes any major investment opportunities, such as a data centre relocation or virtualization project. This is because these investments have to be traced to the delivery of services and the value that is realized. The service pipeline provides a business view of possible future services and is part of the service portfolio that is not normally published to customers.

The service pipeline represents the service provider's growth and strategic outlook for the future and reflects the general health of the provider. It also reflects the extent to which new service concepts and ideas for improvement are being fed by service strategy, service design and continual improvement. Good financial management for IT services is necessary to ensure adequate funding for the pipeline.

There are many ways in which a service can enter the service pipeline, for example:

- A customer requests a new service.
- The service provider's strategy has identified a new opportunity.
- A customer has identified a new business opportunity that will require support from IT.
- A business outcome is under-served by current services.
- A new technology is available and has the potential to create new business opportunities.
- Service management processes (like capacity management, service level management or problem management) identify a better solution to the services that are currently offered.
- Continual service improvement processes identify a gap in the current service portfolio.

The service pipeline ensures that all of these opportunities are properly quantified in terms of investment and return, and then moved through the service design and service transition lifecycle stages until they are available for live use. This ensures that potential opportunities are formally registered and processed and not overlooked in an ever-changing set of customer demands.

Typically, the service pipeline is internal to the service provider, and not visible to its customers – especially in an external service provider. This is because not all services will be built and released; or proposed services may change significantly from what was initially imagined to what was eventually deployed. However, there are many situations where a customer is able to access the service pipeline, for example:

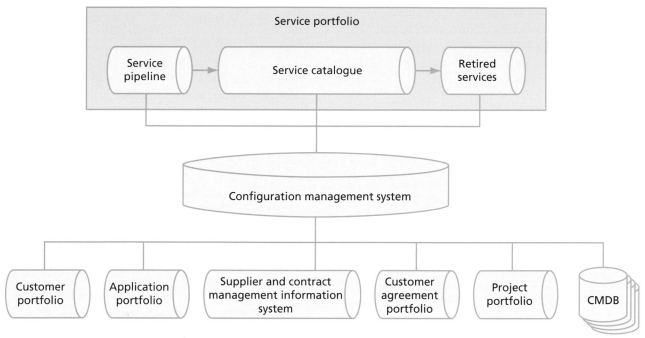

Figure 4.14 The service portfolio

■ If a customer is involved in exploring an opportunity, or is providing requirements for a new service, they are often given access to information about that service in the service pipeline.

■ If it is important for a customer to be able to check on the status of a new service, they should be given access to information about that service in the service pipeline.

■ If it is important to set a customer's expectations about the new service, they might be given information that is in the service pipeline.

In many cases, it is not necessary to give a customer access to the service pipeline, but simply to use information in the service pipeline to provide the customer with updates about upcoming services.

When the service is moved from development and becomes operational it is moved from the service pipeline into the service catalogue.

This does not mean that customers will have no view of the service before it enters the service catalogue – for example, in an internal supplier it might be appropriate for key customers to use the service portfolio to check on progress, or to adjust their planning according to information in the service pipeline. Not all customers will be given access to all services in the service pipeline. Only customers who have been authorized will be able

to access only the services that they are involved with.

External providers tend to keep their service pipeline a closely guarded secret, providing selected information to key customers, but only moving the service into the service catalogue once it has been thoroughly tested and ready for use. It may, however, conduct market research and use focus groups as part of its marketing process for services in the service pipeline.

Service providers that encourage their customers to be engaged in the process of defining and modelling new services will tend to move those services into the service catalogue earlier than service providers who build strictly according to pre-defined requirements.

4.2.4.3 Service catalogue

The service catalogue and service catalogue management are described in detail in *ITIL Service Design*. This section describes the role of the service catalogue in service portfolio management and the relationship between the service portfolio, service pipeline and service catalogue.

The service catalogue is a database or structured document with information about all live IT services, including those available for deployment. The service catalogue is the only part of the service portfolio published to customers, and is used to support the sale and delivery of IT services. The service catalogue includes information about deliverables, prices, contact points, ordering and request processes.

Items can enter the service catalogue only after due diligence has been performed on related costs and risks. Only operational services can be found in the service catalogue and resources are engaged to fully support active services.

The catalogue is useful in developing solutions for customers from one or more services. Items in the catalogue can be configured and suitably priced to fulfil a particular need. The service catalogue is an important tool for service strategy because it represents the service provider's actual and present capabilities. Many customers are only interested in what the provider can commit now, rather than in future.

In addition, the service catalogue serves as a service order and demand channelling mechanism. It defines and communicates the policies, guidelines and accountability required for the service provider to deliver and support services to its customers. The service catalogue details each service and shows the service components that make up each one. It also provides an overview of the assets, processes and systems involved in each service. It acts as the acquisition portal for customers, including pricing and service-level commitments, and the terms and conditions for service provision. Also the service catalogue contains details about standard service requests, enabling users to request those services using the appropriate channels. In automated service catalogues these requests can be initiated in the tool, and then routed to the appropriate request fulfilment procedure.

When service providers have many customers or serve many businesses, there may be multiple service catalogues projected from the service portfolio. In other words, a service catalogue articulates the provider's operational capability within the context of a customer or market space.

The service catalogue is also a tool for service portfolio management decisions. At one level it identifies the linkage between service assets, services and business outcomes. This information is used to identify where existing services are used to meet current business outcomes, and to identify potential gaps in the service portfolio.

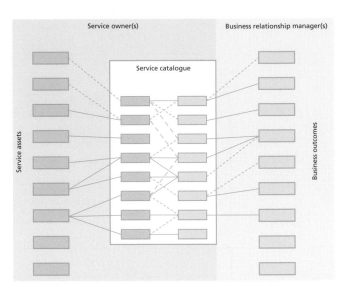

Figure 4.15 The service catalogue and linkages between services and outcomes

Figure 4.15 shows these linkages between the following:

- The boxes on the left are service assets used by the service provider to provide services. These could be servers, databases, applications, network devices etc.
- Services in the service catalogue. There are two layers of services shown in Figure 4.15. The layer on the left shows supporting services, which are usually not seen by the customer directly (contained in a view of the service catalogue called the technical or supporting service catalogue). One example is application hosting (unless it is a Type III service provider offering application-hosting services). The second layer of services is customer-facing services. An example is point of sales.
- The boxes on the right are business outcomes, which the business achieves when it uses these services. An example is the ability to make sales and provide receipts to customers.

At another level, the service catalogue identifies the demand for a service and shows how the service provider will fulfil the demand. Figure 4.16 shows the same relationships, but in terms of demand. Every time the business works to achieve a business outcome, it places demand on the services. Demand management identifies these patterns of business activity and how they are fulfilled by services. In Figure 4.16 demand management has been able to show that some

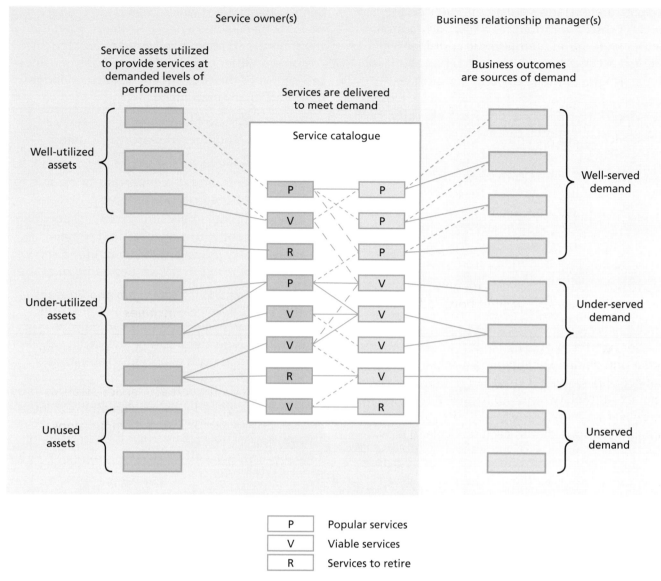

Figure 4.16 Service catalogue and demand management

services are able to meet the level of demand better than others. It is also clear that there is some demand that is not being met at all. Figure 4.16 also shows that there are a number of services that are not properly supported, and capacity management has identified some service assets that are either under-utilized or not utilized at all.

Service portfolio management is able to use this information as follows:

■ Services that are performing well and are popular are identified for allocation of additional resources to ensure continued performance and anticipate increases in demand for those services.

■ Services that are performing in an acceptable manner but are either inefficient or do not address all aspects of the business requirements adequately are deemed viable services. An effort should be made to make them more popular by introducing new attributes, addressing warranty or utility issues, matching them more appropriately to the sources of demand or by new pricing policies.

■ Services that are unused or consistently performing poorly are marked for retirement. A new service transition project is initiated and a transition plan is drafted to phase out the service.

Services with poor financial performance may be retained in the catalogue with adequate justification. Some catalogue services may have strategic use – for example, they might provide an important output to another service, or they might be in an early adoption phase. In this case the service's costs are carried for a few early customers on the understanding that more customers will use it in future, and costs will be recovered at a later stage. Whatever the justification, it must be approved by senior leadership who may choose to subsidize. Internal service providers are often required to maintain a catalogue of service, regardless of their independent financial viability.

A subset of the service catalogue may be third-party or outsourced services. These are services that are offered to customers with varying levels of value addition or combination with other catalogue items (for example, broadband internet access to employees working from home offices). It extends the range of the service catalogue in terms of customers and market spaces. Third-party services may be used to address under-served or unserved demand (Figure 4.16) until items in the service pipeline are phased into operation. They can also be used as a substitute for services being retired from the service catalogue. Sourcing is not only an important strategic option but can also be an operational necessity. Section 3.7 provides more guidance on sourcing strategy.

A comparison of the typical content and purpose of the service portfolio and service catalogue is illustrated in Figure 4.17.

4.2.4.4 Retired services

Some services in the service portfolio are phased out or retired. There is a decision to be made by each organization, following a service review, on when to move a service from catalogue to retired.

Some organizations will do this when the service is no longer available to new customers, even though the service is still being delivered to existing customers. Other organizations will only move the service out of the catalogue when it is no longer delivered to any customers.

Retired services are maintained in the service portfolio for a number of reasons, including:

■ The replacement service might not meet all requirements, and it is important to be able to fall back to the previous service.
■ When defining a new service, service portfolio management might discover that some functionality is available from a retired service. This might result in the service being reinstated as part of a new service.
■ There might be regulatory requirements to maintain archived data that can only be accessed using the previous service, in which case information is exported to a read-only database for future use.

Service portfolio management will define a policy for the length of time that a service will remain in the service portfolio. This could be expressed in time, or how many alternatives are available in the service catalogue.

Retiring services is managed through service transition. This is to ensure that all commitments made to customers are duly fulfilled and service assets are released from contracts. When services are retired the related knowledge and information are stored in a knowledge base for future use. Retired services are not available to new or existing customers or contracts unless a special business case is made. Such services may be reactivated into operation under special conditions and SLAs that are to be approved by senior management. This is necessary because such services may cost a lot more to support and may disrupt economies of scale and scope.

4.2.4.5 Configuration management system

The configuration management system (CMS) is a set of tools and databases that are used to manage an IT service provider's configuration data. The configuration management system also includes information about incidents, problems, known errors, changes and releases, and may contain data about employees, suppliers, locations, business units, customers and users. The configuration

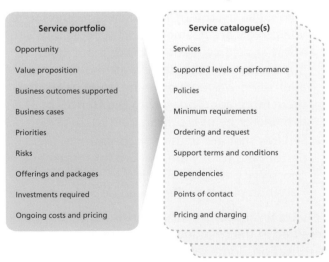

Figure 4.17 Service portfolio and service catalogues

management system includes tools for collecting, storing, managing, updating and presenting data about all configuration items and their relationships. The configuration management system is maintained by configuration management and is used by all IT service management processes.

A configuration management database (CMDB) is a database used to store configuration records throughout their lifecycle. The configuration management system maintains one or more configuration management databases, and each database stores attributes of configuration items, and relationships with other configuration items.

In the context of service portfolio management the configuration management system records and controls data about each service, CIs that make up services, the people and tools that support services and the relationships between all of them. The service portfolio is part of the service knowledge management system (SKMS) and is based on data from sources in the CMS.

4.2.4.6 Application portfolio

The application portfolio is a database or structured document used to manage applications throughout their lifecycle. The application portfolio contains key attributes of all applications. The application portfolio is sometimes implemented as part of the service portfolio or, if this does not yet exist, as part of the service knowledge management system.

One of the most common mistakes is to use the application portfolio as the service portfolio. Although all applications are represented in the service portfolio, they are usually not, in and of themselves, services. For example, a single service might use several applications (a company price list draws data from the manufacturing control application, warehousing and distribution applications and the shipping application). Alternatively, a service might be just one of the many outputs of a single application. For example, the payroll application provides several different services, such as paying employees, tracking benefits, producing tax statements etc. Each of these is viewed as a different service by different people or groups in the organization.

While it may be easy to initiate the service portfolio by using the application portfolio as an input, the application portfolio should be clearly distinguished from the service portfolio as the portfolio is developed.

The application portfolio(s) are usually defined and maintained by application development organizations. Their use by application development includes:

- Tracking investment in the applications.
- Preventing duplication – when a new request is made, application developers can determine whether an existing application will be able to meet the requirements, or estimate how much work would be needed to augment an existing application.
- Tracking who is responsible for a specific application. This is especially important when development teams work on multiple applications and projects.
- Identifying which customers use each application. This is helpful to ensure that requests for change are legitimate and to avoid conflicting requirements or requests being made.
- Identifying which services use each application.

The application portfolio has a very important role to play in service portfolio management. Firstly, it allows strategic service requirements and requests to be linked to specific applications or projects within application development. Any services in the service pipeline can be linked to application development assessment and qualification. This allows both development and operations teams to be able to quantify and evaluate opportunities in the service pipeline in conjunction with one another. Secondly, it enables the organization to track investments in a service at all stages of the service lifecycle. Thirdly, it enables application development and IT operations to coordinate their efforts and facilitates greater cooperation throughout the service lifecycle.

Although service portfolio management does not create and maintain the application portfolio, nothing should be in the application portfolio without first going through the service portfolio management process. Thus every entry in the application portfolio should be linked to one or more entries in the service portfolio.

Application development approaches, methods and processes are outside the scope of ITIL, but application development itself plays an integral role in service management. These processes and functions are responsible for building the applications that are used to achieve business outcomes, and it is vital that their role is recognized and included in all relevant processes. Chapter 5 addresses the nature of the relationship between IT service management and application development. *ITIL Service Operation* provides details about how the software development lifecycle and application management cycle can be linked or integrated.

4.2.4.7 Customer portfolio

The customer portfolio is maintained by the business relationship management process and is covered in more detail in section 4.5. However, it is an important input into the service portfolio management process.

The customer portfolio is a database or structured document used to record all customers of the IT service provider. The customer portfolio is the business relationship manager's view of the customers who receive services from the IT service provider.

Service portfolio management uses the customer portfolio to ensure that the relationship between business outcomes, customers and services is well understood. The service portfolio documents these linkages and is validated with customers through business relationship management.

4.2.4.8 Customer agreement portfolio

The customer agreement portfolio is a database or structured document used to manage service contracts or agreements between an IT service provider and its customers. Each IT service delivered to a customer should have a contract or other agreement that is listed in the customer agreement portfolio.

Although many organizations tend to believe that an agreement only exists when an SLA has been signed, this is not true. Whenever a service provider offers a service and a customer uses that service an agreement comes into existence. The problem with

these agreements is that they are informal and there is often a misalignment between what the customer expects and what the service provider actually delivers.

Best practice has shown that a more formal approach to these agreements, using service level agreements, helps to overcome these misalignments and to control how services change over time to meet changing business needs. However, where SLAs are not being used, the very least that is required is to formally document and link customer expectations to the services provided, and get the customer to agree to what has been documented.

External service providers will use the customer agreement portfolio as a means of tracking all legal contractual requirements and will link them to the service portfolio and customer portfolio. The customer agreement portfolio enables the service provider to track the relationship between customer, service and contractual requirements. It is especially helpful when a single service is used by more than one customer, to ensure that the level of service is provided to meet all contracts, and especially the most stringent of these.

Internal service providers will use the customer agreement portfolio to track SLAs and less formal agreements to ensure ongoing ability to meet customer expectations, or to prevent customer expectations from changing without a justified (and funded) need.

Since the customer agreement portfolio is really an intersection of the service and customer portfolios, it is usually managed as part of service portfolio management. The business relationship management process uses the customer agreement portfolio extensively, and provides important input to its contents.

4.2.4.9 Project portfolio

The project portfolio is a database or structured document used to manage projects that have been chartered (a charter is a document authorizing the project and stating its scope, terms and references). The project portfolio is used to coordinate projects; ensuring objectives are met within time and cost and to specification. The project portfolio also ensures that projects are not duplicated, that they stay within the agreed scope and that resources are available for each project. The project portfolio is the tool used to manage single projects as well as large-scale programmes, consisting of multiple projects.

The project portfolio is typically defined and maintained by a PMO in larger organizations. Although smaller organizations may manage projects singly, it is still important to maintain a project portfolio to track the impact of all projects over time, and to be able to refer back to previous projects for lessons learned. The scope of the project portfolio will depend on the structure of an organization and the way it is managed. Most organizations keep a separate project portfolio for IT projects, but some include both business and IT projects. If there are separate portfolios they should reference each other – for example, a project to change a business process should be linked to the IT project to change the corresponding IT services.

The project portfolio is important to service portfolio management since new services, and many changes to existing services, are managed as projects once they have been chartered. The project portfolio helps service portfolio management to track the status of these projects, compare the expenditure to the expected investment, and ensure that the services are being built and designed as intended. This is especially helpful in setting customer expectations, and in being able to ensure compliance with contracts or agreements in the customer agreement portfolio. In addition, there might be several projects related to a single service. The project portfolio will ensure that these are aligned and coordinated.

4.2.4.10 Service models

The concept of service models is described in detail in section 3.4.7 but forms an integral part of service portfolio management.

Service portfolio management uses service models to analyse the impact of new services or changes to existing services. If a service model does not exist for a service in the pipeline, service portfolio management will ensure that one is defined. Service models are also valuable in assessing which existing service assets can be used to support new services – thus enabling more efficiency through using a principle of 'create once, use many times'.

4.2.4.11 Market spaces and service growth

The service portfolio provides a baseline of all planned services and those currently offered. It also identifies all the customers and market spaces that are currently served and those that are planned to be served.

Market spaces are helpful to service portfolio management to evaluate the impact of a proposed new service or change to an existing service, since they clarify the opportunity that is being served. In addition, whenever a market space is identified within service portfolio management it becomes an important input to strategic assessment to identify changes in the market and address gaps in the current strategy. For more information see sections 3.4 and 4.1.5.4.

4.2.4.12 Aligning service assets, services and business outcomes

Service portfolio management plays an important role in how assets are allocated, deployed and managed. Section 4.1.5.14 explained the importance of aligning service assets to customer outcomes as part of strategy execution. Service portfolio management plays an important role in achieving this since the service portfolio and configuration management system (CMS) documents the relationship between business outcomes, services and service assets. Each service in the service portfolio has to be expressed in the CMS as a set of service assets, performance requirements, standard operating procedures, functions and SLAs.

4.2.4.13 Service portfolio management through the service lifecycle

Although service portfolio management is a process within service strategy, it also plays an important part in every stage in the service lifecycle.

In service design service portfolio management ensures that design work is prioritized according to business needs, and that there is a clear understanding of how the service will be measured by the business. Each service is clearly linked to the agreed business outcomes, providing an understanding of how service assets will be used, and identifying the levels of performance that will be required. This basic and high-level understanding of the service will provide a benchmark against which detailed requirements analysis can be measured. When combined with demand management, service portfolio management provides a clear picture of when these services will be required and what level of demand will be placed upon them.

Service portfolio management also provides input to the teams involved in building the services. This will ensure that the teams remain focused on the objectives, outcomes and priorities of each service. It will also work with the PMO or project manager to monitor the build process to ensure that the services are built on time, to specification and to budget.

Service transition builds and tests the services that will be placed into the service catalogue. The service portfolio provides guidance to service transition in building, testing and evaluating the service. Change management authorization is necessary to move a service into the service catalogue. This is because:

- It is necessary to ensure that the service is a complete product that can be fully supported. This includes technical feasibility, financial viability and operational capability. Incomplete products offered in haste can result in significant losses for service providers and customers.
- Items in the service catalogue entail commitments made to customers, in the form of either agreements or contracts. Any changes to the catalogue have to be evaluated for impact on the ability to meet those commitments.
- Adding items to the service catalogue means that capabilities and resources need to be set aside for present and prospective customers. If those resources cannot be allocated, then a decision has to be made whether to continue providing that service, or whether those resources and capabilities need to be re-prioritized.

Service operation delivers the service in the service catalogue part of the service portfolio. Service portfolio management provides them with an understanding of the services and how and why they need to be delivered. This is an important input to defining standard operating procedures, event management, incident management priorities and escalation procedures.

Continual service improvement evaluates whether the services in the portfolio met the stated objectives, and if not identifies ways in which the situation can be rectified. Continual service improvement also evaluates the business cases and objectives to ensure that they are still valid, and therefore that service portfolio management continues to prioritize services appropriately.

Note on managing portfolios

Although each portfolio discussed in section 4.2.4.13 has its own purpose and specific content, they are often used in conjunction with one another and they may contain overlapping information. It might be more appropriate to consider managing all portfolios using the same process and tools. A project to establish just a service portfolio or project portfolio in isolation may not yield the same results. In addition, investing in several portfolios over time, each isolated from the other, will be more costly in the longer term than taking an integrated approach.

4.2.5 Process activities, methods and techniques

Service portfolio management consists of four main phases of activity, illustrated in Figure 4.18.

- **Define** This phase focuses on documenting and understanding existing services and new services. Each service must have a documented

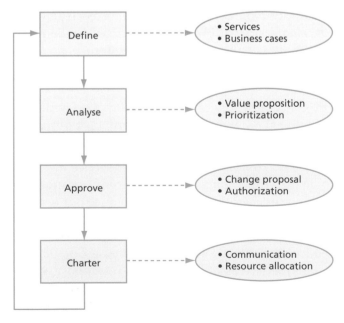

Figure 4.18 Phases of service portfolio management

business case. Data for each service, such as which service assets are required, and where investments are made, needs to be validated.

- **Analyse** The analysis of services in the portfolio will indicate whether the service is able to optimize value, and how supply and demand can be prioritized and balanced.
- **Approve** Every service needs to be approved and the level of investment authorized to ensure sufficient resources to deliver the anticipated levels of service.
- **Charter** A charter is a document authorizing the project and stating its scope, terms and references. Services are not just built on request from anyone in the organization. They have to be formally chartered, and stakeholders need to be kept up to date with information about decisions, resource allocation and actual investments made.

An example of how these four phases can be executed in a process is given in Figure 4.19 and described in detail below. Before defining and executing the process, however, it is important that the service portfolio itself is defined.

Defining the service portfolio begins with collecting information from all existing services as well as every proposed service. The cyclic nature of the SPM process set means that the 'define' phase not only creates an initial inventory of services, but also validates the data on a recurring basis. Different portfolios will have different refresh cycles. Some cycles will be triggered by a particular event or business trend. For example, a merger and acquisition event triggers a portfolio re-examination.

4.2.5.1 Process initiation

Once the service portfolio itself has been established, all new services and changes to existing services will need to go through a formal process of assessment and approval.

New services and changes to existing services can be initiated from a number of sources, and will be presented in a number of different forms. As a result there is no fixed record for inputs to the service portfolio management process. Rather the initiation of the process will often be as a result of changes to plans or the identification of a service improvement plan.

Although there are a variety of different types of input, it is important for service portfolio management to maintain a central record of all plans, requests and suggestions that are submitted. In some organizations these are simply called requests, but this could be confused with standard service requests submitted for request fulfilment. Also, many of the inputs to service portfolio management are not requests, but plans.

4.2.5.2 Process initiation: strategy management for IT services

The primary input to service portfolio management is from strategy management for IT services. This will be in the form of the strategic plans, which outline initiatives for new business opportunities and outcomes, together with the services that are required to deliver them.

Service portfolio management will be responsible for evaluating each initiative to ensure that the required levels of investment and return are feasible, and that the strategy is achievable from a services point of view.

This is just as applicable for internal service providers as it is for external. The ability to provide internal and external IT services will be key to the organization's being able to meet its strategy. Therefore service portfolio management will be involved in setting the organization's overall strategy, as well as its IT strategy.

4.2.5.3 Process initiation: business relationship management

The business relationship management process is a direct interface to customers and users, and it is likely that it will receive a number of different types of request. These range from requests for information about services to requests for training, to requests for new services and changes to existing services.

In many cases these requests can be dealt with through change management, request fulfilment or incident management – but some requests will need to be submitted to service portfolio management. These include requests for new services, added functionality to existing services and performance improvements in existing services.

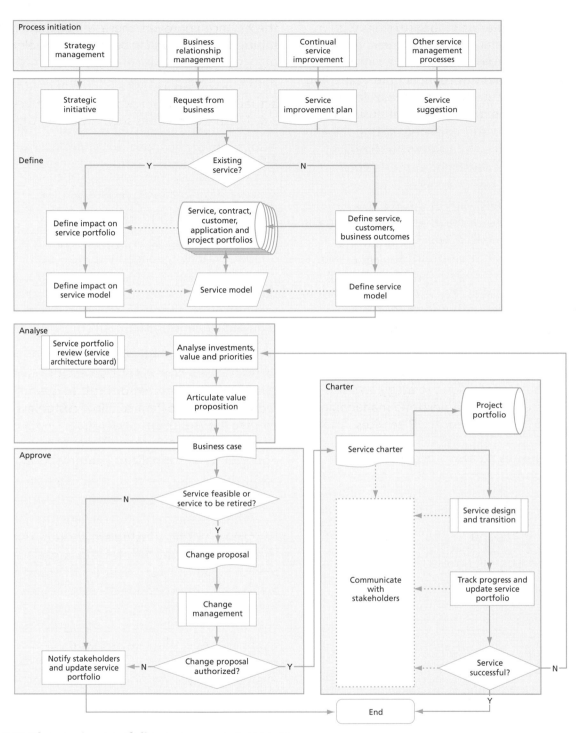

Figure 4.19 The service portfolio management process

4.2.5.4 Process initiation: continual service improvement

Continual service improvement (CSI) initiates three types of input to service portfolio management.

Firstly, opportunities to improve the performance or service level achievements of services in the portfolio. This may mean that the business is not able to achieve the level of business outcomes that

it requires. Each opportunity for improvement (logged in the CSI register) will be assessed in terms of the new level of investment that has been (and will be) made in this service, compared to the overall projected return. In other words, the new investment required, together with the investment already made, may make the service too expensive for what the business will actually achieve.

Secondly, CSI identifies new opportunities within the current strategy, or gaps in the current portfolio of services. For example, the nature of the business outcomes has changed due to market conditions and the current service needs to be adjusted to meet the new patterns of business activity. Another example is where existing services were designed to enable a specific business outcome, but some requirements were omitted during service design.

Thirdly, CSI identifies opportunities for overall improvements in cost, mitigation of risks etc. These may result in projects that are not related to a single service, but affects multiple services or the entire operation of the service provider. These also need to be channelled through service portfolio management since the change in investment and impact on services needs to be properly identified and managed.

If CSI identifies an opportunity or gap that requires a change in the organization's strategy, this will not be submitted to service portfolio management, but to strategy management for IT services instead.

4.2.5.5 Process initiation: other service management processes

Specific service management processes have the task of managing changes to services, or modelling warranty and utility options that can be presented to the customer. Many of these options will impact the levels of investment and it is important that service portfolio management evaluates these suggested changes before they are initiated.

Although many suggestions can be routed through change management, this is not recommended if the suggestion has a significant impact on the existing levels of investment or achievement of business outcomes. Any suggestions that change management considers to be strategic should be immediately referred to service portfolio management.

This means that service portfolio management and change management should define thresholds for what constitutes a strategic issue.

4.2.5.6 Define

This part of the process is about defining desired business outcomes, opportunities, utility and warranty requirements and the services themselves – as well as the anticipated investment to achieve

these. Once approved, these will be moved into the service design stage for design and development.

This section describes the process for managing the definition of services. The approach used to actually define the services is described in section 3.4. These two sections should be read together.

4.2.5.7 Define: strategy

Any new strategy or change to an existing strategy should be submitted to service portfolio management. This will be in the form of strategic plans, identified market spaces and outcomes, priorities and policies. These will be used to identify specific service opportunities and the stakeholders that will be consulted in defining the services.

4.2.5.8 Define: request from business

Requests from the business come in different formats, from informal to detailed proposals. While this makes it somewhat difficult to quantify the request, it is important to allow customers and users to express their initial request in the way that is understandable to them. There will be plenty of opportunity to formalize requirements into standardized formats later in the process.

There is no specific type of record for this type of request, but it is important that each request is registered and that customers are kept up to date on its status. In addition, it is advisable that service portfolio management define a standard method and format of recording requests that come from the business. In this way requests can be formatted into a consistent structure for progressing through the service portfolio management process. Whoever executes the business relationship management process should be responsible for documenting requests on behalf of the customer.

4.2.5.9 Define: service improvement opportunities and plans

Identifying service improvement opportunities and building service improvement plans (SIPs) are described in detail in *ITIL Continual Service Improvement.*

Not all improvement opportunities and SIPs are about changing services. Many relate to the processes, people and tools that support or deliver the services. These opportunities will still be submitted to service portfolio management since they impact the overall investment in providing services, and will need to be allocated to the services at some stage.

4.2.5.10 Define: service suggestion

Many service suggestions would fall under the control of change management. Where a suggestion requires an investment above a defined threshold or where it specifically impacts the agreed utility and warranty of a service, however, it should be submitted to service portfolio management. Examples include:

- Capacity management identifies a new technology that can increase the performance of a service, while making it easier to manage, and will need to be deployed.
- IT service continuity management establishes a new business impact that they have not provided for, and requires a new recovery plan.
- Availability management identifies a new countermeasure that will mitigate service risks, and this will require a significant modification to the data centre.
- Problem management identifies a resolution for an intermittent service disruption, but it will require migration to a new platform.
- Suppliers may make strategic changes to their products or services. This is especially important if the supplier is strategic. Supplier management and capacity management must be sure to channel these as requests to service portfolio management.

4.2.5.11 Define: existing service?

The steps for existing services are different from those for new services, so it is important to establish whether the input is regarding a new or existing service.

This may seem like a simple step, but if the service portfolio is new the service provider may not actually know about every service that is offered. This is especially true for internal service providers where customers do not pay for services, and no formal catalogue has been defined. It may also involve a service that has been built by IT experts in the business units themselves, and so IT would have no record of it.

Whenever in doubt, service portfolio management should treat the service as a new service. In this way the process can be used to bring the service

under formal service management control. Care should be taken, however, to ensure that the new service does not duplicate any existing service in the service portfolio.

4.2.5.12 Define: service, customers, business outcomes (new services)

In this step service portfolio management will define the service based on the information provided. At this stage it will not be possible to produce a detailed architecture for the service (this is done during service design). In fact in this step any attempts to define the service in terms of the technology used to deliver it should be resisted. This could result in a service based on what technology is capable of, and not on what the business or customer actually needs.

The items to be defined at this stage include:

- The purpose of the service (what it must achieve)
- The customers and consumers of the service
- The major inputs and outputs of the service
- High-level performance requirements (for example, when it needs to be available)
- What business activity will it support, and is that activity stable or dynamic?
- Does the service need to comply with (or enable the business to comply with) any regulatory or legal requirements?
- Are there any standards that need to be applied to the service?
- What are the actual business outcomes that the service will be supporting, and who is responsible for these outcomes?
- Are there any other stakeholders that need to be involved in defining and evaluating this service?
- The anticipated level of investments and returns. Although these will not be known, the customer will know what type of return they need, and how much they are prepared to spend to achieve it.
- Are there any constraints that need to be considered (e.g. budget, resources)?

4.2.5.13 Define: service model (new services)

The concept of service models is discussed in section 3.4.7. At this stage service portfolio management will need to understand how the service will be structured. Again this is not a detailed technical architecture, rather a high-level view of all of the components of the service and how they fit together. Some of these components will be customer assets, and some will be service assets.

For example, the service model will need to outline which staff will be using the service, what type of equipment they will be using, and what outputs they will be expecting. It will also specify the need for certain types of IT equipment or services – for example, networking, storage, internet access etc.

At this stage the service model is used to identify the boundaries of the service, and also to identify all the technical stakeholders that will need to be involved in analysing the service. In some cases it will also be possible to identify existing services or service assets that could be used to create the new service. Service portfolio management therefore supports the decision-making process of whether to use the existing infrastructure and applications or invest in the procurement or development of new infrastructure and applications.

4.2.5.14 Define: impact on service portfolio (existing services)

Service portfolio management will already know the details of the customers, utility and warranty of the service, although it would be helpful to double-check that this information is recorded in the service portfolio, and specifically in the service catalogue. The purpose of this stage is to evaluate the impact on the existing utility, warranty and investment in the service.

Although the required investment may not be fully known, it will be possible to identify the people who will be able to make this determination.

The impact on the service portfolio refers to the impact on a number of key areas, including:

- The current business outcomes (will the proposal negatively impact any current commitments to customers or suppliers?)
- Investment levels
- Service level agreements
- Warranty levels
- Contractual obligations
- Existing required utility (for example, changing an existing service may benefit one customer, but it might negatively impact another)

- Is there another existing service that can be combined with this service to deliver the required utility or warranty?
- Patterns of business activity, and levels of demand on the service. (Will this increase or decrease demand on the service, and therefore on key service assets?)

4.2.5.15 Define: impact on service model (existing services)

The concept of service models is discussed in section 3.4.7. At this stage service portfolio management will need to determine whether there is any impact on the existing service model. This will include:

- Will the dynamics of the model change?
- Will the flow of data and information change?
- Will there be any new components?
- Will any of the existing components need to change?
- Will the demand level on any of the components change?
- Are there components from other service models that could be used to support the changes to the existing service?
- Will any constraints be introduced?
- Will any relationships be impacted?

This step will also help to identify all the technical stakeholders that will need to be involved in analysing the service.

4.2.5.16 Analyse

The analysis of each service moving through the service portfolio management process is performed by linking each one to the service strategy. For external service providers this will be a linkage to the organization's overall strategy. For internal service providers it will mean linking to the IT strategy and the strategies of the other business units.

Questions that will help to translate the organization's strategic intent for services include:

- What are the long-term goals of the service organization?
- What services are required to meet those goals?
- What capabilities and resources are required for the organization to achieve those services?
- How will we get there?

In other words, service portfolio management articulates how the perspective, position, plan and patterns will be translated into actual services. The answers to these questions guide not only the analysis but also the desired outcomes of service portfolio management. The ability to satisfactorily answer these questions requires the involvement of senior leaders and subject matter experts.

The way in which services will be analysed needs to be clearly defined before the analysis actually begins. If the organization does not understand what analysis it will perform, it is unlikely to know the right data to collect. Data collection exercises are usually disruptive and should be as streamlined as possible.

The analysis phase requires input from multiple specialized areas. Identifying the correct people to perform analysis for each service can be quite challenging. For this reason, some organizations use a standard pool of senior architects and managers (the service architecture board – SAB) to evaluate each service and assign analysis tasks to specific groups based on the type of knowledge and skills required for that service. This group will also validate the analysis work and ensure that the change proposal is properly prepared.

4.2.5.17 Analyse: service portfolio review

This is an ongoing activity within service portfolio management, which is aimed at regularly reviewing existing services in the service portfolio to determine whether they still meet their objectives, and whether they are still appropriate for the strategy of the organization. The review will also ensure that services in the service pipeline are properly defined, analysed, approved and chartered.

Services are evaluated in terms of:

- Do they still support the achievement of appropriate business outcomes?
- What level of investment has been made since the last review?
- Do the returns still justify the continued investments?
- Does the service provider still have the appropriate resources and capabilities to continue delivering the service?
- Can the service be used to meet any new strategic opportunities?

- Does the service have any potential new uses that would create a strategic opportunity for the organization?

The output of this review will feed into the analysis of investments, value and priorities. In some cases service portfolio management might find that a new opportunity needs to be presented to the organization's executives during the strategy management cycle. This should be done as part of the strategy assessment stage.

4.2.5.18 Analyse: analyse investments, value and priorities

Service portfolio management works with financial management for IT services to use the techniques outlined in section 4.3 and in section 3.6 to quantify the investment and value of each service.

This requires an understanding of the business outcomes to be achieved, how the service will be used to achieve those outcomes, any supporting services that will be used, and how these are linked to the achievement of the business outcomes.

To achieve this mapping of service assets to services to business outcomes, service portfolio management starts to document them in the service portfolio as illustrated in Figure 4.15 in section 4.2.4.3. As the project progresses, these linkages will be formalized and documented in the service catalogue.

Using the techniques outlined in section 3.2.3 to map money spent to value added to value realized, service portfolio management is able to work with the customer to calculate the value of the service. This can then be compared to the value of all services in the current strategy, and the effort to build and deliver them can be prioritized. Section 4.1.5.16 also has a discussion on prioritizing investments for strategy.

The option space tool

A service portfolio is an expression of the provider's service strategy. Executing a service strategy involves making a sequence of major decisions. Some commitments, once made, cannot be undone. Providers can only revise their plans for future commitments. To ensure that decisions about the priority and schedule of service development are sound, service portfolio management sets a framework within which future strategic decisions can be made.

Important note on analysing investments, value and priorities

At this stage of the process there is no detailed service design. Therefore it is not possible to determine the exact amount of money that will need to be spent on the service. The purpose of this activity is to determine what level of investment the organization is prepared to make and when it is prepared to make it – in other words, to determine the feasibility of the service. When the service is approved, the architecture, design and build teams will continually evaluate whether the service meets the investment objectives.

A useful tool for making decisions on the timing and sequencing of investments in a service portfolio is called an option space tool (Figure 4.20). An option space can guide decisions to invest and, if so, when (this section draws on work done by Luehrman, 1998). According to Luehrman, strategy is based on selecting from a range of investment options. He uses the following concepts:

- **Value-to-cost** This is a ratio indicating the relative return on an investment. If the value realized is less than the investment the value-to-cost is less than 1. If the return is the same as the investment the value-to-cost is 1. If the return is greater than the investment the value-to-cost is greater than 1.
- **Volatility** This is the extent to which the conditions being measured are likely to change.

In Figure 4.20, Luehrman uses the example of a tomato garden where tomatoes all ripen at different times. Some are rotten and will need to be discarded (their state of rottenness is unlikely to change, so is not volatile). Others are ripe and ready to pick and sell immediately. All other tomatoes are at some other stage – some will be ready for harvesting soon, and others will never be acceptable for harvest.

Luehrman's concept can be illustrated in Figure 4.20, which illustrates six different options for the tomatoes in the tomato garden.

This tool has been adapted for use in service management. In Figure 4.21 additional criteria have been placed on the axes of the chart to illustrate the variables involved in service strategy,

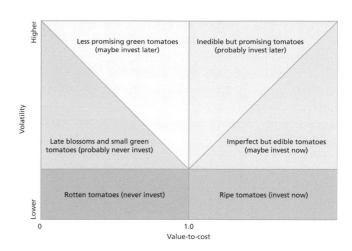

Figure 4.20 Option spaces (tomato garden example)

namely whether market spaces and customers are new or existing, and whether customer needs are currently under- or over-served. These can be calculated together with the value-to-cost ratio to evaluate in which space an option falls – and therefore whether or not it represents a good investment. Please note that this chart can be read with the value-to-cost and any other individual axis or combination of axes.

Financial measures need not be the only measure. Other factors can and should be incorporated such as:

- Mission imperatives
- Compliance
- Trends
- Intangible benefits
- Strategic or business fit
- Social responsibilities
- Innovation.

For example, fulfilling a legal compliance issue may on its own generate a value-to-cost measure of greater than one. Government agencies may generate value-to-cost measures on public policy while military organizations may generate measures based on mission imperatives.

In this way the option space tool can not only indicate which services will yield a favourable financial return on investment, but it can also indicate which services will move the organization closer to achieving other strategic objectives.

The other axes are based on market spaces, customers and customer needs. Each is used as a guide for strategic intent. The desire of a Type I

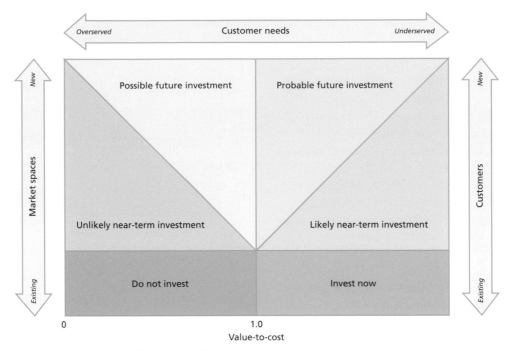

Figure 4.21 The option space tool for IT service management

provider to serve a new business unit, for example, may have less value if the customer needs are already over-served.

Thus Figure 4.21 illustrates that the most favourable investments are on the right of the chart and involve services that are delivered to existing customers and have a high value-to-cost ratio. Services with a moderate value that are provided to new customers represent a reasonably attractive opportunity, but will not take priority.

Services on the left of the chart in Figure 4.21 are less attractive, but may become more so if the internal or external environment changes and they become more cost-effective, or the customer demand for those services becomes very high, in which case the organization can charge a premium for them.

Prioritizing service investments

Once the services have been analysed using techniques similar to the option space tool, executives will need to decide which services will take priority. Services will be classified in one of three strategic categories:

■ **Run the business** (RTB) RTB investments are centred on maintaining service operations.
■ **Grow the business** (GTB) GTB investments are intended to grow the organization's scope of services.

■ **Transform the business** (TTB) TTB investments are moves into new market spaces.

Each of these categories is further classified in terms of the type of budget that will be available for this category of service. Since some types of investment are more risky than others, executives allocate funding so that that there is a balance between higher-risk categories of spending and lower-risk categories. These categories are:

■ **Venture** This is the portion of the budget that is available to create services in a new market space.
■ **Growth** This is the portion of the budget that has been allocated to create new services in existing market space.
■ **Discretionary** This is money in the budget that is available if needed, but which does not have to be spent. This portion of the budget is often used to provide enhancements to existing services.
■ **Non-discretionary** This represents money that has to be spent in order to operate and maintain existing services.
■ **Core** This is the portion of the budget that takes the highest priority, since it is used to operate and maintain business-critical services.

Figure 4.22 illustrates how the budget is allocated to the three service categories.

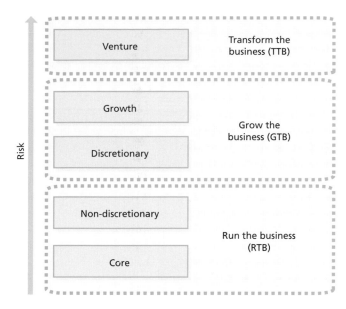

Figure 4.22 How executives allocate budget to strategic categories of service

Figure 4.22 indicates that when a service moves from the RTB category towards the TTB category the risk increases. This is because investment is being made in new services and new customers, both of which are uncertain. The least risk is involved when delivering or modifying existing services to existing customers. In these cases the organization has tested capabilities and good knowledge of the customer requirements and

culture – so they have a very good chance of achieving customer satisfaction and loyalty.

In a market where there is a lot of change, however, services that are low risk today may not be in demand tomorrow. For this reason it is important that executives invest in a portfolio of balanced risk. Thus, if one investment does not achieve its objectives, the others will continue to produce results.

By determining the allocation of budget into run-the-business, grow-the-business or transform-the-business service categories, executives are not only affirming their risk tolerance, but are directly affecting the modes of operation implemented through service design and executed by the operational staff. The distribution of services from RTB to TTB will reflect the nature of the organization: predominantly RTB if IT is a cost centre (back-office), predominantly TTB if IT is an investment centre (commercial provider).

Figures 4.23 and 4.24 use the option space tool to illustrate how two service providers prioritize their investments according to their strategy and level of risk tolerance. Figure 4.23 gives an example of an internal service provider that is focused on maintaining services.

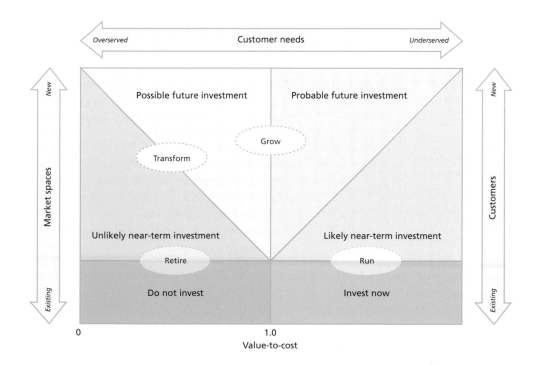

Figure 4.23 An internal service provider focused on maintaining services (RTB)

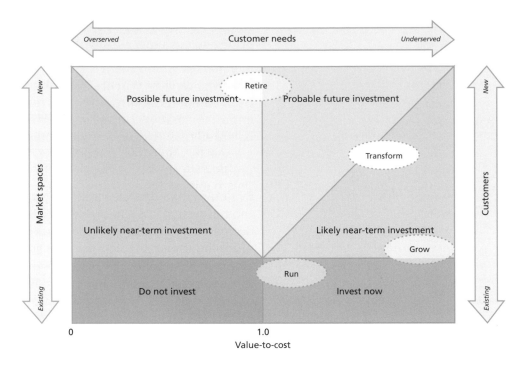

Figure 4.24 An external service provider focused on expanding the scope of services (TTB)

In Figure 4.23 the service provider is making the most of their investments in providing existing services to existing customers that are under-served.

Investment in growth will only be made sometime in the future, if at all, and spending on transformation is unlikely and only to very-well-defined new market spaces. Any services that have a negative value-to-cost ratio and where customers are over-served already will be retired. This example shows a low risk tolerance and a focus on supporting the existing business.

By contrast, the external service provider illustrated in Figure 4.24 is investing heavily in growth and transformation. Existing services to existing customers with a low to moderate value-to-cost ratio will be maintained, and investment will be made in growing services to existing customers and market spaces that are currently under-served. These investments will be made in the current financial year. Transformation investment, in which new services will be delivered to new customers and market spaces, will most likely begin in the current financial year, but most investment will be made after the growth has taken place. Services that are designed for new customers and market spaces, but which have a low value-to-cost ratio, will be retired. This example shows a service provider with a reasonably high tolerance for risk, and with a fairly aggressive expansion strategy.

4.2.5.19 Analyse: articulate value proposition

Once the investment analysis and prioritization has been completed, the results will be formatted and documented in a business case. The business case will describe the opportunity, and provide a description of what the service expected to achieve.

The business case will also provide details of the business outcomes the service will be designed to meet, and the investment the organization is prepared to make in the service. This information will continue to be used to perform return on investment calculations throughout the project.

The business case is the justification for pursuing a course of action to meet stated organizational goals and acts as the link back to service strategy and funding. It is the assessment of a service investment in terms of potential benefits and the resources and capabilities required to provision and maintain it.

Business cases are discussed in more detail in section 3.6 as part of service economics.

4.2.5.20 Approve: is the service or change feasible?

Once the value proposition has been articulated and a business case documented, service portfolio management can work with the customers and business executives to decide whether the service is feasible. This is the first 'go/no-go' decision in the process.

Up to this point service portfolio management has facilitated a good understanding of the desired future state of services in the organization. At this point, decision makers in the organization decide on which aspects of that anticipated future state are feasible. With approvals comes the corresponding authorization for new services and resources. There will be a second 'go/no-go' decision once the detail of the new service has been defined and a more accurate estimate of the investment is understood.

One risk associated with these decisions is the fact that a detailed design has not been completed and the anticipated level of investment may be inaccurate. Each decision maker will need to understand this risk, and must be notified of significant changes to expenditure on the service or change at each major stage of the project.

The decisions about how services will be progressed through the service portfolio management process fall into six categories:

- **Retain/build** Largely self-contained, with well-defined asset, process and system boundaries, these services are aligned with, and are relevant to, the organization's strategy.
- **Replace** These services do not meet minimum levels of technical and functional fitness.
- **Rationalize** Often organizations discover they are offering services that are composed of multiple releases of the same operating system, multiple versions of the same software and/or multiple versions of system platforms providing similar functions. The duplication will have to be removed and a single solution chosen that best fits the strategy and customer or business requirements. Rationalization also applies to service with unclear or overlapping business functionality.
- **Refactor** Often services that meet the technical and functional criteria of the organization display fuzzy process or system boundaries. An example would be a service handling its own authentication or continuity functions. In these cases, the service can often be refactored to include only the core functionality, with common services used to provide the remainder.

Refactoring is also useful when a service embeds potentially reusable services within itself.

- **Renew** These services meet functional fitness criteria, but fail technical fitness. An example may be a service whose fulfilment elements include a mainframe system and frame relay network that still supports business-critical processes where the strategic direction of the organization is to retire the mainframe platform and source an MPLS (Multi-Protocol Label Switching) WAN.
- **Retire** Services that no longer meet a business objective or strategy. These services may be identified by customers or technical groups, but many will only be discovered during the service portfolio review.

A service will not be feasible if it is not able to achieve the required business outcomes, or if the level of investment is too high for the estimated return. Service portfolio management will facilitate the decision to retire the existing service or to stop any further design activity.

In most cases the business and/or customer will have been involved in this decision. However, they may still want to pressure the service provider to move ahead with the service anyway. This will cause the service provider to deviate from the agreed strategy of the organization, and it is also likely to result in the service provider having to deliver services that either they are not capable of delivering, or they have no funding for. It is vital that the service provider is not put into this position, and they will require the full support of the organization's executives once a decision has been made that a service is not feasible.

The service provider has to decide how to respond to such cases. The response is likely to include a combination of the following:

- Explain to the customer why the need cannot be fulfilled.
- Explain what is needed of the customer in terms of commitment, sponsorship or funding for new service development. Customers may reconsider their needs in view of service development costs they may have to bear.
- Develop the service if the customer makes the necessary commitment.
- Decline the opportunity if the customer cannot commit.

- Consider supporting the customer in partnership with third parties.

Under no circumstances should the service provider agree to deliver services without the appropriate funding or without the appropriate service assets. Any attempts to force the situation should be escalated to the organization's executives, who will need to make a decision about the service. If they agree that the service should be developed or retained, they will need to secure the required funding.

4.2.5.21 Approve: change proposal

Once a decision has been made that the new service, or change to an existing service, is feasible, it will need to be submitted through change management for detailed assessment and final authorization.

If it is a simple change, it is likely that it has already come to service portfolio management through change management. However, most new services and complex strategic changes come directly to service portfolio management for assessment and approval before being passed to change management for authorization.

Since the details of the new service or changes have not yet been defined in detail, it will be difficult to submit a simple request for change (RFC). Instead, service portfolio management will submit a change proposal. This allows the design teams to spend money and prioritize resources even though a final decision regarding the change has yet to be made.

The change proposal will allow change management to coordinate the activities of all resources required to investigate the customer and infrastructure requirements; and also ensure that these activities are prioritized in relation to other authorized changes already being built, tested and implemented by the same resources.

Note that the decision to retire a service should also be submitted through change management and that the request for change should document all potential impacts and dependencies affected by the retirement.

The change proposal should include:

- A high-level description of the new or changed service, including business outcomes to be supported, and utility and warranty to be provided
- Full business case including risks, issues and alternatives, as well as budget and financial expectations
- Expected implementation schedule.

Note on legislated changes in government departments

Internal service providers in government departments will not have a choice about implementing changes that have been legislated. In these cases, the change proposal can still be used to analyse the change and its impact before raising an RFC. Some organizations will immediately raise an RFC and perform the analysis as part of the normal change management process.

4.2.5.22 Approve: change management authorization

The change proposal is submitted to change management, which will facilitate a detailed assessment of the proposed design, resource requirements, priorities and investments. The change proposal will be treated in much the same way as an RFC, except that the activity is focused on investigating what the new or changed service will look like and what it will take to design, build and deploy it.

The objective is to obtain enough information that a decision can be made to confirm whether or not the service is feasible, and then to initiate the actual detailed design and deployment of the new or changed service.

Service portfolio management analysis identified the boundaries of what the service needs to achieve, and how much investment is available. Change management will facilitate further investigation and provide a high-level blueprint for the new or changed service.

Why is it necessary to go through two rounds of assessment? The reason is that the work done as part of the change management assessment is fairly detailed and resource-intensive. Service portfolio management should eliminate any work it already knows will have a negative outcome. This saves time and effort, but it will also ensure that resources are not frequently working on ideas that will never be implemented. This is demotivating and counter-productive.

4.2.5.23 Approve: change proposal authorized?

If the change proposal is authorized by change management, service portfolio management will use the feedback collated by change management to draft a service charter (see section 4.2.5.24).

If the change proposal is rejected, service portfolio management will have to notify all stakeholders and update the service portfolio with the status.

For internal service providers it is likely that the stakeholders were already involved in the change management process (if not this may require a review of that process). It is therefore unlikely that a lengthy report and communication campaign needs to be set up to notify them that the change proposal has been rejected. However, it is important that the stakeholders have been formally notified, and that the service provider is able to work with them to devise a plan to continue without the proposed service. Section 4.2.5.20 presents some potential actions.

When a change proposal is rejected by an external provider, it will essentially be telling its customers that it is forgoing the business opportunity, which might result in the customer terminating their relationship with the service provider. This scenario must have been part of the business case, and therefore service portfolio management will have drafted a plan on how to present the answer to the customer, and also how to deal with the situation if the customer is dissatisfied with the outcome.

In any case, service portfolio management should work through business relationship management to ensure that a positive outcome can be achieved if possible. Executives must also sign off on any rejection of a service that they have already approved in principle.

4.2.5.24 Service charter

Charter has two meanings, both of which are relevant here – although this section primarily refers to the second:

- A verb which implies that the new service (or changes to the existing service) has been commissioned by the customer or business executives
- A noun referring to a document which is used to authorize work to meet defined objectives, outputs, schedules and expenditure. Charters are normally used to initiate the design stage of projects. In service portfolio management, services are chartered using a service charter.

The service charter ensures that all stakeholders, development, testing and deployment staff members have a common understanding of what will be built, by when and how much it will cost. The implication of using the term 'charter' is that the changes will be managed using a project management approach, which in larger organizations will be managed using a PMO.

Since this activity will be performed as part of a project, the service charter will also be an input into the project management process (to initiate the design stage of the project), and will be entered into the project portfolio.

Typical contents of a service charter

Project management methodologies include information about the contents of a service charter. This section is not intended to replace this information, but to provide an overview of a service charter for readers who are not familiar with these methodologies.

The structure of a service charter will vary depending on documentation standards in different organizations and cultures (for example, some will contain an executive overview and summary of the background; others will place a lot more emphasis on background and forgo the executive summary). This is not a template for a service charter, rather a checklist of the minimum information that should be included. This list refers to projects, since a charter is often used as part of a standard project management approach.

- Overview:
  - Description of the service being developed or changed
  - Background, providing the reasons for the work (e.g. part of a strategy, or to fulfil a customer request)
  - Project scope and objectives

- Any assumptions, standards or instructions that need to be taken into account during the design, transition and operation of the service
- Sponsorship
- Glossary of technical and business terms if necessary.
- Approach:
  - Project deliverables and quality requirements
  - Organization and responsibilities (which groups will be participating in the project and what will they be doing?)
  - Resource allocated to the project
  - Risks and constraints
  - Stages – for example, there might be a requirements gathering stage, development and procurement stage, testing stage and deployment stage
  - Schedule
  - Project control, how progress will be tracked and communicated and how exceptions will be escalated and managed.
- Project authority:
  - This identifies who is ultimately responsible for the project, who is funding it and who will be able to sign off on the deliverables.

4.2.5.25 Charter: communicate with stakeholders

Stakeholders should be notified of the progress of the project from the time it is chartered to the time the service has been deployed.

This will ensure that stakeholders continue to support the project and also that any delays or other exceptions are communicated in the context of ongoing communication. Stakeholders are far more likely to respond constructively to bad news when they feel that they are involved in the project.

Any actions required of the stakeholders – for example, involvement in testing or to clarify requirements – can be coordinated through the communication channels. If appropriate, communication with business leaders and users can be coordinated through business relationship management (see section 4.5.5). Communication with suppliers can be coordinated through the supplier management process.

4.2.5.26 Charter: service design and transition processes

Although the service charter is used to initiate the work of design and transition, the service charter remains active throughout this phase since it is the formal approval of the scope and requirements of the project. The actual work of designing, developing, building, testing and deploying the service will be done during service design and transition, using the processes and functions outlined in the core ITIL publications of the same name. A very brief summary is provided as follows:

- Service level management ensures that the performance, availability and security requirements are understood and communicated to the build and test teams.
- Service catalogue management ensures that the service catalogue is updated at the appropriate time to show the status of the service, and as a basis for communicating the purpose and availability of the service.
- Capacity management will ensure that the patterns of business activity are understood and related to the technology that will support the service. It will also ensure that the service is designed to meet reliability, maintainability and serviceability requirements.
- Availability management will ensure that the service is designed to meet the levels and times of availability required by the customer.
- IT service continuity management will assess the impact of service failure and design plans to be invoked if there is a major contingency that disrupts the ability of the service provider to function normally.
- Information security management ensures that the service is designed to protect the organization's confidentiality and integrity, and that the service complies with organizational (and sometimes legislated or regulatory) security policies and requirements.
- Supplier management ensures that all third-party suppliers are contracted to provide the levels of service, product and support required to ensure the required performance of the service.
- Change management and change evaluation ensure that the actual changes made to the infrastructure, applications, tools and organization are properly controlled and

managed, to ensure minimal impact when the new service is deployed.

- Service asset and configuration management will identify, control and validate all data and information required by the service provider to manage the service effectively and efficiently.
- Service validation and testing ensures that the service meets the requirements documented in the service charter and requests for change.
- Release and deployment management ensures that the customer and service provider are prepared and trained to manage and use the service, and that the service is deployed in a manner that causes minimal disruption to the business.
- Knowledge management documents how to use information and knowledge about the organization and services to make sound decisions about the management and delivery of the service. Knowledge management also stores, protects, maintains and shares all the documents, information and knowledge needed to design, transition and operate the service.

4.2.5.27 Charter: track progress and update service portfolio

As the design, build and deployment teams progress the work on the service, updates are provided to service portfolio management, and the service portfolio updated. This can be automated by linking project management tools to portfolio management tools.

The purpose of this tracking and updating is to ensure that the estimated levels of investment and capability were accurate. If the cost of the service significantly exceeds the estimate, service portfolio management will escalate the situation to the stakeholders. Since each project is ultimately driven as part of the strategy, the executives will be notified and a decision made as to whether to support the increased level of investment or discontinue the project and re-assess the strategy.

4.2.5.28 Service successful?

This check is similar to the post-implementation review in change management, except it is broader in scope. The question here is whether the service has met the requirements of the strategy, and is contributing to the achievement of business outcomes as specified by the stakeholders.

Important note on tracking and updating

The management of stakeholders and project escalation is part of the project management methodology used. This means that both service portfolio management and the PMO (or project manager) must agree on the logistics of escalation. However, since service portfolio management issues the service charter for the project, it is normal for the first escalation to go to service portfolio management.

The success of a service is determined through a range of measures, but will largely depend on whether it performed in operation as it was designed and tested. Therefore the service operation processes will play an important role, especially:

- **Event management** Did events for the service fall within the normal range of activity? Did informational events indicate normal utilization? Were the alerts related to normal operations intervention, or were they related to exceptions?
- **Incident management** How many incidents were related to this service? What levels of impact and urgency were involved? Were they the result of a service defect or a lack in user training?
- **Problem management** How many defects were found in the service? Was it possible to identify a workaround and/or a permanent solution? Was the solution effective in preventing recurring incidents?

If the service is not successful, it is not simply rebuilt. Rather it will need to be analysed again to determine what additional funding would be required to correct the service. If it is large, the additional investment might reduce the overall value of the service to the extent where the return on investment is negligible. In that case the customers or the organization's executives might decide to modify their strategy. The service would be retired and work will begin on ensuring that the modified strategy can be supported.

4.2.5.29 Retiring services

Retiring a service refers to decommissioning or formally removing the service from live use. At that point it is no longer used by customers or users. It is removed from the service catalogue and cannot be requested. It is also removed from live use through service transition processes.

Services are retired for a number of reasons, including:

- The strategy of the organization has changed.
- The technology used by the business has changed, and the service no longer supports the new technology (see the example below).
- Organizations have merged or been acquired and duplicate services are retired.
- The service no longer supports the achievement of business outcomes.
- The return on the investment made in that service is no longer viable.
- The customer (or business) decides to source the service from an alternative (or external) service provider.

Retired services are usually maintained in case a business need arises that the service can meet, or in case the original business requirement re-emerges. For example, a shipping company communicated exclusively by telex. With the advent of email, the telex service was retired. After some years, the company decided to open a route to a country which still used telexes and faxes as a primary communication medium. The telex service was reinstated and integrated into the email system.

Once the service is retired it is usually maintained for some period of time, or until there are alternative services that would be able to deliver the same functionality if needed.

4.2.5.30 Refreshing the portfolio

Conditions and markets change, invalidating prior ROI calculations. Some services may no longer be optimal due to compliance or regulatory concerns. Events occur such as mergers and acquisitions, divestitures, new public legislation or redeployed missions. The CIO is responsible for the overall balance of investments, and relies on the service portfolio management process for monitoring, measuring and re-assessing these investments. The CIO is then able to make decisions about making trade-offs as business needs change. Not all services need be low risk or high reward. Instead, by seeking an efficient portfolio with optimal levels of ROI and risk, the organization is maximizing the value realization on its constrained and limited resources and capabilities.

This requires a regular, formal review of the portfolio that compares the services and investments with the IT strategy and the overall organizational strategy. The frequency of these reviews should be at a minimum of quarterly, and not just when the strategy is being produced. These reviews can be done as part of regular CSI activities.

4.2.6 Triggers, inputs, outputs and interfaces

4.2.6.1 Triggers

Triggers of service portfolio management include:

- A new strategy has been devised, or an existing strategy is being changed. This does not necessarily have to be in the form of a plan before service portfolio management is involved. A change to a perspective, position or pattern of action might impact existing services or service models. Service portfolio management could be used as part of the analysis of any potential impact.
- Business relationship management receives a request for a new service or a change to an existing service. Service portfolio management helps to define and formalize this request before submitting it to change management in the form of a change proposal.
- Service improvement opportunities from CSI.
- Feedback from design, build and transition teams to indicate the status of the service during the charter stage of the process. If these reports indicate a deviation from the specifications, cost or release time, service portfolio management will be involved in estimating the impact of this, and defining corrective action.
- Service level management reviews that identify a service is not meeting its expected outcomes or that it is not being used in the way it was intended.
- Financial management for IT services indicates that a service costs significantly more or less than anticipated, thus impacting the potential return on investment for that service.

4.2.6.2 Inputs

Inputs to service portfolio management include:

- Strategy plans
- Service improvement opportunities

- Financial reports
- Requests, suggestions or complaints from the business
- Project updates for services in the charter stage of the process.

4.2.6.3 Outputs

Outputs from service portfolio management include:

- An up-to-date service portfolio
- Service charters that authorize the work for designing and building new services or changes to existing services
- Reports on the status of new or changed services
- Reports on the investment made in services in the service portfolio, and the returns on that investment
- Change proposals that are used to allow change management to assess and schedule the work and resources required to charter services
- Identified strategic risks.

4.2.6.4 Interfaces

Major service portfolio management interfaces include:

- Service catalogue management is closely linked with service portfolio management in that the service catalogue is part of the service portfolio. However, service portfolio management determines which services will be placed into the service catalogue, while service catalogue management performs all the activities required for this to be done.
- Strategy management for IT services defines the overall strategy of services, and therefore determines what type of services should be included in the portfolio, and which should not. It also determines the objectives for investments (what levels of investment can be made and what the anticipated returns should be), and the ideal market spaces which will be targeted.
- Financial management for IT services provides information and tools to enable service portfolio management to perform return on investment calculations. In addition financial management for IT services also helps to track the actual costs of services to enable service portfolio management to track the accuracy of

forecasts. This will be used to improve the analysis of services in the future.
- Demand management provides information about the patterns of business activity that is used to determine the utilization and expected return on investment for the service.
- Business relationship management initiates requests and obtains business information and requirements that are used in defining services and evaluating whether they would provide a sufficient return on investment. Business relationship management also keeps customers informed about the status of services in service portfolio management.
- Service level management ensures that services are able to achieve the levels of performance defined in service portfolio management and provides feedback when this is not the case.
- Capacity management and availability management ensure that the capacity and availability requirements of chartered services are designed and built.
- IT service continuity management identifies the business impact of risks associated with delivering the service, and designs counter-measures and recovery plans to ensure that the service is able to achieve the objectives defined during service portfolio management.
- Information security management ensures that the confidentiality, integrity and availability objectives defined during service portfolio management are met.
- The supplier management process indicates that a suppler will no longer be able to supply services or that a supplier relationship is at risk.
- Change management evaluates the resources required to introduce new services or changes to existing services, thus enabling the service to be chartered. Change management also ensures that all changes involved in designing, building and releasing the service are controlled and coordinated.
- Service asset and configuration management provides the tools, information and data upon which the service portfolio is based. It also provides data and information for service models.
- Service validation and testing ensures that the anticipated functionality and returns of each service can be achieved.

- Knowledge management enables IT managers and architects to make informed decisions about the best service options to meet the organization's objectives.
- Continual service improvement provides feedback about the actual use and return of services against their anticipated use and return. This information is used to improve services and make changes about the mix and availability of services in the service portfolio.

4.2.7 Information management

The documentation and information required for effective service portfolio management have been described throughout section 4.2, but an overview of the main sources is as follows:

- The service portfolio, consisting of a service pipeline, service catalogue and retired services.
- The project portfolio to manage services that have been chartered and are being designed and built.
- The application portfolio that allows service portfolio management to understand the relationship between applications and services.
- The customer portfolio and customer agreement portfolio that allows service portfolio management to understand customer requirements, the services that have been designed to meet those services, and the agreements which have been made to deliver the services.
- Service models which allow service portfolio management to understand the composition and dynamics of a service before it moves into expensive design and build activity. Service models also indicate where a service may leverage existing investments.
- The service strategy, which provides a framework of anticipated opportunities, constraints, objectives and desired business outcomes. Service portfolio management is expected to define what mix of services can best meet the strategic objectives of the organization.
- The configuration management system provides data and information that supports the development and assessment of service models and the assessment of new services and changes to existing services.

4.2.8 Critical success factors and key performance indicators

This section provides examples of critical success factors (CSFs). These are the conditions that need to be in place, or things that need to happen, if the service portfolio management process is to be considered successful. Each CSF will include examples of key performance indicators (KPIs). These are metrics that are used to evaluate factors that are crucial to the success of the process. KPIs, as differentiated from general metrics, should be related to CSFs.

The following list includes some sample CSFs for service portfolio management. Each organization should identify appropriate CSFs based on its objectives for the process. Each sample CSF is followed by a small number of typical KPIs that support the CSF. These KPIs should not be adopted without careful consideration. Each organization should develop KPIs that are appropriate for its level of maturity, its CSFs and its particular circumstances. Achievement against KPIs should be monitored and used to identify opportunities for improvement, which should be logged in the CSI register for evaluation and possible implementation.

- **CSF** The existence of a formal process to investigate and decide which services to provide
  - **KPI** A formal service portfolio management process exists under the ownership of the service portfolio management process owner.
  - **KPI** The service portfolio management process is audited and reviewed annually and meets its objectives.
- **CSF** A model to analyse the potential return on investment and acceptable level of risk for new services or changes to existing services
  - **KPI** Every service has a documented statement of the initial investment made in the service.
  - **KPI** Accounting records are produced on a monthly or quarterly basis to show the ongoing investment in each service. These are compared with the business outcomes that have been achieved and the return on investment is calculated.
  - **KPI** Customer surveys indicate a high level of satisfaction with the value they are receiving.

- **KPI** Each service has documented risks associated with it. The service portfolio will identify what mitigation or counter-measures have been taken, and where the customer has decided to live with the risk.
- **CSF** The ability to document each service provided, together with the business need it meets and the business outcome it supports
  - **KPI** A service portfolio exists and is used as the basis for deciding which services to offer. An audit shows that every service is documented in the service portfolio.
  - **KPI** There is a documented process for defining the business need and business outcome, which is formally owned by the service portfolio management process owner.
  - **KPI** Each service in the service portfolio is linked to at least one business outcome. This is verified through a regular review of the service portfolio.
- **CSF** A formal process to review whether services are enabling the organization to achieve its strategy
  - **KPI** Service portfolio management provides regular and structured feedback to strategy management for IT services regarding the performance of each service and its ability to meet stated business outcomes.
  - **KPI** An audit of strategy documents and the service portfolio shows that the business outcomes in the service portfolio are consistent with those stated in the relevant strategy.
- **CSF** The ability to change services in response to changes in the internal and external environments – where appropriate
  - **KPI** Every change to an external or internal environment identified in strategy management for IT services has a corresponding entry to service portfolio management, and each of these has been evaluated and a decision made about the need for change to the relevant services.
  - **KPI** A review of the organization's strategy shows that all changed business objectives and outcomes continue to be met by the services in the service portfolio.
  - **KPI** Customer surveys show continued high levels of satisfaction.

- **CSF** Tools that enable the service provider to track the investment in services throughout their lifecycle
  - **KPI** The investment in each service is quantified in the service portfolio.
  - **KPI** Investment in each service is reported, starting with the initial investment, and followed by monthly, quarterly or annual reporting on ongoing investments.
  - **KPI** The investments made are consistent with the projected return on investment forecasts.
- **CSF** A formal process exists to evaluate the viability of services, and to retire them when they are no longer viable
  - **KPI** Number of services retired.
  - **KPI** Number of services reinstated after being retired (this will indicate the level of accuracy of evaluating viability).

4.2.9 Challenges and risks

4.2.9.1 Challenges

Challenges for service portfolio management include:

- Lack of access to customer business information, which will prevent service portfolio management from understanding the desired business outcomes and strategies.
- Absence of a formal project management approach. This will mean that it is more difficult to charter services and track them through the design and transition stages.
- Absence of a project portfolio – which will make it difficult to assess the impact of new initiatives on new services or proposed changes to services.
- Absence of a customer portfolio and customer agreement portfolio, which will make it difficult to identify the objectives, use and return on investment of services.
- A service portfolio that only focuses on the service provider aspects of services. This will make it difficult to calculate the value of services, model future utilization or validate the customer requirements for the service.
- The lack of a formal change management process, which can be used to control the introduction of new services, or manage changes to existing services.

4.2.9.2 Risks

Service portfolio management risks include:

- Making a decision to offer services without validated or complete information. Often customer pressure to offer a service means that the decision is rushed, and service portfolio management has not completed a full investigation of the risks associated with the service.
- Offering services without defining how they will be measured. It is very difficult to calculate the return on investment of a service that has not been designed around a clear value proposition. In situations where cost cutting is being considered, service providers may find themselves being forced to eliminate services which appear to be valuable, but for which no tangible returns can be demonstrated.

4.3 FINANCIAL MANAGEMENT FOR IT SERVICES

Financial management is a complex process that all organizations use as a basis for conducting business. It is usually owned by a senior executive and managed by a financial management function. Financial management enables the organization to manage its resources, and to ensure that these resources are being used to achieve the organization's objectives.

The IT organization, along with all other departments in the organization, is involved in the organization's financial management process. They apply the organization's financial management procedures and practices to ensure that they are aligned with the organization's objectives and financial policies. In doing so, these departments often create their own financial management processes.

ITIL Service Strategy recognizes that these two layers of financial management exist within most organizations, and refers to financial management as a general process used by the organization, as well as to financial management as it is applied by an IT service provider. In this section, the text will therefore use the term 'financial management' as follows:

- **Financial management** This refers to the generic use of the term.
- **Enterprise financial management** This refers specifically to the process as it is used by the 'corporate' financial department.
- **Financial management for IT services** This refers to the way in which the IT service provider has applied the process.

Financial management for IT services is the process responsible for managing an IT service provider's budgeting, accounting and charging requirements. It is also the process that is used to quantify the value that IT services contribute to the business.

Finance is the common language which allows the service provider to communicate effectively with their customers and other business units. Financial management enables the service provider to develop the capabilities of operational visibility, insight and superior decision-making. Just as business units are able to generate value by analysing product mix and margin data, or customer profiles and product behaviour, financial data continues to increase the importance of financial management for IT and the business as well.

More than any other process, financial management enables an IT service provider to play a strategic role in the business. It helps to quantify IT's value and contributions, and quantifies the business opportunities that IT services enable.

Financial management as a strategic tool is equally applicable to all three service provider types. Internal service providers are increasingly asked to operate with the same levels of financial visibility and accountability as their business unit and external counterparts. Moreover, technology and innovation have become the core revenue-generating capabilities of many companies.

Financial management provides the business and IT with the quantification, in financial terms, of the value of IT services, the value of the assets used to provide those services, and the qualification of operational forecasting. Talking about IT in terms of services is a crucial aspect of changing the perception of IT and its value to the business. Therefore, a significant portion of financial management is working in tandem with IT and the business to help identify, document and agree on the value of the services being received, and the enablement of service demand modelling and management.

Organizations that simply report on how much money was spent by IT and then allocate it back to the business units are finding it increasingly difficult to quantify the value of specific IT services. When customers see the amount of money spent on IT as a lump sum, they tend to forget all the individual services they use and the value they obtain from each one. Instead these customers demand increasing (often unreasonable) levels of service without wanting to pay any additional money. When IT is unable to deliver without asking for more money, they are perceived as a drain on the organization's finances.

Important note on financial management

Financial management is a complex, specialized area and it is beyond the scope of this publication to provide a detailed description of the whole of financial management. Financial management should be managed and performed by skilled and trained professionals, even within the IT environment.

However, all levels of management are required to understand financial management at a high level. Accountants will require information from other managers, and it is helpful if they understand the basic concepts and language of finance. *ITIL Service Strategy* therefore provides an overview of the main practices of financial management as related to service management in general, and IT service management in particular.

4.3.1 Purpose and objectives

The purpose of financial management for IT services is to secure the appropriate level of funding to design, develop and deliver services that meet the strategy of the organization. At the same time financial management for IT services is a gatekeeper that ensures that the service provider does not commit to services that they are not able to provide. Financial management for IT services identifies the balance between the cost and quality of service and maintains the balance of supply and demand between the service provider and their customers.

For example, a customer asks an internal service provider to provide a service at a certain level. If the service provider is able to quantify the initial investment and ongoing costs of that service, the customer can make a decision as to whether that service will provide sufficient value to cover the costs. If the internal service provider is not able to quantify the costs, then they will be put under significant pressure to deliver the service at the highest possible level.

The objectives of financial management for IT services include:

- Defining and maintaining a framework to identify, manage and communicate the cost of providing services.
- Evaluating the financial impact of new or changed strategies on the service provider.
- Securing funding to manage the provision of services.
- Facilitating good stewardship of service and customer assets to ensure the organization meets its objectives. This should be done together with service asset and configuration management and knowledge management.
- Understanding the relationship between expenses and income and ensuring that the two are balanced according to the organization's financial policies.
- Managing and reporting expenditure on service provision on behalf of the organization's stakeholders.
- Executing the financial policies and practices in the provision of services.
- Accounting for money spent on the creation, delivery and support of services.
- Forecasting the financial requirements for the organization to be able to meet its service commitments to its customers, and compliance with regulatory and legislative requirements.
- Where appropriate, defining a framework to recover the costs of service provision from the customer.

4.3.2 Scope

Financial management is normally a well-established and well-understood part of any organization. Professional accountants manage dedicated finance departments, which set financial policies, budgeting procedures, financial reporting standards, accounting practices and revenue generation or cost recovery rules.

In an IT context, financial management is often a separate function either reporting to the CIO or the chief financial officer (CFO), but with some form of functional reporting between the two areas. Regardless of where the function is actually situated in the organization, financial management for IT services is a specialized area that requires an understanding of the world of finance and business as well as the world of technology.

A common misunderstanding is that all accountants are the same – without understanding that there are different specializations in accounting. Specifically, financial management for IT services requires accountants with a good understanding of cost accounting – a discipline often found in manufacturing environments. It is important that the correct skills are specified when hiring a person to manage IT finances.

Financial policies and practices within IT must be consistent with those of the rest of the organization. This is not only a requirement of most financial management legislation, regulations and best practice, but it also facilitates better communication and reporting between IT and other business units.

In internal service providers financial management plays a translational role between corporate financial systems and service management. The result of a service-oriented accounting function is that far greater detail and understanding is achieved regarding service provision and consumption, and the generation of data that feeds directly into the planning process.

Financial management consists of three main processes:

- **Budgeting** This is the process of predicting and controlling the income and expenditure of money within the organization. Budgeting consists of a periodic negotiation cycle to set budgets (usually annual) and the monthly monitoring of the current budgets.
- **Accounting** This is the process that enables the IT organization to account fully for the way its money is spent (particularly the ability to identify costs by customer, by service and by activity). It usually involves accounting systems, including ledgers, charts of accounts, journals etc. and should be overseen by someone trained in accountancy.

- **Charging** This is the process required to bill customers for the services supplied to them. This requires sound IT accounting practices and systems.

Table 4.4 shows that there are two distinct cycles associated with accounting, budgeting and charging:

- A planning cycle (annual), where cost projections and workload forecasting form a basis for cost calculations and price setting
- An operational cycle (monthly or quarterly) where costs are monitored and checked against budgets, bills are issued and revenue collected.

Table 4.4 Budgeting, IT accounting and charging cycles

	Budgeting	IT accounting	Charging
Planning (annual)	Agree overall expenditures	Establish standard unit costs for each IT resource	Establish pricing policy and publish price list
Operational (monthly)	Take actions to manage budget exceptions or changed costs	Monitor expenditure by cost centre	Compile and issue bills

4.3.3 Value to business

The landscape of IT is changing as strategic business and delivery models evolve rapidly, product development cycles shrink and disposable designer products become ubiquitous. These dynamics create what often appears to IT professionals as a dichotomy of priorities: increasing demands on performance and strategic business alignment, combined with greater demand for superior operational visibility and control. Much like their business counterparts, IT organizations are increasingly using financial management to assist in the pursuit of:

- Enhanced decision-making
- Speed of change
- Service portfolio management
- Financial compliance and control
- Operational control
- Value capture and creation.

Internal IT organizations are conceding that they are quite similar to market-facing companies. They share the need to analyse, package, market and deliver services just as any other business. They also share a common and increasing need to understand and control factors of demand and supply, and to provide services as cost-effectively as possible while maximizing visibility into related cost structures.

Financial management provides information that is valuable in generating strategies, and in moving from the way in which assets are used currently to how they need to be used to achieve new strategic initiatives. Rigorously applied, financial management generates meaningful critical performance information used to answer important questions for an organization:

- Is our differentiation strategy resulting in higher profits or revenues, lower costs or greater service adoption?
- Which services cost us the most, and why?
- What are our volumes and types of consumed services, and what is the correlating budget requirement?
- How efficient are our service provision models in relation to alternatives?
- Does our strategic approach to service design result in services that can be offered at a competitive 'market price', substantially reduce risk or offer superior value?
- Where are our greatest service inefficiencies?
- Which functional areas represent the highest priority opportunities for us to focus on as we generate a CSI strategy?

Without meaningful operational financial information, it is not possible to answer these questions correctly, and strategic decisions become little more than instinctive responses to flawed or limited observations and information, often from a single organizational unit. Such methods can often incorrectly steer strategy, service design and tactical operational decisions.

Specific benefits to the business include:

- The ability to conduct business in a financially responsible manner and to comply with regulatory and legislative requirements and generally accepted accounting principles. This will allow the business to operate legally and avoid heavy penalties for non-compliance.

- Accurate planning and forecasting of the budget needed to cover the cost of service.
- An understanding of the cost of IT to each business unit will allow IT service providers to recover the costs through their services and (for Type III service providers) maintain profitability. Many organizations fail to account for IT costs when doing business, and find their profit margins shrinking uncontrollably when IT costs are allocated at the end of each financial period.
- Better matching of IT services to business outcomes results in more appropriate and controllable spending models, and more predictable profitability.
- The ability to make sound business decisions regarding the use of and investment in IT.

4.3.4 Policies, principles and basic concepts

4.3.4.1 Enterprise financial management policies

Each organization applies the rules, practices and local laws of financial management according to their specific business, structure and culture. Financial management for IT services is an application of the financial management policies and practices of the organization as a whole and must therefore follow the policies and practices of the organization as a whole.

Example of the value of financial management in decisions regarding cloud

When making a decision to source services from a cloud service provider, an organization is essentially changing its capital expenditure (where large infrastructure investments are made and depreciated over time) into operational expenditure (where money is spent on services that have no asset value).

A cloud service provider will experience exactly the converse. In order to provide services, it will need to make a significant capital investment in infrastructure, applications etc.

Exactly how these decisions impact each organization will be impossible to measure without an adequate financial management approach and systems. Financial management is therefore key to the strategy of service providers.

The enterprise financial management policies provide a framework within which IT must work to manage all financial aspects of its services and organization. Policies that impact an IT service provider might include:

- What level of financial expenditure needs to be tracked (e.g. cost per desktop device, or the total cost of all desktops)
- Which configuration items need to be recorded as financial assets and how they should be classified
- How fixed assets are depreciated
- How taxes are managed (for example, an IT service that is sold externally is reported differently from an IT service that is only used internally)
- How costs are reported
- How revenue is accounted for (and linked to IT services)
- Whether the cost of services will be accounted for individually, or whether the overall cost of IT will be calculated and allocated back to the business units
- Requirements to comply with legislative or other regulatory requirements.

An important policy decision to be made is whether IT will be a profit or cost centre. This is a decision made by the organization's executives, not by IT management. This is because IT, as a business unit, is subject to the same governance as any other business unit. Although IT executives may be asked to participate in making that decision, this is ultimately a matter of enterprise financial policy. Definitions of these two options are:

- **Cost centre** Two definitions for the term 'cost centre' are commonly used in business. Although they appear close in meaning, they are different. In this context the term is used to indicate a business unit or department to which costs are assigned, but which does not charge for services provided. It is, however, expected to account for the money it spends, and may be expected to show a return on the business's investment in it. A cost centre is able to focus awareness on costs and enable investment decisions to be better founded, without the overheads of billing. However, it is less likely to shape users' behaviour and does not give the IT organization the full ability to choose how to financially manage itself (for example, in

funding IT investment). The other definition for the term 'cost centre' is used in the context of accounting, and is described in section 4.3.5.4. Care should be taken to read the context of the term to ensure the correct meaning is inferred.

- **Profit centre** A business unit that charges for providing services. A profit centre can be created with the objective of making a profit, recovering costs or running at a loss. As a profit centre IT is able to exercise greater autonomy, even to the extent that it can be operated as a separate business entity, under the ownership and direction of the corporate entity. IT will also be able to achieve better cost control over service provision and calculate the true costs of IT by customers. Charging other business units in the same organization can be useful in demonstrating the value that the service provider delivers, and in ensuring that funding is obtained from an appropriate source (i.e. the customer that uses the services).

A Type III service provider is a profit centre, since it is a business in its own right. However, the different units within the company (IT, HR, sales, marketing etc.) will be seen as either cost or profit centres, just as they would in any enterprise.

4.3.4.2 Funding

Funding is the sourcing and allocation of money for a specific purpose or project. For IT service management funding refers to the means whereby an IT service provider obtains financial resources that pay for the design, transition, operation and improvement of IT services.

Funding comes from two sources, external and internal:

- **External funding** Comes from revenue that is received from selling services to external customers. External funding for IT services is not the same as revenue, however, since revenue can be used to fund multiple projects or departments. For example, an application hosting service is provided to external customers and earns revenue of £100,000. That revenue might be used to partially fund the HR department, the sales department and the customer service department as well as the IT organization that actually delivers the service. Ultimately, how the money is allocated is a function of the enterprise financial management policies.

- **Internal funding** Comes from other business units inside the same organization. Internal funding, however, is not truly internal. All funding ultimately comes from outside the organization – in the form of revenue from business services, investments from shareholders, grants from donors (for charitable organizations) or allocation from government funding (government agencies). Failure to recognize the true source of funding often results in incorrectly prioritized services, or services that are simply inappropriate for the organization's mission.

The decision of how IT services will be funded is an important one, and will ultimately impact the makeup of services in the service portfolio, the quality of services and the models used to design, transition, operate and improve those services.

How IT is funded will also depend on whether IT will be viewed as a cost or a profit centre. As a cost centre funding is based only on replenishing actual costs expended to deliver service. By contrast, a profit centre is often funded based on the actual costs plus a perceived value-added amount. The capture of this additional value above actual cost is not confined to external providers, as internal service providers also need to continually expand their offerings and fund the analysis of provision alternatives and service quality enhancements.

Funding models

Funding models help to define how and when the IT service provider will be funded. Each model uses the same financial data, adapted to the organizational culture and enterprise financial management policies. In each case the aim is to provide the organization with clarity about how IT is funded and what it achieves with that funding. The funding model chosen should always take into account and be appropriate for the current business culture and expectations. Funding models include:

- **Rolling plan funding** A rolling plan is a plan for a fixed number of months, years or other cycles. At the end of the first cycle, the plan is simply extended by one more cycle. In effect this means that the plan always covers the same amount of time or number of cycles, and is continually adjusted to meet changing

conditions. This type of planning is used in more volatile or dynamic environments. The advantage of this type of funding model is that it allows the service provider to adjust funding requirements as necessary and also to obtain funding more readily (since they do not always have to wait until the beginning of the next financial year to obtain funding). However, most organizations only use this type of planning and funding for specific projects, not the ongoing provision of all IT services.

- **Trigger-based funding** In this model a plan is initiated and funding is provided when a specific situation or event occurs. For example, the change management process would be a trigger to the planning process for all authorized changes that have financial impacts. Another trigger might be capacity planning where capacity utilization might indicate that an upgrade or migration is required.

- **Zero-based funding** Most internal service providers are funded using this model, since it is based on ensuring that IT breaks even. In this model IT is allowed to spend up to the agreed budget amount, or get special approval to spend over the amount, and at the end of the financial period (monthly, quarterly or annually) the money is recovered from the other business units through cost transfers. This equates to funding only the actual costs to deliver the IT services.

4.3.4.3 Financial management for IT services and value

Chapter 3 discusses the concept of value and services in detail. This paragraph simply reminds the reader that it is impossible to calculate the value of services without clearly defined and properly executed practices for financial management for IT services.

However, this does not mean that the whole responsibility for demonstrating value should be the responsibility of the service provider. The appropriate financial management models and practices need to be in place in both the service provider and their customers – since the calculation of value is a joint responsibility of both the service provider and the customer. If they have a different understanding of how costs and returns are calculated it will be impossible to demonstrate the value of IT services.

For more information on value, calculating value and the roles of the service provider and customer in defining value see the discussion on service economics in section 3.6.

4.3.4.4 Compliance

Compliance relates to the ability to demonstrate that proper and consistent accounting methods and/or practices are being employed. This includes financial asset valuation, capitalization practices, revenue recognition, access and security controls etc. If proper practices are documented and known, compliance can be easily addressed. However, it is important that enterprise financial management policies clearly outline what legislative and other regulatory requirements apply to the service provider and the customer's organization.

Over the past decade a number of important regulatory and standards-related issues and opportunities have been introduced that impact financial management. Certain legislation has had enormous impact on financial audit and compliance activities. The public demand for accurate, meaningful data regarding the value of a company's transactions and assets places greater pressure on enterprise financial management. There are wide variations in the impact of such legislation that should be considered.

Public frameworks such as COBIT and the advice and consent of public accountants and auditors are valuable to service management. The implementation of public frameworks and standards such as COBIT, ISO/IEC 20000, Management of Risk (M_o_R); and regulations such as Basel II and Sarbanes-Oxley, and other industry-specific regulation may appear to be pure costs with no tangible benefits. However, regulatory compliance tends to improve data security and quality processes, creating a greater need for understanding the costs of compliance. Services provided to one industry at a certain price may not necessarily be provided at the same price to a different industry segment. There are instances where the cost of compliance has been large enough to have an impact on the pricing of a service.

4.3.5 Process activities, methods and techniques

It should be stressed once again that this section does not cover every aspect of financial management. It is aimed at providing an overview of best practices with which IT managers will be expected to be involved. Also, note that financial management practices vary from country to country and organization to organization. It is important to adapt any guidance provided in this publication to local laws, policies and practices.

The major inputs, outputs and activities of financial management for IT services are illustrated in Figure 4.25 and described in the rest of section 4.3.

4.3.5.1 Major inputs

Each of the inputs in Figure 4.25 also receives outputs from financial management for IT services. For ease of reference these are described here and referred to again in section 4.3.6.

Regulatory requirements

Financial management is subject to legislation and requirements from other regulatory bodies. The aim of these requirements is to prevent fraudulent activity, ensure that the stakeholders' interests are protected and facilitate ethical and legal activity by the organization and its leaders.

Regulatory requirements (such as Sarbanes-Oxley) and good financial practices, such as Generally Accepted Accounting Practices (GAAP), will form the basis for enterprise financial management policies. An important role of financial management is to ensure compliance with regulatory requirements.

Enterprise financial management policies

Enterprise financial management policies should be documented by the organization's senior finance executives and made available to all staff members managing financial functions and processes. These policies will define how the activities in enterprise financial management work and how they relate to similar activities at an enterprise level.

These policies will, in turn, have to be refined based on the specific accounting, budgeting and charging requirements of the service provider.

Service management processes

Each service management process provides financial information about how money is spent, what services are provided and what commitments have been made to customers. This information is used to analyse the most appropriate funding and accounting models for the service provider to ensure that the appropriate levels of service are provided at the appropriate cost.

Financial management provides each service management process with input about how money should be spent, what returns are expected and

how to record their activity so that it can be measured from a financial perspective.

Service, contract, customer, application and project portfolios

Each of these portfolios contains financial information that is used to analyse investments in services and the corresponding returns.

Financial management for IT services helps to define the boundaries of what services can be

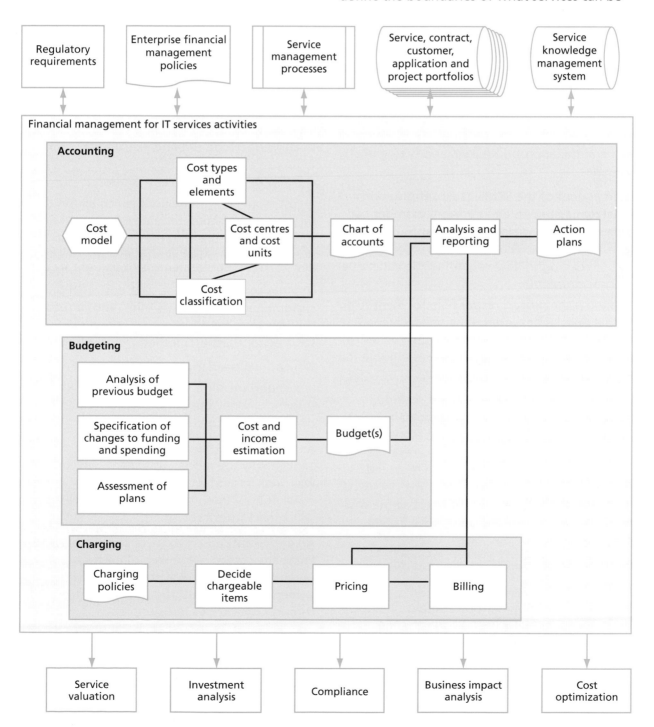

Figure 4.25 Major inputs, outputs and activities of financial management for IT services

offered, and under what terms and conditions. Financial management for IT services ensures that the service provider only commits to deliver services that meet the required levels of return. In other words, financial management input to the portfolios prevents over-commitment by the service provider.

Service knowledge management system

The SKMS provides specific information about the service assets and any related investments. This information helps financial management for IT services to align specific assets to a service, or services, so that they can be appropriately accounted for and, where necessary, priced.

Financial management for IT services will provide data that is used as part of the SKMS to support decision-making about the balance of cost and quality, and the appropriate level and timing of investments.

One component of the SKMS, the configuration management system, is an important provider of data about the financial aspects of configuration items.

4.3.5.2 Accounting

Accounting is the process responsible for identifying the actual costs of delivering IT services, comparing these with budgeted costs and managing variance from the budget. Accounting is also responsible for tracking any income earned by services.

It should be noted that income is not recorded against services where revenue was earned indirectly. For example, if IT delivers a service to a business unit that uses the service to perform a revenue-producing activity, the income will be recorded against the business unit activity, not the IT service. In these cases the business unit will record the cost of the IT service and link the cost to the income it earned.

Accounting enables the service provider to:

- Track actual costs against budget
- Support the development of a sound investment strategy which recognizes and evaluates the options and flexibility available from modern technology
- Provide cost targets for service performance and delivery
- Facilitate prioritization of resource usage

- Make decisions with full understanding of the cost implications and hence the minimum of risk
- Support the introduction, if required, of charging for IT services
- Review the financial consequences of previous strategic decisions to enable the organization to learn and improve.

As accounting processes and practices mature and become more service-oriented, they provide more evidence of the contribution and performance of the IT organization. As accounting enables IT to track financial information according to services (service account) rather than as a set of expenses and investments (cost account), it dramatically changes the dynamics and visibility of service management, enabling a higher level of service strategy development and execution.

4.3.5.3 Accounting: cost model

A cost model is a framework which allows the service provider to determine the costs of providing services and ensure that they are allocated correctly. Cost models also enable the service provider to understand the impact of proposed changes to the current service, customer and customer agreement portfolios, and proposed changes to current financial management for IT services approaches, methods and techniques.

Why do we need a cost model?

It is important for a service provider to know what it spends money on, but that information on its own is not enough.

Knowing where money has been spent does not explain why the money was spent, which services it was used for and whether the customer received value. It also doesn't explain how business demand will impact future spending.

An important reason to understand costs is to know the cost of ownership of each service, and to understand what things make that cost of ownership rise or fall, and how to control that through the various decisions made in portfolio management, change management etc.

A cost model provides a framework that identifies where money is being spent, but also links that expenditure to specific services and/or customers. If financial management for IT services is able to link specific costs to specific services and customers, then it will be able to predict how changes to those services will impact the cost of IT. Alternatively, changes to technology or increases in the price of an item can be accurately communicated to the customer of the affected services. With this type of information service provider managers and customers are able to make better decisions about their service requirements and delivery options.

Another reason for using cost models is that there are different types of cost, and they all behave differently. Some costs will increase, some will decrease, while others will fluctuate. Some costs are spread over several years, while others will only ever happen once. A cost model makes it easy to identify these dynamics and make sense of them, so that the service provider can accurately forecast its expenditure, understand the relative cost and value of services and communicate effectively with customers about the terms and conditions under which services will be delivered and supported.

Another major issue for many organizations is that most IT investments are shared across multiple services and/or multiple customers. The fundamental question is 'how do we split these shared costs fairly?'. If too much is allocated to a specific service, it will become uncompetitive; if too little is allocated, it makes a loss every time it is used. This allocation needs to be well planned and implemented, and based on accurate information. The cost model provides a financial baseline that is used as input into how the service provider will identify charges or service pricing – and thus prevent unfair cost recovery models, which could result in a dispute with customers.

A cost model is not just a more sophisticated financial classification framework; it allows the service provider to structure financial information into a format that supports its strategy, tactics and operations. A cost model creates a standard format that will be used to analyse and report on the services it delivers, requests for new or changed services and the customers it supports. That format will translate all the factors involved in providing services into terms that are meaningful for the business, and which will facilitate good decision-making by both the service provider and the customer.

Cost models enable a service provider to calculate and communicate the cost of ownership of a service. This is a fundamental tool in understanding

the value of IT and ensuring that the business is able to influence its investment in IT.

It is possible for a service provider to define more than one cost model, especially where groups of services or customers are distinct from one another. For example, an organization that provides services to the military at the same time as providing services to commercial customers will need different approaches to finance.

The cost model defines the following policies and practices:

- How expenditure items will be recorded and tracked
- How each item will be classified in accounting terms
- How costs will be allocated to services and/or customers
- How costs will be reported.

There are a number of cost models to choose from, depending on the type of organization and the financial objectives. For IT service providers the five most commonly used are discussed below. However, please note that the diagrams and accompanying descriptions are examples only – there are any number of ways in which these cost models can be defined.

Cost by IT organization

This model is typically only used in internal service providers with multiple IT organizations. In this model each IT organization accounts for its costs and reports them to the enterprise financial management function. These costs are analysed and then allocated to various business units and other functions based on one or more of a number of factors. These include number of users, number of PCs, percentage of overall utilization of IT services etc.

This cost model is illustrated in Figure 4.26.

In Figure 4.26 all costs are accounted for by the IT organization that spends the money. In this cost model direct costs are any costs that are incurred by a single IT organization (for example, salaries of employees in that department). Indirect costs are costs that are shared by multiple departments (for example, the costs of the network backbone). Direct and indirect costs, and methods of allocating these costs, are discussed in section 4.3.5.6.

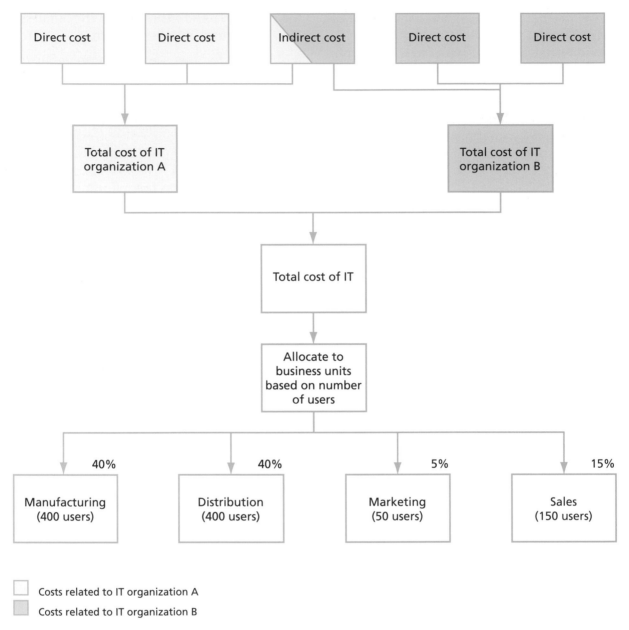

Figure 4.26 Cost by IT organization

Once the total cost of all IT organizations is added up, the total cost of IT is allocated to the business units. In Figure 4.26 the number of users in each business unit is used as a way of allocating the cost of IT and the percentage of costs allocated to each business unit is indicated above the name of the business unit. In this example the following calculation was used:

Percentage of IT costs allocated to business unit = Number of users in business unit / Total number of users ×100

The advantages of the 'cost by IT organization' model are:

■ It is cheap, since all that is being used are the organization's existing accounting tools and staff.
■ It is easy to calculate and allocate costs.
■ It is easy to track IT expenditure and measure changes in spending patterns over time. This may indicate areas of inefficiency over time.

However, the disadvantages far outweigh the above. These include:

■ The business is able to see the cost of IT, but cannot quantify the cost of the services they use. This makes it difficult to quantify the value of the services.

■ There is no assurance that the number of users is a fair reflection of how a business unit uses IT services. In the above example, although Manufacturing and Distribution have the same number of users, Manufacturing only uses IT half as much as Distribution. This means that Manufacturing is paying double for IT, and the price of products will have to be set higher than necessary to cover that cost. This could make the products uncompetitive.

■ The only way IT can demonstrate a direct contribution to profitability is to cut costs, which might actually reduce IT's ability to deliver vital services.

■ If the business is not aware of the price of services, it tends to be more unreasonable in its demand for services – in terms of both the number and the quality of services. This places IT in a very difficult position. Business users keep demanding higher levels of service (often increasing costs), while managers keep trying to reduce the cost of IT (often reducing quality). Because IT costs are not linked to services, IT managers find it very difficult to demonstrate their actual business contributions.

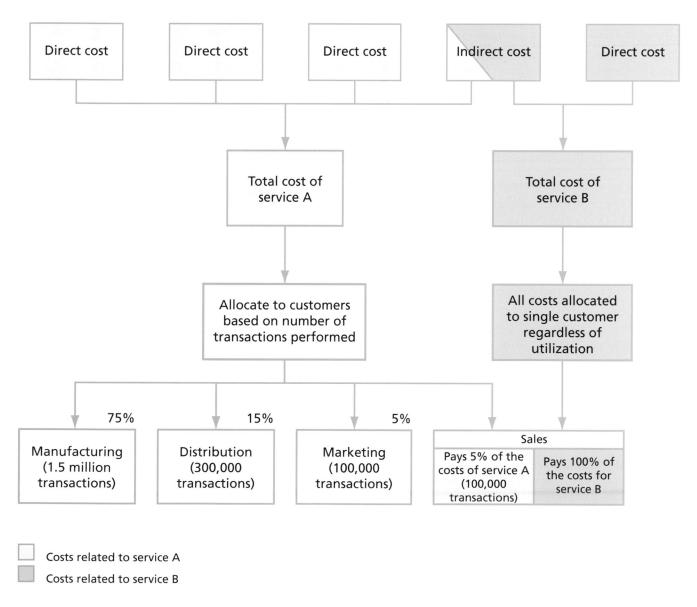

Figure 4.27 Cost by service

- Organizations using this type of model often cost projects separately, but there is no way of determining whether the services implemented by the project teams actually achieved the required levels of return.
- Service portfolio management cannot be fully effective since investments in services cannot be tracked through the lifecycle. In addition, there is no effective way of filtering services in the service pipeline, since it is almost impossible to evaluate the effect of a new service on the existing cost structures.

Although this cost model is cheap and easy, and is the most widely used type of cost model, it is of little real value to IT as a service provider. It provides only the minimum information required by the enterprise accounting policies, and does not enable IT to be seen as a contributor of value. Although the business understands the cost of IT, returns on investments cannot be calculated. It is not recommended for any but the smallest and homogeneous types of organizations, which have no more than a handful of services and a small number of users.

Cost by service

This type of cost model is essential for Type III service providers, especially those that position themselves using variety-based positioning, since they are in the business of selling services. However, it is also one of the most valuable types of cost model for internal service providers. In this type of cost model the costs of IT are reported according to service, which makes it possible to inform customers about the cost or price of a specific service. The customer is able to use this information to determine if the service will add value to them or whether it is too expensive for the outcomes they are trying to achieve.

This cost model is illustrated in Figure 4.27.

Figure 4.27 shows an internal service provider offering services to a number of business units in an organization. Costs are accounted for according to the services offered by the service provider. Service A is shared by four business units (internal customers), while service B is dedicated to only one business unit. Direct costs are any costs that are incurred when delivering a single service (for example, a specific application that is only used to provide a single service). Indirect costs are costs that are shared across multiple services (for

example, the cost of a server that is used to support more than service; and the cost of its server administrator). Direct and indirect costs, and methods of allocating these costs, are discussed in section 4.3.5.6.

Once the total cost of each service has been calculated, it is allocated to the business unit. In Figure 4.27 service A is provided to four different business units and the cost is allocated to each, based on how much they used it during the accounting period. Service B is provided to a single business unit, sales, which pays the total cost of providing the service. At the end of the accounting period, the IT service provider will report the allocated costs of all services that each customer uses. Sales uses two services, covering 5% of the costs of service A (based on utilization) and 100% of the cost of service B (since they are the only customer).

If charging has been implemented, the allocation will be the basis for billing in internal service providers. If not, the allocation is simply reported so that each business unit is able to add it to their other costs and calculate their overall costs. The allocation also allows the business to link the cost of each service to business outcomes and thereby calculate the value of the service.

This cost model is used differently by Type III suppliers to calculate pricing. Customers are not allocated a charge based on how much the service cost, rather they are charged according to a price list – and recovery has to be more than the cost of the service to continue funding the service provider. A 'cost by service' model for Type III suppliers is discussed and illustrated in section 4.3.5.6.

Advantages of the 'cost by service' model include:

- Customers are able to understand the balance between the cost and quality of a service and decide what investment is appropriate for the type of business outcomes they wish to achieve.
- It is easier to set customer expectations about the level of service they will receive, thus resulting in greater levels of customer satisfaction.
- The service provider is able to ensure that it has the necessary funding to provide the agreed levels of service.
- Both the service provider and the customer are more easily able to quantify the value of the

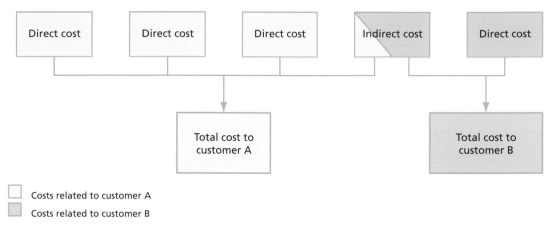

Costs related to customer A
Costs related to customer B

Figure 4.28 Cost by customer

service and the contribution it makes to the business.

■ Knowing the costs of IT services that are used to create and deliver services and products to external customers can help business units to price these services or products correctly – ensuring that the organization does not make an unintentional loss.

■ The impact of changes to existing services can be more easily quantified and assessed.

Disadvantages of the 'cost by service' model include:

■ It is more expensive to use this cost model since it relies on specialized cost accountancy skills and tools. In addition it requires a clear understanding of configuration items and how they relate to each other and the services being delivered.

■ The allocation of indirect costs can be quite difficult, and could require sophisticated measurement tools to ensure that costs are correctly apportioned to cost centres.

■ Allocating costs to services may influence the utilization of the service. While this may reduce costs over time, it creates difficulties in the short term. This is because the costs do not simply disappear when a user stops using a service.

Cost by customer

This type of cost model is rarely used on its own, since it involves communicating the actual costs of components within the service provider to the customer. This is a type of 'pass through' model, where the service is paid for by the service provider and then immediately allocated to the customer.

This type of cost model is difficult to use when costing items that are not visible to the customer, since most customers are not willing to pay for items that they do not use directly. However, it is often used effectively for providing desktop equipment and support, and software licensing for personal productivity software. This cost model works well where the customer is able to relate the price to the item that has been delivered.

More frequently, costs are first allocated to a service or other cost centre before being allocated to customers. This is discussed in the section about hybrid cost models (see below).

This cost model is illustrated in Figure 4.28.

In this example items that are visible to customers are allocated to those customers in internal service providers. Whenever a cost is shared between more than one customer, agreement is reached between the service provider and the customer about how that cost will be divided between them. Direct and indirect costs, and methods of allocating these costs, are discussed in section 4.3.5.6.

Advantages of the 'cost by customer' model include:

■ It is a simple and transparent method of helping the customer understand and influence the way they use individual units of a service.

■ It creates a forum for discussion of finances between the business and IT, although this could also be a disadvantage (see below).

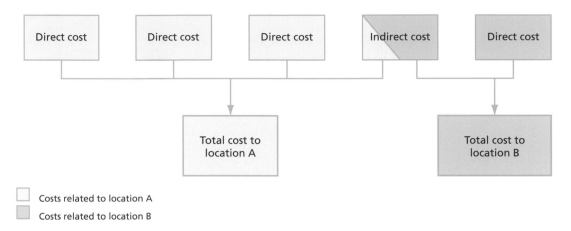

Figure 4.29 Cost by location

■ When used together with other cost models, it helps solve difficulties with those services – for example, PCs are used to access almost every IT service, but it is not feasible to try to allocate the cost of every PC across all services. It is much easier to see the PC itself as a cost that can be allocated directly to the customer.

Disadvantages of the 'cost by customer' model include:

■ The cost of IT can be exposed to business managers who do not understand what it takes to manage IT, and they might insist on IT reducing those costs without understanding the impact.
■ It is not appropriate to communicate the costs of IT to customers using technical categories – unless the technology itself is the service (e.g. storage).

Cost by location

As with the 'cost by customer' this type of cost model is rarely used on its own, since it involves communicating the actual costs of components within the service provider to a group of customers at a particular location. This is also a type of 'pass through' model, where the service is paid for by the service provider and then immediately allocated to a location. The location will then decide how to allocate the costs across the local business units.

This type of cost model is suitable when different locations use services differently, or where the service delivery mechanisms are different. For example, one location might use second-line support from the corporate IT organization. Another location is smaller and more remote, and

is serviced by a third-party support company. In this case, the cost of support will need to be allocated to the location. The local manager will either reflect that cost as part of the cost of doing business in that location, or else allocate it back to the business units in the local office.

More frequently, costs are first allocated to a service or other cost centre before being allocated to customers. A specific example is given in the section about hybrid cost models (see below).

In Figure 4.29 direct costs refer to the cost of any item that is only used for one location, regardless of which customers are present at that location and what services they use, for example a third-party support contract for PCs for a remote location. Indirect costs are costs of items that are shared by more than one location – for example, a database server which is used to upload receipts from ten retail stores. Direct and indirect costs, and methods of allocating these costs, are discussed in section 4.3.5.6.

Advantages of the 'cost by location' model include:

■ When combined with other cost models it can help to account for locations that need to report their costs separately.
■ It can help to determine the viability of the business in a particular location.
■ It ensures that any unique local requirements are properly evaluated and delivered, without setting unrealistic expectations that services will be exactly the same as in headquarters.
■ It ensures that the requirements of remote locations are properly accounted for and not forgotten.

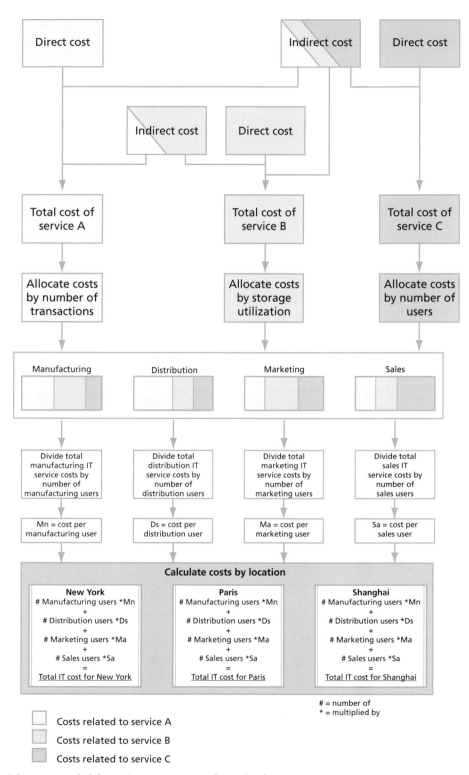

= number of
* = multiplied by

☐ Costs related to service A

☐ Costs related to service B

■ Costs related to service C

Figure 4.30 Hybrid cost model (service, customer, location)

Disadvantages of the 'cost by location' model include:

■ Some services that are critical for supporting remote locations might be more expensive, even though the business in that location justifies the expense. On learning the true costs some locations might be tempted to source the service from another supplier. For example, one office might choose a public internet service provider instead of a dedicated link to headquarters. This has security and performance implications and might impact on the overall business of that office.

■ Understanding the cost of a location might be good for business managers who want to ensure each location's continued viability, but it does not help local managers understand the cost of individual services and how the quality and cost can be influenced.

Hybrid cost models

As stated in the previous sections, it is unlikely that the cost model used by any organization will consist of just one method. Most cost models employ a number of different types of cost model for various purposes and situations. The aim of this is to ensure that every stakeholder has the right information to ensure wise investment in IT, correct balance between cost and quality and, most important, whether services support the achievement of business outcomes in a cost-optimized manner.

Most organizations will not need a fully hybridized model, but an example is provided below.

In Figure 4.30 an example is given of a business that has the following needs:

■ The business manufactures, markets, distributes and sells a range of products.

■ Three business-critical services are used to support four business units in three locations.

■ Each business unit must understand the costs of the services they use, so that they can find the optimal balance between cost (as low as possible) and quality (production and distribution must be able to operate at a set pace) – every outage has a cost and there is a set limit to the amount of outage that will be tolerated.

■ The cost of each service can be applied to the business units so that their products can be manufactured, distributed, marketed and sold at a competitive price.

■ Each location is measured on its production and sales, and profit margins, so the cost of IT for every location needs to be quantified.

This example uses a hybrid model of cost by service, customer and location. Using this cost model, the organization goes through the following steps:

■ IT costs are analysed and allocated to the three service cost centres.

■ Since each service needs to know the cost of the services that they will be using, the cost of each service must be allocated to the four business units, using some measure that is meaningful for the type of service.

■ Once each customer knows the cost of each service they are able to work with IT to ensure that they are able to influence the quality of the service. If they need more quality, they will be able to understand the additional cost and assess the impact of that cost on the pricing of the product.

■ The next step is to allocate the IT costs of the four business units to the three locations. Each business unit will add the costs of all three services so that they know the total cost that has to be allocated.

■ They then divide the total cost of all three services by the total number of users in each business unit. They could use any measure – for example, number of products produced, revenue adjusted for local currency etc. In this example, the number of employees was chosen because it was easy to calculate and will ensure a proportionate cost allocation.

■ Finally the number of employees from each business unit in each location is counted and multiplied by the cost per employee per business unit. These are added together for the four business units in each location to provide the total cost of IT per region.

In this way, costs are allocated fairly and managers at every level of the organization have meaningful information about the cost of IT.

Dealing with unallocated costs

No cost model can fully account for all indirect costs or allocations. For example, it is fairly easy to calculate direct and indirect costs for items that are used to deliver services. But what about costs that are not easily related to services? For example, overheads, such as the cost of the CIO and general IT management – how are the costs of IT management allocated?

The enterprise financial management policies will define policies for how to deal with costs that remain after the identified direct and indirect costs have been allocated. Unallocated indirect costs are also sometimes called overheads or unabsorbed costs.

In the case of overheads such as IT management an agreed formula is used to allocate a portion of the cost of IT management to every cost centre, whether that is a service, a user, a customer or a location. This 'uplift' is normally calculated so that it is proportional to the distribution of costs across the cost centres. For example, if 80% of IT's costs are allocated to service A and 20% to service B, then the uplift for IT management would also be 80% to service A and 20% to service B.

4.3.5.4 Accounting: cost centres and cost units
Cost centres

Two definitions for the term 'cost centre' are commonly used in business. Although they appear close in meaning, they are different. Depending on the context, the term might refer to a function or department which does not charge for services or contribute directly to the profit of an organization – for example, by selling services externally (see section 4.3.4.1).

In the context of cost models and accounting systems, however, a cost centre is anything to which a cost can be allocated – for example, a service, location, department, business unit etc. That cost centre might become the basis for a charging policy or billing method. For example, some accounting systems use the concept of cost location codes to indicate where the costs will be accounted for. The cost location code is the cost centre. Care should be taken to read the context of the term to ensure the correct meaning is inferred.

This means that even a profit centre will have cost centres associated with it, since it needs to record its costs in order to understand how to calculate its margins.

Cost centres are used to determine which costs are direct and which are indirect (see section 4.3.5.6). They also provide meaningful categories for allocating and reporting costs so that they can be understood and influenced by a wide audience.

For example, if an IT organization is told to reduce its costs, where does it start? Just looking at the list of expenses doesn't help to identify which costs are necessary, which are inflated and which are unnecessary. If those costs can be allocated to a service or business unit then the IT manager has the basis for a meaningful discussion with the stakeholders. Do they need that level of service?

Are there any aspects of the service or IT expenses that they are currently using that can be removed?

In this way cost centres make it possible for IT managers to work with their customers and other managers in the organization to assess the impact of cost cutting or investment on the customer.

Cost units

Allocating costs to a cost centre is helpful in understanding the total cost of that cost centre. It helps to answer a number of questions (such as 'What is each business unit's share of the cost of service A?'), but it leaves even more unanswered – for example, if the cost centre is a service:

- Can a customer decrease costs by using less of the service?
- How is the cost of the service different for customers who use the service differently?
- When providing services to internal customers, can the service provider communicate the cost of a service in terms that are meaningful to the customers?
- When providing services to external customers, does the service provider have a baseline cost for each component of the service that the customer buys, thus ensuring profitability?

A cost unit is the lowest level category to which costs will be allocated. Cost units are usually things that can be easily measured and communicated in terms to which customers can relate. Cost units enable the service provider to break down the costs of a high-level cost centre into smaller categories that can be used to link the customer's use of the service to the level of expenditure. Cost units help to increase the accuracy of forecasting and make it easier to link costs to items that customers actually use.

An example and diagram (Figure 4.31) will help to clarify the relationship between cost centres and cost units. The IT organization in a manufacturing company provides a service called Inventory Control to two business units, Manufacturing and Warehousing. Following a cost model where costs are allocated to services, the IT organization allocated costs to the Inventory Control cost centre. From here, the IT organization could simply look at the number of transactions or number of users, and allocate the total cost of the Inventory Control cost centre to the two customers.

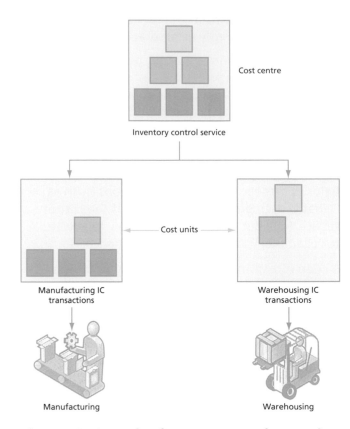

Figure 4.31 Example of cost centres and cost units

However, that would not be fair. Although the Inventory Control service is used five times per manufactured item by each department, it is used differently by each customer. Manufacturing uses it to track the location and stock levels of every component used on the assembly line (thousands of items), and to place orders when stock runs low. Warehousing only uses it to track the number and location of manufactured items in the warehouse (hundreds of items). Although the number of transactions is similar, the complexity of the transactions is different. How should IT communicate this to the customers?

One option is to use the CPU seconds, memory utilization and network bandwidth utilization as a basis, but this can be confusing. Instead the IT organization created two cost units, Manufacturing IC Transaction and Warehousing IC Transaction. Based on resource utilization IT was able to determine that Manufacturing used twice as many resources as Warehousing. They explained the difference in non-technical terms and customers were able to get an accurate understanding of the cost of the service for them.

4.3.5.5 Accounting: cost types and cost elements

Once the cost model has been defined, the work of defining how to record and track expenses can begin. The first step is to define the categories that will be used to record expenses. These should be meaningful for the type of services being provided and the resources that are used to deliver the services, and should reflect the practices, procedures and culture of the organization.

Cost units and unit costs

It is not the intention of this publication to detail all aspects of accounting, but there is a potential for confusion between two terms and this brief explanation is aimed at preventing any confusion.

A **cost unit** is a category within a cost centre that enables a service provider to break down the high-level costs of the cost centre into more specific terms. The term **'unit cost'** is more frequently used for the manufacturing environment than for services. It refers to the standard cost of producing one unit. Unit costs are used to set a baseline for pricing, and for detecting any unplanned cost variance.

Unit costs are most effective when the unit being measured is consistent – for example, when an assembly line produces 100,000 of exactly the same item. In this case the unit cost is the total cost of the assembly line and raw materials, divided by the number of products.

Most services are not constant, they are dynamic. The number of service units delivered is based on demand, and often the amount of resources used to deliver the service varies with each delivery. IT should try to quantify the unit cost for each cost unit, but this will often be more a guideline than a fixed amount. There are accounting methods for dealing with this variability, but they are outside the scope of *ITIL Service Strategy* since they involve advanced accountancy skills. Unit costs can effectively be calculated for 'commoditized' services, which have a constant demand, and use a fixed set of resources consistently.

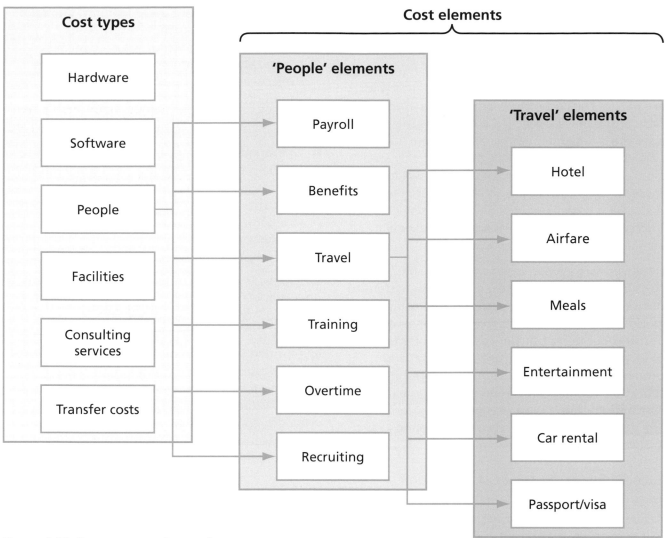

Figure 4.32 Cost types and cost elements

There are at least two levels of category used to define costs, cost types and cost elements, which may be further broken down into sub-categories. These are illustrated in Figure 4.32 and described below. Please note that the categories used in the examples are not prescribed. Each service provider should use categories that are appropriate for its situation and practices.

Cost types are the highest level of category to which costs are assigned in budgeting and accounting – for example, hardware, software, people, consulting services and facilities.

Cost elements are the sub-categories to which costs are assigned in budgeting and accounting. Cost elements are sub-categories of cost types. For example, the cost type 'people' could have cost elements of payroll, staff benefits, expenses, training, overtime etc. In general, cost elements are

the same as budget line items where the purpose of the model is simple recovery of costs.

Cost elements can be broken downs into several hierarchies of sub-category. Figure 4.32 shows three levels of detail. However, the number of categories, and how they are organized will need to be appropriate for each organization. Some may need two levels, others three, while some may need more.

A special cost type that should always be included in cost models is the transfer cost. This is any cost that involves internal movement or re-allocation of costs from one department to another and may include similar categories to the cost types and elements (for example, people costs can be transferred from a department to a specific project, based on the amount of time they spend working on the project). Transfer costs are helpful in quantifying the contributions made by one department to another.

Transfer costs should be visible in the cost model because people may forget that internal goods and services represent a cost to the organization and are part of the cost of providing service. Hence a false figure may be reached when assessing costs if a service is dependent upon activity from another part of the organization but this cost is excluded from calculations. Some organizations will insist on these transfer costs being accounted for in each part of the organization while others may only use them when modelling costs and no money will actually pass across the organization.

However, care should be taken not to view transfer costs in the same way as revenue or expenditure to or from third parties. For example, one company mandated all departments to 'sell' their services to one another using transfer costs. The intention was to increase awareness of costs and value, and promote better quality. But the actual result was that some business units reduced sales to external customers because it was easier to sell internally. The end result was that the company made losses in several lines of business.

4.3.5.6 Accounting: cost classification

Once the cost types, elements and units have been defined it is necessary to determine how each one will be managed, analysed and reported. Another way of thinking about this is to understand how the costs will behave. For example, are they likely to change, go up, come down or fluctuate? Most cost elements behave in a predictable way if financial management for IT services is able to classify them correctly and link them to business activity.

Although this is a complex area, there are six major classifications, grouped in three pairs of options (each cost element will be classified as one or the other of each of these pairs). A special type of cost classification (depreciation) is also discussed. The classifications are as follows:

Capital or operational

The first classification is whether the cost is capital or operational. All costs are either capital or operational:

- **Capital costs** or capital expenditure (Capex) is the cost of purchasing something that will become a financial asset – for example,

computer equipment and buildings. Capital costs are used to purchase fixed assets, information about which is stored in the organization's asset register, and which are subject to the asset management process. The values of fixed assets are depreciated over multiple accounting periods. The concept of depreciation is discussed in more detail below.
- **Operational costs** or operational expenditure (Opex) is the cost resulting from running the IT services, which often involves repeating payments – for example, staff costs, hardware maintenance and electricity. Operational expenses are also known as current expenditure or revenue expenditure.

Why does IT need to classify costs as capital or operational?

Simply put, if a cost is classified as operational, the entire cost of that item has to be accounted for and funded in the current financial year. If this is a large investment that is not going to show any returns in the current year, it will be very difficult to show value and it is very likely that IT will be viewed as too expensive, or that an alternative service needs to be found. Additionally, the organization's tax liabilities are different for operational and capital expenses.

If a cost is defined as capital, it will be spread over more than one year. Only the portion of the cost that is allocated to the current year will need to be allocated or recovered from the business. This makes it easier to demonstrate the value of the service, even when the overall investment is higher than the first year's return.

The decision about whether to classify costs as capital or operational is not an arbitrary one. It is determined by enterprise financial policies based on generally accepted accounting practices, tax legislation and the organization's own decisions about how IT will be funded. Tax legislation will provide rules about the minimum cost that qualifies as a capital cost, the number of years over which the investment can be spread and by how much the cost may be depreciated each year.

Accountants in the organization are qualified to understand these laws, policies and funding decisions, and to provide advice and guidance to IT about how to apply them.

Many organizations choose to identify certain types of major expenditure as capital to reduce the

Example 1

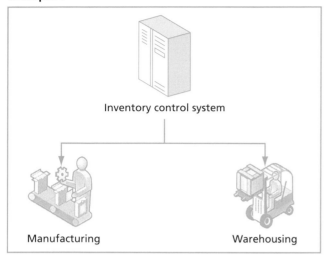

In a cost model where cost is allocated by customer the inventory control system is an indirect cost since it is shared by two customers

Example 2

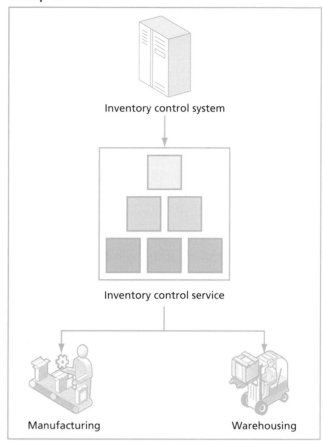

In a cost model where cost is allocated by service the inventory control system is a direct cost since it is dedicated to a single service

Figure 4.33 A cost can be classified as direct or indirect in different cost models

impact on the current financial year of such expenditure. This is referred to as 'capitalization'. The most common item for this to be applied to is software, whether developed in-house or purchased.

The reason for this is that a business that is investing in a major software development, which provides service for a number of years, does not want to show all of the costs in a single year (and so, potentially, an operating loss). The board wants the value of the company and its shares to reflect the investment made but adding the cost of the item to the assets of the company without adjusting cash flow in some way would also give a false picture. The agreed method is to show capital and operational expenditure separately but to apply rules of depreciation, described later in this section, to provide a balance. This system allows an organization to spread the cost of a major

purchase over a number of years although, as with all systems, many additional rules (and laws) have to be written to prevent fraud or misleading of investors.

An example of which cost elements would be considered as capital or operational costs, and which could be either, is provided in Table 4.5.

Direct or indirect

The second cost classification is whether the cost is direct or indirect:

■ **Direct costs** refer to any cost in providing an IT service which can be allocated in full to a specific customer, service, cost centre, project etc. (for example, the cost of providing dedicated servers or personal computers).

■ **Indirect costs** refer to any cost of providing an IT service which cannot be allocated in full to a specific cost centre, such as customer, service,

Table 4.5 Examples of capital and operational costs

Typical capital costs	Typical operational costs	Costs that could be either capital or operational, depending on level of investment, tax laws and enterprise policy
Hardware above a specific financial value Buildings (e.g. data centre facilities)	Maintenance costs Software licensing fees Consulting Salaries Office rental Hardware below a defined cost Utilities (power and water)	Software Remodelling of existing facilities PCs (some organizations or countries allow calculation of the total investment in PCs rather than the individual cost of each PC)

location, project etc. (for example, the cost of providing shared servers or shared software licences). Where indirect costs are not easily allocated to a cost centre, they are sometimes known as overheads, and allocated using a separate 'uplift' calculation.

Whether a cost is classified as direct or indirect depends on the cost model used, and which costs will be allocated to which cost centres (for example, service, customer, location, project etc.). This is covered in detail in the section on cost models (section 4.3.5.3). Figure 4.33 gives an example of how the same cost could be classified as direct and indirect, depending on the cost model used.

Why does IT need to classify costs as direct or indirect?

Direct and indirect costs are allocated differently. Direct costs are allocated to a single cost centre, while indirect costs have to be shared across more than one cost centre. If costs are allocated incorrectly the information provided to customers will be misleading, especially if they are using that information to price their own products and services.

Classifying costs as direct or indirect helps IT to be more accurate when it communicates the actual cost of IT to another business unit. It also helps the business unit to be more accurate when calculating the return on its IT investment, and the pricing of its good and services.

A large manufacturing company had several plants, each manufacturing a different line of products. The company decided to enter a new market with a line of luxury products requiring precision manufacturing. To support this strategy they

invested in an expensive integrated manufacturing control and enterprise resource management solution. Instead of treating this as a direct investment for that line of products, IT decided to treat it as an indirect cost and allocated it evenly across all plants. This sudden increase in the cost of IT to all plants had a devastating effect on one plant. This plant manufactured a line of low-cost, high-volume products. These products were now expected to cover the costs of the new IT solution, which meant that product prices had to be increased, which made them uncompetitive. Sales declined, the plant started losing money and that line of products was discontinued.

Allocation of costs

Once a cost has been defined as indirect, the next decision is how it will be allocated. This is a complex area of accountancy, and a qualified professional will need to ensure that the appropriate methods are chosen and properly used. However, accountants will need the assistance of IT professionals to provide input to these methods, and so this publication provides a very brief definition of four of the most commonly used allocation methods:

- **Activity-based costing** This method analyses all the activities required to produce a product or deliver a service. The resources required to perform each activity (time and materials) are documented. The amount of each activity performed for each cost centre is measured, and the agreed costs of that activity allocated to the cost centre. This is an accurate, but expensive and complex, method.
- **Utilization-based allocation** In this method the cost of a resource used by multiple cost centres

is allocated based on how much the cost centre uses the resource. For example, if five business units (cost centres) use storage, the cost of the storage is allocated using the percentage of the total space used by each business unit. Utilization-based allocation should be carefully used, as it could discourage customers from using a resource. For example, if the service desk is allocated by utilization, people will stop calling it, and the impact of incidents will increase. This emphasizes the need to apply utilization-based allocation by service usage.

■ **Agreed basis for allocation** In some cases there is no straightforward method for allocation, and IT and the business will agree criteria that are easy to measure, and considered fair by the business units. This could be number of users, number of PCs or something else. The most important factor here is that all parties agree that this is a fair way of allocating costs, and that the costs being allocated are visible to the business units. For example, this is often used to allocate the costs of a service desk to the business.

■ **Indirect cost rate** Regardless of what method of allocation is used, there are always costs that cannot be easily allocated. The indirect cost rate method sets a consistent rate to allocate these costs:

- Step 1: For each cost centre, add up the direct costs (*d*) and allocated indirect costs (*i*): $d + i = a$
- Step 2: Calculate the total of all cost centres' direct and allocated indirect costs ($\sum a = t$)
- Step 3: Place all unallocated indirect costs into a pool (*u*)
- Step 4: For each cost centre calculate the percentage (*p*) of total direct and indirect costs allocated to them: $(a/t) \times 100 = p$
- Step 5: Use that rate to allocate the remaining indirect costs to each cost centre: $u \times p = r$
- Step 6: Calculate the total costs allocated to each cost centre: *total costs per cost centre = a + r.*

An example of this calculation in spreadsheet format is shown in Table 4.6.

Fixed or variable

The third cost classification is whether the cost is fixed or variable:

■ **Fixed costs** are costs that do not vary with IT service usage – for example, the cost of server hardware.

■ **Variable costs** are costs that depend on how much an IT service is used, how many products are produced, the number and type of users, electricity or something else that cannot be fixed in advance.

Table 4.6 Example of indirect cost rate calculation

	Direct and allocated indirect costs			Allocating unallocated indirect costs			
Symbol	*d*	*i*	*a*	*p*	*u*	*r*	
Description	Total direct costs	Total allocated indirect costs	Total direct and allocated costs	Allocation percentage	Unallocated indirect costs	Allocation of *u*	Total cost
Calculation			d + i	a/t		u × p	a + r
					80,000		
Cost centre 1	250,000	150,000	400,000	25%		20,000	420,000
Cost centre 2	150,000	75,000	225,000	14%		11,250	236,250
Cost centre 3	80,000	25,000	105,000	7%		5,250	110,250
Cost centre 4	500,000	20,000	520,000	33%		26,000	546,000
Cost centre 5	300,000	50,000	350,000	22%		17,500	367,500
Sub-total(s) (*t*)			1,600,000			80,000	1,680,000

A simpler alternative to detailed tracking

It is not always possible or viable to track this level of detail. Instead of using tools or people to try to monitor and find out how much time people spend on activities, and instead of having them fill in detailed timesheets, a better way is to ask each person or team as part of a budgeting process to say what proportion of their time they spend on the activities they do/services they support. This is a very simple but powerful method used by some organizations to understand how much services cost. Where activities cover several services, additional information can be used – e.g. on a service desk where operatives spend 50% of their time dealing with calls, the call statistics can allocate this across services. It's also invaluable information for resource management, HR etc.

It is important to note that fixed costs can change. The price of maintenance may go up halfway through the year, an employee may get a salary increase, the cost of insurance may decrease because of some risk mitigation measures that have been implemented. This does not make the costs variable. The difference between fixed and variable costs is based on a specific factor, such as usage or time, and not simply because the price goes up.

Why does IT need to classify costs as fixed or variable?

There are two main reasons why IT should know whether a cost is variable or fixed.

The first reason is that IT should be able to forecast expenditure. Fixed costs are easier to predict since they generally stay the same. If there is a price increase or decrease for a fixed cost, the timing and amount are usually fairly predictable within a particular industry. Variable costs are more difficult to predict because they depend on the customers' demand for the service. The better an IT organization understands its customers' patterns of business activity, the better it will be able to predict the amount of funding they will need to cover their costs.

The second reason is that uncontrolled variable costs can result in issues between the IT organization and the other business units. For example, at the beginning of the year, a business unit predicts a certain level of service utilization.

The IT organization budgets for a certain amount of storage, processor power, printing costs etc. Most of these costs are variable. About two-thirds of the way through the year, the customer exceeds their annual predicted usage. Now there is no budget for additional storage, servers etc. Even worse, if the IT organization did not track this expenditure as a variable cost linked to that specific service and that specific business unit, there is no way it can obtain additional funding from that customer, and it is left with the task of trying to re-allocate budget from other services and business units, or requesting additional funding from all business units at the end of the year to cover its losses. In either case, IT's credibility suffers, and it becomes even more difficult to obtain funding the following year.

What about costs that stay the same within a certain range of usage, and then go up as soon as usage crosses a threshold? For example, a printer can print up to 20,000 pages per day. If usage consistently exceeds that threshold another printer, or a larger replacement printer, may need to be purchased. This type of variation, somewhere between a fixed and a variable cost, is called a stepped fixed cost, and is illustrated in Figure 4.34.

Understanding how fixed and variable costs 'behave' will assist the service provider to understand and predict the level of cost incurred at different levels of customer activity. This will ensure that they are able to forecast funding requirements more accurately. Examples of fixed and variable costs are provided in Table 4.7.

Table 4.7 Examples of fixed and variable costs

Fixed costs	Variable costs
Salaries (salaries stay the same regardless of how many hours the employee works)	Cost of hourly or daily contractors (the more they are utilized the more money is spent on them)
Benefits (health insurance, retirement, company car etc.)	Overtime (the more an employee works overtime, the more money they are paid)
Printers	Paper and toner/ink
Building loan repayments	Electricity and water
Insurance premiums	Travel costs

Depreciation

Depreciation is a measure of the reduction in value of an asset over its life, and is predetermined by enterprise financial management policies or tax legislation. The reduction in value is based on wearing out, consumption or other reduction in the useful economic value. Useful economic value means that the asset is directly or indirectly contributing to the objectives of the organization. In other words, the asset is still producing a return on its investment. Please note that this is an accounting (or book) calculation and it may be possible that an asset continues to contribute in the real world even after its asset value has been reduced to zero.

Although depreciation is not a cost classification as such, it is a special consideration applied only to fixed assets. Depreciation allows an organization to account for the cost of an asset over several years, and also allows them to build reserves for replacing that asset after it is no longer useful – without being punished with taxation for assets that no longer have any value.

Why does IT need to account for depreciation?

Many services require a significant investment in service assets. However, these assets are often designed to last longer than the current financial year and they are also designed to deal with growth in demand over a number of years. These service assets are designed to deliver value over a number of years – and their cost is therefore much higher than the return on investment they deliver in the first year.

If the service provider demanded that the customer pays the entire amount of the investment in the

Paper – variable cost

Printer – fixed cost

Printer 2 – increases the fixed cost

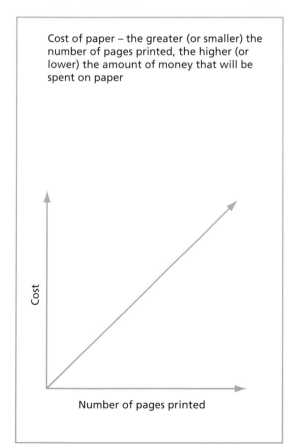

Cost of paper – the greater (or smaller) the number of pages printed, the higher (or lower) the amount of money that will be spent on paper

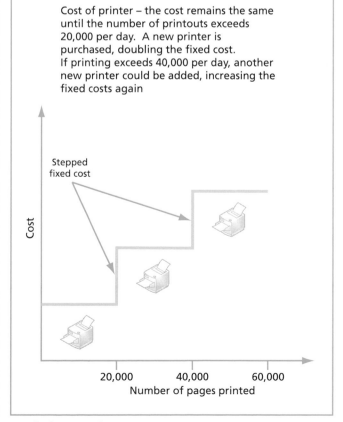

Cost of printer – the cost remains the same until the number of printouts exceeds 20,000 per day. A new printer is purchased, doubling the fixed cost. If printing exceeds 40,000 per day, another new printer could be added, increasing the fixed costs again

Figure 4.34 Example – fixed and variable costs in a printing service

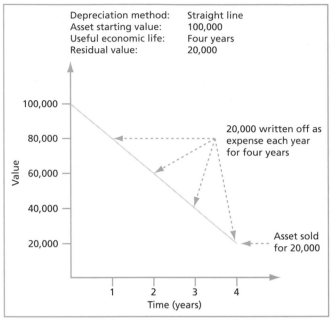

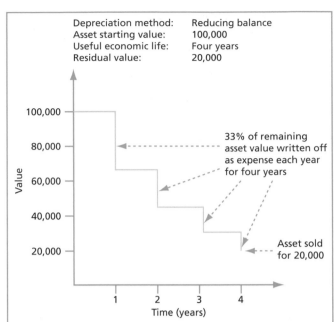

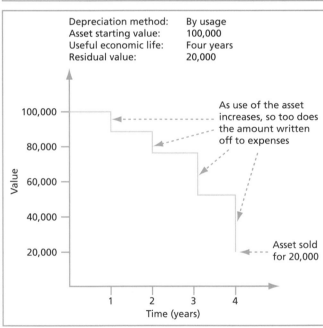

Figure 4.35 Common depreciation methods

first year, this would be a skewed assessment of the value of the service. Firstly the customer might not be able to afford the service, or they might have to price their products or services too high, or they might simply go bankrupt trying to pay for the service.

Secondly, if the first customers pay for the entire investment, the cost to subsequent customers will be minimal. This is also not an accurate quantification of the true cost and value of the service.

Depreciation allows IT to account for the cost of large service assets over a number of years, allowing them to demonstrate a more accurate return on investment, and ensuring that the business has a valid basis for calculating the value of the service.

Calculating depreciation

Calculating depreciation involves three factors:

■ The current cost (or valuation) of the asset
■ The length of the asset's expected useful economic life, having due regard to the

incidence of obsolescence

■ The estimated residual value of the asset at the end of its useful economic life.

The useful economic life of an asset may be:

■ Predetermined by financial policies or tax legislation
■ Dependent on its physical deterioration through use, time or wear and tear
■ Reduced by economic or technological obsolescence.

The depreciation methods used should be the ones most appropriate having regard to the types of assets and their use in the business. Enterprise financial management policies give guidance in this. The most common methods of assessing depreciation are described below and illustrated in Figure 4.35:

■ **Straight line method** Where an equal amount is written off the value of the asset each year. Usually a fixed percentage of purchase cost, this results in the item having zero net book value after a pre-set number of years (although it may continue to be used).
■ **Reducing balance method** Where a set percentage of the capital cost is written off the net book value each year. Often this is of the form 40% in the first year, 30% in the second year and 30% in the last year. The net book value is the capital cost minus the depreciation written off to date.
■ **By usage** Where depreciation is written off according to the extent of usage during a period. It is usual to estimate the total useful 'life' of a device and to calculate the proportion of this that has been 'used' during the year. For example, a laser printer may be estimated to have a useful 'life' of 5,000,000 pages. If the average usage is 1,000,000 pages in a year, it can be depreciated by 20% in that year.

Financial management for IT services may require IT assets to be 'written off' before the end of their useful life, increasing the apparent cost of services but facilitating a charging system that generates revenue for the early replacement of systems.

4.3.5.7 Accounting: chart of accounts

The chart of accounts is a list of all the accounts that are used to record income and expenses. The chart of accounts is defined and managed by enterprise financial management. In a Type III provider, it is likely that the chart of accounts is set up according to the types of services delivered and their customers.

In internal service providers, however, it is more likely that the chart of accounts has been defined according to the type of business the organization conducts. For this reason the chart of accounts is sometimes difficult for IT managers to understand, and it is therefore difficult to communicate well with the business on financial matters.

For this reason, financial management for IT services needs to align the chart of accounts with its own cost models, services and expenditure. More IT organizations are creating their own charts of accounts and then aligning them with the enterprise chart of accounts. An example of this is provided in Figure 4.36. This allows IT management to analyse the cost of services in terms that facilitate IT decisions and management, and then translate the implications of their cost analysis in terms that enable business processes to be more effective.

However, care should be taken not to duplicate or become independent of enterprise financial management. This can be costly and does not add much value. The idea is to use these IT-oriented tools and financial management systems to support enterprise financial management.

4.3.5.8 Accounting: analysis and reporting

Analysis and reporting in financial management for IT services have the following aims:

■ To build an organization-wide understanding of the service provider's income, expenses and investments
■ To communicate the cost of services to all stakeholders
■ To provide a basis for controlling expenditure according to the stated strategies, objectives and business outcomes of the organization and its customers
■ To ensure that funding of the service provider is adequate. Without analysis and reporting it is not possible to fully understand the service provider's funding needs
■ To ensure that the methods, risks and returns of the service provider's financial management practices are fully understood by the officers of

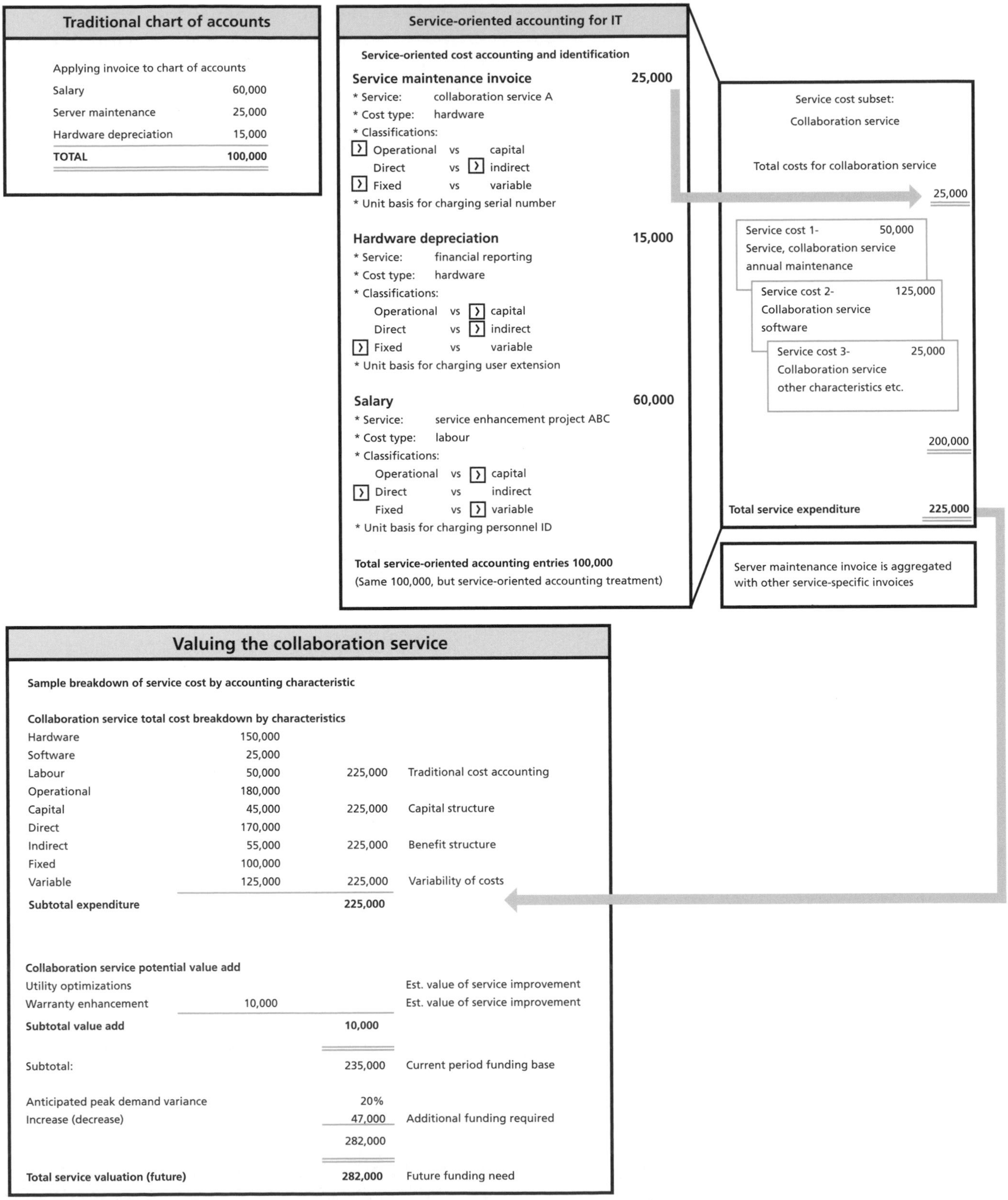

Traditional chart of accounts

Applying invoice to chart of accounts

Salary	60,000
Server maintenance	25,000
Hardware depreciation	15,000
TOTAL	**100,000**

Service-oriented accounting for IT

Service-oriented cost accounting and identification

Service maintenance invoice   **25,000**
* Service: collaboration service A
* Cost type: hardware
* Classifications:
  - ⟩ Operational   vs   capital
  - Direct   vs   ⟩ indirect
  - ⟩ Fixed   vs   variable
* Unit basis for charging serial number

Hardware depreciation   **15,000**
* Service: financial reporting
* Cost type: hardware
* Classifications:
  - Operational   vs   ⟩ capital
  - Direct   vs   ⟩ indirect
  - ⟩ Fixed   vs   variable
* Unit basis for charging user extension

Salary   **60,000**
* Service: service enhancement project ABC
* Cost type: labour
* Classifications:
  - Operational   vs   ⟩ capital
  - ⟩ Direct   vs   indirect
  - Fixed   vs   ⟩ variable
* Unit basis for charging personnel ID

Total service-oriented accounting entries 100,000
(Same 100,000, but service-oriented accounting treatment)

Service cost subset:

Collaboration service

Total costs for collaboration service

    25,000

Service cost 1-   50,000
Service, collaboration service
annual maintenance

Service cost 2-   125,000
Collaboration service
software

Service cost 3-   25,000
Collaboration service
other characteristics etc.

    200,000

Total service expenditure   **225,000**

Server maintenance invoice is aggregated
with other service-specific invoices

Valuing the collaboration service

Sample breakdown of service cost by accounting characteristic

Collaboration service total cost breakdown by characteristics

Hardware	150,000		
Software	25,000		
Labour	50,000	225,000	Traditional cost accounting
Operational	180,000		
Capital	45,000	225,000	Capital structure
Direct	170,000		
Indirect	55,000	225,000	Benefit structure
Fixed	100,000		
Variable	125,000	225,000	Variability of costs
Subtotal expenditure		**225,000**	

Collaboration service potential value add

Utility optimizations			Est. value of service improvement
Warranty enhancement	10,000		Est. value of service improvement
Subtotal value add		**10,000**	
Subtotal:		235,000	Current period funding base
Anticipated peak demand variance	20%		
Increase (decrease)	47,000		Additional funding required
		282,000	
Total service valuation (future)		**282,000**	Future funding need

Figure 4.36 Translation of cost account data to service account information

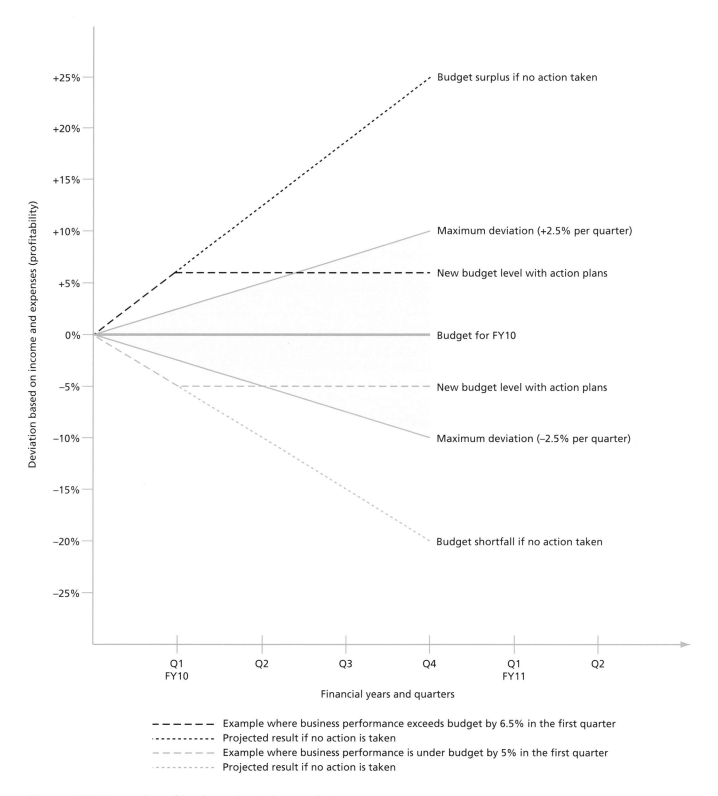

Figure 4.37 Examples of budget deviation analysis

the organization, so that they can initiate any remedial action required by law or regulation

■ To build appropriate and fair cost allocation methods that ensure that each service is properly priced so that the business can ensure that the service is competitive, and that the

service provider is able to retain value for funding

■ To help customers calculate the value of services in terms of return on their investment in each service that they use

■ To review strategic decisions to ensure that predicted financial outcomes were actually realized.

As with other components of financial management, analysis and reporting are well understood and implemented within formal accounting systems and generally accepted accounting practices. What is often missing, however, is the perspective of the internal IT service provider.

Although most financial reporting has some standard reports, these may not be fully tuned to IT's requirements, or to communicating the value of IT services. Accountants will need to understand what IT has to know in order to deliver and manage services. IT has to know what the accountants need to know in order to produce that information.

There are several types of analysis and reporting, but one which is worthy of mention here is budget deviation analysis. This is because it is a common tool used by all business units, and it links the activities of the service provider to those of the customer. Although the primary use of this technique is between internal service providers and customers, it can also be used to analyse external customer activity and compare it to the forecast financial dynamics (income, expenditure etc.).

The basic premise of budget deviation analysis is that any deviation from a budget represents a potential risk. The budget represents the optimal levels of expenditure to achieve a specific set of business outcomes. If there is no further input, the organization will continue to spend on the assumption that the strategy has been set and all the business units have to do is execute.

In reality, budgets are hardly ever accurate. They are forecasts based on a set of assumptions and historical trends. If the actual performance differs from the forecast, the organization may need to change the way it works to adapt to the changes in the business. If actual income levels are too low, the organization's strategy may have been ineffectual, and there is a risk that the organization makes a loss, or that IT will not be properly funded. If income levels are too high, this implies a higher demand for services, and the organization may not have adequate capacity to meet the demand.

Contrary to popular belief, budgets do not exist just to authorize or limit spending. They are a valuable tool in ensuring that the level of spending is appropriate for the level of business activity. If income exceeds expectation, it is likely that spending may need to be increased.

Figure 4.37 illustrates budget deviation analysis. The following aspects are illustrated:

■ A budget is set for the next financial year – this is the central thick line. If everything were to go according to plan the actual performance of the organization would mirror the budget.

■ However, the organization knows that budgets are not always accurate, and have set upper and lower deviation thresholds of 2.5% per quarter. This means that if there is a deviation of less than 2.5% no action is required, since the levels of expenditure and capacity will be able to address the level of business activity without any adaptation. The acceptable level of deviation (at + or – 2.5% per quarter) is illustrated by the coloured triangle. As long as the actual performance is within that area, no further action is required.

■ If, however the deviation exceeds that level, the budget needs to be re-assessed and an action plan put in place. In Figure 4.37 both a positive and negative deviation are illustrated.

■ The negative deviation (–5%) requires that an action plan be put in place that will usually identify which costs need to be reduced, or how to increase income. If it is possible to revert to the original budget, then the situation has been resolved. If it is not possible to revert to the previous budget, the action plan will result in a new budget for the remainder of the year, and all business units will have to realign their budgets.

■ The positive deviation (+6.5%) is just as dangerous for the business, but the action plan will focus on either increasing capacity and expenditure, or (less likely) on reducing the levels of business activity. Please note that actually achieving a budget surplus of 25% is very unlikely unless the organization has a huge amount of spare resources, and some market dynamic that the organization has no control over is at play.

4.3.5.9 Accounting: action plans

If financial analysis and reports show that the organization is on track to achieve its financial targets, little action is required but to continue executing the original plans and strategies. However, if there is significant deviation from agreed financial targets, an action plan needs to be put in place and executed. These action plans are normally short term, and are aimed at restoring the organization to its planned path within a month or quarter, or else getting the stakeholders to agree to change the original plans and targets.

Reporting budget deviation on its own achieves little but awareness. A budget deviation with an associated action plan is a powerful management tool.

Typical triggers that cause a service provider to initiate action plans in financial management for IT services include:

- **Unexpected increase or decrease in costs** For example, the cost of maintenance or hardware.
- **Under-utilization of services by customers** This means that the investments made were higher than necessary, which is especially problematic if the customer is being charged for the services, and the service provider now stands to make a loss. It is also a problem if related assets are being depreciated by usage.
- **Over-utilization of services by customers** This means that the investment made was lower than necessary. Money will have to be found to purchase additional resources to meet the increased demand. This is problematic where an IT organization is expected to break even, and is now on track to make a significant 'profit'. It is also a problem if related assets are being depreciated by usage, since higher levels of depreciation costs have to be recovered in that financial period.
- **Inaccurate business planning** There are occasions where a customer has overlooked some aspect of their business, or failed to communicate with IT about a project which will increase IT's costs.
- **Unexpected changes to the external environment** These include any event that impacts the service provider's costs, and over which they have no control. For example, a supplier goes out of business, or is acquired by another company and a new product has to be purchased. Economic downturns also put stress on the organization to anticipate a slowdown in business by cutting costs and planned projects.
- **Unexpected changes to the internal environment** Organizations are always in a state of flux. People are promoted or leave the organization, business units get reorganized, new products and services are added and old ones retired. Every one of these changes will impact the way in which the organization uses and pays for IT.

Close monitoring of financial reporting will often indicate that a change has taken place and that the service provider needs to take action. Sometimes the situation will be unexpected, and will require a quick response to assess what the cause is, and then develop a plan to deal with it. In addition the action plan should include continual improvement activities to help prevent recurrence.

In other cases the possibility of the situation arising was anticipated and the service provider already has a plan defined that can be adapted to the specific events that have occurred. Examples of this type of plan include:

- Obtain and allocate additional funding. There are many ways of doing this, for example:
  - Many service providers specifically put aside budget to deal with cost increases. Although they may not know exactly where these cost increases will occur, they know that it is very likely that such increases will occur, and are prepared for some variation to the budget.
  - Some service providers have an agreement with their customer to cover any cost increases up to a certain level. In this case the service provider meets with the customer, explains the situation and agrees to the increase.
  - If IT costs are allocated from a central budget, there will be a plan to notify enterprise financial management of the situation and have them change the allocation details.
  - The cost increase may be posted to, and recovered in, the following financial year – although there are a number of risks and regulatory issues around this option, depending on where the organization is based.
- Change the price of the service (where customers are charged for the service). The

main problem with this plan occurs when the customer is not able to afford the increased price, or if the contract prevents mid-term price increases. This should have been provided for in the agreement or contract at the beginning of the financial year but, if not, the business relationship manager (BRM) will have to engage with the customer to reach an agreement on how the new costs will be recovered.

- Plans should be in place for when a customer is over- or under-utilizing a service, especially for internal service providers which are required to break even. Plans could involve adjusting the rate to prevent an unacceptable profit or loss; or else posting the profit or loss to a central account where it will be offset against other expenses.

- External service providers should also have a plan for financial under-performance. This could be because the service was not as successful as anticipated (not enough customers purchased it), or because the organization lost customers or contracts. These plans will involve a review of the services, customers and contract performance. There might be a problem with marketing, sales or service quality, and executives of the organization should drive corrective action. The same plans should be in place for Type I and II providers, but interestingly the trigger is usually customer satisfaction rather than financial performance.

4.3.5.10 Budgeting

Budgeting is the activity of predicting and controlling the spending of money. Budgeting consists of a periodic negotiation cycle to set future budgets (usually annual) and the routine monitoring and adjusting of current budgets.

Budget planning typically begins at least one quarter before the current financial year end. This is to ensure that all departments have a good understanding of how the organization will end the year, thus also providing a more accurate starting point for the next year. This also provides enough time for each business unit to gather the data required to create the budget.

Budgeting begins with either the CFO or the financial controller providing budgetary guidelines, including growth expectations and cost limitations. Each department or business unit uses these to create a draft budget which is returned to the CFO or financial controller's office. All budgets are compared, assessed in the light of the overall strategy of the organization and returned to each business unit for revisions. This negotiation might happen two or three times before the budget is finalized and the new financial year begins.

Most managers are familiar with the activity of producing and approving an annual budget, and then reviewing the budget regularly to ensure that the targets are being met. What many fail to appreciate, however, is the importance of budgeting as a business tool.

Budgeting is the mechanism that marshals the resources necessary to meet the strategic and tactical objectives of the organization. Budgeting answers fundamental business questions, and then goes on to ensure that the answers are properly executed. For example:

- Does the organization have the resources needed to meet the objectives?
- Where will those resources come from?
- How many/much of the resources will we need and when?
- What commitment can we expect from every business unit to meet these objectives?
- Every month and quarter, where should the organization be in meeting its objectives?
- Where do we increase costs to keep up with performance that is better than expected?
- Where do we cut costs if performance is worse than expected?

Budgeting is the basis for a number of key reports and financial reporting tools and is a critical component of financial management. For example, see section 4.3.5.8 for a description of how budget deviation analysis can help the organization gear its services and expenditure to business performance.

4.3.5.11 Budgeting: analysis of previous budget

The budgeting cycle starts with two steps. The first of these is an analysis of the previous year's budget to detect any trends of expenditure or income that were too tactical or operational to be detected during a strategy assessment. In addition, the analysis will also look for mistakes made during the previous year's planning (for example, where costs or projected business performance were incorrectly estimated).

Who does budgeting belong to?

Budgeting is executed by all managers who have responsibility for any level of expenditure or income. Since each manager understands their part of the organization best, they will define their plans, and the budgets that will enable them to execute those plans.

However, the budgeting process, policies and documents are defined and managed by enterprise financial management. IT does not 'own' the budgeting process, although when they submit a budget they make a commitment to achieve the levels of performance that are reflected in that budget.

Each level of management will define budgets for their area of responsibility and then submit those budgets to their managers, who will use them as input into their budgets. This process is repeated until budgets at the level of senior management are submitted to enterprise financial management, where they are compared with the strategy, business and other plans.

Any errors in the planning process should also be identified – for example, the exclusion of any key stakeholders, or incorrect assumptions made because information was not available.

The results of the analysis should be documented and used when defining the budget for the next year.

4.3.5.12 Budgeting: assessment of plans

Budgets are impacted by several initiatives and plans. Each of these plans should be assessed to determine its impact on the budget, and to ensure that the budget is updated to enable each department to execute their role in each plan.

Typical plans that should be assessed within IT include:

- The organization's strategy
- All plans that involve executing the organization's strategy
- Project plans for any project planned for the next financial year
- Plans for changes in the customer environment (relocation, workforce reduction, new marketing campaigns etc.)
- Planned new services in the service pipeline

- Technology update or refresh plans
- The IT capacity and availability plans
- Service improvement plans
- Services to be retired.

4.3.5.13 Budgeting: specification of changes to funding and spending

Many of the changes that will impact the budget are not in formal plans. Nevertheless, they have to be specified so that any funding or expenditure required during the year is taken into account. Typical changes include:

- Review and revision of existing contracts
- Changes to service utilization forecasts
- Changes to financial management policies about how costs or income will be accounted for
- Changes in financial reporting requirements
- Revision of an existing charging policy.

4.3.5.14 Budgeting: cost and income estimation

After analysing the plans, preceding budget and any known changes it is now possible to begin compiling the budget for the next financial year. This involves going through the budget, typically a spreadsheet defined by enterprise financial management, and estimating the values for each item for each month and quarter.

In most cases the costs of items in the spreadsheet are known because of the preparation work done in analysing plans, previous budgets etc. However, the cost of some budget items may not be known – for example, overtime payments, contractor payments, consumables, external network charges. These have to be estimated, usually based on the previous year's budget, or on a forward prediction of the costs of the estimated workload.

Some costs may vary from the estimates, depending on usage. An example of this is software licences that may increase (in steps) as further users are introduced. Other costs may need to be estimated to cover out-of-hours support or major equipment relocation.

Finance management must be cautious in estimating changes in costs where they do not fully control them. For example, planning a reduction of 20% in computer accommodation usage by removing old disk drives and closing one room is unlikely to result in 20% saving in costs, as the rental for the space may be fixed by the lease.

4.3.5.15 Budgeting: budget(s)

A budget is a list of all the money an organization or business unit plans to receive, and plans to pay out, over a specified period of time. It will take into account all existing spending, and how this will change during the next financial year (for example, if the cost of maintenance is increased, or more people are employed).

In addition the budget must forecast any investments in planned new services or changes to existing services. This information will be provided by strategy management for IT services and service portfolio management.

The IT organization will also have plans to update, replace or invest in technology to decrease overall costs or increase performance. These will also have to be forecast in the budget. Each department head will provide a list of investments they plan to make during the next financial year and these will be recorded in the budget, and preferably linked to the services they support.

A budget is typically documented as a spreadsheet with the rows indicating the items of expenditure and a column indicating when that expenditure will take place. Budgets typically consist of the following items:

- Expenses listed according to the categories in the chart of account, usually grouped by department
- Some budgets keep each cost type on a separate spreadsheet, especially if the budget is very complex
- An indication of which service the item supports
- Items for operational expenses are normally listed separately from items for capital investment
- Projects will be listed separately, together with a brief description of the project and its purpose
- Expected income and sources of the income
- A column for each month and quarter to record the planned income and expenditure and the actual income and expenditure.

4.3.5.16 Charging

Charging is the activity whereby payment is required for services delivered. For internal service providers charging is optional, and many organizations choose to treat their IT service provider as a cost centre (see section 4.3.4.1). In this situation charging is often referred to as 'chargeback' since the costs of the service provider are simply re-allocated back to other business units by the central financial function using an internal charging method.

Type III service providers do not have any option but to charge for their services, since this is where the organization obtains the revenue which keeps it in business. This is not 'chargeback' since services are generally sold at a profit.

The CFO or financial controller in organizations with internal service providers has an important decision to make – should they charge for their services?

The argument in favour of charging includes:

- Charging places the customer in control of their IT spend. They decide which services to use and how much of each service to take based upon a known understanding of what the consumption will cost them.
- Charging for services provides the business with more accurate information, allowing business leaders to make more informed decisions about their use of technology.
- IT is able to operate with greater transparency and accountability.
- Customers have a greater appreciation of the value of the services they use, since they can compare the costs of the services with the business outcomes they can achieve.
- Charging can encourage better, or different, use of IT services to support business outcomes at optimal cost.
- Charging ensures that requests for a particular type or level of service are tempered by an understanding of the financial implications of each request.
- Charging can result in changes in behaviour – for example, ensuring that users use high-demand services at off-peak times.

The arguments against charging include:

- Charging can be a complex and bureaucratic process, involving expensive accounting tools.

- Charging could change the politics of the organization negatively, especially if IT is the only department charging for its services.
- If financial reporting adequately represents the costs of providing services in business terms, there is less need for charging.

Ultimately the decision about whether to charge for services is determined by the culture of the organization and the policies of enterprise financial management. While IT may influence this decision, it is not their decision to make.

Unless the IT service organization has the support of the whole organization in introducing charging, it will fail. It has to be simple, fair and realistic:

- **Simple** The overheads of cost management must deliver the benefits of an improved overall cost effectiveness without the bureaucracy commonly associated with IT accounting systems.
- **Fair** 'I can obtain the services cheaper elsewhere and that's what I'll do.' The system must be fair and realistic; services which are not cost-effective need to be reviewed and hard decisions taken. Each business should pay the same money for the same service.
- **Realistic** 'I'm saving money, even though it must be costing the company more.' Anomalies in the charging system will be exploited by businesses. The charging mechanisms must be designed to achieve optimal behaviour.

The image of the IT service provider is likely to change; they may be seen initially as demanding money without providing the required service, as having become bureaucratic and focused on trivial accounting. To limit this risk, IT organizations considering the implementation of charging should:

- Publicize the programme and work with the businesses to define charging policy.
- Ensure that service level agreements are in place and representative of actual service.
- Ensure that the benefits are quantifiable and demonstrable.

4.3.5.17 Charging: charging policies

Charging policies determine how charging will work, and are defined by the office of the CFO or financial controller. The first policy decision is

whether or not to charge. This is discussed in section 4.3.5.16.

The second policy decision is what level of cost recovery needs to be achieved. These can be summarized as:

- **Cost recovery or break-even** In this case IT will only seek to recover its costs. It will not make a profit or loss.
- **Recovery with an additional margin** In this case IT will seek to recover more than its actual costs. This policy raises a number of questions, which must be answered and agreed before charging is introduced:
  - **What will IT do with the additional funding?** In some cases the money is placed in a separate account earmarked for refreshing technology or covering the costs of unanticipated projects. In other cases it is used to offset the costs of new investments that are lightly used in the first year or two.
  - **How will the margin be perceived?** It is important to note that this is not a profit. Since the money is being transferred internally it does not increase or reduce the revenue of the organization as a whole. Viewing excess charging as a profit could actually result in undesirable behaviour – for example, cost cutting of expensive items to increase the margin, even though they are used to support vital business functions.
- **Cross-subsidization** This is where a subset of services is charged with an additional margin, which is then applied to offset the cost of another subset of services. This policy is often used to fund services to business units that have run out of budget, or whose business performance is lower than expected. The danger here is that temporary subsidies have a way of becoming permanent. When that happens, one business unit might be charged too little and may not sell their products at a price that covers their true costs. Another business unit pays too much for their services, resulting in the pricing of their products or services being uncompetitive.
- **Notional charging** This is not really a type of charging at all, but a type of financial reporting. Notional charging is a way of telling an internal customer how much a service would cost them if they were paying for it directly. The reason notional charging is used is to make

customers aware of the true costs of the services they are using. It can also be used to compare the costs of outsourcing versus insourcing. Finally notional charging is often used as a six-month or year-long interim measure when implementing charging for the first time. This gives the service provider an opportunity to correct any errors in their financial system, and also gives customers the opportunity to plan budgets for when charging goes live.

The third policy decision is how behaviour should be managed. Whether intended or not, when people are charged for services their behaviour will change. In some cases charging is deliberately used to influence behaviour, such as ensuring more efficient use of resources (for example, charging more for using a service at peak times encourages people to use the service at off-peak hours). In other cases charging results in unforeseen (often undesired) behaviour. Whenever charging is implemented, it should include a conscious policy to monitor the impact of charging on behaviour and tune the charging system to deal with each situation.

The fourth policy decision is how the organization will deal with customers who decide that they can purchase IT services from another service provider at a lower cost. There are a number of factors here, including:

- Are the business units free to seek services outside the organization? If introducing charging for the first time, business units should not be able to change service providers for at least the first year, and then only with special authorization from the CEO or CFO. This will ensure that any errors can be rectified, and will also prevent decisions being made on the basis of emotions or politics, rather than actual business value.
- How will IT cover the costs of new services or additional capacity? Some investments are designed to support an IT service over several years. This will mean that the first year of the service might be overly expensive, and customers might be tempted to look outside the organization for cheaper services. A good accounting system should be able to use depreciation or other accounting practices to defer some of these costs.

- Are services really cheaper and better outside the organization? Many customers do not understand all the resources required to deliver and support services. It is easy to look outside the organization to find a cheaper alternative, but these investigations are usually superficial and do not take into account all aspects of the service provided. It is important that financial management for IT services and service portfolio management are closely aligned so that the business units can get a more objective assessment of exactly what is included in the cost of the service.
- If a service really is cheaper from an external provider, should the business unit be encouraged to change service providers? There is no easy answer to this, but there are some cautions. For example, external service providers can offer services more cost-effectively because they have more paying customers that use the service. When there is a problem with the service, or contention for the shared resources, which customer has priority? Also, how easy is it to get the service provider to customize the service for each individual customer? Finally, the level of investment is not reduced just because a customer goes to an external customer. This also has to be accounted for in the decision.
- How will the organization cover the costs of both the external supplier and the investments made for the business unit that sourced its services externally? The whole discussion about external service providers is often an academic one. In reality, a comparison of an internal transfer charge with external expenditure to a third party cannot be made at face value. The comparison is a complex financial matter, and should not be taken lightly. Often, when these simplistic comparisons are made, it is an attempt by the business unit to convince the IT organization to commit to higher levels of service or to lower costs.
- The internal IT organization will be involved in some way in managing the external supplier and that has a cost which needs to be included.
- The price of the warranty as well as the utility – customers may well only consider the latter; external providers may well price low to get into the account and then it emerges that expensive add-ons are required to make the service work properly.

- Lack of flexibility and responsiveness – if the service is provided to several customers, it will be more difficult and expensive to get changes authorized.
- The fact that internal spend on IT is very different from money spent with an external provider. The cost associated with this will need to be defined.

The final policy decision is based on current monitoring capabilities. If it is not possible to monitor system or service usage, then it will not be possible to allocate costs or provide a reasonable explanation of the charges. Therefore the charging policies have to articulate what level of measurement will be performed, and what investments are required to enhance monitoring where required.

4.3.5.18 Charging: decide chargeable items

Successful charging requires that the customer understands exactly what they are being charged for. This enables them to quantify the value of the service, and to work with IT to optimize the balance between the cost of the service and its quality. It also helps to set expectations about the level of service that will be received.

Chargeable items have to be items which can be perceived and controlled by the customer (for example, PCs connected to the network or number of transactions performed). The customer can then manage their budget by controlling their demand for these items. The more closely the chargeable items relate to the organization's business deliverables the better the interface to the customers. Only a lack of information should force charging to be directly based on resource usage; this lack of information must be dealt with and it is important that in the analysis phase steps are taken to ensure the future availability of the information.

Chargeable items are similar to cost units in that they are the lowest level at which a cost (or charge) is measured. The main difference is that cost units are measured from an IT point of view, and chargeable items are measured from a customer point of view. Charging therefore relies on having accurate cost models and pricing models.

The reason for having two different categories (cost units and chargeable items) is that the cost of the item might be different from its price. Also, chargeable items may consist of more than one

cost unit. Figure 4.38 illustrates the relationship between cost units and chargeable items.

In Figure 4.38 a customer requests a report using an IT service. As far as the customer is concerned, the report is the service that is being delivered and what the customer is paying for. Explanations about the cost of transactions do not make much sense. Instead, the costs allocated to the transaction are combined with the costs allocated to the printouts and recovered by charging for the report.

In non-IT terms, airlines sell tickets for a flight; they do not issue a bill covering usage of aircraft, fuel, food, proportional crew costs and so on. The flight is the chargeable item.

Often, business deliverables are not suitable as chargeable items because they require too detailed a measurement of the resources consumed. For example, a customer may require a service to produce sales analyses but calculating the individual cost of one analysis or even of many types of analysis could add to the total costs

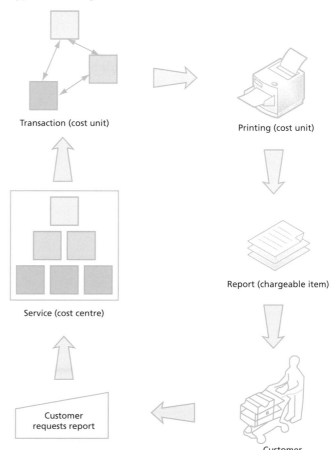

Figure 4.38 Cost units and chargeable items

unacceptably. In such cases, a structure may have to be established in which the service is charged for as a whole.

Often, business deliverables cannot be easily attributed to single processes or applications. Applications are rarely written to produce single logical business deliverables: often many customers utilize portions of a multitude of programmes, each of which contributes to the production of parts of many business deliverables.

Where a customer requires charges to be variable, dependent upon usage, the chargeable items have to be more specific to that customer and easily attributable to that customer. The more freedom the customer has to define their own service, the more detailed the charging structure required.

4.3.5.19 Charging: pricing

Pricing is the activity for establishing how much customers will be charged.

The decision about how much to charge depends on what the chargeable item is, which cost units are associated with the chargeable item and the policies about cost recovery (see section 4.3.5.17). The decision also depends on expected value of the service sale and trends of consumption over the fiscal year – it is not just a linear relationship.

> #### Charging and value
>
> For external service providers, charging is less tied to the cost, and more to the value of the service and relative costs of similar services provided by competitors. In these cases the cost models will indicate the lowest level of charging before causing an impact on profitability.

Several options exist for deciding how much to charge. No matter which methodology is used, or none or all, it is more important to make certain that the overriding substantiation comes from providing value to the business. Options include:

Cost

This option is based on a break-even or cost recovery model. The chargeable item is priced as close as possible to the actual cost of the cost units.

The main difficulty with this approach is that the cost of the chargeable item might vary with volatile demand, leading to an unexpected profit or loss, which has to be allocated using enterprise financial management policies.

Take the following (simplified) example: a business unit uses a service which consists of a shared server, and an application. The business unit agreed to pay for the application since it is the only user. However, the cost of the server was shared with two customers. IT and the customers agreed to a price per transaction.

IT calculated the price of the transaction based on the cost of the server and the number of transactions predicted by the customers. The price was calculated as follows:

- Cost of server = £100,000 (to be recovered by the end of the year)
- Projected number of transactions from both customers: 500,000
- Cost per transaction: £100,000 / 500,0000 = £0.20.

During the third quarter, over £150,000 had already been charged for the server, with IT earning a £50,000 profit. What happened?

The cost of the server is a fixed cost, and the £100,000 would only be recovered if the number of transactions was exactly what the customers said it would be. The number of transactions was 750,000 but the allocation of the cost of the server to the transaction was not adjusted along with the new utilization figures, resulting in the profit.

This type of situation can be resolved in a number of ways. For example, the price could have been adjusted when the utilization rate started escalating; or the additional funds could be used to purchase a new server to deal with the additional demand. Regardless of which method is chosen, it needs to be agreed with the customer, and it has to comply with enterprise financial management policies.

Cost plus

There are a number of cost-plus pricing models. The basic form is:

Price = cost + x%

The mark-up (x%) can be either set by the organization to match returns on other business investments, or allocated by the IT organization to meet strategic business needs, e.g. encouraging the use of strategic applications but discouraging the use of legacy applications.

Cost plus may be used for large one-off original projects where the costs cannot be easily predicted.

Going rate

The price is comparable with similar service providers in similar organizations.

Market price

The price is the same as that charged by external suppliers. Care should be exercised in asking external suppliers to quote prices – they may well disguise a discount to gain the business. Also it is not always appropriate to compare internal financial transfers with external expenditure.

At the same time, it is not sufficient to simply evaluate the price. Sourcing services externally offsets some of the commercial risk from the customer to the supplier, i.e. the supplier is taking risk (and cost) associated with their estimate that they will sell sufficient quantities of the service to cover their fixed costs. If the service is provided internally the internal IT organization has to take this risk.

Fixed price

The IT organization sets a price based upon negotiation with the customer, which covers a set period and a predicted consumption.

However the prices are determined, it is essential that they are visible to customers so that they can tailor their budget forecasts and service requirements to match the likely costs.

Tiered subscription

This method of pricing involves a service being priced differently according to the service package option that has been selected. The varying prices cover the cost of the additional layers of warranty and utility.

For example, a silver subscription to PC support only offers support during office hours and is the cheapest since no overtime or shift allowances have to be paid to support staff. Platinum subscriptions offer 24-hour support, seven days a week. The higher price covers the cost of additional support staff, overtime and call-out allowances.

The main problem with this approach arises if only a small number of customers choose platinum, but in insufficient numbers to cover the cost of the higher level of service. Although it might seem fair to say that they should all take a lower tier of

service, the business impact for those users might be high.

Differential charging

Setting different charges for different usage of the same or similar services enables an organization to reward some usage patterns over others. For instance the use of differential charging to increase charges for service usage during peak daytime processing periods may encourage changes in customer behaviour which reduce overall costs, often without the IT organization being blamed for poor value of service. This can result in smoothing demand for capacity and reducing the overall capacity required.

4.3.5.20 Charging: billing

Whereas charging refers to the process of recovering money for services directly from the customer, billing is the process of producing and presenting an invoice for services to a customer. Billing is therefore a sub-process of charging. There are three main options for billing.

No billing

In this option the service provider decides not to produce an invoice of any type. This is normally the case when IT simply allocates its costs to other business units. This is not an option for Type III service providers, which are required to submit invoices in order to receive payment. Failure to produce an invoice will result in non-payment.

Informational billing (notional charging)

This option is also restricted to Type I and II service providers, and is used as part of a notional charging policy. In this case the service provider produces an invoice but does not actually go through the process of collecting revenue.

Informational billing is used either to create awareness of the true cost of services (and to influence customer behaviour in some way), or to prepare the customer for the situation when real charging is implemented.

Since informational billing requires a fully functional financial system for internal customers, it tends to be a very expensive way of creating awareness, unless the organization will be implementing real charging.

Billing and collection (real charging)

This type of billing is used when the customer pays a Type III service provider in revenue (external customer) or a Type I or II service provider by internal transfer (internal customer). This type of billing requires a dedicated IT financial system that can handle invoicing, collection, debtors, creditors and age analysis (how long a payment has been outstanding).

As with informational billing, there should be a good business reason for a Type I or II service provider to make this investment. This is normally done in organizations with autonomous business units, each of which carries its own profit and loss.

One of the disadvantages of using this billing approach internally is that many employees lose sight of the fact that all business units have the same set of overall business objectives, and start withholding payment or critical services due to budgetary constraints or lack of communication. There is also the danger that employees start thinking of themselves as an external customer, rather than as a steward of the organization's resources.

4.3.6 Triggers, inputs, outputs and interfaces

4.3.6.1 Triggers

Triggers of financial management for IT services include:

- Monthly, quarterly and annual financial reporting cycles are mandated and form part of the standard financial management policies and standards of any organization. An example of a regularly triggered financial process is budgeting.
- Audits will indicate actions that need to be taken to adjust some aspect of the accounting, budgeting or charging system.
- Requests for financial information from other service management processes – for example, return on investment information for services in the service portfolio, or information to determine the cost of making a change.
- Investigation into a new service opportunity, either during the definition of a strategy (high-level financial value of the opportunity), or during service portfolio management where a more specific financial assessment is required.
- The introduction of charging for IT services (internal service provider) or the need to

determine the price of a service (external service provider).
- A request for change will trigger the need for financial information about the cost of making changes, and the ongoing financial impact of the change.

4.3.6.2 Inputs

The major inputs to financial management for IT services are illustrated in Figure 4.25 and discussed in more detail in section 4.3.5.1. Inputs include:

- Policies, standards and practices defined by legislation, regulators and enterprise financial managers
- Generally Accepted Accounting Practices (GAAP) and local variations
- All data sources where financial information is stored, including the supplier database, configuration management system, the service portfolio, customer agreement portfolio, application portfolio and project portfolio
- The service portfolio provides the structure of services that will be provided, which in turn will be the basis for the accounting system – since all costs (and returns) will ultimately be expressed in terms of the services provided.

4.3.6.3 Outputs

The major outputs of financial management for IT services are illustrated in Figure 4.25 and discussed in Chapter 3, but are listed here for ease of reference.

- **Service valuation** This is the ability to understand the costs of a service relative to its business value. This involves a combination of accounting methods described above and return on investment approaches (section 3.6.1).
- **Service investment analysis** Financial management for IT services provides the information and history to enable the service provider to determine the value of the investment in a service. This information is used by the business to demonstrate the value they have realized in using the service to achieve their desired outcomes. Without accounting and financial reporting, there would be no ability to track the level of investment or the return on that investment. It is important to note that financial management for IT services must be able to track and compare both IT

financial data and that of the business unit in order to perform service investment analysis.

- **Compliance** Regardless of the location of a service provider, or whether they are internal or external, financial data is subject to regulation and legislation. Financial management for IT services helps implement and enforce policies that ensure the organization is able to store and archive financial data, secure and control it and make sure that it is reported to the appropriate people. IT financial management data specifically allows the executives of the organization to track the levels of investment in IT and ensure that the money is being used to achieve the overall organizational strategy, mitigate risks and achieve the appropriate returns in a legal and ethical manner.

- **Cost optimization** Cost optimization should not always be equated with cost savings. The goal of cost optimization is to make sure that investments are appropriate for the level of service that the customers demand, and the level of returns that are being projected. In other words, cost optimization may result in increased levels of spending if demand and potential returns increase. Cost optimization is about gearing expenditure to the expected levels of activity and return. At the same time, cost optimization is also about preventing unnecessary expenditure. Every opportunity should be investigated from two perspectives. Firstly, is it possible and cost-effective to use existing services or technology to achieve the outcomes? Secondly, what is the most cost-effective investment (not always the cheapest) that needs to be made if the existing technology will not be able to work?

- **Business impact analysis (BIA)** Business impact analysis (BIA) is covered in section 3.6.2, and involves understanding the effect on the business if a service were not available. This enables the business to prioritize investments in services and service continuity. Financial management for IT services contributes to BIA by providing financial data and information to quantify the potential effect on the business. It also helps to quantify and prioritize the actions that need to be taken to prevent the impact from becoming reality.

- **Planning confidence** Planning confidence is not a tangible output or plan – rather it refers to the level of confidence that service stakeholders have in the service provider being able to accurately forecast costs and returns. A lack of planning confidence results in a lack of confidence in the service provider, and in many cases an unwillingness by the business to invest in IT unless absolutely necessary. The more the service provider communicates appropriate and meaningful financial information the more it will be used in the planning and investment analysis processes. The more that happens, the more the stakeholders will focus on making sure that the information is accurate and available.

4.3.6.4 Interfaces

Major interfaces with financial management for IT services include:

- All service management processes use financial management to determine the costs and benefits of the process itself. In addition many of them use financial management information or activities to support the execution of their process activities.

- Strategy management for IT services works with enterprise financial management to determine the financial objectives for the organization. In internal service providers, financial management for IT services is used to translate the organizational strategy into specific objectives for the service provider. Strategy management for IT services also defines expected returns on investment, based on information and tools provided by financial management for IT services, and financial management for IT services in turn will be expected to track and report on the achievement of these.

- Service portfolio management provides the service structure which will be used to define cost models, accounting and budgeting systems and the basis for charging.

- Business relationship management provides information to financial management for IT services about the way in which the business measures the value of services and what they are prepared to pay for services. This is especially important in external service providers, where service management processes will use this information to define services that provide a good balance between price, functionality and cost. In addition, business relationship management is a valuable channel of communication to customers about financial policies and pricing. In internal service providers, business relationship management can help to arbitrate on which customers will provide funding for services which are shared across multiple business units, each with different requirements for performance.

■ Capacity and availability management are able to provide valuable information to financial management for IT services about the various options of technology and service performance. This in turn will be used to calculate costs and to provide costing reports to various other processes, and ultimately the customers themselves.

■ Change management uses financial management for IT services to help determine the financial impact or requirements of changes.

■ Service asset and configuration management documents financial data about assets and configuration items. This data is used as the basis for financial analysis and reporting. Enterprise financial management also provides the policies that are used as the basis for managing financial assets of the organization (such as depreciation).

■ Continual service improvement uses financial management for IT services to determine whether the return of a proposed improvement is worth the investment required to make the improvement.

4.3.7 Information management

The documentation and information required for effective financial management for IT services have been described throughout section 4.3, but an overview of the main sources is as follows:

■ Financial management systems, such as accounting, budgeting and charging systems
■ Financial management policies, legislation and regulations defined by external parties, as well as the internal enterprise finance managers
■ Financial reporting structures, templates and spreadsheets (e.g. budgets), as well as the reports themselves, which are the basis of

compliance and also a major output to other service management processes
■ The organization's chart of accounts
■ The service knowledge management system (of which financial management for IT services is an integral part).

4.3.8 Critical success factors and key performance indicators

This section provides examples of critical success factors (CSFs). These are the conditions that need to be in place, or things that need to happen, if the financial management for IT services process is to be considered successful. Each CSF will include examples of key performance indicators (KPI). These are metrics that are used to evaluate factors that are crucial to the success of the process. KPIs, as differentiated from general metrics, should be related to CSFs.

The following list includes some sample CSFs for financial management for IT services. Each organization should identify appropriate CSFs based on its objectives for the process. Each sample CSF is followed by a small number of typical KPIs that support the CSF. These KPIs should not be adopted without careful consideration. Each organization should develop KPIs that are appropriate for its level of maturity, its CSFs and its particular circumstances. Achievement against KPIs should be monitored and used to identify opportunities for improvement, which should be logged in the CSI register for evaluation and possible implementation.

■ **CSF** There is an enterprise-wide framework to identify, manage and communicate financial information, and this includes the cost of and associated return on services
  ● **KPI** Enterprise financial management has established standards, policies and charts of accounts which it requires all business units to use and comply with. Audits will indicate the extent of compliance.
  ● **KPI** The financial management for IT services framework specifies how services will be accounted for, and regular reports are submitted and used as a basis for measuring the service provider's performance.
  ● **KPI** Timely and accurate submission of financial reports by each organizational unit.

- **CSF** Financial management for IT services is a key component of evaluating strategies
  - **KPI** All strategies have a comprehensive analysis of investment and returns, conducted with information from financial management for IT services.
  - **KPI** Review of strategies indicates that financial forecasts were accurate to within an acceptable percentage.
  - **KPI** Timely and accurate provision of financial information for service analysis during service portfolio management.
- **CSF** Funding is available to support the provision of services
  - **KPI** Internal service providers receive the funding required to provide the agreed services – showing a break-even at the end of the financial planning period.
  - **KPI** External service providers are able to sell services at the required levels of profitability.
  - **KPI** Funding is made available for research and development of new services, or improvements to existing services.
- **CSF** Service asset and configuration management work together with financial management for IT services to ensure good stewardship of service and customer assets
  - **KPI** Customer and service assets are recorded in the configuration management system, and all required financial information is complete.
  - **KPI** Regular reports are produced on the costs and utilization of customer and service assets and action plans are targeted for any deviations from required performance or utilization.
- **CSF** The service provider must understand the relationship between expenses and income and ensure that the two are balanced according to the organization's financial policies
  - **KPI** For internal service providers: the expenditure of the service provider is recorded in a timely and accurate fashion, according to enterprise financial management requirements.
  - **KPI** For external service providers: the expenditure and income of each business unit is reported in a timely and accurate fashion, according to enterprise financial management requirements.

- **KPI** The cost of each service is reported on a monthly, quarterly and/or annual basis, and compared with the return achieved by that service (either in terms of income, or in terms of meeting some other business objective).
- **CSF** Financial management for IT services must provide reporting to the organization's stakeholders that enables them to make sound decisions and to comply with regulatory reporting requirements
  - **KPI** Standard financial reports (as determined by policy or regulation) are produced on time and provided to the appropriate stakeholder.
  - **KPI** Deviations in expenditure or income above a specified percentage must be reported to the appropriate level of management, together with an action plan to rectify the situation. Action plans will be measured by whether they achieved the result agreed.
  - **KPI** No penalties or fines are incurred due to non-compliance with regulatory or legislative requirements.
  - **KPI** Each major decision will be reviewed in terms of the accuracy of the outcome compared to what was forecast.
- **CSF** The service provider must be able to account for the money spent on the creation, delivery and support of services
  - **KPI** The service provider uses an accounting system, and this is configured to report on its costs by service.
  - **KPI** Regular reports are provided on the costs of services in design, transition and operation.
- **CSF** Financial management for IT services is able to report on, and accurately forecast, the financial requirements to meet service commitments to customers
  - **KPI** Financial reports are structured according to the service in the service portfolio.
  - **KPI** Financial forecasts are accurate to within an agreed percentage of the forecast amount.
- **CSF** The service provider is able to charge for services where appropriate

- **KPI** Charging for IT services is conducted as agreed with customers (accurately and on time).
- **KPI** Complaints or queries about charges raised occur below an agreed percentage, and are resolved within an agreed time.
- **KPI** Charges are calculated so as to allow the service provider to meet its recovery targets (break-even or profitability).

4.3.9 Challenges and risks

4.3.9.1 Challenges

Challenges for financial management for IT services include:

- Financial reporting and cost models that are focused on the cost of infrastructure and applications rather than the cost of services. This will make it very difficult to communicate the value of services, and customers will often demand higher levels of service than the service provider can provide. External service providers will not be able to price their services accurately.
- While financial management for IT services needs to comply with enterprise standards and policies, its chart of accounts and reporting should be appropriate for an IT service provider. Categories should be meaningful to the IT organizations, but should also be mapped to the enterprise financial systems.
- If the organization focuses on cost saving rather than cost optimization, financial management for IT services will find itself having to identify cost-cutting measures rather than demonstrating return on investment and value – often resulting in demands to cut costs even further or customers choosing other service providers, since there is a low perception of the value of the service provider.
- When financial management for IT services is first introduced or formalized, it may be difficult to find where financial data is located and how it is controlled, especially if IT organizations have operated relatively independently of one another. Financial management for IT services relies on planning information provided by other processes, both within and outside of service management, which may not be available routinely.

- Internal service providers may find it difficult to introduce charging. This will require a change in culture, changes to the way in which IT's success is measured and the need to articulate value in relation to alternative service providers. In addition the IT organization may not be able to respond to changes in users' demands resulting from being charged – although the behaviour may change, the basic cost of providing the services remains the same.
- External service providers will need to balance the cost of services with the perceived value of those services to ensure the correct pricing models. Getting the balance right is not just about ensuring that the price is higher than the cost. The service has to be priced to reflect the value to the customer (what the customer is prepared to pay for the service).

4.3.9.2 Risks

Financial management for IT services risks include:

- Introducing dedicated financial management processes for an internal service provider, when finances are already being managed at an enterprise level, may be viewed as unnecessary and a waste of money and time. However, there is a real risk that a lack of dedicated financial management for IT services will result in poor decisions about the type and level of services offered to the business. The cost of a bad investment decision can far outweigh the costs of implementing financial management for IT services.
- Organizations that do not have adequate financial management processes for IT services may find themselves exposed to penalties for non-compliance with legislative or regulatory requirements.
- Staff need to be available who understand the world of the service provider (in this case IT), as well as the world of cost accounting.

4.4 DEMAND MANAGEMENT

Demand management is the process that seeks to understand, anticipate and influence customer demand for services and the provision of capacity to meet these demands.

Demand management is a critical aspect of service management. Poorly managed demand is a source of risk for service providers because of uncertainty in demand. Excess capacity generates cost without creating value that provides a basis for cost recovery. Customers are reluctant to pay for idle capacity unless it has value for them.

In some cases a certain amount of unused capacity is necessary to deliver service levels. This capacity creates value because it enables a higher level of assurance. This capacity cannot be considered idle capacity because it has been designed into the service on purpose.

Insufficient capacity has impact on the quality of services delivered and limits the growth of the service. Service level agreements, forecasting, planning and tight coordination with the customer can reduce the uncertainty in demand but cannot entirely eliminate it.

Service management faces the additional problem of synchronous production and consumption. Service production cannot occur without the concurrent presence of demand that consumes the output. It is a pull-system in which consumption cycles stimulate production cycles.

Demand management techniques such as off-peak pricing, volume discounts and differentiated service levels can influence the arrival of demand in specific patterns. However, demand still pulls capacity. Demand cannot exist simply because capacity exists.

4.4.1 Purpose and objectives

The purpose of demand management is to understand, anticipate and influence customer demand for services and to work with capacity management to ensure the service provider has capacity to meet this demand. Demand management works at every stage of the lifecycle to ensure that services are designed, tested and delivered to support the achievement of business outcomes at the appropriate levels of activity.

This is where the service provider has the opportunity to understand the customer needs and feed these into the service strategies to realize the service potential of the customer and to differentiate the services to the customers.

The objectives of demand management are to:

■ Identify and analyse patterns of business activity to understand the levels of demand that will be placed on a service

■ Define and analyse user profiles to understand the typical profiles of demand for services from different types of user

■ Ensure that services are designed to meet the patterns of business activity and the ability to meet business outcomes

■ Work with capacity management to ensure that adequate resources are available at the appropriate levels of capacity to meet the demand for services, thus maintaining a balance between the cost of service and the value that it achieves

■ Anticipate and prevent or manage situations where demand for a service exceeds the capacity to deliver it

■ Gear the utilization of resources that deliver services to meet the fluctuating levels of demand for those services.

4.4.2 Scope

The scope of the demand management process is to identify and analyse the patterns of business activity that initiate demand for services, and to identify and analyse how different types of user influence the demand for services.

Demand management activities should include:

■ Identifying and analysing patterns of business activity associated with services

■ Identifying user profiles and analysing their service usage patterns

■ Identifying, agreeing and implementing measures to influence demand together with capacity management. This is sometimes called the 'management of demand'. This could be in situations where service demand exceeds capacity, and where capacity increases are not feasible (e.g. differential charging, incentives, penalties). It could also be in situations where a new service has been launched and IT wishes to encourage users to use it more. Also, it could be used to reduce demand in peak utilization times and shift it to less active times – thus more efficiently balancing overall utilization levels.

Demand management is active in every stage of the service lifecycle, and works closely with several other processes. One of the closest of these is capacity management. Although the exact nature of this relationship is discussed in section 4.4.6, it is important to note the difference in scope between these two processes.

At first glance the scopes of capacity and demand management seem to overlap, and it might appear that demand management is just one aspect of capacity management. However, this is an over-simplification of both processes. Both are concerned with achieving the same business outcomes, and both are concerned with optimizing investment, but the processes themselves are different. To generalize, demand management focuses primarily on the business and user aspects of providing services, whereas capacity management focuses primarily on the resourcing and technology aspects.

The fundamental differences between demand management and capacity management are summarized in Table 4.8.

4.4.3 Value to business

The main value of demand management is to achieve a balance between the cost of a service and the value of the business outcomes it supports. The other service strategy processes define the linkage between (and the investment required for) business outcomes, services, resources and capabilities. Demand management refines the understanding of how, when and to what level these elements interact. This enables executives to evaluate the real investment required to achieve business outcomes at varying levels of activity.

Example of how demand management could have improved business outcomes

A large retailer made a significant investment in point-of-sale technology to reduce the time to check out customers, and increase the accuracy of the checkout procedure. The anticipated outcome was increased customer satisfaction, and the ability to increase store turnover by 5% per day. A review of the project revealed that the investment only achieved its objectives at the larger stores. Smaller stores had fewer customers with fewer items to purchase and the new technology added significant overhead to these stores without any noticeable increase in customer satisfaction or turnover.

Demand management could have anticipated this situation and identified two user profiles with different patterns of business activity and different technology requirements, saving the retailer a significant amount of unnecessary investment. This information would be used in conjunction with capacity management to improve the design of the service to better meet the desired business outcomes.

Table 4.8 Comparison of demand management and capacity management

	Demand management	Capacity management
Purpose	Identify, analyse and influence customer demand for services and the capacity to meet this demand	Ensure that current and future capacity requirements of services are provided cost-effectively, and that services are performing at the agreed level
Focus	Anticipating the demand for services based on user profiles and patterns of business activity, and identifying the means to influence that demand to achieve an optimal balance between investment and business outcome achievement	Understanding the current and future requirements for resources and capabilities and ensuring that these are designed, tested and managed to meet the demand on services
Major activities	Identifying patterns of business activity, user profiles and the resulting demand on services. Anticipating increases or decreases in demand, and identifying strategies for dealing with these. Influencing demand through incentives, penalties or differential charging	Producing a capacity plan to ensure the investment in the appropriate levels of capacity. Ensuring optimal use and performance of resources. Evaluating the impact of new or changed resources and capabilities on existing performance levels

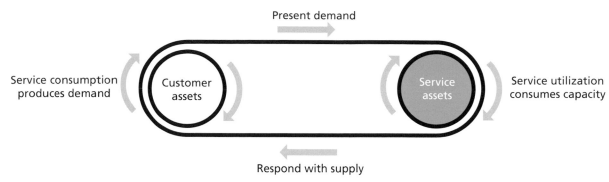

Figure 4.39 Present demand — Service consumption produces demand — Customer assets — Service assets — Service utilization consumes capacity — Respond with supply

Figure 4.39 Tight coupling between demand, capacity and supply

4.4.4 Policies, principles and basic concepts

4.4.4.1 Supply and demand

From a strategic perspective demand management is about matching supply to demand.

Consumption produces demand and production consumes demand in a highly synchronized pattern (Figure 4.39). Unlike goods, services cannot be manufactured in advance and stocked in a finished goods inventory in anticipation of demand. Demand and capacity are far more tightly coupled in service systems even when compared with just-in-time (JIT) manufacturing.

In Figure 4.39 customer assets present a pattern of demand to the service provider. Each time a user consumes a service demand is presented to the service provider, and this consumes capacity of the service assets. This, in turn, results in the service being supplied to meet the consumer's demand. The greater the consumption of the service, the higher the demand, the higher the consumption of capacity, and the more of the service is supplied.

This cycle of demand and supply will only function effectively while the service assets have available capacity. As soon as capacity is no longer available, the service provider will not be able to supply enough of the services to satisfy customer demand.

For this reason, a major part of demand management is to understand the potential demand, and the impact of the demand on the service assets. This allows capacity management to manage service assets (and investments) towards optimal performance and cost.

The productive capacity of resources available to a service is adjusted according to demand forecasts and patterns. Some types of capacity can be quickly increased as required and released when not in use. The arrival of demand can be influenced using pricing incentives. However, it is not possible to produce and stock service output before demand actually materializes.

4.4.4.2 Gearing service assets

The balance of supply and demand is achieved by gearing the service assets to meet the dynamic patterns of demand on services. This is not just a case of responding to demand as it presents itself, but it involves anticipating the demand, identifying the signals of increasing or decreasing demand and defining a mechanism to scale investment and supply as required.

Managing service assets according to demand involves a number of service management actions, including the following:

■ Identifying the services (through service portfolio management)
■ Quantifying the patterns of business activity (see section 4.5.1)
■ Specifying the appropriate architecture to deal with the type and quantity of demand (for example, deciding on dedicated versus virtualized processing environment)
■ Capacity and availability planning to ensure that the right service assets are available at the right time and are performing at the right levels
■ Performance management and tuning service assets to deal with variations in demand.

4.4.4.3 Demand management through the lifecycle

To be fully effective, demand management needs to be active throughout the service lifecycle. It might be tempting to assume that processes that are active in each stage of the lifecycle will address demand issues. However, if demand management is not consciously coordinated and managed, this will only tend to happen on an *ad hoc*, reactive basis.

The activities of demand management in each stage of the lifecycle will include:

■ **Service strategy** Identify the services and outcomes, and the patterns of business activity that are generated by achieving these outcomes. Forecast demand based on service utilization scenarios and communicate to design teams. Support service portfolio management by estimating activity levels to achieve specific outcomes.

■ **Service design** Confirm customer requirements regarding availability and performance, and validate that the service assets are designed to meet those requirements. In this stage the primary process interfaces are capacity management and availability management, although demand management will also contribute to sizing of service continuity options.

■ **Service transition** Demand management is involved in testing and validating services for forecast utilization and patterns of business activity. The ability to influence and manage demand for a service should also be tested.

■ **Service operation** Technical, application and operations management functions will monitor service assets and service utilization levels to ensure that demand is within normal levels and, if not, will initiate performance tuning or corrective action.

■ **Continual service improvement** Demand management will work to identify trends in patterns of business activity and to initiate changes to the capabilities of the service provider, or changes to the behaviour of customers where appropriate.

4.4.5 Process activities, methods and techniques

The following activities, methods and techniques can be selected and applied as needed to perform demand management.

4.4.5.1 Identify sources of demand forecasting

Demand management is based on a good understanding of business activity and how that activity impacts the demand for services. Demand management must therefore identify any documents, reports or information that can provide insight to these activities, and assist in forecasting the levels of demand. These sources will be used to define, monitor and refine the other components of demand management described in this section.

Potential sources of information that can assist demand management to forecast demand include:

■ Business plans
■ Marketing plans and forecasts
■ Production plans (in manufacturing environments)
■ Sales forecasts
■ New product launch plans.

4.4.5.2 Patterns of business activity

Services are designed to enable business activities, which in turn achieve business outcomes. Thus every time a business activity is performed, it generates demand for services. Customer assets such as people, processes and applications all perform business activities, and because of the way these assets are organized or because of the tasks they are completing, this activity will tend to be performed in patterns. These patterns of business activity (PBA) represent the dynamics of the business and include interactions with customers, suppliers, partners and other stakeholders.

Since PBA operate in a dynamic environment, they are often dynamic themselves. However, since services often directly support one or more PBA, and since PBA achieve business outcomes it is important that they are properly understood and aligned to services. This requires that they have to be properly defined and documented and changes properly controlled.

Once a PBA has been identified, a PBA profile should be drawn up and details about the PBA documented. The following items need to be documented:

■ **Classification** This indicates the type of PBA, and could refer to where it originates (user or automated), the type and impact of outcomes supported, and the type of workload supported.

■ **Attributes** Such as frequency, volume, location and duration.

■ **Requirements** Such as performance, security, availability, privacy, latency or tolerance for delays.

■ **Service asset requirements** Design teams will draft a utilization profile for each PBA in terms of what resources it uses, when and how much

of each resource. If the quantity of resources is known, and the pattern of utilization is known, the capacity management process will be able to ensure that resources are available to meet the demand – provided it stays within the forecast range.

Figure 4.40 illustrates three PBA. Example A shows the pattern of sales for a greeting card company in the USA. Customers buy greeting cards for major holidays or events. The different volumes of sales

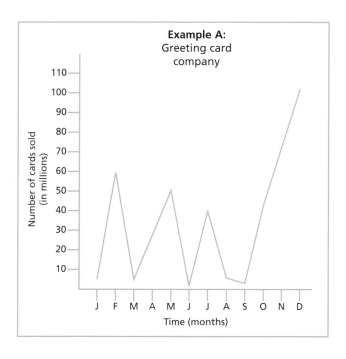

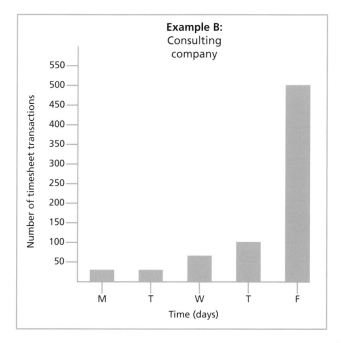

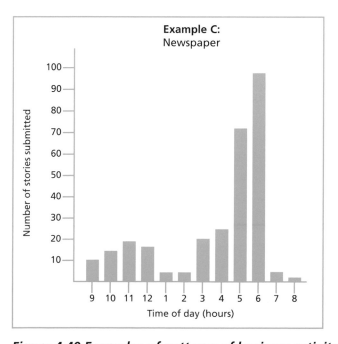

Each chart shows patterns of business activity (PBA). Each activity relies on IT services and each places a demand on the IT service provider's assets.

Example A – annual PBA: Greeting cards need to be designed, manufactured and distributed for each major holiday. The fluctuation in sales will result in a fluctuation in demand for IT services.

Example B – weekly PBA: Consultants need access to a timesheet system to track their activities so that customers can be billed. Most consultants wait until the end of the week to complete their timesheets. Some consultants record their activities daily.

Example C – daily PBA: Journalists have to meet the deadline of 6pm to submit their stories for publication. After the deadline, only high-impact corrections are made. The later in the day, the more critical the IT services become, and also the more utilized. Most journalists use the lunch hour to interview people for stories.

Figure 4.40 Examples of patterns of business activity

Table 4.9 User profiles matched with patterns of business activity (example)

User profile	Applicable pattern of business activity (PBA)	PBA code
Senior executive (UP1)	Moderate travel – domestic and overseas; highly sensitive information; zero latency on service requests; high need for technical assistance; need to be highly available to the business	45F 45A 35D
Highly mobile executive (UP2)	Extensive travel – domestic and overseas; sensitive information; low latency on service requests; moderate need for technical assistance; high customer contact; need to be highly available to customers	45A 35D 22A
Office-based staff (UP3)	Office-based administrative staff; low travel – domestic; medium latency on service requests; low need for technical assistance; full-featured desktop needs; moderate customer contact; high volume of paperwork; need to be highly productive during work hours	22A 14B 3A
Payment processing system (UP4)	Business system; high volume; transaction-based; high security needs; low latency on service requests; low seasonal variation; mailing of documents by postal service; automatic customer notification; under regulatory compliance; need for low unit costs; need to be highly secure and transparent (audit control)	12F
Customer assistance process (UP5)	Business process; moderate volume; transaction-based; moderate security needs; very low latency on service requests; medium seasonal variation; mailing of replacement parts by express; automatic customer notification; need to be highly responsive to customers	24G 10G

require different levels of IT service utilization. The IT service provider has to be able to anticipate the business activity before each major holiday so the company can be sure to prepare and ship the greeting cards in time. In addition, the online ordering systems will be in high demand in the two weeks prior to the holiday. This will require the service provider either to invest in spare capacity which will be idle at other times of the year, or to be able to balance the workload across multiple resources. In this way, processing lower-priority services will make way for the volumes of the higher-priority seasonal activity.

In example B of Figure 4.40 a consulting company relies on a timesheet service to bill consultants' time. Since most consultants complete their timesheets for the entire week at the end of the week, the later it is in the week the more critical the service, and the more it is utilized. Consultants may need to be encouraged to log their time at the end of each day, or the beginning of the next day.

Example C of Figure 4.40 shows how journalists use a word-processing and editorial service. Workloads tend to be light early in the day, but the closer to the deadline they move, the more the service is

utilized. It is unlikely that the behaviour of the journalists will be changed, since the PBA reflect established working practices. In these cases, measures will have to be taken to ensure that resources are available to match the PBA.

4.4.5.3 User profiles

User profiles (UPs) are based on roles and responsibilities within organizations. As suggested earlier, business processes and applications are treated as users in many business contexts. Many processes are not actively executed or controlled by staff or personnel. Process automation allows for processes to consume services on their own. Processes and applications can have user profiles.

Each UP can be associated with one or more PBA, as shown in Table 4.9. This allows aggregations and relations between diverse PBAs connected by the interactions between their respective UPs. User profiles are constructed using one or more pre-defined PBA. They are also under change control. UPs represent patterns that are persistent and correlated.

Pattern matching using PBA and UPs ensures a systematic approach to understanding and

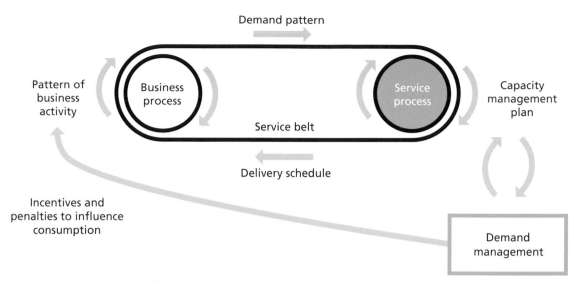

Figure 4.41 Business activity influences patterns of demand for services

managing demand from customers. They also require customers to better understand their own business activities and view them as consumers of services and producers of demand.

When PBA and UPs are used to communicate demand, service providers have the information necessary to sort and serve the demand with appropriately matched services, service levels and service assets. This leads to improved value for both customers and service providers by eliminating waste and poor performance.

UPs communicate information on the roles, responsibilities, interactions, schedules, work environments and social context of related users.

4.4.5.4 Activity-based demand management

Business processes are the primary source of demand for services. Patterns of business activity (PBA) influence the demand patterns seen by the service providers (Figure 4.41). It is very important to study the customer's business to identify, analyse and classify such patterns to provide sufficient basis for capacity management. Visualize the customer's business activity and plans in terms of the demand for supporting services.

For example, the fulfilment of a purchase order (business activity) may result in a set of requests (demand) generated by the order-to-cash process (business process of customer). Analysing and tracking the activity patterns of the business process makes it possible to predict demand patterns for services in the catalogue that support the process. It is also possible to predict demand

for underlying service assets that support those services. Every additional unit of demand generated by business activity is allocated to a unit of service capacity. Demand patterns occur at multiple levels. Activity-based demand management can daisy-chain demand patterns to ensure that the business plans of customers are synchronized with the service management plans of the service provider. See Figure 4.42 for an example of activity-based demand management.

If a business plan calls for the allocation of human resources, the addition of an employee can be translated into additional demand for the service desk function in terms of service requests and service incidents. Similarly, new instances of business processes can be used as predictors of demand for the service demand in terms of incidents and requests. After validating the activity/demand model it is possible to make adjustments to account for variations such as new employees, changes to business processes and technology upgrades on the customer's side.

Some of the benefits for analysing PBA are in the form of inputs to service management functions and processes such as the following:

■ Service design can optimize designs to suit demand patterns.
■ Capacity management translates the PBA into workload profiles so that the appropriate resources can be made available to support the levels of service utilization.

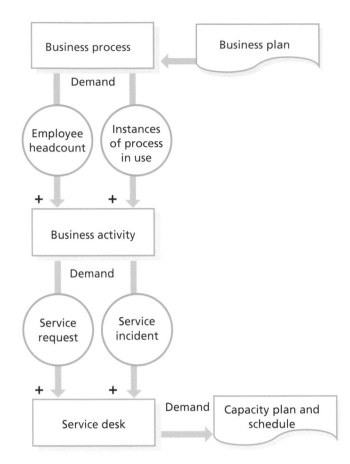

Figure 4.42 Example of activity-based demand management

- Service catalogue can map demand patterns to appropriate services.
- Service portfolio management can approve investments in additional capacity, new services or changes to services.
- Service operation can adjust allocation of resources and scheduling.
- Service operation can identify opportunities to consolidate demand by grouping closely matching demand patterns.
- Financial management for IT services can approve suitable incentives to influence demand.

4.4.5.5 Develop differentiated offerings

When analysing the PBA, it may become apparent that different levels of performance are required at different times, or different combinations of utility. In these cases, it is important to work with service portfolio management to define service packages that meet the variations in PBA.

For example, a company that produces seasonal goods may vary its sales process during periods of peak demand. During quieter times, sales staff may complete the entire order process (log the sale, check for inventory, initiate shipping and bill the customer), thus using all the utility of the service each time an order is placed.

During periods of peak activity, the sales people may only log the sale and check for inventory, passing the order to temporary staff for shipping and billing, and then moving to the next order. In this case there might be two differentiated offerings to reflect the two PBA.

Service packages are described in more detail in section 3.4.8.

4.4.5.6 Management of operational demand

One of the activities of demand management during service operation is to manage or influence the demand where services or resources are being over-utilized. Typically this would occur in the following situations:

- The patterns of business activity were inaccurate, resulting in over- or under-utilization of the service. Demand management could assist by providing penalties or incentives for users to reduce service usage, to use it at off-peak periods or (where the service is being under-utilized) to increase utilization. An example of a measure to influence demand is differential charging, where customers are billed higher rates for using the service during peak times. This is normally done in conjunction with capacity management, service level management and financial management for IT services.
- The business environment changed, resulting in a change to the pattern of business activity. This should be dealt with in conjunction with service level management and capacity management to understand the new utilization patterns, and to gear the resources and capabilities of the service provider appropriately. The new service requirements should also be reflected in the service portfolio.
- The service provider's forecast for resources was inaccurate, and there is insufficient budget to increase capacity. This situation is dealt with in more detail in the section on capacity management in *ITIL Service Design*.

It is important to note that demand management does not work in isolation when influencing demand. This is a complex situation involving changes to services, the service provider's ability to meet customer demand and the achievement of business outcomes. As a result, demand management always works in conjunction with capacity management, service level management, service portfolio management and financial management for IT services.

4.4.6 Triggers, inputs, outputs and interfaces

4.4.6.1 Triggers

Triggers of demand management include:

■ A request from a customer for a new service, or change to an existing service. This will be initiated through business relationship management and service portfolio management.
■ A new service is being created to meet a strategic initiative – this will be initiated through service portfolio management.
■ A service model needs to be defined, and patterns of business activity and/or user profiles must be defined.
■ Utilization rates are causing potential performance issues, or a potential breach of an SLA.
■ An exception has occurred to forecast patterns of business activity.

4.4.6.2 Inputs

Inputs to demand management include:

■ Initiative to create a new service, or to change an existing service. These inputs can come from service portfolio management or from change management.
■ Service models need to be validated and patterns of business activity associated with each service model will need to be defined.
■ The customer portfolio, service portfolio and customer agreement portfolio, all of which will contain information about demand and supply for services.

■ Charging models will be assessed to ensure that under- or over-recovery does not occur in internal service providers; or that pricing will be profitable for external service providers.
■ Chargeable items will need to be validated to ensure that customers actually perceive them and use them as defined.
■ Service improvement opportunities and plans will need to be assessed in terms of their impact on demand.

4.4.6.3 Outputs

Outputs of demand management include:

■ User profiles
■ Patterns of business activity will be formally documented and included in the service and customer portfolios
■ Policies for management of demand when resources are over-utilized
■ Policies for how to deal with situations where service utilization is higher or lower than anticipated by the customer
■ Documentation of options for differentiated offerings that can be used to create service packages.

4.4.6.4 Interfaces

Major interfaces with demand management include:

■ Strategy management for IT services will identify the key business outcomes and business activities that will be used to establish patterns of business activity and user profiles.
■ Service portfolio management uses information from demand management to create and evaluate service models, to establish and forecast utilization requirements and to identify the different types of user of the service. In addition, SPM will be able to develop service packages based on the information about patterns of business activity and user profiles.
■ Financial management for IT services will help to forecast the cost of providing the demand based on forecast patterns of business activity. In addition, it will work with demand management to identify measures to regulate demand when there is over-utilization of the service (e.g. through differential charging).

Financial management for IT services will also identify the relative costs of each differentiated offering.

- Business relationship management is the primary source of information about the business activities of the customer. Business relationship management will also be useful in validating the user profiles and differentiated service offerings before they are confirmed in the customer and service portfolios.
- Service level management will help to formalize agreements in which the customer commits to levels of utilization, and the service provider commits to levels of performance. Actual levels of performance and utilization will be reviewed at the regular service level review meetings (using information from demand management and capacity management) and any deviations noted. Demand management will work with service level management to define policies for how to deal with variances in supply and demand.
- Capacity management will work closely with demand management to define exactly how to match supply and demand in the design and operation of the service. Capacity management will monitor the actual utilization of service and work with demand management to understand trends of utilization and how to adjust the services for future use.
- Availability management uses information about patterns of business activity to determine when service availability is most important. This information is also helpful for performing service outage analysis and project service availability reporting.
- IT service continuity management will use demand management information to perform business impact analysis. It will be able to determine which workloads are impacted, and what volume of work is impacted by major outages at different times. Demand management information is also helpful in sizing recovery options to be able to deal with the minimum levels of business activity to ensure business continuity.
- Change management will work with demand management and capacity management to assess the impact of changes on how the business uses services. This is helpful in confirming the impact of the change and also

in evaluating the true cost of changing the service (a 'simple' change may push demand over a threshold where significant additional investment is required).

- Service asset and configuration management will identify the relationship between the demand placed on services and the demand placed on systems and devices. This is an essential link in ensuring that operational teams are able to execute what was anticipated during strategy and design.
- Service validation and testing will ensure that the service has correctly dealt with patterns of demand, and that measures taken to prevent over-utilization are effective.
- Event management, if instrumented correctly, can provide information about actual patterns of service utilization and validate the anticipated patterns of business activity for a service. Any deviation can be assessed and adjustments made to the service through service portfolio management.

4.4.7 Information management

The documentation and information required for effective demand management have been described throughout section 4.4, but an overview of the main sources is as follows:

- The service portfolio
- The customer portfolio to obtain information about customers and the opportunities that they represent
- The project portfolio to ensure that all projects have included demand management as a component
- Minutes of meetings between business relationship managers and customers
- Service level agreements are used to set a baseline for previous demand levels, and to define limits and policies for future utilization
- The configuration management system to map service assets, customer assets and business outcomes.

4.4.8 Critical success factors and key performance indicators

This section provides examples of critical success factors (CSFs). These are the conditions that need to be in place, or things that need to happen, if the demand management process is to be considered successful. Each CSF will include examples of key performance indicators (KPIs). These are metrics that are used to evaluate factors that are crucial to the success of the process. KPIs, as differentiated from general metrics, should be related to CSFs.

The following list includes some sample CSFs for demand management. Each organization should identify appropriate CSFs based on its objectives for the process. Each sample CSF is followed by a small number of typical KPIs that support the CSF. These KPIs should not be adopted without careful consideration. Each organization should develop KPIs that are appropriate for its level of maturity, its CSFs and its particular circumstances. Achievement against KPIs should be monitored and used to identify opportunities for improvement, which should be logged in the CSI register for evaluation and possible implementation.

- **CSF** The service provider has identified and analysed the patterns of business activity and is able to use these to understand the levels of demand that will be placed on a service.
  - **KPI** Patterns of business activity are defined for each relevant service.
  - **KPI** Patterns of business activity have been translated into workload information by capacity management.
- **CSF** The service provider has defined and analysed user profiles and is able to use these to understand the typical profiles of demand for services from different types of user.
  - **KPI** Documented user profiles exist and each contains a demand profile for the services used by that type of user.
- **CSF** A process exists whereby services are designed to meet the patterns of business activity and meet business outcomes.
  - **KPI** Demand management activities are routinely included as part of defining the service portfolio.
- **CSF** An interface with capacity management to ensure that adequate resources are available at the appropriate levels of capacity to meet the demand for services
  - **KPI** Capacity plans include details of patterns of business activity and corresponding workloads.

- **KPI** Utilization monitors show balanced workloads. Minimal over-utilization and a maximum amount of unused capacity (this is to prevent technical groups from over-investing in capacity to avoid being blamed for over-utilization).
- **CSF** There is a means to manage situations where demand for a service exceeds the capacity to deliver it.
  - **KPI** Techniques to manage demand have been documented in capacity plans and, where appropriate, in service level agreements.
  - **KPI** Differential charging (as an example of one such technique) has resulted in a more even demand on the service over time.

4.4.9 Challenges and risks

4.4.9.1 Challenges

Challenges for demand management include:

- The availability of information about business activities – especially if demand management is not included in the overall set of requirements and has to be collected separately. Customers have a limited tolerance for how many people gather information about their service requirements.
- Customers might find it difficult to break down individual activities that make sense to the service provider. Business relationship management should be able to assist in making this translation.
- Lack of a formal service portfolio management process or service portfolio. This will make it difficult to understand the business requirements, relative value and priority of services, and will mean that demand management information might be recorded on an *ad hoc* basis, often with little coordination and duplicate effort.

4.4.9.2 Risks

Demand management risks include:

- Lack of, or inaccurate, configuration management information, which makes it difficult to estimate the impact of changing demand on the service provider's infrastructure and applications.

- Service level management is not able to obtain commitments to minimum or maximum utilization levels, and it is therefore difficult to commit to levels of service. This situation often results in higher than necessary levels of investment to enable the service provider to keep ahead of demand – even when not essential.

4.5 BUSINESS RELATIONSHIP MANAGEMENT

For many organizations, the role of the business relationship manager (BRM) was established to execute certain customer-facing activities in various processes, such as service level management. However, as the role matured it became clear that there was a discernible process to support that role.

Business relationship management is the process that enables BRMs to provide links between the service provider and customers at the strategic and tactical levels. The purpose of these links is to ensure that the service provider understands the business requirements of the customer and is able to provide services that meet these needs. The primary measure of whether this purpose is being achieved is the level of customer satisfaction.

4.5.1 Purpose and objectives

The purpose of the business relationship management process is two-fold:

- To establish and maintain a business relationship between the service provider and the customer based on understanding the customer and their business needs.
- To identify customer needs and ensure that the service provider is able to meet these needs as business needs change over time and between circumstances. Business relationship management ensures that the service provider understands these changing needs. Business relationship management also assists the business in articulating the value of a service. Put another way, business relationship management ensures that customer expectations do not exceed what they are willing to pay for, and that the service provider is able to meet the customer's expectations before agreeing to deliver the service.

The objectives of business relationship management include:

- Ensure that the service provider understands the customer's perspective of service, and is therefore able to prioritize its services and service assets appropriately
- Ensure high levels of customer satisfaction, indicating that the service provider is meeting the customer's requirements
- Establish and maintain a constructive relationship between the service provider and the customer based on understanding the customer and their business drivers
- Identify changes to the customer environment that could potentially impact the type, level or utilization of services provided
- Identify technology trends that could potentially impact the type, level or utilization of services provided
- Establish and articulate business requirements for new services or changes to existing services
- Ensure that the service provider is meeting the business needs of the customer
- Work with customers to ensure that services and service levels are able to deliver value
- Mediate in cases where there are conflicting requirements for services from different business units
- Establish formal complaints and escalation processes for the customer.

4.5.2 Scope

For internal service providers business relationship management is typically executed between a senior representative from IT (larger organizations may have dedicated BRMs) and senior managers (customers) from the business units. Here the emphasis is on aligning the objectives of the business with the activity of the service provider.

In external service providers business relationship management is often executed by a separate and dedicated function of BRMs or account managers – each one dedicated to a customer, or group of smaller customers. The emphasis here is on maximizing contract value through customer satisfaction.

Business relationship management focuses on understanding how services meet customer requirements. To achieve this, the process must focus on understanding and communicating:

- Business outcomes that the customer wants to achieve
- Services that are currently offered to the customer, and the way in which they are used by the customer
- The way in which services are currently offered including who is responsible for the services, what levels of service have been agreed, the quality of services delivered and any changes that are anticipated
- Technology trends that could impact current services and the customer, and the nature of the potential impact
- Levels of customer satisfaction, and what action plans have been put in place to deal with the causes of dissatisfaction
- How to optimize services for the future
- How the service provider is represented to the customer. This at times means raising concerns around commitments that the business made to IT but is not meeting.

From the above points, it is clear that business relationship management depends on a number of other service management processes and functions. For example, the mapping of business outcomes and services is done in service portfolio management. Service level management provides information about the levels of services agreed and achieved. Configuration management provides a mapping of infrastructure, applications, services, service owners and customers. Capacity management provides information about utilization levels and the potential impacts of new technologies.

Unless the relationships between business relationship management and other service management processes are clearly identified, there is potential for confusion about the boundaries between them. The main criterion for setting these boundaries is that business relationship management focuses on the actual relationship between the service provider and its customers and the levels of customer satisfaction, whereas the other processes focus on the services themselves, and the extent to which they meet the stated requirements.

This does not mean that business relationship management is unconcerned with the services

themselves, but that it focuses on the overall extent to which the service provider is meeting the customer's needs.

It also does not mean that other processes are not concerned with customer satisfaction, but that they focus on the quality of services and on specific actions they can take to meet customer expectations for those services.

A good example of the difference between business relationship management and other service management processes is that of service level management.

Both these processes involve regular interfaces with customers and both are concerned with ongoing reviews of service and service quality. However, the two processes have different purposes and the nature and content of the customer interface is different. These differences are summarized in Table 4.10.

It should also be noted that business relationship management is not just concerned with service delivery and support, but also with the design and building of services. This means that business relationship management is the primary process for strategic communication with customers for all departments in the service provider, including application development teams within the service provider's organization.

4.5.2.1 Processes and roles for business relationship management and SLM

This section is about the scope of the business relationship management process, and how it differs from other processes, especially service level management (SLM). It should be noted that the processes are similar in that they both involve significant interface with customers. For this reason, many organizations use a single person or group to execute both processes. Some organizations refer to them as service level managers, while others refer to them as business relationship managers (BRMs).

At the same time there are clear differences between the processes, and care should be taken that the people executing them understand when they are performing a role based on building customer relationships and defining customer requirements; and when they are defining and

Table 4.10 Differences between business relationship management and service level management

	Business relationship management	Service level management
Purpose	To establish and maintain a business relationship between the service provider and the customer based on understanding the customer and their business needs. To identify customer needs (utility and warranty) and ensure that the service provider is able to meet these needs.	To negotiate service level agreements (warranty terms) with customers and ensure that all service management processes, operational level agreements and underpinning contracts are appropriate for the agreed service level targets.
Focus	Strategic and tactical – the focus is on the overall relationship between the service provider and their customer, and which services the service provider will deliver to meet customer needs.	Tactical and operational – the focus is on reaching agreement on the level of service that will be delivered for new and existing services, and whether the service provider was able to meet those agreements.
Primary measure	Customer satisfaction, also an improvement in the customer's intention to better use and pay for the service. Another metric is whether customers are willing to recommend the service to other (potential) customers.	Achieving agreed levels of service (which leads to customer satisfaction).

Table 4.11 Business relationship management process activities and other service management processes

Scenario	Primary process being executed	Other processes involved
Developing high-level customer requirements for a proposed new service	Business relationship management	Service portfolio management
Building a business case for a proposed new service	Business relationship management	Service portfolio management
Confirming customer's detailed functionality requirements for a new service	Design coordination	Business relationship management
Confirming a customer requirement for service availability for a new service	Service level management	Business relationship management, availability management
Establishing patterns of business activity	Demand management	Business relationship management
Evaluating business case for new service request from customer and deciding go/no go	Service portfolio management	Business relationship management, financial management for IT services
Report service performance against service level targets	SLM	Business relationship management

coordinating the tactical levels of performance of specific services.

4.5.3 Value to business

The value of business relationship management is in the ability of the service provider to articulate and meet the business needs of its customers.

Business relationship management creates a forum for ongoing, structured communication with its customers. This enables business relationship management to achieve better alignment and integration of services in the future, as well as to achieve the current business outcomes.

With that communication comes a greater understanding by the service provider of their customer's business, and greater understanding by the customer of the service provider's capabilities and services. It helps to set realistic customer expectations, and puts a human face on the service provider.

When there are disagreements about what should be delivered, business relationship management enables both groups to reach agreement quickly and without speculation about motives that often occurs when two parties do not know each other. The end result is higher levels of trust that the service provider is going to deliver value in future, and a greater willingness to work together as strategic partners.

The focus on customer satisfaction enables the service provider and customer alike to gauge how effectively the business objectives are being met.

Without business relationship management services will still be delivered and will still meet delivery targets, but it is difficult to quantify the value of the services, and there is no guarantee that the appropriate business needs are being fully met, that services are prioritized correctly, or that the customers the service provider meets with are truly representing the business needs of the customer. Service provision without business relationship management is possible, but it is costly, erratic and filled with mistrust.

4.5.3.1 Business relationship management and other service management processes

While most other service management processes focus on making sure the service provider can execute, the business relationship management process focuses on making sure the customer gets what they need. The business relationship management process is acting as a check and balance. This ensures that the customer is properly represented within the service provider, and that the service provider does not lose focus on the customer requirements while striving for efficiency and ease of management.

Some organizations assume that if all processes are working then business relationship management will automatically be performed. That assumption, however, will result in individual activities being performed in an isolated manner, some getting

The importance of knowing the 'right' customer

An external service provider was asked to build and deliver a set of processes and services to move web applications from development into production. The customer was the manager of a group of web developers in a large bank. After six months of hard work the processes were ready and the services had been tested, using criteria provided by the customer. The first package of web applications was released, and immediately crashed several business-critical online services. Although the outage was brief and the change was rolled back, the damage was significant and the service provider was blamed and fired.

The truth of the situation was that the web applications were never approved by the bank. The web developers worked for a business unit that was trying to split away from the internal IT service provider. Their applications (supposedly only for use by their business unit) inadvertently replaced some key functionality on the bank's intranet, which resulted in the failure of key external services.

The service provider had a relationship with the wrong customer. Had they had an ongoing relationship with the bank, they would have known the appropriate decision makers, and would have had a better understanding of the impact of their actions on other CIs in the bank. They would have known of the politics of the situation, and taken the appropriate action. As it was, they were blamed for the situation and prevented from doing business with the bank in future.

neglected because of other priorities and ultimately many of the activities of business relationship management never actually being performed – even if there is a person playing the role of BRM.

However, it is important to understand that in a single situation the same team may be executing activities for the business relationship management process and other processes. Table 4.11 provides some examples.

4.5.4 Policies, principles and basic concepts

4.5.4.1 Business relationship management and the business relationship manager

The process of business relationship management is often confused with the business relationship manager (BRM) role. This is because the role is high profile and many customers identify the process activities with the person playing the role.

The role of the BRM can also cause confusion about the process. This is because the BRM often represents other processes when engaged in business relationship management – for example, when obtaining information about customer requirements and business outcomes, the BRM is also providing this input to service portfolio management, demand management and capacity management. Thus, it may seem unclear as to which process the BRM role is executing.

The role of many BRMs is broader than the business relationship management process because they are executing more processes than just business relationship management. In many cases a process may call upon the person in the BRM role to initiate communication with a customer – for example, a project manager needs help in communicating a revised project schedule to the business. A person in the role of business relationship management can easily facilitate this communication as part of the project management process – this does not necessarily mean that project management has initiated the business relationship management process.

The business relationship management role is described in detail in Chapter 6.

4.5.4.2 Customer portfolio

The customer portfolio is a database or structured document used to record all customers of the IT service provider. The customer portfolio is business relationship management's view of the customers who receive services from the IT service provider.

The customer portfolio is used in several processes, especially service portfolio management, but it is defined and maintained in the business relationship management process. The customer portfolio allows the service provider to quantify

their commitments, investments and risks relative to each customer. For example:

- The customer portfolio makes it possible to understand who the customers of a service are. This might sound obvious, but many organizations find it difficult to know who the real customer is, especially when services are used by multiple business units or customers. For example, one organization did not know that a certain business unit was using an application until it failed and caused a major impact to the business. This was because access and usage was controlled by the application development team directly.
- Without a customer portfolio, it is easy for anybody in a business unit to place demands on the service provider. Defining who the customer is, and who in the customer's organization has the authority to make decisions about what services are required, is an important step in making sure that the service provider does not over-commit.
- A customer portfolio makes it easier to quantify the use and value of each service. Without a customer portfolio service delivery is often reduced to an unquestioning production of outputs. This means that staff in the service provider will simply deliver what they have been told to deliver, regardless of whom the customer is and what they use the service for. This approach might be acceptable with highly commoditized services that never change, but it can be very damaging when the service is dependent on customer-specific situations that require different levels of service or priorities at different times.
- Without a customer portfolio it is possible to understand the investment in a service, but not how that investment relates to each customer.
- A customer portfolio will also enable the service provider to document customer leads (especially relevant for external service providers) and follow up on these opportunities.

Each customer relationship carries with it an element of risk. This should be expected because the service provider and customer work differently, and have different competencies, knowledge and capabilities. The customer portfolio helps the service provider to quantify and manage risks. Most risks in working with a particular customer can be mitigated through negotiation, or changing some aspect of the service or the way it is delivered and supported. However, in some cases the service provider might even consider that a particular opportunity is too risky, and use the customer portfolio to identify customers with whom they will not do business. Typical risks include:

- The customer's business (and therefore demand for services) is volatile. It is therefore difficult for them to commit to consistent utilization levels, and difficult for the service provider to plan and execute a consistent quality of service.

- A customer that is extremely cost-sensitive may force the service provider's margins so low that any variation results in a loss, especially if that is the only customer using a particular service. Although this seems like a problem that only applies to external service providers, many internal service providers are forced into situations where they have to deliver a set of services without being able to recover the cost of those services. These service providers are often unfairly perceived to provide sub-standard service quality while draining the organization's resources. The best approach would be to negotiate with the customer to ensure that they are prepared to commit to the appropriate funding (or revenue) model. If not the service provider should refuse the business, but this is not always possible for internal service providers.

- Customers that share the same service might have different expectations. Catering to the highest expectation is expensive to the service provider (especially if the customer is paying the same as everyone else). Catering to the average expectation will satisfy some customers, while leaving others wanting more. Catering to the lowest expectation will be most cost-effective, but leave the majority of customers dissatisfied.

- A customer may decide to change service providers – for example, to outsource various aspects of the internal service provider.

Another important contribution of the customer portfolio is that it makes it possible for the service provider to analyse market spaces for growth opportunities. If the customer portfolio identifies that the service provider is very good at delivering services to a specific type of customer, they can embark on a strategy to expand their market space to similar customers. They may also be able to

identify additional services that can be delivered to existing customers by comparing the current service portfolio and customer portfolio. For more information on expanding market spaces, see section 3.4.

Typical contents of a customer portfolio include:

- Customer name
- Authorized customer representative
- Business relationship manager name
- Description of customer's business, and key business outcomes
- List of services provided to the customer (link to the service portfolio) along with any specific commitments for those services (link to agreements or contracts in the customer agreement portfolio)
- Historic and projected revenue (and margins for external service providers). This is essential to understand who the key customers are. In reality no organization ever has enough resources to give equal focus to all customers. Key customers have to be identified and prioritized for special attention by BRMs
- List of regular meetings with a description of the content and expected attendees at each meeting
- Description of the reports that are produced, who receives those reports and what action will be taken as a result of the reports
- Description of how and when performance will be reviewed
- Overview of past performance, major issues or events and how these were handled
- Outline of planned future services for this customer
- Schedule of agreement or contract reviews. These include a formal status report on the performance of all services, any exceptions handled and future planning for services. The result of these reviews will be a renewal or renegotiation of the contract. These reviews are typically coordinated with service level management.

4.5.4.3 Customer agreement portfolio

The customer agreement portfolio is a database or structured document used to manage service contracts or agreements between an IT service provider and its customers. Each IT service delivered to a customer should have a contract or other agreement that is listed in the customer agreement portfolio.

The customer agreement portfolio is an important tool for business relationship management, but it is usually defined and maintained as part of service level management. This is to ensure alignment of services to the agreements at the most fundamental levels of service. It is very difficult to achieve economies of scale, and to deliver shared services, if each contract is managed from a different baseline. It is therefore very important to coordinate all commitments across all agreements from a central point. This also makes it difficult for a BRM or account manager to promise a service to the customer that the service provider is unable to deliver.

Conversely, the contracts or SLAs themselves will need to be negotiated and managed separately for each customer. For internal service providers SLAs are negotiated and maintained by service level management, involving BRMs where these exist (see section 4.5.4.1). For external service providers the process is more complex, involving legal specialists, service level management and dedicated BRMs.

For a Type III service provider with large numbers of consumer-type customers there will be a different approach still, with standard contracts that are offered to large numbers of customers without the option to negotiate. Business relationship management will tend to be in the form of marketing activities, such as focus groups or customer satisfaction surveys.

4.5.4.4 Customer satisfaction

Section 3.5 covers how services are designed and delivered to ensure customer satisfaction, and references the Kano model. These are central to effective business relationship management, since business relationship management is primarily responsible for ensuring that customers are satisfied with the service they receive.

Business relationship management measures customer satisfaction and compares service provider performance with customer satisfaction targets and previous scores. The most common form of measuring customer satisfaction is a regular survey, which should be designed to be easy to complete in a short time. This is different from the customer satisfaction survey performed by many service desks to ensure that incidents were closed and that the service desk analysts were professional in their approach. Business relationship management surveys have to do with whether the service achieves its objectives at every level. It may reference the service desk surveys, but only as a subset of the overall measurement of customer satisfaction.

Business relationship management should launch an investigation into any significant variations in satisfaction levels so that the reasons are understood. Business relationship management should also trend customer satisfaction metrics, taking care to ensure that similar measurement instruments were used, to ensure consistent metrics. Any issues with customer satisfaction should be investigated and discussed with the customer. Where appropriate, opportunities for improvement should be logged in the CSI register in conjunction with service level management, for later review and prioritization.

Care should be taken to validate the customer satisfaction scores, as a worse-than-normal score may not be the result of poor service by the service provider. For example, one organization found that poor performance in the customer organization had resulted in poor bonuses being paid out, reducing the overall level of satisfaction of employees. This was reflected in poor scores for the service provider, which had met its service targets! Even where the service provider is not to blame, however, a poor customer satisfaction score reflects a negative perception of the service, and business relationship management should still discuss this with the customer.

To ensure customer satisfaction business relationship management works throughout the service lifecycle to understand customer requirements and expectations, and ensure that they are being met or exceeded:

■ In service strategy, business relationship management ensures that the service provider understands the customer's objectives and overall requirements. Information about the customer is identified and documented in the customer catalogue, and business relationship management ensures that this is appropriately linked to all potential services and agreements in the service and customer agreement portfolios. As agreement is reached about the type and level of service required, business relationship management will initiate a service portfolio management evaluation of whether a service currently in the service catalogue or pipeline will meet that need. At all stages of the service pipeline, through development and operation, business relationship management will represent the customer's perspective and requirements. Business relationship management also ensures that the customer is aware of the service provider's constraints and requirements.

■ In service design, business relationship management provides guidance to both the customer and the design teams about who to communicate with, and what the content of that communication will be. Business relationship management also ensures that the service provider has properly understood the customer's detailed requirements, and initiates corrective action if this is not the case. In addition, business relationship management will work with service level management to ensure that the customer's expectations of the new service are set at the appropriate level, based on constraints faced by the service provider.

■ In service transition, business relationship management ensures that the customer is involved in change, release and deployment activities that impact their services, ensuring that their feedback has been taken into due consideration. Service validation and testing will need customer input for customer and user acceptance testing, and will need the customer to provide (or authorize the use of) suitable test data. Business relationship management provides a valuable communication channel to ensure that customers are involved whenever necessary, and also to keep customers apprised of any changes or developments. The BRM may represent the customer on the CAB, or they may arrange for the customer to be at CAB meetings and change evaluation meetings when appropriate. In service operation business relationship management works with service level management, incident management and the service desk to ensure that services have been delivered according to the contract or SLA. This does not mean that every process owner will be involved in every (or even many) incidents or changes – rather that each of these processes have interests which intersect at the service desk. Roles should be clearly defined

and separated so that all processes are represented by a single interface to prevent multiple calls to the service desk for each major incident. Each of these processes or functions will also measure the level of customer satisfaction regularly and report this to business relationship management. Any customer satisfaction issues will be raised directly with the customer through business relationship management, and the appropriate resolution defined in concert with other service management processes.

■ In continual service improvement, business relationship management monitors service reports and is given frequent updates about levels of customer satisfaction, exceptions to service levels or specific requests or complaints from the customer. Working together with other processes and functions, business relationship management will help to identify appropriate remedial action and agree this with the customer.

Important note regarding customer and user satisfaction

There is ongoing debate about the difference between customer and user satisfaction. On the one side of the debate, the argument is that the customer is paying for the service, and has therefore defined the level of service that will be offered to the customer. The only relevant metric is therefore customer satisfaction. User satisfaction is not really relevant since the users do not pay for the service.

On the other side of the debate, the argument is that customers are ultimately investing in the service on behalf of the users who will be using it. Therefore user satisfaction is just as, if not more, important than customer satisfaction. If one ignores user satisfaction it is very likely that the users will cause the service to fail, or complain so much about the service that the customers will be forced to reconsider their decision.

In truth, this is a very complex discussion and often says more about the culture of the customer than that of the service provider. However, there are some factors that the service provider needs to be aware of and should do its best to influence.

- Both customer and user satisfaction are important, since both can influence decisions about which services are used and which service provider can deliver those services. This is well understood in retail environments – if a parent (customer) buys a cereal that their child (consumer or user) refuses to eat, how likely are they to buy it again? By the same token if a toy company markets a video game using graphic images of horror and carnage, how many parents will buy it for their children? Providing a service that satisfies both the customer and user is key, and business relationship

management is at the heart of helping the customer to make that decision.

- At the same time, there are situations where the customer is only prepared to pay for a certain level of service, but when it is delivered to the user they demand more. If the service provider accedes to this demand they could find themselves with satisfied users, but an unprofitable business. Sayings like 'the customer is always right' may be helpful in focusing the attitude and behaviour of the service provider staff, but there is a flip side to the coin – 'The customer pays for the service'.

Table 4.12 What satisfies customers and users?

Customers	Users	Conflict
Pricing Is it cost-effective? Does it compare favourably with similar services from other service providers? Is there anything we can cut out to make it cheaper?	*Performance* How fast is it? How quick is response time? Will it always be there when I need it?	The better the performance, the more expensive the service. Users need to be educated about the level of performance they can expect. If a decision has been made to go with a cheaper service, business relationship management should equip customers with information and messaging to explain the decision.
Profitability/value Will this service provide us with a return on investment? Will it help us to meet our business objectives?	*Ease of use* How intuitive is the user interface? How many screens do I have to go through to complete a transaction? Will I get training on how to use it? Will it make my job easier?	Ease of use may require additional investments in a more well-rounded or mature service. It could also mean that more training and greater levels of support from the service provider are required. Additional investments may lengthen the return, or make the value more difficult to justify. The BRM should work with the customer to demonstrate how ease of use can increase profitability in the long run or result in greater value through better ability of users to meet organizational objectives.
Service impact What will this service actually achieve? Will it increase productivity? Will it enable us to improve our services? Where will we be in six months, one year, three years after having used this service?	*Quality* How does this service actually work? Will it do everything I need it to do? Will it solve some of the problems I'm currently experiencing?	Customers are not as concerned about service quality as long as it gets the job done at a reasonable price – although it may be more difficult for the user to work with the service. A higher-quality service that gets the same job done may be more popular with users, but will be difficult to sell to the customer. The BRM can work with customers and users to help them evaluate the balance between net result and quality. There might be some additional value that quality brings that the customer has overlooked.
Innovation Will this service enable me to identify new opportunities? Will it help me to grow the business? Will it open new markets, or will it enable us to expand what we deliver?	*Consistency* Will I be able to use this service to do my work as long as I stay in this job? Will it do what I need it to do the same way every time?	This conflict is ever-present in business. Services can actually help resolve it by automating routine tasks, putting more inexperienced staff in positions that perform those tasks and focusing the attention of more experienced staff on innovation. The BRM can help to bring about this change in culture as the service is introduced by educating customers about best practices in using the service.

Business relationship management is key to keeping this balance.

- User satisfaction should not start with the delivery of service. Even where the customer does not engage with its users during the strategy stage, business relationship management should make every effort to convince the customer to include users in the service design and transition stage.

- There is a significant difference between customers of external service providers and those of internal service providers. An external service provider is contractually bound to provide services to their customers, provided they are paid to do so, and that it is legal and possible to do. Customer satisfaction is generally high provided the customer and users get what they paid for or a little better.

- Internal service providers deliver services to business units in their own organization. Real money does not change hands, and the motivation to provide service is that the organization as a whole meets its objectives. Internal business units have been known to abuse this situation by demanding crippling levels of service from IT on the pretext that they are paying customers. Even worse, some organizations have been seriously compromised because any manager in a business unit is able to demand any service from IT, and not even pay for it because IT is centrally funded. This mindset that IT needs to do whatever the business tells it to is no longer valid. IT is not only a service provider, it is also a business unit with a responsibility to work with other business units to meet the objectives of their organization. The BRM plays a very important role in ensuring that this mindset is understood, and that the relationship between service provider, customer and user is balanced with the overall objectives of the organization.

- It is important to understand that customers and users measure service differently. Table 4.12 illustrates this. The BRM is key to understanding what drives satisfaction in both customers and users, and ensuring a good balance of both is designed, delivered and communicated to both customers and users.

The BRM has a unique challenge in ensuring customer and user satisfaction. Although it is important that both customers and users are satisfied with the service they receive, they are often satisfied by different aspects of the service. Table 4.12 illustrates how customers are satisfied by different (often opposing) factors. The BRM has to ensure that the customer has decided on the trade-off between each set of conflicting factors, and then communicate to each group how the service has been delivered from that group's point of view.

4.5.4.5 Service requirements

Throughout the service lifecycle business relationship management is involved in defining and clarifying requirements for service. This involves investigating the business need or opportunity, validating it, defining a business case and evaluating both the warranty and utility needed. The main processes involved here are service portfolio management in service strategy and design coordination and service level management in service design.

This type of activity is specialized and will require expertise in business analysis. Customers do not always know how to articulate requirements, especially when they have to be translated into the language and format that the service provider can understand and use to design and build the service, and to define metrics to determine success.

In some cases, customers attempt to define requirements that they think will make sense to the service provider. In other cases customers may distrust the service provider, and attempt to dictate a solution rather than requirements – making it difficult for the service provider to understand and deliver the real value.

There are four common categories of information that are gathered and presented (incorrectly) as objectives or requirements (Ulwick, 2005):

- **Solutions** Customers present their requirements in the form of a solution to a problem. Customers may lack the technical expertise to be able to arrive at the best possible solution. Customers may ultimately be disappointed by the very solution they present. To mitigate this risk, rather than looking to customer ideas about the service itself, look for the criteria they use to measure the value of a service.

- **Specifications** Customers present their requirements in the form of specifications – vendor, product, architectural style, computing platform etc. By accepting specifications, a provider needlessly prevents its own organization from devising optimal services.

■ **Needs** Customers present their requirements as high-level descriptions of the overall quality of the service. By their nature, high-level descriptions do not include a specific benefit to the customer. For example, '… service will be available 99.9% of the time'. These inputs are frequently ambiguous and imprecise. They leave the provider wondering what customers really mean: '99.9% of business hours? 99.9% of a calendar year? Does this include maintenance windows? Can the 0.1% be used all at once?' By leaving room for interpretation, the provider leaves too much to chance. Business relationship management should ensure all input is measurable and actionable.

■ **Benefits** Customers present their requirements in the form of benefit statements. Again, the risk is in the ambiguity or imprecision of the statements. 'Highly reliable', 'faster response' and 'better security' take on many meanings and present different implications for the organization.

The BRM can help to avoid any confusion by helping to articulate and validate the requirements and explain to customers how this will make it easier for the service provider to deliver what the customer needs.

Part of the problem is that many service providers obtain requirements without providing any guidelines. Customers will then respond in any way that is convenient to them, and they will also respond as if there are no limitations on what they can ask for. The service provider has created a difficult situation – firstly they have to translate the requirements without knowing the thought process that created them, and secondly they have already set expectations that they may not be able to meet simply by accepting the requirements from the customer.

Service providers should take on more 'marketing mindset'. Here the service provider changes its thinking from 'what should we deliver?' to 'what value is the customer trying to achieve?'. In other words, instead of getting the customer to specify the service, they should focus on the outcome and then work their way back to defining the service. Table 4.13 contains a number of leading indicators,

or common business objectives, that can be used to define better requirements.

Table 4.13 Customer tasks, outcomes and constraints

Type of objective data	Data
Customer tasks	What task or activity is the service to carry out? What job is the customer seeking to execute?
Customer outcomes	What outcomes is the customer attempting to obtain? What is the desired outcome?
Customer constraints	What constraints may prevent the customer from achieving the desired outcome? How can the provider remove these constraints?

4.5.4.6 Business relationship management as facilitator of strategic partnerships

Some service providers are so important to their customer that they are included in strategic discussions about the customer's business, even forming part of the CEO or CIO steering group. Business relationship management is the process that facilitates this, and ensures that the right person is included in these meetings.

Business relationship management will also ensure that relevant information about the strategic direction of the customer is communicated back into the appropriate processes and people within the service provider organization. This will enable them to re-assess their own strategy, market spaces, future opportunities and service portfolio.

This facilitation is valid for internal and external service providers, although the legal and confidentiality issues for external service providers are significantly more complex due to potential conflicts of interest. It is up to the executives of the customer, and good standards of business conduct of the service provider, to ensure that conflicts of interest are avoided. The service provider should not be present in discussions that could place them in a compromising position, and should not communicate compromising information back into their organization if they happen to obtain it while performing this role.

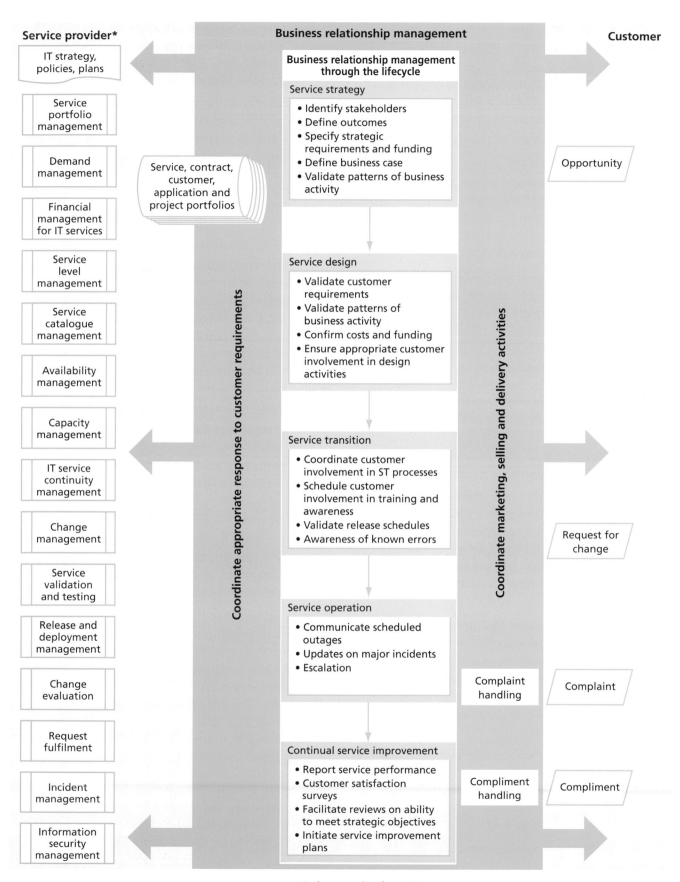

Figure 4.43 Business relationship management activities

4.5.5 Process activities, methods and techniques

The context and activities of business relationship management are illustrated in Figure 4.43. This diagram shows the position of the business relationship management process as providing a bridge between the world of the customer and the world of the service provider.

Figure 4.43 shows the world of the service provider on the left, the world of the customer on the right and the business relationship management process bridging the two. The two overarching activities of the business relationship management process are:

- To represent the service provider to its customers through coordinated marketing, selling and delivery activities
- To work with service portfolio management and design coordination to ensure that the service provider's response to customers' requirements is appropriate. Thus the process facilitates customer advocacy throughout the service lifecycle.

4.5.5.1 The nature of the business relationship management process

The business relationship management process itself consists of activities in every stage of the service lifecycle, but it is rarely executed as a single end-to-end process. The exact activities that are executed will depend on the situation that has caused the service provider or customer to initiate the process.

For example, if a customer has identified a new business need, the business relationship management process will be initiated to help document the opportunity and business requirements and then execute the activities identified in the service strategy and service design boxes in Figure 4.43.

If, on the other hand, a customer wishes to order a standard service, the business relationship management process will be initiated to execute the activities in the service operation and service transition boxes in Figure 4.43.

Business relationship management also interfaces with a number of other service management processes throughout the service lifecycle. As a result it is difficult to define a single end-to-end process with a single beginning and end. Rather,

business relationship management as a process consists of a number of key activities that are linked together and executed as sub-processes throughout the lifecycle.

The business relationship management process has distinct groups and sequences of activities, even if they are not all performed from beginning to end every time the process is initiated. For example, the process can be initiated in the service design stage of the lifecycle by service level management, without first going through service strategy.

4.5.5.2 Process initiation

The business relationship management process is initiated either by the customer or by service management processes and functions – usually by contacting the BRM (role). The BRM is usually responsible for executing the business relationship management process – although some aspects could be automated or delegated. For example, a service level manager could play the role of BRM in many situations.

The BRM must maintain a register of all opportunities, requests, complaints and compliments to track them and ensure that they do not fall between different processes and functions.

4.5.5.3 Initiation by customers

Customers need a way to communicate with the service provider about their needs, opportunities and requirements, and to have these taken care of in a formal, organized manner.

It is not optimal for customers to interface directly with service developers and technical staff whenever they need something. Firstly, if more than one customer requests something similar from two different groups, this causes wasted effort and investment. The BRM overcomes this by maintaining a central register of requests through service portfolio management. Secondly, there is no guarantee that the service provider will be able to consistently offer the service once it has been developed. Thirdly, the service provider environment can be complex and the customer may find themselves being referred from one group to another without any action being taken.

The business relationship management process provides a point of coordination for all customer requirements, so that customers are able to deal with the appropriate staff at the appropriate time without having to worry about whether their requirements will be followed through. The only exceptions are the routine interfaces between service provider and customer staff during the delivery of services; and the coordination provided by the service desk in resolving incidents or standard service requests (although in specific cases standard service requests, such as requests by VIPs, could be routed through business relationship management instead – as shown in Figure 4.43).

Also, customers should not have to be concerned about how to engage with the service provider. They should not have to wonder whether to log a request for change or how to initiate the design of a new service. These are mechanisms created by the service provider to facilitate their internal processes, and customers should not be expected to understand the peculiarities of the service provider's processes. (At the same time, customers often find it helpful to learn how to use standard documentation for frequently used services, so that they save time in completing the documentation and getting it processed without rework. For example, travel agencies become experts in submitting passport applications to the appropriate government agency – their service provider.)

The business relationship management process ensures that customers have a single point of contact for dealing with any kind of requirement, and that their requirements are documented in the correct format for the service provider's processes. Business relationship management will also coordinate any customer involvement in the service provider's processes – for example, in testing a new service or documenting a business case.

Opportunity

Customers engage with the BRM when they identify an opportunity that the service provider can help them to exploit, or when they need additional services from the service provider. Sometimes, during regular review meetings, the customer raises some issue that they are working on and the BRM can assist in defining the opportunity.

In these cases the business relationship management process will ensure that the opportunity or need is documented and then passed to the appropriate service management process to manage it further. What is important is that business relationship management is not just a

mechanism to document the opportunity. The BRM also monitors its progress on behalf of the customer and, where necessary, coordinates between processes and expedites the opportunity if it gets held up by any service provider process or function.

In external service providers, business relationship management, managed by a BRM (sometimes called an account manager), will treat this kind of opportunity as a sales scoping opportunity. They will coordinate all activities required to produce a proposal and bid, progress it through the sales cycle until the deal is concluded and then hand over to a delivery manager to ensure that the service is deployed and delivered. However, it is important to note that the BRM will continue to communicate with the customer to make sure that the delivery organization is delivering what was agreed.

Request for change

Requests for change (RFC) are used to initiate the change management process. However, customers may not be familiar with the process or how to complete the request. The business relationship management process will ensure that the customer is assisted in completing and submitting the request.

However, the BRM will also continue to monitor the change through the change management process, providing status updates to the customer, or requesting additional information if necessary. The BRM also represents the customer in change advisory board meetings, and coordinates any other activity that the customer will be involved in – for example, pilots, deployment testing and scheduling. The business relationship management process facilitates this interaction.

Other requests

Many requests are not as specific as requests for change, or defining a specific new opportunity. In some cases a customer needs help to understand a new service opportunity, or would like to know whether a new technology represents a new business opportunity for them. They may be requests about how individuals in the customer organization can benefit from discounted products or services from the service provider (e.g. 'can I get a copy of my office automation software at a discounted rate for my own personal use?'). If there is a formal process to deal with this type of request (e.g. service portfolio management) then business relationship management will redirect the request and follow up to make sure that it is properly dealt with and that the customer is satisfied.

If there is not a formal process to deal with the request, then business relationship management will initiate any activity required to action that request, possibly using multiple processes or different departments in the service provider organization. Again, the key is not to fulfil every request received, but to ensure that the customer's requests are actioned appropriately and that the customer is satisfied with the outcome, whether negative or positive.

It is important to note that it will not always be possible to accede to every request. In these cases business relationship management is an important factor in whether the customer will perceive the negative answer in a positive light, and remain satisfied with the outcome. For example, providing an alternative – 'We are not able to do what you have asked because …, however, we understand that this is important to you, have you thought about …?' Or agreeing to the request, but putting a price to it that will ensure that, if the customer insists on it, the service provider will be able to deliver it effectively.

Complaint

Customer complaints in business relationship management should not be confused with incident management.

Incident management is a formal process whereby specific service disruptions are reported to the service provider (usually through a service desk). The service provider will then attempt to restore the service within the agreed time. This may involve escalating the incident to higher levels of technical expertise or management to ensure that the incident is resolved in a timely manner.

The BRM should not have to deal with most incidents. If they find that this is the case, it implies that the incident management process is not working effectively, or the time agreed to resolve incidents has not been defined correctly.

There are four situations when the BRM should be involved with incidents, but this does not imply that the BRM is responsible for incident management. It merely implies that there is an

additional level of customer support provided in these situations (please note that in terms of role, either the BRM or a service level manager could be involved):

- When a major incident occurs. The BRM ensures that communication is taking place with the customer, and prevents technical staff from being disrupted by the customer while the incident is being resolved. The BRM also ensures that customers are kept updated with information about the *post mortem* review and facilitates any service level management review if appropriate.

- When repeated incidents occur, making the customer feel that their priorities are not being taken seriously or that the service provider is incompetent. The BRM, often together with service level management, provides relevant information back to the customer, reassuring them of their importance to the service provider and outlining any corrective actions that are proposed by service level management. The BRM has an important diplomatic role to play here, because in some cases the incidents may not be caused by the service provider, but by the customer (for example, by over-utilization or introducing unauthorized changes to client computers etc.). The involvement of the BRM to focus on the customer relationship aspects often makes it easier for the service level management process to introduce proposed changes to the contract or agreement.

- Incidents related to new services. This could be viewed as part of early life support (see *ITIL Service Transition*), where a customer is reassured that any early issues with the service are resolved and customer priorities are being taken seriously. Care should be taken to set customer expectations that this level of support will only be provided in the short term, although they are always free to raise complaints in future. The BRM can tactfully redirect incidents to the service desk when reported after the early life support phase. Please note that this does not imply that the BRM will be involved in driving early life support for every project, but it should be considered for major or high-profile projects.

■ When a customer has reported an incident to the service desk, but has not received any information about the incident, or feels that it has not been prioritized correctly. In these cases the business relationship management process would be able to provide up-to-date information to the customer and possibly get the incident escalated, or get the customer to accept a longer resolution time. Alternatively, the service desk may be experiencing very high numbers of high-priority incidents, and realize that it will not be able to resolve all incidents in time. Usually this situation is escalated to service level management, but the incident may be serious enough that additional diplomacy may be required to mollify the customer, and the BRM is involved.

Nevertheless complaints about the service or the relationship with the service provider should be expected. Complaints that could be handled by business relationship management include:

■ The functionality of a new service is not what the customer wanted.

■ The customer is not satisfied with the overall level of service received. This might be because the number of incidents is too high (even if they are fixed on time), or because the customer's situation has changed, or because they have become accustomed to the standard level of service and think that they should get something better.

■ A service provider's staff member has not been respectful, or did not treat a situation seriously enough. This request will require further investigation and potentially a meeting with the staff member's manager and an apology to the customer.

■ The service provider is not giving the customer information that they need. This is usually due to the service provider not knowing that the customer needed the service, or simply not having the information. Again, the BRM should investigate the situation, update the customer, contract or service portfolio as necessary and ensure that the information is either provided as required, or the customer is advised that it cannot be provided, and an alternative worked out.

■ A competitor is offering better service, cheaper rates etc. This will require an in-depth investigation of the situation through strategy management for IT services, service portfolio management, service level management, financial management for IT services etc. If feasible these processes should evaluate whether the new level of service or different pricing is feasible and work with the BRM to renegotiate the contract. If it is not feasible, the customer should be notified and a decision made about whether to terminate the current relationship.

Complaint handling

Complaints should not be dealt with as if it is the first time the service provider has received a complaint. No relationship is perfect, and a good service provider recognizes that there will be complaints, and establishes a formal procedure to handle them. This will ensure that all parties are clear about what constitutes a complaint and how it will be handled. The BRM is responsible for recording and managing complaints from the time they are made to the time they have been dealt with, regardless of which process or function was used to resolve the complaint.

The BRM should review outstanding complaints regularly and, if acceptable progress is not being made, should escalate them following the appropriate procedure. Customers should be kept advised as to the status of the complaint and any action required to resolve it. Business relationship managers should bear in mind that resolving a complaint might require some action from the customer, and should be able to tactfully manage the situation with them.

It is also helpful for the BRM to analyse the complaints over time to determine if there are any trends. Please note that this is not the same as problem management, where incidents are trended with the aim of discovering and fixing the root cause. The complaints managed by the BRM are concerned with the overall quality and relevance of the service to the customer, and the ability of the service provider to meet customer requirements.

The BRM will work with service level management and the customer to develop a plan for improving services as part of continual service improvement.

It is important to provide formal feedback to customers about their complaint. Feedback is usually in the form of a letter or email, and should:

- Thank the customer for making the effort to report the situation.
- Apologize for the situation and the inconvenience caused.
- Provide a brief summary of the situation to show that it has been correctly noted, and any action that has been taken – if appropriate. If the action involves disciplining an employee this should not be specifically mentioned, but some mention of the fact that the situation with the individual has been approached and the appropriate action taken.
- Assure the customer that steps have been taken to rectify the situation, and to prevent recurrence. If appropriate, a brief summary of these steps should be provided to reassure the customer that the complaint has been taken seriously.
- Thank the customer for raising the complaint and assure them of the service provider's commitment to service and customer satisfaction.
- Encourage the customer to contact the BRM should the situation not be resolved satisfactorily.

Finally, the BRM should put all significant resolved complaints on the agenda for the next review meeting to check whether the resolution was effective. Minor complaints can be dealt with by telephone or email.

Compliments

While most service providers have sophisticated processes and tools to deal with customer complaints and incidents, fewer have a formal process for dealing with compliments. It is true that customers are more likely to report dissatisfaction with service, and that each complaint creates an opportunity to improve customer satisfaction. It is just as important, however, to listen to customers when they are pleased with a service.

Compliments in this context refer to unsolicited positive feedback from a customer regarding the quality of service and the way the service was provided. This does not include the results of a customer satisfaction survey, which is a structured method of obtaining specific types of feedback.

Compliments indicate that the service provider is meeting, and often exceeding, the customer's expectations. These calls can help to validate the effectiveness of new services or service improvement plans. Compliments also indicate some of the less tangible aspects of a service that are important to a customer.

Feedback to staff members about compliments can be used to encourage desired behaviours and to increase morale. A well-timed compliment to a deserving team can often do more to improve attitudes towards work and customers than several complaints.

Compliments usually involve:

- The positive actions or attitude of a staff member or team. Interestingly, positive attitudes and actions do not attract as many compliments during normal service delivery as they do when performed during some type of service exception. Customers expect that a basic level of positivity is part of the service provider's job and therefore does not warrant special mention. In these cases the achievement of service level agreements and business outcomes is used to maintain staff morale and motivation.
- The quality of a service. This is especially true if the quality of service was better than expected, or the customer is pleased with some new feature of the service – usually with the intention of making sure the feature is retained.
- The effective resolution of an incident. Compliments are usually given when the incident was managed smoothly, but not often if the incident was not initially handled well, and resulted in initial frustration for the customer, or if the incident occurred several times before being resolved.

Handling compliments

Compliments are a valuable input to a number of processes because they contain unsolicited feedback in the customer's own words. Compliments therefore offer a unique insight into the real priorities and values of the customer.

Compliments can be used to determine if the appropriate level of service is being delivered, but they can also indicate where the service provider is increasing expectation beyond sustainable levels.

For example, care should be taken not to overemphasize compliments about heroic efforts. While staff should be encouraged to provide good customer service, and to provide additional assistance during unusual situations, too much emphasis on this aspect may encourage people to try to offer higher than required levels of service when there is no need to do so. This could result in escalating costs, and increasing levels of expectation from the customer.

In cases where customers are commenting on a feature of a service, the compliment should be documented and submitted to service portfolio management as part of ongoing review of the achievement of service objectives.

Compliments about the outcome of processes (for example, incident and change management) should be documented and forwarded to those processes as part of the process evaluation. Since customers will often not know which team or process is responsible for the positive outcome, the BRM provides a central access and coordination point for documenting and following through on compliments.

When customers call the service desk with compliments, these should be logged as part of the business relationship management process.

It is always a good idea to provide feedback to customers about their compliments. Feedback is usually in the form of a letter or email, and should:

- Thank the customer for the compliment
- Mention if it resulted in any type of action
- Contain a statement of how important both complaints and compliments are to the process of assuring good levels of service
- Contain an invitation to contact the BRM with any complaint or compliment in future.

4.5.5.4 Initiation by the service provider

The service provider is also able to initiate the business relationship management process if they need input from customers, or if they need to initiate the creation of a new service or changes to an existing service.

Some common scenarios in which the service provider will initiate the business relationship management process include:

- Strategy management for IT services has identified new opportunities that will require a new service or changes to existing services. Business relationship management is initiated to execute the activities in the service strategy and service design boxes of Figure 4.43.
- Service level management is revising existing, or drafting new, service level agreements. Business relationship management will be required to execute activities in the service design and service transition boxes of Figure 4.43.
- Demand management and capacity management need to quantify patterns of business activity as part of defining the organization's capacity plan.
- Financial management for IT services needs to define cost models that align to the desired business outcomes and services, and which can be used to assess the return on investment in services.
- As part of a marketing or sales campaign for a new service.
- Customer input is needed for service transition – for example, to provide users for user acceptance testing or to authorize the use of sensitive test data.

4.5.5.5 The business relationship management process through the lifecycle

This is the core of the business relationship management process, which enables the service provider's internal process to align, interface and, where necessary, integrate with the customer's business. The activities in each stage are not always all executed, and they are not always executed in the same sequence.

The exact number and combination of activities will vary depending on the scenario that has initiated the business relationship management process. This makes it even more important to register each initiation, and then design a response to each one.

Some scenarios will recur frequently (for example, those mentioned in section 4.5.5.4), and business relationship management will have a standard procedure defined and documented for each of these. The procedures will document exactly which business relationship management activities will be executed, in which sequence and which other process will be involved in the procedure.

The main tools used by business relationship management in executing the process are:

- A central register of all the cases that have been initiated. This is likely to be in the form of a customer relationship management tool. In external service providers these are likely to be part of the enterprise resource management suite of tools. In internal service providers, they are usually part of the service management suite of tools.

- The customer portfolio, which is used to track business outcomes, opportunities etc. The customer portfolio can also be used as a contact management database for progressing opportunities and strategies, for communication planning and to identify key stakeholders for service provider projects.

- The service portfolio, which is used to enable the BRMs to log new opportunities, and also to identify all customer-related activities required of business relationship management as part of evaluating and approving new services or changes to existing services. Business relationship managers will also use the service portfolio to enter and track investments required from the customer. The service portfolio provides information that the BRM can use to identify if an existing service can meet a new opportunity. The service portfolio also provides status information used by the BRM to keep the customer updated with the status of the service.

- The customer agreement portfolio, which is used to quantify the opportunities that have been identified as part of the service strategy, or that have been requested by the customer.

- The application portfolio will identify the existing functionality available, as well as the application development and management teams that the BRM will need to communicate with to explore each opportunity.

- The project portfolio will provide the BRM will information about project schedules, current priorities and the status of any new service or changes to existing services.

Service strategy

In service strategy business relationship management will primarily work to apply strategies, policies and plans to coordinate the service provider's processes with customer requirements and opportunities. Strategy management for IT services will have identified the key market spaces and business opportunities. The BRM will ensure that these are appropriately defined and executed from a customer perspective.

The main areas business relationship management will work with in this stage are:

- **IT strategy, policies and plans** These identify strategic opportunities, outcomes, priorities and any action plans that have already been agreed and approved. In addition, the policies will define some of the parameters within which business relationship management should work for approved and new opportunities (for example, which opportunities would be viewed as moving the organization away from its strategy, and with which standards the organization needs to comply).

- **Service portfolio management** Wherever feasible, existing services should be leveraged to meet new market spaces, customers or customer requirements. These often exist in the form of existing lines of service or service packages (see section 3.4.8). Business relationship management will identify the most suitable combination of lines of service and service packages to meet each business outcome. If these do not exist, a new service may need to be defined. The main business relationship management activities executed to achieve this include:
  - Work with service portfolio management to identify all the stakeholders for the project
  - Define the outcomes that need to be met. Although these may have been stated in the strategy, they may need to be defined in more detail
  - In the case of a new opportunity identified by the customer, the BRM will need to define the strategic requirements (these should already exist in services that have been identified in the service strategy. If not the BRM will work with the customer to identify them)
  - Ensure that funding is available for the new service, or any changes to the existing service. If funding is not available, either the service will not be provided (and the BRM will need to inform the customer), or the situation will need to be escalated to the organization's executives, since the agreed strategy is at risk

- Define the business case for the new or changed service. The BRM will need to work with the customer to understand the business outcomes and anticipated returns for the service.
- **Demand management** The BRM will identify patterns of business activity that are anticipated for each opportunity, and also the factors that influence these patterns.
- **Financial management for IT services** The BRM will help to validate the cost models to be used for each opportunity (for external service providers, this will relate to pricing models rather than cost models) and provide information to be used in financial forecasting. Financial management for IT services will assist in identifying and evaluating investments for the opportunity.

Service design

In service design business relationship management will work to ensure that the detailed design and development of services continue to meet the requirements of the customer, and that they are valid for the business outcomes that have been identified. Although business relationship management focuses primarily on the functionality (utility) requirements of the services, it will need to be able to assure customers of the warranty of the services as well.

The main processes they will work with include:

- **Project management** Every project will need to interface with business relationship management. The BRM will work to confirm or clarify customer requirements and obtain more detailed requirements where necessary. The BRM will also assist in ongoing communication planning and liaison with the customer. Whenever resources are required from the customer, the BRM will ascertain who the appropriate resources are, get agreement from the customer and coordinate the resource scheduling.
- **Financial management for IT services** Business relationship management will need to ensure that the costs identified in the design are in line with the investment anticipated in the strategy. Financial management for IT services will notify them of any deviations and the BRM will work with the customer to gain acceptance of these, or to modify the design requirements.

- **Service level management** For existing services business relationship management will work with service level management to determine the current levels of service for existing services and how these are likely to change. Business relationship management will ensure that the customer is aware of these and that they are acceptable. For new services, the BRM will ensure that all service level requirements are communicated to service level management. The BRM will also facilitate the negotiation of the service level agreements for the new or changed services, and initiate action to resolve any differences between the service provider and customer.
- **Demand management** If not already defined, the BRM will work with the customers to define the patterns of business activity for the service. If these have already been defined in service strategy, the BRM will confirm or refine them. Additional information or clarification may become available during the project, and may become lost or ignored by project teams focused on producing their deliverables. Business relationship management will ensure that any changes are properly dealt with and either specifically accepted into the scope of work, or else formally rejected and the customers notified.
- **Service catalogue management** The BRM will work with the customers to define the description of the service in the service catalogue and service request catalogue.
- **Availability management** Approaches that design availability purely on the basis of device or system availability often fail to meet the customer requirements. The BRM plays an important role in defining exactly when the service needs to be available, and how this will be measured by the users.
- **Capacity management** Some of the work with capacity management will be done through demand management and service level management, and in some cases there will be no need for business relationship management to interface directly with capacity management. However, it is important for capacity management to ensure that they understand the type of transactions being performed by the customer, and how important system and device performance is for those transactions. Business relationship management will be able to

ascertain this information and ensure that it is built into the service requirements and testing plans.

■ **IT service continuity management** Identifying business impacts and recovery objectives cannot be done without involvement from the customer. The BRM will facilitate this and ensure that IT service continuity management retains a focus on service continuity as a whole, and not just IT recovery.

Service transition

The BRM will coordinate customer involvement in the processes active during service transition. They will also ensure that all changes and releases meet the requirements set by the customer.

■ **Change management** Many opportunities that depend on existing services and technology will be initiated through change management. The BRM will raise the request for change and ensure that the customer is appropriately represented throughout the change management process. The BRM will also sign-off on successful implementation of the change. The BRM ensures that the customer is represented in assessing the impact and scheduling of changes, as well as involving the customer in any appropriate change management activity, such as assessing the impact of changes.

■ **Knowledge management** The BRM makes sure that customer needs for knowledge and information are included in knowledge management plans, and that knowledge and information about the customer and their business processes are available in the SKMS as required.

■ **Service testing and validation** The final authority on whether the service does what it was required to do is the customer. The BRM ensures that the testing plans have been properly designed to test the customer requirements, and then coordinates the customer involvement in the plans. The BRM coordinates customer activity during testing, including allocation of users for UAT and negotiating for use of test data.

■ **Release and deployment management** The BRM coordinates the schedule of releases with other business priorities, and ensures that all customers and users have received adequate

training for the new or changed service. Any concerns or questions raised by the customers and users will be communicated back to the release team to ensure that they can be addressed in the release documentation. The BRM will also receive information about known errors in the service, and will ensure that the customer knows about them and can work with those errors. They will also communicate any plans, costs (if appropriate) and schedules for resolving those known errors. The BRM also works with the customer to ensure appropriate participation and coverage of pilots.

■ **Change evaluation** The BRM is able to assist in coordinating change evaluation activities, and will also coordinate logging and coordinating any action arising from the evaluation.

Service operation

Many organizations feel that once a service has been deployed (i.e. a solution sold to the customer), the business relationship management process is no longer required for that service – until a new requirement is raised. This is not true for two reasons. Firstly, the way in which customers use services changes over time, and the BRM needs to be able to detect that and feed it back to the service provider, so that they can continue to be relevant. Secondly, no service is perfect and although the service desk is able to deal with most incidents and requests, some require a higher level of involvement and communication than others.

■ **Request fulfilment** In some cases the BRM will need to work with customers to educate them on how to request standard services from the service request catalogue. In other cases, the BRM is actually the point of contact for requesting these services. This is usually done for certain key people in the customer environment and is used as a way of enhancing the customer relationship.

■ **Incident management** Business relationship management is usually involved during major incidents to provide focused communication to the customer about the status of the incident, and to keep incident management up to date with customer impacts. In extreme cases, the BRM will be involved in the decision to invoke disaster recovery plans. Business relationship management is also used by customers to escalate incidents that they feel are not being treated with the appropriate level of urgency by the service desk or technical teams. The BRM's role in these cases is to support both the customer and incident management by providing incident management with business information that will help in evaluating the relative priority of incidents, and reaching agreement on which will be dealt with first.

Continual service improvement

Business relationship management facilitates continual service improvement by helping to identify improvement opportunities and then coordinating both service provider and customer activities to achieve this improvement. Once opportunities have been identified, the process begins again in service strategy. One of the fundamental business relationship management activities in this stage is conducting customer satisfaction surveys, which are instrumental in identifying areas for improvement and new opportunities.

Processes and activities that business relationship management interfaces with in this stage of the service lifecycle include:

- **Service reporting** Business relationship management is key to identifying what will be reported to the customer, and what the customer will be expected to do with the reports they receive. Business relationship management will also use the reports to influence customer perception of the service provider and the quality of services. Service reporting also identifies what items need to be monitored, and can also be used to define how event management needs to be configured. Information from service reporting is a central component of regular business relationship management reviews with the business.
- **Service level management** Business relationship management works with service level management to schedule and conduct service reviews with the customers and users. Any actions agreed in those meetings will be coordinated and monitored by the BRM, whether the actions apply to customers or the service provider.

- **Seven-step improvement process** Business relationship management helps to identify and communicate proposed improvement to services, or to the service strategy, design, transition and operation processes of the supplier. Business relationship management will also facilitate the involvement of the customer in defining requirements and business cases for improvements.

4.5.6 Triggers, inputs, outputs and interfaces

4.5.6.1 Triggers

Triggers of business relationship management include:

- A new strategic initiative
- A new service, or a change to an existing service, has been initiated
- A new opportunity has been identified
- A service has been chartered by service portfolio management
- Customer requests or suggestions
- Customer complaints
- A customer meeting has been scheduled
- A customer satisfaction survey has been scheduled.

4.5.6.2 Inputs

Inputs to business relationship management include:

- Customer requirements
- Customer requests, complaints, escalations or compliments
- The service strategy
- Where possible, the customer's strategy
- The service portfolio
- The project portfolio to ensure that requirements are gathered in a timely fashion, and that all projects include business relationship management activity where appropriate
- Service level agreements
- Requests for change
- Patterns of business activity and user profiles defined by demand management, and which need to be validated through business relationship management.

4.5.6.3 Outputs

Outputs of business relationship management include:

- Stakeholder definitions
- Defined business outcomes
- Agreement to fund (internal) or pay for (external) services
- The customer portfolio
- Service requirements for strategy, design and transition
- Customer satisfaction surveys, and the published results of these surveys
- Schedules of customer activity in various service management process activities
- Schedule of training and awareness events
- Reports on the customer perception of service performance.

4.5.6.4 Interfaces

Major interfaces with business relationship management include:

- Strategy management for IT services works closely with business relationship management to identify market spaces with information gleaned from customers. Business relationship management is also instrumental in gathering strategic requirements, identifying desired business outcomes and securing funding (internal) or pursuing deals (external).
- Service portfolio management and business relationship management work closely together to identify more detailed requirements and information about the customer environment required to create service models and assess proposed services. The BRM obtains requests and suggestions about services in the service portfolio and keeps customers up to date about the progress of services being assessed and chartered.
- Business relationship management helps financial management for IT services to obtain information about the financial objectives of the customer and helps the service provider to understand what level of funding or pricing the customer is prepared to accept. For internal service providers, return on investment calculations can only be performed with information about how the service has benefited the customer. The BRM is instrumental in helping customers to understand and accept charging policies, especially when first introduced. In some cases customer information may be required to calculate the cost of services, and the BRM will help to ascertain which information is required and how it will be obtained.
- Business relationship management assists demand management to identify and validate patterns of business and user profiles. Business relationship management will also be able to help identify changes to those patterns or the priorities of specific business activities. If demand needs to be managed, the BRM will be able to work with demand management to communicate this to the customer and agree on an appropriate mechanism to manage the demand.
- Service level management is able to use information about customers and service requirements gathered during the business relationship management process to understand the customer's priorities regarding service performance and deliverables. This can be very helpful in providing background before any SLA is finalized. In addition, the BRM will ensure that any SLA is updated in the customer agreement portfolio.
- Service catalogue management provides the basis for many discussions, reviews and requests that are initiated through business relationship management. It is important that the BRM is involved in communication with customers as services move from the service pipeline in the service catalogue. This will keep customers up to date, and ensure that expectations about the service are managed throughout the design and transition stages of the service lifecycle.
- Capacity and availability management rely on information about business outcomes and service requirements gathered through business relationship management. Business relationship management will also be used to validate information about proposed levels of performance and availability, especially as it relates to whether customers are prepared to pay for these levels.
- Business relationship management provides valuable perspectives and information on business priorities and outcomes for IT service continuity management. Business relationship management is also instrumental in ensuring

that counter-measures, recovery plans and tests accurately represent the world of the customer – and thus increase the level of assurance of the services to be provided.

■ Business relationship management is often the initiating point for requests for change and will also be involved with assessing the impact and priority of changes. Business relationship management also ensures the appropriate level of customer involvement in the change management process.

■ Business relationship management also ensures the appropriate level of customer involvement in release and deployment management, and service validation and testing.

■ Service improvements and the seven-step improvement process are an important part of business relationship management – from the point of view of both improvement opportunities, as well as validating, prioritizing and communicating improvement opportunities and plans with the customer in conjunction with service level management.

4.5.7 Information management

The documentation and information required for effective business relationship management have been described throughout section 4.5, but an overview of the main sources is as follows:

■ The service portfolio, project portfolio and application portfolio are all important references to enable business relationship management to communicate between the customer and the service provider regarding the services that are being provided currently and what will be provided in future.

■ The customer portfolio and customer agreement portfolio are updated and validated as part of business relationship management.

■ Customer satisfaction surveys need to be properly defined, tested and administered. The results will also need to be stored so that they are available to provide benchmarks, trending and improvement metrics.

■ The service catalogue is an important reference in communicating consistently with customers about the quality and performance of services, as well as requirements for changes to existing services.

4.5.8 Critical success factors and key performance indicators

This section provides examples of critical success factors (CSFs). These are the conditions that need to be in place, or things that need to happen, if the business relationship management process is to be considered successful. Each CSF will include examples of key performance indicators (KPIs). These are metrics that are used to evaluate factors that are crucial to the success of the process. KPIs, as differentiated from general metrics, should be related to CSFs.

The following list includes some sample CSFs for business relationship management. Each organization should identify appropriate CSFs based on its objectives for the process. Each sample CSF is followed by a small number of typical KPIs that support the CSF. These KPIs should not be adopted without careful consideration. Each organization should develop KPIs that are appropriate for its level of maturity, its CSFs and its particular circumstances. Achievement against KPIs should be monitored and used to identify opportunities for improvement, which should be logged in the CSI register for evaluation and possible implementation.

■ **CSF** The ability to document and understand customer requirements of services, and the business outcomes they wish to achieve
  ● **KPI** Business outcomes and customer requirements are documented and signed off by the customer as input into service portfolio management and service design processes.
■ **CSF** The ability to measure customer satisfaction levels, and to know what action to take with the results
  ● **KPI** Customer satisfaction levels are consistently high and are used as feedback into service portfolio management and strategy management for IT services. Any score lower than a defined level results in an investigation into the cause and corrective action – involving service level management, problem management, capacity management etc.
■ **CSF** The ability to identify changes to the customer environment that could potentially impact the type, level or utilization of services provided

- **KPI** Customer satisfaction and customer retention rates are consistently high.
- **KPI** Business relationship management provides input about changes to the customer environment that result in changes to services and strategy, resulting in improved customer satisfaction scores (and for external service providers, increased revenue).
- **CSF** The ability to identify technology trends that could potentially impact the type, level or utilization of services provided (this will be done together with capacity management)
  - **KPI** Opportunities leveraging new technologies have been identified with the business and included in the service portfolio. Each opportunity's return on investment has been measured and a decision made to keep or retire the service based on how effectively it met its objectives.
- **CSF** The ability to establish and articulate business requirements for new services or changes to existing services
  - **KPI** Every new service has a comprehensive set of requirements defined by business managers and staff, and these have been signed off by both business and IT leadership at the strategy, design and transition stages.
  - **KPI** The reasons for, expected results and detailed requirements for changes to services are documented and signed off at the strategy, design and transition stages.
- **CSF** Business relationship management must be able to measure that the service provider is meeting the business needs of the customer
  - **KPI** The service provider is consistently rated above a defined minimum level in a structured customer satisfaction survey.
  - **KPI** Service performance is matched to business outcomes, and reported to the customer. Deviations from expected achievements are documented and an improvement opportunity is logged in the CSI register or a change to the service portfolio is initiated as appropriate.
- **CSF** Formal complaints and escalation processes are available to customers
  - **KPI** Number of complaints and escalations are measured and trended over time and by customer. Escalations must reduce over time. Number of complaints will vary, but care should be taken to investigate changes in trends – services are getting worse (more complaints), services are improving (fewer complaints) or the process is not being used (fewer complaints).

4.5.9 Challenges and risks

4.5.9.1 Challenges

Challenges for business relationship management include:

- If business relationship management is attempted simply as a means of working on levels of customer satisfaction, it will probably fail. Business relationship management needs to be involved in defining services, and tracking that they are delivered according to the agreed levels of service. They are more than just 'window dressing' to make the IT organization look customer-friendly.
- A history of poor service may make it difficult for business relationship management to function effectively – as it will have to deal with the lack of credibility, which sometimes results in customers not being willing to share requirements, feedback and opportunities.
- Confusion between the role of business relationship manager (BRM) and the process of business relationship management. BRMs are often required to execute activities from other processes simply because of their customer-facing position. This does not make those activities part of the business relationship management process.

4.5.9.2 Risks

Business relationship management risks include:

- Because business relationship management is closely related to a number of other processes, confusion about the boundaries between these processes will mean that there is potential for duplication of activity, interference or for activities to be neglected. For example, it is counter-productive for multiple processes to try to escalate the same issue (for example, an incident) in the same way. As an example, the incident manager will find themselves inundated with calls from business relationship management, service level management etc. which will actually prevent them from being able to deal with the incident. It is important that these boundaries are clearly defined.

■ If there is a disconnect between the customer-facing processes, such as business relationship management, and those focusing more on technology, such as capacity management, it is likely that the service provider will become ineffectual. Both are critical for success, and they need to be properly integrated.

Service strategy, governance, architecture and ITSM implementation strategies

5

5 Service strategy, governance, architecture and ITSM implementation strategies

The purpose of this chapter is to explore various aspects of service strategy as they relate to the business, and the overall implementation of IT service management (ITSM). Specifically, it will provide an overview of corporate governance of IT, a service management system, the relationship between ITSM and enterprise architecture and the relationship between ITSM and application development.

Chapters 3 and 4 cover the concepts and processes of service strategy in detail, but they do not explain an ITSM implementation strategy – or how to go about implementing the ITSM processes described in the core ITIL publications. This chapter will provide an overview of what such an implementation strategy could look like.

5.1 GOVERNANCE

Governance is the single overarching area that ties IT and the business together, and services are one way of ensuring that the organization is able to execute that governance. Governance is what defines the common directions, policies and rules that both the business and IT use to conduct business.

Many IT service management strategies fail because they try to build a structure or processes according to how they would like the organization to work instead of working within the existing governance structures.

Changing the organization to meet evolving business requirements is a positive move, but project sponsors have to ensure that governance of the organizations recognizes and accepts these changes. Failure to do this will result in a break between the organization's governance policies and its actual processes and structure. This results in a dysfunctional organization, and a solution that will ultimately fail.

5.1.1 What is governance?

Corporate governance refers to the rules, policies and processes (and in some cases, laws) by which businesses are operated, regulated and controlled. These are often defined by a board of directors or shareholders, or the constitution of the organization; but they can also be defined by legislation, regulation, standards bodies or consumer groups.

Governance is important in the context of service strategy, since the strategy of the organization forms a foundation for how that organization is governed and managed.

The standard for corporate governance of IT is ISO/IEC 38500. This publication references the concepts of this standard and how it has been applied.

Governance is expressed in a set of strategies, policies and plans, as illustrated in Figure 5.1.

Figure 5.1 Strategy, policy and plan

Figure 5.1 shows how governance works to apply a consistently managed approach at all levels of the organization – firstly by ensuring a clear strategy is set, then by defining the policies whereby the strategy will be achieved. The policies also define boundaries, or what the organization may not do as part of its operations. For example, stating that

IT services will be delivered to internal business units only, and will not be sold externally as an outsourcing company would. The policies also clearly identify the authority structures of the organization. This is indicated in how decisions are made, and what the limits of decision-making will be for each level of management. The plans ensure that the strategy can be achieved within the boundaries of the policies.

It should be noted here that, while plans are ultimately part of governance, governors themselves do not define or produce the plans themselves. Rather, managers will use governance to define plans that are consistent with, and approved by, the executive and governors. However, governors will review the progress and implementation of plans.

5.1.1.1 Setting the strategy, policies and plans

Defining strategy, policies and plans is a rigorous process, and consists of three main activities: evaluation, directing and monitoring. Although the governance process itself is out of the scope of this publication, it is helpful to provide an overview, and to demonstrate the links between service strategy and governance. Figure 5.2 highlights the main activities of governance.

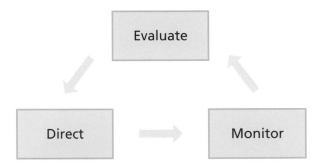

Figure 5.2 Governance activities

Governance needs to be able to evaluate, direct and monitor the strategy, policies and plans. These activities can be summarized as follows.

5.1.1.2 Evaluate

This refers to the ongoing evaluation of the organization's performance and its environment. This evaluation will include an intimate knowledge of the industry, its trends, regulatory environment and the markets the organization serves. The strategic assessment (section 4.1.5.1) is typical of the type of input that is used in this evaluation.

Items that are used to evaluate the organization include:

- Financial performance
- Service and project portfolios
- Ongoing operations
- Escalations
- Opportunities and threats
- Proposals from managers, shareholders, customers etc.
- Contracts
- Feedback from users, customers and partners.

5.1.1.3 Direct

This activity relates to communicating the strategy, policies and plans to, and through, management. It also ensures that management is given the appropriate guidelines to be able to comply with governance.

This activity includes:

- Delegation of authority and responsibility
- Steering committees to communicate with management, and to discuss feedback (also used during 'evaluate')
- Vision, strategies and policies are communicated to managers, who are expected to communicate and comply with them
- Decisions that have been escalated to management, or where governance is not clear.

5.1.1.4 Monitor

In this activity, the governors of the organization are able to determine whether governance is being fulfilled effectively, and whether there are any exceptions. This enables them to take action to rectify the situation, and also provides input to further evaluate the effectiveness of current governance measures.

Monitoring requires the following areas to be established:

- A measurement system, often a balanced scorecard
- Key performance indicators
- Risk assessment
- Compliance audit
- Capability analysis, which will ensure that management has what they need to comply with governance.

5.1.2 Who governs?

In this section the term 'governor' refers to any person or group that is responsible for the governance of an organization. In some organizations this could be a board of directors, appointed by the shareholders or members of the organization specifically to ensure that the organizations fulfils its mission. In government organizations these might be senior officials (e.g. cabinet ministers or secretaries), or a legislative or executive body (e.g. Congress, Houses of Parliament, Department of Public Administration etc.).

'The executive' refers to the group of senior managers of the organization that is responsible for the day-to-day governance of the organization on behalf of the governors. The executive, generally led by the chief executive officer (CEO), provides the link between the governors and the managers of the organization. Members of the executive have both a governance and management role, and are an overlap or an intersection of the two, specifically so that the terms of governance can be translated into what needs to be done to fulfil and comply with governance.

5.1.3 What is the difference between governance and management?

Governance is performed by governors. Governors are concerned with ensuring that the organization adheres to rules and policies; but even more, that the desired end results are being achieved in doing so.

Management is performed by executives and people who report to them. Their job is to execute the rules, processes and operations of the organization according to the governance policies, and to achieve the strategies defined by the governors. Managers coordinate and control the work that is required to meet the strategy, within the defined policies and rules. The executive ensures that governance and management are aligned and that management is executing the right activities in the right way, as required by governance.

Governors (those who create and ensure governance) are often not managers in the same organization. Governance and accountability are created by the governors. Management is the execution of the rules and authority granted by governance. This enables a system of checks and balances to be maintained and thus maximizes the

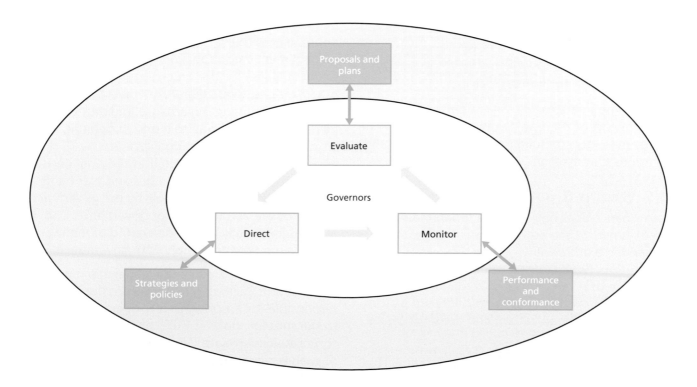

Figure 5.3 Governance and management activities

integrity of the organization. Exceptions include situations where the chairperson (governor) of the board is also the chief executive officer or managing director (manager).

Figure 5.3 shows the role of managers relative to the activities of governance.

The governance of IT service management will generally be determined by people with management responsibility in the organization. For example, it is important to determine how processes and functions are managed, and how they relate to one another, especially in terms of who is accountable and responsible for each area. However, it is important to remember that service strategies, and strategies for organizing service management, should be a subset of the overall strategies, policies and plans defined above.

5.1.4 The governance framework

A governance framework is a categorized and structured set of documents that clearly articulate the strategy, policies and plans of the organization. ISO/IEC 38500 outlines the following six principles that are used to define domains of governance (or areas that need to be governed):

■ Establish responsibilities
■ Strategy to set and meet the organization's objectives
■ Acquire for valid reasons
■ Ensure performance when required
■ Ensure conformance with rules
■ Ensure respect for human factors.

Each of these domains will have high-level policies that form part of the framework, and which will be used by managers to build procedures, services and operations that meet the organization's objectives.

5.1.5 What is IT governance?

IT governance does not exist as a separate area. Since IT is part of the organization, it cannot be governed in a different way from the rest of the organization. ISO/IEC 38500 refers to 'corporate governance of IT' and not IT governance. This implies that IT complies with and fulfils the policies and rules of the organization, and does not create a separate set for itself.

As mentioned several times in this publication, IT and the other business units share the same objectives and corporate identity and are required to follow the same governance rules.

What is normally called IT governance is usually a matter of the CIO, or senior IT manager, enforcing corporate governance through a set of applied strategies, policies and plans. Nevertheless, as a member of the executive, the CIO participates in how governance is defined and translated for management.

5.1.6 How is corporate governance of IT defined, fulfilled and enforced?

Although IT governance is not separate from corporate governance, it is important that IT executives have input into how corporate governance will specify how IT is governed. This is usually done through an IT steering committee, which also defines IT strategy and is involved in all major decisions regarding IT and its role in the organization.

As a member of the executive of directors, the CIO will ensure that the corporate strategies, policies, rules and plans include a high-level overview of how IT will be governed. If the CIO is not a member of the board of directors, it is the responsibility of the member who is responsible for IT to ensure that the CIO is consulted on what needs to be included.

In most cases, the governors will need assistance in defining governance for IT. This can be provided by management consultants or by engagement with senior IT leaders in the organization. In many organizations, the IT department will be heavily involved in defining governance and may even have a dedicated group to work on defining, enforcing and monitoring governance for IT. It is important to note, however, that the final decision about the strategy, policies, rules and plans and how they are enforced is made by the governors, since they are accountable for governance. This accountability may not be delegated to managers, who are required to comply with governance.

Governance is fulfilled by the leadership of each business unit, including IT. Therefore the CIO is responsible for ensuring that IT operates according to the strategy, policies, rules and plans defined in corporate governance. Since IT is an integral part of each business unit, however, it is important that the leaders of other business units are also engaged in defining how governance of IT will be fulfilled and enforced.

This is usually achieved by establishing an IT steering committee, also called an IT steering group. The purpose of the steering committee is to establish how IT will comply with and fulfil corporate governance. In addition it also represents how IT works with other business units to help them comply with corporate governance.

An example of the IT steering group in relation to other governance bodies is shown in Figure 5.4. The names and specific roles of each of these groups may differ from organization to organization.

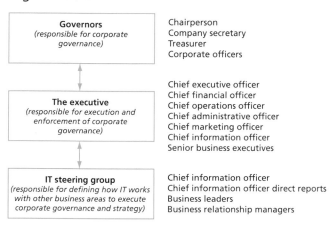

Figure 5.4 Governance bodies

The composition of the IT steering committee makes it an ideal platform to discuss and agree a number of other areas too. These include:

- The discussion and recommendation of the IT strategy, and IT strategy-planning documents, to the governors
- Clarification of strategic-requirements from other business units
- Ensuring the contents and consequences of the IT strategy are clearly understood by other business leaders
- Major decisions requiring funding from other business units
- Settling disputes about IT service priorities
- Reaching agreement about the minimum level of service for shared services (usually when one business unit wants a much higher level of service, but cannot afford to cover the costs themselves, and requires the agreement of all other business units to move to the higher level)

- Discussing IT service issues that require senior management intervention
- Negotiating changes to policies in other business units that impede IT's ability to meet its objectives (for example, an IT organization is asked to reduce costs, but users insist on the most expensive solution).

5.1.7 How does service strategy relate to governance?

From sections 5.1.1 to 5.1.5 it appears that all strategy is strictly contained within the role of the governors. This is not the case. Instead, the governors are responsible for the strategy of the organization, and for ensuring that all parts of the organization are aligned to that strategy. Every part of the organization must, however, produce its own strategy that enables it to fulfil the overall corporate strategy. Each strategy must be grounded in the corporate strategy and must be approved by the governors.

Section 4.1 covers the process of strategy management for IT services. That section discussed two levels of strategy – service strategy in general, and service strategy for IT as an internal service provider (section 4.1.5.20). In general strategy management is the responsibility of the board of directors. In larger organizations this is performed by a dedicated department reporting to the CEO or managing director – often called the strategy and planning department or something similar.

Strategy management for an internal IT service provider will be overseen by the CIO and the IT steering committee. Again in larger organizations, this might be a dedicated function reporting to the CIO.

The service portfolio is also an integral part of fulfilling governance, since the nature of services, their content and the required investment are directly related to whether the strategy is achievable. The current and planned services in the service portfolio are an important part of strategy analysis and execution.

Financial management for IT services is also a critical element of evaluating what investment is required to execute service strategies, ensuring that strategies are executed within the appropriate costs, and then measuring whether the strategy was achieved within the defined limits.

Demand management provides a mechanism for identifying tolerance levels for effective strategy execution. Each strategy approved by the governors must include the boundaries within which that strategy will be effective. Demand management assists in defining these boundaries in terms of business activity and service performance.

Business relationship management is instrumental in defining the requirements and performance of services to customers. This makes it possible for those customers to comply with corporate governance in their organizations.

5.2 ESTABLISHING AND MAINTAINING A SERVICE MANAGEMENT SYSTEM

Governance works to apply a consistently managed approach at all levels of the organization. Areas of specialization and processes within the organization are managed by management systems.

Definition: management system (taken from ISO 9001)

A system to establish policy and objectives and to achieve those objectives.

A system can be further defined as a set of processes, technology and people working cohesively to achieve a set of common goals. Note that the management system of an organization can include different management systems, such as a quality management system, a financial management system or an environmental management system.

A service management system (SMS) is used to direct and control the service management activities to enable effective implementation and management of the services. Processes are established and continually improved to support delivery of service management.

The SMS includes all service management strategies, policies, objectives, plans, processes, documentation and resources required to deliver services to customers. It also identifies the organizational structure, authorities, roles and responsibilities associated with the oversight of service management processes. For service providers that are aiming to achieve and maintain certification to ISO/IEC 20000, the SMS meets the requirements of ISO/IEC 20000-1. Coordinated integration and implementation of an SMS provides ongoing control, greater effectiveness, efficiency and opportunities for continual improvement.

The adoption of a SMS should be a strategic decision for an organization. The SMS, its processes and the relationships between the processes are implemented in a different way by different service providers. The design and implementation of the SMS will be influenced by the service provider's needs and objectives, requirements, processes and the size and structure of the organization. The SMS should be scalable. For example, a service provider may start with a simple situation that requires a simple SMS solution. Over time, the service provider may grow and require changes to the SMS, perhaps to cope with different market spaces, the different nature of relationships with customers, organizational changes, new suppliers or changes in technology.

As referenced in Chapter 2, an organization may implement several management systems such as:

- A quality management system (ISO 9001)
- An environmental management system (ISO 14000)
- A service management system (ISO/IEC 20000-1)
- An information security management system (ISO/IEC 27001).

As there are common elements between management systems, many organizations manage these systems in an integrated way rather than having separate management systems. To meet the requirements of a specific management system standard an organization needs to analyse the requirements of the relevant management standard in detail; and compare them with those that have already been incorporated in the existing integrated management system.

5.3 IT SERVICE STRATEGY AND THE BUSINESS

This section has been covered to some extent in Chapters 3 and 4, but the components have been summarized and repeated here for ease of reference.

Aligning the IT service strategy with the business is an important exercise that involves both parties.

Successful strategies are typically anchored top to bottom in the business vision, mission and core values. The overarching IT service strategy and underpinning service provider strategies should be examined and validated with the business to ensure that they serve the desired business outcome.

When it comes to the overarching business strategy, IT organizations typically are in general alignment with the rest of the business. As the overarching strategy is translated into strategies for individual business units, however, it becomes more difficult to achieve alignment, especially if the business units themselves are fairly autonomous. The level for business unit strategies will vary from organization to organization but it is best to avoid assumptions when it comes to defining these underpinning strategies.

Examining the IT service strategies at a more detailed level allows for the organization to be 'fit for purpose' and 'fit for use', which ultimately translates to value in the form of business outcomes.

An organization may have an IT strategy for service operations, which includes the service desk function. Considering that the service desk is the front-end to service operations, it is vitally important that the strategy clearly articulates what the expectations and desired outcomes of the service desk are. If superior customer service, accountability or customer advocacy are important differentiators for the business, the service desk should be designed, resourced and empowered to make one or more of those a reality.

5.3.1 Using service strategy to achieve balance

Building an overarching IT service strategy that is underpinned by a set of more targeted service strategies can require some careful consideration and planning. It often includes objectively considering a service's current state, future state, competition, opportunity, risk and, most importantly, talking with the business.

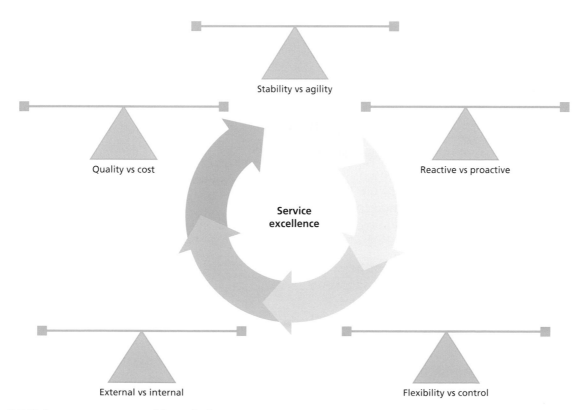

Figure 5.5 Using strategy to achieve balance

A good assessment of the effectiveness of a given service in supporting the overall business outcome and strategy is to evaluate how it impacts the balance of the organization. These are discussed in detail in *ITIL Service Operation* (see also Figure 5.5).

This might include a review of current investments, successes, failures, volumes, trends, costs, values etc. Achieving a perfect balance here is not only unlikely; it may be unbalanced by design. For example, the leadership team in a start-up organization may have greater appetite for risk than that of the market leader. Therefore, adjusting the balances should be done intentionally and be fully supported by the business. The service providers cannot lose sight of the overarching IT strategy, their position as an integrated business partner or their role of supporting the overall business vision/mission.

5.3.2 Integrated partners

Alignment of IT strategies with the business is something that should be done with the business leaders. IT leadership can contribute intelligence about technology trends, open market services, opportunities, risks and threats but, in the end, the IT strategies should represent the business they serve, and should be understood and agreed to by the business.

One method for creating and evolving these strategies is to create an IT steering committee with representation from the business, IT, enterprise architecture and governance. Examining the business value of IT services and aligning IT strategies helps IT begin to think about services in the context of value creation rather than components, technology and organization. Now IT service providers can begin to retool and think about all of the potential service options rather than just the ones built or provided internally.

IT can begin to transition away from specific technology discussions with the customers to value-based discussions anchored with the desired business outcome. When IT becomes an integrated strategic business partner, it starts to seek out the best possible solution for the business even if that means recommending a service provider other than itself.

5.4 IT SERVICE STRATEGY AND ENTERPRISE ARCHITECTURE

Enterprise architecture refers to the description of an organization's enterprise and associated components. It describes the organizational relationship with systems, sub-systems and external environments along with the interdependencies that exist between them. Enterprise architecture also describes the relationship with enterprise goals, business functions, business processes, roles, organizational structures, business information, software applications and computer systems – and how each of these interoperate to ensure the viability and growth of the organization.

Service strategy and enterprise architecture are complementary while both serving different purposes in the organization. When examined from a pure framework perspective, there can sometimes appear to be overlapping elements and/or activities. Part of developing a sound strategy is to examine the relevant industry frameworks and fabricate a model that is most likely to position the organization for the greatest degree of success. This isn't an exercise of choosing one framework over another but it is a case for selecting the components, activities or solutions that best serve the desired outcome. In the end, an organization is likely to be leveraging several industry frameworks, rather than adopting a single specific framework in its entirety.

Put another way, enterprise architecture identifies how to achieve separation of concerns (thus achieving a set of checks and balances), and how to define architectural patterns (or the rules of how systems communicate with one another). See section 5.3.8 in *ITIL Service Design* for more information on separation of concerns (SoC).

Enterprise architecture injects valuable intelligence into service strategy with clear definitions around business processes and solid engineering design principles. Enterprise architecture also plays a key role in the creation, use, maintenance and modelling of a reusable set of architectures for the organization. These architecture domains might include business architecture, information architecture, technology architecture, governance architecture and others. IT and service strategy development/maintenance should include representation from enterprise architecture to ensure seamless integration and alignment across an organization's enterprise and associated components. Development and maintenance of this is typically done by the IT steering committee.

The enterprise architecture team should have established models and criteria for designing services, processes and functions within the enterprise. IT process and function design may require additional detail but there should be a sense of alignment with the overall enterprise. These models are typically designed to be extensible so that new business processes and functions can easily be added, extended or discontinued. The IT service management team can subsequently create a service management implementation model that snaps into the broader enterprise architecture model in the form of decision support.

Figure 5.6 represents a generic open source architecture model that includes four primary architecture layers (business, application, technical, information), which are linked to the underlying decision support elements via the IT strategy. This model may be slightly different depending on the organization's preferred enterprise architecture framework but the concepts are applicable. Each architecture layer has three different perspectives that represent a conceptual, logical and physical view. The conceptual view represents the 'What' or the high-level capabilities of the corresponding architecture layer. The logical view represents 'How' the 'What' will be achieved, while the physical view represents the specific elements that will enable the 'How' and 'What' from an architecture perspective. The next layer of the model is the IT strategy, which should underpin the enterprise architecture layers. The IT strategy should fully support the enterprise architecture principles so that IT is effectively acting as a fully integrated business partner. In this model, the ITSM elements act as decision support system for the IT strategy to ensure service decisions, whether they be 'service portfolio' or 'change management', are fully aligned with the high-level capabilities as defined by the enterprise architecture. In summary, the enterprise architecture, IT strategy and decision support need to be fully integrated to ensure that the desired business outcomes are realized and the associated enterprise architecture systems and sub-systems are optimized. The ITSM processes that make up decision support can serve as a check and

balance to minimize drift from the desired business outcome.

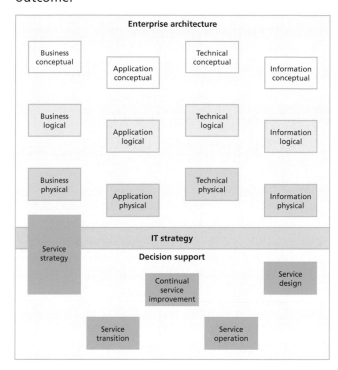

Figure 5.6 Enterprise architecture, strategy and service management

The extensibility of this model should include support for both internal and external service providers' need to develop elementary processes within a given IT function or process. There are many functions that are simply not defined in a single industry framework. Therefore, establishing an extensible model that enables service providers to integrate seamlessly is important and will minimize the number of orphaned processes and functions in the organization. Failure to address this can result in inconsistencies, attempts to fit everything into a single framework and overlapping processes in the organization.

Examples of enterprise architecture frameworks include:

■ **TOGAF** The Open Group Architecture Framework, which defines a framework for the design, planning, implementation and governance of an enterprise. TOGAF defines the structure of components in the organization, their relationships with one another and the principles and guidelines governing their design and evolution.

- **The Zachman Framework** This is a two-dimensional matrix that can be used to view and define an enterprise. It is a taxonomy for organizing architectural artefacts (e.g. documents and models) that takes into account both whom the artefact targets and what particular issue is being addressed.

5.5 IT SERVICE STRATEGY AND APPLICATION DEVELOPMENT

IT strategy and service strategy are both directly linked with application development in a number of different areas. The IT strategy combined with the underpinning service strategy lifecycle will serve as a primary feed into governance and application development. Decisions such as build vs. buy can also be influenced by IT strategy and the service strategy lifecycle. One of the main activities within the service strategy lifecycle is the classification of service assets. A well-defined service strategy combined with service asset classifications can empower business and IT leaders to make informed decisions without being intimately familiar with every aspect of a given service.

Application development teams should maintain alignment with service strategy by incorporating it into individual product line strategies and internal development efforts. While service strategy is created to drive the fulfilment of the desired business objectives, application development plans should be aligned to support service and IT strategy. In a sense, the application development strategy will have its own 4 Ps of strategy (perspective, position, plans and patterns) but it derives the overall direction from the service and IT strategy. This can also play a key role in helping the organization achieve the appropriate balance of innovation vs. operations.

Like other IT service providers, the application development providers should examine and validate their strategy (4 Ps of service strategy) within the context of the overarching IT strategy. If 'time to market' with new offerings is a primary objective or strategy, then the application development team can begin to align or position itself for that strategy from a people, process and technology perspective.

The service and IT strategy combined with the results from continual service improvement (CSI) can also play an important role in the design of upstream application development processes, the software development lifecycle and the associated service delivery tracks. For example, if the IT service strategy includes moving the organization to a certain mix of 'Commercial Off the Shelf' (COTS) solutions, there may be incentives or mandates built into the decision support processes that begin to lean the organization that way.

5.6 CREATING A STRATEGY FOR IMPLEMENTING SERVICE MANAGEMENT PROCESSES

This publication has focused primarily on how a service provider defines a service strategy, and how it defines strategies for services themselves. However, the way in which services are managed is also a critical success factor for the service provider.

This section therefore focuses on how to define a strategy for implementing service management processes. It is very important that organizations should not simply try to 'implement service management' as an entire framework in a single project or programme. The objectives of the organization must be clearly defined and then the components of service management that will support those objectives carefully scoped and implemented.

In addition, it is important to note that this section is a guide, not a mandatory set of techniques and methods. Many organizations will have their own approaches to conducting activities like defining a mission and vision, and for identifying risk. If these are in place in the reader's organization, section 5.6 might not be as relevant as it is to those readers who do not have formally established approaches for implementing this type of initiative.

ITIL will identify the major dependencies and linkages between processes, so that the organization can define how the processes they are implementing today will evolve and interface with processes that may be implemented in the future.

The implementation strategy for implementing service management processes will be defined and executed using the same lifecycle as the services, i.e. strategy, design, transition, operation and continual improvement. The tools and approaches defined in each stage will also be helpful in defining and executing an implementation strategy for service management processes, especially the seven-step improvement process of continual service improvement.

It must also be emphasized that simply implementing a set of processes and tools will not automatically be successful. There are a number of areas that need to be addressed, including:

- Clearly defining the business needs and objectives, which will determine the strategy. Without these, it will be difficult to sustain the implementation of the processes and tools through their lifecycle.
- Only those processes and tools that support these business needs and objectives should be implemented, rather than an indiscriminate implementation of processes, simply because they exist in ITIL.
- The implementation itself will be executed using formal project and programme management methodologies and tools. Thus the strategy will identify the projects that will be initiated and how they will be managed, and will also identify an overall project or programme manager (depending on the size and scope of implementation).
- A service management programme will change the culture and politics (and possibly the structure) of the organization. Management should be aware of this, and should be prepared to support, and sometimes enforce, these changes. Every implementation strategy should therefore include a clear strategy on how these changes will be managed.
- Simply implementing processes and assigning owners to these will not guarantee successful implementation or ongoing operation of the processes. A successful service management strategy will need a formal service management system – which identifies all the interrelationships between the processes, resources and tools, and which ensures that controls are properly defined and enforced.

It is important to note that an implementation strategy for ITSM processes does not follow the same steps as the strategy management process in section 4.1. This is because it forms part of the execution of the corporate and IT strategies. In the larger organizational context this implementation strategy is a tactical project or programme plan, and not a strategy in and of itself – even if it is considered strategic by the IT organization staff.

5.6.1 Types of service management implementation

There are almost as many strategies for service management as there are organizations that have implemented it. However, they typically conform to one of four patterns, based on the current situation of the organization. This section is based on ideas from *Strategic Selling* (Miller *et al.*, 1995).

5.6.1.1 Even keel mode

'Even keel' is a sailing term used to describe a sailing boat that is in calm weather and does not need any special techniques or tactics to move forward. Winds are favourable and sailing is straightforward.

Decision makers feel that their organizations are well managed and on track to meet their organizational objectives. Although there may be some minor difficulties within IT, these are not significant enough to initiate any projects aimed at changing the way IT is managed.

In many cases their position is correct. If IT is a component of the organization's strategy and has drafted and executed plans that meet the organization's requirements, it is unlikely that they will need to make any fundamental changes to their current practices. It is also very likely that they are using basic IT service management practices to a greater or lesser degree.

The appropriate service management strategy in these cases is to continue to focus on CSI and ensure that the organization continues to grow good service management practices over time.

The appropriate strategy for service management is the same as the performance projected by the organization's leaders, in other words, IT should continue to do exactly what is in the existing plans.

In other cases, decision makers in IT may feel that everything is fine, whereas they are actually out of touch with the business, and are not part of the overall business strategy. Unfortunately, this is a very difficult situation in which to introduce IT service management. Decision makers often feel threatened by any attempts to change the current situation or challenge their perceptions – which is why they are in this situation in the first place.

In these cases the person wishing to introduce service management to resolve the situation has limited options, including:

- Being promoted into a leadership position and initiating a comprehensive assessment of the current situation, effectively moving the organization into trouble or growth mode.
- Convincing the current leaders that an assessment is necessary. Experience shows that this option is not very effective, unless the person requesting the assessment is very influential. In most cases the assessment will result in further denial by the decision makers and make them more entrenched in the existing practices. This could also result in the person requesting the assessment losing their position.
- Maintaining silence, monitoring the situation and waiting for a significant failure to introduce IT service management. This could also have negative consequences – decision makers could blame the individual for having had the solution and withholding it. In addition, it may take a long time for an appropriate situation to arise, which is frustrating and demotivating for the individual.
- Resigning and joining an organization more suited to their enthusiasm and skills, especially if they are passionate about IT service management.

5.6.1.2 Trouble mode

These organizations have recognized that there is a significant weakness or problem with the way in which IT is managed. This is usually seen in repeated outages, unreliable changes, customer dissatisfaction, capacity shortages, uncontrolled spending etc. Whatever the symptom, decision makers understand that they need to take significant action. Initially they might have invested in some short-term fix that has not been successful, and now recognize the need for a more comprehensive management approach.

This is a good situation to initiate a service management programme, since the decision makers recognize the need for it, and the business will often only find a rigorous, proven approach to be credible. In addition, there is usually a greater willingness to spend money to resolve the situation.

Figure 5.7 illustrates the appropriate strategy for organizations in trouble mode. This diagram shows the IT service management strategy will focus on building a solution that solves the immediate problem and moves the organization out of trouble. For example, if the problem is unreliable changes, the project will focus on building a centralized change management process, configuring and implementing the appropriate tools, and ensuring that all IT personnel are trained to use the new processes and tools.

In this type of situation, it is often not helpful to talk about ITIL or proprietary frameworks. The decision makers know that they are vulnerable, and that some vendors may attempt to exploit the situation by tying them into a large, complex solution that goes far beyond their immediate needs. All the decision makers want to see is that they have resolved the problem, and have restored stability and their credibility. The project team should therefore focus on the specific service management actions needed to resolve the problem, rather than try to 'sell' the decision makers on ITIL. Although the team should be open and mention that their approach is based on industry standards and best practices, they should emphasize the nature of the solution.

However, there are dangers to the approach of using service management to move an organization out of trouble. Fixing the immediate problem may provide stability in the short term, but it might highlight (or even create) additional problems later. For example introducing change management solves one set of problems, but it is unlikely that poorly controlled changes are the only problem, since poor change management is only a symptom of a broader lack of control and service management. Continued performance problems or repeated incidents will result in even greater levels of dissatisfaction from users and customers who thought that these were a thing of the past.

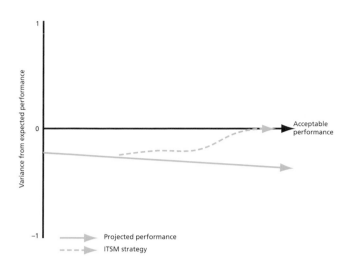

Figure 5.7 Strategy for organizations in trouble

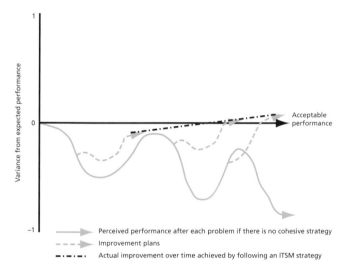

Figure 5.8 Dealing with repeated trouble

The result is a pattern of repeated trouble. Figure 5.8 illustrates this pattern. Over time, IT reacts to a series of problems, using service management to fix each one. The overall impression of the organization (represented by the solid coloured line – perceived performance) is that IT service management does not address all their requirements and in fact has been making the organization progressively worse. In addition, IT loses credibility at an increasing rate.

Of course, this is not true, since failure to take any action in the first place would have resulted in even more catastrophic outcomes – but perception is very powerful, and invariably IT service management, ITIL and the project team will get the blame for the situation.

To prevent this situation Figure 5.8 illustrates a series of actions aimed at dealing with each progressive problem, while over time increasing the level of control and service quality. The key to success is to define an overall ITSM strategy that uses ITIL techniques to identify each subsequent trouble area before it develops and implement the solution before the problem manifests itself. The strategy follows an incremental implementation cycle, where each initiative builds on the previous, and each initiative results in continual growth of the IT organization's performance.

After the first few problem situations are resolved (usually no more than three), the organization will revert to either even keel (see section 5.6.1.1) or growth mode.

Where to start when dealing with trouble

The starting point will be different in every organization, depending on the initial problem being experienced. Most organizations tend to start with incident and problem management, since the ability to deal with outages tends to be one of the first challenges that presents itself – no matter what is wrong behind the scenes.

The next most common starting point is change management, since problems are often a reflection of siloed groups being unable to coordinate their activities effectively. This is most visible when changes are deployed.

The most important guideline is to start in the area that is causing the most pain to the organization. While working on a solution to that problem, the team should already be assessing the situation to identify the next problem that will emerge. For example, starting with incident management will almost always result in detailed work on improving communication between the technical management, application management and operations management functions. This will almost always result in defining better change management processes, which will almost always result in the need for a more cohesive approach to configuration management.

Projects in this type of organization tend to be more 'bottom up' and tend to focus first on the areas contained in *ITIL Service Operation* and *ITIL Service Transition*.

Importantly, no matter which area is implemented first, they will all require a basic understanding of what services are delivered by IT. This means that most projects include the definition of a basic service catalogue as an integral component.

5.6.1.3 Growth mode

Organizations in growth mode have made a strategic decision to improve or change the organization significantly over the planning period. For example, they might be expanding into new markets, establishing new lines of business or improving the performance of the organization as a whole.

The organization's strategy recognizes that IT is part of the solution to achieving this level of growth. Decision makers will look for a comprehensive, strategic approach, such as IT service management, to achieve this growth.

In these situations it is appropriate to talk about IT service management as a framework and to articulate each of the components and how they will enable the overall strategy. The implementation strategy for service management processes will be to implement the whole of the framework over time.

Figure 5.9 illustrates an organization in growth mode. The organization's strategy requires a significant improvement in IT's performance (the coloured line). The IT service management project team needs to define an approach in which all service management processes and functions are deployed to the appropriate levels over time. Figure 5.9 shows that there is a time lapse between the definition of the organization's strategy and the IT service management implementation. This is because it will take a significant amount of time to conduct the ITSM assessment, set the strategy, prepare resources etc.

Unlike trouble mode, it is important to stress the fact that IT's strategy is based on a comprehensive framework, based on best practices like ITIL or standards such as ISO/IEC 20000. This will reassure the organization's executives that IT's plan is more likely to address the overall organizational strategy and that IT has a good chance of succeeding. In other words, emphasizing the framework reduces the organization's perception of IT risk.

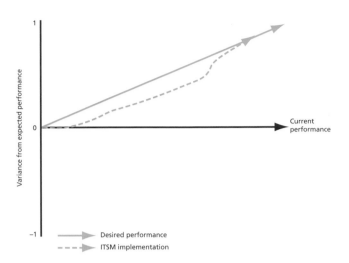

Figure 5.9 Strategy for organizations in growth mode

Where to start to achieve growth

Growth-based projects generally tend to start with a comprehensive assessment of all aspects of their organization, ranging from existing processes, tools and technology, to the culture and structure of the organization. This is then compared to the growth strategy and the most significant gaps or adjustments are addressed first. There is no correct approach to this, but the early stages of the project will include cataloguing every aspect of the organization and marking those that will need to change, and how they will need to change.

These projects generally have a 'top-down' approach that focuses on structural and architectural changes first. Any ITSM processes or functions that are necessary to achieve this are implemented first. This implies that the processes in *ITIL Service Strategy* and *ITIL Service Design* tend to be the first processes that will be changed or implemented.

5.6.1.4 Radical change mode

These are organizations that are going through a fundamental change as an organization – for example, they might be outsourcing IT or going through a merger or acquisition.

These projects are similar to those for organizations in growth mode, with two major differences:

■ The first phases of the project (assessment, planning, designing and implementing the solution) all need to happen very quickly. This is followed by a long and intensive programme of entrenching the new practices into the new organization.

■ The project is managed by a small group of people who may not disclose the details of the project until an appropriate time, usually around the implementation phase. This demands a less participative implementation style and makes it difficult to ensure that the requirements are comprehensive and accurate at operational levels.

These two differences usually mean that the project is structured as an overall programme with a comprehensive strategy, and several projects – each aimed at building a different aspect of the new organization. It also requires that the project is driven more directly by senior managers since the plans need to be changed when unforeseen situations arise – and this is very likely to happen. For a short time during the transition, the overall programme becomes the governance of the changing organization.

Figure 5.10 illustrates the type of strategy required for organizations in radical change mode. The actual change is preceded by a significant amount of preparation activity. This often goes beyond planning and includes the actual implementation of key processes (such as service portfolio management and business relationship management) and functions (such as a new financial management function for restructured organization and services). The project will also focus on preparing for new standard operating procedures for vital business functions, and new documentation and reporting standards.

When the actual change occurs, there is a period when the rest of the organization is educated about the new processes and functions and how they will work in future. At that time, the project team will no longer be restricted by confidentiality requirements, and will begin working on the more detailed operational processes, such as change, incident and problem management.

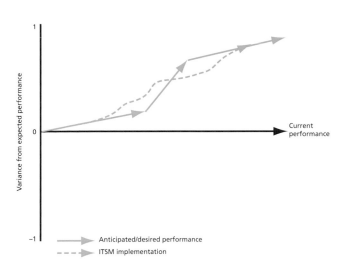

Figure 5.10 Strategy for organizations planning radical change

5.6.2 Defining a vision and mission for the service management implementation

Once the planning team understands the overall strategy of the organization, and what business or IT management issues they need to address, they should define a vision and mission. This is the 'perspective' in the 4 Ps of service strategy.

A clear vision enables the implementation project team and all of its stakeholders to understand the strategic value initiative and thus achieve greater support. A good vision statement has four main purposes:

■ To clarify the direction of an initiative
■ To motivate people to take action that moves the organization to make the vision reality
■ To coordinate the actions of different people or groups
■ To represent the view of senior management as they direct the organization towards its overall objectives.

5.6.2.1 Defining the vision and mission

The planning team should be very careful to take the organizational vision and strategy into account as they develop the vision and mission for the service management process implementation. This section deals with the vision and mission for the service management process implementation, not for the entire organization. It may well be that the vision of the organization will change if the project is successful, but that is something that needs to be handled by the organizational executives as part of a separate exercise.

One of the most common ways of developing a vision and mission is to conduct a workshop with key stakeholders. The outcome of the workshop is to have a vision statement that each individual is prepared to support and that they can explain convincingly.

This seems to be fairly simple, but in reality this is probably one of the most difficult things to achieve. Every person in the workshop has their own opinion about what is wrong and how to solve the problem. In the beginning stages of the workshop it is not uncommon to find that every person there believes that the other people are the ones with a problem, and he or she has just been asked to attend to give the rest of the group the benefit of their experience!

In addition, each person has their own set of objectives and aspirations, which are sometimes in conflict with those of other people in the meeting.

It is common for the group to argue about single words in the statement that, to an outsider, seem to be insignificant. This is not because the word is wrong, but is an attempt by the participant to negotiate the terms whereby they will accept the vision statement.

A good facilitator will be sensitive to the need of each of the people involved, but will also drive them towards a negotiated settlement. In a sense the actual statement that is documented is less important than the fact that everyone in the room is prepared to work together on achieving the same objective.

It is therefore not always crucial to achieve consensus – just moving someone from being opposed to where they are prepared to live with the outcome is a win.

The nature of individual agendas and the negotiation that occurs in these workshops introduces a whole range of group dynamics, which a facilitator should ideally be able to see face to face. These dynamics could include:

- An individual verbally stating that they agree with the vision, but their body language indicating otherwise. If they leave the meeting without this being resolved they will work to undermine the project

- An individual being a little emotional about the direction the meeting is taking because it threatens their sense of security or conflicts with their personal aspirations
- The group feeling bullied by a person with strong views or a power base that is not immediately obvious
- Some individuals in the group needing to be drawn out before they contribute
- A lack of focus in some individuals distracting the group.

The very nature of the workshop makes it difficult to run virtually, unless the participants know each other well. Most workshops take two to three days, and it is recommended that all participants meet in the same physical location. It is also advisable to run the workshop off-site to ensure minimal disruption to the participants.

Step 1 – Where have we come from?

Vision and mission statements do not occur in isolation. There has to be a reason for the team getting together to discuss the need for IT service management. The first phase of defining a vision and mission is to understand the events and dynamics that have led us to this point.

This part of the workshop documents the factors that have led to this meeting. These could include:

- Significant events
- Key people, actions and decisions
- Environmental factors
- Locations (e.g. is this relevant to a specific site or does it relate to multiple sites?)
- Previous objectives and projects and their success or failure.

Note: Some of these factors may have been negative. The facilitator should ensure that these are documented, but that the meeting is not side-tracked into a detailed discussion about the effects, personalities or assigning of blame.

Step 2 – Assessing the context

In this section of the workshop the team will attempt to capture all relevant environmental factors that could influence what the vision and mission will be. Ideally, the assessment should have been conducted and will have identified most of these areas; however, it is still necessary for the team to consider these areas when defining the vision and mission.

Whereas the previous section focused on what happened in the past, this section focuses on what could affect the future. These factors could include:

- External environment:
  - Technology
  - Economic
  - Political
  - Legislation
- Internal environment:
  - Business plans and objectives
  - Political
  - Financial
  - Requirements expressed by any stakeholders or potential stakeholders.

This part of the workshop is best done using brainstorming techniques where participants are able to contribute items freely. What may seem to be irrelevant at first may turn out to be significant at one of the later stages of the workshop.

Step 3 – Situational analysis

This part of the workshop is an extension of the previous one, except that here the team will review what other organizations have done in the area being considered. Potential inputs to this discussion are:

- Projects undertaken by a competitor
- Case studies (the itSMF conferences have a wealth of case study presentations)
- White papers
- Industry research (e.g. benchmark reports).

This part of the workshop will document any relevant factors about what these organizations have done including:

- Any environmental factors that influenced the organization
- Which vendor organizations were involved
- What tools or technologies were used
- What alternatives were considered and why they were rejected
- What mistakes were made
- Key outcomes.

In this part of the workshop the facilitator should ensure that relevant factors are documented, but should prevent the workshop from becoming a detailed discussion about competitive technologies, vendors or companies. The aim is to understand what influenced the other organization's vision, not to debate the merits of various approaches.

At this stage, the team should take into account any SWOT analysis outputs. If this was not done during the assessment, it should be done here. To recap, a SWOT analysis analyses the Strengths, Weaknesses, Opportunities and Threats currently facing the team. It is also a helpful tool for the facilitator to summarize Steps 2 and 3 on one page.

Key things to remember in SWOT analysis are:

- Strengths can be built upon
- Weaknesses need to be dealt with or turned into strengths
- Opportunities should be exploited
- Threats need to be minimized.

These items will assist in articulating the vision and mission and ensuring that they are more realistic.

Step 4 – Define the possibilities

Now that the analysis has been completed the workshop becomes creative. In this step, the team is asked to imagine a future state in which the issues in the previous three steps have all been dealt with.

This part of the workshop is likely to result in all kinds of ideas and suggestions, often uncoordinated and in no particular order. It is important to note that that this is not the step where the vision and mission are defined. This is where the team has free rein to imagine what could be possible. This provides the raw materials from which the vision and mission will eventually be built.

It is important not be too restrictive, but at the same time to maintain some sort of structure to the responses so that they do not get lost or minimized. A number of techniques can be helpful here, but one that combines many of those techniques is the newspaper technique.

Here participants work as individuals or small groups and create a newspaper front page to describe the outcome of the project. Each front page should contain:

- One or more articles
- At least one headline
- At least one article describing the successful outcome of the project

- A picture illustrating the article (this is important to capture symbolism that may not be easy to express in words)
- Some of the more creative groups will also create adverts and 'related stories' to fill up their front page.

Note: This stage also provides input to the awareness campaign.

Step 5 – Restating values, policies and guiding principles

After Step 4 the team will be fairly excited about the vision that is emerging. One of two things can happen at this point:

- The team could get carried away by their enthusiasm and start creating a vision that is not feasible or practical.
- Some members of the team, realizing this, may start to negate the visions of other members, resulting in a kind of team despondency – and a vision that is not ambitious enough.

A skilled facilitator deals with this by revisiting the objective of the meeting and getting the team to restate any values or guiding principles of the organization that may be relevant to this project. Please note that this may relate to the organization as a whole, or just to a single department or group within the organization.

The values, policies and guiding principles provide input to creating the vision, but they are also the basis for the mission statement, which will also need to be articulated at this stage.

This part of the workshop should not take too long and the facilitator should be careful not to labour the point too much. All they really need to determine is whether their thinking is consistent with the purpose and culture of the organization.

Step 6 – Stating the vision and mission (getting agreement)

The facilitator will now work with the group to define the vision and mission statements. This is normally done in two steps:

- Summarize the vision and mission themes. The individuals or small groups in Step 4 will have created a number of different views of the vision and mission. However, there will be common themes running through each of these. These themes should be summarized by

the facilitator, although the wording should be agreed by the team.
- Merge the themes into vision and mission statements. Again, this will be done by the facilitator with the team agreeing to the final wording.

Having the facilitator summarize the themes into vision and mission statements externalizes them from the team and ensures that they think of it as a team effort. This is important in ensuring that each of the team members feels equally responsible for the vision and willing to take ownership of it.

It is important that the group then obtains buy-in from senior management to demonstrate their commitment to the vision and mission. If they do not achieve this senior management buy-in then the risk of project failure will be increased.

Vision killers

The National Association of School Boards (NASB), on its website, encourages facilitators to watch out for the following factors which could derail the visioning process:

- Tradition
- Fear of ridicule
- Stereotypes of people, conditions, roles and governing councils
- Complacency of some stakeholders
- Fatigued leaders
- Short-term thinking
- 'Naysayers' (people who disagree with all ideas from the team, even when they have none of their own).

Confirming the direction

Although the visioning workshop should have taken into account the business objectives and strategy, it is always possible that the team created elements of the vision that may be in conflict with the strategy and direction of the rest of the organization.

If the senior managers who determined the strategy of the organization do not support the changes required to meet the ITSM vision, then it will not succeed.

The team should confirm that the vision and mission are in line with the organization's strategies by discussing it with the appropriate level of management, as well as by consulting any documents related to the organization's strategy.

5.6.3 Service management assessment

Once the organization knows what type of strategy it needs to follow, it is necessary to do an assessment to confirm the strategic approach and define a more detailed service management implementation strategy. An assessment will confirm the current situation, identify strengths and weaknesses and propose an approach for service management implementation. Many organizations prefer to define the mission and vision for service management (as part of the service strategy) before conducting the assessment.

Please note that, while the assessment will mirror the strategic assessment performed in strategy management, it is a different assessment. The strategic assessment focuses on the overall strategy of the organization, and how that relates to services. The service management assessment is a tactical assessment focused specifically on what elements of service management are required to meet a specific set of business issues and IT management challenges. A service management assessment forms part of the execution of the overall service strategy.

Although the subject of assessments is covered in *ITIL Continual Service Improvement*, this section contains a brief overview of assessments for the sake of completeness.

The assessment will identify areas of strengths (that can be built upon) and weaknesses (that need to be addressed) specifically related to the challenges that the organization is attempting to solve. The output of the assessment will be a report which will be submitted to the team defining the strategy. They will use it as an input to defining the strategy, and will use extracts or summaries to raise stakeholder awareness. Trying to define a strategy without an assessment would be like trying to run a race without knowing where the starting line is.

Another reason for conducting the assessment is to establish a baseline for the measurement of improvements. When implementing a service management process, there may be a temporary loss incurred during the implementation of a new process or change to a process. Once overcome, this temporary loss should be replaced with measurable improvement.

A good assessment will enable the team defining the implementation strategy for service management processes to understand the variables that can make or break the success of the project. These variables form the basis for the rest of this section and can be summarized as follows:

- **External reference** An ITSM project or programme will usually refer to an external reference as a guideline – in the same way as a driver would refer to a map to ensure that they are on the correct road. Most assessments are tied to a specific standard, framework, reference model or methodology. Understanding that no assessment is objective is an important step in a successful ITSM implementation. Even ITIL-based assessments tend to vary in how best practice is interpreted.
- **The stakeholders** Everyone has a different perception about what needs to be done. In addition, regardless of what an assessment recommends, the stakeholders will decide how to move forward. Often this is done in the worst possible way – as people pay lip service to the assessment results while working behind the scenes to promote their own agendas.
- **The existing situation** The assessment will not be conducted in a sterile environment. Some ITSM processes may be in place already, and this will impact the findings and recommendations of the assessment. This will also impact how people in the organization feel about the assessment. If there are negative perceptions about past ITSM projects, the assessment may have to adjust its recommendations to ensure that future action is accepted. The assessment should also be used to challenge preconceived ideas about how effective the current situation is.
- **Other projects** Several ITSM projects have failed simply because they did not take into account that there were other projects competing for budget, people and executive support.
- **Organizational dynamics and objectives** Experience has shown that the solution that is eventually deployed rarely looks anything like the original plan. There are a number of reasons for this, including the following:

- ITSM is not widely understood and supported in many organizations – it's often seen as an internal IT project. Of course this is not true – ITSM is dependent on a complex set of relationships and processes, many of which are controlled by other groups in the organization. Projects that fail to identify these and get the relevant groups involved in the project will find that changes in other parts of the organization keep affecting its scope and deliverables.
  - The culture of an organization may require that things work differently from the framework they are using as an external reference. Projects that attempt to impose external standards on an organization are poor projects and will find that the deliverables change every time an obstacle is met. This extends the duration and cost of the project.
  - Politics play an extremely important role in most organizations. The informal politics are the most dangerous because they are often unseen. The ability to determine the direction and nature of organizational politics is a critical success factor.
- **Changes in the external environment should also be noted** A good example of this was the introduction of Sarbanes-Oxley legislation. Many projects changed direction and scope as soon as this legislation was announced.
- **The type of assessment that is available** There are a number of assessments in the market, ranging from short and inexpensive self-assessments, to complex, detailed and expensive investigations. The team should be careful to evaluate which assessment will yield the best result for their current situation. A complex, detailed assessment is overkill for an organization just starting out on their ITSM journey, whereas a high-level self-assessment will not be suitable for an organization looking for detailed guidance on how to implement a specific subset of processes.
- **The organization's maturity level** A more mature organization will need a different type of assessment from an organization that is just starting out on its ITSM journey.
- **The availability of resources** The appropriate skills and experience levels are crucial for the project's success. The assessment should enable the project team to identify what skills and experience are needed and whether they exist in the organization today or whether they need to be hired or contracted in.

- **Technology** This covers a range of variables, for example:
  - Is there a strategic partnership with a vendor (usually a contract already in existence, which requires the IT organization to include the vendor in the initiative), and does this require some knowledge of the management processes or methodologies that they use?
  - Does the strategy have to address a specific technology or platform, and if so are there any specific requirements that this strategy should take note of?
  - Is the strategy constrained by the architecture standards of the organization?
  - Does the strategy include implementing tools or, if it addresses a specific technology, will this require additional skills and experience not assessed by a technology-independent assessment?
- **Assessment** The assessment should provide the organization with a comprehensive view of its current situation, including shortcomings and potential areas for improvement.

5.6.3.1 What should be assessed?

There are many different types of assessment, and each approaches the task differently. At the very least, the strategy team should ensure that the assessment they choose (or conduct themselves) should include the following areas:

Processes

Since IT service management is a process-based approach it makes sense that the first thing to be assessed is which processes are in place and how functional they are currently. The following can be used as references to map which processes exist in the organization:

- **Best-practice guidelines** Publications such as ITIL are useful in that they provide a fair amount of detail about how ITSM processes should work and how they should be structured. At the same time they contain a number of alternatives and options – it is impossible to comply with all of these at the same time! The advantage of using ITIL is that it uses a standard terminology and is based on good 'common sense' so people can identify with it fairly easily.

- **Standards (e.g. ISO/IEC 20000, ISO/IEC 27001)** These are useful in checking whether certain processes are being performed in the organization, and whether the ITIL process objectives are being met. They cannot, however, assess whether the way in which they are being done is efficient or effective.

- **Proprietary frameworks** Several vendors have developed more detailed guidance, frameworks and reference models. These are valuable since they provide detailed, and more prescriptive, guidance than that contained in ITIL, and have also demonstrated how the ITIL guidelines will work in applied situations. However, it is important to ensure that the vendor's approach is consistent with that to be used in the customer organization.

Note on external references

Using an external reference is necessary, but it can also cause problems if approached in the wrong way.

External references were not written for your organization's specific requirements, structure, culture and objectives. Although they provide a good reference point, they should be used exactly as that – a reference point.

Processes are often not clearly identifiable as a single entity. They may have grown over time and across several departments. The people who work with them may view them as 'something we have to do', not realizing that they are part of a process. Using an external reference helps to identify all the iterations of a process, but it can also create confusion if people are not familiar with the terminology and objectives of the reference model.

The organization

The second thing to check is the organization itself. The primary objective of the assessment is to understand the objectives of the organization and then to check whether it is structured to meet these objectives optimally.

This is easier said than done, since an ITSM project rarely has the opportunity to address the overall structure, objectives and culture of the organization. Rather, the purpose of the

assessment is more to identify what the constraints are so that the project can be more successful.

There are a few obvious things to look for, and a few that are more difficult to define. This section lists some examples of items to be assessed regarding the structure and operation of an organization:

- **Duplication** One of the easiest things to determine is whether an activity is being performed by more than one group (even if it is for different reasons). These are usually clear, quick efficiency wins, although care should be taken not to simply start cutting headcount. The first question the project team will be asked when they have completed the assessment is 'Where are we going to get all the people to implement this and make it work?'. The answer is to reassign the people who were gained when duplication was reduced.

- **Quality of communication** The assessment needs to include questions and checks for whether communication takes place, in what form and whether the messages are known and acted upon.

- **Clarity** This refers to people's understanding of their roles and how they contribute to the organization's objectives.

- **Centralized vs. decentralized structure and decision-making** There is no right or wrong way to manage an organization, but the project will need to know how authority is manifested in the organization if it is to be successful.

In addition to the structural aspects, it is important that the assessment considers the cultural aspects of the organization. Examples of what the assessment might consider are as follows:

- **Trust and cohesiveness** This refers to the extent that each person supports the organization's goals, and their belief that managers and executives are communicating appropriately and taking the appropriate actions for the organization.

- **Mode of working** Some organizations work by meeting, others prefer matrixed work teams, yet others prefer a traditional hierarchy. Again, there is no correct way of doing things, but the answers will determine how the solution is defined and implemented.

- **Learning culture** This refers to the extent to which the organization is prepared to evolve the way that it works. Some organizations discourage learning, emphasizing their successful track record over the past years. The predominant culture is reluctant to change anything that's working – even if it's not!
- **Skills and experience** Many organizations already have sophisticated skills catalogues or skills matrices. In these cases it is important to evaluate these to ensure that the skills required for this project are part of those systems. In other organizations, the assessment will help to identify the skills and experience required for the project as well as who has them.

Technology

It is important that, in addition to considering processes, the assessment also focuses on technology. Even if the strategy is not primarily about looking for tools, technology is ultimately going to play an important role in the solution – either because it needs to be managed, or because it provides tools that support the solution.

Most technology assessments are used to assess tools to determine whether they will support a specific process or processes, e.g. a detailed assessment of three configuration management tools to determine which one suits our organization's requirements best.

However, a good initial ITSM assessment will also take into account several technology factors, including the following:

- **The IT strategy** (see section 4.1) Does this exist, and if so are we going to be constrained by specific vendor organizations or platforms?
- **Technology projects** Implementing a configuration management project just as the organization is about to consolidate 50 data centres into 5 will not be well accepted unless it forms part of the data centre project.
- **Duplication** As with people, it is common to find two tools performing the same function in two groups. This creates quick-win opportunities, but care should be taken that key functionality is not sacrificed. However, the role and scope of these tools should be carefully considered. There may be a valid reason for the duplication, and the assessment should determine whether this is the case or not.

- **'Shelfware'** Many organizations have more tools than they could ever possibly use, many of them still on someone's shelf in its original packaging. In other cases a tool was purchased, but is only being used for one aspect of its functionality.
- **Integration** It is important to consider the amount of integration needed between tools that will support service management in the organization. The assessment should identify at what point solutions exist, and how well integrated they are. In some cases, the strategy might identify the need to replace multiple point solutions with a suite (or vice versa if the organization needs to be more flexible in the way different units operate). If new technologies are to be considered, the amount of integration with existing technologies (or between parts of the new technologies) should be assessed.
- **Technology trends in the IT and service management industries** The assessment should look for game-changing technologies – these are often most helpful when it is possible to make radical changes. A good example was when dependency mapping tools started emerging and greatly changed configuration management implementations.

External environment

A comprehensive assessment should also take into account any environmental factors that are likely to affect the service management implementation strategy directly or indirectly. At the same time, for a limited-scope implementation this may not be as relevant. Examples of external environmental factors are:

- **Socio-economic factors** These may affect the growth of the company and increase or reduce the demands on the solution over time. Although many of these factors may not be relevant to defining an implementation strategy, there are some that are: for example, typical salary structures and standards of living in a particular region (which is being considered as a service desk location).
- **The business environment** These include trends in outsourcing certain types of activity or organization. An example of this has been the outsourcing of service desk organizations to offshore companies.

- **Legislation** Legislation such as Sarbanes-Oxley creates additional reporting or auditing requirements.
- **Technology** This refers to how technology developments may change the way in which the solution works. For example, help desks used to be purely telephone-based. As use of the internet grew, a whole series of solutions emerged to expand the services provided by these organizations, while reducing their cost.

5.6.3.2 Compliance- and maturity-based assessments

Assessments based on checking compliance are different from those that are based on a maturity model of some kind. This section examines some of these differences and considers the circumstances under which each should be used. It also looks at some hybrid assessment approaches.

Compliance-based assessments

Compliance-based assessments are aimed at evaluating whether an organization meets some type of external criteria or not. These criteria could be in the form of standards (e.g. ISO/IEC 20000), proprietary frameworks, legislation or methodologies. The aim is to see whether an organization matches some external standards or specifications. Also included are internal audits on a regular basis (see DIN EN ISO 19011).

Compliance-based assessments might be helpful in defining an implementation strategy for service management processes if a strategic objective is compliance with a particular standard. In other cases, however, these assessments are more useful as tactical assessments to identify non-compliance and remedial action.

It is also possible to run compliance-based assessments using internal standards. For example, the assessment of a department's documentation to ensure that it meets corporate policy requirements. Again, the emphasis is simply on identifying whether the target organization matches a standard or specification.

Compliance-based assessments are really snapshots of an organization, and have the following characteristics or limitations:

- They do not take into account the individual objectives or future direction of the organization.

- They are generally binary – you either comply or you do not. Some assessments will attempt to make this a little more meaningful by evaluating whether that specific item needs to be in compliance or not, and others will add in some other categories (partially present, planned for etc.), but the bottom line is still about whether the organization is in compliance or not, and if not – what is it doing about it?

The most common reason for using compliance-based assessments is to obtain a standards certification. A related reason is to comply with legislative requirements or contractual terms and conditions (e.g. outsourcing agreements).

In these projects there are three distinct phases:

- **Preparing for certification** Any vendor can help to prepare an organization for certification. The main emphasis of this phase is to determine the gaps that will prevent certification, and then implement measures to address the gaps – usually within one year.
- **The certification audit** This is done by a specialized agency or certification auditor who has been accredited by the standards body to conduct these audits. To prevent conflict of interest, the auditor does not typically offer preparation services – and certainly not in the same organization.
- **Regular audits** After certification, regular audits are conducted by the certification agency to ensure that the processes are being maintained and improved. Again, any vendor can help to maintain and improve the processes, and they can conduct interim assessments, but only an accredited auditor can conduct the re-certification audit.

Some organizations also use these assessments as a starting point for their service management projects. While this has some value, there are some problems with this approach. For example:

- Compliance-based assessments do not evaluate whether a specific discipline is right for the organization at that time. For example, implementing service level management simply because we don't have it yet could cause a lot of damage in an organization that is still trying to stabilize the performance of some key infrastructure components.

■ Standards compliance on its own is not usually a good value proposition for executives – unless the organization uses standards as a competitive advantage. Most executives are more concerned with saving costs and improving the quality of services. Although this can be done through compliance, it is an indirect route and costs more money in the short term.

Important note on compliance

Compliance with a standard does not guarantee that an organization will meet its objectives effectively and efficiently. All that the certificate means is that the prescribed processes are present in the organization and that they are being managed – it does not evaluate the validity of the outputs or the extent to which the business is enhanced by those processes.

In addition, organizations have been known to create documentation or artefacts (such as request for change forms) just to get through the certification, although they never actually use them in practice.

Maturity-based assessments

Maturity-based assessments evaluate where an organization is located on a journey from one state to another. They usually start with a base state of zero (i.e. nothing is in place) and end at a state of 5 (i.e. everything that needs to be done is in place and is working perfectly – the only thing the organization needs to do is anticipate changes and adjust the system accordingly).

Each component of the reference model or framework is assessed and the organization is awarded a score for that area (in increments of 0.5 between 0 and 5). Usually the organization as a whole is awarded an aggregate score that reflects the overall level of maturity in the area being assessed.

The assumption of these assessments is that there is a trade-off between the benefits of operating at a higher level of maturity, and the costs of implementing and managing this level.

A further assumption is made that the costs of moving to a higher level are offset by a reduction in waste and duplicate efforts. An argument can often be made, however, that the cost of operating at the highest level of maturity is far greater than

any savings. This means that most organizations tend to aim for a maturity level just higher than the middle of the range, unless there is an overarching reason for moving further (e.g. legislation, contract requirements, or the fact that our competitive advantage comes from being the best).

Maturity-based assessments can be more intensive and take longer to conduct than compliance-based assessments because they have to evaluate the organization on several different sets of criteria.

Maturity-based assessments are useful for defining a tailored solution that builds incremental improvements over time. These assessments help an organization to identify which areas are weakest and strongest and then evaluate which improvements can be achieved in the short term, and which would be better left to the longer term.

Comparison of compliance- and maturity-based assessments

Some similarities between compliance- and maturity-based assessments are as follows:

■ Both measure the organization according to a pre-defined (usually external) set of specifications and standards
■ Both are very structured, and require rigorous and extensive programmed questioning to determine the organization's position, often using standardized questionnaires
■ Both are repeated on a regular basis to determine the effect of changes in the organization.

Some differences between compliance- and maturity-based assessments are illustrated in Table 5.1.

Exception-based assessments

Compliance- and maturity-based assessments are both based on measuring the organization against an external standard or best practice. An exception-based assessment accumulates evidence of business failures (including outages) caused by poor service management and uses these to justify a deeper analysis.

This is a good method to focus attention on specific trouble spots. At the same time, it is sometimes difficult for stakeholders to be objective about the results of such investigations. For this reason, it is often helpful for these assessments to be facilitated by a specialist, often an outside consultant.

Table 5.1 Differences between compliance- and maturity-based assessments

Compliance-based assessments	Maturity-based assessments
Tend to be binary – either the organization complies or it does not.	Break the standard into different areas and assess levels of compliance.
Assign an overall rating of compliance, usually in the form of a certificate.	Assign a numeric rating of the level of maturity in each of the areas being evaluated, and often also a numeric aggregate (or sometimes minimum) score for the organization.
Result in a snapshot of the organization as it currently exists.	Result in a plan of how to move from one level to the next.
Help to assess the costs and benefits of compliance.	Help to assess the cost and benefits of improvement over time.
Repeated assessments determine whether the organization is still in compliance (or closer to compliance). If not, certification may be revoked.	Repeated assessments evaluate whether the action plans to move from one level of maturity to another have been successful, and whether the cost/benefit forecasts were accurate.
Good for achieving standards certification.	Good for defining an implementation strategy.

5.6.4 Objectives for implementing service management

5.6.4.1 Using assessment outputs to define objectives

One of the most obvious inputs for defining the objectives of the project is the assessment report. Once the assessment has investigated the current situation, interviewed all stakeholders and examined relevant artefacts, it will be possible to provide a good idea of what needs to be done.

The assessment can help the team to identify where to start, what needs to be done and in what sequence. Thus the assessment is a valuable tool to determine the scope and objectives of the project.

There are many ways to use the assessment report, but most involve the following steps:

- All issues or gaps and recommendations are listed – usually in a spreadsheet.
- The issues are weighted (using a value of 1 to 10 or high, medium, low etc.) according to:
  - Their current impact on the organization
  - The effect on the organization if they were dealt with/not dealt with
  - Their relevance to the vision statement.
- The recommendations are weighted (using the same values as above) according to:
  - Cost to implement (time, people and money)

- What would happen if we did not implement them
  - Their relevance to the mission statement.
- Values are assigned to the issues and the recommendations and a top 10 or 20 list of each is generated.
- The two lists are compared to ensure that they are consistent. For example, a problem may not be addressed by the recommendations – in which case a new recommendation has to be defined or an existing one promoted. Alternatively, a recommendation may exist without a corresponding problem. This may indicate that the recommendation is really about fixing something that is not broken, or it may indicate that the problem is much larger than originally thought.
- The list of problems and recommendations is finalized.
- A catalogue of all the ITIL components or processes that will enable the team to address the problems and implement the recommendations is drawn up. This list will be the basis for the objectives to be defined in the next section.
- The catalogue is compared with the vision statement to ensure that the project is still in alignment.

Please note that in this process it is possible that the vision and mission will be re-assessed. This is not necessarily a bad thing as the assessment may have uncovered some factors that affect the direction of the project. However, it will mean re-assessing the expectations of the stakeholders. This is often not a major problem, since the stakeholders are expecting the assessment to act as a change catalyst. However, the revised vision and mission statements must be approved by all stakeholders before moving any further.

5.6.4.2 Setting and managing objectives

The vision statement and the assessment results will indicate the desired outcome of the service management process implementation and a strategy on what gaps or obstacles exist that prevent that outcome from being achieved. The objectives of the project will indicate how the outcome will be achieved.

By this stage defining the objectives should be quite straightforward, but it is important not to assume that everyone understands or accepts them. For this reason, it is mandatory that all stakeholders play a role in defining or signing off on the objectives. Many organizations find that a workshop approach is helpful here – and this could be run at the end of the assessment, although experience indicates that it is better to allow a week or two for the assessment results to sink in before defining the objectives.

The guidelines for defining objectives are the same as in section 4.1.5.6, and readers should refer to this section for guidance. It covers why objectives are so difficult to meet, and suggests some controls to ensure a greater 'hit rate' for objectives. The next section (section 5.6.5) will deal with some more general techniques that will ensure that the project meets its objectives.

> **Key message**
>
> It is easier to state an objective than it is to meet it.

5.6.5 Identifying and managing risk

ITIL contains several references to risk management. Appendix E also deals with risk management frameworks. These frameworks can be used to manage risk associated with a service management implementation, which would normally be undertaken as part of a project. Each project management methodology will also have an approach for identifying and managing risks.

ITIL Service Strategy does not cover these methodologies in any detail, but it does provide a high-level discussion for a typical ITSM project.

5.6.5.1 Planning for risk management

Depending on the scope and complexity of the service management implementation strategy, the team may need to have a separate plan to deal with the identified risks. This plan will become part of any overall project plan that is part of executing the strategy and will be reviewed at regular control points. Some projects will assign an individual to monitor and manage the risks associated with the project.

In general, though, it is the project manager's responsibility to ensure that risks are identified and that measures are put in place to mitigate them. Usually the project team will jointly identify and document the risks, including the potential impacts and – if known – the probability of the risk occurring.

Identifying the risks

This part of risk management involves naming the risk. When first identifying the risk it is not necessary to try to explain or quantify the risk, but just to get as many ideas as possible about what might threaten the success of a project or strategy. Brainstorming is probably the best way of doing this, since ideas that are raised tend to uncover risks that were not obvious at first.

Each identified or suspected risk should be documented together with its potential consequences – e.g. if the network team is not able to upgrade the network by 13 January, then we will have to delay the pilot implementation by two weeks.

Analysing the risks

Once the team has identified the risks, they can start quantifying the impact and probability of the risk.

The impact is the effect on a strategy or project (and its customers) if the risk should become reality, and the consequences are experienced.

Most risk management approaches use both qualitative and quantitative descriptions of these areas. This means that the consequences and impacts are defined in words, and then a numeric value is associated with them. The numbers are used to calculate the ranking of the risk, while the description is used to define how to deal with the risk.

Please note that a risk with a probability of 100% is not a risk; it is a certainty and therefore an issue. These risks should be taken off the risk plan and dealt with as issues. Likewise a risk with a probability of 0 should be removed from the plan.

5.6.5.2 Managing risks

Once the risks have been assessed and documented, together with their action plans, the risk management plan must be reviewed regularly to ensure that appropriate actions have been taken and are working as expected.

It is important to note that any of the risks may change status throughout the project. For example, we may have totally avoided a risk, or a mitigation action is so successful that the risk is downgraded or even retired. On the other hand, a situation may arise which causes some risks to become more probable, thus increasing their ranking.

These changes must be monitored and built into the normal project control mechanisms – e.g. every project meeting should include a review of the risk management plan and the assessment of any new risks.

Risk management is a repetitive activity and it is likely that the entire process will be completed several times.

5.6.6 Preparing a business case

This section outlines the purpose of the business case, explores how to overcome some difficulties in preparing the business case and then discusses some of the approaches used in calculating the value of the solution. Please note that the business case can be produced and refined throughout the process of defining a service management implementation strategy. It is being discussed here because it refers to concepts that are described earlier, not because it has to be done in this particular sequence.

The concept of the business case and its use are described in section 3.6.1.1 as it refers to calculating the return on investment for services. This section considers business cases in the context of defining a strategy for service management process implementations.

5.6.6.1 The business case as a sales tool

The primary reason for writing a business case is to 'sell' the project. A good sales document has the following characteristics:

- It is easy to read. People don't buy products or services when there is too much fine print.
- It is easy to understand. A business case that is filled with technical language and complex calculations will not be read, and often not approved without considerable political 'pull' being exerted by the sponsor.
- It is concise. A good business plan makes its point and its arguments quickly and clearly, with enough detail to convince the appropriate audience.
- It is complete. If the project team has completed the visioning and the assessment (and they have defined the objectives and risks properly), they should be able to address the most important stakeholder concerns and questions in this document.
- It is convincing. The business case is not just a form to be filled out and presented. It needs to articulate convincing arguments for the organization to support the project. Start with the most important reasons and deal with the most important objections first.

A good executive sponsor will help the team to understand what to emphasize in the business case, and also what arguments to avoid.

5.6.6.2 Preparing a business case

The purpose of a business case is to demonstrate the net benefit of the project to the organization. This involves analysing the cost of the project and then comparing it with the benefits of the project. The business case typically also contains an analysis of what would happen if the project did not go ahead.

There are three main challenges with preparing a business case:

- **Estimating the costs** The amount of work involved in a project is always an estimate, and there are very few guidelines available regarding the number and type of resources that are going to be needed for ITSM implementation projects. Some guidelines are given in the next module, but these will vary depending on the scope of the project, how many processes are going to be implemented, whether they are going to be implemented concurrently or sequentially etc.

- ■ **Quantifying indirect and intangible benefits** Since ITSM processes are often concerned with 'maintenance and control' type activities, it is often difficult to show a direct benefit to the functionality of the organization. In addition, benefits like improved staff morale and customer satisfaction are difficult to demonstrate. The business case will therefore need extra effort to link some of the indirect and intangible benefits to direct business outcomes.
- ■ **Obtaining accurate information about the business and IT performance** Organizations that are implementing ITSM often do not have metrics and complete historical data to help them demonstrate potential benefits. In addition, business performance data may not be available for similar reasons – or if it is available it may be confidential.

This section suggests some high-level guidelines for dealing with these challenges and for preparing a business case.

Estimating the cost

The cost of a project is relatively easy to calculate, provided the inputs, resource requirements and timescales are known.

The difficulty with estimating the cost of ITSM projects is three-fold:

Firstly, there are no established formulae to calculate how many resources of what type will need to be available and for how long. There are many guidelines, but none of these is absolute.

Secondly, the complexity of ITSM projects tends to change over time. As each project is completed, the benefits become visible to more groups, who want to participate in future projects, or who want to participate in the existing project. While this may seem like poor project management, it is often the reality of the situation in fragmented or siloed organizations.

While it's easy to say that these dependencies are clearly outlined in ITIL, the politics of the organization are not. So why not wrap up phase 1 and then initiate a new project to link in the other two teams? Simply because the involvement of the other two teams fundamentally changes the design

of the processes, the tools and the skills required of the staff.

These changes are almost impossible to forecast, and make a firm costing very difficult. Until ITSM becomes a science that is clearly understood and practised across all areas of an IT organization, this will continue to be a problem.

Thirdly, most of the costs of an IT project are not in the implementation of the solution, but in what happens afterwards. Most projects tend to estimate the costs involved in implementing the solution, but the ongoing management and improvement is very difficult to estimate.

Quantifying indirect and intangible benefits

Many management decision approaches have worked out methods for accounting for items that may seem to be intangible. For example, how can the following ITSM benefits be quantified:

- ■ Improved staff morale
- ■ Better relationship between IT and the business
- ■ Increased productivity of IT staff (some would argue that this is a tangible calculation, but if you really look at their calculations, they are often based on assumptions about intangible items). In addition, how would non-technical people know when an IT person was being more productive?
- ■ Better control over IT assets.

There are often well-established ways of measuring these intangible items. It is best to include them in the business case with some examples and allow the business to place a value on them.

Obtaining accurate information

A credible business case needs to be based on information that stakeholders are familiar with, or that they can verify if they are not.

Sources of information include:

- ■ Business plans
- ■ Marketing plans
- ■ Departmental action plans and meeting minutes
- ■ Intranet web pages – especially those dedicated to a specific department, group or project
- ■ Performance reports – usually related to a department or project.

Techniques for obtaining information include:

- A general principle for obtaining information is that most people are more than willing to provide you with information that you need (providing it does not breach confidentiality) – but you have to know what to ask for.
- Direct interviews. These are really only effective if you know exactly what information you're looking for. Questions that are too open or vague can be frustrating for the interviewee, and may reflect poorly on the interviewer's credibility.
- Awareness campaign. These are mainly seen as an opportunity to sell the solution, but if meetings and presentations are facilitated well, they can also be used to solicit information that we may not have.
- Scouring internal websites regularly. This is a good way of scoping what information you need to find. For example, an internal website may give you some high-level details about a marketing project and who is on the team, but you will still have to interview the team members directly to get any specific details that you are looking for.
- Speaking to third parties (vendor sales people often have access to information about what is happening in other parts of your organization).

5.6.7 The project charter

All project management methodologies use the concept of a project charter, although it is sometimes known by other names (e.g. terms of reference). The charter is the document that authorizes the project team to execute the project and allows the project manager to assign tasks and responsibilities to individuals on the project even if they report in to other managers.

The project charter is a consolidated overview of the project, outlining the objectives and organization of the project, together with reference to the background, scope and reason for the project. It allows all stakeholders of the project to document what has been agreed about the objective, scope and deliverables of the project. This means that it is a valuable communication tool as well as providing the mandate for the project team to define and execute the project plan.

A project charter should consist of the following information (in no specific order):

- The project name
- The vision of the project
- A brief description of the problem being solved
- The objectives of the project
- The names of the project team, and a brief description of their roles. If appropriate the document could also contain a project organization chart
- The name and signature of the person approving the project
- A list of assumptions and policies upon which the project is based
- An outline of the key deliverables of the project and, if known, the timescales involved
- A summary of the project requirements (this would probably be an attachment)
- A summary of the project risks and action plans (this would probably be an attachment)
- The approved budget for the project.

There are no rules regarding the content and length of the project charter except that it should be short enough that people will actually read it. Experience shows that this means fewer than five pages.

5.6.8 Go/no go

The final step of the service management process implementation strategy is to obtain agreement to proceed. If agreement is not obtained, this will require the planning team to make changes if funding exists, or seek additional funding to change the strategy, or else stop the project altogether. Please note that the strategy should also identify key stages at which a go/no go decision can be made for each aspect of the implementation.

A 'go' decision for the strategy usually depends on the following factors:

- A good awareness campaign
- Effective communication of the vision to all stakeholders
- A business case that outlines the appropriate level of benefit to the organization
- A realistic assessment and communication of the threats and how they will be mitigated
- A clear alignment between the project charter and the strategy of the organization as a whole.

Organizing for
service strategy

6

6   Organizing for service strategy

'I was in a warm bed, and suddenly I'm part of a plan.' Woody Allen in *Shadows and Fog*

This chapter describes the general concepts of organizing for service management in relation to service strategy and the related practices. It includes generic roles, responsibilities and competencies that apply across the service lifecycle and specific aspects for the processes described in this publication.

Section 2.2.3 describes the basic concepts of organization, function, group, team, department, division and role that are used in this chapter.

Definition: organization

Organizations are goal-directed, boundary-maintaining and socially constructed systems of human activity (Aldrich, 1999).

Organizations are designed and built for a purpose. These goals drive the behaviours of an organization's many agents who dynamically interact with each other. The many interactions produce emergent macro-level patterns of organizational behaviour. IT organizations are complex systems embedded within the larger complex system of their business, customers and industry.

The transaction costs principle is a simple and yet powerful means for explaining organizations. It argues that, in certain circumstances, organizations are more efficient mechanisms for cooperation than contracting or sourcing. IT organizations are subject to transaction costs. They must search for, negotiate, monitor, coordinate and govern resources in order to produce services. As people come together in an organization, they must learn what to do and how to work with others to perform. If this cooperation is done ineffectively, transaction costs rise. The better the organization manages its transaction costs, the better it justifies its existence. Further, certain risks are better mitigated through organizations than through contracts:

- **Incomplete contracts** No contract can ever cover every possible contingency. The greater and more complex the cooperation needed with

Figure 6.1 Organizational value creation cycle

external contractors, the greater the possibility of an incomplete contract (Williamson and Winter, 1993).

- **The hold-up problem** Services often require investments in specific assets such as infrastructure or facilities. The problem of incomplete contracts implies that there is always a possibility that contracts will unravel. Contractors are then stuck with these hard-to-reverse assets and may then withhold access as they seek better terms (Holmstrom and Roberts, 1998).

- **Change endurance** Organizations create structures that outlive the participation of their agents. These cooperative structures allow an organization to strive for complex strategies that may require years to enact.

- **Collective learning** Much like individuals, organizations are capable of learning. Despite changes in individuals, organizations act as a stabilizing and collective storehouse for knowledge while in pursuit of their goals (Camazine *et al.*, 2001).

Adequate scarce resources, a well-considered strategy and distinctiveness allow an organization to provide superior performance versus competing alternatives, in turn justifying the acquisition of still more scarce resources. This virtuous cycle is illustrated in Figure 6.1.

6.1 ORGANIZATIONAL DEVELOPMENT

When senior managers adopt a service management orientation, they are adopting a vision for the organization. Such a vision provides a model toward which staff can work. Organizational change, however, is not instantaneous. Senior managers often make the mistake of thinking that announcing the organizational change is the same as making it happen.

There is no one best way to organize. Elements of an organizational design, such as scale, scope and structure, are highly dependent on strategic objectives. Over time, an organization will likely outgrow its design. There is the underlying problem of structural fit. Certain organizational designs fit while others do not. The design challenge is to identify and select among often distinct choices. Thus the problem becomes much more solvable when there is an understanding of the factors that influence fit and the trade-offs involved, such as control and coordination.

When the organization performs well, the structure tends to drift towards a decentralized model where local managers possess greater autonomy (Figure 6.2). When problems persist, the tendency is to shift to a centralized model. This pendulum swing represents a lack of confidence in local decision-making. Despite the extreme difficulties, there is a persistent belief that an organization is controlled from the top. But giving orders is not the same as being in control. There are no guarantees, however, that local managers will appreciate the impact of their decisions on the larger organization. Their decisions can be short term and short-sighted. This wavering between

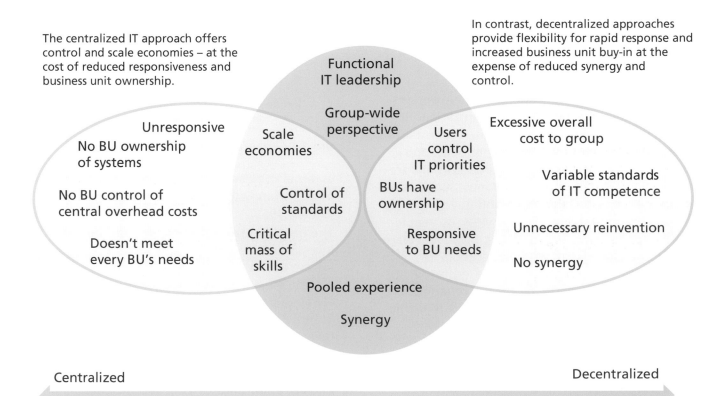

Figure 6.2 The centralized-decentralized spectrum

centralized and decentralized management is attributed as the source of long-term organizational problems and has been described as 'the illusion of being in control'. How then does an organization decide how best to manage its current organization and where to land along the design spectrum?

The process for major organizational change involves many events and can be a matter of years rather than months. Leading this change is difficult and should not be reduced to quick or simple fixes. The ability to lead this change is an important competence for senior executives and managers. Understanding when a service strategy is too complicated and rigid is as important as any support process.

Outside forces greatly influence an organization's service strategy, which in turn determines the organizational structure. Where the lines are drawn depends on what the organization is attempting to accomplish. A service strategy then becomes an implicit blueprint for an organization's design, shaping scale and scope. Scale refers to size. Scope refers not only to the broadness of service offerings – it also describes the range of activities the organization performs. When an organization decides on a make-or-buy strategy, for example, it is determining the scope of its activities. The trade-offs are control versus coordination.

An organization's age and size affect its structure. As the organization grows and matures, changes in roles and relationships must be made or problems will arise. This is particularly important for organizations adopting a service orientation, as pressures for efficiency and discipline inevitably lead to greater formalization and complexity. The risk over time is that the organization becomes too bureaucratic and rigid.

Most IT organizations tend to grow for prolonged periods without severe setbacks. The term evolution describes the quieter periods while the term revolution describes the upheaval of management practices.

6.1.1 Stages of organizational development

Organizations are generally characterized by a dominant management style: network, directive, delegative, coordinated or collaborative (Greiner,

1998) (Figure 6.3). Each style serves the needs of the organization for a period of time. As service requirements evolve, the organization encounters a dominant management challenge that must be resolved before growth can continue. The organization can no longer address its service challenge with its current management style. Nor can it be successful by retreating to a previous style – it must move ahead.

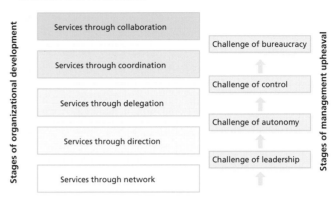

Figure 6.3 Stages of organizational development

6.1.1.1 Stage 1: Network

The focus of a Stage 1 organization is on the rapid, informal and *ad hoc* delivery of services. The organization is highly technology-oriented, perhaps entrepreneurial, and is reluctant to adopt formal structures. Innovation and entrepreneurship are important organizational values. The organization learns which processes and services work and adjusts accordingly. The organization believes that informal structures are far better suited to the resources required to deliver services. Past successes reinforce this belief. As the service demands grow, this model is not sustainable. It requires great local knowledge and intense dedication on the part of the staff. Conflict is created as staff members resist the creation of service structures.

As the organization grows and the need for efficient resources increases, leaders are confronted with the task of having to manage an organization. This is a very different skill from technology and entrepreneurship and often a task for which leaders find themselves ill prepared.

The global CIO of a multinational automotive company built an IT organization in an unusual manner. He hires divisional CIOs to correspond to business divisions: North America, Europe, Asia-Pacific, Latin America, Africa, the Middle East and finance. At the same time, he hires process information officers (PIOs) to work horizontally in different specialities across all divisions around the world: product development, supply chain management, production, customer experience and business services (HR, legal and so on).

The IT organization for one of the most popular sports leagues in North America flourishes under a culture of speed and entrepreneurship. Sunday game results and media events often dictate service activities with short time frames. Service processes are minimally structured, with room for improvisation and adaptation.

What are these organizational structures called?

Answer (see sections 6.1.1.1 to 6.1.1.5)

Stage 5 or collaboration/matrix: a matrix structure is a very difficult form of lateral process to implement, and it is used for stronger collaboration with the business.

Stage 1 or network: the focus of this organization is on the rapid, informal and *ad hoc* delivery of services. Informal structures are far better suited for success.

A common structure in this stage is called a network (Figure 6.4). A network structure is a cluster whose actions are coordinated by agreements rather than through a formal hierarchy of authority. The members work closely together to complement each other's activities. The goal of the organization is to share its skills with the customer in order to allow them to become more efficient, reduce costs or improve quality.

The key advantages of a network structure are:

- It avoids the high bureaucratic costs of operating a complex organizational structure.
- The organization can be kept flat with fewer managers required.
- The organization can quickly adapt or alter its structure.

The practical disadvantages of a network structure are:

- Managers must ensure the activities of the staff are integrated.
- The coordination problems are significant.
- There are difficulties in externally sourcing functional activities.

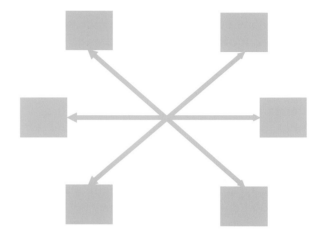

Figure 6.4 Services through network

Guidance

To grow past this challenge requires a significant change in leadership style. While this is accomplished through a variety of human performance techniques and methods, the desired outcome is a cadre of strong managers skilled and experienced in service management structures. Their influence and business focus are essential for moving to the next stage.

6.1.1.2 Stage 2: Directive

The Stage 1 crisis of leadership ends with a strong management team. They take responsibility for directing strategy and direct low-level managers to assume functional responsibilities (Figure 6.5).

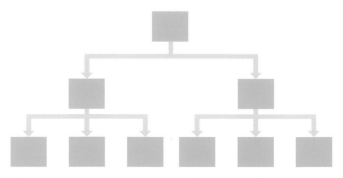

Figure 6.5 Services through direction

The focus of a Stage 2 organization is on hierarchical structures that separate functional activities. Communication is more formal and basic processes are in place. Although effort and energy are diligently applied to services, they are likely to be inefficient. Functional specialists are frequently faced with the difficult decision of whether to follow the process or take the initiative on their own.

A crisis of autonomy arises because the centralization limits decision-making and the freedom to experiment or innovate. Entrepreneurial motivation is degraded. For example, high-level approval is needed to start new projects, while successful performance at the lower levels goes unnoticed or unrewarded. Staff members become frustrated with their lack of autonomy. By not solving this crisis, the organization limits its ability to grow and prosper.

Guidance

To grow past this challenge requires a shift to greater delegation. Responsibility for service processes should be driven lower in the organization, allowing process owners to be responsible for lower-level decision-making and service accountability.

6.1.1.3 Stage 3: Delegation

The Stage 2 crisis ends with the delegation of authority to lower-level managers, linking their increased control to a corresponding reward structure (Figure 6.6). Growth through delegation allows the organization to strike a balance between technical efficiency and the need to provide room for innovation in the pursuit of new means to reduce costs or improve services.

The focus of a Stage 3 organization is on the proper application of a decentralized organizational structure. More responsibility shifts from functional owners to process owners. Process owners focus on process improvement and customer responsiveness. The challenge here is when functional and process objectives clash. Functional owners feel a loss of control and seek to regain it. At this stage, top managers intervene in decision-making only when necessary.

Guidance

Rather than the frequent reaction of returning to a functionally centralized model, the recommended approach is to enhance the organization's coordination techniques and solutions. The most common approach is through formal systems and programmes. There are occasions when an organization attempts to resolve the coordination challenge by centralizing on a process, rather than a functional model. Rather than creating a white space between functions, this leads to white space between processes. In other words, a pure process model is as problematic as a purely functional organizational model. A balance should be sought or the organization will revert back to a crisis of autonomy.

6.1.1.4 Stage 4: Coordination

The focus of a Stage 4 organization is on the use of formal systems in achieving greater coordination (Figure 6.7). Senior executives acknowledge the criticality of these systems and take responsibility for success of the solutions. The solutions lead to planned service management structures that are intensely reviewed and continually improved. Each service is treated as a carefully nurtured and monitored investment. Technical functions remain

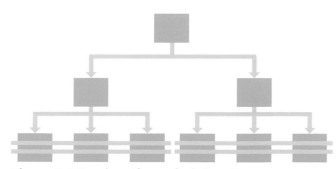

Figure 6.6 Services through delegation

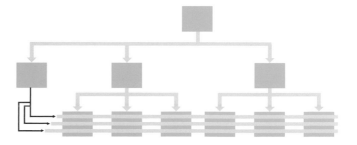

Figure 6.7 Services through coordination

centralized while service management processes are decentralized.

Guidance

The challenge here is the ability to respond to business needs in an agile manner. The business often adopts a perception that IT, despite its service orientation, has become too bureaucratic and rigid. While the linkages to the business may be well understood, innovation is dampened and service procedures have taken precedence over business agility.

6.1.1.5 Stage 5: Collaboration

The focus of a Stage 5 organization is on stronger collaboration with the business (Figure 6.8). Relationship management is more flexible, while managers are highly skilled in teamwork and conflict resolution. The organization responds to changes in business conditions and strategy in the form of teams across functions. Experiments in new practices are encouraged. A matrix-type structure is frequently adopted in this phase.

A matrix structure is a rectangular grid that shows the vertical flow of functional responsibility and a horizontal flow of product or customer responsibility. The provider effectively has two (or more) line organizations with dual lines of authority and a balance of power, and two (or more) bosses, each actively participating in strategy setting and governance.

An organization with a matrix structure adopts whatever functions the organization requires to achieve its goals. Functional personnel report to the heads of their respective functions but do not work under their direct supervision. Rather, the work of the functional staff is primarily determined by the leadership of the respective cross-functional product or customer team. The matrix relies on minimal formal vertical control and maximum horizontal control from the use of integrated teams.

The key advantages of a matrix structure are:

- Reduces and overcomes functional barriers
- Increases responsiveness to changing product or customer needs
- Opens up communication between functional specialists
- Provides opportunities for team members from different functions to learn from each other
- Uses the skills of specialized employees who move from product to product, or customer to customer, as needed.

In practice, there can be many problems with a matrix structure. The disadvantages are:

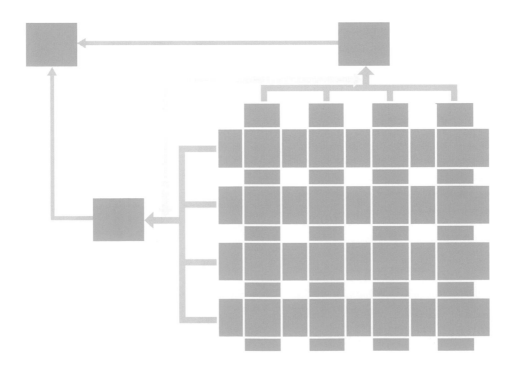

Figure 6.8 Services through collaboration

- Lacks a control structure that allows staff to develop stable expectations of each other
- Staff can be put off by the ambiguity and role conflict produced
- Potential conflict between functions and product or customer teams over time.

6.1.1.6 Deciding on a structure

Notice how each phase influences the other over time. The sequences are not always inevitable or linear. Each phase is neither right nor wrong. They are signposts to guide the organization. By understanding the current state, senior executives are better able to decide in what direction, and how far, to move along the centralized-decentralized spectrum.

The key to applying service management organizational development is understanding the following:

- Where the organization is in the sequence
- The range of appropriate options
- Each solution will bring new challenges.

6.2 ORGANIZATIONAL CHANGE

No matter what type of change the organization decides on, there remains the problem of getting the organization to change. Implementing change can be thought of as a three-step process, as in Figure 6.9.

Figure 6.9 Three-step change process

Resistance to change will force the organization to revert to previous behaviours unless steps are taken to refreeze the new changes. Role and task changes are not enough. Managers must actively manage the process:

- The first step to change is diagnosis. Namely, acknowledge the need for change and the factors prompting it. For example, complaints about service quality have increased or operating costs have escalated. Or morale is low while turnover is high. There is little point in focusing on improving costs if the customer is concerned about quality.

- The second step is determining the desired state. While this can be a difficult planning process with alternative courses of action, it begins with the organization's strategy and desired structure. Is the strategy based on reducing costs or improving quality? Should the organization adopt a product or geographic structure?

- The third step is implementation. This three-step process begins with identifying possible impediments to change. What obstacles are anticipated? For example, functional managers may resist reductions in power or prestige. The more severe the change then the greater the difficulties encountered. Next, decide who will be responsible for implementing changes and controlling the change process. These change agents can be external, as in consultants, or internal, as in knowledgeable managers. External change agents tend to be more objective and less likely to be perceived to be influenced by internal politics, while internal agents tend to have greater local knowledge. Last, decide on which change strategy will most effectively unfreeze, change and refreeze the organization. These techniques fall into two categories: top-down and bottom-up. Top-down is a dramatic restructuring by senior managers while bottom-up is a gradual change by low-level employees. Example techniques include:
  - Education and communication
  - Participation and empowerment
  - Facilitation
  - Bargaining and negotiation
  - Process consultation
  - Team building and inter-group training.

Section 3.1.1 in *ITIL Continual Service Improvement* provides further guidance on moving towards a desired state.

6.3 ORGANIZATIONAL DEPARTMENTALIZATION

It is common to think of organizational hierarchies in terms of functions. As the functional groups become larger, think of them in terms of departmentalization. A department might loosely be defined as an organizational activity involving more than a certain number of people. When a functional group grows to departmental size, the organization can reorient the group to one of the following areas or a hybrid thereof:

- **Function** Preferred for specialization, the pooling of resources and reducing duplication
- **Product** Preferred for servicing businesses with strategies of diverse and new products, usually manufacturing businesses
- **Market space or customer** Preferred for organizing around market structures. Provides differentiation in the form of increased knowledge of and response to customer preferences
- **Geography** The use of geography depends on the industry. By providing services in close geographical proximity, travel and distribution costs are minimized while local knowledge is leveraged
- **Process** Preferred for an end-to-end coverage of a process.

Certain basic structures are preferred for certain service strategies, as shown in Table 6.1.

6.4 ORGANIZATIONAL DESIGN

The starting point for organizational design is strategy (Figure 6.10). It sets the direction and guides the criteria for each step of the design process.

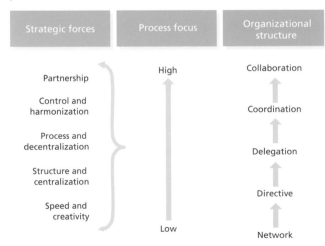

Figure 6.10 Matching strategic forces with organizational development

It is recommended to decide on a departmentalization structure prior to designing key processes. For example, if the provider's organization will be structured by geography or aligned by customers, the process design will be

guided by this criterion. Once key processes are understood, it is appropriate to begin organizational design (Figure 6.11).

The flow depends on clearly articulated strategic criteria. Processes can be thought of as organizational software – configurable to the requirements of a service strategy. Organizational designers should see each step as an iterative cycle: create basic processes and structures, learn about current and new conditions and adjust as learning evolves.

6.5 ORGANIZATIONAL CULTURE

Organizational culture is the set of shared values and norms that control the IT organization's internal and external interactions. Just as an organizational structure can improve performance, so too can an organization's culture increase organizational effectiveness.

There are two types of organizational values – terminal and instrumental:

- **Terminal values** are desired outcomes or end-states. IT organizations can adopt any of the following as terminal values: quality, excellence, reliability, innovativeness or profitability. Terminal values are often reflected in the organization's strategic perspective.
- **Instrumental values** are desired modes of behaviour. IT organizations can adopt any of the following as instrumental values: high standards, respecting tradition and authority, acting cautiously and conservatively or being frugal.

Terminal and instrumental values are key shapers of behaviour and can therefore produce very different responses in an IT organization. Many mergers and acquisitions fail because of these differences. Culture is transmitted to staff through socialization, training programmes, stories, ceremonies and language.

A service management organizational culture can be analysed through the following steps:

- Identify the terminal and instrumental values of the organization.
- Determine whether the goals, norms and rules of the organization are properly transmitting the value of the organizational culture to staff members. Are there areas for improvement?

Table 6.1 Basic organizational structures

Basic structure	Strategic considerations
Functional	Specialization Common standards Small size
Product	Product focus Strong product knowledge
Market space or customer	Service unique to segment Customer service Buyer strength Rapid customer service
Geography	On-site services Proximity to customer for delivery and support Organization perceived as local
Process	Need to minimize process cycle times Process excellence

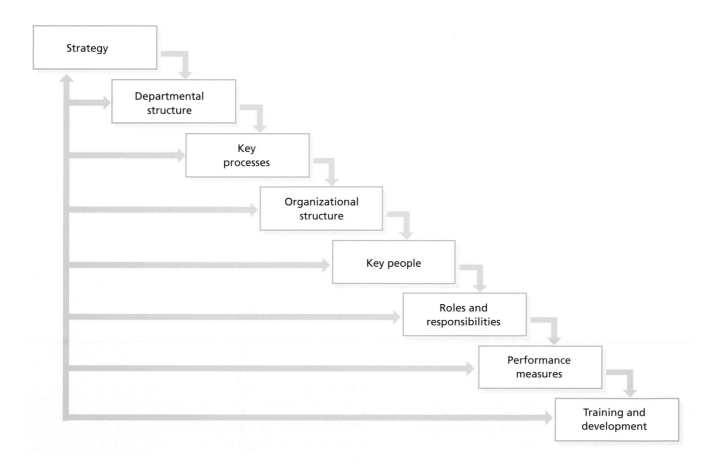

Figure 6.11 Organizational design steps

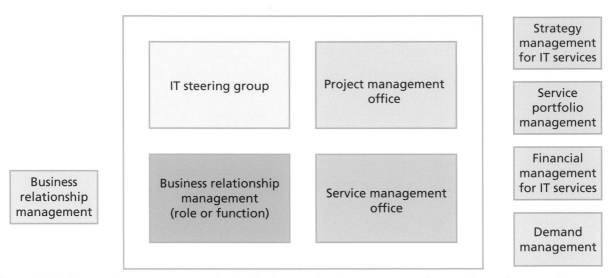

Figure 6.12 Strategic components of a logical organization structure for an IT service provider

■ Assess the methods the IT organization uses to introduce new staff. Do these practices help newcomers learn the organization's culture? (Van Maanen and Schein (1979) identified 12 socialization tactics that are useful in orienting newcomers to an organization's culture.)

6.6 FUNCTIONS

A function is a team or group of people and the tools or other resources they use to carry out one or more processes or activities. In larger organizations, a function may be broken out and performed by several departments, teams and groups, or it may be embodied within a single organizational unit (e.g. the service desk). In smaller organizations, one person or group can perform multiple functions – e.g. a technical management department could also incorporate the service desk function.

For service strategy to be successful, an organization will need to clearly define the roles and responsibilities required to undertake the processes and activities identified in Chapters 4 and 5. These roles will need to be assigned to individuals, and an appropriate organization structure of teams, groups or functions established and managed.

6.7 A LOGICAL ORGANIZATION STRUCTURE FOR AN IT SERVICE PROVIDER

Service provider organization structures will vary significantly depending on the culture, governance,

decision-making process etc. However, it is possible to create a logical structure to illustrate the major organizational aspects, processes and the way in which major roles are related to each other. One possible logical structure is shown in the following series of figures. Please note that this is just an example and may not be the best organizational structure for a particular organization. Care should be taken to apply these principles rather than attempting to replicate the structure exactly.

Figure 6.12 illustrates the major strategic components within a service provider.

Figure 6.12 illustrates the components of a logical organization structure that need to be in place to drive a successful service strategy. It is impossible to draw all the various groups and interactions, and so these diagrams are focused on highlighting the main organizational dynamics.

The IT steering group consists of executives from the business and IT service provider. The IT steering group will ensure that the enterprise strategy is appropriately represented in the service provider. It also evaluates initiatives within the service provider that might influence or change the current strategy positively in future. The IT steering group is also concerned with the investments being made by the service provider, and with ensuring that they will result in the desired levels of return.

The project management office (PMO) ensures that all projects and programmes are evaluated, managed and reported according to the enterprise and IT service provider's strategy.

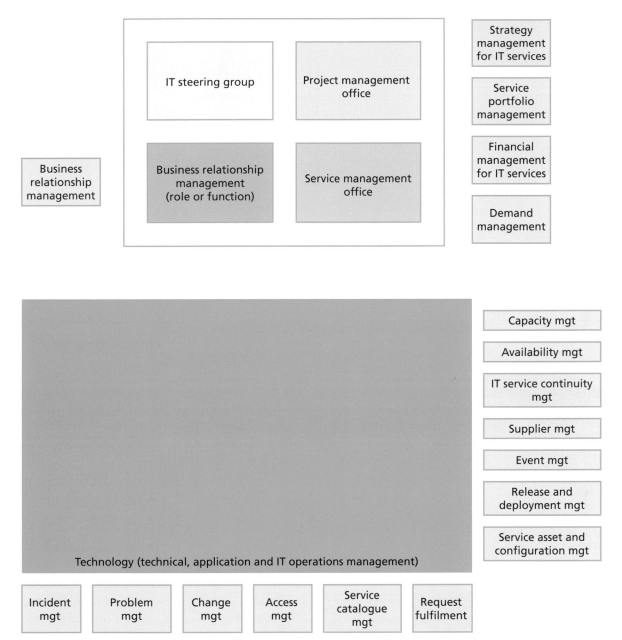

Figure 6.13 Strategic, tactical and operational components of an IT service provider's logical organization structure

The service management office (SMO) coordinates all processes and functions that manage the service provider's services throughout their lifecycle. All light-coloured boxes in Figures 6.12, 6.13 and 6.14 are processes that are coordinated by the SMO. These form part of the logical organization structure because each process has a process owner that is accountable for its effectiveness and efficiency. Not all process owners report directly into the manager of the SMO, and some could also be executives, operational managers or IT staff, with a functional reporting line to the SMO. Some processes may be managed by a function (for example, financial management).

Business relationship management has been identified as a process as well as a role or function because, as an advocate of the customer, it plays an important role in articulating and communicating the strategy of the customer and the strategy of the service provider. In external service providers, where customer executives are not part of the IT steering group, business relationship managers (BRMs) will represent their interests.

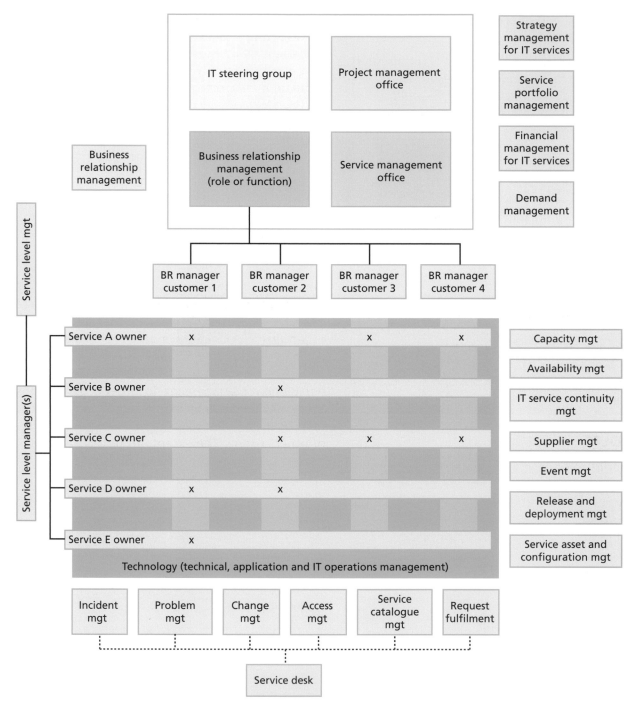

Figure 6.14 Linkage between customers and the service provider's logical organization structure

Figure 6.13 illustrates the tactical and operational components of the IT service provider, at a high level.

In Figure 6.13 the large dark-coloured box represents the technology (service assets) of the service provider, and includes infrastructure, applications and IT technical staff. They take direction from the strategic components, and use the processes around the dark-coloured box to execute the strategies, through designing,

transitioning and operating (delivering) services. It is in this box that the actual design, build, transition and operation of the services takes place.

Again, each light-coloured box is coordinated by the SMO, although the process owner may work for one of the operational or tactical departments in IT.

What is missing from this diagram is the linkage between the customer and the service provider at a strategic, tactical and operational level. This is illustrated in Figure 6.14.

Figure 6.14 shows how the customer is represented at every level of the logical structure through BRMs, the service level manager(s) and service owners. Each customer is represented by a BRM who works with the service owner and service level manager for each service used by the customer (indicated by an X). Together they will gather and analyse customer requirements and strategies; and then define the appropriate levels of service, ensuring that they are designed, transitioned and delivered appropriately. They will also monitor the customer and technology environment for changes and communicate these back into the strategic and technology components.

The users interface mainly through a set of processes at the bottom of the technology box. They may also be represented in meetings or research being conducted by the BRM, although the BRM primarily works with the customers rather than users.

6.8 ROLES

A number of roles need to be performed in support of service strategy. Please note that this section provides guidelines and examples of role descriptions. These are not exhaustive or prescriptive, and in many cases roles will need to be combined or separated. Organizations should take care to apply this guidance in a way that suits their own structures and objectives.

A role is a set of responsibilities, activities and authorities granted to a person or team. A role is defined in a process or function. One person or team may have multiple roles; for example, the roles of configuration manager and change manager may be carried out by a single person.

Roles are often confused with job titles, but it is important to realize that they are not the same. Each organization will define appropriate job titles and job descriptions that suit its needs, and individuals holding these job titles can perform one or more of the required roles.

It should also be recognized that a person may, as part of their job assignment, perform a single task that represents participation in more than one process. For example, a technical analyst who submits a request for change (RFC) to add memory

to a server to resolve a performance problem is participating in activities of the change management process at the same time as taking part in activities of the capacity management and problem management processes.

Roles fall into two main categories – generic roles such as process manager and process owner, and specific roles that are involved within a particular lifecycle stage or process such as a change administrator or knowledge management process owner. Roles can be combined in a number of different ways, depending on the organizational context. For example, in many organizations there will be someone with the job title of change manager who combines the roles of the change management process owner, change management process manager, change administrator and chair of a change advisory board (CAB). In a small organization the change manager role may be combined with roles from service asset and configuration management or release and deployment management. In larger organizations there may be many different people carrying out each of these roles, split by geography, technology or other criteria. The exceptions to this are that there must be only one process owner for each process and one service owner for each service.

Roles are accountable or responsible for an activity. They may also be consulted or informed about something: for example a service owner may be consulted about a change during an impact assessment activity. The RACI model, described in section 6.9, provides a useful way of defining and communicating roles and responsibilities.

What is a service manager?

Service manager is a generic term for any manager within the service provider. The term is commonly used to refer to a business relationship manager, a process manager or a senior manager with responsibility for IT services overall. A service manager is often assigned several roles such as business relationship management, service level management and continual service improvement.

6.8.1 Generic service owner role

To ensure that a service is managed with a business focus, the definition of a single point of accountability is absolutely essential to provide the level of attention and focus required for its delivery.

The service owner is accountable for the delivery of a specific IT service. The service owner is responsible to the customer for the initiation, transition and ongoing maintenance and support of a particular service and accountable to the IT director or service management director for the delivery of the service. The service owner's accountability for a specific service within an organization is independent of where the underpinning technology components, processes or professional capabilities reside.

Service ownership is as critical to service management as establishing ownership for processes which cross multiple vertical silos or departments. It is possible that a single person may fulfil the service owner role for more than one service.

The service owner has the following responsibilities:

- Ensuring that the ongoing service delivery and support meet agreed customer requirements
- Working with business relationship management to understand and translate customer requirements into activities, measures or service components that will ensure that the service provider can meet those requirements
- Ensuring consistent and appropriate communication with customer(s) for service-related enquiries and issues
- Assisting in defining service models and in assessing the impact of new services or changes to existing services through the service portfolio management process
- Identifying opportunities for service improvements, discussing these with the customer and raising RFCs as appropriate
- Liaising with the appropriate process owners throughout the service lifecycle
- Soliciting required data, statistics and reports for analysis and to facilitate effective service monitoring and performance
- Providing input in service attributes such as performance, availability etc.
- Representing the service across the organization
- Understanding the service (components etc.)
- Serving as the point of escalation (notification) for major incidents relating to the service

- Representing the service in change advisory board (CAB) meetings
- Participating in internal service review meetings (within IT)
- Participating in external service review meetings (with the business)
- Ensuring that the service entry in the service catalogue is accurate and is maintained
- Participating in negotiating service level agreements (SLAs) and operational level agreements (OLAs) relating to the service
- Identifying improvement opportunities for inclusion in the continual service improvement (CSI) register
- Working with the CSI manager to review and prioritize improvements in the CSI register
- Making improvements to the service.

The service owner is responsible for continual improvement and the management of change affecting the service under their care. The service owner is a primary stakeholder in all of the underlying IT processes which enable or support the service they own. For example:

- **Incident management** Is involved in (or perhaps chairs) the crisis management team for high-priority incidents impacting the service owned
- **Problem management** Plays a major role in establishing the root cause and proposed permanent fix for the service being evaluated
- **Release and deployment management** Is a key stakeholder in determining whether a new release affecting a service in production is ready for promotion
- **Change management** Participates in CAB decisions, authorizing changes to the services they own
- **Service asset and configuration management** Ensures that all groups which maintain the data and relationships for the service architecture they are responsible for have done so with the level of integrity required
- **Service level management** Acts as the single point of contact for a specific service and ensures that the service portfolio and service catalogue are accurate in relation to their service
- **Availability management and capacity management** Reviews technical monitoring data from a domain perspective to ensure that the needs of the overall service are being met

- **IT service continuity management** Understands and is responsible for ensuring that all elements required to restore their service are known and in place in the event of a crisis
- **Information security management** Ensures that the service conforms to information security management policies
- **Financial management for IT services** Assists in defining and tracking the cost models in relation to how their service is costed and recovered.

6.8.2 Generic process owner role

The process owner role is accountable for ensuring that a process is fit for purpose. This role is often assigned to the same person who carries out the process manager role, but the two roles may be separate in larger organization's. The process owner role is accountable for ensuring that their process is performed according to the agreed and documented standard and meets the aims of the process definition.

The process owner's accountabilities include:

- Sponsoring, designing and change managing the process and its metrics
- Defining the process strategy
- Assisting with process design
- Ensuring that appropriate process documentation is available and current
- Defining appropriate policies and standards to be employed throughout the process
- Periodically auditing the process to ensure compliance to policy and standards
- Periodically reviewing the process strategy to ensure that it is still appropriate and change as required
- Communicating process information or changes as appropriate to ensure awareness
- Providing process resources to support activities required throughout the service lifecycle
- Ensuring that process technicians have the required knowledge and the required technical and business understanding to deliver the process, and understand their role in the process
- Reviewing opportunities for process enhancements and for improving the efficiency and effectiveness of the process

- Addressing issues with the running of the process
- Identifying improvement opportunities for inclusion in the CSI register
- Working with the CSI manager and process manager to review and prioritize improvements in the CSI register
- Making improvements to the process.

6.8.3 Generic process manager role

The process manager role is accountable for operational management of a process. There may be several process managers for one process, for example regional change managers or IT service continuity managers for each data centre. The process manager role is often assigned to the person who carries out the process owner role, but the two roles may be separate in larger organizations.

The process manager's accountabilities include:

- Working with the process owner to plan and coordinate all process activities
- Ensuring that all activities are carried out as required throughout the service lifecycle
- Appointing people to the required roles
- Managing resources assigned to the process
- Working with service owners and other process managers to ensure the smooth running of services
- Monitoring and reporting on process performance
- Identifying improvement opportunities for inclusion in the CSI register
- Working with the CSI manager and process owner to review and prioritize improvements in the CSI register
- Making improvements to the process implementation.

6.8.4 Generic process practitioner role

A process practitioner is responsible for carrying out one or more process activities.

In some organizations, and for some processes, the process practitioner role may be combined with the process manager role; in others there may be large numbers of practitioners carrying out different parts of the process.

The process practitioner's responsibilities typically include:

- Carrying out one or more activities of a process
- Understanding how their role contributes to the overall delivery of service and creation of value for the business
- Working with other stakeholders, such as their manager, co-workers, users and customers, to ensure that their contributions are effective
- Ensuring that inputs, outputs and interfaces for their activities are correct
- Creating or updating records to show that activities have been carried out correctly.

6.8.5 Strategy management for IT services roles

This section describes a number of roles that need to be performed in support of the strategy management process. These roles are not job titles, and each organization will have to define appropriate job titles and job descriptions for their needs.

Many organizations will have a person with the job title 'IT strategy manager'. This job typically combines the roles of strategy management for IT services process owner and strategy management for IT services process manager.

6.8.5.1 Strategy management for IT services process owner

The strategy management for IT services process owner's responsibilities typically include:

- Carries out the generic process owner role for the strategy management for IT services process (see section 6.8.2 for more details)
- Works with other process owners to ensure that the organization's overall IT strategy is effectively reflected in their processes.

6.8.5.2 Strategy management for IT services process manager

The strategy management for IT services process manager's responsibilities typically include:

- Carries out the generic process manager role for the strategy management for IT services process (see section 6.8.3 for more details)

- Formulates, documents and maintains the organization's overall IT strategy, so as to best underpin the business strategy
- Assists in informing, publicizing and marketing of the key aspects of the IT strategy so that all customers, potential customers, staff members, suppliers and other relevant groups are aware of the IT strategy and how it will be taken forward
- Responsible to the IT steering group for the successful implementation and operation of the IT strategy
- Reviews the operation and performance of the IT strategy and makes any necessary changes or adjustments to the IT strategic plans or the way they are implemented or operated
- Plans and manages support for strategy management tools and processes
- Coordinates interfaces between strategy management for IT services and other processes.

6.8.6 Other roles involved in the strategy management for IT services process

In addition to the specific roles and activities described above, many important roles and activities are performed by senior managers of the service provider and in the wider organization. Examples of some important individuals and groups and the role they play in service strategy are discussed below, although their actual titles may differ between organizations.

6.8.6.1 Business strategy manager

The business strategy manager's responsibilities typically include:

- Formulates, documents and maintains the organization's overall business strategy
- Assists in informing, publicizing and marketing of the key aspects of the business strategy so that all customers, potential customers, staff members, suppliers and other relevant groups are aware of the strategy and how it will be taken forward
- Responsible to the organization's owners, shareholders, chief officers etc. for the successful implementation and operation of the business strategy

- Reviews the operation and performance of the business strategy and makes any necessary changes or adjustments to the strategic plans or the way they are implemented or operated.

6.8.6.2 IT steering group

The IT steering group will be made up of company owners, board directors, chief officers, senior managers or others appointed on their behalf. In most organizations this will also include one or more enterprise architects.

The IT steering group's responsibilities typically include:

- Steers the overall direction of the IT strategy, its implementation and the ongoing activities within the IT organization, so as to best underpin the organization's business strategy and meet the desired business outcomes
- Approves the IT financial budgets and decides how they will be broadly spent
- Plans the future for IT by prioritizing, deciding and scheduling proposed projects, infrastructure upgrades and major changes
- Has overall responsibility for IT governance.

6.8.6.3 IT director or service management director

Medium and larger organizations may wish to appoint an IT director or service management director to be responsible for all of its ITSM processes and/or to establish a service management office. These role titles will vary based on the culture of the organization (e.g. vice president or manager may be more appropriate than director).

The IT director or service management director's responsibilities typically include:

- Takes overall responsibility for the successful implementation and operation of the organization's overall ITSM processes
- Proposes, initiates and manages any ITSM service improvement initiatives
- Works with individual process owners and managers to identify issues, performance levels and potential improvements
- Manages resources between the ITSM processes and functions
- Takes responsibility for ITSM staff development and training.

6.8.7 Service portfolio management roles

This section describes a number of roles that need to be performed in support of the service portfolio management process. These roles are not job titles, and each organization will have to define appropriate job titles and job descriptions for their needs.

6.8.7.1 Service portfolio management process owner

The service portfolio management process owner's responsibilities typically include:

- Carries out the generic process owner role for the service portfolio management process (see section 6.8.2 for more details)
- Works with other process owners to ensure there is an integrated approach to the design and implementation of service portfolio management.

6.8.7.2 Service portfolio management process manager

The service portfolio management process manager's responsibilities typically include:

- Carries out the generic process manager role for the service portfolio management process (see section 6.8.3 for more details)
- Manages and maintains the organization's service portfolio
- Manages the surrounding processes for keeping the portfolio attractive to customers and up to date
- Markets the portfolio, and in particular the service catalogue, so that customers and potential customers are aware of the services available
- Helps formulate service packages and associated options, so that services can be combined in logical groupings to produce products that can be marketed, sold and consumed to best meet customers' needs.

6.8.8 Business relationship management roles

This section describes a number of roles that need to be performed in support of the business relationship management process. These roles are not job titles, and each organization will have to define appropriate job titles and job descriptions for their needs.

6.8.8.1 Business relationship manager

Many organizations will have a person with the job title 'business relationship manager' (BRM). This job may combine the roles of business relationship management process owner and business relationship management process manager and allocate it to one person.

'Business relationship manager' may also represent a number of individuals working within business relationship management and focused on different customer segments or groups. In some organizations, this role may be combined with the role of service level manager.

There can also be confusion between the role of the BRM, and the process of business relationship management. Business relationship managers are often required to execute activities from other processes simply because of their customer-facing position. This does not make those activities part of the business relationship management process.

6.8.8.2 Business relationship management process owner

The business relationship management process owner's responsibilities typically include:

- Carries out the generic process owner role for the business relationship management process (see section 6.8.2 for more details)
- Works with other process owners to ensure there is an integrated approach to the design and implementation of business relationship management.

6.8.8.3 Business relationship management process manager

The business relationship management process manager's responsibilities typically include:

- Carries out the generic process manager role for the business relationship management process (see section 6.8.3 for more details)
- Identifies customer needs and ensures that the service provider is able to meet these needs with an appropriate catalogue of services
- Ensures that customer expectations do not exceed what they are willing to pay for, and that the service provider is able to meet the customer's expectations before agreeing to deliver the service
- Ensures high levels of customer satisfaction, indicating that the service provider is meeting the customer's requirements
- Establishes and maintains a constructive relationship between the service provider and the customer based on understanding the customer and their business drivers
- Identifies changes to the customer environment that could potentially impact the type, level or utilization of services provided
- Identifies technology trends that could potentially impact the type, level or utilization of services provided
- Establishes and articulates business requirements for new services or changes to existing services
- Ensures that the service provider is meeting the business needs of the customer
- Mediates in cases where there are conflicting requirements for services from different business units.

6.8.8.4 Customers/users

The customers and users of the IT services are the other side of business relationship management, and will need to engage with business relationship management to voice their needs and to participate in the ongoing relationship to help ensure business outcomes are supported.

6.8.9 Financial management for IT services roles

This section describes a number of roles that need to be performed in support of the financial management for IT services process. These roles are not job titles, and each organization will have to define appropriate job titles and job descriptions for their needs.

Many organizations will have a person with the job title 'IT financial manager'. This job typically combines the roles of financial management for IT services process owner and financial management for IT services process manager.

6.8.9.1 Financial management for IT services process owner

The financial management for IT services process owner's responsibilities typically include:

- Carries out the generic process owner role for the financial management for IT services process (see section 6.8.2 for more details)
- Works with other process owners to ensure there is an integrated approach to the design and implementation of financial management for IT services.

6.8.9.2 Financial management for IT services process manager

The financial management for IT services process manager's responsibilities typically include:

- Carries out the generic process manager role for the financial management for IT services process (see section 6.8.3 for more details)
- Compiles and formulates the annual IT budgets and submits them for scrutiny and approval by the IT steering group
- Manages the IT budgets on a daily, monthly and annual basis, initiating corrective actions to balance income and expenditure in line with the budgets
- Produces regular statements of accounts for management information and to allow relevant managers to manage their own areas of the budgets
- Formulates and manages any recharging systems for IT customers
- Examines and reports on value-for-money of all major activities, projects and proposed expenditure items within IT.

6.8.9.3 Budget holders

Various IT managers may be nominated as budget holders, to estimate, agree and manage the budgets for their own particular area(s).

Budget holder responsibilities typically include:

- Submits annual budget estimate
- Negotiates and agrees their annual budget
- Manages their budget on an ongoing basis
- Reports budget activities and outcomes on a regular basis.

6.8.10 Demand management roles

This section describes a number of roles that need to be performed in support of the demand management process. These roles are not job titles, and each organization will have to define appropriate job titles and job descriptions for their needs.

6.8.10.1 Demand management process owner

The demand management process owner's responsibilities typically include:

- Carries out the generic process owner role for the demand management process (see section 6.8.2 for more details)
- Works with other process owners to ensure there is an integrated approach to the design and implementation of demand management.

6.8.10.2 Demand management process manager

The demand management process manager's responsibilities typically include:

- Carries out the generic process manager role for the demand management process (see section 6.8.3 for more details)
- Identifies and analyses patterns of business activity to understand the levels of demand that will be placed on a service
- Defines and analyses user profiles to understand the typical profiles of demand for services from different types of user
- Helps design services to meet the patterns of business activity and the ability to meet business outcomes
- Ensures that adequate resources are available at the appropriate levels of capacity to meet the demand for services, thus maintaining a balance between the cost of service and the value that it achieves
- Anticipates and prevents or manages situations where demand for a service exceeds the capacity to deliver it
- Gears the utilization of resources that deliver services to meet the fluctuating levels of demand for those services.

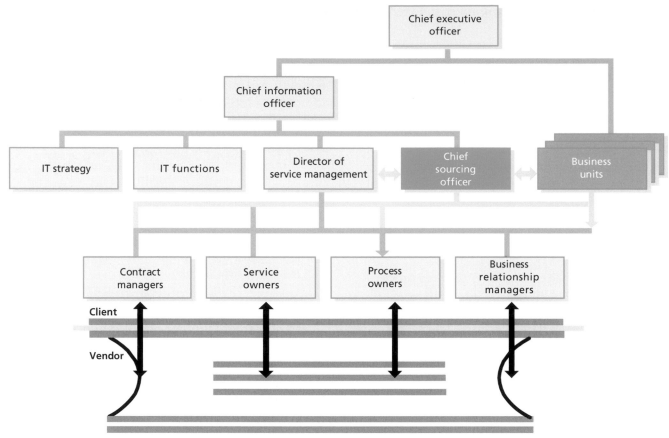

Figure 6.15 Chief sourcing officer – an example

6.8.11 Sourcing roles

Sourcing roles are defined more or less formally in different organizations. In the most formal, a sourcing office may be established and the role of chief sourcing officer defined. Whether this is represented as a full-time function or not, the key aspects of the role should be formalized and assigned to an individual or team to manage.

Any sourcing strategy should involve and be executed through supplier management (see *ITIL Service Design*).

Figure 6.15 illustrates how this role could be defined as a formal position within the client organization. Please note that this is only one example. Depending on the type of sourcing, this could be quite different. For example, if the organization is using a cloud service provider (such as Software as a Service or Platform as a Service – see Appendix C, section C.2), the chief sourcing officer (CSO) could report into another organization altogether – like into the general manager of one of the business units.

The chief sourcing officer:

- Promotes the sourcing strategy and the sourcing office
- Works closely with the CIO to develop a sourcing strategy that will determine which roles and responsibilities are best assumed by internal personnel and in which areas external resources should be deployed; sets guiding principles for governance
- Coordinates and rallies a mix of external and internal people towards goals through an empowerment-and-trust style, rather than the command-and-control hierarchical structure used with internal resources
- Is an integrator, coordinator, communicator, leader, coach: creates a shared identity among external and internal sources so that team members identify themselves first and foremost with the initiative at hand
- Has the ability to interact at the executive level, and to inspire and lead at the delivery level.

Other key sourcing roles should be clearly defined for coordinating activities across multiple service providers, as shown in Table 6.2.

Table 6.2 Examples of sourcing roles and responsibilities

Role	Description	Key competencies
Director of service management	Senior executive who understands the business and defines, plans, purchases and manages all aspects of service delivery on behalf of business units.	Authority and seniority to prioritize and define services for business units Large-scale service and operations management Financial and commercial management Governance, negotiation and contract management
Contract manager	Constructs, negotiates, monitors and manages the legal and commercial contract on behalf of the sourcing organization.	Contract management for large-scale service provision Negotiation and conflict resolution Service definition and management Translation of business into contractual requirements
Service owner	Defines, plans, and manages sourced elements of the service and performance on behalf of sourcing organization.	Authority and seniority to prioritize and define sourcing needs for specific elements of the service
Process owner	Interfaces with business users and functions to review, define and authorize current and future process models. Aim to identify and standardize best practices.	Capability and process definition Process mapping Service monitoring Managing user forums, e.g. joint application development, conference room pilot Best-practice identification, capture and deployment
Business representatives	Primary service recipients on behalf of each business unit who define business requirements, monitor service, raise service requests and own budgets.	Knowledge of specific business functions Requirements gathering, definition and prioritization Service monitoring Managing user forums

6.9 RESPONSIBILITY MODEL – RACI

Clear definitions of accountability and responsibility are essential for effective service management. To help with this task the RACI model or 'authority matrix' is often used within organizations to define the roles and responsibilities in relation to processes and activities. The RACI matrix provides a compact, concise, easy method of tracking who does what in each process and it enables decisions to be made with pace and confidence.

RACI is an acronym for the four main roles of being:

- **Responsible** The person or people responsible for correct execution – for getting the job done
- **Accountable** The person who has ownership of quality and the end result. Only one person can be accountable for each task

- **Consulted** The people who are consulted and whose opinions are sought. They have involvement through input of knowledge and information
- **Informed** The people who are kept up to date on progress. They receive information about process execution and quality.

When using RACI, there is only one person accountable for an activity for a defined scope of applicability. Several people may be responsible for executing parts of the activity. In this model, accountable means end-to-end accountability for the process. Accountability should remain with the same person for all activities of a process.

The RACI chart in Table 6.3 shows the structure and power of RACI modelling. The rows represent a number of required activities and the columns identify the people who make the decisions, carry out the activities or provide input.

Table 6.3 An example of a simple RACI matrix

	Director service management	Service level manager	Problem manager	Security manager	Procurement manager
Activity 1	AR	C	I	I	C
Activity 2	A	R	C	C	C
Activity 3	I	A	R	I	C
Activity 4	I	A	R	I	
Activity 5	I	R	A	C	I

Whether RACI or some other tool or model is used, the important thing is to not just to leave the assignment of responsibilities to chance or leave it to the last minute to decide. For example, if there is a transfer of a service from one service provider to another, RACI models should be designed in the service design lifecycle stage, and tested and deployed in service transition. In service operation, people assigned to specific roles will perform the activities in the RACI matrix.

Further details on the RACI matrix are provided in Chapter 3 of *ITIL Service Design*.

6.10 COMPETENCE AND TRAINING

6.10.1 Competence and skills for service management

Delivering service successfully depends on personnel involved in service management having the appropriate education, training, skills and experience. People need to understand their role and how they contribute to the overall organization, services and processes to be effective and motivated. As changes are made, job requirements, roles, responsibilities and competencies should be updated if necessary.

Each service lifecycle stage depends on appropriate skills and experience of people and their knowledge to make key decisions. In many organizations, personnel will deliver tasks appropriate to more than one lifecycle stage. They may well find themselves allocated (fully or partially) from operational tasks to support a design exercise and then follow that service through service transition. They may then, via early life support activities, move into support of the new or changed services that they have been involved in designing and implementing into the live environment.

The specific roles within ITIL service management all require specific skills, attributes and competences from the people involved to enable them to work effectively and efficiently. However, whatever the role, it is imperative that the person carrying out that role has the following attributes:

- Awareness of the business priorities, objectives and business drivers
- Awareness of the role IT plays in enabling the business objectives to be met
- Customer service skills
- Awareness of what IT can deliver to the business, including latest capabilities
- The competence, knowledge and information necessary to complete their role
- The ability to use, understand and interpret the best practice, policies and procedures to ensure adherence.

The following are examples of attributes required in many of the roles, dependent on the organization and the specific roles assigned:

- Management skills – both from a person management perspective and from the overall control of process
- Ability to handle meetings – organizing, chairing, and documenting meetings and ensuring that actions are followed up
- Communication skills – an important element of all roles is raising awareness of the processes in place to ensure buy-in and conformance. An ability to communicate at all levels within the organization will be imperative
- Articulateness – both written (e.g. for reports) and verbal

- Negotiation skills are required for several aspects, such as procurement and contracts
- An analytical mind – to analyse metrics produced from the activity.

Many people working in service management are involved with continual service improvement. *ITIL Continual Service Improvement* provides specific guidance on the skill levels needed for CSI activities.

6.10.2 Competence and skills framework

Standardizing job titles, functions, roles and responsibilities can simplify service management and human resource management. Many service providers use a common framework of reference for competence and skills to support activities such as skill audits, planning future skill requirements, organizational development programmes and resource allocation. For example, resource and cost models are simpler and easier to use if jobs and roles are standard.

The Skills Framework for the Information Age (SFIA) is an example of a common reference model for the identification of the skills needed to develop effective IT services, information systems and technology. SFIA defines seven generic levels at which tasks can be performed, with the associated professional skills required for each level. A second dimension defines core competencies that can be combined with the professional skills. SFIA is used by many IT service providers to identify career development opportunities.

More information on SFIA can be found at www.sfia.org.uk

6.10.3 Training

Training in service management helps service providers to build and maintain their service management capability. Training needs must be matched to the requirements for competence and professional development.

The official ITIL qualification scheme enables organizations to develop the competence of their personnel through approved training courses. The courses help students to gain knowledge of ITIL best practices, develop their competencies and gain a recognized qualification. The scheme has four levels:

- Foundation level

- Intermediate level
- ITIL Expert
- ITIL Master.

More information on ITIL qualifications can be found at www.itil-officialsite.com

Technology considerations

7

7   Technology considerations

Herbert A. Simon of Carnegie Mellon University won the 1978 Nobel Prize in economics for his work on decision-making processes within economic organizations. According to Simon's concept of bounded rationality there are limits to the decision-making capabilities of human agents in formulating and solving complex problems and in processing information. Even the most dedicated, motivated and talented groups and individuals have limited capacity for dealing with the inherent complexity, uncertainty and conflicts or trade-offs in most socio-technical systems.

Services are socio-technical systems with service assets as the operating elements. People and processes act as concentrators of other assets in social and technical sub-systems respectively (Figure 7.1). The performance of one sub-system affects the performance of the other in positive and negative ways.

The interactions between the two sub-systems are in the form of dependencies (passive) and influences (active) critical to the performance of service management as a value-creating system. The following are just a few examples of how each of these interactions matter:

■ Improvements in design and engineering of activities, tasks and interfaces can compensate for limitations of people

■ Improvements in knowledge, skills, attitudes and experience can partly compensate for poorly designed or inadequate processes, applications and infrastructure

■ Automation of routine processes can reduce variation, allow quick adjustments to process capacity and relieve stress on service staff during peak demand and off-hours. In some countries, automation can reduce the cost of operations attributable to expensive human resources

■ Productivity tools can make efficient use of human resources. Communications and collaboration tools can increase the effectiveness of knowledge sharing and problem solving

■ Analytical modelling, simulation and visualization tools are useful to analyse the impact of strategies, tactics and operations. They are useful to construct hypotheses, evaluate options and plan scenarios.

The effectiveness of service strategy relies on a loosely coupled but balanced and strong relationship between the social and technical subsystems. It is essential to identify and control these dependencies and influences. Reviews in service design, service transition, service operation and continual service improvement should include

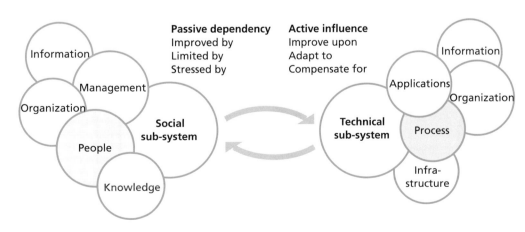

Figure 7.1 Services as socio-technical systems with people and processes as pivots

analysis of possible dysfunction or lack of synchronization between the two sub-systems.

The design of socio-technical systems is an important consideration in service management. It is important to recognize that services are much more than a series of activities that produce intangible value. They are systems with complex interactions between various factors of production or service assets. The methods and principles of operations research, systems dynamics and statistical process control are very useful within the context of improving the reliability of services.

7.1 SERVICE AUTOMATION

Automation can have particularly significant impact on the performance of service assets such as management, organization, people, process, knowledge and information. Applications by themselves are a means of automation but their performance can also be improved where they need to be shared between people and process assets. Advances in artificial intelligence, machine learning and rich-media technologies have increased the capabilities of software-based service agents to handle a variety of tasks and interactions.

Automation is considered to improve the utility and warranty of services. It may offer advantages in many areas of opportunity, including the following:

- The capacity of automated resources can be more easily adjusted in response to variations in demand volumes.
- Automated resources can handle capacity with fewer restrictions on time of access; they can therefore be used to serve demand across time zones and during after-hours.
- Automated systems present a good basis for measuring and improving service processes by holding constant the factor of human resources. Conversely, they can be used to measure the differential impact on service quality and costs due to varying levels of knowledge, skills and experience of human resources.
- Many optimization problems such as scheduling, routeing and allocation of resources require computing power that is beyond the capacity of human agents.

- Automation is a means for capturing the knowledge required for a service process. Codified knowledge is relatively easy to distribute throughout the organization in a consistent and secure manner. It reduces the depreciation of knowledge when employees move within the organization or permanently leave.

When judiciously applied, the automation of service processes helps improve the quality of service, reduce costs and reduce risks by reducing complexity and uncertainty, and by *efficiently* resolving trade-offs. (This is the concept of Pareto efficiency, where the solution or bargain is efficient when one side of the trade-off cannot be better off without making the other side worse off.)

The following are some of the areas where service management can benefit from automation:

- Design and modelling
- Service catalogue
- Pattern recognition and analysis
- Classification, prioritization and routeing
- Detection and monitoring
- Optimization.

Demand for services can be captured from simple interactions customers have with items in an automated service catalogue. There is a need to hide the complexity in the relationships between customer outcomes and the service assets that produce them, and present only the information the customers need to specify the utility and warranty needed with respect to any particular outcome. However, customers need choice and flexibility in presenting demand.

It is possible to handle routine service requests with some level of automation. Such requests should be identified, classified and routed to automated units or self-service options. This requires the study of patterns of business activity that exist with each customer.

The variation in the performance of individuals with time, workload, motivation and nature of the task at hand can be a disadvantage in many situations. The variation in the knowledge, skills and experience of individuals can lead to variation in the performance of processes. Variations in processing times across service transactions, jobs or cycles can result in degradation of service levels, usually in the form of delays and congestion (Figure 7.2).

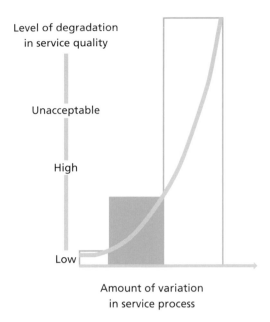

Figure 7.2 Degrading effect of variation in service processes

7.1.1 Preparing for automation

Applying automation indiscriminately can create more problems or exacerbate existing ones. The following guidelines should be applied:

- Simplify the service processes before automating them. By itself, simplification of processes can reduce variations in performance because there are fewer tasks and interactions for variations to enter. Simplification should not adversely affect the outcome of the process. Removal of necessary information, tasks or interactions makes the processes simpler but less useful. There are limits to simplification. Begin the analysis for automation at this limit.
- Clarify the flow of activities, allocation of tasks, need for information and interactions. All service agents and users should be clear about what they need to do so that the required inputs for a service transaction are available and complete. Automation itself makes the clarification easier through messaging, interactive terminals and websites.
  So automate, clarify, test, modify and then automate again.
- In self-service situations, reduce the surface area of the contact users have with the underlying systems and processes. Needless interactions with the internals of the system can introduce avoidable variation because of mental overload and slower learning curves. Simplify the

interfaces so that users see the attributes needed to present demand and extract utility.
- Do not be in a hurry to automate tasks and interactions that are neither simple nor routine in terms of inputs, resources and outcomes. Recurring patterns are more suited for automation than less consistent and infrequent activities.

7.1.2 Service analytics and instrumentation

Information is necessary but not sufficient for answering questions such as why certain data is the way it is and how it is likely to change in the future. Information is static. It only becomes knowledge when placed in the context of patterns and their implications. Those patterns give a high level of predictability and reliability about how the data will change over time. By understanding patterns of information we can answer 'How?' questions such as:

- How does this incident affect the service?
- How is the business impacted?
- How do we respond?

This is service analytics.

To understand things literally means to put them into a context. Service analytics involves both analysis, to produce knowledge, and synthesis, to provide understanding. This is called the DIKW structure (Figure 7.3).

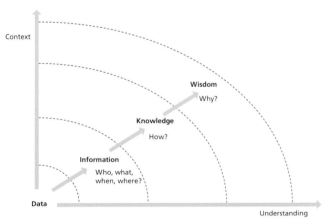

Figure 7.3 The flow from data to wisdom

While data does not answer any questions, it is a vital resource. Most organizations consider this capability in the form of instrumentation. The term instrumentation describes the technologies and techniques for measuring the behaviours of infrastructure elements. Instrumentation reports actual or potential problems and provides feedback after adjustments. Most organizations already have an installed base of instrumentation monitoring infrastructure elements similar to those in Table 7.1.

Table 7.1 Instrumentation techniques

Technique	Action
Asynchronous capture	Passive listeners scan for alerts.
External source	Compile data from external sources, such as service desk tickets, suppliers or systems – e.g. enterprise resource planning (ERP).
Manual generation	Manually create or alter an event.
Polling	Monitoring systems actively interrogate functional elements.
Synthetic transactions	Simulate the end-user experience through known transactions.

While data from element instrumentation is absolutely vital, it is insufficient for monitoring services. A service's behaviour derives from the aggregate behaviour of its supporting elements. While instrumentation can collect large amounts of raw data, greater context is needed to determine the actual relevance of any data. Information is the understanding of the relationships between pieces of data. Information answers four questions: Who, What, When and Where? This can be thought of as event, fault and performance management. The event management function refines instrumentation data into those that require further attention. While the line between instrumentation and event management can vary, the goal remains the same: create usable and actionable information. Table 7.2 describes common event management techniques.

A fault is an abnormal condition that requires action to repair, while an error is a single event. A fault is usually indicated by excessive errors. A fault can result from a threshold violation or a state change. Performance, on the other hand, is a measure of how well something is working. The function of the operations group begins with fault management. But as this function matures from reactive to proactive, the challenge becomes performance management. Fault management systems usually display topology maps with

coloured indicators. Typically they have difficulties in dealing with complex objects that span multiple object types and geographies. Further context is needed to make this information useful for services. Begin by transitioning from information to knowledge.

Table 7.2 Event management techniques

Technique	Action
Compression	Consolidate multiple identical alarms into a single alarm.
Correlation	See if multiple alert sources occurring during a short period of time have any relationship.
Filtering	Apply rules to a single alert source over some period of time.
Intelligent monitoring	Apply adaptive instrumentation.
Roll-up	Compress alerts through the use of hierarchical collection structures.
Verification	Actively confirm an actual incident.

Service analytics is useful to model existing infrastructure components and support services to the higher-level business services. This model is built on dependencies rather than topology – causality rather than correlation. Infrastructure events are then tied to corresponding business processes. The component-to-system-to-process linkage – also known as the service model – allows us to clearly identify the business impact of an event. Instead of responding to discrete events, managers can characterize the behaviour of a service. This behaviour is then compared to a baseline of the normal behaviour for that time of day or business cycle.

With service analytics, not only can an operations group do a better job of identifying and correcting problems from the user's standpoint, it can also predict the impact of changes to the environment. This same model can be turned around to show business demand for IT services. This is a high leverage point when building an on-demand environment.

This is as far along the DIKW structure as modern technologies allow. It is well understood that no computer-based technology can provide wisdom. It requires people to provide evaluated understanding, to answer and appreciate the

'Why?' questions. Moreover, the application of intelligence and experience is more likely to be found in the organizational processes that define and deliver service management than in applied technologies. Section 9.1.4 outlines some of the challenges in measurement that can be addressed by service analytics.

7.2 SERVICE INTERFACES

7.2.1 Characteristics of good service interfaces

The design of service interfaces is critical to service management. Highly usable service interfaces are necessary for service orientation. The principles of specialization and coordination are possible because of effective interfaces between service assets and customer assets. Service interfaces are typically present at the point of utilization or service access points (Figure 7.4).

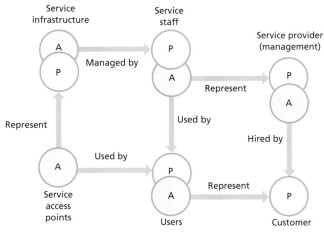

Key
P = principals
A = agents

Figure 7.4 The critical role of service interfaces

Service access points are associated with one or more channels of service. User interfaces include those provided for the customer's employees and other agents, as well as process-to-process interfaces. The service interfaces should meet the basic requirements of warranty:

■ They should be easily located or ubiquitous enough, or simply embedded in the immediate environment or business context, as in the case of interfaces to software applications.
■ They should be available in forms or media that allow choice and flexibility for users. For

example, there should be choice between staffed locations and automated self-service options, and choice between a browser and a mobile phone as access points.
■ They should be available with enough capacity to avoid queuing or backlog when supporting concurrent use by many users. The presence of other users should not be noticeable (non-rival use).
■ They should accommodate users with varying levels of skills, competencies, backgrounds and disabilities.
■ The principle of ubiquity should be traded off with the need to keep interfaces low-profile and low-overhead to avoid undue stress on the customer's use context or the business environment.
■ They should be simple and reliable, having only the functions required for users to tap the utility of the service.
■ Service interfaces should be self-reliant, requiring little or no intervention from service agents other than the dialogue necessary to carry out the service transaction.

7.2.2 Types of service technology encounters

Advances in communication technologies are having a profound effect on the manner in which service providers interact with customers. Airport kiosks, for example, have changed the interaction between airlines and their customers. There are five modes in which technology interacts with a service provider's customers (Figure 7.5):

■ **Mode A: technology-free** Technology is not involved in the service encounter. Consulting services, for example, may be Mode A.
■ **Mode B: technology-assisted** A service encounter where only the service provider has access to the technology. For example, an airline representative who uses a terminal to check in passengers is Mode B.
■ **Mode C: technology-facilitated** A service encounter where both the service provider and the customer have access to the same technology. For example, a planner in consultation with a customer can refer to 'what if' scenarios on a personal computer to illustrate capacity and availability modelling profiles.

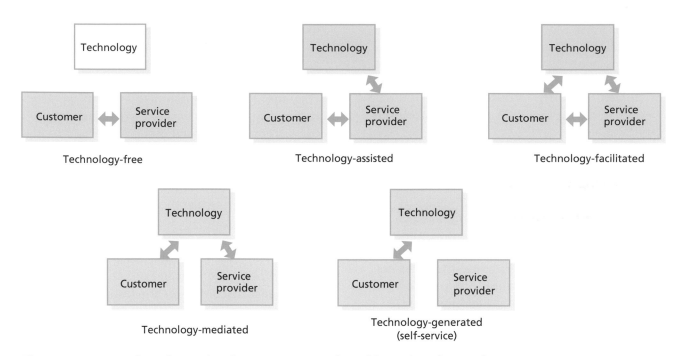

Figure 7.5 Types of service technology encounters (Froehle and Roth, 2004)

- **Mode D: technology-mediated** A service encounter where the service provider and the customer are not in physical proximity. Communication may be through a phone. For example, a customer who receives technical support services from a service desk is Mode D.
- **Mode E: technology-generated** A service encounter where the service provider is represented entirely by technology, commonly known as self-service. For example, bank ATMs, online banking and distance learning are Mode E.

Encounters should be designed while considering customer assets.

- Are customer employees technical or non-technical?
- What are the implications of the technology encounter to the customer?
- What are the customer expectations and perceptions?

For example, Mode E may be less effective than Modes B or C in cases where the encounter is complex or ambiguous. When the encounter is routine and explicit, as in password resets, Mode E may be preferred. Other modes may have secondary considerations. Mode D, for example, may have language or time-zone implications.

7.2.3 Self-service channels

Automation is useful to supplement the capacity of services. Self-service channels are increasingly popular among users now accustomed to human–computer interactions, devices and appliances. The ubiquitous channel of service delivery is the internet, with browsers acting as service access points that are widely distributed, standardized and highly familiar through constant use. Advances in artificial intelligence and speech recognition have improved the capabilities of software-based service agents in conducting dialogue with customers. The richness of the dialogue and the complexity of the interaction continue to increase.

The capacity of self-service channels has very low marginal cost, is highly scalable, does not suffer from fatigue, offers highly consistent performance and is offered on a 24/7 basis at a relatively low cost. Additionally, users perceive the following disadvantages with human-to-human interactions with respect to incidents and problems:

- The emotional burden that the user is asked to carry in complaining about the service
- Variability in the experience, competence and emotional state of human agents
- Limited capacity of human resources, which causes uncertainty in wait times
- The need to schedule certain interactions with staff

■ The fees associated with certain human resources.

Self-service channels are effective when appropriate knowledge and service logic is embedded into the self-service terminal. Service design should ensure that use case analysis is performed to ensure usability, efficiency and ease in interactions through the automated interface.

Another example would be the use of the productive capacity of customers through self-service channels. Advances in human-computer interaction and the richness of interaction technologies, such as touch-screens, scanners and signature capture devices, allow for certain service activities to be completed without the presence or intervention of service staff (Rayport and Jaworski, 2004). This is a very intelligent way to adjust capacity that is highly sensitive to the presence of demand. Each customer brings one additional unit of productive capacity, instantly added and removed from the system without inventory-carrying costs to the service provider.

It is necessary to evaluate the level of control users are expected to assume with self-service options. The level of control should be commensurate with the proficiency and experience level of the users (Lidwell et al., 2003). In almost every population of users there are differences in levels of experience, skills, aptitudes and work environments that determine preferences for methods and modes of interaction. The attributes and functions of service interfaces should take these differences into account. There will be trade-offs as different segments of users expect to be served according to their preferences. Some prefer step-by-step guidance while others prefer efficiency and flexibility. Advances in artificial intelligences and machine learning are creating a new level of sophistication for service interfaces, which are context-aware, forgiving of new users and capable of dialogue embedded with enquiry. The principle of forgiveness requires that the design of a service helps users avoid errors. When errors do occur, the design should minimize negative consequences.

7.2.4 Technology-mediated service recovery

According to the peak-end rule, whereby the service providers recover well from service incidents, customers may actually retain a more positive perception of service quality than they had before the incident. This behaviour provides justification for investment in superior service support systems, processes and staff. While the strategic intent may be to reduce the occurrence of service incidents, the tactical goal would be to recover well from service incidents that are not avoided or foreseen.

Under certain conditions, the use of automation allows for quicker service recovery through fast resolution of service incidents. Users often expect nothing more than quick resolution of their problems without tedious policies and procedures. This provides a business case for simplifying, standardizing and automating certain service activities or interactions. However, when poorly designed or implemented, automated or self-service options can be especially aggravating for a user who may have suffered from a service incident. The challenge is to pick the right type of interface for a particular interaction.

Simple and routine incidents should be recovered using automation when all other factors are equal. Software-agents with diagnostic capabilities can interact with users to resolve basic technical problems. Online knowledge bases with search and navigation capabilities are useful examples of such recovery.

Example of leveraging intangible assets

The product installation and maintenance system of a major internet and telecom solutions provider generated £0.75 billion in savings (1996–1998). The company made an extensive amount of technical knowledge about its solutions freely available online to its customers. Large amounts of workload were diverted away from its technical support staff and engineers, who could focus on tougher problems needing escalation. Most of the customers were themselves technical staff willing to attempt to fix problems on their own to the extent possible. This online knowledge base could be concurrently used by a large number of customers without degradation of quality or inordinate waiting times (from Lev, 2001).

The approach processes knowledge from service management processes into automated solutions such as online technical support, self-service terminals, IVR units and software applications. Users are then presented with the self-service option as the first line of support to solve the most routine of problems. It also helps to raise the level of technical knowledge of users through well-designed documentation and self-help kits. Over time, this reduces the number of incidents that have to be handled by human resources (see example in Figure 7.4).

The idea of making it convenient, quick and courteous for users to report service incidents and receive compensation is an important principle that should shape policies and guidelines. Good service culture requires it to be easy and fair for customers to file a complaint and have problems resolved, without undue burden on their time, effort, or emotion, all of which are forms of indirect costs and psychological costs of being a customer (Tax and Brown, 1998). The need for that becomes particularly important where the customer or users will not receive any financial compensation. At this level of maturity, the service provider has institutionalized the true meaning of providing warranty to the customer. Preventing simple failures from turning into negative feelings will help maintain higher levels of customer satisfaction. Such service providers also demonstrate to their customers certain ethics that contribute to long-term success in the relationship.

7.3 TOOLS FOR SERVICE STRATEGY

7.3.1 Simulation

IT organizations often exhibit counter-intuitive behaviour resulting from many agents interacting over time. Long-term behaviour can be surprisingly different from short-term behaviour. System dynamics is a methodology for understanding and managing the complex problems of IT organizations. It offers a means to capture and model the feedback processes, stocks and flows, time delays and other sources of complexity associated with IT organizations. It is a tool for evaluating the consequences of new policies and structures before putting them into action.

Just as an airline uses flight simulators to help pilots learn, system dynamics offers simulation

methods and tools available to help senior managers understand their organizations. These management flight simulators, based on mathematical models and computer simulation, can deliver useful insights for decision makers faced with enormous complexity and policy resistance.

The application of system dynamics in the service and process domains has yielded remarkable insight for IT organizations. Some examples are:

- **The capability trap** By pressuring staff to work harder, an organization unwittingly triggers a scenario where ever-increasing levels of effort are required to maintain the same level of performance (Repenning and Sterman, 2001a).
- **The tool trap** Although technology tools offer very useful help to an organization, they often require the development of knowledge and experience. When an organization adopts new tools, it triggers lower productivity in the short term. The increase in workload from training, learning and practice activities may unwittingly push a resource-constrained organization over its tipping point. (Repenning and Sterman, 2001b).
- **The fire-fighter trap** When an organization rewards managers for excellence in fire-fighting, they may unwittingly create a dynamic harming the long-term performance of the organization. The long-term performance is instead improved by not rewarding excellence in fire-fighting (Repenning and Sterman, 2001b).

7.3.2 Analytical models

Analytical models are very useful where the complexity is manageable, and there is no policy resistance or interacting feedback loops. They are effective when objectives are clear, the options are well defined and the critical uncertainties are measurable. They are easy to develop when there is a fair amount of clarity on a problem or situation, the cause and effect relationships are clear and persistent, and patterns are recognizable. They also need enough historical information for assumptions on certain variables, such as costs, processing times and the load factors of resources.

Good examples of the use of analytical models are service desk and call centre staffing, which can be visualized as a system of queues. It is possible to gather data on the rate of arrival of requests (or

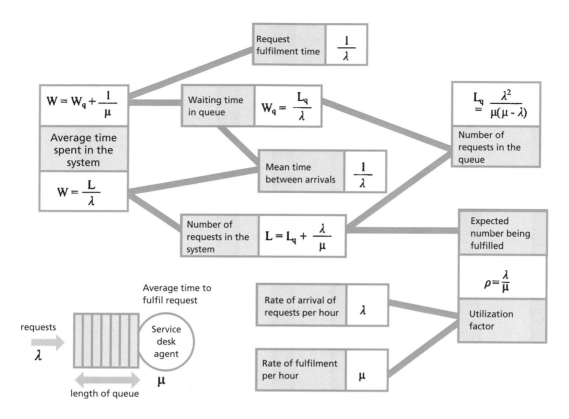

Figure 7.6 Example of a simple analytical model for the service desk

incidents), how long it takes to process them on average, and how many requests are waiting to be handled. This level of knowledge is sufficient to build simple analytical models. Figure 7.6 shows an example for a single-stage, single-agent queue at a service desk, with certain assumptions about the arrival pattern of requests and the processing time.

Service desk modelling can become quite complex with the addition of numbers of service channels, multi-stage processes, dependencies and delays. However, it is useful to start with basic models and progressively elaborate them to reflect closely the reality of a problem or situation.

The following are commonly used sets of tools useful for decision-making in service strategy:

■ Decision trees, payoff matrices, analytic hierarchy process etc.
■ Linear programming (Figure 7.7) and integer programming, goal programming etc.
■ Queuing and network flow models (Figure 7.8)
■ Clustering, forecasting, time-series analysis etc.
■ Analysis of variance, design of experiments etc.

These methods can be applied to solve a variety of problems such as:

■ Allocation of resources between services and contracts
■ Analysis of demand patterns and segmentation of users
■ Compression, correlation and filtering (Table 7.2)
■ Scheduling of jobs, tasks and staff
■ Location and layout of facilities and infrastructure elements
■ Capital budgeting, pricing and purchase decisions
■ Portfolio optimization
■ Contingency planning and redundancy (coverage problems).

There is depth and diversity in analytical models, some of which have been in use for decades and have been instrumental to the maturity of disciplines such as operations management, project management and financial analysis. Service sectors such as telecommunications, transportation, logistics and financial services have achieved high

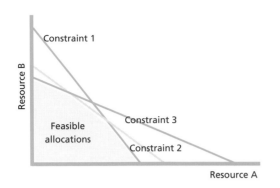

Figure 7.7 Simple LP model

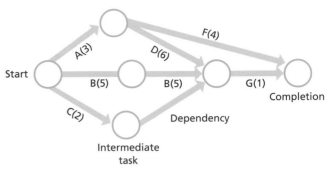

Figure 7.8 Simple network model

levels of performance from the application of systems and industrial engineering concepts, methodologies and quality control processes to service functions and processes (National Academy of Engineering, 2003).

There is a range of automation tools available for analytical modelling. The simplest tool available is a computer spreadsheet such as Microsoft Excel with its built-in solver function. Models with a fair amount of sophistication can be built using spreadsheets. More sophisticated models can be constructed using tools, special-purpose optimization programming languages (OPL) and optimization engines. Several commercial solutions for automation in service management include functions and modules for analytical modelling and visualization.

Service strategy and other functions and processes in the service lifecycle can benefit similarly from such knowledge to improve performance in the presence of technical, financial and time constraints. Six Sigma™, PMBOK and PRINCE2 offer well-tested sets of methods based on analytical models. These should be evaluated and adopted within the context of service strategy and service management.

Implementing service strategy

8

8   Implementing service strategy

8.1   IMPLEMENTATION THROUGH THE LIFECYCLE

Strategic positions and perspectives are converted into strategic plans and patterns with goals and objectives for execution through the service lifecycle. The positions are driven by the need to serve specific customers and market spaces and influenced by strategic perspectives as a service provider (Figure 8.1). Plans are a means of achieving those positions. Plans include projects and programmes and result in ongoing revision of the service catalogue, service pipeline, customer agreement portfolio, financial budgets and delivery schedules and the implementation of improvement programmes.

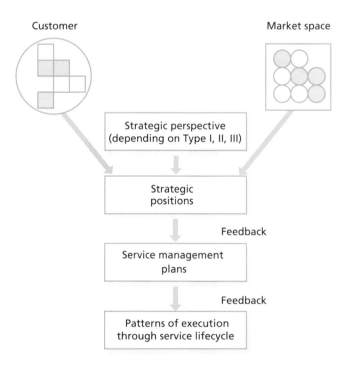

Figure 8.1 Strategic planning and control process (Simons, 1995)

Plans identify specific actions that need to be undertaken within each stage of the lifecycle in order to develop and deploy the capabilities and resources required to reach strategic positions.

Plans translate the intent of strategy into action through service design, service transition, service operation and continual service improvement. Service strategy provides input to each stage of the service lifecycle. Continual service improvement provides the feedback and learning mechanism by which the execution of strategy is controlled throughout the lifecycle.

8.1.1   Top down

For any given market space, service strategy defines the portfolio of services to be offered and the customers to be serviced. This in turn determines the customer agreement portfolio that needs to be supported with design, transition and operation capabilities. Lifecycle capabilities are defined in terms of the systems, processes, knowledge, skills and experience required at each stage to effectively support the customer agreement portfolios. Interactions between service management capabilities are clearly defined and managed for an integrated and systematic approach to service management. Service design and operation capabilities determine the type of transition capabilities required. They determine the portfolio of service designs and the operating range of the service provider in terms of models and capacities.

How quickly a service is transitioned from design to operations depends on the capabilities of the service transition stage. Transition capabilities reduce the costs and risks for customers and service providers throughout the lifecycle by maintaining visibility and control over all service management systems and processes. In this manner, transition capabilities not only act as filters but also as amplifiers that increase the effectiveness of design and operation. They interact with service designs to provide new and improved service models. They interact with operation models and capacity to increase the operational effectiveness of plans and schedules. The net effect is reflected in the service levels delivered to customers in fulfilment of contracts.

Customers and service providers both face strategic risks from uncertainties. It is impossible to either control or predict all the factors in a business environment. The risks may translate into challenges or into opportunities depending on alignment between service management capabilities and the emergent needs of customers.

Service strategy requires continual service improvement to drive feedback through the lifecycle elements to ensure that challenges and opportunities are not mismanaged.

New strategic positions are adopted based on patterns that emerge from executing the service lifecycle. This bottom-up development of service strategy is combined with the traditional top-down approach to form a closed-loop planning and control system for service strategies. Such feedback and learning is a critical success factor for service management to drive changes and innovation.

8.2 SERVICE STRATEGY IMPLEMENTATION ACTIVITIES FOLLOWING A LIFECYCLE APPROACH

The strategy of a service provider has to be continually adjusted and refined to meet changing customer requirements and strategies. As a result it is important that service strategy processes and tools are implemented to enable this dynamic environment.

Implementing service strategy is not just a case of designing and deploying a set of static processes and then making sure that the same actions are performed consistently year after year. As services move through the service lifecycle, so too must the implementation and improvement of the service strategy processes.

Further, just as the strategy of the service provider is owned and directed by the senior executives of the organization, so too are the service strategy processes. Although process owners and implementation resources may be assigned by senior executives, the executives themselves are the main stakeholders and users of the processes, and they should therefore be closely involved throughout the lifecycle.

In addition, service strategy determines how the service lifecycle functions, and how services are designed, transitioned, operated and improved. As a result, it is critical that the implementation of service strategy processes follow the same stages that other processes do. This section therefore shows how service strategy implementations follow the service lifecycle stages, and how it influences those stages as it is implemented.

8.2.1 Setting the implementation strategy

Ironically, even though the formal service strategy processes do not yet exist, it is important that a formal strategy for the initiative be defined and executed. This is best done using the organization's programme and project management approaches, since the initiative should be managed as a formal project or series of projects.

The strategy for the implementation should, at a minimum, include the following areas:

- **Current state assessment** Definition of the current environment
- **Target state definition** Description of the end-state, in terms of strategic perspective and position
- **Gap analysis** Description of the differences (gaps) between the current state and the desired target state
- **Project identification** Logical groupings of activities, with specific objectives, that need to be undertaken to close identified gaps
- **Project estimation** Analysis of the project's scope, scale, interdependencies, risks, costs and resource requirements
- **Project consolidation** Logical grouping of identified projects into 'streams' or initiatives that address key aspects of the implementation, such as 'governance', 'people', 'process', 'technologies' and 'management of change' (the organizational change management)
- **Roadmap** Development of the time-bound action plan that will provide the instruction on sequence of the initiatives and projects required to close the gaps.

When reading a book on strategy, it is tempting to approach the task as if nothing of this nature has been attempted before. This is probably not true. Even if there is no existing formal service strategy, the existing culture of the organization and the way decisions are made are a *de facto* strategy. The initiative needs to take this into account and ensure that the existing environment is considered. A significant amount of organizational change management will need to be included in the initiative to address the fundamental change to the culture of the organization.

One of the most important aspects to be defined is how the initiative will impact the current direction of the organization. For example, if the service strategy will introduce new processes, how will these impact the operations of the enterprise, and how will this impact the overall competitive advantage of the organization?

The strategy must also include mechanisms for feedback during the implementation process, so that decision makers can evaluate whether plans need to be deferred or adjusted according to factors discovered during the design, transition and operation stages.

Finally, the executive ownership of the initiative and the resulting processes cannot be emphasized enough. Some organizations have treated this as a tactical exercise aimed purely at IT operations. This is a recipe for failure. Service strategy is at the heart of the business of the service provider, and is one of the key responsibilities of the organization's executives. Regardless of how the executives perceived their roles prior to service strategy processes being implemented, these will now become a core part of their responsibility and accountability. This needs to be fully understood, approved and executed if the implementation is to be successful.

8.2.2 Designing service strategy

In this stage of the lifecycle the actual processes, tools and organizational structure (if required) will be designed. Design will include the collection of detailed requirements for the areas to be implemented as well as the actual design of the tools and procedures to be used. The following areas will potentially be included in this design:

- Process design for strategy management, service portfolio management, financial management for IT services, demand management and / or business relationship management
- Definition of roles for these processes
- For strategy management, an agreed assessment method, forecasting and planning tools, document control tools, identified sources for industry information etc.
- The service portfolio, customer portfolio and customer agreement portfolio
- A standard for defining service models and assessing business impact of new services or changes to existing services
- Financial management tools, policies, charts of accounts (if these do not already exist), cost

model definitions, charging strategies and methods etc.
- Demand management procedures, techniques and tools
- The interfaces between all service strategy process and other processes. However, due to the intricate interrelationship between business relationship management and other processes, this will deserve even more careful design.

8.2.2.1 Special note on implementing service portfolio management

Some organizations implement service portfolio management because they need to better define services. However, it is important that implementing service portfolio management and defining services are clearly differentiated.

In the first instance the initiative should address the design of the process and tools to be used for service portfolio management. Once these processes and tools have been defined, it is then possible to go about defining and formalizing the services.

Attempting to define the services in the absence of service portfolio management could result in a lack of consistency of service definition, poorly defined service models (with the associated inaccurate forecasting of service requirements) and a lack of formal gatekeeping. This will result in services moving into the lifecycle without the appropriate business cases, authorization and impact assessments.

8.2.3 Transitioning service strategy

During the transition stage the designed service strategy processes and tools will be built or purchased (and customized if necessary), tested and deployed.

This stage will include the following high-level activities:

- Training of the project teams to ensure consistent and appropriate level of knowledge about the processes being implemented
- Development or purchase of any tools needed to support the processes, and their configuration
- Training tool administrators how to manage the tools

- Training process managers how to manage the process
- Testing the tools to ensure that they are able to provide the required utility and warranty
- Testing the processes to ensure that they can be executed as planned, and that they will achieve the desired results
- A pilot deployment of the tools and/or processes that have been built
- Training of users of the tools and staff who are expected to execute or comply with the processes
- Deployment of the tools and/or processes
- Post-implementation review to ensure that the tools and processes have been deployed correctly, and to provide feedback to the initiative's strategists and designers regarding the success of the project.

8.2.4 Operating service strategy

During this stage, the service strategy processes described in Chapter 4 will be executed. Please note that this does not mean that service strategy becomes the responsibility of IT operations. It remains the responsibility of the executives of the service provider organization, and they retain accountability even if they delegate the responsibility for certain aspects of execution.

The following generic activities will be included in this stage:

- Execution of process activities as defined in the process documentation, and according to the defined policies for that process
- Maintenance of the tools used to support these processes
- Monitoring the performance of the processes and the quality of the output of those processes
- Identifying and resolving process exceptions
- Monitoring the overall success of the strategy, services and customer relationships.

8.2.5 Continual improvement of service strategy

The role of continual service improvement will include:

- Assessment of the metrics of each process and evaluation of the effectiveness and efficiency of each process

- Revision of the requirements for metrics and information as the processes mature
- Identification of opportunities for improvement of processes
- Evaluation of whether the strategy and services are meeting the objectives set, and plans to address the situation if they are not.

8.3 THE IMPACT OF SERVICE STRATEGY ON OTHER LIFECYCLE STAGES

Although all lifecycle stages interface with one another, service strategy provides the direction, policies and standards whereby each stage is executed, and in which services move through the lifecycle. This section highlights the major impact which service strategy has on the other four stages.

8.3.1 Service strategy and service design

Service strategy sets the broad direction for the design of services and the objectives that services need to achieve, but it also defines the specific outcomes that the designed services need to achieve. Service strategy therefore provides the initiation for services that need to be designed, and will ultimately be able to determine whether the service provider was successful. Service strategy defines what will be needed to ensure the competitiveness of the service provider and the satisfaction of its customers. Service design will define, in detail, how the service provider will achieve that.

On the one hand, service strategy enables design. It charters the services and provides input about what services need to be created, how they will be funded and what they need to achieve.

On the other hand, service strategy creates boundaries within which that design must be undertaken. For example, it creates policies and standards to which service design must adhere. It specifies how far the design teams can allow their creativity to go in creating and changing services.

The service strategy tools and procedures that impact service design the most are described below.

8.3.1.1 Outcomes and constraints

It is critical that the design of a service is based on the outcomes that the customer desired, expressed in terms of utility and warranty. The service design

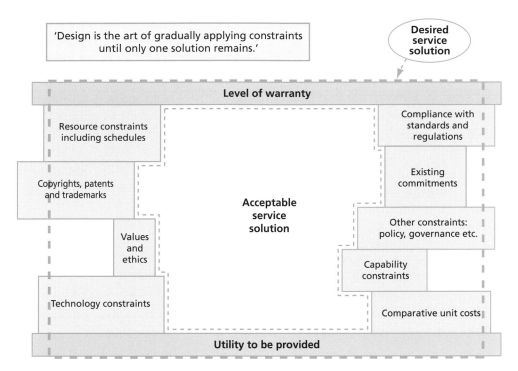

'Design is the art of gradually applying constraints until only one solution remains.'

Desired service solution

Level of warranty

Resource constraints including schedules

Compliance with standards and regulations

Copyrights, patents and trademarks

Existing commitments

Values and ethics

Acceptable service solution

Other constraints: policy, governance etc.

Capability constraints

Technology constraints

Comparative unit costs

Utility to be provided

Figure 8.2 Design constraints driven by strategy

will validate, clarify and expand the exact attributes of the service that are needed to support these outcomes. Determining which attributes of a service are essential, which add value and which are purely 'nice to have' is an important part of designing a service, and a part that will have been made clearer by the work done during service strategy.

In addition, service strategy will identify the constraints under which the service needs to be developed. These may cover a broad range of areas including funding, resource availability, legislation etc. When formally assessed and quantified, these constraints create a set of boundaries within which the design must take place. This is illustrated in Figure 8.2. The area inside the boundaries represents the space within which service design must take place.

Proposals to exceed any of these boundaries in order to complete the design would require authorization at the appropriate level in the organization. In giving this authorization the potential consequences for organization strategy should be taken into account. This may be as simple as requesting additional funding (thus altering the investment model) or as complex as launching a legal campaign to change legislation or obtain a waiver from legislative requirements.

If the solution space needs to be expanded, there may well be a need to add additional architectural building blocks into the architecture continuum.

8.3.1.2 Service models

Service models provide the basic architecture that is used to develop services during service design. These are the starting point for defining and developing a service design package. Service models will not only inform the designers about the market space that the service is being designed for, but also the type of asset that will need to be put in place to deliver and support the service.

Service models also aid in communicating the intent of the service strategy, and the dynamics of the service, to a broad range of teams involved in the design of the service. This will assist in maintaining consistency of both understanding and design.

8.3.1.3 Patterns of business activity

Design activities related to the utilization, performance, capacity and availability of the service will rely heavily on the identification and validation of patterns of business activity (PBA) through demand management. For more information on PBA please see section 4.4.5.2.

8.3.1.4 Business impact analysis

The design teams might be aware of the relative importance of services, based on an understanding of the outcomes and their knowledge of the customers. Nevertheless, it is important that the business importance of the service is objectively defined and held as a standard for design prioritization.

This is important from two points of view. Firstly, the design needs to incorporate appropriate levels of availability, service continuity, security and performance. Business impact analysis (BIA) is an important input for this activity. Secondly, the design teams will need to prioritize their own activities. BIA will help the teams to be able to judge where their efforts are best spent, especially where there is a resource conflict. For more information on BIA, please see section 3.6.2.

8.3.1.5 Business relationship management

Business relationship management is an important source of information about the customer, their objectives, environment and requirements. It is especially important to continue to validate and clarify customer requirements throughout the service design stage.

Any changes to requirements or design that impact the overall service model, investment or strategy will need to be validated against the strategy for the service and the service provider. Business relationship management plays an invaluable role in ensuring that this is done.

8.3.2 Service strategy and service transition

Service transition is often seen as a purely tactical stage, in which services are moved from design and build into operation. In fact, service transition is critical for the organization to be able to change its strategy. It is through service transition that the necessary cultural, organizational and service changes occur that allow the organization to meet its changing objectives.

Service strategy therefore has a key impact on service transition from three points of view.

Firstly, service strategy assists in moulding the strategy for how services should be transitioned (together with transition planning and support). For example, how involved should customers be in the transition process; what mechanisms are appropriate for release and deployment of new services; what levels of training are required to prepare for a new or changed service?

Secondly, service strategy is instrumental in defining what needs to change, when and to what extent. If changes were not managed within the context of service strategy, it would be very easy for hundreds of small changes, each controlled in its own right, to result in a major change to the strategy of the organization over time. Through service portfolio management and strategy management, service transition is able to ensure that all changes contribute to the achievement of the service provider's overall strategy, as well as the strategy of individual services.

Thirdly, service transition will test and validate that the services being introduced and changed are able to achieve the objectives and outcomes that have been defined during service strategy and service design. Thus service strategy provides the basis for which tests are run and services evaluated.

8.3.3 Service strategy and service operation

Strategies are ultimately realized through service operation. Well-crafted strategies with great potential can never be realized without proper support from operations. Strategies must be mindful of operational capabilities and constraints. Operations, on the other hand, should clearly understand the outcomes necessary for a given strategy and provide adequate support with effectiveness and efficiency.

For example, some businesses have large-scale operations in several countries or regions with high levels of business activity driven by the needs of their own customers. The end-customers may be a cost-conscious but highly dependable source of revenue for the business. Many government agencies operate in similar business conditions though with different mandates. Such high-volume, low-margin, steady-stream business strategies depend on service providers being able to support them with adequate availability and capacity but at low unit costs.

Service operation is where the value that was anticipated and designed is finally realized. It is critical that operational activities are designed and measured using the strategic objectives and outcomes as a basis. Although operational activities are not strategic, they are what enable the organization to achieve its strategy. It should be possible to define the linkage between strategic outcomes and operational activities. This is discussed in detail in *ITIL Service Operation*.

In addition, it should be possible to measure how successfully the strategy is being executed, and how well it is achieving its objectives by measuring operational activities – but only if these metrics have been anticipated in the design of the service (see section 4.1.4.3 on instrumentation of services in *ITIL Service Operation*).

8.3.4 Service strategy and continual service improvement

Continual service improvement takes its lead from service strategy in that it uses the defined strategies and desired outcomes as a basis for evaluating whether services are successful.

At the same time, continual service improvement acts as an initiator of strategy. Through continual assessment and measurement, it assists in determining where a strategy needs to be changed and how it can be made more effective. It detects changes in the use and outcomes of services, and determines the ongoing relevance of services.

Challenges, risks and critical success factors

9

9 Challenges, risks and critical success factors

9.1 CHALLENGES

9.1.1 Complexity

IT organizations are complex systems, with many components (people, processes, technology etc.) needing to interact with other components. Hence they are interdependent.

This complexity explains why some service organizations resist change. They are self-stabilizing and policy resistant. Their complexity overwhelms our ability to understand them. The result: the more you try to change them, the more they resist.

The natural tendency is to break services down into discrete processes managed by different groups with specialized knowledge, experience and resources. This approach is useful. However, the more divided a system, the greater the need for coordination between components.

An automobile, for example, is more than a collection of parts. The parts themselves do not have a life of their own. The most significant recent breakthrough in braking systems for automobiles was not achieved by simply enhancing the performance of brake pads or rotors, but from extending the braking system to include not only the brake components, but also road and weather conditions, driver behaviour and the dynamic interactions between these elements. This bigger-picture view led designers to move beyond simply continual improvements in materials science and manufacturing to the counter-intuitive idea of anti-lock braking systems (ABS), which compensate for variations in weather conditions and driver skills.

Similarly, breaking services and service management down into specific processes is a suitable tactic – providing that their interconnectedness is not lost. Service management processes are a means and not the end. They are necessary because working together they produce the characteristics of service that define value for the customer. Treated separately, some of the most significant consequences of decisions and actions may remain hidden until after major problems and incidents. Service strategy must therefore ensure

that the bigger picture is always examined and taken into account.

9.1.2 Coordination and control

Decision makers in general have limited time, attention span and personal capacity. They delegate roles and responsibilities to teams and individuals who specialize in specific systems, processes, performance and outcomes. Specialization allows for development of in-depth knowledge, skills and experience. It also allows for innovation, improvements and changes to occur within a controlled space.

However, an increase in the level of specialization leads to a corresponding increase in the need for coordination. This is a major challenge in service management because of the level of specialization needed for various stages of the service lifecycle, processes and functions. Coordination can be improved with cooperation and control between teams and individuals, and with suppliers.

9.1.3 Preserving value

It is important that the value of services to the customer is preserved, and that the customer's perception of the services is maintained at a high level. This should be achieved through:

- Eliminating or reducing deviations in performance
- Maintaining operational effectiveness and efficiency
- Reducing hidden costs (e.g. high transaction costs incurred when changes are made to services, service levels or demand levels in a trial-and-error manner)
- Publicizing and substantiating hidden benefits (e.g. reduced lock-in through leasing assets rather than buying them)
- Use of automation, web-based functionality, support tools etc. to reduce the cost of providing service and better allow scalability without commensurate cost increases.

9.1.4 Effective measurement

Organizations have long understood the Deming principle: if you cannot measure it, you cannot manage it. Yet despite significant investments in products and processes, many IT organizations fall short in creating a holistic service analytics capability. Performance measurements in service organizations are frequently out of step with the business environments they serve. This misalignment is not for the lack of measurements. Rather, traditional measurements focus more on internal goals than the external realities of customer satisfaction. Even the measurements of seasoned organizations emphasize control at the expense of customer response. While every organization differs, there are some common rules that are useful in designing effective measurements, as shown in Table 9.1.

Measurements focus the organization on its strategic goals, tracking progress and providing feedback. Be sure to change measurements when needed as strategy evolves. When they conflict, older measurements will usually beat new goals because measurements, not strategic goals, generally determine rewards and promotions.

Crafting new strategic goals without changing the related measurements is no change at all.

Current monitoring solutions often result in the capture of only a small percentage of failures. Practice shows that monitoring discrete components is not enough. An approach that integrates with service management and promotes cross-domain coordination is more likely to afford success. Unfortunately, the common techniques are not completely satisfactory. They work well in restricted problem domains, where they focus on a particular sub-system or individual application; they don't work as well in a service management context.

The holy grail of monitoring is often referred to as 'end-to-end' visibility. Yet many IT organizations have little or no visibility into the business processes. One cannot exist without the other. Indeed, the endpoints in 'end-to-end' are often misunderstood. Imagine the increased relevance that IT would gain if they could answer questions like the following:

Table 9.1 Measurement principles

Principle	Guidance
Begin on the outside, not the inside of the service organization	A service organization should ask itself, 'What do customers really want and when?' and 'What do the best alternatives give our customers that we do not?' Customers, for example, frequently welcome discussion on ways to make better use of their service providers. They may also welcome personal relationships in the building of commitment from providers.
Responsiveness to customers beats all other measurement goals	Care is taken not to construct control measures that work against customer responsiveness. For example, organizations sometimes measure change management process compliance by the number of RFCs rejected. While this measurement may be useful, it indirectly rewards slow response. An improved measurement strategy would include the number of RFCs authorized in a set period of time as well as the percentage of changes that do not generate unintended consequences. Throughput, as well as compliance, is directly rewarded.
Think of process and service as equals	Focusing on services is important but be careful not to do so at the expense of process. It is easy to lose sight of process unless measurements make it equally explicit to the organization. Reward those who fix and improve process.
Numbers matter	Use a numerical and timescale that can go back far enough to cover the explanation of the current situation. Financial metrics are often appropriate. For non-commercial settings, adopt the same principle of measuring performance for outcomes desired (for example 'beneficiaries served').
Compete as an organization. Don't let overall goals get lost among the many performance measures	Be mindful of losing track of overall measures that tell you how the customer perceives your organization against alternatives. Train the organization to think of the service organization as an integrated IT system for the customer's benefit.

- What is the delay, together with business impact, on the supply chain due to an IT problem?
- How long does it take to process procurement orders, and where are the worst delays?
- When is more than £1,000,000 worth of orders waiting to go through the distribution systems?

It is not uncommon for the business or senior managers to ask 'How?' and 'Why?' when the monitoring solution can only answer 'What?' and 'When?' Most IT organizations have deployed analytic technologies that primarily focus on the collection of monitoring data and while they are extremely effective at data collection they are ineffective in providing insight into services. This is where the knowledge management DIKW structure is so important to translate the Data-to-Information-to-Knowledge-to-Wisdom.

9.2 RISKS

9.2.1 Definition of risk

Risk is defined as a possible event that could cause harm or loss, or affect an organization's ability to achieve its objectives. A risk is measured by the probability of a threat, the vulnerability of the asset to that threat, and the impact it would have if it occurred. Risk can also be defined as uncertainty of outcome, and can be used in the context of measuring the probability of positive outcomes as well as negative outcomes.

Every organization manages its risk, but not always in a way that is visible, repeatable and consistently applied to support decision-making. The task of risk management is to ensure that the organization makes cost-effective use of a risk framework that has a series of well-defined steps. The aim is to support better decision-making through a good understanding of risks and their likely impact. There are two distinct phases in dealing with risk: risk assessment and risk management:

- **Risk assessment** This is concerned with gathering information about exposure to risk so that the organization can make appropriate decisions and manage risk appropriately.
- **Risk management** This involves having processes in place to monitor risks, access to reliable and up-to-date information about risks, the right balance of control in place to deal with those risks, and decision-making processes supported

by a framework of risk assessment and evaluation.

Risk management covers a wide range of topics, including business continuity management (BCM), security, programme/project risk management and operational service management. These topics need to be placed in the context of an organizational framework for the management of risk. Some risk-related topics, such as security, are highly specialized and this guidance provides only an overview of such aspects.

Risk management is discussed in more detail in section 5.6.5, and Appendix E identifies a number of industry frameworks that can be used to formalize an approach to risk management.

9.2.2 Inaccurate information

In 2006 Mark Hurd, then chairman and CEO at HP, said 'the number one risk factor in any organization is lack of accurate information'.

All organizations must strive to gather and validate the information needed for accurate and appropriate business decisions to be made. This relates back to the earlier section 9.1.4 regarding the need for accurate measurement and how this measurement should be translated through the DIKW structure, but goes much wider than this. It includes the need for building good relationships and communication channels within all business units and with customers and suppliers, and using these channels to gain timely, accurate business information including business strategy and tactics, customer needs, service and performance requirements, demand patterns and volumetrics, market intelligence and technical capabilities.

9.2.3 Risk of taking, or failing to take, opportunities

Risk is normally perceived as something to be avoided because of its association with threats. While this is generally true, risk is also to be associated with opportunity. Failure to take opportunities can be a risk in itself. The opportunity costs of under-served market spaces and unfulfilled demand is a risk to be avoided. The service portfolio can be mapped to an underlying portfolio of risks that are to be managed. When service management is effective, services in the catalogue and pipeline represent opportunities to create value for customers and capture value for stakeholders. Otherwise, those services can be threats from the possibility of failure associated with the demand patterns they attract, the commitments they require and the costs they generate. Implementing strategies often requires changes to the service portfolio, which means managing associated risks.

Decisions about risk need to be balanced so that the potential benefits are worth more to the organization than it costs to address the risk. For example, innovation is inherently risky but could achieve major benefits in improving services. The ability of the organization to limit its exposure to risk will also be of relevance. The aim should be to make an accurate assessment of the risks in a given situation, and analyse the potential benefits. The risks and opportunities presented by each course of action should be defined in order to identify appropriate responses.

9.2.4 Design risks

Customers expect services to have a beneficial impact on the performance of their assets, which is utility from their perspective. There is always a risk that services as designed fail to deliver the expected benefits in utility. A major cause for poor performance is poor design. There is also a risk that the utility of a service diminishes with a significant change in the pattern of demand. For example, some services are designed in ways that prevent them from being scalable. In the short term, terms and conditions related to demand in service level agreements might protect the service provider from penalties. It does not protect them from changes in customer perception about the suitability of the service.

Organizations should institutionalize a systematic approach to service design so that opportunities and resources are not wasted early in the lifecycle. Service design processes and methods are a means to reduce the performance risks and demand risks of services. They take into account the type of customer assets to be supported, how those assets generate returns for customers and the characteristics of demand they impose on the service to be designed. Service design defines the best configuration of service assets that can provide the necessary performance potential and accept not only a specific pattern of demand but also tolerate variations within a specified range.

Good designs also ensure that services are economical to operate and flexible enough to modify and improve.

9.2.5 Operational risks

There are two levels of risk that must be considered from a service management perspective: risks faced by the business, and the business services it uses, and risks to the IT services that underpin the business and its processes. For a complete view of risk, both levels must be considered simultaneously as they constantly interact with each other.

The systems and processes of service transition should filter and negate such risks. The capabilities in service operation convert operational risks into opportunities to create value for customers. Their effect of removing risks from the customer's business is the core value proposition of many services.

Procedures in service transition must be robust enough to ensure that this filtering capability is achieved: schedule pressures are likely to lead to demands for early delivery of new capability without the agreed level of warranty, leading to tensions when the service falls below the agreed quality.

Value to customers is realized in the service operation stage of the lifecycle when actual demand for services arrives. Warranty commitments require every unit of demand to be met with a unit of capacity that is available, secure and continuous within a frame of reference.

9.2.6 Market risks

A common source of risk for all types of service provider is the choice that their customers have on sourcing decisions. In recent years, Type I providers have faced the risk of outsourcing when customers sign contracts with external providers in pursuit of strategic objectives. Customers are willing to make that switch when benefits outweigh the costs and risks of switching from one type to another.

While outsourcing and shared services are the dominant trend, insourcing (or perhaps the affirmation of status quo) continues to be a valuable strategic option for customers. This is the risk faced primarily by Type III providers and to a limited extent by Type II providers.

Effective service management helps reduce the levels of competitive risks faced by service providers by increasing the scale and scope of demand for a service catalogue. Other ways of reducing market risks include:

- Reducing the total cost of utilization (TCU), giving customers financial incentives not to switch to other options
- Differentiation: providing services that are unique, novel or difficult for competitors to replicate
- Consolidation: concentrating demand from several customers or customer groups onto a single service rather than offering a lot of diverse but similar services – thus reducing costs to help retain customers.

9.3 CRITICAL SUCCESS FACTORS

To a large extent all of the challenges and risks already mentioned can be inverted to become critical success factors (CSFs). For example, achieving accurate measurement is a challenge; lack of accurate measurement is a risk; having accurate measurement in place is a critical success factor – without it successful services are impossible to achieve.

In addition there are a number of other factors critical to the success of a service management organization:

- Experienced, skilled and trained staff with the strategic vision and decision-making skills needed for success
- Adequate support (and, importantly, funding) from the business which must recognize the potential value IT service management can offer
- Appropriate and effective support tools to allow the processes to be quickly and successfully implemented and operated in a cost-effective way.

Afterword

Afterword

ITIL Service Strategy encourages exercises in strategic thinking much needed by IT organizations and others vying to be service providers preferred by customers. It has established a strategic context for service management in the real world. But that world is about change and uncertainty. Commercial pressures, competition, legislation and environmental factors all affect business priorities and consequently also the strategies that support the business. Public sector and non-profit organizations may not have to make profits for shareholders, but they share many of the same concerns as companies and corporations. Public sector organizations, for example, have to deliver cost-effective services, and at the top level or at the internal department level run the risk of being shut down, merged or outsourced if they are not effective. This publication is about being prepared for possible scenarios, and turning threats into opportunities.

We all want to be 'not optional'. To survive and flourish, every organization, department, branch, section and individual has to understand how they create value for themselves and for their customers and the way that their suppliers enhance that value. They must appreciate the strategic choices both for their own services and for those they receive from providers. Because of the environment of constant change, strategy is not something to do once, and service strategies need to be developed, applied and continually reviewed, just like all the other parts of the service lifecycle. If the strategy is effective, then the effort in all the other stages of the lifecycle will be applied appropriately and successfully.

Services are a predominant form in which value is created and transferred between organizations, and service management is in time maturing as a discipline. A wealth of knowledge and best practice is available for use if there is clarity on why services may be used to support the customer's business. Clarity is attained if there is a willingness to take a long-term view, to search for patterns among the noisy detail, and to be guided by business fundamentals rather than technical possibilities. Best practice is rooted in hard facts and sound principles, which are often dismissed under the pretext of being practical. Poor practice is often the blind pursuit of success in the footsteps of early champions and leaders who, unbeknownst to their followers, have been far more diligent. *ITIL Service Strategy* encourages its readers to adopt a practical but principled approach to finding long-term success and durable capabilities in service management.

Appendix A: Present value of an annuity

Appendix A: Present value of an annuity

Use Table A.1 to find the present value of an annuity of £1 in arrears.

Find the column under your discount rate (or cost of capital). Then find the horizontal row corresponding to the last year of the investment.

The point at which the column and the row intersect is the present value of a series of £1 payments. Multiply this value by the number of pounds you expect to receive in each payment in order to find the present value of the series.

Table A.1 Present value of an annuity

Present worth of £1 per period payable at end of each period

Years	3%	3.5%	4%	4.5%
1	£0.970874	£0.966184	£0.961538	£0.956938
2	£1.913470	£1.899694	£1.886095	£1.872668
3	£2.828611	£2.801637	£2.775091	£2.748964
4	£3.717098	£3.673079	£3.629895	£3.587526
5	£4.579707	£4.515052	£4.451822	£4.389977
6	£5.417191	£5.328553	£5.242137	£5.157872
7	£6.230283	£6.114544	£6.002055	£5.892701

Years	5%	5.5%	6%	6.5%
1	£0.952381	£0.947867	£0.943396	£0.938967
2	£1.859410	£1.846320	£1.833393	£1.820626
3	£2.723248	£2.697933	£2.673012	£2.648476
4	£3.545951	£3.505150	£3.465106	£3.425799
5	£4.329477	£4.270284	£4.212364	£4.155679
6	£5.075692	£4.995530	£4.917324	£4.841014
7	£5.786373	£5.682967	£5.582381	£5.484520

Years	7%	7.5%	8%	8.5%
1	£0.934579	£0.930233	£0.925926	£0.921659
2	£1.808018	£1.795565	£1.783265	£1.771114
3	£2.624316	£2.600526	£2.577097	£2.554022
4	£3.387211	£3.349326	£3.312127	£3.275597
5	£4.100197	£4.045885	£3.992710	£3.940642
6	£4.766540	£4.693846	£4.622880	£4.553587
7	£5.389289	£5.296601	£5.206370	£5.118514

Years	9%	9.5%	10%	10.5%
1	£0.917431	£0.913242	£0.909091	£0.904977
2	£1.759111	£1.747253	£1.735537	£1.723961
3	£2.531295	£2.508907	£2.486852	£2.465123
4	£3.239720	£3.204481	£3.169865	£3.135858
5	£3.889651	£3.839709	£3.790787	£3.742858
6	£4.485919	£4.419825	£4.355261	£4.292179
7	£5.032953	£4.949612	£4.868419	£4.789303

Table A.1 continued

Present worth of £1 per period payable at end of each period

Years	11%	11.5%	12%	12.5%
1	£0.900901	£0.896861	£0.892857	£0.888889
2	£1.712523	£1.701221	£1.690051	£1.679012
3	£2.443715	£2.422619	£2.401831	£2.381344
4	£3.102446	£3.069614	£3.037349	£3.005639
5	£3.695897	£3.649878	£3.604776	£3.560568
6	£4.230538	£4.170294	£4.111407	£4.053839
7	£4.712196	£4.637035	£4.563757	£4.492301

Years	13%	13.5%	14%	14.5%
1	£0.884956	£0.881057	£0.877193	£0.873362
2	£1.668102	£1.657319	£1.646661	£1.636124
3	£2.361153	£2.341250	£2.321632	£2.302292
4	£2.974471	£2.943833	£2.913712	£2.884098
5	£3.517231	£3.474743	£3.433081	£3.392225
6	£3.997550	£3.942505	£3.888668	£3.836005
7	£4.422610	£4.354630	£4.288305	£4.223585

Years	15%	16%	17%	18%
1	£0.869565	£0.862	£0.855	£0.847
2	£1.625709	£1.605	£1.585	£1.566
3	£2.283225	£2.246	£2.210	£2.174
4	£2.854978	£2.798	£2.743	£2.690
5	£3.352155	£3.274	£3.199	£3.127
6	£3.784483	£3.685	£3.589	£3.498
7	£4.160420	£4.039	£3.922	£3.812

Years	19%	20%	21%	22%
1	£0.840	£0.833	£0.826	£0.820
2	£1.547	£1.528	£1.509	£1.492
3	£2.140	£2.106	£2.074	£2.042
4	£2.639	£2.589	£2.540	£2.494
5	£3.058	£2.991	£2.926	£2.864
6	£3.410	£3.326	£3.245	£3.167
7	£3.706	£3.605	£3.508	£3.416

Appendix B: Description of asset types

B

Appendix B: Description of asset types

B.1 MANAGEMENT

Management is a system that includes leadership, administration, policies, performance measures and incentives. This layer cultivates, coordinates and controls all other asset types. Management includes idiosyncratic elements such as philosophy, core beliefs, values, decision-making style and perceptions of risk. It is also the most distinctive and inimitable type of asset which is deeply rooted in the organization.

The term organization is used here to refer to the enterprise or firm rather than the organization asset type. The most likely manner in which management assets can be partially extracted from an organization is by the poaching of key individuals who were instrumental in defining and developing a particular management system.

Service management itself is a type of specialized management asset like others such as project management, research and development, and manufacturing management.

B.2 ORGANIZATION

Organization assets are active configurations of people, processes, applications and infrastructure that carry out all organizational activities through the principles of specialization and coordination (see section 2.4.1). This category of assets includes the functional hierarchies, social networks of groups, teams and individuals, as well as the systems they use to work together towards shared goals and incentives. Organization assets include the patterns that people, applications, information and infrastructure deploy, either by design or by self-adaptive process, to maximize the creation of value for stakeholders. Some service organizations are superior to others simply by virtue of their organization – for example, networks of wireless access points, storage systems, point-of-sale terminals, databases, hardware stores and remote backup facilities. Strategic location of assets by itself is a basis for superior performance and competitive advantage.

B.3 PROCESS

Process assets are made of algorithms, methods, procedures and routines that direct the execution and control of activities and interactions. There is a great diversity in process assets, which are specialized to various degrees from generic management processes to sophisticated low-level algorithms embedded in software applications and other forms of automation. Process assets are the most dynamic of asset types. They signify action and transformation. Some of them are also the means by which organization and management assets coordinate and control each other and interact with the business environment. Process, people and application assets execute them; knowledge and information assets enrich them; and applications and infrastructure assets enable them. Examples of process assets are order fulfilment, accounts receivable, incident management, change management and testing.

B.4 KNOWLEDGE

Knowledge assets are accumulations of awareness, experience, information, insight and intellectual property that are associated with actions and context. Management, organization, process and applications assets use and store knowledge assets. People assets store tacit knowledge in the form of experience, skills and talent. Such knowledge is primarily acquired through experience, observation and training. Movement of teams and individuals is an effective way to transfer tacit knowledge within and across organizations (Argote, 2000). Knowledge assets in tacit form are hard for rivals to replicate but easy for owners to lose. Organizations seek to protect themselves from loss by codifying tacit knowledge into explicit forms such as knowledge embedded in process, applications and infrastructure assets. Knowledge assets are difficult to manage but can be highly leveraged with increasing returns and virtually zero opportunity costs (Lev, 2001). Knowledge assets include policies, plans, designs, configurations, architectures, process definitions, analytical methods, service definitions, analyses, reports and surveys. They may be owned as intellectual property and protected by copyrights, patents and trademarks. Knowledge assets can also be rented for use under licensing arrangements and service contracts.

B.5 PEOPLE

The value of people assets is the capacity for creativity, analysis, perception, learning, judgement, leadership, communication, coordination, empathy and trust. Such capacity is in teams and individuals within the organization, due to knowledge, experience and skills. Skills can be conceptual, technical and social. People assets are also the most convenient absorbers and carriers of all forms of knowledge. They are the most versatile and potent of all asset types because of their ability to learn and adapt. People assets represent an organization's capabilities and resources. If capabilities are the capacity for action, people assets are the actors. From the capabilities' perspective, people assets are the only type that can create, combine and consume all other asset types. Their tolerance of ambiguity and uncertainty also compensates for the limitations of processes, applications and infrastructure. Because of their enormous potential, people assets are often the most expensive in terms of development, maintenance and motivation. They are also assets that can be hired or rented but cannot be owned. Customers highly value services that enhance the productivity or potential of people assets.

People assets are also resources with productive capacity. Units of cost, time and effort measure their capacity as teams and individuals. They are mobile, multi-purpose and highly adaptive with the innate ability to learn. Staffing contracts, software agents and customers using self-service options augment the capacity of people assets.

B.6 INFORMATION

Information assets are collections, patterns and meaningful abstractions of data applied in contexts such as customers, contracts, services, events, projects and operations. They are useful for various purposes including communication, coordination and control of business activities. Information assets exist in various forms such as documents, records, messages and graphs. All asset types produce them but management, processes, knowledge, people and applications primarily consume them. The value of information assets can vary with time, location

and format, and depreciate very quickly. Some services create value by processing information and making it available as needed by management, processes, people and applications assets. The criteria of effectiveness, efficiency, availability, integrity, confidentiality, reliability and compliance can be used to evaluate the quality of information assets (ITGI, 2005).

B.7 APPLICATIONS

Applications assets are diverse in type and include artefacts, automation and tools used to support the performance of other asset types. Applications are composed of software, hardware, documents, methods, procedures, routines, scripts and instructions. They automate, codify, enable, enhance, maintain or mimic the properties, functions and activities of management, organization, processes, knowledge, people and information assets. Applications derive their value in relation to these other assets. Process assets in particular commonly exist inside applications. Applications assets consume, produce and maintain knowledge and information assets. They can be of various types such as general purpose, multi-purpose and special purpose. Some applications are analogous to industrial tools, machinery and equipment because they enhance the performance of processes. Others are analogous to office equipment and consumer appliances because they enhance the personal productivity of people assets. Examples of applications are accounting software, voicemail, imaging systems, encryption devices, process control, inventory tracking, electronic design automation, mobile phones and bar code scanners. Applications are themselves supported by infrastructure, people and process assets. One of the most powerful attributes of applications is that they can be creatively combined and integrated with other asset types, particularly other applications to create valuable new assets.

B.8 INFRASTRUCTURE

Infrastructure assets have the peculiar property of existing in the form of layers defined in relation to the assets they support, especially people and applications. They include information technology assets such as software applications, computers, storage systems, network devices, telecommunication equipment, cables, wireless links, access control devices and monitoring systems. This category of assets also includes traditional facilities such as buildings, electricity, heating, ventilation and air conditioning (HVAC) and water supply, without which it would be impossible for people, applications and other infrastructure assets to operate. Infrastructure assets by themselves may be composed mostly of applications and other infrastructure assets. Assets viewed as applications at one level can be utilized as infrastructure at another. This is an important principle that allows service orientation of assets.

B.9 FINANCIAL CAPITAL

Financial assets are required to support the ownership or use of all types of asset. They also measure the economic value and performance. Financial assets include cash, cash equivalents and other assets such as marketable securities, and receivables that are convertible into cash with degrees of certainty and ease. Adequacy of financial assets is an important concern for all organizations including government agencies and non-profit organizations. The promise and potential of other assets are not realized in full without financial assets.

Appendix C: Service strategy and the cloud

Appendix C: Service strategy and the cloud

At the time of writing, a major new trend has been emerging. Known by various names and taking various forms – including 'the cloud', 'converging infrastructure' and 'hybrid delivery' – this trend will play a vital role in forming the strategy of IT service providers in the future.

It is clear that this trend is significant, but it is still too early to write an authoritative set of best practice guidance about how to define, manage and deliver service in the cloud. Many approaches have focused on the technology needed in order to embark on a cloud strategy (e.g. virtualization), and not on the strategic implications of using these technologies. Instead, this publication includes a brief overview of the major themes and issues surrounding this complex area, drawing on the work of Ewald Comhaire, Lee Kedrie, Ed Mangiaratti and Peter Gilis (all cloud strategists within HP).

The basic principle of the cloud is that whatever IT service or utility a customer needs can be provided directly using the internet (or intranet) on a pay-per-use basis. Customers do not see, nor do they care, how the services are created and delivered. All they care about is that each service meets a specific need at a specified price – and that it is scalable and accessible whenever and wherever they need it.

Cloud services are elastic, in that they can expand and contract (seemingly intuitively) to meet variable customer needs. Customers can demand and customize these services almost at will, and mix and match different components, all through easy-to-use self-service interfaces.

C.1 CHARACTERISTICS OF CLOUD SERVICES

Cloud services share the following five characteristics:

- **On demand** Customers can access them whenever and wherever they need them through the internet (or intranet).
- **Ubiquitous access** Any client can access these services, even thin clients, because they use standard networking mechanisms and protocols.
- **Resource pooling** Cloud services are provided by pooled resources which, because they are based on internet access, can be located anywhere. Physical and virtual devices are dynamically assigned and reassigned according to customer demand. Although customers do not have control over the exact location of these devices, they are able to specify high-level requirements. For example, they can specify that customer data be located in a specific country to comply with data privacy legislation.
- **Rapid elasticity** Services can be provisioned to rapidly scale up or down to meet real-time customer demand.
- **Measured services** Since cloud services are pay-per-use, it is important that their usage be metered, and that a financial model exists to be able to bill for these services. Resource usage is monitored, controlled and reported.

From these characteristics it is clear that service portfolio management plays a very important role in defining the service models, services and service packages that the service provider provides.

The main feature of cloud services is that the services in the service portfolio can be selected, combined and used in a number of packages – in real time as demanded by the customer. A cloud portfolio consists of clearly defined building blocks, each of which is a service in its own right, but customers determine how these services will be constructed and used.

Demand forecasting is essentially a function of market research, although the emphasis is not so much on anticipating demand as being able to respond to it rapidly. Resources are deployed and redeployed continuously for a variety of workloads.

Another key difference identified through these characteristics is the role of the customer. In more traditional service models, customer requirements are gathered and worked into clearly defined, single-purpose services. In cloud models, the customer is able to define and use services as their requirements evolve. Cloud service providers are able to respond quickly to changes in demand for both utility and warranty.

The pay-per-use aspect of cloud services requires sophisticated and flexible financial management processes and models. Profitable services are more easily identified, and non-profitable services discontinued, based on a response to customer demand. In many traditional service funding models it is almost impossible to determine the cost of an individual service, let alone whether it is contributing to the profitability of the organization. Cloud services are therefore easily perceived as having value because customers can link their outcomes to the cost of the service immediately.

C.2 TYPES OF CLOUD SERVICE

Apart from individual services provided to consumers and customers, cloud providers are able to offer the following types of service to IT organizations, providing them with flexibly priced sourcing options and reducing the need for high levels of investment in unused capacity. These types of service include:

- **Software as a Service** (SaaS) This is where a service provider enables a customer to use software without having to purchase the actual software itself. The customer is therefore able to benefit from the utility of the software, while paying only for the level of utilization that they require. An example of this is a service desk that uses third-party owned and hosted incident management software to log and resolve incidents over the internet. The brand of software is often irrelevant, as long as it provides the functionality and reporting required by the customer. It may not have the full custom functionality that suits every aspect of the customer's requirements, but it meets enough of their requirements to be acceptable for the price paid. In this way the service provider can reach a broader range of companies with standardized functionality.
- **Platform as a Service** (PaaS) In this type of service, the service provider sells an environment and tools which can be used by customers to develop their own applications and services. Although the customer does not control the infrastructure and they do not own

the tools and programming languages, they have full control over the applications.
- **Infrastructure as a Service** (IaaS) Here the service provider sells the use of infrastructure resources, such as storage or processing power. Users can deploy applications on this infrastructure, and use the infrastructure as a basis for internal or external services to their customers.

There is a danger with these types of service, however. Some IT service providers have used these options as a means to abdicate the responsibility and risks of the IT service to the customer. For example, one IT organization decided that it could not understand the business of its internal customers. They knew that the customer needed servers and storage, and so decided to offer these as services. In this way, they reasoned, they did not have to be concerned with funding, service level agreements or capacity management. What happened, however, was that the customer began insisting on control of their own 'cloud' services and investment in technology reached unprecedented levels. In addition, much of the equipment and storage provided did not meet customer needs because of the varying requirements for speed, refresh rates and flexibility. Had the IT organization understood its customers better, it would have been able to properly gear each cloud to their specific requirements.

C.3 TYPES OF CLOUD

There is not just one type of cloud. Service providers will need to decide which type of cloud service provider they want to be. Options include:

- **Private cloud** These are clouds provided by a cloud service provider to a single organization over a network that is owned by that organization or its service provider. The cloud could be provided by an internal service provider (internal private cloud) or an outsourcer (external private cloud). This type of cloud has many of the benefits of cloud (on demand flexible services) without many of the disadvantages (risk and security).
- **Community cloud** The cloud infrastructure is owned and operated by or on behalf of a group of organizations that share common concerns or practices. An example is a group of

universities that provide a similar range of services to their students and academic staff.

- **Public cloud** The cloud infrastructure is owned by a service provider who sells a standard range of services to a number of organizations or to the general public.
- **Hybrid cloud** This type of cloud is where two or more of the types of cloud infrastructure, generally owned by different organizations, are combined for the specific purpose of porting data, applications or services.

C.4 COMPONENTS OF A CLOUD ARCHITECTURE

In order for a cloud service to be successful, there are at least four components that need to be in place. These are:

- **Service catalogue and portal** It is critical that customers and users know exactly what services are available and can access them easily. They must also know what the cost of the service is, and any terms of use. The service desk plays an important role in informing customers of information that is not readily available through the portal, and assists in providing access. In addition, some form of SLA dashboard will help to articulate what level of service can be expected for the money paid.
- **Service governance** This defines, communicates and automates the policies, standards and principles applied to the service provider in providing cloud services. Governance is defined and enforced through the cloud architecture, financial management, and service portfolio management.
- **Service delivery management** The most important part of this area is the ability to monitor and report on the utilization of the services, since this is how the cloud services are funded. In addition, service operation processes, capacity and availability management, and security and business continuity management are critical for the success of this component of the cloud architecture.

- **Infrastructure and service delivery** Here the emphasis is on the services themselves. This component of the architecture includes the service delivery mechanisms and service content, the middleware, the virtualized infrastructure and the facilities in which all these need to be housed.

Service strategy is key in defining the standards, governance, models and content of these architectures.

Appendix D:
Related guidance

Appendix D: Related guidance

This is a common appendix across the ITIL core publications. It includes frameworks, best practices, standards, models and quality systems that complement and have synergy with the ITIL service lifecycle.

Section 2.1.7 describes the role of best practices in the public domain and references some of the publications in this appendix. Each core publication references this appendix where relevant.

Related guidance may also be referenced within a single ITIL core publication where the topic is specific to that publication.

D.1 ITIL GUIDANCE AND WEB SERVICES

ITIL is part of the Best Management Practice (BMP) portfolio of best-practice guidance (see section 1.3). BMP products present flexible, practical and effective guidance, drawn from a range of the most successful global business experiences. Distilled to its essential elements, the guidance can then be applied to every type of business and organization.

The BMP website (www.best-management-practice.com) includes news, reviews, case studies and white papers on ITIL and all other BMP best-practice guidance.

The ITIL official website (www.itil-officialsite.com) contains reliable, up-to-date information on ITIL – including information on accreditation and the ITIL software scheme for the endorsement of ITIL-based tools.

Details of the core publications are as follows:

- Cabinet Office (2011). *ITIL Service Strategy*. TSO, London.
- Cabinet Office (2011). *ITIL Service Design*. TSO, London.
- Cabinet Office (2011). *ITIL Service Transition*. TSO, London.
- Cabinet Office (2011). *ITIL Service Operation*. TSO, London.
- Cabinet Office (2011). *ITIL Continual Service Improvement*. TSO, London.

The full ITIL glossary, in English and other languages, can be accessed through the ITIL official site at: www.itil-officialsite.com/InternationalActivities/ITILGlossaries.aspx

The range of translated glossaries is always growing, so check this website for the most up-to-date list.

Details of derived and complementary publications can be found in the publications library of the Best Management Practice website at: www.best-management-practice.com/Publications-Library/IT-Service-Management-ITIL/

D.2 QUALITY MANAGEMENT SYSTEM

Quality management focuses on product/service quality as well as the quality assurance and control of processes to achieve consistent quality. Total Quality Management (TQM) is a methodology for managing continual improvement by using a quality management system. TQM establishes a culture involving all people in the organization in a process of continual monitoring and improvement.

ISO 9000:2005 describes the fundamentals of quality management systems that are applicable to all organizations which need to demonstrate their ability to consistently provide products that meet customer and applicable statutory and regulatory requirements. ISO 9001:2008 specifies generic requirements for a quality management system.

Many process-based quality management systems use the methodology known as 'Plan-Do-Check-Act' (PDCA), often referred to as the Deming Cycle, or Shewhart Cycle, that can be applied to all processes. PDCA can be summarized as:

- **Plan** Establish the objectives and processes necessary to deliver results in accordance with customer requirements and the organization's policies.
- **Do** Implement the processes.
- **Check** Monitor and measure processes and product against policies, objectives and requirements for the product and report the results.

■ **Act** Take actions to continually improve process performance.

There are distinct advantages of tying an organization's ITSM processes, and service operation processes in particular, to its quality management system. If an organization has a formal quality management system that complies with ISO 9001, then this can be used to assess progress regularly and drive forward agreed service improvement initiatives through regular reviews and reporting.

Visit www.iso.org for information on ISO standards.

See www.deming.org for more information on the W. Edwards Deming Institute and the Deming Cycle for process improvement.

D.3 RISK MANAGEMENT

A number of different methodologies, standards and frameworks have been developed for the assessment and management of risk. Some focus more on generic techniques widely applicable to different levels and needs, while others are specifically concerned with risk management relating to important assets used by the organization in the pursuit of its objectives. Each organization should determine the approach to risk management that is best suited to its needs and circumstances. It is possible that the approach adopted will leverage the ideas reflected in more than one of the recognized standards and/or frameworks.

Appendix E gives more information on risk management. See also:

■ Office of Government Commerce (2010). *Management of Risk*: *Guidance for Practitioners*. TSO, London.
■ ISO 31000:2009 Risk management – principles and guidelines.
■ ISO/IEC 27001: 2005 Information technology – security techniques – information security management systems – requirements.
■ ISACA (2009). *The Risk IT Framework* (based on COBIT, see section D.5).

D.4 GOVERNANCE OF IT

Corporate governance refers to the rules, policies, processes (and in some cases, laws) by which businesses are operated, regulated and controlled. These are often defined by the board or shareholders, or the constitution of the organization; but they can also be defined by legislation, regulation or consumer groups.

ISO 9004 (Managing for the sustained success of an organization – a quality management approach) provides guidance on governance for the board and executive of an organization.

The standard for corporate governance of IT is ISO/IEC 38500. The purpose of this standard is to promote effective, efficient and acceptable use of IT in all organizations by:

■ Assuring stakeholders (including consumers, shareholders and employees) that, if the standard is followed, they can have confidence in the organization's corporate governance of IT
■ Informing and guiding directors in governing the use of IT in their organization
■ Providing a basis for objective evaluation of the corporate governance of IT.

Typical examples of regulations that impact IT include: financial, safety, data protection, privacy, software asset management, environment management and carbon emission targets.

Further details are available at www.iso.org

Section 5.1.4 references the concepts of ISO/IEC 38500 and how the concepts can be applied.

D.5 COBIT

The Control OBjectives for Information and related Technology (COBIT) is a governance and control framework for IT management created by ISACA and the IT Governance Institute (ITGI).

COBIT is based on the analysis and harmonization of existing IT standards and good practices and conforms to generally accepted governance principles. It covers five key governance focus areas: strategic alignment, value delivery, resource management, risk management and performance management. COBIT is primarily aimed at internal and external stakeholders within an enterprise who wish to generate value from IT investments; those who provide IT services; and those who have a control/risk responsibility.

COBIT and ITIL are not 'competitive', nor are they mutually exclusive – on the contrary, they can be used in conjunction as part of an organization's overall governance and management framework. COBIT is positioned at a high level, is driven by business requirements, covers the full range of IT activities, and concentrates on *what* should be achieved rather than *how* to achieve effective governance, management and control. ITIL provides an organization with best-practice guidance on *how* to manage and improve its processes to deliver high-quality, cost-effective IT services. The following COBIT guidance supports strategy management and continual service improvement (CSI):

- COBIT maturity models can be used to benchmark and drive improvement.
- Goals and metrics can be aligned to the business goals for IT and used to create an IT management dashboard.
- The COBIT 'monitor and evaluate' (ME) process domain defines the processes needed to assess current IT performance, IT controls and regulatory compliance.

Further details are available at www.isaca.org and www.itgi.org

D.6 ISO/IEC 20000 SERVICE MANAGEMENT SERIES

ISO/IEC 20000 is an internationally recognized standard for ITSM covering service providers who manage and deliver IT-enabled services to internal or external customers. ISO/IEC 20000-1 is aligned with other ISO management systems standards such as ISO 9001 and ISO/IEC 27001.

One of the most common routes for an organization to achieve the requirements of ISO/IEC 20000 is by adopting ITIL best practices. ISO/IEC 20000-1 is based on a service management system (SMS). The SMS is defined as a management system to direct and control the service management activities of the service provider. ISO/IEC 20000 includes:

- ISO/IEC 20000-1:2005 – Information technology – Service management – Part 1: Specification

- ISO/IEC 20000-1:2011 – Information technology – Service management – Part 1: Requirements for a service management system (the most recent edition of the ISO/IEC 20000 standard)
- ISO/IEC 20000-2:2005 – Information technology – Service management – Part 2: Code of practice (being updated to include guidance on the application of service management systems and to support ISO/IEC 20000-1:2011)
- ISO/IEC 20000-3:2005 – Information technology – Service management – Part 3: Scope and applicability
- ISO/IEC TR 20000-4 – Information technology – Service management – Part 4: Process reference model
- ISO/IEC TR 20000-5:2010 – Information technology – Service management – Part 5: Exemplar implementation plan for ISO/IEC 20000-1.

A closely related publication that is under development is ISO/IEC TR 15504-8 – Process assessment model for IT service management.

Further details can be found at www.iso.org or www.isoiec20000certification.com

Organizations using ISO/IEC 20000-1: 2005 for certification audits will transfer to the new edition, ISO/IEC 20000-1: 2011.

ITIL guidance supports organizations that are implementing service management practices to achieve the requirements of ISO/IEC 20000-1: 2005 and the new edition ISO/IEC 20000-1: 2011.

Other references include:

- Dugmore, J. and Lacy, S. (2011). *Introduction to ISO/IEC 20000 Series: IT Service Management.* British Standards Institution, London.
- Dugmore, J. and Lacy, S. (2011). *BIP 0005: A Manager's Guide to Service Management* (6th edition). British Standards Institution, London.

D.7 ENVIRONMENTAL MANAGEMENT AND GREEN/SUSTAINABLE IT

The transition to a low-carbon economy is a global challenge. Many governments have set targets to reduce carbon emissions or achieve carbon neutrality. IT is an enabler for environmental and cultural change that will help governments to achieve their targets – for example, through enabling tele- and video-conferencing, and remote and home working. However, IT is also a major user of energy and natural resources. Green IT refers to environmentally sustainable computing where the use and disposal of computers and printers are carried out in sustainable ways that do not have a negative impact on the environment.

Appendix E in *ITIL Service Design* includes further information on environmental architectures and standards. Appendix E in *ITIL Service Operation* also provides useful considerations for facilities management, including environmental aspects.

The ISO 14001 series of standards for an environment management system is designed to assure internal and external stakeholders that the organization is an environmentally responsible organization. It enables an organization of any size or type to:

■ Identify and control the environmental impact of its activities, products or services
■ Improve its environmental performance continually
■ Implement a systematic approach to setting and achieving environmental objectives and targets, and then demonstrating that they have been achieved.

Further details are available at www.iso.org

D.8 ISO STANDARDS AND PUBLICATIONS FOR IT

ISO 9241 is a series of standards and guidance on the ergonomics of human system interaction that cover people working with computers. It covers aspects that impact the utility of a service (whether it is fit for purpose) such as:

■ ISO 9241-11:1999 Guidance on usability
■ ISO 9241-210:2010 Human-centred design for interactive systems
■ ISO 9241-151:2008 Guidance on world wide web user interfaces.

ISO/IEC JTC1 is Joint Technical Committee 1 of ISO and the International Electrotechnical Commission (IEC). It deals with information technology standards and other publications.

SC27 is a subcommittee under ISO/IEC JTC1 that develops ISO/IEC 27000, the information security management system (ISMS) family of standards. For further details, Appendix E includes information on

ISO/IEC 27001. SC7 is a subcommittee under ISO/IEC JTC1 that covers the standardization of processes, supporting tools and supporting technologies for the engineering of systems, services and software. SC7 publications include:

■ ISO/IEC 20000 Information technology – service management (see section D.6)
■ ISO/IEC 19770-1 Information technology – software asset management processes. ISO/IEC 19770-2:2009 establishes specifications for tagging software to optimize its identification and management
■ ISO/IEC 15288 Systems and software engineering – systems life cycle processes. The processes can be used as a basis for establishing business environments – e.g. methods, procedures, techniques, tools and trained personnel
■ ISO/IEC 12207 Systems and software engineering – software life cycle processes
■ ISO/IEC 15504 Process assessment series. Also known as SPICE (software process improvement and capability determination), it aims to ensure consistency and repeatability of the assessment ratings with evidence to substantiate the ratings. The series includes exemplar process assessment models (PAM), related to one or more conformant or compliant process reference model (PRM). ISO/IEC 15504-8 is an exemplar process assessment model for IT service management that is under development
■ ISO/IEC 25000 series – provides guidance for the use of standards named Software product Quality Requirements and Evaluation (SQuaRE)
■ ISO/IEC 42010 Systems and software engineering — recommended practice for architectural description of software-intensive systems.

SC7 is working on the harmonization of standards in the service management, software and IT systems domains. Further details are available at www.iso.org

D.9 ITIL AND THE OSI FRAMEWORK

At around the time that ITIL V1 was being written, the International Standards Organization launched an initiative that resulted in the Open Systems Interconnection (OSI) framework. Since this initiative covered many of the same areas as ITIL

V1, it is not surprising that there was considerable overlap.

However, it is also not surprising that they classified their processes differently, used different terminology, or used the same terminology in different ways. To confuse matters even more, it is common for different groups in an organization to use terminology from both ITIL and the OSI framework.

The OSI framework made significant contributions to the definition and execution of ITSM programmes and projects around the world. It has also caused a great deal of debate between teams that do not realize the origins of the terminology that they are using. For example, some organizations have two change management departments – one following the ITIL change management process and the other using the OSI installation, moves, additions and changes (IMAC) model. Each department is convinced that it is completely different from the other, and that it is performing a different role. Closer examination will reveal that there are several areas of commonality.

In service operation, the management of known errors may be mapped to fault management. There is also a section related to operational capacity management, which can be related to the OSI concept of performance management.

Information on the set of ISO standards for the OSI framework is available at: www.iso.org

D.10 PROGRAMME AND PROJECT MANAGEMENT

Large, complex deliveries are often broken down into manageable, interrelated projects. For those managing this overall delivery, the principles of programme management are key to delivering on time and within budget. Best management practice in this area is found in *Managing Successful Programmes* (MSP).

Guidance on effective portfolio, programme and project management is brought together in *Portfolio, Programme and Project Offices* (P3O), which is aimed at helping organizations to establish and maintain appropriate business support structures with proven roles and responsibilities.

Structured project management methods, such as PRINCE2 (PRojects IN Controlled Environments) or the Project Management Body of Knowledge (PMBOK) developed by the Project Management Institute (PMI), can be used when improving IT services. Not all improvements will require a structured project approach, but many will, due to the sheer scope and scale of the improvement. Project management is discussed in more detail in *ITIL Service Transition*.

Visit www.msp-officialsite.com for more information on MSP.

Visit www.p3o-officialsite.com for more information on P3O.

Visit www.prince-officialsite.com for more information on PRINCE2.

Visit www.pmi.org for more information on PMI and PMBOK.

See also the following publications:

- Cleland, David I. and Ireland, Lewis R. (2006). *Project Management: Strategic Design and Implementation* (5th edition). McGraw-Hill Professional.
- Haugan, Gregory T. (2006). *Project Management Fundamentals*. Management Concepts.
- Office of Government Commerce (2009). *Managing Successful Projects with PRINCE2*. TSO, London.
- Cabinet Office (2011). *Managing Successful Programmes*. TSO, London.
- Office of Government Commerce (2008). *Portfolio, Programme and Project Offices*. TSO, London.
- The Project Management Institute (2008). *A Guide to the Project Management Body of Knowledge* (PMBOK Guide) (4th edition). Project Management Institute.

D.11 ORGANIZATIONAL CHANGE

There is a wide range of publications that cover organizational change including the related guidance for programme and project management referred to in the previous section.

Chapter 5 in *ITIL Service Transition* covers aspects of organizational change elements that are an essential part of, or a strong contributor towards, service transition. *ITIL Service Transition* and *ITIL*

Continual Service Improvement refer to Kotter's 'eight steps for organizational change'.

Visit www.johnkotter.com for more information. See also the following publications:

- Kotter, John P. (1996). *Leading Change*. Harvard Business School Press.
- Kotter, John P. (1999) *What Leaders Really Do*. Harvard Business School Press.
- Kotter, J. P. (2000). Leading change: why transformation efforts fail. *Harvard Business Review* January–February.
- Kotter, John P. and Cohen, Dan S. (2002). *The Heart of Change: Real-Life Stories of How People Change their Organizations*. Harvard Business School Press.
- Kotter, J. P. and Schlesinger, L. C. (1979). Choosing strategies for change. *Harvard Business Review* Vol. 57, No. 2, p.106.
- Kotter, John P., Rathgeber, Holger, Mueller, Peter and Johnson, Spenser (2006). *Our Iceberg Is Melting: Changing and Succeeding Under Any Conditions*. St. Martin's Press.

D.12 SKILLS FRAMEWORK FOR THE INFORMATION AGE

The Skills Framework for the Information Age (SFIA) enables employers of IT professionals to carry out a range of human resource activities against a common framework including a skills audit, planning future skill requirements, development programmes, standardization of job titles and functions, and resource allocation.

SFIA provides a standardized view of the wide range of professional skills needed by people working in IT. SFIA is constructed as a simple two-dimensional matrix consisting of areas of work on one axis and levels of responsibility on the other. It uses a common language and a sensible, logical structure that can be adapted to the training and development needs of a very wide range of businesses.

Visit www.sfia.org.uk for further details.

D.13 CARNEGIE MELLON: CMMI AND ESCM FRAMEWORK

The Capability Maturity Model Integration (CMMI) is a process improvement approach developed by the Software Engineering Institute (SEI) of Carnegie Mellon University. CMMI provides organizations with the essential elements of effective processes. It can be used to guide process improvement across a project, a division or an entire organization. CMMI helps integrate traditionally separate organizational functions, sets process improvement goals and priorities, provides guidance for quality processes, and suggests a point of reference for appraising current processes. There are several CMMI models covering different domains of application.

The eSourcing Capability Model for Service Providers (eSCM-SP) is a framework developed by ITSqc at Carnegie Mellon to improve the relationship between IT service providers and their customers.

Organizations can be assessed against CMMI models using SCAMPI (Standard CMMI Appraisal Method for Process Improvement).

For more information, see www.sei.cmu.edu/cmmi/

D.14 BALANCED SCORECARD

A new approach to strategic management was developed in the early 1990s by Drs Robert Kaplan (Harvard Business School) and David Norton. They named this system the 'balanced scorecard'. Recognizing some of the weaknesses and vagueness of previous management approaches, the balanced scorecard approach provides a clear prescription as to what companies should measure in order to 'balance' the financial perspective. The balanced scorecard suggests that the organization be viewed from four perspectives, and it is valuable to develop metrics, collect data and analyse the organization relative to each of these perspectives:

- The learning and growth perspective
- The business process perspective
- The customer perspective
- The financial perspective.

Some organizations may choose to use the balanced scorecard method as a way of assessing and reporting their IT quality performance in general and their service operation performance in particular.

Further details are available through the balanced scorecard user community at www.scorecardsupport.com

D.15 SIX SIGMA

Six Sigma is a data-driven process improvement approach that supports continual improvement. It is business-output-driven in relation to customer specification. The objective is to implement a measurement-oriented strategy focused on process improvement and defects reduction. A Six Sigma defect is defined as anything outside customer specifications.

Six Sigma focuses on dramatically reducing process variation using statistical process control (SPC) measures. The fundamental objective is to reduce errors to fewer than 3.4 defects per million executions (regardless of the process). Service providers must determine whether it is reasonable to expect delivery at a Six Sigma level given the wide variation in IT deliverables, roles and tasks within IT operational environments.

There are two primary sub-methodologies within Six Sigma: DMAIC (Define, Measure, Analyse, Improve, Control) and DMADV (Define, Measure, Analyse, Design, Verify). DMAIC is an improvement method for existing processes for which performance does not meet expectations, or for which incremental improvements are desired. DMADV focuses on the creation of new processes. For more information, see:

- George, Michael L. (2003). *Lean Six Sigma for Service: How to Use Lean Speed and Six Sigma Quality to Improve Services and Transactions*. McGraw-Hill.
- Pande, Pete and Holpp, Larry (2001). *What Is Six Sigma?* McGraw-Hill.
- Pande, Peter S., Neuman, Robert P. and Cavanagh, Roland R. (2000). *The Six Sigma Way: How GE, Motorola, and Other Top Companies are Honing their Performance*. McGraw-Hill.

Appendix E:
Risk assessment
and management

E

Appendix E: Risk assessment and management

This appendix contains basic information about several broadly known and used approaches to the assessment and management of risk. It is not intended to be a comprehensive study of the subject, but rather to provide an awareness of some of the methods in use.

E.1 DEFINITION OF RISK AND RISK MANAGEMENT

Risk may be defined as uncertainty of outcome, whether a positive opportunity or negative threat. It is the fact that there is uncertainty that creates the need for attention and formal management of risk. After all, if an organization were absolutely certain that a negative threat would materialize, there would be little difficulty in determining an appropriate course of action. Likewise, if an organization could be guaranteed that the positive opportunity would be realized, then its path would be clear. Managing risks requires the identification and control of the exposure to those risks which may have an impact on the achievement of an organization's business objectives.

Every organization manages its risk, but not always in a way that is visible, repeatable and consistently applied to support decision-making. The purpose of formal risk management is to enable better decision-making based on a sound understanding of risks and their likely impact on the achievement of objectives. An organization can gain this understanding by ensuring that it makes cost-effective use of a risk framework that has a series of well-defined steps. Decision-making should include determining any appropriate actions to take to manage the risks to a level deemed to be acceptable by the organization.

A number of different methodologies, standards and frameworks have been developed for risk management. Some focus more on generic techniques widely applicable to different levels and needs, while others are specifically concerned with risk management relating to important assets used by the organization in the pursuit of its objectives. Each organization should determine the approach to risk management that is best suited to its needs and circumstances, and it is possible that the approach adopted will leverage the ideas reflected in more than one of the recognized standards and/or frameworks.

In this appendix the following approaches to managing risks are briefly explained:

- Management of Risk (M_o_R)
- ISO 31000
- ISO/IEC 27001
- Risk IT.

E.2 MANAGEMENT OF RISK (M_o_R)

Management of Risk (M_o_R) is intended to help organizations put in place an effective framework for risk management. This will help them take informed decisions about the risks that affect their strategic, programme, project and operational objectives.

M_o_R provides a route map of risk management, bringing together principles, an approach, a process with a set of interrelated steps and pointers to more detailed sources of advice on risk management techniques and specialisms. It also provides advice on how these principles, approach and process should be embedded, reviewed and applied differently depending on the nature of the objectives at risk.

The M_o_R framework is illustrated in Figure E.1.

The M_o_R framework is based on four core concepts:

- **M_o_R principles** Principles are essential for the development and maintenance of good risk management practice. They are informed by corporate governance principles and the international standard for risk management, ISO 31000: 2009. They are high-level and universally applicable statements that provide guidance to organizations as they design an appropriate approach to risk management as part of their internal controls.

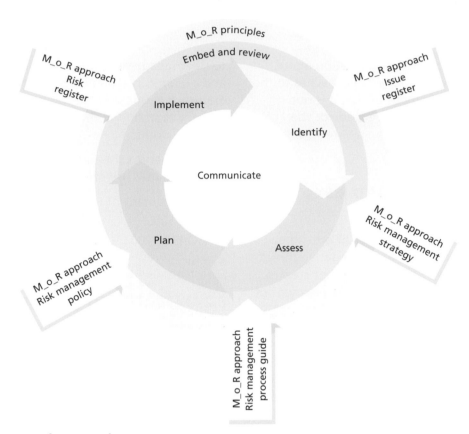

Figure E.1 The M_o_R framework

- **M_o_R approach** Principles need to be adapted and adopted to suit each individual organization. An organization's approach to the principles needs to be agreed and defined within a risk management policy, process guide and strategies.
- **M_o_R process** The process is divided into four main steps: identify, assess, plan and implement. Each step describes the inputs, outputs, tasks and techniques involved to ensure that the overall process is effective.
- **Embedding and reviewing M_o_R** Having put in place an approach and process that satisfy the principles, an organization should ensure that they are consistently applied across the organization and that their application undergoes continual improvement in order for them to be effective.

There are several common techniques which support risk management, including a summary risk profile. A summary risk profile is a graphical representation of information normally found in an existing risk register, and helps to increase the visibility of risks. For more information on summary

risk profiles and other M_o_R techniques, see *Management of Risk: Guidance for Practitioners* (OGC, 2010).

E.3 ISO 31000

ISO 31000 was published in November 2009 and is the first set of international guidelines for risk management, intended to be applicable and adaptable for 'any public, private or community enterprise, association, group or individual.' ISO 31000 is a process-oriented rather than a control-oriented approach to risk management, and provides guidance on a broader, more conceptual basis, rather than specifying all aspects of an organization's risk assessment and management approach. For example, ISO 31000 does not define how an organization will create risk data or measure risk, nor does it ensure that an organization will include a review of all risk areas relevant to the achievement of their objectives. ISO 31000 was published as a standard without certification.

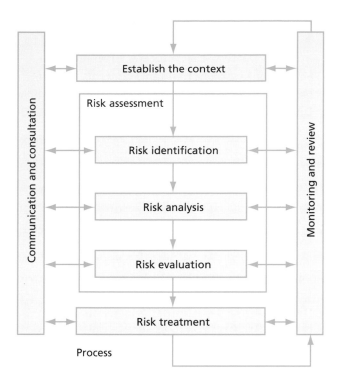

Figure E.2 ISO 31000 risk management process flow

ISO 31000 defines risk as 'the effect of uncertainty on objectives'. Risk management should be performed within a framework that provides the foundations and provisions which will embed the management of risk throughout all levels of the organization. ISO 31000 identifies the necessary components of such a framework as:

■ Mandate and commitment
■ Design of framework for managing risk
■ Understanding the organization and its context
■ Establishing risk management policy
■ Accountability
■ Integration into organizational processes
■ Resources
■ Establishing internal communication and reporting mechanisms
■ Establishing external communication and reporting mechanisms
■ Implementing risk management
■ Monitoring and review of the framework
■ Continual improvement of the framework.

Within this context the risk management process is seen at a high level in Figure E.2.

Once the framework has been established and the context understood, risk assessment is undertaken. This consists of three steps: risk identification, risk analysis and risk evaluation. The risk identification

step is intended to create a comprehensive list of risks based on those events that might create, enhance, prevent, degrade, accelerate or delay the achievement of the organization's objectives. Risk analysis involves developing a full understanding of the risks as an input to risk evaluation and the decisions regarding the plan for treating the risks. Risk evaluation is to make decisions about which risks require treatment and the relative priorities amongst them.

Risk treatment involves the modification of risks using one or more approaches. These approaches are not necessarily mutually exclusive and may include:

■ Avoiding the risk by deciding not to start or continue with the activity that gives rise to the risk
■ Taking or increasing the risk in order to pursue an opportunity
■ Removing the risk source
■ Changing the likelihood
■ Changing the consequences
■ Sharing the risk with another party or parties (including contracts and risk financing)
■ Retaining the risk by informed decision.

The approach described in ISO 31000 provides broad scope for each organization to adopt the high-level principles and adapt them to their specific needs and circumstances.

E.4 ISO/IEC 27001

ISO/IEC 27001 was published in October 2005 and is an information security management system (ISMS) standard which formally specifies a management system that is intended to bring information security under explicit management control. While ISO/IEC 27001 is a security standard, not a risk management standard, it mandates specific requirements for security, including requirements relating to risk management. The risk management methods described in this context may be applied to general risk management activities as well.

ISO/IEC 27001 requires that management:

■ Systematically examines the organization's information security risks, taking account of the threats, vulnerabilities and impacts
■ Designs and implements a coherent and comprehensive suite of information security

controls and/or other forms of risk treatment (such as risk avoidance or risk transfer) to address those risks that are deemed unacceptable

- Adopts an overarching management process to ensure that the information security controls continue to meet the organization's information security needs on an ongoing basis.

The key risk management-related steps described in ISO/IEC 27001 include:

- Define the risk assessment approach of the organization
- Identify a risk assessment methodology that is suited to the ISMS, and the identified business information security, legal and regulatory requirements
- Develop criteria for accepting risks and identify acceptable levels of risk
- Identify the risks
- Identify the assets within the scope of the ISMS, and the owners of these assets
- Identify the threats to these assets
- Identify the vulnerabilities that might be exploited by the threats
- Identify the impact that losses of confidentiality, integrity and availability may have on these assets
- Analyse and evaluate the risks
- Assess the business impacts on the organization that might result from security failures, taking into account the consequences of a loss of confidentiality, integrity or availability of the assets
- Assess the realistic likelihood of security failures occurring in the light of prevailing threats and vulnerabilities, and impacts associated with these assets, and the controls currently implemented
- Estimate the levels of risk
- Determine whether the risks are acceptable or require treatment using the previously established criteria for accepting risks
- Identify and evaluate options for the treatment of risks. Possible actions may include:
  - Applying appropriate controls
  - Knowingly and objectively accepting risks, providing they clearly satisfy the organization's policies and the criteria for accepting risks

  - Avoiding risks
  - Transferring the associated business risks to other parties, e.g. insurers, suppliers
- Select control objectives and controls for the treatment of risks
- Obtain management approval of the proposed residual risks
- Obtain management authorization to implement and operate the ISMS.

During the implementation and operation of the ISMS, a plan for risk treatment is formulated (identifying the appropriate management action, resources, responsibilities and priorities for managing information security risks) and implemented. ISO/IEC 27001 also calls for the ongoing monitoring and reviewing of the risks and risk treatment and the formal maintenance of the ISMS to ensure that the organization's goals are met.

This approach is focused specifically on the assets involved in organizational information security, but the general principles can be applied to overall service provision.

E.5 RISK IT

Risk IT is part of the IT governance product portfolio of ISACA that provides a framework for effective governance and management of IT risk, based on a set of guiding principles. Risk IT is about IT risk, including business risk related to the use of IT. The publications in which Risk IT is documented include *The Risk IT Framework* (ISACA, 2009) and *The Risk IT Practitioner Guide* (ISACA, 2009) (available from www.isaca.org).

The key principles in Risk IT are that effective enterprise governance and management of IT risk:

- Always connect to the business objectives
- Align the management of IT-related business risk with overall enterprise risk management
- Balance the costs and benefits of managing IT risk
- Promote fair and open communication of IT risk
- Establish the right tone from the top while defining and enforcing personal accountability for operating within acceptable and well-defined tolerance levels
- Are continuous processes and part of daily activities.

The framework provides for three domains, each containing three processes, as shown in Figure E.3. *The Risk IT Framework* describes the key activities of each process, the responsibilities for the process, information flows between the processes and the performance management of each process.

Risk governance ensures that IT risk management practices are embedded in the enterprise, enabling it to secure optimal risk-adjusted return. Risk evaluation ensures that IT-related risks and opportunities are identified, analysed and presented in business terms. Risk response ensures that IT-related risk issues, opportunities and events are addressed in a cost-effective manner and in line with business priorities.

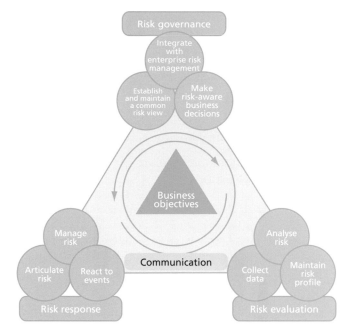

Figure E.3 ISACA Risk IT process framework

Appendix F:
Examples of inputs
and outputs across
the service lifecycle

F

Appendix F: Examples of inputs and outputs across the service lifecycle

This appendix identifies some of the major inputs and outputs between each stage of the service lifecycle. This is not an exhaustive list and is designed to help understand how the different lifecycle stages interact. See Table 3.21 for more detail on the inputs and outputs of the service strategy stage.

Lifecycle stage	Examples of inputs from other service lifecycle stages	Examples of outputs to other service lifecycle stages
Service strategy	Information and feedback for business cases and service portfolio Requirements for strategies and plans Inputs and feedback on strategies and policies Financial reports, service reports, dashboards, and outputs of service review meetings Response to change proposals Service portfolio updates including the service catalogue Change schedule Knowledge and information in the service knowledge management system (SKMS)	Vision and mission Strategies, strategic plans and policies Financial information and budgets Service portfolio Change proposals Service charters including service packages, service models, and details of utility and warranty Patterns of business activity and demand forecasts Updated knowledge and information in the SKMS Achievements against metrics, KPIs and CSFs Feedback to other lifecycle stages Improvement opportunities logged in the CSI register
Service design	Vision and mission Strategies, strategic plans and policies Financial information and budgets Service portfolio Service charters including service packages, service models, and details of utility and warranty Feedback on all aspects of service design and service design packages Requests for change (RFCs) for designing changes and improvements Input to design requirements from other lifecycle stages Service reports, dashboards, and outputs of service review meetings Knowledge and information in the SKMS	Service portfolio updates including the service catalogue Service design packages, including: ■ Details of utility and warranty ■ Acceptance criteria ■ Updated service models ■ Designs and interface specifications ■ Transition plans ■ Operation plans and procedures Information security policies Designs for new or changed services, management information systems and tools, technology architectures, processes, measurement methods and metrics SLAs, OLAs and underpinning contracts RFCs to transition or deploy new or changed services Financial reports Updated knowledge and information in the SKMS Achievements against metrics, KPIs and CSFs Feedback to other lifecycle stages Improvement opportunities logged in the CSI register

Lifecycle stage	Examples of inputs from other service lifecycle stages	Examples of outputs to other service lifecycle stages
Service transition	Vision and mission Strategies, strategic plans and policies Financial information and budgets Service portfolio Change proposals, including utility and warranty requirements and expected timescales RFCs for implementing changes and improvements Service design packages, including: ■ Details of utility and warranty ■ Acceptance criteria ■ Service models ■ Designs and interface specifications ■ Transition plans ■ Operation plans and procedures Input to change evaluation and change advisory board (CAB) meetings Knowledge and information in the SKMS	New or changed services, management information systems and tools, technology architectures, processes, measurement methods and metrics Responses to change proposals and RFCs Change schedule Known errors Standard changes for use in request fulfilment Knowledge and information in the SKMS (including the configuration management system) Financial reports Updated knowledge and information in the SKMS Achievements against metrics, KPIs and CSFs Feedback to other lifecycle stages Improvement opportunities logged in the CSI register
Service operation	Vision and mission Strategies, strategic plans and policies Financial information and budgets Service portfolio Service reports, dashboards, and outputs of service review meetings Service design packages, including: ■ Details of utility and warranty ■ Operations plans and procedures ■ Recovery procedures Service level agreements (SLAs), operational level agreements (OLAs) and underpinning contracts Known errors Standard changes for use in request fulfilment Information security policies Change schedule Patterns of business activity and demand forecasts Knowledge and information in the SKMS	Achievement of agreed service levels to deliver value to the business Operational requirements Operational performance data and service records RFCs to resolve operational issues Financial reports Updated knowledge and information in the SKMS Achievements against metrics, KPIs and CSFs Feedback to other lifecycle stages Improvement opportunities logged in the CSI register
Continual service improvement	Vision and mission Strategies, strategic plans and policies Financial information and budgets Service portfolio Achievements against metrics, key performance indicators (KPIs) and critical success factors (CSFs) from each lifecycle stage Operational performance data and service records Improvement opportunities logged in the CSI register Knowledge and information in the SKMS	RFCs for implementing improvements across all lifecycle stages Business cases for significant improvements Updated CSI register Service improvement plans Results of customer and user satisfaction surveys Service reports, dashboards, and outputs of service review meetings Financial reports Updated knowledge and information in the SKMS Achievements against metrics, KPIs and CSFs Feedback to other lifecycle stages

References and further reading

References and further reading

The following authors are either cited directly in the text, or have influenced the thinking of the authors and shaped the contents of this publication. They are indicative of the breadth and depth and diversity of knowledge available to interested readers. Some of these are seminal works in their respective fields, notable for their enduring influence several decades after publication. Others are contemporary works addressing new challenges and opportunities facing organizations.

Note that this list does not include the publications in the Best Management Practice (BMP) portfolio which are cited in full in Appendix D.

Argote, L. (2000). Knowledge transfer: a basis for competitive advantage in firms. *Organizational Behaviour and Human Decision Processes*. Vol. 82, No. 1, pp. 150–69.

Allee, Verna (2003). *The Future of Knowledge: Increasing Prosperity Through Value Networks*. Butterworth-Heinemann.

Breene, T., Mulani, N.P. and Nunes, P.F. (2005). Marks of distinction. *Outlook Journal*, No. 2.

Bryson, J.R., Daniels, P.W. and Warf, B. (2004). *Service Worlds: People, Organisations, Technologies*. Routledge.

Burner, Mike (2004). *Service Orientation and its Role in your Connected Systems Strategy*. Microsoft. http://msdn2.microsoft.com/en-us/library/ms954826.aspx

Camazine, S., Deneubourg, J. L., Franks, N. R., Sneyd, J., Theraulaz, G. and Bonabeau, E. (2001). *Self-Organization in Biological Systems*. Princeton University Press.

Carr, Nicholas (2005). The end of corporate computing. *MIT Sloan Management Review*. Vol. 46(3), 67–73.

Chan, Kim W. and Mauborgne, Renée (2005). *Blue Ocean Strategy: How to Create Uncontested Market Space and Make Competition Irrelevant*. Harvard Business School Press.

Cherbakov, L., Galambos, G., Harishankar, R., Kalyana, S. and Rackham, G. (2005). Impact of service orientation at the business level. *IBM Systems Journal*, Vol. 44, No. 4.

Coase, Ronald (1937). The nature of the firm. *Economica*, 4(16), 386–405.

Easton, G. and Jarrell, S. (1998). The effects of total quality management on corporate performance: an empirical investigation. *Journal of Business*, 71(2), 253–307.

Edmondson, A. and Frei, F. (2002). *Transformation at the IRS*. Harvard Business School.

Forrester, Jay W. (1961). *Industrial Dynamics*. MIT Press.

Forrester, Jay W. (1971). *Principles of Systems*. Wright-Allen Press.

Froehle, C. and Roth, A.V. (2004). New measurement scales for evaluating perceptions of the technology-mediated customer service experience. *Journal of Operations Management*, 22(1), 1–21.

Goold, Michael and Campbell, Andrew (2002). *Designing Effective Organizations: How to Create Structured Networks*. Jossey-Bass.

Grant, Robert M. (1991). The resource-based theory of competitive advantage: implications for strategy formulation. *California Management Review*, Vol. 33, No. 3.

Gratton, Lynda and Ghoshal, Sumantra (2005). Beyond best practice. *MIT Sloan Management Review*, 46(3).

Greiner, Larry E. (1998, orig. 1972). Evolution and revolution as organizations grow. *Harvard Business Review*, May–June.

Grönroos, Christian (2001). *Service Management and Marketing: A Customer Relationship Management Approach*. John Wiley and Sons.

Hill, Peter (1977). On goods and services. *The Review of Income and Wealth*, 23: 315–38.

Holmstrom, B. and Roberts, J. (1998). The boundaries of the firm revisited. *Journal of Economic Perspectives*, 12, 73–94.

Iqbal, Majid (2004). Getting students excited about services: providing a context for applying their newly acquired knowledge ITSqc Working Paper CMU-ITSQC-WP-04-001a. Carnegie Mellon University, Pittsburgh, PA, USA.

Iravani, Seyed M., Van Oyen, Mark P. and Sims, Katharine T. (2005). Structural flexibility: a new perspective on the design of manufacturing and service operations. *Management Science*, Vol. 51, No. 2, 151–66.

ITGI (2005). COBIT 4.0: *Control OBjectives, Management Guidelines and Maturity Models*. IT Governance Institute.

Jones, Gareth R. (2007). *Organizational Theory, Design and Change*. Pearson Prentice Hall.

Judd, R.C. (1964). The case for redefining services. *Journal of Marketing*, Vol. 28, 58–9.

Kano, N., Seraku, N., Tsuji, S. and Takahashi, F. (1984). Attractive Quality and Must-be Quality. *Hinshitsu (Quality, The Journal of Japanese Society for Quality Control)*, 14(2), 39–48.

Keating, E. K., Oliva, R., Repenning, N. P., Rockart, S. and Sterman, J. D. (1999). Overcoming the improvement paradox. *European Management Journal*, 17(2), 120–34.

Lev, B. (2001). *Intangibles: Management, Measurement and Reporting*. The Brookings Institution.

Lidwell, W., Holden, K. and Butler, J. (2003). *Universal Principles of Design*. Rockport Publishers.

Lovelock, Christopher and Gummesson, Evert (2004). Whither services marketing? In search of a new paradigm and fresh perspectives. *Journal of Service Research*, 7 (August), 20–41.

Luehrman, T.A. (1998). Strategy as a portfolio of real options. *Harvard Business Review*, 76(5), 89–99.

Luftman, Jerry and Brier, Tom (1999). Achieving and sustaining business–IT alignment. *California Management Review*, Vol. 42, No. 1.

Magretta, J. (2002). *What Management Is: How it Works and Why it's Everyone's Business*. The Free Press, New York.

Malone, T. W., Crowston, K. and Herman, G. A. (eds) (2003). *Organizing Business Knowledge: The MIT Process Handbook*. MIT Press, Cambridge, MA.

McNeillis, Paul (2005). ITNOW 2005 47(6), 14–15; British Computer Society. doi:10.1093/itnow/bwi114

Milgrom, Paul and Roberts, John (1992). *Economics, Organization and Management*. Prentice-Hall.

Miller, R. B., Heiman, S.E. and Tuleja, T. (1995). *The New Strategic Selling*. Grand Central.

Mintzberg, Henry (1994). *The Rise and Fall of Strategic Planning*. Basic Books.

Morecroft, John, Sanchez, Ron and Heene, Aime (2002). *Systems Perspective on Resources, Capabilities, and Management Processes*. Elsevier Science.

National Academy of Engineering (2003). *The Impact of Academic Research on Industrial Performance*. The National Academies Press.

Nagle, T.N. and Holden, R.K. (2002). *Strategy and Tactics of Pricing: A Guide to Profitable Decision-making* (3rd edition). Prentice-Hall.

Porter, Michael E. (1996). What is strategy? *Harvard Business Review*, November–December.

Rathmell, J.M. (1966). What is meant by services? *Journal of Marketing*, Vol. 30, 32–6.

Rayport, J.F. and Jaworski, B.J. (2004). Best face forward. *Harvard Business Review*, December.

Repenning, Nelson P. and Sterman, John D. (2001a). Nobody ever gets credit for fixing problems that never happened: creating and sustaining process improvement. *California Management Review*, 43(4).

Repenning, Nelson P., Goncalves, Paulo and Black, Laura (2001b). Past the tipping point: the persistence of firefighting in product development. *California Management Review*, 43(4).

Rummler, Geary (1995). *Improving Performance: How to Manage the White Space on the Organization Chart*. Jossey-Bass.

Seely Brown, John and Hagel III, John (2005). Innovation blowback: disruptive management practices from Asia. *The McKinsey Quarterly*, No. 1.

Senge, Peter (1990). *The Fifth Discipline*. Currency Doubleday.

Simons, Robert (1995). *Levers of Control: How Managers Use Innovative Control Systems to Drive Strategic Renewal*. Harvard Business School Press, Boston, Massachusetts.

Sterman, John D. (2000). *Business Dynamics. Systems Thinking and Modeling for a Complex World*. McGraw-Hill.

Tapscott, Don, Ticoll, David and Lowy, Alex (2000). *Digital Capital: Harnessing the Power of Business Webs*. Harvard Business School Press.

Tax, S.S. and Brown, S.W. (1998). Recovering and learning from service failure. *Sloan Management Review*, 75–88.

Toomey, Mark (2009). *Waltzing with the Elephant*. Infonomics.

Ulwick, Anthony (2005). *What Customers Want: Using Outcome-driven Innovation to Create Breakthrough Products and Services*. McGraw-Hill.

Van Maanen, J. and Schein, E.H. (1979). Toward a theory of organizational socialization. *In* B. Staw (ed.), *Research in Organizational Behavior 1*. JAI Press, Greenwich, 209–264.

Williamson, O.E. and Winter, S.G. (1993). *The Nature of the Firm: Origins, Evolution and Development*. Oxford University Press.

Abbreviations and
glossary

Abbreviations

ACD	automatic call distribution	FTA	fault tree analysis
AM	availability management	IRR	internal rate of return
AMIS	availability management information system	ISG	IT steering group
		ISM	information security management
ASP	application service provider	ISMS	information security management system
AST	agreed service time		
BCM	business continuity management	ISO	International Organization for Standardization
BCP	business continuity plan		
BIA	business impact analysis	ISP	internet service provider
BMP	Best Management Practice	IT	information technology
BRM	business relationship manager	ITSCM	IT service continuity management
BSI	British Standards Institution	ITSM	IT service management
CAB	change advisory board	itSMF	IT Service Management Forum
CAPEX	capital expenditure	IVR	interactive voice response
CCM	component capacity management	KEDB	known error database
CFIA	component failure impact analysis	KPI	key performance indicator
CI	configuration item	LOS	line of service
CMDB	configuration management database	MIS	management information system
CMIS	capacity management information system	M_o_R	management of risk
		MTBF	mean time between failures
CMM	capability maturity model	MTBSI	mean time between service incidents
CMMI	Capability Maturity Model Integration	MTRS	mean time to restore service
CMS	configuration management system	MTTR	mean time to repair
COBIT	Control OBjectives for Information and related Technology	NPV	net present value
		OLA	operational level agreement
COTS	commercial off the shelf	OPEX	operational expenditure
CSF	critical success factor	PBA	pattern of business activity
CSI	continual service improvement	PDCA	Plan-Do-Check-Act
CTI	computer telephony integration	PFS	prerequisite for success
DIKW	Data-to-Information-to-Knowledge-to-Wisdom	PIR	post-implementation review
		PMBOK	Project Management Body of Knowledge
DML	definitive media library		
ECAB	emergency change advisory board	PMI	Project Management Institute
ELS	early life support	PMO	project management office
eSCM-CL	eSourcing Capability Model for Client Organizations	PRINCE2	PRojects IN Controlled Environments
		PSO	projected service outage
eSCM-SP	eSourcing Capability Model for Service Providers	QA	quality assurance
		QMS	quality management system

RACI	responsible, accountable, consulted and informed
RCA	root cause analysis
RFC	request for change
ROA	return on assets
ROI	return on investment
RPO	recovery point objective
RTO	recovery time objective
SAC	service acceptance criteria
SACM	service asset and configuration management
SAM	software asset management
SCM	service capacity management
SCMIS	supplier and contract management information system
SDP	service design package
SFA	service failure analysis
SIP	service improvement plan
SKMS	service knowledge management system
SLA	service level agreement
SLM	service level management
SLP	service level package
SLR	service level requirement
SMART	specific, measurable, achievable, relevant and time-bound
SMIS	security management information system
SMO	service maintenance objective
SoC	separation of concerns
SOP	standard operating procedure
SOR	statement of requirements
SOX	Sarbanes-Oxley (US law)
SPI	service provider interface
SPM	service portfolio management
SPOF	single point of failure
TCO	total cost of ownership
TCU	total cost of utilization
TO	technical observation

TOR	terms of reference
TQM	total quality management
UC	underpinning contract
UP	user profile
VBF	vital business function
VOI	value on investment
WIP	work in progress

Glossary

The core ITIL publications (*ITIL Service Strategy*, *ITIL Service Design*, *ITIL Service Operation*, *ITIL Service Transition*, *ITIL Continual Service Improvement*) referred to in parentheses at the beginning of a definition indicate where a reader can find more information. Terms without such a reference may either be used generically across all five core publications, or simply may not be explained in any greater detail elsewhere in the ITIL series. In other words, readers are only directed to other sources where they can expect to expand on their knowledge or to see a greater context.

acceptance

Formal agreement that an IT service, process, plan or other deliverable is complete, accurate, reliable and meets its specified requirements. Acceptance is usually preceded by change evaluation or testing and is often required before proceeding to the next stage of a project or process. *See also* service acceptance criteria.

access management

(*ITIL Service Operation*) The process responsible for allowing users to make use of IT services, data or other assets. Access management helps to protect the confidentiality, integrity and availability of assets by ensuring that only authorized users are able to access or modify them. Access management implements the policies of information security management and is sometimes referred to as rights management or identity management.

account manager

(*ITIL Service Strategy*) A role that is very similar to that of the business relationship manager, but includes more commercial aspects. Most commonly used by Type III service providers when dealing with external customers.

accounting

(*ITIL Service Strategy*) The process responsible for identifying the actual costs of delivering IT services, comparing these with budgeted costs, and managing variance from the budget.

accounting period

(*ITIL Service Strategy*) A period of time (usually one year) for which budgets, charges, depreciation and other financial calculations are made. *See also* financial year.

accredited

Officially authorized to carry out a role. For example, an accredited body may be authorized to provide training or to conduct audits.

activity

A set of actions designed to achieve a particular result. Activities are usually defined as part of processes or plans, and are documented in procedures.

agreement

A document that describes a formal understanding between two or more parties. An agreement is not legally binding, unless it forms part of a contract. *See also* operational level agreement; service level agreement.

alert

(*ITIL Service Operation*) A notification that a threshold has been reached, something has changed, or a failure has occurred. Alerts are often created and managed by system management tools and are managed by the event management process.

analytical modelling

(*ITIL Continual Service Improvement*) (*ITIL Service Design*) (*ITIL Service Strategy*) A technique that uses mathematical models to predict the behaviour of IT services or other configuration items. Analytical models are commonly used in capacity management and availability management. *See also* modelling; simulation modelling.

application

Software that provides functions which are required by an IT service. Each application may be part of more than one IT service. An application runs on one or more servers or clients. *See also* application management; application portfolio.

application management

(*ITIL Service Operation*) The function responsible for managing applications throughout their lifecycle.

application portfolio

(*ITIL Service Design*) A database or structured document used to manage applications throughout their lifecycle. The application portfolio contains key attributes of all applications. The application portfolio is sometimes implemented as part of the service portfolio, or as part of the configuration management system.

application service provider (ASP)

(*ITIL Service Design*) An external service provider that provides IT services using applications running at the service provider's premises. Users access the applications by network connections to the service provider.

architecture

(*ITIL Service Design*) The structure of a system or IT service, including the relationships of components to each other and to the environment they are in. Architecture also includes the standards and guidelines that guide the design and evolution of the system.

assembly

(*ITIL Service Transition*) A configuration item that is made up of a number of other CIs. For example, a server CI may contain CIs for CPUs, disks, memory etc.; an IT service CI may contain many hardware, software and other CIs. *See also* build; component CI.

assessment

Inspection and analysis to check whether a standard or set of guidelines is being followed, that records are accurate, or that efficiency and effectiveness targets are being met. *See also* audit.

asset

(*ITIL Service Strategy*) Any resource or capability. The assets of a service provider include anything that could contribute to the delivery of a service. Assets can be one of the following types: management, organization, process, knowledge, people, information, applications, infrastructure or financial capital. *See also* customer asset; service asset; strategic asset.

asset management

(*ITIL Service Transition*) A generic activity or process responsible for tracking and reporting the value and ownership of assets throughout their lifecycle. *See also* service asset and configuration management; fixed asset management; software asset management.

asset register

(*ITIL Service Transition*) A list of fixed assets that includes their ownership and value. *See also* fixed asset management.

asset specificity

(*ITIL Service Strategy*) One or more attributes of an asset that make it particularly useful for a given purpose. Asset specificity may limit the use of the asset for other purposes.

attribute

(*ITIL Service Transition*) A piece of information about a configuration item. Examples are name, location, version number and cost. Attributes of CIs are recorded in a configuration management database (CMDB) and maintained as part of a configuration management system (CMS). *See also* relationship; configuration management system.

audit

Formal inspection and verification to check whether a standard or set of guidelines is being followed, that records are accurate, or that efficiency and effectiveness targets are being met. An audit may be carried out by internal or external groups. *See also* assessment; certification.

authority matrix

See RACI.

availability

(*ITIL Service Design*) Ability of an IT service or other configuration item to perform its agreed function when required. Availability is determined by reliability, maintainability, serviceability, performance and security. Availability is usually calculated as a percentage. This calculation is often based on agreed service time and downtime. It is best practice to calculate availability of an IT service using measurements of the business output.

availability management (AM)

(*ITIL Service Design*) The process responsible for ensuring that IT services meet the current and future availability needs of the business in a cost-effective and timely manner. Availability management defines, analyses, plans, measures and improves all aspects of the availability of IT services, and ensures that all IT infrastructures, processes, tools, roles etc. are appropriate for the agreed service level targets for availability. *See also* availability management information system.

availability management information system (AMIS)

(*ITIL Service Design*) A set of tools, data and information that is used to support availability management. *See also* service knowledge management system.

availability plan

(*ITIL Service Design*) A plan to ensure that existing and future availability requirements for IT services can be provided cost-effectively.

backup

(*ITIL Service Design*) (*ITIL Service Operation*) Copying data to protect against loss of integrity or availability of the original.

balanced scorecard

(*ITIL Continual Service Improvement*) A management tool developed by Drs Robert Kaplan (Harvard Business School) and David Norton. A balanced scorecard enables a strategy to be broken down into key performance indicators. Performance against the KPIs is used to demonstrate how well the strategy is being achieved. A balanced scorecard has four major areas, each of which has a small number of KPIs. The same four areas are considered at different levels of detail throughout the organization.

baseline

(*ITIL Continual Service Improvement*) (*ITIL Service Transition*) A snapshot that is used as a reference point. Many snapshots may be taken and recorded over time but only some will be used as baselines. For example:

- An ITSM baseline can be used as a starting point to measure the effect of a service improvement plan
- A performance baseline can be used to measure changes in performance over the lifetime of an IT service
- A configuration baseline can be used as part of a back-out plan to enable the IT infrastructure to be restored to a known configuration if a change or release fails.

See also benchmark.

benchmark

(*ITIL Continual Service Improvement*) (*ITIL Service Transition*) A baseline that is used to compare related data sets as part of a benchmarking exercise. For example, a recent snapshot of a process can be compared to a previous baseline of that process, or a current baseline can be compared to industry data or best practice. *See also* benchmarking; baseline.

benchmarking

(*ITIL Continual Service Improvement*) The process responsible for comparing a benchmark with related data sets such as a more recent snapshot, industry data or best practice. The term is also used to mean creating a series of benchmarks over time, and comparing the results to measure progress or improvement. This process is not described in detail within the core ITIL publications.

best management practice (BMP)

The Best Management Practice portfolio is owned by the Cabinet Office, part of HM Government. Formerly owned by CCTA and then OGC, the BMP functions moved to the Cabinet Office in June 2010. The BMP portfolio includes guidance on IT service management and project, programme, risk, portfolio and value management. There is also a management maturity model as well as related glossaries of terms.

best practice

Proven activities or processes that have been successfully used by multiple organizations. ITIL is an example of best practice.

billing

(*ITIL Service Strategy*) Part of the charging process. Billing is the activity responsible for producing an invoice or a bill and recovering the money from customers. *See also* pricing.

brainstorming

(*ITIL Service Design*) (*ITIL Service Operation*) A technique that helps a team to generate ideas. Ideas are not reviewed during the brainstorming session, but at a later stage. Brainstorming is often used by problem management to identify possible causes.

british standards institution (BSI)

The UK national standards body, responsible for creating and maintaining British standards. See www.bsi-global.com for more information. *See also* International Organization for Standardization.

budget

A list of all the money an organization or business unit plans to receive, and plans to pay out, over a specified period of time. *See also* budgeting; planning.

budgeting

The activity of predicting and controlling the spending of money. Budgeting consists of a periodic negotiation cycle to set future budgets (usually annual) and the day-to-day monitoring and adjusting of current budgets.

build

(*ITIL Service Transition*) The activity of assembling a number of configuration items to create part of an IT service. The term is also used to refer to a release that is authorized for distribution – for example, server build or laptop build. *See also* configuration baseline.

business

(*ITIL Service Strategy*) An overall corporate entity or organization formed of a number of business units. In the context of ITSM, the term includes public sector and not-for-profit organizations, as well as companies. An IT service provider provides IT services to a customer within a business. The IT service provider may be part of the same business as its customer (internal service provider), or part of another business (external service provider).

business capacity management

(*ITIL Continual Service Improvement*) (*ITIL Service Design*) In the context of ITSM, business capacity management is the sub-process of capacity management responsible for understanding future business requirements for use in the capacity plan. *See also* service capacity management; component capacity management.

business case

(*ITIL Service Strategy*) Justification for a significant item of expenditure. The business case includes information about costs, benefits, options, issues, risks and possible problems. *See also* cost benefit analysis.

business continuity management (BCM)

(*ITIL Service Design*) The business process responsible for managing risks that could seriously affect the business. Business continuity management safeguards the interests of key stakeholders, reputation, brand and value-creating activities. The process involves reducing risks to an acceptable level and planning for the recovery of business processes should a disruption to the business occur. Business continuity management sets the objectives, scope and requirements for IT service continuity management.

business customer

(*ITIL Service Strategy*) A recipient of a product or a service from the business. For example, if the business is a car manufacturer, then the business customer is someone who buys a car.

business impact analysis (BIA)

(*ITIL Service Strategy*) Business impact analysis is the activity in business continuity management that identifies vital business functions and their dependencies. These dependencies may include suppliers, people, other business processes, IT services etc. Business impact analysis defines the recovery requirements for IT services. These requirements include recovery time objectives, recovery point objectives and minimum service level targets for each IT service.

business objective

(*ITIL Service Strategy*) The objective of a business process, or of the business as a whole. Business objectives support the business vision, provide guidance for the IT strategy, and are often supported by IT services.

business operations

(*ITIL Service Strategy*) The day-to-day execution, monitoring and management of business processes.

business perspective

(*ITIL Continual Service Improvement*) An understanding of the service provider and IT services from the point of view of the business, and an understanding of the business from the point of view of the service provider.

business process

A process that is owned and carried out by the business. A business process contributes to the delivery of a product or service to a business customer. For example, a retailer may have a purchasing process that helps to deliver services to its business customers. Many business processes rely on IT services.

business relationship management

(*ITIL Service Strategy*) The process responsible for maintaining a positive relationship with customers. Business relationship management identifies customer needs and ensures that the service provider is able to meet these needs with an appropriate catalogue of services. This process has strong links with service level management.

business relationship manager (BRM)

(*ITIL Service Strategy*) A role responsible for maintaining the relationship with one or more customers. This role is often combined with the service level manager role.

business service

A service that is delivered to business customers by business units. For example, delivery of financial services to customers of a bank, or goods to the customers of a retail store. Successful delivery of business services often depends on one or more IT services. A business service may consist almost entirely of an IT service – for example, an online banking service or an external website where product orders can be placed by business customers. *See also* customer-facing service.

business service management

The management of business services delivered to business customers. Business service management is performed by business units.

business unit

(*ITIL Service Strategy*) A segment of the business that has its own plans, metrics, income and costs. Each business unit owns assets and uses these to create value for customers in the form of goods and services.

call

(*ITIL Service Operation*) A telephone call to the service desk from a user. A call could result in an incident or a service request being logged.

call centre

(*ITIL Service Operation*) An organization or business unit that handles large numbers of incoming and outgoing telephone calls. *See also* service desk.

capability

(*ITIL Service Strategy*) The ability of an organization, person, process, application, IT service or other configuration item to carry out an activity. Capabilities are intangible assets of an organization. *See also* resource.

Capability Maturity Model Integration (CMMI)

(*ITIL Continual Service Improvement*) A process improvement approach developed by the Software Engineering Institute (SEI) of Carnegie Mellon University, US. CMMI provides organizations with the essential elements of effective processes. It can be used to guide process improvement across a project, a division or an entire organization. CMMI helps integrate traditionally separate organizational functions, set process improvement goals and priorities, provide guidance for quality processes, and provide a point of reference for appraising current processes. See www.sei.cmu.edu/cmmi for more information. *See also* maturity.

capacity

(*ITIL Service Design*) The maximum throughput that a configuration item or IT service can deliver. For some types of CI, capacity may be the size or volume – for example, a disk drive.

capacity management

(*ITIL Continual Service Improvement*) (*ITIL Service Design*) The process responsible for ensuring that the capacity of IT services and the IT infrastructure is able to meet agreed capacity- and performance-related requirements in a cost-effective and timely manner. Capacity management considers all resources required to deliver an IT service, and is concerned with meeting both the current and future capacity and performance needs of the business. Capacity management includes three sub-processes: business capacity management, service capacity management, and component capacity management. *See also* capacity management information system.

capacity management information system (CMIS)

(*ITIL Service Design*) A set of tools, data and information that is used to support capacity management. *See also* service knowledge management system.

capacity plan

(*ITIL Service Design*) A plan used to manage the resources required to deliver IT services. The plan contains details of current and historic usage of IT services and components, and any issues that need to be addressed (including related improvement activities). The plan also contains scenarios for different predictions of business demand and costed options to deliver the agreed service level targets.

capacity planning

(*ITIL Service Design*) The activity within capacity management responsible for creating a capacity plan.

capital budgeting

(*ITIL Service Strategy*) The present commitment of funds in order to receive a return in the future in the form of additional cash inflows or reduced cash outflows.

capital cost

(*ITIL Service Strategy*) The cost of purchasing something that will become a financial asset – for example, computer equipment and buildings. The value of the asset depreciates over multiple accounting periods. *See also* operational cost.

capital expenditure (CAPEX)

See capital cost.

capitalization

(*ITIL Service Strategy*) Identifying major cost as capital, even though no asset is purchased. This is done to spread the impact of the cost over multiple accounting periods. The most common example of this is software development, or purchase of a software licence.

category

A named group of things that have something in common. Categories are used to group similar things together. For example, cost types are used to group similar types of cost. Incident categories are used to group similar types of incident, while CI types are used to group similar types of configuration item.

certification

Issuing a certificate to confirm compliance to a standard. Certification includes a formal audit by an independent and accredited body. The term is also used to mean awarding a certificate to provide evidence that a person has achieved a qualification.

change

(*ITIL Service Transition*) The addition, modification or removal of anything that could have an effect on IT services. The scope should include changes to all architectures, processes, tools, metrics and documentation, as well as changes to IT services and other configuration items.

change advisory board (CAB)

(*ITIL Service Transition*) A group of people that support the assessment, prioritization, authorization and scheduling of changes. A change advisory board is usually made up of representatives from: all areas within the IT service provider; the business; and third parties such as suppliers.

change evaluation

(*ITIL Service Transition*) The process responsible for formal assessment of a new or changed IT service to ensure that risks have been managed and to help determine whether to authorize the change.

change management

(*ITIL Service Transition*) The process responsible for controlling the lifecycle of all changes, enabling beneficial changes to be made with minimum disruption to IT services.

change model

(*ITIL Service Transition*) A repeatable way of dealing with a particular category of change. A change model defines specific agreed steps that will be followed for a change of this category. Change models may be very complex with many steps that require authorization (e.g. major software release) or may be very simple with no requirement for authorization (e.g. password reset). *See also* change advisory board; standard change.

change proposal

(*ITIL Service Strategy*) (*ITIL Service Transition*) A document that includes a high level description of a potential service introduction or significant change, along with a corresponding business case and an expected implementation schedule. Change proposals are normally created by the service portfolio management process and are passed to change management for authorization. Change management will review the potential impact on other services, on shared resources, and on the overall change schedule. Once the change proposal has been authorized, service portfolio management will charter the service.

change request

See request for change.

change schedule

(*ITIL Service Transition*) A document that lists all authorized changes and their planned implementation dates, as well as the estimated dates of longer-term changes. A change schedule is sometimes called a forward schedule of change, even though it also contains information about changes that have already been implemented.

chargeable item

(*ITIL Service Strategy*) A deliverable of an IT service that is used in calculating charges to customers (for example, number of transactions, number of desktop PCs).

charging

(*ITIL Service Strategy*) Requiring payment for IT services. Charging for IT services is optional, and many organizations choose to treat their IT service provider as a cost centre. *See also* charging process; charging policy.

charging policy

(*ITIL Service Strategy*) A policy specifying the objective of the charging process and the way in which charges will be calculated. *See also* cost.

charging process

(*ITIL Service Strategy*) The process responsible for deciding how much customers should pay (pricing) and recovering money from them (billing). This process is not described in detail within the core ITIL publications.

charter

(*ITIL Service Strategy*) A document that contains details of a new service, a significant change or other significant project. Charters are typically authorized by service portfolio management or by a project management office. The term charter is also used to describe the act of authorizing the work required to complete the service change or project. *See also* change proposal; service charter; project portfolio.

classification

The act of assigning a category to something. Classification is used to ensure consistent management and reporting. Configuration items, incidents, problems, changes etc. are usually classified.

client

A generic term that means a customer, the business or a business customer. For example, client manager may be used as a synonym for business relationship manager. The term is also used to mean:

- A computer that is used directly by a user – for example, a PC, a handheld computer or a work station
- The part of a client server application that the user directly interfaces with – for example, an email client.

closed

(*ITIL Service Operation*) The final status in the lifecycle of an incident, problem, change etc. When the status is closed, no further action is taken.

closure

(*ITIL Service Operation*) The act of changing the status of an incident, problem, change etc. to closed.

COBIT

(*ITIL Continual Service Improvement*) Control OBjectives for Information and related Technology (COBIT) provides guidance and best practice for the management of IT processes. COBIT is published by ISACA in conjunction with the IT Governance Institute (ITGI). See www.isaca.org for more information.

code of practice

A guideline published by a public body or a standards organization, such as ISO or BSI. Many standards consist of a code of practice and a specification. The code of practice describes recommended best practice.

commercial off the shelf (COTS)

(*ITIL Service Design*) Pre-existing application software or middleware that can be purchased from a third party.

compliance

Ensuring that a standard or set of guidelines is followed, or that proper, consistent accounting or other practices are being employed.

component

A general term that is used to mean one part of something more complex. For example, a computer system may be a component of an IT service; an application may be a component of a release unit. Components that need to be managed should be configuration items.

component capacity management (CCM)

(*ITIL Continual Service Improvement*) (*ITIL Service Design*) The sub-process of capacity management responsible for understanding the capacity, utilization and performance of configuration items. Data is collected, recorded and analysed for use in the capacity plan. *See also* business capacity management; service capacity management.

component CI

(*ITIL Service Transition*) A configuration item that is part of an assembly. For example, a CPU or memory CI may be part of a server CI.

confidentiality

(*ITIL Service Design*) A security principle that requires that data should only be accessed by authorized people.

configuration

(*ITIL Service Transition*) A generic term used to describe a group of configuration items that work together to deliver an IT service, or a recognizable part of an IT service. Configuration is also used to describe the parameter settings for one or more configuration items.

configuration baseline

(*ITIL Service Transition*) The baseline of a configuration that has been formally agreed and is managed through the change management process. A configuration baseline is used as a basis for future builds, releases and changes.

configuration item (CI)

(*ITIL Service Transition*) Any component or other service asset that needs to be managed in order to deliver an IT service. Information about each configuration item is recorded in a configuration record within the configuration management system and is maintained throughout its lifecycle by service asset and configuration management. Configuration items are under the control of change management. They typically include IT services, hardware, software, buildings, people and formal documentation such as process documentation and service level agreements.

configuration management

See service asset and configuration management.

configuration management database (CMBD)

(*ITIL Service Transition*) A database used to store configuration records throughout their lifecycle. The configuration management system maintains one or more configuration management databases, and each database stores attributes of configuration items, and relationships with other configuration items.

configuration management system (CMS)

(*ITIL Service Transition*) A set of tools, data and information that is used to support service asset and configuration management. The CMS is part of an overall service knowledge management system and includes tools for collecting, storing, managing, updating, analysing and presenting data about all configuration items and their relationships. The CMS may also include information about incidents, problems, known errors, changes and releases. The CMS is maintained by service asset and configuration management and is used by all IT service management processes. *See also* configuration management database.

configuration record

(*ITIL Service Transition*) A record containing the details of a configuration item. Each configuration record documents the lifecycle of a single configuration item. Configuration records are stored in a configuration management database and maintained as part of a configuration management system.

continual service improvement (CSI)

(*ITIL Continual Service Improvement*) A stage in the lifecycle of a service. Continual service improvement ensures that services are aligned with changing business needs by identifying and implementing improvements to IT services that support business processes. The performance of the IT service provider is continually measured and improvements are made to processes, IT services and IT infrastructure in order to increase efficiency, effectiveness and cost effectiveness. Continual service improvement includes the seven-step improvement process. Although this process is associated with continual service improvement, most processes have activities that take place across multiple stages of the service lifecycle. *See also* Plan-Do-Check-Act.

contract

A legally binding agreement between two or more parties.

control

A means of managing a risk, ensuring that a business objective is achieved or that a process is followed. Examples of control include policies, procedures, roles, RAID, door locks etc. A control is sometimes called a countermeasure or safeguard. Control also means to manage the utilization or behaviour of a configuration item, system or IT service.

Control OBjectives for Information and related Technology

See COBIT.

control perspective

(*ITIL Service Strategy*) An approach to the management of IT services, processes, functions, assets etc. There can be several different control perspectives on the same IT service, process etc., allowing different individuals or teams to focus on what is important and relevant to their specific role. Examples of control perspective include reactive and proactive management within IT operations, or a lifecycle view for an application project team.

control processes

The ISO/IEC 20000 process group that includes change management and configuration management.

core service

(*ITIL Service Strategy*) A service that delivers the basic outcomes desired by one or more customers. A core service provides a specific level of utility and warranty. Customers may be offered a choice of utility and warranty through one or more service options. *See also* enabling service; enhancing service; IT service; service package.

cost

The amount of money spent on a specific activity, IT service or business unit. Costs consist of real cost (money), notional cost (such as people's time) and depreciation.

cost benefit analysis

An activity that analyses and compares the costs and the benefits involved in one or more alternative courses of action. *See also* business case; internal rate of return; net present value; return on investment; value on investment.

cost centre

(*ITIL Service Strategy*) A business unit or project to which costs are assigned. A cost centre does not charge for services provided. An IT service provider can be run as a cost centre or a profit centre.

cost element

(*ITIL Service Strategy*) The middle level of category to which costs are assigned in budgeting and accounting. The highest-level category is cost type. For example, a cost type of 'people' could have cost elements of payroll, staff benefits, expenses, training, overtime etc. Cost elements can be further broken down to give cost units. For example, the cost element 'expenses' could include cost units of hotels, transport, meals etc.

cost management

(*ITIL Service Strategy*) A general term that is used to refer to budgeting and accounting, and is sometimes used as a synonym for financial management.

cost model

(*ITIL Service Strategy*) A framework used in budgeting and accounting in which all known costs can be recorded, categorized and allocated to specific customers, business units or projects. *See also* cost type; cost element; cost unit.

cost type

(*ITIL Service Strategy*) The highest level of category to which costs are assigned in budgeting and accounting – for example, hardware, software, people, accommodation, external and transfer. *See also* cost element; cost unit.

cost unit

(*ITIL Service Strategy*) The lowest level of category to which costs are assigned, cost units are usually things that can be easily counted (e.g. staff numbers, software licences) or things easily measured (e.g. CPU usage, electricity consumed). Cost units are included within cost elements. For example, a cost element of 'expenses' could include cost units of hotels, transport, meals etc. *See also* cost type.

cost effectiveness

A measure of the balance between the effectiveness and cost of a service, process or activity. A cost-effective process is one that achieves its objectives at minimum cost. *See also* key performance indicator; return on investment; value for money.

countermeasure

Can be used to refer to any type of control. The term is most often used when referring to measures that increase resilience, fault tolerance or reliability of an IT service.

course corrections

Changes made to a plan or activity that has already started to ensure that it will meet its objectives. Course corrections are made as a result of monitoring progress.

crisis management

Crisis management is the process responsible for managing the wider implications of business continuity. A crisis management team is responsible for strategic issues such as managing media relations and shareholder confidence, and decides when to invoke business continuity plans.

critical success factor (CSF)

Something that must happen if an IT service, process, plan, project or other activity is to succeed. Key performance indicators are used to measure the achievement of each critical success factor. For example, a critical success factor of 'protect IT services when making changes' could be measured by key performance indicators such as 'percentage reduction of unsuccessful changes', 'percentage reduction in changes causing incidents' etc.

CSI register

(*ITIL Continual Service Improvement*) A database or structured document used to record and manage improvement opportunities throughout their lifecycle.

culture

A set of values that is shared by a group of people, including expectations about how people should behave, their ideas, beliefs and practices. *See also* vision.

customer

Someone who buys goods or services. The customer of an IT service provider is the person or group who defines and agrees the service level targets. The term is also sometimes used informally to mean user – for example, 'This is a customer-focused organization.'

customer asset

Any resource or capability of a customer. *See also* asset.

customer agreement portfolio

(*ITIL Service Strategy*) A database or structured document used to manage service contracts or agreements between an IT service provider and its customers. Each IT service delivered to a customer should have a contract or other agreement that is listed in the customer agreement portfolio. *See also* customer-facing service; service catalogue; service portfolio.

customer portfolio

(*ITIL Service Strategy*) A database or structured document used to record all customers of the IT service provider. The customer portfolio is the business relationship manager's view of the customers who receive services from the IT service provider. *See also* customer agreement portfolio; service catalogue; service portfolio.

customer-facing service

(*ITIL Service Design*) An IT service that is visible to the customer. These are normally services that support the customer's business processes and facilitate one or more outcomes desired by the customer. All live customer-facing services, including those available for deployment, are recorded in the service catalogue along with customer-visible information about deliverables, prices, contact points, ordering and request processes. Other information such as relationships to supporting services and other CIs will also be recorded for internal use by the IT service provider.

dashboard

(*ITIL Service Operation*) A graphical representation of overall IT service performance and availability. Dashboard images may be updated in real time, and can also be included in management reports and web pages. Dashboards can be used to support service level management, event management and incident diagnosis.

Data-To-Information-To-Knowledge-To-Wisdom (DIKW)

(*ITIL Service Transition*) A way of understanding the relationships between data, information, knowledge and wisdom. DIKW shows how each of these builds on the others.

deliverable

Something that must be provided to meet a commitment in a service level agreement or a contract. It is also used in a more informal way to mean a planned output of any process.

demand management

(*ITIL Service Design*) (*ITIL Service Strategy*) The process responsible for understanding, anticipating and influencing customer demand for services. Demand management works with capacity management to ensure that the service provider has sufficient capacity to meet the required demand. At a strategic level, demand management can involve analysis of patterns of business activity and user profiles, while at a tactical level, it can involve the use of differential charging to encourage customers to use IT services at less busy times, or require short-term activities to respond to unexpected demand or the failure of a configuration item.

Deming cycle

See Plan-Do-Check-Act.

dependency

The direct or indirect reliance of one process or activity on another.

deployment

(*ITIL Service Transition*) The activity responsible for movement of new or changed hardware, software, documentation, process etc. to the live environment. Deployment is part of the release and deployment management process.

depreciation

(*ITIL Service Strategy*) A measure of the reduction in value of an asset over its life. This is based on wearing out, consumption or other reduction in the useful economic value.

design

(*ITIL Service Design*) An activity or process that identifies requirements and then defines a solution that is able to meet these requirements. *See also* service design.

design coordination

(*ITIL Service Design*) The process responsible for coordinating all service design activities, processes and resources. Design coordination ensures the consistent and effective design of new or changed IT services, service management information systems, architectures, technology, processes, information and metrics.

detection

(*ITIL Service Operation*) A stage in the expanded incident lifecycle. Detection results in the incident becoming known to the service provider. Detection can be automatic or the result of a user logging an incident.

development

(*ITIL Service Design*) The process responsible for creating or modifying an IT service or application ready for subsequent release and deployment. Development is also used to mean the role or function that carries out development work. This process is not described in detail within the core ITIL publications.

diagnosis

(*ITIL Service Operation*) A stage in the incident and problem lifecycles. The purpose of diagnosis is to identify a workaround for an incident or the root cause of a problem.

differential charging

A technique used to support demand management by charging different amounts for the same function of an IT service under different circumstances. For example, reduced charges outside peak times, or increased charges for users who exceed a bandwidth allocation.

direct cost

(*ITIL Service Strategy*) The cost of providing an IT service which can be allocated in full to a specific customer, cost centre, project etc. For example, the cost of providing non-shared servers or software licences. *See also* indirect cost.

directory service

(*ITIL Service Operation*) An application that manages information about IT infrastructure available on a network, and corresponding user access rights.

document

Information in readable form. A document may be paper or electronic – for example, a policy statement, service level agreement, incident record or diagram of a computer room layout. *See also* record.

downtime

(*ITIL Service Design*) (*ITIL Service Operation*) The time when an IT service or other configuration item is not available during its agreed service time. The availability of an IT service is often calculated from agreed service time and downtime.

driver

Something that influences strategy, objectives or requirements – for example, new legislation or the actions of competitors.

early life support (ELS)

(*ITIL Service Transition*) A stage in the service lifecycle that occurs at the end of deployment and before the service is fully accepted into operation. During early life support, the service provider reviews key performance indicators, service levels and monitoring thresholds and may implement improvements to ensure that service targets can be met. The service provider may also provide additional resources for incident and problem management during this time.

economies of scale

(*ITIL Service Strategy*) The reduction in average cost that is possible from increasing the usage of an IT service or asset. *See also* economies of scope.

economies of scope

(*ITIL Service Strategy*) The reduction in cost that is allocated to an IT service by using an existing asset for an additional purpose. For example, delivering a new IT service from an existing IT infrastructure. *See also* economies of scale.

effectiveness

(*ITIL Continual Service Improvement*) A measure of whether the objectives of a process, service or activity have been achieved. An effective process or activity is one that achieves its agreed objectives. *See also* key performance indicator.

efficiency

(*ITIL Continual Service Improvement*) A measure of whether the right amount of resource has been used to deliver a process, service or activity. An efficient process achieves its objectives with the minimum amount of time, money, people or other resources. *See also* key performance indicator.

enabling service

(*ITIL Service Strategy*) A service that is needed in order to deliver a core service. Enabling services may or may not be visible to the customer, but they are not offered to customers in their own right. *See also* enhancing service.

enhancing service

(*ITIL Service Strategy*) A service that is added to a core service to make it more attractive to the customer. Enhancing services are not essential to the delivery of a core service but are used to encourage customers to use the core services or to differentiate the service provider from its competitors. *See also* enabling service; excitement factor.

enterprise financial management

(*ITIL Service Strategy*) The function and processes responsible for managing the overall organization's budgeting, accounting and charging requirements. Enterprise financial management is sometimes referred to as the 'corporate' financial department. *See also* financial management for IT services.

environment

(*ITIL Service Transition*) A subset of the IT infrastructure that is used for a particular purpose – for example, live environment, test environment, build environment. Also used in the term 'physical environment' to mean the accommodation, air conditioning, power system etc. Environment is used as a generic term to mean the external conditions that influence or affect something.

error

(*ITIL Service Operation*) A design flaw or malfunction that causes a failure of one or more IT services or other configuration items. A mistake made by a person or a faulty process that impacts a configuration item is also an error.

escalation

(*ITIL Service Operation*) An activity that obtains additional resources when these are needed to meet service level targets or customer expectations. Escalation may be needed within any IT service management process, but is most commonly associated with incident management, problem management and the management of customer complaints. There are two types of escalation: functional escalation and hierarchic escalation.

eSourcing Capability Model for Client Organizations (eSCM-CL)

(*ITIL Service Strategy*) A framework to help organizations in their analysis and decision-making on service sourcing models and strategies. It was developed by Carnegie Mellon University in the US. *See also* eSourcing Capability Model for Service Providers.

eSourcing Capability Model for Service Providers (eSCM-SP)

(*ITIL Service Strategy*) A framework to help IT service providers develop their IT service management capabilities from a service sourcing perspective. It was developed by Carnegie Mellon University in the US. *See also* eSourcing Capability Model for Client Organizations.

estimation

The use of experience to provide an approximate value for a metric or cost. Estimation is also used in capacity and availability management as the cheapest and least accurate modelling method.

event

(*ITIL Service Operation*) A change of state that has significance for the management of an IT service or other configuration item. The term is also used to mean an alert or notification created by any IT service, configuration item or monitoring tool. Events typically require IT operations personnel to take actions, and often lead to incidents being logged.

event management

(*ITIL Service Operation*) The process responsible for managing events throughout their lifecycle. Event management is one of the main activities of IT operations.

excitement attribute

See excitement factor.

excitement factor

(*ITIL Service Strategy*) An attribute added to something to make it more attractive or more exciting to the customer. For example, a restaurant may provide a free drink with every meal. *See also* enhancing service.

external customer

A customer who works for a different business from the IT service provider. *See also* external service provider; internal customer.

external service provider

(*ITIL Service Strategy*) An IT service provider that is part of a different organization from its customer. An IT service provider may have both internal and external customers. *See also* outsourcing; Type III service provider.

facilities management

(*ITIL Service Operation*) The function responsible for managing the physical environment where the IT infrastructure is located. Facilities management includes all aspects of managing the physical environment – for example, power and cooling, building access management, and environmental monitoring.

failure

(*ITIL Service Operation*) Loss of ability to operate to specification, or to deliver the required output. The term may be used when referring to IT services, processes, activities, configuration items etc. A failure often causes an incident.

fault

See error.

fault tolerance

(*ITIL Service Design*) The ability of an IT service or other configuration item to continue to operate correctly after failure of a component part. *See also* countermeasure; resilience.

financial management

(*ITIL Service Strategy*) A generic term used to describe the function and processes responsible for managing an organization's budgeting, accounting and charging requirements. Enterprise financial management is the specific term used to describe the function and processes from the perspective of the overall organization. Financial management for IT services is the specific term used to describe the function and processes from the perspective of the IT service provider.

financial management for IT services

(*ITIL Service Strategy*) The function and processes responsible for managing an IT service provider's budgeting, accounting and charging requirements. Financial management for IT services secures an appropriate level of funding to design, develop and deliver services that meet the strategy of the organization in a cost-effective manner. *See also* enterprise financial management.

financial year

(*ITIL Service Strategy*) An accounting period covering 12 consecutive months. A financial year may start on any date (for example, 1 April to 31 March).

fit for purpose

(*ITIL Service Strategy*) The ability to meet an agreed level of utility. Fit for purpose is also used informally to describe a process, configuration item, IT service etc. that is capable of meeting its objectives or service levels. Being fit for purpose requires suitable design, implementation, control and maintenance.

fit for use

(*ITIL Service Strategy*) The ability to meet an agreed level of warranty. Being fit for use requires suitable design, implementation, control and maintenance.

fixed asset

(*ITIL Service Transition*) A tangible business asset that has a long-term useful life (for example, a building, a piece of land, a server or a software licence). *See also* service asset; configuration item.

fixed asset management

(*ITIL Service Transition*) The process responsible for tracking and reporting the value and ownership of fixed assets throughout their lifecycle. Fixed asset management maintains the asset register and is usually carried out by the overall business, rather than by the IT organization. Fixed asset management is sometimes called financial asset management and is not described in detail within the core ITIL publications.

fixed cost

(*ITIL Service Strategy*) A cost that does not vary with IT service usage – for example, the cost of server hardware. *See also* variable cost.

fulfilment

Performing activities to meet a need or requirement – for example, by providing a new IT service, or meeting a service request.

function

A team or group of people and the tools or other resources they use to carry out one or more processes or activities – for example, the service desk. The term also has two other meanings:

- An intended purpose of a configuration item, person, team, process or IT service. For example, one function of an email service may be to store and forward outgoing mails, while the function of a business process may be to despatch goods to customers.
- To perform the intended purpose correctly, as in 'The computer is functioning.'

gap analysis

(*ITIL Continual Service Improvement*) An activity that compares two sets of data and identifies the differences. Gap analysis is commonly used to compare a set of requirements with actual delivery. *See also* benchmarking.

governance

Ensures that policies and strategy are actually implemented, and that required processes are correctly followed. Governance includes defining roles and responsibilities, measuring and reporting, and taking actions to resolve any issues identified.

guideline

A document describing best practice, which recommends what should be done. Compliance with a guideline is not normally enforced. *See also* standard.

identity

(*ITIL Service Operation*) A unique name that is used to identify a user, person or role. The identity is used to grant rights to that user, person or role. Example identities might be the username SmithJ or the role 'change manager'.

impact

(*ITIL Service Operation*) (*ITIL Service Transition*) A measure of the effect of an incident, problem or change on business processes. Impact is often based on how service levels will be affected. Impact and urgency are used to assign priority.

incident

(*ITIL Service Operation*) An unplanned interruption to an IT service or reduction in the quality of an IT service. Failure of a configuration item that has not yet affected service is also an incident – for example, failure of one disk from a mirror set.

incident management

(*ITIL Service Operation*) The process responsible for managing the lifecycle of all incidents. Incident management ensures that normal service operation is restored as quickly as possible and the business impact is minimized.

incident record

(*ITIL Service Operation*) A record containing the details of an incident. Each incident record documents the lifecycle of a single incident.

indirect cost

(*ITIL Service Strategy*) The cost of providing an IT service which cannot be allocated in full to a specific customer – for example, the cost of providing shared servers or software licences. Also known as overhead. *See also* direct cost.

information security management (ISM)

(*ITIL Service Design*) The process responsible for ensuring that the confidentiality, integrity and availability of an organization's assets, information, data and IT services match the agreed needs of the business. Information security management supports business security and has a wider scope than that of the IT service provider, and includes handling of paper, building access, phone calls etc. for the entire organization. *See also* security management information system.

information security management system (ISMS)

(*ITIL Service Design*) The framework of policy, processes, functions, standards, guidelines and tools that ensures an organization can achieve its information security management objectives. *See also* security management information system.

information system

See management information system.

information technology (IT)

The use of technology for the storage, communication or processing of information. The technology typically includes computers, telecommunications, applications and other software. The information may include business data, voice, images, video etc. Information technology is often used to support business processes through IT services.

infrastructure service

A type of supporting service that provides hardware, network or other data centre components. The term is also used as a synonym for supporting service.

insourcing

(*ITIL Service Strategy*) Using an internal service provider to manage IT services. The term insourcing is also used to describe the act of transferring the provision of an IT service from an external service provider to an internal service provider. *See also* service sourcing.

integrity

(*ITIL Service Design*) A security principle that ensures data and configuration items are modified only by authorized personnel and activities. Integrity considers all possible causes of modification, including software and hardware failure, environmental events, and human intervention.

internal customer

A customer who works for the same business as the IT service provider. *See also* external customer; internal service provider.

internal rate of return (IRR)

(*ITIL Service Strategy*) A technique used to help make decisions about capital expenditure. It calculates a figure that allows two or more alternative investments to be compared. A larger internal rate of return indicates a better investment. *See also* net present value; return on investment.

internal service provider

(*ITIL Service Strategy*) An IT service provider that is part of the same organization as its customer. An IT service provider may have both internal and external customers. *See also* insourcing; Type I service provider; Type II service provider.

International Organization for Standardization (ISO)

The International Organization for Standardization (ISO) is the world's largest developer of standards. ISO is a non-governmental organization that is a network of the national standards institutes of 156 countries. See www.iso.org for further information about ISO.

International Standards Organization

See International Organization for Standardization.

internet service provider (ISP)

An external service provider that provides access to the internet. Most ISPs also provide other IT services such as web hosting.

ISO 9000

A generic term that refers to a number of international standards and guidelines for quality management systems. See www.iso.org for more information. *See also* International Organization for Standardization.

ISO 9001

An international standard for quality management systems. *See also* ISO 9000; standard.

ISO/IEC 20000

An international standard for IT service management.

ISO/IEC 27001

(*ITIL Continual Service Improvement*) (*ITIL Service Design*) An international specification for information security management. The corresponding code of practice is ISO/IEC 27002. *See also* standard.

IT accounting

See accounting.

IT infrastructure

All of the hardware, software, networks, facilities etc. that are required to develop, test, deliver, monitor, control or support applications and IT services. The term includes all of the information technology but not the associated people, processes and documentation.

IT operations

(*ITIL Service Operation*) Activities carried out by IT operations control, including console management/ operations bridge, job scheduling, backup and restore, and print and output management. IT operations is also used as a synonym for service operation.

IT operations control

(*ITIL Service Operation*) The function responsible for monitoring and control of the IT services and IT infrastructure. *See also* operations bridge.

IT operations management

(*ITIL Service Operation*) The function within an IT service provider that performs the daily activities needed to manage IT services and the supporting IT infrastructure. IT operations management includes IT operations control and facilities management.

IT service

A service provided by an IT service provider. An IT service is made up of a combination of information technology, people and processes. A customer-facing IT service directly supports the business processes of one or more customers and its service level targets should be defined in a service level agreement. Other IT services, called supporting services, are not directly used by the business but are required by the service provider to deliver customer-facing services. *See also* core service; enabling service; enhancing service; service; service package.

IT service continuity management (ITSCM)

(*ITIL Service Design*) The process responsible for managing risks that could seriously affect IT services. IT service continuity management ensures that the IT service provider can always provide minimum agreed service levels, by reducing the risk to an acceptable level and planning for the recovery of IT services. IT service continuity management supports business continuity management.

IT service management (ITSM)

The implementation and management of quality IT services that meet the needs of the business. IT service management is performed by IT service providers through an appropriate mix of people, process and information technology. *See also* service management.

IT Service Management Forum (itSMF)

The IT Service Management Forum is an independent organization dedicated to promoting a professional approach to IT service management. The itSMF is a not-for-profit membership organization with representation in many countries around the world (itSMF chapters). The itSMF and its membership contribute to the development of ITIL and associated IT service management standards. See www.itsmf.com for more information.

IT service provider

(*ITIL Service Strategy*) A service provider that provides IT services to internal or external customers.

IT steering group (ISG)

(*ITIL Service Design*) (*ITIL Service Strategy*) A formal group that is responsible for ensuring that business and IT service provider strategies and plans are closely aligned. An IT steering group includes senior representatives from the business and the IT service provider. Also known as IT strategy group or IT steering committee.

ITIL

A set of best-practice publications for IT service management. Owned by the Cabinet Office (part of HM Government), ITIL gives guidance on the provision of quality IT services and the processes, functions and other capabilities needed to support them. The ITIL framework is based on a service lifecycle and consists of five lifecycle stages (service strategy, service design, service transition, service operation and continual service improvement), each of which has its own supporting publication. There is also a set of complementary ITIL publications providing guidance specific to industry sectors, organization types, operating models and technology architectures. See www.itil-officialsite.com for more information.

job description

A document that defines the roles, responsibilities, skills and knowledge required by a particular person. One job description can include multiple roles – for example, the roles of configuration manager and change manager may be carried out by one person.

Kano model

(*ITIL Service Strategy*) A model developed by Noriaki Kano that is used to help understand customer preferences. The Kano model considers attributes of an IT service grouped into areas such as basic factors, excitement factors, performance factors etc.

key performance indicator (KPI)

(*ITIL Continual Service Improvement*) (*ITIL Service Design*) A metric that is used to help manage an IT service, process, plan, project or other activity. Key performance indicators are used to measure the achievement of critical success factors. Many metrics may be measured, but only the most important of these are defined as key performance indicators and used to actively manage and report on the process, IT service or activity. They should be selected to ensure that efficiency, effectiveness and cost effectiveness are all managed.

knowledge base

(*ITIL Service Transition*) A logical database containing data and information used by the service knowledge management system.

knowledge management

(*ITIL Service Transition*) The process responsible for sharing perspectives, ideas, experience and information, and for ensuring that these are available in the right place and at the right time. The knowledge management process enables informed decisions, and improves efficiency by reducing the need to rediscover knowledge. *See also* Data-to-Information-to-Knowledge-to-Wisdom; service knowledge management system.

known error

(*ITIL Service Operation*) A problem that has a documented root cause and a workaround. Known errors are created and managed throughout their lifecycle by problem management. Known errors may also be identified by development or suppliers.

lifecycle

The various stages in the life of an IT service, configuration item, incident, problem, change etc. The lifecycle defines the categories for status and the status transitions that are permitted. For example:

- The lifecycle of an application includes requirements, design, build, deploy, operate, optimize
- The expanded incident lifecycle includes detection, diagnosis, repair, recovery and restoration
- The lifecycle of a server may include: ordered, received, in test, live, disposed etc.

line of service (LOS)

(*ITIL Service Strategy*) A core service or service package that has multiple service options. A line of service is managed by a service owner and each service option is designed to support a particular market segment.

live

(*ITIL Service Transition*) Refers to an IT service or other configuration item that is being used to deliver service to a customer.

live environment

(*ITIL Service Transition*) A controlled environment containing live configuration items used to deliver IT services to customers.

maintainability

(*ITIL Service Design*) A measure of how quickly and effectively an IT service or other configuration item can be restored to normal working after a failure. Maintainability is often measured and reported as MTRS. Maintainability is also used in the context of software or IT service development to mean ability to be changed or repaired easily.

major incident

(*ITIL Service Operation*) The highest category of impact for an incident. A major incident results in significant disruption to the business.

manageability

An informal measure of how easily and effectively an IT service or other component can be managed.

management information

Information that is used to support decision making by managers. Management information is often generated automatically by tools supporting the various IT service management processes. Management information often includes the values of key performance indicators, such as 'percentage of changes leading to incidents' or 'first-time fix rate'.

management information system (MIS)

(*ITIL Service Design*) A set of tools, data and information that is used to support a process or function. Examples include the availability management information system and the supplier and contract management information system. *See also* service knowledge management system.

Management of Risk (M_o_R)

M_o_R includes all the activities required to identify and control the exposure to risk, which may have an impact on the achievement of an organization's business objectives. See www.mor-officialsite.com for more details.

management system

The framework of policy, processes, functions, standards, guidelines and tools that ensures an organization or part of an organization can achieve its objectives. This term is also used with a smaller scope to support a specific process or activity – for example, an event management system or risk management system. *See also* system.

marginal cost

(*ITIL Service Strategy*) The increase or decrease in the cost of producing one more, or one less, unit of output – for example, the cost of supporting an additional user.

market space

(*ITIL Service Strategy*) Opportunities that an IT service provider could exploit to meet the business needs of customers. Market spaces identify the possible IT services that an IT service provider may wish to consider delivering.

maturity

(*ITIL Continual Service Improvement*) A measure of the reliability, efficiency and effectiveness of a process, function, organization etc. The most mature processes and functions are formally aligned to business objectives and strategy, and are supported by a framework for continual improvement.

maturity level

A named level in a maturity model, such as the Carnegie Mellon Capability Maturity Model Integration.

metric

(*ITIL Continual Service Improvement*) Something that is measured and reported to help manage a process, IT service or activity. *See also* key performance indicator.

middleware

(*ITIL Service Design*) Software that connects two or more software components or applications. Middleware is usually purchased from a supplier, rather than developed within the IT service provider. *See also* commercial off the shelf.

mission

A short but complete description of the overall purpose and intentions of an organization. It states what is to be achieved, but not how this should be done. *See also* vision.

model

A representation of a system, process, IT service, configuration item etc. that is used to help understand or predict future behaviour.

modelling

A technique that is used to predict the future behaviour of a system, process, IT service, configuration item etc. Modelling is commonly used in financial management, capacity management and availability management.

monitoring

(*ITIL Service Operation*) Repeated observation of a configuration item, IT service or process to detect events and to ensure that the current status is known.

near-shore

(*ITIL Service Strategy*) Provision of services from a country near the country where the customer is based. This can be the provision of an IT service, or of supporting functions such as a service desk. *See also* offshore; onshore.

net present value (NPV)

(*ITIL Service Strategy*) A technique used to help make decisions about capital expenditure. It compares cash inflows with cash outflows. Positive net present value indicates that an investment is worthwhile. *See also* internal rate of return; return on investment.

normal change

(*ITIL Service Transition*) A change that is not an emergency change or a standard change. Normal changes follow the defined steps of the change management process.

notional charging

(*ITIL Service Strategy*) An approach to charging for IT services. Charges to customers are calculated and customers are informed of the charge, but no money is actually transferred. Notional charging is sometimes introduced to ensure that customers are aware of the costs they incur, or as a stage during the introduction of real charging.

objective

The outcomes required from a process, activity or organization in order to ensure that its purpose will be fulfilled. Objectives are usually expressed as measurable targets. The term is also informally used to mean a requirement.

off the shelf

See commercial off the shelf.

Office of Government Commerce (OGC)

OGC (former owner of Best Management Practice) and its functions have moved into the Cabinet Office as part of HM Government. See www.cabinetoffice.gov.uk

offshore

(*ITIL Service Strategy*) Provision of services from a location outside the country where the customer is based, often in a different continent. This can be the provision of an IT service, or of supporting functions such as a service desk. *See also* near-shore; onshore.

onshore

(*ITIL Service Strategy*) Provision of services from a location within the country where the customer is based. *See also* near-shore; offshore.

operate

To perform as expected. A process or configuration item is said to operate if it is delivering the required outputs. Operate also means to perform one or more operations. For example, to operate a computer is to do the day-to-day operations needed for it to perform as expected.

operation

(*ITIL Service Operation*) Day-to-day management of an IT service, system or other configuration item. Operation is also used to mean any predefined activity or transaction – for example, loading a magnetic tape, accepting money at a point of sale, or reading data from a disk drive.

operational

The lowest of three levels of planning and delivery (strategic, tactical, operational). Operational activities include the day-to-day or short-term planning or delivery of a business process or IT service management process. The term is also a synonym for live.

operational cost

The cost resulting from running the IT services, which often involves repeating payments – for example, staff costs, hardware maintenance and electricity (also known as current expenditure or revenue expenditure). *See also* capital expenditure.

operational expenditure (OPEX)

See operational cost.

operational level agreement (OLA)

(*ITIL Continual Service Improvement*) (*ITIL Service Design*) An agreement between an IT service provider and another part of the same organization. It supports the IT service provider's delivery of IT services to customers and defines the goods or services to be provided and the responsibilities of both parties. For example, there could be an operational level agreement:

- Between the IT service provider and a procurement department to obtain hardware in agreed times
- Between the service desk and a support group to provide incident resolution in agreed times.

See also service level agreement.

operations bridge

(*ITIL Service Operation*) A physical location where IT services and IT infrastructure are monitored and managed.

operations control

See IT operations control.

operations management

See IT operations management.

opportunity cost

(*ITIL Service Strategy*) A cost that is used in deciding between investment choices. Opportunity cost represents the revenue that would have been generated by using the resources in a different way. For example, the opportunity cost of purchasing a new server may include not carrying out a service improvement activity that the money could have been spent on. Opportunity cost analysis is used as part of a decision-making process, but opportunity cost is not treated as an actual cost in any financial statement.

optimize

Review, plan and request changes, in order to obtain the maximum efficiency and effectiveness from a process, configuration item, application etc.

organization

A company, legal entity or other institution. The term is sometimes used to refer to any entity that has people, resources and budgets – for example, a project or business unit.

outcome

The result of carrying out an activity, following a process, or delivering an IT service etc. The term is used to refer to intended results as well as to actual results. *See also* objective.

outsourcing

(*ITIL Service Strategy*) Using an external service provider to manage IT services. *See also* service sourcing.

overhead

See indirect cost.

Pareto principle

(*ITIL Service Operation*) A technique used to prioritize activities. The Pareto principle says that 80% of the value of any activity is created with 20% of the effort. Pareto analysis is also used in problem management to prioritize possible problem causes for investigation.

partnership

A relationship between two organizations that involves working closely together for common goals or mutual benefit. The IT service provider should have a partnership with the business and with third parties who are critical to the delivery of IT services. *See also* value network.

pattern of business activity (PBA)

(*ITIL Service Strategy*) A workload profile of one or more business activities. Patterns of business activity are used to help the IT service provider understand and plan for different levels of business activity. *See also* user profile.

performance

A measure of what is achieved or delivered by a system, person, team, process or IT service.

performance management

Activities to ensure that something achieves its expected outcomes in an efficient and consistent manner.

pilot

(*ITIL Service Transition*) A limited deployment of an IT service, a release or a process to the live environment. A pilot is used to reduce risk and to gain user feedback and acceptance. *See also* change evaluation; test.

plan

A detailed proposal that describes the activities and resources needed to achieve an objective – for example, a plan to implement a new IT service or process. ISO/IEC 20000 requires a plan for the management of each IT service management process.

Plan-Do-Check-Act (PDCA)

(*ITIL Continual Service Improvement*) A four-stage cycle for process management, attributed to Edward Deming. **Plan**-Do-Check-Act is also called the Deming Cycle. Plan – design or revise processes that support the IT services; **Do** – implement the plan and manage the processes; **Check** – measure the processes and IT services, compare with objectives and produce reports; **Act** – plan and implement changes to improve the processes.

planning

An activity responsible for creating one or more plans – for example, capacity planning.

policy

Formally documented management expectations and intentions. Policies are used to direct decisions, and to ensure consistent and appropriate development and implementation of processes, standards, roles, activities, IT infrastructure etc.

post-implementation review (PIR)

A review that takes place after a change or a project has been implemented. It determines if the change or project was successful, and identifies opportunities for improvement.

practice

A way of working, or a way in which work must be done. Practices can include activities, processes, functions, standards and guidelines. *See also* best practice.

pricing

(*ITIL Service Strategy*) Pricing is the activity for establishing how much customers will be charged.

PRINCE2

See PRojects IN Controlled Environments.

priority

(*ITIL Service Operation*) (*ITIL Service Transition*) A category used to identify the relative importance of an incident, problem or change. Priority is based on impact and urgency, and is used to identify required times for actions to be taken. For example, the service level agreement may state that Priority 2 incidents must be resolved within 12 hours.

problem

(*ITIL Service Operation*) A cause of one or more incidents. The cause is not usually known at the time a problem record is created, and the problem management process is responsible for further investigation.

problem management

(*ITIL Service Operation*) The process responsible for managing the lifecycle of all problems. Problem management proactively prevents incidents from happening and minimizes the impact of incidents that cannot be prevented.

procedure

A document containing steps that specify how to achieve an activity. Procedures are defined as part of processes. *See also* work instruction.

process

A structured set of activities designed to accomplish a specific objective. A process takes one or more defined inputs and turns them into defined outputs. It may include any of the roles, responsibilities, tools and management controls required to reliably deliver the outputs. A process may define policies, standards, guidelines, activities and work instructions if they are needed.

process control

The activity of planning and regulating a process, with the objective of performing the process in an effective, efficient and consistent manner.

process manager

A role responsible for the operational management of a process. The process manager's responsibilities include planning and coordination of all activities required to carry out, monitor and report on the process. There may be several process managers for one process – for example, regional change managers or IT service continuity managers for each data centre. The process manager role is often assigned to the person who carries out the process owner role, but the two roles may be separate in larger organizations.

process owner

The person who is held accountable for ensuring that a process is fit for purpose. The process owner's responsibilities include sponsorship, design, change management and continual improvement of the process and its metrics. This role can be assigned to the same person who carries out the process manager role, but the two roles may be separate in larger organizations.

production environment

See live environment.

profit centre

(*ITIL Service Strategy*) A business unit that charges for services provided. A profit centre can be created with the objective of making a profit, recovering costs, or running at a loss. An IT service provider can be run as a cost centre or a profit centre.

programme

A number of projects and activities that are planned and managed together to achieve an overall set of related objectives and other outcomes.

project

A temporary organization, with people and other assets, that is required to achieve an objective or other outcome. Each project has a lifecycle that typically includes initiation, planning, execution, and closure. Projects are usually managed using a formal methodology such as PRojects IN Controlled Environments (PRINCE2) or the Project Management Body of Knowledge (PMBOK). *See also* charter; project management office; project portfolio.

project charter

See charter.

Project Management Body of Knowledge (PMBOK)

A project management standard maintained and published by the Project Management Institute. See www.pmi.org for more information. *See also* PRojects IN Controlled Environments (PRINCE2).

Project Management Institute (PMI)

A membership association that advances the project management profession through globally recognized standards and certifications, collaborative communities, an extensive research programme, and professional development opportunities. PMI is a not-for-profit membership organization with representation in many countries around the world. PMI maintains and publishes the Project Management Body of Knowledge (PMBOK). See www.pmi.org for more information. *See also* PRojects IN Controlled Environments (PRINCE2).

project management office (PMO)

(*ITIL Service Design*) (*ITIL Service Strategy*) A function or group responsible for managing the lifecycle of projects. *See also* charter; project portfolio.

project portfolio

(*ITIL Service Design*) (*ITIL Service Strategy*) A database or structured document used to manage projects throughout their lifecycle. The project portfolio is used to coordinate projects and ensure that they meet their objectives in a cost-effective and timely manner. In larger organizations, the project portfolio is typically defined and maintained by a project management office. The project portfolio is important to service portfolio management as new services and significant changes are normally managed as projects. *See also* charter.

PRojects IN Controlled Environments (PRINCE2)

The standard UK government methodology for project management. See www.prince-officialsite.com for more information. *See also* Project Management Body of Knowledge (PMBOK).

qualification

(*ITIL Service Transition*) An activity that ensures that the IT infrastructure is appropriate and correctly configured to support an application or IT service. *See also* validation.

quality

The ability of a product, service or process to provide the intended value. For example, a hardware component can be considered to be of high quality if it performs as expected and delivers the required reliability. Process quality also requires an ability to monitor effectiveness and efficiency, and to improve them if necessary. *See also* quality management system.

quality assurance (QA)

(*ITIL Service Transition*) The process responsible for ensuring that the quality of a service, process or other service asset will provide its intended value. Quality assurance is also used to refer to a function or team that performs quality assurance. This process is not described in detail within the core ITIL publications. *See also* service validation and testing.

quality management system (QMS)

(*ITIL Continual Service Improvement*) The framework of policy, processes, functions, standards, guidelines and tools that ensures an organization is of a suitable quality to reliably meet business objectives or service levels. *See also* ISO 9000.

quick win

(*ITIL Continual Service Improvement*) An improvement activity that is expected to provide a return on investment in a short period of time with relatively small cost and effort. *See also* Pareto principle.

RACI

(*ITIL Service Design*) A model used to help define roles and responsibilities. RACI stands for responsible, accountable, consulted and informed.

real charging

(*ITIL Service Strategy*) A charging policy where actual money is transferred from the customer to the IT service provider in payment for the delivery of IT services. *See also* notional charging.

record

A document containing the results or other output from a process or activity. Records are evidence of the fact that an activity took place and may be paper or electronic – for example, an audit report, an incident record or the minutes of a meeting.

recovery

(*ITIL Service Design*) (*ITIL Service Operation*) Returning a configuration item or an IT service to a working state. Recovery of an IT service often includes recovering data to a known consistent state. After recovery, further steps may be needed before the IT service can be made available to the users (restoration).

recovery option

(*ITIL Service Design*) A strategy for responding to an interruption to service. Commonly used strategies are manual workaround, reciprocal arrangement, gradual recovery, intermediate recovery, fast recovery, and immediate recovery. Recovery options may make use of dedicated facilities or third-party facilities shared by multiple businesses.

redundancy

(*ITIL Service Design*) Use of one or more additional configuration items to provide fault tolerance. The term also has a generic meaning of obsolescence, or no longer needed.

relationship

A connection or interaction between two people or things. In business relationship management, it is the interaction between the IT service provider and the business. In service asset and configuration management, it is a link between two configuration items that identifies a dependency or connection between them. For example, applications may be linked to the servers they run on, and IT services have many links to all the configuration items that contribute to that IT service.

release

(*ITIL Service Transition*) One or more changes to an IT service that are built, tested and deployed together. A single release may include changes to hardware, software, documentation, processes and other components.

release and deployment management

(*ITIL Service Transition*) The process responsible for planning, scheduling and controlling the build, test and deployment of releases, and for delivering new functionality required by the business while protecting the integrity of existing services.

release package

(*ITIL Service Transition*) A set of configuration items that will be built, tested and deployed together as a single release. Each release package will usually include one or more release units.

reliability

(*ITIL Continual Service Improvement*) (*ITIL Service Design*) A measure of how long an IT service or other configuration item can perform its agreed function without interruption. Usually measured as MTBF or MTBSI. The term can also be used to state how likely it is that a process, function etc. will deliver its required outputs. *See also* availability.

remediation

(*ITIL Service Transition*) Actions taken to recover after a failed change or release. Remediation may include back-out, invocation of service continuity plans, or other actions designed to enable the business process to continue.

repair

(*ITIL Service Operation*) The replacement or correction of a failed configuration item.

request for change (RFC)

(*ITIL Service Transition*) A formal proposal for a change to be made. It includes details of the proposed change, and may be recorded on paper or electronically. The term is often misused to mean a change record, or the change itself.

request fulfilment

(*ITIL Service Operation*) The process responsible for managing the lifecycle of all service requests.

requirement

(*ITIL Service Design*) A formal statement of what is needed – for example, a service level requirement, a project requirement or the required deliverables for a process. *See also* statement of requirements.

resilience

(*ITIL Service Design*) The ability of an IT service or other configuration item to resist failure or to recover in a timely manner following a failure. For example, an armoured cable will resist failure when put under stress. *See also* fault tolerance.

resolution

(*ITIL Service Operation*) Action taken to repair the root cause of an incident or problem, or to implement a workaround. In ISO/IEC 20000, resolution processes is the process group that includes incident and problem management.

resource

(*ITIL Service Strategy*) A generic term that includes IT infrastructure, people, money or anything else that might help to deliver an IT service. Resources are considered to be assets of an organization. *See also* capability; service asset.

response time

A measure of the time taken to complete an operation or transaction. Used in capacity management as a measure of IT infrastructure performance, and in incident management as a measure of the time taken to answer the phone, or to start diagnosis.

responsiveness

A measurement of the time taken to respond to something. This could be response time of a transaction, or the speed with which an IT service provider responds to an incident or request for change etc.

restore

(*ITIL Service Operation*) Taking action to return an IT service to the users after repair and recovery from an incident. This is the primary objective of incident management.

retire

(*ITIL Service Transition*) Permanent removal of an IT service, or other configuration item, from the live environment. Being retired is a stage in the lifecycle of many configuration items.

return on assets (ROA)

(*ITIL Service Strategy*) A measurement of the profitability of a business unit or organization. Return on assets is calculated by dividing the annual net income by the total value of assets. *See also* return on investment.

return on investment (ROI)

(*ITIL Continual Service Improvement*) (*ITIL Service Strategy*) A measurement of the expected benefit of an investment. In the simplest sense, it is the net profit of an investment divided by the net worth of the assets invested. *See also* net present value; value on investment.

review

An evaluation of a change, problem, process, project etc. Reviews are typically carried out at predefined points in the lifecycle, and especially after closure. The purpose of a review is to ensure that all deliverables have been provided, and to identify opportunities for improvement. *See also* change evaluation; post-implementation review.

rights

(*ITIL Service Operation*) Entitlements, or permissions, granted to a user or role – for example, the right to modify particular data, or to authorize a change.

risk

A possible event that could cause harm or loss, or affect the ability to achieve objectives. A risk is measured by the probability of a threat, the vulnerability of the asset to that threat, and the impact it would have if it occurred. Risk can also be defined as uncertainty of outcome, and can be used in the context of measuring the probability of positive outcomes as well as negative outcomes.

risk assessment

The initial steps of risk management: analysing the value of assets to the business, identifying threats to those assets, and evaluating how vulnerable each asset is to those threats. Risk assessment can be quantitative (based on numerical data) or qualitative.

risk management

The process responsible for identifying, assessing and controlling risks. Risk management is also sometimes used to refer to the second part of the overall process after risks have been identified and assessed, as in 'risk assessment and management'. This process is not described in detail within the core ITIL publications. *See also* risk assessment.

role

A set of responsibilities, activities and authorities assigned to a person or team. A role is defined in a process or function. One person or team may have multiple roles – for example, the roles of configuration manager and change manager may be carried out by a single person. Role is also used to describe the purpose of something or what it is used for.

root cause

(*ITIL Service Operation*) The underlying or original cause of an incident or problem.

Sarbanes-Oxley (SOX)

US law that regulates financial practice and corporate governance.

scalability

The ability of an IT service, process, configuration item etc. to perform its agreed function when the workload or scope changes.

scope

The boundary or extent to which a process, procedure, certification, contract etc. applies. For example, the scope of change management may include all live IT services and related configuration items; the scope of an ISO/IEC 20000 certificate may include all IT services delivered out of a named data centre.

security

See information security management.

security management

See information security management.

security management information system (SMIS)

(*ITIL Service Design*) A set of tools, data and information that is used to support information security management. The security management information system is part of the information security management system. *See also* service knowledge management system.

security policy

See information security policy.

separation of concerns (SoC)

An approach to designing a solution or IT service that divides the problem into pieces that can be solved independently. This approach separates what is to be done from how it is to be done.

server

(*ITIL Service Operation*) A computer that is connected to a network and provides software functions that are used by other computers.

service

A means of delivering value to customers by facilitating outcomes customers want to achieve without the ownership of specific costs and risks. The term 'service' is sometimes used as a synonym for core service, IT service or service package. *See also* utility; warranty.

service acceptance criteria (SAC)

(*ITIL Service Transition*) A set of criteria used to ensure that an IT service meets its functionality and quality requirements and that the IT service provider is ready to operate the new IT service when it has been deployed. *See also* acceptance.

service analytics

(*ITIL Service Strategy*) A technique used in the assessment of the business impact of incidents. Service analytics models the dependencies between configuration items, and the dependencies of IT services on configuration items.

service asset

Any resource or capability of a service provider. *See also* asset.

service asset and configuration management (SACM)

(*ITIL Service Transition*) The process responsible for ensuring that the assets required to deliver services are properly controlled, and that accurate and reliable information about those assets is available when and where it is needed. This information includes details of how the assets have been configured and the relationships between assets. *See also* configuration management system.

service capacity management (SCM)

(*ITIL Continual Service Improvement*) (*ITIL Service Design*) The sub-process of capacity management responsible for understanding the performance and capacity of IT services. Information on the resources used by each IT service and the pattern of usage over time are collected, recorded and analysed for use in the capacity plan. *See also* business capacity management; component capacity management.

service catalogue

(*ITIL Service Design*) (*ITIL Service Strategy*) A database or structured document with information about all live IT services, including those available for deployment. The service catalogue is part of the service portfolio and contains information about two types of IT service: customer-facing services that are visible to the business; and supporting services required by the service provider to deliver customer-facing services. *See also* customer agreement portfolio; service catalogue management.

service catalogue management

(*ITIL Service Design*) The process responsible for providing and maintaining the service catalogue and for ensuring that it is available to those who are authorized to access it.

service change

See change.

service charter

(*ITIL Service Design*) (*ITIL Service Strategy*) A document that contains details of a new or changed service. New service introductions and significant service changes are documented in a charter and authorized by service portfolio management. Service charters are passed to the service design lifecycle stage where a new or modified service design package will be created. The term charter is also used to describe the act of authorizing the work required by each stage of the service lifecycle with respect to the new or changed service. *See also* change proposal; service portfolio; service catalogue.

service continuity management

See IT service continuity management.

service contract

(*ITIL Service Strategy*) A contract to deliver one or more IT services. The term is also used to mean any agreement to deliver IT services, whether this is a legal contract or a service level agreement. *See also* customer agreement portfolio.

service culture

A customer-oriented culture. The major objectives of a service culture are customer satisfaction and helping customers to achieve their business objectives.

service design

(*ITIL Service Design*) A stage in the lifecycle of a service. Service design includes the design of the services, governing practices, processes and policies required to realize the service provider's strategy and to facilitate the introduction of services into supported environments. Service design includes the following processes: design coordination, service catalogue management, service level management, availability management, capacity management, IT service continuity management, information security management, and supplier management. Although these processes are associated with service design, most processes have activities that take place across multiple stages of the service lifecycle. *See also* design.

service design package (SDP)

(*ITIL Service Design*) Document(s) defining all aspects of an IT service and its requirements through each stage of its lifecycle. A service design package is produced for each new IT service, major change or IT service retirement.

service desk

(*ITIL Service Operation*) The single point of contact between the service provider and the users. A typical service desk manages incidents and service requests, and also handles communication with the users.

service hours

(*ITIL Service Design*) An agreed time period when a particular IT service should be available. For example, 'Monday–Friday 08:00 to 17:00 except public holidays'. Service hours should be defined in a service level agreement.

service improvement plan (SIP)

(*ITIL Continual Service Improvement*) A formal plan to implement improvements to a process or IT service.

service knowledge management system (SKMS)

(*ITIL Service Transition*) A set of tools and databases that is used to manage knowledge, information and data. The service knowledge management system includes the configuration management system, as well as other databases and information systems. The service knowledge management system includes tools for collecting, storing, managing, updating, analysing and presenting all the knowledge, information and data that an IT service provider will need to manage the full lifecycle of IT services. *See also* knowledge management.

service level

Measured and reported achievement against one or more service level targets. The term is sometimes used informally to mean service level target.

service level agreement (SLA)

(*ITIL Continual Service Improvement*) (*ITIL Service Design*) An agreement between an IT service provider and a customer. A service level agreement describes the IT service, documents service level targets, and specifies the responsibilities of the IT service provider and the customer. A single agreement may cover multiple IT services or multiple customers. *See also* operational level agreement.

service level management (SLM)

(*ITIL Service Design*) The process responsible for negotiating achievable service level agreements and ensuring that these are met. It is responsible for ensuring that all IT service management processes, operational level agreements and underpinning contracts are appropriate for the agreed service level targets. Service level management monitors and reports on service levels, holds regular service reviews with customers, and identifies required improvements.

service level package (SLP)

See service option.

service level requirement (SLR)

(*ITIL Continual Service Improvement*) (*ITIL Service Design*) A customer requirement for an aspect of an IT service. Service level requirements are based on business objectives and used to negotiate agreed service level targets.

service level target

(*ITIL Continual Service Improvement*) (*ITIL Service Design*) A commitment that is documented in a service level agreement. Service level targets are based on service level requirements, and are needed to ensure that the IT service is able to meet business objectives. They should be SMART, and are usually based on key performance indicators.

service lifecycle

An approach to IT service management that emphasizes the importance of coordination and control across the various functions, processes and systems necessary to manage the full lifecycle of IT services. The service lifecycle approach considers the strategy, design, transition, operation and continual improvement of IT services. Also known as service management lifecycle.

service management

A set of specialized organizational capabilities for providing value to customers in the form of services.

service manager

A generic term for any manager within the service provider. Most commonly used to refer to a business relationship manager, a process manager or a senior manager with responsibility for IT services overall.

service model

(*ITIL Service Strategy*) A model that shows how service assets interact with customer assets to create value. Service models describe the structure of a service (how the configuration items fit together) and the dynamics of the service (activities, flow of resources and interactions). A service model can be used as a template or blueprint for multiple services.

service operation

(*ITIL Service Operation*) A stage in the lifecycle of a service. Service operation coordinates and carries out the activities and processes required to deliver and manage services at agreed levels to business users and customers. Service operation also manages the technology that is used to deliver and support services. Service operation includes the following processes: event management, incident management, request fulfilment, problem management, and access management. Service operation also includes the following functions: service desk, technical management, IT operations management, and application management. Although these processes and functions are associated with service operation, most processes and functions have activities that take place across multiple stages of the service lifecycle. *See also* operation.

service option

(*ITIL Service Design*) (*ITIL Service Strategy*) A choice of utility and warranty offered to customers by a core service or service package. Service options are sometimes referred to as service level packages.

service owner

(*ITIL Service Strategy*) A role responsible for managing one or more services throughout their entire lifecycle. Service owners are instrumental in the development of service strategy and are responsible for the content of the service portfolio. *See also* business relationship management.

service package

(*ITIL Service Strategy*) Two or more services that have been combined to offer a solution to a specific type of customer need or to underpin specific business outcomes. A service package can consist of a combination of core services, enabling services and enhancing services. A service package provides a specific level of utility and warranty. Customers may be offered a choice of utility and warranty through one or more service options. *See also* IT service.

service pipeline

(*ITIL Service Strategy*) A database or structured document listing all IT services that are under consideration or development, but are not yet available to customers. The service pipeline provides a business view of possible future IT services and is part of the service portfolio that is not normally published to customers.

service portfolio

(*ITIL Service Strategy*) The complete set of services that is managed by a service provider. The service portfolio is used to manage the entire lifecycle of all services, and includes three categories: service pipeline (proposed or in development), service catalogue (live or available for deployment), and retired services. *See also* customer agreement portfolio; service portfolio management.

service portfolio management (SPM)

(*ITIL Service Strategy*) The process responsible for managing the service portfolio. Service portfolio management ensures that the service provider has the right mix of services to meet required business outcomes at an appropriate level of investment. Service portfolio management considers services in terms of the business value that they provide.

service potential

(*ITIL Service Strategy*) The total possible value of the overall capabilities and resources of the IT service provider.

service provider

(*ITIL Service Strategy*) An organization supplying services to one or more internal customers or external customers. Service provider is often used as an abbreviation for IT service provider. *See also* Type I service provider; Type II service provider; Type III service provider.

service provider interface (SPI)

(*ITIL Service Strategy*) An interface between the IT service provider and a user, customer, business process or supplier. Analysis of service provider interfaces helps to coordinate end-to-end management of IT services.

service reporting

(*ITIL Continual Service Improvement*) Activities that produce and deliver reports of achievement and trends against service levels. The format, content and frequency of reports should be agreed with customers.

service request

(*ITIL Service Operation*) A formal request from a user for something to be provided – for example, a request for information or advice; to reset a password; or to install a workstation for a new user. Service requests are managed by the request fulfilment process, usually in conjunction with the service desk. Service requests may be linked to a request for change as part of fulfilling the request.

service sourcing

(*ITIL Service Strategy*) The strategy and approach for deciding whether to provide a service internally, to outsource it to an external service provider, or to combine the two approaches. Service sourcing also means the execution of this strategy. *See also* insourcing; internal service provider; outsourcing.

service strategy

(*ITIL Service Strategy*) A stage in the lifecycle of a service. Service strategy defines the perspective, position, plans and patterns that a service provider needs to execute to meet an organization's business outcomes. Service strategy includes the following processes: strategy management for IT services, service portfolio management, financial management for IT services, demand management, and business relationship management. Although these processes are associated with service strategy, most processes have activities that take place across multiple stages of the service lifecycle.

service transition

(*ITIL Service Transition*) A stage in the lifecycle of a service. Service transition ensures that new, modified or retired services meet the expectations of the business as documented in the service strategy and service design stages of the lifecycle. Service transition includes the following processes: transition planning and support, change management, service asset and configuration management, release and deployment management, service validation and testing, change evaluation, and knowledge management. Although these processes are associated with service transition, most processes have activities that take place across multiple stages of the service lifecycle. *See also* transition.

service validation and testing

(*ITIL Service Transition*) The process responsible for validation and testing of a new or changed IT service. Service validation and testing ensures that the IT service matches its design specification and will meet the needs of the business.

service valuation

(*ITIL Service Strategy*) A measurement of the total cost of delivering an IT service, and the total value to the business of that IT service. Service valuation is used to help the business and the IT service provider agree on the value of the IT service.

serviceability

(*ITIL Continual Service Improvement*) (*ITIL Service Design*) The ability of a third-party supplier to meet the terms of its contract. This contract will include agreed levels of reliability, maintainability and availability for a configuration item.

seven-step improvement process

(*ITIL Continual Service Improvement*) The process responsible for defining and managing the steps needed to identify, define, gather, process, analyse, present and implement improvements. The performance of the IT service provider is continually measured by this process and improvements are made to processes, IT services and IT infrastructure in order to increase efficiency, effectiveness and cost effectiveness. Opportunities for improvement are recorded and managed in the CSI register.

shared service unit

See Type II service provider.

shift

(*ITIL Service Operation*) A group or team of people who carry out a specific role for a fixed period of time. For example, there could be four shifts of IT operations control personnel to support an IT service that is used 24 hours a day.

simulation modelling

(*ITIL Continual Service Improvement*) (*ITIL Service Design*) A technique that creates a detailed model to predict the behaviour of an IT service or other configuration item. A simulation model is often created by using the actual configuration items that are being modelled with artificial workloads or transactions. They are used in capacity management when accurate results are important. A simulation model is sometimes called a performance benchmark. *See also* analytical modelling; modelling.

single point of contact

(*ITIL Service Operation*) Providing a single consistent way to communicate with an organization or business unit. For example, a single point of contact for an IT service provider is usually called a service desk.

SMART

(*ITIL Continual Service Improvement*) (*ITIL Service Design*) An acronym for helping to remember that targets in service level agreements and project plans should be specific, measurable, achievable, relevant and time-bound.

snapshot

(*ITIL Continual Service Improvement*) (*ITIL Service Transition*) The current state of a configuration item, process or any other set of data recorded at a specific point in time. Snapshots can be captured by discovery tools or by manual techniques such as an assessment. *See also* baseline; benchmark.

software asset management (SAM)

(*ITIL Service Transition*) The process responsible for tracking and reporting the use and ownership of software assets throughout their lifecycle. Software asset management is part of an overall service asset and configuration management process. This process is not described in detail within the core ITIL publications.

source

See service sourcing.

specification

A formal definition of requirements. A specification may be used to define technical or operational requirements, and may be internal or external. Many public standards consist of a code of practice and a specification. The specification defines the standard against which an organization can be audited.

stakeholder

A person who has an interest in an organization, project, IT service etc. Stakeholders may be interested in the activities, targets, resources or deliverables. Stakeholders may include customers, partners, employees, shareholders, owners etc. *See also* RACI.

standard

A mandatory requirement. Examples include ISO/IEC 20000 (an international standard), an internal security standard for Unix configuration, or a government standard for how financial records should be maintained. The term is also used to refer to a code of practice or specification published by a standards organization such as ISO or BSI. *See also* guideline.

standard change

(*ITIL Service Transition*) A pre-authorized change that is low risk, relatively common and follows a procedure or work instruction – for example, a password reset or provision of standard equipment to a new employee. Requests for change are not required to implement a standard change, and they are logged and tracked using a different mechanism, such as a service request. *See also* change model.

standard operating procedures (SOP)

(*ITIL Service Operation*) Procedures used by IT operations management.

statement of requirements (SOR)

(*ITIL Service Design*) A document containing all requirements for a product purchase, or a new or changed IT service. *See also* terms of reference.

status

The name of a required field in many types of record. It shows the current stage in the lifecycle of the associated configuration item, incident, problem etc.

strategic

(*ITIL Service Strategy*) The highest of three levels of planning and delivery (strategic, tactical, operational). Strategic activities include objective setting and long-term planning to achieve the overall vision.

strategic asset

(*ITIL Service Strategy*) Any asset that provides the basis for core competence, distinctive performance or sustainable competitive advantage, or which allows a business unit to participate in business opportunities. Part of service strategy is to identify how IT can be viewed as a strategic asset rather than an internal administrative function.

strategy

(*ITIL Service Strategy*) A strategic plan designed to achieve defined objectives.

strategy management for IT services

(*ITIL Service Strategy*) The process responsible for defining and maintaining an organization's perspective, position, plans and patterns with regard to its services and the management of those services. Once the strategy has been defined, strategy management for IT services is also responsible for ensuring that it achieves its intended business outcomes.

supplier

(*ITIL Service Design*) (*ITIL Service Strategy*) A third party responsible for supplying goods or services that are required to deliver IT services. Examples of suppliers include commodity hardware and software vendors, network and telecom providers, and outsourcing organizations. *See also* supply chain; underpinning contract.

supplier and contract management information system (SCMIS)

(*ITIL Service Design*) A set of tools, data and information that is used to support supplier management. *See also* service knowledge management system.

supplier management

(*ITIL Service Design*) The process responsible for obtaining value for money from suppliers, ensuring that all contracts and agreements with suppliers support the needs of the business, and that all suppliers meet their contractual commitments. *See also* supplier and contract management information system.

supply chain

(*ITIL Service Strategy*) The activities in a value chain carried out by suppliers. A supply chain typically involves multiple suppliers, each adding value to the product or service. *See also* value network.

supporting service

(*ITIL Service Design*) An IT service that is not directly used by the business, but is required by the IT service provider to deliver customer-facing services (for example, a directory service or a backup service). Supporting services may also include IT services only used by the IT service provider. All live supporting services, including those available for deployment, are recorded in the service catalogue along with information about their relationships to customer-facing services and other CIs.

SWOT analysis

(*ITIL Continual Service Improvement*) A technique that reviews and analyses the internal strengths and weaknesses of an organization and the external opportunities and threats that it faces. SWOT stands for strengths, weaknesses, opportunities and threats.

system

A number of related things that work together to achieve an overall objective. For example:

- A computer system including hardware, software and applications
- A management system, including the framework of policy, processes, functions, standards, guidelines and tools that are planned and managed together – for example, a quality management system
- A database management system or operating system that includes many software modules which are designed to perform a set of related functions.

tactical

The middle of three levels of planning and delivery (strategic, tactical, operational). Tactical activities include the medium-term plans required to achieve specific objectives, typically over a period of weeks to months.

technical management

(*ITIL Service Operation*) The function responsible for providing technical skills in support of IT services and management of the IT infrastructure. Technical management defines the roles of support groups, as well as the tools, processes and procedures required.

technical support

See technical management.

terms of reference (TOR)

(*ITIL Service Design*) A document specifying the requirements, scope, deliverables, resources and schedule for a project or activity.

test

(*ITIL Service Transition*) An activity that verifies that a configuration item, IT service, process etc. meets its specification or agreed requirements. *See also* acceptance; service validation and testing.

third party

A person, organization or other entity that is not part of the service provider's own organization and is not a customer – for example, a software supplier or a hardware maintenance company. Requirements for third parties are typically specified in contracts that underpin service level agreements. *See also* underpinning contract.

threat

A threat is anything that might exploit a vulnerability. Any potential cause of an incident can be considered a threat. For example, a fire is a threat that could exploit the vulnerability of flammable floor coverings. This term is commonly used in information security management and IT service continuity management, but also applies to other areas such as problem and availability management.

threshold

The value of a metric that should cause an alert to be generated or management action to be taken. For example, 'Priority 1 incident not solved within four hours', 'More than five soft disk errors in an hour', or 'More than 10 failed changes in a month'.

throughput

(*ITIL Service Design*) A measure of the number of transactions or other operations performed in a fixed time – for example, 5,000 e-mails sent per hour, or 200 disk I/Os per second.

total cost of ownership (TCO)

(*ITIL Service Strategy*) A methodology used to help make investment decisions. It assesses the full lifecycle cost of owning a configuration item, not just the initial cost or purchase price. *See also* total cost of utilization.

total cost of utilization (TCU)

(*ITIL Service Strategy*) A methodology used to help make investment and service sourcing decisions. Total cost of utilization assesses the full lifecycle cost to the customer of using an IT service. *See also* total cost of ownership.

total quality management (TQM)

(*ITIL Continual Service Improvement*) A methodology for managing continual improvement by using a quality management system. Total quality management establishes a culture involving all people in the organization in a process of continual monitoring and improvement.

transaction

A discrete function performed by an IT service – for example, transferring money from one bank account to another. A single transaction may involve numerous additions, deletions and modifications of data. Either all of these are completed successfully or none of them is carried out.

transfer cost

(*ITIL Service Strategy*) A cost type which records expenditure made on behalf of another part of the organization. For example, the IT service provider may pay for an external consultant to be used by the finance department and transfer the cost to them. The IT service provider would record this as a transfer cost.

transition

(*ITIL Service Transition*) A change in state, corresponding to a movement of an IT service or other configuration item from one lifecycle status to the next.

transition planning and support

(*ITIL Service Transition*) The process responsible for planning all service transition processes and coordinating the resources that they require.

tuning

The activity responsible for planning changes to make the most efficient use of resources. Tuning is most commonly used in the context of IT services and components. Tuning is part of capacity management, which also includes performance monitoring and implementation of the required changes. Tuning is also called optimization, particularly in the context of processes and other non-technical resources.

Type I service provider

(*ITIL Service Strategy*) An internal service provider that is embedded within a business unit. There may be several Type I service providers within an organization.

Type II service provider

(*ITIL Service Strategy*) An internal service provider that provides shared IT services to more than one business unit. Type II service providers are also known as shared service units.

Type III service provider

(*ITIL Service Strategy*) A service provider that provides IT services to external customers.

underpinning contract (UC)

(*ITIL Service Design*) A contract between an IT service provider and a third party. The third party provides goods or services that support delivery of an IT service to a customer. The underpinning contract defines targets and responsibilities that are required to meet agreed service level targets in one or more service level agreements.

unit cost

(*ITIL Service Strategy*) The cost to the IT service provider of providing a single component of an IT service. For example, the cost of a single desktop PC, or of a single transaction.

urgency

(*ITIL Service Design*) (*ITIL Service Transition*) A measure of how long it will be until an incident, problem or change has a significant impact on the business. For example, a high-impact incident may have low urgency if the impact will not affect the business until the end of the financial year. Impact and urgency are used to assign priority.

usability

(*ITIL Service Design*) The ease with which an application, product or IT service can be used. Usability requirements are often included in a statement of requirements.

use case

(*ITIL Service Design*) A technique used to define required functionality and objectives, and to design tests. Use cases define realistic scenarios that describe interactions between users and an IT service or other system.

user

A person who uses the IT service on a day-to-day basis. Users are distinct from customers, as some customers do not use the IT service directly.

user profile (UP)

(*ITIL Service Strategy*) A pattern of user demand for IT services. Each user profile includes one or more patterns of business activity.

utility

(*ITIL Service Strategy*) The functionality offered by a product or service to meet a particular need. Utility can be summarized as 'what the service does', and can be used to determine whether a service is able to meet its required outcomes, or is 'fit for purpose'. The business value of an IT service is created by the combination of utility and warranty. *See also* service validation and testing.

validation

(*ITIL Service Transition*) An activity that ensures a new or changed IT service, process, plan or other deliverable meets the needs of the business. Validation ensures that business requirements are met even though these may have changed since the original design. *See also* acceptance; qualification; service validation and testing; verification.

value chain

(*ITIL Service Strategy*) A sequence of processes that creates a product or service that is of value to a customer. Each step of the sequence builds on the previous steps and contributes to the overall product or service. *See also* value network.

value for money

An informal measure of cost effectiveness. Value for money is often based on a comparison with the cost of alternatives. *See also* cost benefit analysis.

value network

(*ITIL Service Strategy*) A complex set of relationships between two or more groups or organizations. Value is generated through exchange of knowledge, information, goods or services. *See also* partnership; value chain.

value on investment (VOI)

(*ITIL Continual Service Improvement*) A measurement of the expected benefit of an investment. Value on investment considers both financial and intangible benefits. *See also* return on investment.

variable cost

(*ITIL Service Strategy*) A cost that depends on how much the IT service is used, how many products are produced, the number and type of users, or something else that cannot be fixed in advance.

variance

The difference between a planned value and the actual measured value. Commonly used in financial management, capacity management and service level management, but could apply in any area where plans are in place.

verification

(*ITIL Service Transition*) An activity that ensures that a new or changed IT service, process, plan or other deliverable is complete, accurate, reliable and matches its design specification. *See also* acceptance; validation; service validation and testing.

version

(*ITIL Service Transition*) A version is used to identify a specific baseline of a configuration item. Versions typically use a naming convention that enables the sequence or date of each baseline to be identified. For example, payroll application version 3 contains updated functionality from version 2.

vision

A description of what the organization intends to become in the future. A vision is created by senior management and is used to help influence culture and strategic planning. *See also* mission.

vital business function (VBF)

(*ITIL Service Design*) Part of a business process that is critical to the success of the business. Vital business functions are an important consideration of business continuity management, IT service continuity management and availability management.

vulnerability

A weakness that could be exploited by a threat – for example, an open firewall port, a password that is never changed, or a flammable carpet. A missing control is also considered to be a vulnerability.

warranty

(*ITIL Service Strategy*) Assurance that a product or service will meet agreed requirements. This may be a formal agreement such as a service level agreement or contract, or it may be a marketing message or brand image. Warranty refers to the ability of a service to be available when needed, to provide the required capacity, and to provide the required reliability in terms of continuity and security. Warranty can be summarized as 'how the service is delivered', and can be used to determine whether a service is 'fit for use'. The business value of an IT service is created by the combination of utility and warranty. *See also* service validation and testing.

work instruction

A document containing detailed instructions that specify exactly what steps to follow to carry out an activity. A work instruction contains much more detail than a procedure and is only created if very detailed instructions are needed.

workaround

(*ITIL Service Operation*) Reducing or eliminating the impact of an incident or problem for which a full resolution is not yet available – for example, by restarting a failed configuration item. Workarounds for problems are documented in known error records. Workarounds for incidents that do not have associated problem records are documented in the incident record.

workload

The resources required to deliver an identifiable part of an IT service. Workloads may be categorized by users, groups of users, or functions within the IT service. This is used to assist in analysing and managing the capacity, performance and utilization of configuration items and IT services. The term is sometimes used as a synonym for throughput.

Index

Index

Page numbers in *italic* refer to figures and tables.